CHARLES R. SWINDOLL

# SWINDOLL'S LIVING INSIGHTS

NEW TESTAMENT COMMENTARY

# 1 & 2 CORINTHIANS

*Tyndale House Publishers*
*Carol Stream, Illinois*

Swindoll's Living Insights New Testament Commentary, Volume 7

Visit Tyndale online at tyndale.com.



Designed by Nicole Grimes

Published in association with Yates & Yates, LLP (www.yates2.com).



**Library of Congress Cataloging-in-Publication Data**
Names: Swindoll, Charles R., author.
Title: Insights on 1 & 2 Corinthians / Charles R. Swindoll.
Other titles: Insights on First and Second Corinthians
Description: Carol Stream, Illinois : Tyndale House Publishers, Inc., 2017. |
Series: Swindoll's living insights New Testament commentary : volume 7 |
Includes bibliographical references.
Identifiers: LCCN 2016035394 | ISBN 9781414393711 (hc)
Subjects: LCSH: Bible. Corinthians—Commentaries.
Classification: LCC BS2675.53 .S95 2017 | DDC 227/.207—dc23 LC record available at
https://lccn.loc.gov/2016035394

Printed in China
28 27 26 25 24
9 8 7 6 5

# CONTENTS

## List of Features and Images

# AUTHOR'S PREFACE

For more than sixty years I have loved the Bible. It was that love for the Scriptures, mixed with a clear call into the gospel ministry during my tour of duty in the Marine Corps, that resulted in my going to Dallas Theological Seminary to prepare for a lifetime of ministry. During those four great years I had the privilege of studying under outstanding men of God, who also loved God's Word. They not only held the inerrant Word of God in high esteem, they taught it carefully, preached it passionately, and modeled it consistently. A week never passes without my giving thanks to God for the grand heritage that has been mine to claim! I am forever indebted to those fine theologians and mentors, who cultivated in me a strong commitment to the understanding, exposition, and application of God's truth.

For more than fifty years I have been engaged in doing just that—*and how I love it!* I confess without hesitation that I am addicted to the examination and the proclamation of the Scriptures. Because of this, books have played a major role in my life for as long as I have been in ministry—especially those volumes that explain the truths and enhance my understanding of what God has written. Through these many years I have collected a large personal library, which has proven invaluable as I have sought to remain a faithful student of the Bible. To the end of my days, my major goal in life is to communicate the Word with accuracy, insight, clarity, and practicality. Without informative and reliable books to turn to, I would have "run dry" decades ago.

Among my favorite and most well-worn volumes are those that have enabled me to get a better grasp of the biblical text. Like most expositors, I am forever searching for literary tools that I can use to hone my gifts and sharpen my skills. For me, that means finding resources that make the complicated simple and easy to understand, that offer insightful comments and word pictures that enable me to see the relevance of sacred truth in light of my twenty-first-century world, and that drive those truths home to my heart in ways I do not easily forget. When I come across such books, they wind up in my hands as I devour them and then place them in my library for further reference . . . and, believe me, I often return to them. What a relief it is to have these resources to turn to when I lack fresh insight, or when I need just the right story or illustration, or when I get stuck in the tangled text and cannot find my way out. For the serious expositor, a library is essential. As a mentor of mine once said, "Where else can you have ten thousand professors at your fingertips?"

In recent years I have discovered there are not nearly enough resources like those I just described. It was such a discovery that prompted me to consider becoming a part of the answer instead of lamenting the problem. But the solution would result in a huge undertaking. A writing project that covers all of the books and letters of the New Testament seemed overwhelming and intimidating. A rush of relief came when I realized that during the past fifty-plus years I've taught and preached through most of the New Testament. In my files were folders filled with notes from those messages that were just lying there, waiting to be brought out of hiding, given a fresh and relevant touch in light of today's needs, and applied to fit into the lives of men and women who long for a fresh word from the Lord. *That did it!* I began to work on plans to turn all of those notes into this commentary on the New Testament.

I must express my gratitude to Mike Svigel for his tireless and devoted effort, serving as my hands-on, day-to-day editor. He has done superb work as we have walked our way through the verses and chapters of all twenty-seven New Testament books. It has been a pleasure to see how he has taken my original material and helped me shape it into a style that remains true to the text of the Scriptures, at the same time interestingly and creatively developed, and all the while allowing my voice to come through in a natural and easy-to-read manner.

I need to add sincere words of appreciation to the congregations I have served in various parts of these United States for more than five decades. It has been my good fortune to be the recipient of their love, support, encouragement, patience, and frequent words of affirmation as I have fulfilled my calling to stand and deliver God's message year after year. The sheep from all those flocks have endeared themselves to this shepherd in more ways than I can put into words . . . and none more than those I currently serve with delight at Stonebriar Community Church in Frisco, Texas.

Finally, I must thank my wife, Cynthia, for her understanding of my addiction to studying, to preaching, and to writing. Never has she discouraged me from staying at it. Never has she failed to urge me in the pursuit of doing my very best. On the contrary, her affectionate support personally, and her own commitment to excellence in leading Insight for Living for more than three and a half decades, have combined to keep me faithful to my calling "in season and out of season." Without her devotion to me and apart from our mutual partnership throughout our lifetime of ministry together, Swindoll's Living Insights would never have been undertaken.

I am grateful that it has now found its way into your hands and, ultimately, onto the shelves of your library. My continued hope and prayer is that you will find these volumes helpful in your own study and personal application of the Bible. May they help you come to realize, as I have over these many years, that God's Word is as timeless as it is true.

> The grass withers, the flower fades,
> But the word of our God stands forever. (Isa. 40:8, NASB)

*Chuck Swindoll*
Frisco, Texas

# THE STRONG'S NUMBERING SYSTEM

Swindoll's Living Insights New Testament Commentary uses the Strong's word-study numbering system to give both newer and more advanced Bible students alike quicker, more convenient access to helpful original-language tools (e.g., concordances, lexicons, and theological dictionaries). The Strong's numbering system, made popular by the *Strong's Exhaustive Concordance of the Bible*, is used with the majority of biblical Greek and Hebrew reference works. Those who are unfamiliar with the ancient Hebrew, Aramaic, and Greek alphabets can quickly find information on a given word by looking up the appropriate index number. Advanced students will find the system helpful because it allows them to quickly find the lexical form of obscure conjugations and inflections.

When a Greek word is mentioned in the text, the Strong's number is included in square brackets after the Greek word. So in the example of the Greek word *agapē* [26], "love," the number is used with Greek tools keyed to the Strong's system.

On occasion, a Hebrew word is mentioned in the text. The Strong's Hebrew numbers are completely separate from the Greek numbers, so Hebrew numbers are prefixed with a letter "H." So, for example, the Hebrew word *kapporet* [H3727], "mercy seat," comes from *kopher* [H3722], "to ransom," "to secure favor through a gift."

# INSIGHTS ON 1 CORINTHIANS

*Paul sought to address a growing number of problems dividing the church—effects of its diverse membership of Jews and Gentiles, its rocky beginnings of persecution, and the corrupt religious and moral culture in which it ministered. As the lights dim on our own culture and our churches begin to look more and more like the disheveled, self-serving church in Corinth, Paul's words to that fragmented church take on greater import and more urgent practicality.*

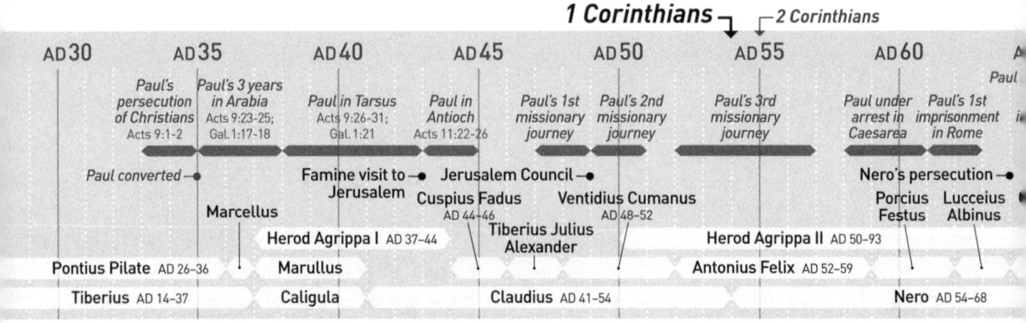


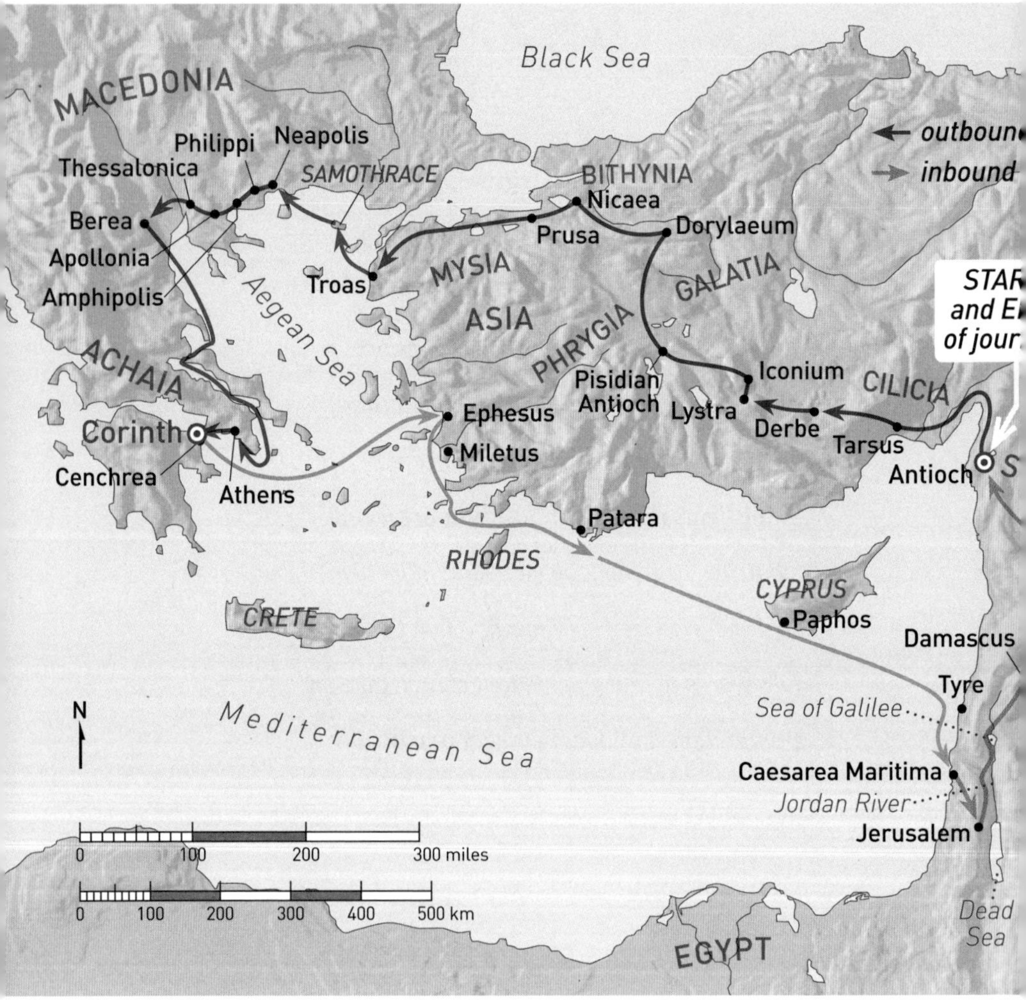


**Paul's Second Missionary Journey.** Paul and Silas left from Antioch to return to several of the cities where Paul had planted churches on his first missionary journey around AD 47 to 48. They proceeded through Asia to Greece, all the way to Corinth, where Paul would meet Priscilla and Aquila and minister in a church of new Christians in the home of Titius Justus.

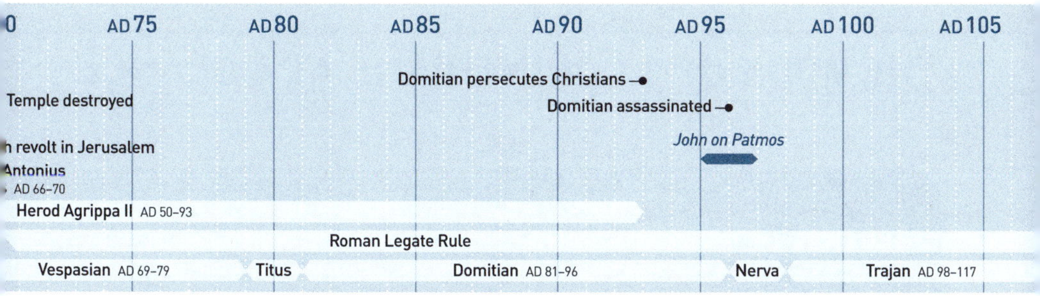


# 1 CORINTHIANS

## INTRODUCTION

During the last few months of 1957, my wife and I were located in San Francisco. To say we were residents would be a bit of an overstatement, because we were *lost* most of the time! It was decades before GPS navigation, and we were faced with unpredictable roads—some running perpendicular, others diagonally, and still others that felt like navigating through a giant platter of spaghetti. We had to constantly keep a lookout for one-way signs or risk being rammed by a trolley, which often just leaped out of nowhere. Those roller-coaster hills, twisted streets, and fading street signs rendered city maps almost useless. The old, strange buildings and side-by-side houses looked like somebody copied and pasted the same design over and over along the city blocks. As a result, we couldn't find our way around by obvious landmarks. Add to all this confusion a thick peninsula fog with a malicious will of its own. After a few hours of playing hide-and-seek with yourself, you start looking for Alice and the Mad Hatter because you conclude, "This city can't possibly exist on *this* side of the looking glass!"

It didn't take long before Cynthia and I devised a means to feel our way around that city. She would sit in the passenger seat, open up a map, and never look up as she would gently voice commands like a flesh-and-blood GPS: "Second street, turn right. . . . First street, turn left. . . . Oops, wrong way, turn around." I didn't know where I was, but I believed her. Most of the time as we traveled from point A to point B (often taking unplanned detours through points C, D, and E), we were both in survival mode, hoping the street cars and impatient drivers wouldn't overtake us.

Well, things changed for us late that fall. We were with some friends atop the new San Francisco Hilton, over twenty stories above the

# THE BOOK OF 1 CORINTHIANS AT A GLANCE

| SECTION | OPENING GREETING AND PRAYER | REBUKING DIVISIONS AND FOLLY | CORRECTING AND IMMORA |
|---|---|---|---|
| PASSAGE | 1:1-9 | 1:10–3:23 | 4:1–6:20 |
| THEMES | Prayer<br>Blessing<br>Greeting | Divisions and Catastrophes<br>Rebuke for Sinful Conditions:<br>"Now I exhort you, brethren . . ." (1:1 | |
| | | Plea for Unity<br>Rebuke for Folly | Plea for Pu<br>Rebuke fo<br>Immorali |
| KEY TERMS | | Spiritual | Fleshly |
| | Grace<br>Called | Wisdom<br>Folly | Steward<br>Immorality |

| ENGTHENING AMILY AND LLOWSHIP | ORDERING CHURCH AND WORSHIP | CONCERNING DEATH AND RESURRECTION | CONCLUDING INSTRUCTIONS AND WARNINGS |
|---|---|---|---|
| 1–10:33 | 11:1–14:40 | 15:1-58 | 16:1-24 |
| Difficulties and Controversies<br>Reply to Specific Questions:<br>"Now concerning the things about which you wrote . . ." (7:1) | | | |
| rriage and Divorce<br>berty and License | Women and Worship<br>Gifts and Ministry | Gospel and Faith<br>Dying and Rising | Giving and Receiving<br>Reproof and Exhortation |
| | Love | Wisdom | |
| Marry<br>owledge | Edification<br>Gift | Gospel<br>Resurrection | Collection<br>Maranatha |

streets, and suddenly the layout of that city fell into place. There we stood, gazing over the peninsula with a bird's-eye view, discovering the interconnectedness of it all—the inner logic of the system that was San Francisco. Off in that direction was the Golden Gate. Over there was the Bay Bridge. Between the two was Fisherman's Wharf, and behind us, Nob Hill and Chinatown. Farther south were Daly City and other significant points down the peninsula. Here were the main thoroughfares, parkways, and boulevards. Once we got above the city to see the whole thing at once, San Francisco suddenly made better sense.

Paul's first letter to the church in Corinth can be just as perplexing as a Texan's first drive through the streets of San Francisco—if one doesn't first take time for a bird's-eye view of the whole and place it in its biblical and historical context. Believe me, the twists and turns in the chapters and verses of 1 Corinthians can lose even the most skilled preachers and teachers. Many expositors get snared by the fatal flaw of immersing themselves in the details of the book before getting an overview. This principle holds true for every book of the Bible, but it's especially vital for 1 Corinthians. So, let me be your guide as we look at the first-century city of Corinth and Paul's ministry there, and then survey the letter. Once we learn the major boulevards and landmarks of this grand letter, we'll be ready to explore the interesting streets, intersections, and neighborhoods without getting lost.

## KEY TERMS IN 1 CORINTHIANS

***agapē* (ἀγάπη)** [26] "love," "benevolence"

The Greek noun *agapē* is rarely found outside Jewish and Christian writings, though verbal forms of the word were used of love in general. The Greek culture celebrated *erōs*, which, while used in various contexts, often connoted the intoxicating, impulsive romantic love between men and women. They also honored *philia* [5373], the warm, noble affection of deep friendship. But *agapē* remained an undeveloped term in Greek literature. Its use, especially of God's love in Jewish and Christian literature, marked it as an unconditional love that rests on a decision to seek another's highest and greatest good. This unmerited and selfless affection describes God's love toward people as well as Christians' responsibility to reflect that love toward others (see 4:21; 8:1; 13:1-13; 14:1; 16:14). Paul's "love chapter" (13:1-13) paints a vivid and beautiful picture of what *agapē* is and is not.

**pneumatikos (πνευματικός)** [4152] "spiritual"
**sarkikos (σαρκικός)** [4559] "fleshly"

Though the adjective *pneumatikos* can refer to other nonmaterial things (Eph. 6:12), in the New Testament it most often relates to the Holy Spirit. Thus, things that come from the Holy Spirit such as gifts, blessings, or revelations are called "spiritual" (Rom. 1:11; 7:14; 1 Cor. 2:13; Eph. 1:3), and people who are empowered by the Holy Spirit in their lifestyle are called "spiritual" (1 Cor. 2:15; 3:1; 14:37; Gal. 6:1). It is sometimes contrasted with *sarkikos* or the related word *sarkinos* [4560] (both meaning "fleshly"; cf. 1 Cor. 3:1, 3) to emphasize a heavenly, divine origin as opposed to an earthly, human origin. Paul uses these opposites to illustrate the carnal, immature condition of the Corinthians, who should have been striving for spiritual maturity.

**sophia (σοφία)** [4678] "wisdom"

Not only was *sophia*, "wisdom," sought after and praised in the Greek mind, but "wisdom" had a rich meaning in the Hebrew Scriptures as well. Wisdom involves far more than mere knowledge of facts. It advances even beyond skillful living or the emphasis on practical virtue as seen in Greek philosophy. Rather, "wisdom" in the Christian sense is a gift from God (Jas. 1:5) closely associated with the presence and working of the Holy Spirit, producing supernatural discernment and prudence. Because true wisdom comes from God, it is often regarded as "folly" by Gentiles.

## CORINTH

In New Testament times, Corinth governed the Roman province of Achaia, which comprised almost the entirety of Greece. As a locus of political power, it hosted the residence of the regional governor, or proconsul.[1] The city had been rebuilt by Julius Caesar in 44 BC and repopulated with freedmen from around the Roman Empire, ending the desolation the city had endured at the hand of the Romans when it had been destroyed in 146 BC.

This influx of outside ethnicities made Corinth very diverse and pluralistic—one of the early cosmopolitan cities. It was a booming place of commerce where many religions existed side by side, and many syncretistic belief systems resulted. The city housed numerous temples to various deities, including a temple to Aphrodite, the fertility goddess. Corinth featured both the cult prostitution associated with such temples and the street prostitution that one frequently finds in such booming port cities.

Corinth was extremely wealthy because of its strategic geographical location. It lay on the isthmus connecting the southern mainland of

Greece, the Peloponnesian Peninsula, to the northern border of Greece and the provinces of Macedonia and Epirus, thus commanding access both to the Adriatic Sea on the west and the Aegean Sea on the east. Due to the turbulent waters south of the Peloponnesian Peninsula, many merchants either dry-docked their ships in the harbor on one side to unload their goods and transport them overland to the other harbor, or they paid to have the ship hauled overland—no insignificant task. Corinth's strategic location along both the overland and marine trade routes brought the city great commercial prosperity, increased even more by the city's own industries, such as its bronze and terra-cotta works.[2] As an indication of its commercial importance, in the first century the city boasted a marketplace larger than any in Rome itself.[3] The cream of prosperity flowed into Corinth's cup.

Along with economic prosperity came peace. Upon regaining financial stability, Corinth again began to host the Isthmian Games, in which Greeks and Romans from all over the Empire competed not only in athletics but also in drama, music, and oratory. The Isthmian contests were held every two years and lasted several days, being conducted in Corinth's huge stadium as well as in its two theaters—one outdoors that seated eighteen thousand people and another indoors that held three thousand. These games were not only popular but also known for their extravagance and licentiousness. The games, of course, brought tourism, which, combined with trade and travel, necessitated

Barry Beitzel

Ruins of Corinth along Lechaion Road with the Acrocorinth in the background the establishment of a banking system that further increased the city's wealth. Archaeological research in the past century has provided abundant evidence of the city's splendor, revealing the existence of wealthy neighborhoods, public and private dining, recreational facilities, and upscale rental properties.[4]

## PAUL'S MINISTRY IN CORINTH

The year was AD 50. After a full year of hard travel over land and sea from Antioch, across Asia Minor, and through Macedonia, preaching the gospel with Silas and Timothy, Paul pressed ahead into Athens, the center of Greek philosophy and culture (Acts 15:40–17:15). Having just escaped the ire of Jewish agitators who had hounded him since he was in Thessalonica (Acts 17:1-13), the battle-weary apostle's arrival in Athens could have brought him some much-needed R & R—had he not felt driven by an inescapable passion for proclaiming the risen Lord.

Observing the army of idols assembled in all the public places of Athens, Paul felt "provoked" in his heart and immediately began engaging Jews and Gentiles alike with the truth of Jesus Christ (Acts 17:16-17). Among his listeners were Epicurean and Stoic philosophers—the intellectual elites of the day. They arranged an ad hoc hearing at the Areopagus, also known as "Mars Hill" (Acts 17:19-21). There Paul's preaching gained a number of new believers in Christ, including Dionysius the Areopagite, a member of the city's cultural and social elite (Acts 17:34).

From the famous city of Athens, where even Paul's critics exhibited common courtesies, Paul crossed the narrow Isthmus of Corinth. That two-day journey along the coast of the Saronic Gulf marked a transition from the famous to the infamous—from what most consider the center of Greek intellectual culture to what we would see as the pit of Greek immoral corruption: *from Athens to Corinth*. Nevertheless, Paul's zeal to spread the gospel far outweighed whatever apprehensions he may have had about the abject depravity he was sure to find in that cesspool of self-indulgence.

At the beginning of what could have easily become a dark and demoralizing ministry in Corinth, God provided two bright lights—Aquila and Priscilla. Paul met this Jewish couple, who recently had left Italy when the emperor Claudius ordered all Jews out of Rome (Acts 18:2). In God's providence, the two men shared the trade of tentmaking (Acts 18:3). Drawn together by their Jewish heritage, common trade, and status as displaced residents, Paul, Aquila, and Priscilla struck up

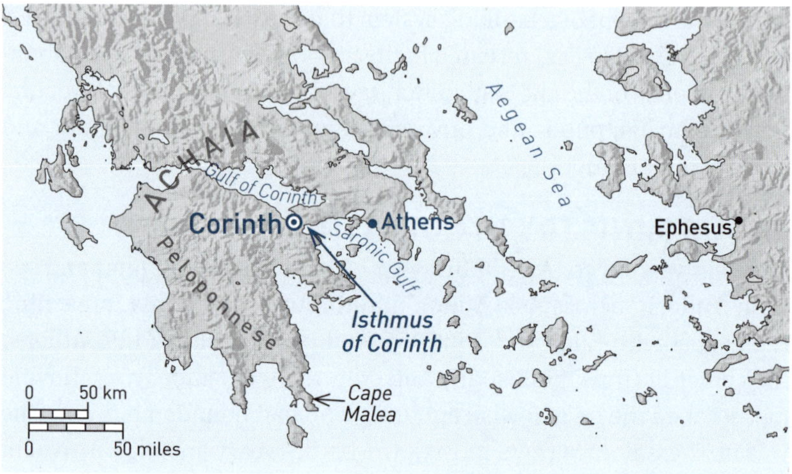


Rome prized **Corinth** because it controlled a strategic intersection of trade. Rather than brave the treacherous journey around Capel Malea, shipowners preferred to drag their ships, cargo and all, across the narrow Isthmus of Corinth. When Paul traveled from Athens to Corinth, he made a similar journey.

a friendship that would last the rest of Paul's life (see Rom. 16:3; 1 Cor. 16:19; 2 Tim. 4:19). Paul discipled them during the week and preached every Sabbath in the synagogue, "trying to persuade Jews and Greeks" that the Messiah anticipated by the Jews was, in fact, Jesus of Nazareth (Acts 18:4-5). Before long the Jewish leaders turned against Paul and he left the synagogue (Acts 18:6-7).

Among Paul's first disciples in Corinth was a Gentile, Titius Justus, a God-fearer whose home hosted the first Corinthian congregation of Christians (Acts 18:7). Also among this group was Crispus, the president of the synagogue, who converted to Christ with his entire household. So, from the very beginning, both Jews and Gentiles comprised the foundational leadership of the church in Corinth (Acts 18:8). Not wanting this budding work to perish and encouraged to press on by a vision of the Lord (Acts 18:9-10), Paul spent a year and a half "teaching the word of God among them" (Acts 18:11).

The bourgeoning work in Corinth, however, soon caught the eye of the enemy, who once again stirred up religious opposition from Jewish legalists (Acts 18:12). Likely believing they would find an ally in Gallio, the newly appointed proconsul of Achaia, Paul's Jewish adversaries brought Paul before the tribunal, charging him with preaching an illegal religion. Yet their hopes at a hearing were dashed when Gallio told the Jews that he refused to meddle in matters of "words and names and your own law" (Acts 18:15). This resulted in a frustrated outbreak of violence against believers in Corinth, which Gallio ignored (Acts 18:16-17).

In the fall of AD 51, Paul left Corinth with Aquila and Priscilla, setting sail for Ephesus (Acts 18:18-19). Those disciples-turned-colleagues remained in Ephesus to carry on their budding ministry while Paul himself traveled on to Caesarea, Jerusalem, and then to his home church in Antioch (Acts 18:22). Aquila and Priscilla's heart for their Corinthian brothers and sisters only grew stronger during their time in Ephesus. In fact, when a well-educated Jew named Apollos arrived in Ephesus boldly preaching what he knew about Jesus, the missionary couple discipled that young teacher, equipping him for a fruitful ministry in Corinth. Acts 18:26-28 describes how Apollos was prepared and sent to Corinth to serve as an influential teacher and apologist in that city:

> But when Priscilla and Aquila heard him, they took him aside and explained to him the way of God more accurately. And when he wanted to go across to Achaia, the brethren encouraged him and wrote to the disciples to welcome him; and when he had arrived, he greatly helped those who had believed through grace, for he powerfully refuted the Jews in public, demonstrating by the Scriptures that Jesus was the Christ.

Barry Beitzel

The *bēma*, or "judgment seat" in Corinth, is the place where cases were decided by Roman law.

While Apollos served in Corinth, Paul returned to Ephesus (Acts 19:1) and began to correspond with the Corinthian church sometime between AD 53 and 55. Paul had written an initial letter to the Corinthian church not long before the letter we call 1 Corinthians. That letter, probably brief, warned the believers "not to associate with immoral people" (1 Cor. 5:9). The teaching of that first letter apparently was misunderstood or misapplied, however, because Paul saw the need to clarify what he meant (5:10-13). We don't have the prequel to 1 Corinthians, probably because 1 Corinthians itself contains all the information originally written in the first letter, but in greater depth. Yet Paul also sought to address a growing number of problems dividing the church—effects of its diverse membership of Jews and Gentiles, its rocky beginnings of persecution, and the corrupt religious and moral culture in which it ministered.

As the lights dim on our own culture and our churches begin to look more and more like the disheveled, self-serving church in Corinth, Paul's words to that fragmented church take on greater import and more urgent practicality.

## OVERVIEW OF FIRST CORINTHIANS

Paul's first letter to the Corinthians consists of seven parts, including a brief introduction. In contrast to 2 Corinthians, which focuses on themes related to ministry and Paul as a gospel minister, 1 Corinthians focuses on healthy church life—both by addressing problems and by calling believers onward in sanctification and the exercise of spiritual gifts. Let's familiarize ourselves with a broad overview of the letter.

*Opening Greeting and Prayer* (1:1-9). As is typical with Paul's letters, 1 Corinthians begins with a general greeting from Paul and Sosthenes (1:1), quite likely the one-time leader of the synagogue in Corinth (Acts 18:17), but now Paul's ministry companion. In this introduction, Paul extends praise where praise is due (1 Cor. 1:4-7), expressing his confidence that God ultimately will confirm their faith to the end (1:8-9). This brief opening, however, quickly leads to a sudden and desperate plea for unity.

*Rebuking Divisions and Folly* (1:10–3:23). In the first of many rebukes, Paul takes aim at the divisions that had formed among the believers in Corinth. He writes, "Now I exhort you, brethren, by the name of our Lord Jesus Christ, that you all agree and that there be no divisions among you, but that you be made complete in the same mind and in the same judgment" (1:10). Part of the problem with the Corinthians was their failure to realize that Christianity is not based on human wisdom, but on revelation from God, given through the person and work of Jesus Christ and through the Holy Spirit (2:1-16). The wisdom of God makes human wisdom seem like folly. And because the ministry of the gospel is ultimately the work of God, not men, the formation of parties based on personalities such as Paul, Peter, and Apollos is rendered ridiculous, as all these men are merely co-laborers through whom God works His miraculous building project (3:1-23).

*Correcting Ills and Immorality* (4:1–6:20). Regrettably, disunity was not the only problem in Corinth. After reasserting his authority as an apostle of Christ (4:1-21), Paul challenges the Corinthians on an issue of gross sexual immorality: "that someone has his father's wife" (5:1). In what follows, Paul outlines the principles and process of church discipline, intended to purge the church of wickedness and purify its people (5:11-13). Besides this, the Corinthian Christians didn't hesitate to sue one another in secular court (6:1-8), and some failed to accompany their conversion to Christianity with a converted lifestyle of sexual purity (6:9-20). In other words, in many ways those churchgoers in Corinth were living more like Corinthians and less like Christians!

*Strengthening Family and Fellowship* (7:1–10:33). Chapter 7 transitions from urgent matters that had come to Paul's attention through messengers (1:11; 5:1) to important matters concerning which the Corinthians themselves had written (7:1). First he addresses issues regarding marriage, singleness, and divorce (7:1-40). Then he answers their questions regarding consuming meat sacrificed to idols and concern for the weaker brother (8:1-13). Using his own lifestyle as an example, Paul urges the Corinthians to selflessly surrender their personal rights for the sake of the gospel (9:1-27). He concludes this section with a reminder of the utter incompatibility of the worship of God through Jesus Christ with the worship of idols and their demonic false gods (10:1-33).

*Ordering Church and Worship* (11:1–14:40). Paul then focuses his attention on the chaotic character of their worship. The Corinthians had failed to exhibit proper order through submission to Christ and to one another (11:1-16), which resulted in self-centered divisions and factions even in the observance of the Lord's Supper (11:17-34). Unsurprisingly, the Corinthians had also exercised spiritual gifts in ways that exhibited personal pride rather than humble deference for one another—the exact opposite of the purpose for which the Holy Spirit gives His gifts (12:1–14:40). Only an attitude of true, selfless, unconditional love could cure their self-centered approach to the Christian life (13:1-13).

*Concerning Death and Resurrection* (15:1-58). If the love chapter in 1 Corinthians 13 is the practical pinnacle of the letter, without a doubt the theological summit of Paul's treatise is 1 Corinthians 15. He begins by reiterating that which is "of first importance"—the message of the gospel of the person and work of Jesus Christ (15:1-11). From this fountainhead of Christian theology—the atoning death and life-giving resurrection of Christ—Paul dives into the depths of the doctrine of our own future resurrection (15:12-58). So vital is this treatment of the faith of the gospel and the hope of the resurrection that this chapter comprises a complete section in our outline of Paul's book.

*Concluding Instructions and Warnings* (16:1-24). Finally, Paul concludes with a few minor matters, concerning neither rebukes nor controversies. He directs them on the proper collection for the saints in Jerusalem (16:1-4). With a few personal remarks, Paul speaks of Timothy's coming to the church in Corinth—emphasizing the value he placed on personal presence and face-to-face interaction (16:5-12) in addition to his authoritative letter. He concludes this great epistle of strong reproofs with an exhortation to stand firm in the faith, with love for the Lord and hope for His coming (16:13-24).

# OPENING GREETING AND PRAYER (1 CORINTHIANS 1:1-9)

We catch the first glimpse of the riches of the church in Corinth in the greeting of the book (1:1-9). Here we learn of the writer and his recipients (1:1-3), the original riches of the church (1:4-7), and then the promised reward for their endurance (1:8-9). When we see the depths to which the church had declined even in the midst of such spiritual wealth, however, this positive description serves merely as a solemn preamble to a sobering tragedy.

## KEY TERMS IN 1 CORINTHIANS 1:1-9

***klētos* (κλητός)** [2822] "called," "named," "invited"
***kaleō* (καλέω)** [2564] "to call," "to name," "to invite"

A noun or verb with the root *kal-* is found four times in the opening greeting and prayer of 1:1-9. It refers to an effectual calling, naming, or summons. Paul was "called" (*klētos*) into service as an apostle (1:1; cf. Rom. 1:1), and the Corinthian believers were "called" (*klētos*) to be holy saints (1 Cor. 1:2) by "calling on" (*epikaleō* [1941]) the name of Jesus Christ (1:2), with whom they were "called" (*kaleō*) into fellowship (1:9). Paul's multiple uses of this term are intended to reinforce the authenticity of the Corinthians' place of salvation in the body of Christ.

***charis* (χάρις)** [5485] "grace," "undeserved or unmerited favor," "cause of delight"

In Greek literature other than the New Testament, this term is closely associated with the word for "joy" and designates good will, favor, pleasure, or delight, as well as the qualities that elicit such dispositions and the actions generated as a result. Much of the New Testament uses the word in this basic sense. Paul, however, uses the word to describe God's unending goodness toward His chosen people and His loyal, abiding love that translates into His faithfulness despite His people's disobedience. In this technical use, "grace" for Paul—who uses this word more than any other New Testament author—specifically refers to undeserved and superabundant blessings that God bestows upon His people—it is this grace that brings salvation and sanctification.

# Starting with Spiritual Riches
## 1 CORINTHIANS 1:1-9

**NASB**

1 Paul, called *as* an apostle of Jesus
Christ [a]by the will of God, and Sos-
thenes our brother,
2 To the church of God which is
at Corinth, to those who have been
sanctified in Christ Jesus, [a]saints by
calling, with all who in every place
call on the name of our Lord Jesus
Christ, their *Lord* and ours:
3 Grace to you and peace from God
our Father and the Lord Jesus Christ.
4 I thank [a]my God always concern-
ing you for the grace of God which
was given you in Christ Jesus, 5 that
in everything you were enriched in
Him, in all speech and all knowledge,
6 even as the testimony concerning
Christ was confirmed [a]in you, 7 so
that you are not lacking in any gift,
awaiting eagerly the revelation of
our Lord Jesus Christ, 8 who will also
confirm you to the end, blameless
in the day of our Lord Jesus Christ.
9 God is faithful, through whom you
were called into fellowship with His
Son, Jesus Christ our Lord.

**1:1** [a]Lit *through* **1:2** [a]Or *holy ones* **1:4** [a]Two early mss do not contain *my* **1:6** [a]Or *among*

**NLT**

1 This letter is from Paul, chosen by
the will of God to be an apostle of
Christ Jesus, and from our brother
Sosthenes.
2 I am writing to God's church
in Corinth,* to you who have been
called by God to be his own holy
people. He made you holy by means
of Christ Jesus,* just as he did for all
people everywhere who call on the
name of our Lord Jesus Christ, their
Lord and ours.
3 May God our Father and the
Lord Jesus Christ give you grace and
peace.
4 I always thank my God for you
and for the gracious gifts he has
given you, now that you belong to
Christ Jesus. 5 Through him, God
has enriched your church in every
way—with all of your eloquent
words and all of your knowledge.
6 This confirms that what I told you
about Christ is true. 7 Now you have
every spiritual gift you need as you
eagerly wait for the return of our
Lord Jesus Christ. 8 He will keep you
strong to the end so that you will be
free from all blame on the day when
our Lord Jesus Christ returns. 9 God
will do this, for he is faithful to do
what he says, and he has invited you
into partnership with his Son, Jesus
Christ our Lord.

**1:2a** *Corinth* was the capital city of Achaia, the southern region of the Greek peninsula. **1:2b** Or *because you belong to Christ Jesus.*

The life of Edgar Allan Poe is one of the most tragic of all American writers. Within a brief span of forty years he literally went from riches to rags. Raised by foster parents who loved him deeply, he received an education that matched his genius in his field of interest. He attended private schools in England, studied at the University of Virginia, and even spent a period of time as a cadet at West Point.

In his heyday, few rivaled Poe's genius as a literary critic, editor, poet, and author of short stories, especially his dramatic thrillers. Most of us have read his spine-tingling tales, *The Pit and the Pendulum*, *The Tell-Tale Heart*, and *The Raven*. Indeed, Poe's works have left their mark on American literature and life.

Yet the mark left by his lifestyle is another tale worth telling. Losing his young bride to tuberculosis, Poe descended into a deep pit of despair, which he attempted to assuage through drugs, alcohol, and the occult. Depression and insanity plagued his short life, eventually leaving him unconscious in the gutter of a windswept street in Baltimore. He never regained consciousness, and four days later he died.

Poe began his life with brilliance, giftedness, opportunity, fame, and riches. Yet the end of his life overflowed with bitterness, poverty, moral depravity, and spiritual destitution. From prestigious bard to penniless bum—that was the tragic tale of Edgar Allan Poe.

This ruinous journey from riches to rags happens not only to individuals but also to churches. The church at Corinth stands as a tragic example. Its rich beginning made it seem invincible: a dynamic and diverse membership gilded with spiritual gifts at a crossroads of commerce and culture that poised them for a powerful impact in world missions. Yet like Poe, within a brief period of time the church at Corinth declined into mediocrity and chaos, as the weight of sin pulled its members deep into the mire of shame.

## — 1:1-3 —

As is typical in his epistles, Paul identifies himself in the opening of the letter, reminding the Corinthians of his position as an apostle of Jesus Christ (1:1). No doubt just the mention of his name, "Paul," would have caused the believers in Corinth to flash back to years before, when he helped them take their first baby steps in the faith. They knew him quite well; so why would Paul need to remind them that he had been "called (*klētos* [2822]) as an apostle"? The occasion of this letter would necessitate a series of severe criticisms, rebukes, words of strong admonition, and detailed instructions. By reminding the Corinthians that he was not only their founding pastor of yesteryear but also an apostle of the universal church, he would firm up his authority at a time when it most likely would be resisted.

The apostle Paul had seen the resurrected Christ with his own eyes and received his apostolic commission directly from the Savior Himself (Acts 26:13-19), who confirmed it also to the prophet Ananias

(Acts 9:15). Afterward, Paul had the authority and power to heal, to discern good and evil, and to speak boldly, free from doctrinal error (Acts 9:22; 13:9-10; 19:11-12; 1 Cor. 2:13). As an apostle, Paul answered to no higher human authority, only to God directly. He manifested a healthy independence. He valued God's favor far more than the favor of men (Gal. 1:10).

In his greeting, Paul also includes "Sosthenes our brother" (1 Cor. 1:1); the Greek text says simply, "Sosthenes the brother." We can't be sure what role Sosthenes played in writing 1 Corinthians. Some believe he served as Paul's secretary, called an *amanuensis*, who wrote Paul's dictated words.[1] The name appears in Acts 18:17 as "the leader of the synagogue" in Corinth. If this is the same person, he obviously had been converted to Christ and later joined Paul in Ephesus. In any case, the Christians in Corinth knew this man by name. Throughout the letter, Paul mostly refers to himself in the first person singular, "I," indicating that he meant the letter to be understood as coming from him, not from Sosthenes or from both of them as a ministry team.[2]

Following a style typical of ancient epistles, Paul next identifies the recipients of the letter (1 Cor. 1:2). He first calls them "the church of God" (1:2). The Greek word for church, *ekklēsia* [1577], refers to an "assembly." It can sometimes mean a general social or political assembly (Acts 19:32, 41), but from the tip of Paul's pen that generic term for an ordered gathering carries significant theological weight. It most often refers to a local membership of a church in a particular city—the people of a specific congregation (Rom. 16:1; 1 Thes. 1:1; Rev. 2:1, 8, 12, etc.), but it can also indicate the "regional church" made up of all the believers and local churches in a named region (Acts 9:31; 1 Cor. 16:19). The term is also used for the entirety of Christianity spread throughout the whole world (Eph. 1:22–23; 3:10; Col. 1:18, 24). Clearly, the church in Paul's mind is not brick and mortar, stained glass, pipe organs, and padded pews, but the body of people saved through faith in Christ and called together to live in community with one another. In fact, at its root the Greek word *ekklēsia* means "called out." In application to the church, the idea is of a special group called out from the world to be part of a new corporate body under the headship of Christ. So, in a very real sense, we bring the church with us when we enter our places of worship; and we take the church with us when we return to the world. We believers *are* the church.

Paul also addresses the Corinthians as "sanctified in Christ Jesus" (1 Cor. 1:2). This means they were "set apart by God to be his holy people."[3] For the sake of clarity, theologians speak of "justification" as the past, one-time event of our salvation; "sanctification" as the ongoing transformation that continues throughout a believer's life; and "glorification" as the future consummation of our salvation when we are resurrected in glorified, imperishable bodies. Though the Bible clearly portrays these past, present, and future aspects of salvation, it does not always use consistent language to describe each of these phases. Paul uses the term "sanctification" (1:2) to refer to the initial, unrepeated "setting apart" of people in the eyes of God, also called "positional sanctification." The result of this permanent setting apart is that believers are now "saints by calling" (1:2).[4] Related to "sanctified," the saint is one who is devoted, consecrated, pure, and holy in God's eyes, uniquely set apart for His use regardless of the saint's practical holiness from day to day.

Paul acknowledges that his letter to the Corinthians would have a much broader application to "all who in every place call on the name of our Lord Jesus Christ, their Lord and ours" (1:2). Because every believer throughout the world is part of the same universal body of Christ and because the Holy Spirit that spoke through Paul's letter to the Corinthians speaks to all believers of every age, Paul's words to the local church in Corinth are able to transcend the geographical and historical boundaries in which they were originally written. In other words, this letter is as much for you and me in the twenty-first century as it was for the Corinthians in the first.

Paul reveals the Corinthians' deepest needs: "grace to you and peace from God our Father and the Lord Jesus Christ" (1:3). Though this is a common greeting in Paul's epistles (Rom. 1:7; 2 Cor. 1:2; Gal. 1:3; etc.), the blessing of "grace" and "peace" would have had particular meaning for Christians and for the Corinthian church in particular. Paul is not referring to the saving grace that transferred them from spiritual death to spiritual life (as in Eph. 2:8-9; Col. 1:13), nor to the eternal peace a saved sinner has with God through justification by faith in the finished work of Jesus Christ (Rom. 5:1). The "grace and peace" Paul mentions should have brought to mind those virtues of the Christian life that must be present to maintain church harmony. As the rest of this letter will demonstrate, Paul wants the Corinthians to be known as gracious saints who lived at peace with one another.

In the next section (1 Cor.1:10-17), we'll see exactly why the Corinthian Christians especially needed a measure of grace and peace from the hand of God. Yet before reprimanding them for the things they did wrong, Paul first praised the troubled church for the things they did right.

## — 1:4-7 —

A well-known principle of interpersonal communication skills says that whenever we need to confront or correct someone, we should begin by pointing out the things we appreciate about that individual.[5] For expert communicators, this kind of approach flows naturally because they have a genuine concern for the person's well-being. It shouldn't surprise us to see this wise, tactful approach exhibited in the writing of the apostle Paul. In view of Paul's sincere estimation of the spiritual goodness of the church in Corinth, one commentator writes:

> Paul looks at the Corinthian church as it is *in Christ* before he looks at anything else that is true of the church. That disciplined statement of faith is rarely made in local churches. The warts are examined and lamented, but often there is no vision of what God has already done in Christ. If the first nine verses of this letter were excised from the text, it would be impossible for any reader to come to anything but a fairly pessimistic view of the church at Corinth.[6]

Paul isn't just blowing smoke when he lists the five positives of the church in Corinth. As the church's founding apostle, Paul had spent considerable time teaching, preaching, training, and shepherding those new believers. He knew many of their strengths firsthand, and he had learned of their more recent failures and shortcomings only by word of mouth. So, before launching into his letter of strong rebuke, Paul writes, "I thank my God always concerning you" (1:4), and then proceeds to name some things about the Corinthian church for which he was very grateful.

First, *the Corinthians were genuinely saved* (1:4). The basis of Paul's gratitude is grace (*charis* [5485])—the goodness and favor God lavished on the Corinthians even though they could never earn it or repay it. Whereas the "grace and peace" from God and Christ mentioned in 1:3 refers to the ongoing grace needed to live the Christian life, the "grace of God" in 1:4 is something that had been given to the Corinthians in the past. The Greek grammar indicates that this particular gift of God's grace *was given* "in Christ Jesus." This means that Paul had full confidence that the Corinthians had genuinely experienced God's unmerited *saving* grace, receiving His gift of salvation by trusting in Jesus Christ.

Second, *the Corinthians were liberally endowed* (1:5). Not only were they saved, but they also were endowed with eloquence and knowledge. They knew the gospel of Jesus Christ. They understood it clearly and could articulate it effectively. If you or I lived in that day and stepped into a meeting of the church in Corinth, we could count on a well-presented message from God's Word. In fact, Paul uses the word "enriched" to describe their condition. This term often refers to monetary wealth, but here it refers to spiritual riches. Imagine having the apostle Paul as the founder of *your* church. Then suppose Apollos, a man "mighty in the Scriptures," continued the work among you. What if Peter himself contributed to your spiritual growth along the way? That's what we would call spiritual riches!

Third, *the Corinthians were securely established* (1:6). Paul says, "The testimony concerning Christ was confirmed in you." *Confirmed* means "established," "made sure," "authenticated." Elsewhere in the New Testament the same Greek word refers to the miraculous signs and wonders that God used to *confirm* the gospel preached by the apostles (Mark 16:20; Heb. 2:3). Paul had personally spent a year and a half of his life establishing a firm foundation for their faith (1 Cor. 3:10). This is the real tragedy of Corinth. It's not as if they had never heard the apostolic testimony concerning Jesus Christ. In fact, they had heard it from the best, and Paul had personally authenticated the earlier soundness of their faith.

Fourth, *the Corinthians were spiritually gifted* (1:7). Don't miss the "so that" at the beginning of the verse. That little connective refers to the result of the previous verse. As a result of the Corinthians' genuine saving faith, they did not lack any spiritual gifts. That must have been something to behold! Not a single gift was absent, and the positive tone of this section suggests that they had at times been exercising those gifts properly.

Fifth, *the Corinthians were prophetically alert* (1:7). As they exercised their spiritual gifts, Paul says they were also "awaiting eagerly the revelation of our Lord Jesus Christ." They knew Christ's coming could occur at any moment, so they were engaged in an urgent ministry in light of that prophetic reality. Because eternity drew nearer every day, they lived in earnest anticipation of that moment when they would see His face (compare Rom. 8:19, 23; Phil. 3:20).

## — 1:8-9 —

The kind of vitality that characterized the Corinthian church results in two rewards that Paul mentions in 1:8-9. The first reward deals with the believer's future: Christ "will also confirm you to the end, blameless in the day of our Lord Jesus Christ" (1:8). Despite our current status as unrelenting sinners, in eternity we will be *blameless*. The word means to be beyond accusation. This will occur "in the day" Christ returns—that is, at the very time of His coming. We know from other Scriptures that this coincides with the believers' resurrection, when our earthly bodies, subject to sin, suffering, and death, will be miraculously transformed into perfect, immortal bodies like Christ's resurrection body (Phil. 3:21; 1 Thes. 4:16-17; 1 Cor. 15:51-54). In our new, glorified state, nobody in heaven or in hell will be able to hold anything over our heads. We will be perfect and blameless before Him (Jude 1:24).

As we wait eagerly for that glorious day, we can enjoy the second blessing in the here and now: "God is faithful, through whom you were called into fellowship with His Son, Jesus Christ our Lord" (1 Cor. 1:9). Based solely on His sovereign grace (Eph. 2:8-9), God called us into an eternal relationship with Christ that began the moment we first believed. The permanence of this relationship is based not on our own efforts, but wholly on the faithfulness of God. God will "confirm" believers "to the end" (1 Cor. 1:8), and Paul reminds us that "God is faithful" (1:9). So, a second reward of enduring fellowship can be experienced every day of our Christian lives with the promise that He will never desert us nor forsake us (Rom. 8:38-39; Heb. 13:5).

## APPLICATION: 1 CORINTHIANS 1:1-9

### Starting Great, Finishing Well

We could focus on numerous practical principles based on this opening salutation of 1 Corinthians. But let me emphasize one in particular we need to remember: *a rich and impressive beginning does not guarantee the same kind of ending.*

We all know the saying, "The bigger they are, the harder they fall," but you may not have heard the similar slogan: the bigger they *think* they are, the harder they fall. As Proverbs 16:18 says, "Pride goes before destruction, and a haughty spirit before stumbling."

The Corinthian church began the marathon of the Christian life ahead of the pack in many ways. Nobody in that age could measure up to the church's level of giftedness, enthusiasm, and breadth of diversity.

These, however, resulted in opportunities for a colossal pride, which led to selfishness and envy, which in turn ended in division and conflict. The Corinthians had let their spiritual vitality go to their heads. The result? They got knocked off their high horses by their own pride.

All of us have the same potential for inflated self-importance. Many of God's people have been endowed with great spiritual gifts, magnetic personalities, material wealth, privileged experiences, exceptional training, and excellent opportunities. Rather than taking these things as gifts from God for the purpose of serving Him through building up His church, we listen instead as the world, the flesh, and the devil sing a different song in perfect harmony: "Look what you've accomplished! It's time you get some recognition! Let people know what you're capable of! Show them who's number one!"

Let this be a warning to us. Just as the Corinthian church crumbled into calamity, so can we. If our God-given possessions or positions lead us to pride, God may step in and take these things away. The fact that we may have started out well on our Christian walk doesn't mean that we will finish well. Yes, we will always have the promise of eternal salvation, which can never be taken away (John 10:28), but each day we must renew our commitment to pursue a holy life, free from poisonous pride and crippling carnality.

# REBUKING DIVISIONS AND FOLLY (1 CORINTHIANS 1:10–3:23)

"God is faithful, through whom you were called into fellowship with His Son, Jesus Christ our Lord" (1:9). After these inspiring words from Paul's greeting to the church in Corinth, the letter could have taken any number of turns. The apostle could have penned a magnificent treatise on the gospel of grace, as he did in the letter to the Romans. Or he could have defended the true grace of God against the works-mongering Judaizers, as in the brief but powerful letter to the Galatians. His words could have touched on practical living in light of the coming of Christ, as they did in the first letter to the church in Thessalonica. With the glowing praise we see in 1:1-9, the original readers might have expected a positive, encouraging, even inspiring epistle from the hand of their founding apostle.

This letter, however, was not addressed to the church in Rome, Galatia, or Thessalonica, but to the church in Corinth, which was in deep trouble. So Paul's positive appraisal in his introductory greeting suddenly gives way to a strong rebuke against divisions and worldly folly (1:10–3:23).

With a few exceptions, the next sixteen chapters of 1 Corinthians march like a parade of strong reproofs for a scandalous church. In this first section, Paul takes aim at the divisions that had formed among the believers in Corinth: "Now I exhort you, brethren . . . that you all agree and that there be no divisions among you, but that you be made complete in the same mind and in the same judgment" (1:10). A major source of many of their problems was their tendency toward exalting human wisdom rather than exulting in the revelation of God in Jesus Christ (2:1-16). Had the Corinthians embraced the church as a work of God rather than the work of mere humans, the parties that had formed around Paul, Peter, and Apollos would have been seen for the folly they were (3:1-23).

## KEY TERMS IN 1 CORINTHIANS 1:10–3:23

***mōros* (μωρός)** [3474] "foolish"
***mōria* (μωρία)** [3472] "foolishness"
Our English word "moron" comes from the Greek word for "foolish," *mōros*. The word is always a term of reproach and can mean "stupid," "irrational," or "lacking foresight." In Paul's use of the term in 1 Corinthians, the sense of the word becomes a matter of one's perspective, as the crucified Christ (1:23) and the things of the Spirit (2:14) are foolishness to unbelievers. Likewise, the message of the cross appears senseless to Greek philosophy (1:18). On the other hand, the greatest wisdom of the world is "foolishness" (*mōria*) from God's perspective (3:19).

***sophia* (σοφία)** [4678] "wisdom"
***sophos* (σοφός)** [4680] "wise man"
Though "wisdom" was most often used in a positive sense among both Jews and Greeks, Paul sometimes uses the words *sophia* ("wisdom") and *sophos* ("wise man") in a negative sense with regard to worldly or secular wisdom pursued apart from God (1:20), and in phrases such as "cleverness (*sophia*) of speech," implying tricky rhetorical strategies devoid of substance (1:17). Yet Paul makes it clear that not all wisdom is suspect—only the "wisdom of the world" that sets itself up against the "wisdom of God" (1:20-21). Care must be taken that believers follow the truly wise, who are enlightened by divine wisdom rather than the worldly wise, who are, in fact, "foolish."

# How to Split a Church

## 1 CORINTHIANS 1:10-17

NASB

10 Now I exhort you, brethren, by the
name of our Lord Jesus Christ, that
you all [a]agree and that there be no
[b]divisions among you, but that you
be [c]made complete in the same mind
and in the same judgment. 11 For
I have been informed concerning
you, my brethren, by Chloe's *people*,
that there are quarrels among you.
12 Now I mean this, that each one of
you is saying, "I am of Paul," and
"I of Apollos," and "I of Cephas,"
and "I of Christ." 13 [a]Has Christ been

NLT

10 I appeal to you, dear brothers and
sisters,* by the authority of our Lord
Jesus Christ, to live in harmony with
each other. Let there be no divisions
in the church. Rather, be of one
mind, united in thought and purpose. 11 For some members of Chloe's
household have told me about your
quarrels, my dear brothers and sisters. 12 Some of you are saying, "I am
a follower of Paul." Others are saying, "I follow Apollos," or "I follow
Peter,*" or "I follow only Christ."
13 Has Christ been divided into

**NASB**

divided? Paul was not crucified for
you, was he? Or were you baptized
[b]in the name of Paul? 14 [a]I thank God
that I baptized none of you except
Crispus and Gaius, 15 so that no one
would say you were baptized [a]in my
name. 16 Now I did baptize also the
household of Stephanas; beyond
that, I do not know whether I bap-
tized any other. 17 For Christ did not
send me to baptize, but to preach the
gospel, not in [a]cleverness of speech,
so that the cross of Christ would not
be made void.

**1:10** [a]Lit *speak the same thing* [b]Lit *schisms* [c]Or *united* **1:13** [a]Or *Christ has been divided!* or *Christ is divided!* [b]Lit *into* **1:14** [a]Two early mss read *I give thanks that* **1:15** [a]Lit *into* **1:17** [a]Lit *wisdom*

**NLT**

factions? Was I, Paul, crucified for
you? Were any of you baptized in
the name of Paul? Of course not!
14 I thank God that I did not bap-
tize any of you except Crispus and
Gaius, 15 for now no one can say they
were baptized in my name. 16 (Oh
yes, I also baptized the household
of Stephanas, but I don't remember
baptizing anyone else.) 17 For Christ
didn't send me to baptize, but to
preach the Good News—and not with
clever speech, for fear that the cross
of Christ would lose its power.

**1:10** Greek *brothers;* also in 1:11, 26. **1:12** Greek *Cephas.*

When I was a young man, people spoke of divorce in the most hushed tones . . . a dark and secret tragedy in the same category as teenage pregnancies or mental illnesses—something that happened only to a distant relative or the unfaithful neighbor down the street. Times have certainly changed! Many of us have felt the devastating fallout from this domestic explosion. Debris from the impact of two colliding wills flies indiscriminately and often lands on the most innocent—the children.

Like the breakup of a marriage, so a congregational divorce is painful and tragic—especially for babes in the Lord who look to their spiritual family for security and stability. I'm convinced that nothing breaks the heart of God like the splintering of a church. Nothing cuts to the quick more than disharmony, unrest, and division among God's people. You and I can count over the past ten years literally dozens of once thriving churches that are now split, divided, filled with dissension. Hate has replaced love. Chaos has driven out peace.

In Paul's day, the church at Corinth teetered on the brink of congregational divorce. From a distance, Paul discerned those cracks of conflict that ultimately could lead to a collapse. He felt so vexed by the news of the church's distressed condition that he couldn't keep silent. The result? A passionate plea for the Corinthians to reconcile—to leave their selfish desires and renew their vows of commitment by cleaving to each other in the Lord Jesus Christ.

## — 1:10 —

We've all heard the word "exhortation." Sometimes we confuse the term with "sharp rebuke," but the Greek word *parakaleō* [3870], which it often translates, simply means "to call to one's side" for the purpose of counsel or encouragement. In other words, rather than approach the wayward Corinthians with the attitude of a father about to take his child out behind the woodshed, he's calling them aside to speak words of wise counsel, encouraging them toward the right path before it is too late. We need to read Paul's words as motivated by genuine love and concern, not by anger and frustration.

This is why Paul reminds his readers of his love by calling them, "brethren" (1:10). He reaches out to them tenderly, as if drawing them together for a family meeting. Yet his words also carry the authority of an older brother charged with being head of the household. As an apostle, Paul could exhort them "by the name of our Lord Jesus Christ"—that is, based on the Lord's authority and power. Compelled by his love for them and using his authority to speak in Christ's name, Paul urgently calls on the Corinthians to put an end to their divisions and to reconcile with one another.

Paul's passionate exhortation has two sides—they are to stop being divided and instead, be united. He urges them to rid themselves of the "divisions" among them. The word "divisions" is the Greek word *schisma* [4978], from which we get English words like "schisms" or "scissors." It refers to a tear, cleft, or split. The same word is used in Matthew 9:16 in reference to a tear in a garment. The Corinthian church suffered from rupture, division, and brokenness.

Paul addresses the worsening problem of schism with two positive exhortations: "that you all agree . . . [and] that you be made complete in the same mind and in the same judgment" (1 Cor. 1:10). Notice the emphasis on the internal realm of the mind. Paul desires that even in the midst of diversity, there would be harmony of attitude, agreement on the essentials of the faith, and single-mindedness of purpose. In this way they would be "complete." The verb *katartizō* [2675], translated "be made complete," is the same word used in Matthew 4:21 for mending nets. What a perfect image for mending the broken relationships that had been torn apart through disagreement, disharmony, and unresolved conflict.

Before we move on, we need to remind ourselves about taking this verse to an extreme. Paul recognized the impossibility of establishing complete uniformity of belief and practice in any church (see Rom. 14:1-5). In fact, 1 Corinthians 12–14 makes it clear that God never intended for the church to reflect a rigid uniformity. God is not interested in manufacturing tin soldiers who look exactly alike. The goal is unity, not uniformity. Variety in the ranks reflects the power and glory of God. Neither division and conflict on the one hand, nor zombie-like uniformity on the other, can reflect God's ideal for a local church. He longs for unity in diversity.

## — 1:11-16 —

Paul moves swiftly from generalities in 1:10 to specifics in 1:11-16. Basing his admonition on the account he received from "Chloe's people" (1:11), he addresses three major problems in Corinth: their quarrels (1:11), their cliques (1:12), and finally their conceit (1:13-16). Let's look at the details of each of these sources of division.

*Their quarrels* (1:11). In the first place, Paul mentions the frequent squabbling among the believers in Corinth. The Greek for "quarrels" is *eris* [2054], which means strife, discord, or wrangling. Yet Paul's use goes beyond mere bickering or minor disagreements. In fact, the word *eris* is condemned in the vice list of Galatians 5:19-21 among serious sins such as immorality, idolatry, and drunkenness; Paul states that "those who practice such things will not inherit the kingdom of God" (Gal. 5:21). In other words, Paul viewed quarreling as a severe spiritual problem, which, if not dealt with decisively, would lead to ruin for the church.

Paul, however, doesn't blame Satan for their quarrelling. Too often the devil gets credit for sins we humans accomplish by our own fleshly desires. Ultimately Satan is behind all evil as its originator (Gen. 3), but people frequently forget that the world and the flesh also contribute to our sinfulness. No wonder Paul places the blame at the Corinthians' feet, pointing out that their spiritual immaturity had created the conflict: "For since there is jealousy and strife among you, are you not fleshly, and are you not walking like mere men?" (1 Cor. 3:3). James also highlighted the source of the kinds of quarrels and conflicts experienced at Corinth: "What is the source of quarrels and conflicts among you? Is not the source your pleasures that wage war in your members? You lust and do not have; so you commit murder. You are envious and cannot obtain; so you fight and quarrel" (Jas. 4:1-2).

The intense quarrelling of the carnal Corinthians led to the second major problem.

*Their cliques* (1 Cor. 1:12). Paul names four factions that were tearing the Corinthians apart. It's understandable that many at Corinth aligned themselves with the "Paulite Party." From Paul's lips they first heard the good news about Jesus Christ (15:3). Because Paul's preaching emphasized freedom from the Law, however, it is possible that this group had begun to turn grace into a green light for the flesh. In any case, those "Paulites" in Corinth were doing something similar to those today who might emphasize just a few verses from Paul's letters, neglecting the fuller teaching we get from James, John, Peter, and the rest of the Bible.

Though the followers of Paul may have enjoyed a majority in Corinth, after Paul left the church, Apollos arrived and "helped greatly those who had believed through grace, for he powerfully refuted the Jews in public, demonstrating by the Scriptures that Jesus was the Christ" (Acts 18:27-28). Apollos was not only intellectually astute; he was verbally eloquent. Greeks especially would have flocked to him, enamored as they were with the skills of keen logic and impressive rhetoric. Thus was born what we might call the "Apollos Fan Club." In light of such an articulate teacher, even Paul's style would have appeared crude and unsophisticated (2 Cor. 10:10; 11:6). Although Paul and Apollos were colleagues rather than competitors (1 Cor. 3:6-9), some overzealous followers held up Apollos as their highbrowed hero, creating friction in the Corinthian congregation (1:12).

The situation, though, had grown more complex than an imaginary duel between two gifted teachers. Paul mentions a third group—let's call them the "Cephas Clan"—followers of the apostle Peter. Peter was perhaps the most prominent among the original twelve disciples, and he exercised considerable influence in the Aramaic-speaking Jewish Christian community. In fact, it may be that Paul uses the Aramaic version of the name "Peter" ("Cephas") in order to highlight that this particular clan of Peter-followers was a contingent of Jewish Christians in Corinth, as Peter was the missionary entrusted with the gospel for the Jews (Gal. 2:7-9). For them, Paul's views on the Law would likely have been perceived as too "progressive," and Apollos's teaching style would have been regarded as too "Gentile." With Peter's credentials as an eyewitness to Christ, no wonder a faithful following would have formed around him (1 Cor. 1:12).

As if three competing sects in the Corinthian church weren't enough to wreak havoc, Paul adds a fourth to his catalogue of clubs. The "Christ Faction" had no need for mere men—neither Paul, nor Apollos, nor Peter. Instead, they were simple followers of Christ. At first glance, we might think, *What's wrong with that? Shouldn't they all have been striving for that?* But because Paul lists them among the other unacceptable sects, the group of Christ followers must have taken their single devotion to Christ to an unhealthy extreme by rejecting all other church authorities, including those appointed by Christ. Perhaps they forgot that though the church was founded with Christ as the "corner stone," the apostles and prophets constituted the church's "foundation" (Eph. 2:20). Nobody could claim independent devotion to Christ while breaking from His chosen apostles. It may be that the Christ Faction had unwittingly begun to behave as though *Christ* belonged only to *them*, while claiming that *they alone* belonged to *Christ*.

After mentioning these cliques, Paul points out the root of these sinful divisions: pride.

*Their conceit* (1 Cor. 1:13-16). Pride fueled the embers of the Corinthians' quarrels and cliques, fanning them into a flame that could easily have consumed that young congregation. They expressed their pride by boasting about who had baptized them (1:13). Apparently they had come to believe that the authenticity of their faith rested not only on baptism, but also on their baptizer. Amazingly, in the midst of conflict, this ordinance of Christ that should have marked the believers' *unity* in one body (Eph. 4:4-6) had deteriorated into a basis for arrogant *boasting*.

Paul sharply challenges their bragging. Contesting his very own "Paulite Party," he points out two obvious points: Paul had not died for their sins, and no one had been baptized in the name of Paul (1 Cor. 1:13). Paul had personally baptized very few of the converts in Corinth: only Crispus, Gaius, and the household of Stephanas (1:14, 16), and here he thanks God that he had *not* baptized any others. Paul is not bad-mouthing baptism, putting it down, or declaring it a useless ritual; rather, he expresses relief that he hadn't personally baptized many of the new Christians because of the specific situation in Corinth: "so that no one would say you were baptized in my name" (1:15).

Pride exhibits itself in so many astonishing ways! Of all things to brag about—the Corinthians puffed up their chests over who laid their hands on them and spoke the name "of the Father and the Son and the Holy Spirit" (cf. Matt 28:19). Clearly, they had lost focus. They allowed the act of baptism as their visible response to the gospel message to overshadow the message of the Father who sent His Son to die for their sins, rise from the dead, and give them new life by the Spirit. When conceited, quarrelling cliques erupt into controversy in a local church, pride stops at nothing.

## Picking Nits

**1 CORINTHIANS 1:13**

*I once learned of two congregations of differing denominations located only a few blocks from each other in a small community. They thought it might be better if they would merge and become one united body, larger and more effective, rather than two struggling churches. A good idea, but both churches proved too petty to pull it off. The problem? They couldn't agree on how they would recite the Lord's Prayer! One group wanted "forgive us our trespasses" while the other demanded "forgive us our debts." So the newspaper reported that one church went back to its trespasses while the other returned to its debts!*

*Several years ago I read of two unmarried sisters who lived together. Because of a slight disagreement over an insignificant issue, they stopped speaking to each other. Unable and unwilling to move out of their small house, they continued to use the same rooms, eat at the same table, and sleep in the same bedroom, all without speaking one word to each other. A chalk line divided the sleeping area into two halves, separating a doorway and fireplace. Each could come and go, cook and eat, sew and read without crossing over into her sister's domain, and neither was willing to take the first step to forgiveness and reconciliation.*

*Such silly skirmishes would be funny if they weren't so prevalent in our own churches and in our own relationships with brothers and sisters in Christ. It's one thing to stand firm on major issues clearly set forth in Scripture; it's another thing to pick fights over jots and tittles. I never cease to be amazed at how petty we Christians can act over things that really don't amount to a hill of beans. But there we stand, ramrod rigid, nose to nose, as if heaven were holding its breath.*

*While ministering at a Bible conference one summer, I waded into this touchy subject. Afterwards it concerned me to hear from*

(continued on next page)

*many in attendance that they had similar convictions but didn't feel free to say so since their pastors kept fanning personal flames and picking scabs off old sores. We preachers can be awfully petty, taking pot shots in sermons when we know nobody can answer back, or shooting jabs and pounding the pulpit on minor matters that make our real adversary (the devil) yawn and smile! Instead of equipping and edifying the saints with solid, well-documented, carefully applied truth from the Book, many would rather promote an exclusive emphasis that is divisive, argumentative, and blindly opinionated.*

*So long as our knowledge is imperfect, our preferences vary, and our opinions differ, we should leave a lot of room in areas that don't really matter. Diversity and variety provide the body with a beautifully blended balance. But a squint-eyed, severe spirit is a killer, strangling its victims with a noose of caustic criticism.*

*All of this calls for a direct and significant question: How much freedom do you allow others to enjoy?*

## —1:17—

At the climax of this sharp exhortation to forsake their quarrelling, their cliques, and their conceit, Paul redirects their attention to the most central thing—the thing that should hold them together in one mind: the gospel. "For Christ did not send me to baptize, but to preach the gospel, not in cleverness of speech, so that the cross of Christ would not be made void" (1:17). Paul didn't go to Corinth to put on a show. He didn't parade his abilities. He didn't turn the spotlight onto himself. In fact, he delegated the work of baptism to others in order to free himself up to keep doing what he was called to do: preach the gospel. Paul also reminds them that he didn't preach that message with eloquent words, rhetorical skill, or "cleverness of speech." To do so would have turned their attention away from the message and onto the messenger.

One commentator wisely notes, "To decorate the story of the cross with rhetoric and cleverness would have been to make people think more of the language than of the facts."[1]

The gospel of Christ's person and work should stand at the center of everything we think, say, and do. Sadly, too many of us have lost sight of this all-important truth. Today, people are mesmerized by "rock-star preachers" who can attract a crowd, rev up the audience, and put on a good show. In our entertainment-driven culture, the Word of God often gets banished to the backstage while flash and jazz take center stage, forcing their way into the limelight. What a tragedy! The apostle Paul couldn't have been clearer: When you glorify the messenger, you distract people from the message.

## APPLICATION: 1 CORINTHIANS 1:10-17

### Turning Your Eyes upon Jesus

As the church in Corinth began to go up in flames of controversy and conflict, the apostle Paul stepped in and began to douse the flames with an urgent plea. As we look back from our twenty-first-century vantage point to observe how Paul handled that first-century crisis, we can learn some vital lessons for our own day. Rising from the ashes of that congregation's smoldering relationships, there is a vital practical truth that will help us avoid the disaster of disunity in our local church bodies: *We must focus fully on Christ.*

When we take our focus off Christ, our gaze necessarily fixes on something else—selfish pursuits, personal opinions, marginal issues, or favorite personalities, to name a few. This misplaced focus leads to divisions. Divisions produce quarrels. Quarrels bring cliques. And cliques are just platoons awaiting orders to strike! In other words, when church members fail to focus fully on Christ, the result will be controversy and conflict. Our response to this truth? The old chorus puts it best:

> Turn your eyes upon Jesus,
> Look full in His wonderful face,
> And the things of earth will grow strangely dim
> In the light of His glory and grace.[2]

Hebrews 12:1-2 says, "Let us also lay aside every encumbrance and the sin which so easily entangles us, and let us run with endurance the race that is set before us, fixing our eyes on Jesus, the Author and Perfecter of faith."

Where is your focus today? Is Christ the center of the picture, or is His image beginning to blur? Take time to refocus your life as you consider these four common distractions that turn our eyes away from Him, leading to selfish ambition, division, and conflict. Pause and ask yourself these questions:

First, *have I fixed my eyes on mere things?* This invariably leads to materialism, the unquenchable lust for *more*: more money, more gadgets, an overabundance of plastic, chrome, metal, silicon, and digital images. If this is your focus, you will continually feel dissatisfied. Paul urged those with means "not to be conceited or to fix their hope on the uncertainty of riches, but on God" (1 Tim. 6:17).

Second, *have I fixed my eyes on my circumstances?* This is a great way to promote either self-pity or pride. Good circumstances tend to give a false sense of security; bad ones nudge us to feel anxious or depressed. We must turn our gaze from this world to Christ, "on the things above, not on the things that are on earth" (Col. 3:2).

Third, *have I fixed my eyes on myself?* When we adore the "trinity" of "me, myself, and I," our concern for others suffers, leading to disunity in the church. To correct this tendency toward an inward focus, Paul wrote, "Do not merely look out for your own personal interests, but also for the interests of others" (Phil. 2:4). To reinforce this, he urged his readers to look to Christ as a model of selfless humility (Phil. 2:5-8).

Finally, *have I fixed my eyes on others?* The Corinthians excelled at turning their attention from Christ to Christ's workers. They bronzed people into idols, set them up on pedestals, and made them objects of worship. This kind of personality-driven ministry always leads to disillusionment because every frail, fallen human will ultimately fall short and bring disappointment. As the psalmist says, "It is better to take refuge in the LORD than to trust in man" (Ps. 118:8).

After answering these questions, take time to "sanctify [set apart] Christ as Lord in your hearts [the center and source of your life]" (1 Pet. 3:15). By turning the eyes of your heart upon Jesus, you'll find that the things of this world will begin to fade, and most of the seemingly irreconcilable differences we have with others in the body of Christ will melt away into irrelevance.

# The Foolishness of the Cross
## 1 CORINTHIANS 1:18-31

**NASB**

18 For the word of the cross is foolish-
ness to those who [a]are perishing, but
to us who [b]are being saved it is the
power of God. 19 For it is written,

"I WILL DESTROY THE WISDOM OF
THE WISE,
AND THE CLEVERNESS OF THE
CLEVER I WILL SET ASIDE."

20 Where is the wise man? Where is
the scribe? Where is the debater of
this age? Has not God made fool-
ish the wisdom of the world? 21 For
since in the wisdom of God the
world through its wisdom did not
*come to* know God, God was well-
pleased through the foolishness of
the [a]message preached to save those
who believe. 22 For indeed Jews ask
for [a]signs and Greeks search for wis-
dom; 23 but we preach [a]Christ cruci-
fied, to Jews a stumbling block and
to Gentiles foolishness, 24 but to
those who are the called, both Jews
and Greeks, Christ the power of God
and the wisdom of God. 25 Because
the foolishness of God is wiser than
men, and the weakness of God is
stronger than men.

26 For [a]consider your calling, breth-
ren, that there were not many wise
according to [b]the flesh, not many
mighty, not many noble; 27 but God
has chosen the foolish things of the
world to shame the wise, and God
has chosen the weak things of the
world to shame the things which are
strong, 28 and the base things of the
world and the despised God has cho-
sen, the things that are not, so that

**NLT**

18 The message of the cross is foolish
to those who are headed for destruc-
tion! But we who are being saved
know it is the very power of God. 19 As
the Scriptures say,

"I will destroy the wisdom of the
wise
and discard the intelligence of
the intelligent."*

20 So where does this leave the
philosophers, the scholars, and the
world's brilliant debaters? God has
made the wisdom of this world look
foolish. 21 Since God in his wisdom
saw to it that the world would never
know him through human wisdom,
he has used our foolish preaching to
save those who believe. 22 It is fool-
ish to the Jews, who ask for signs
from heaven. And it is foolish to the
Greeks, who seek human wisdom.
23 So when we preach that Christ was
crucified, the Jews are offended and
the Gentiles say it's all nonsense.

24 But to those called by God to
salvation, both Jews and Gentiles,*
Christ is the power of God and the
wisdom of God. 25 This foolish plan
of God is wiser than the wisest of
human plans, and God's weakness is
stronger than the greatest of human
strength.

26 Remember, dear brothers and
sisters, that few of you were wise
in the world's eyes or powerful or
wealthy* when God called you. 27 In-
stead, God chose things the world
considers foolish in order to shame
those who think they are wise. And
he chose things that are powerless
to shame those who are powerful.
28 God chose things despised by the
world,* things counted as nothing
at all, and used them to bring to

**NASB**

He may nullify the things that are,
29 so that no [a]man may boast before
God. 30 But [a]by His doing you are in
Christ Jesus, who became to us wis-
dom from God, [b]and righteousness
and sanctification, and redemption,
31 so that, just as it is written, "LET
HIM WHO BOASTS, BOAST IN THE
LORD."

**1:18** [a]Or *perish* [b]Or *are saved* **1:21** [a]Lit *preaching* **1:22** [a]Or *attesting miracles* **1:23** [a]I.e. Messiah **1:26** [a]Lit *see* [b]I.e. human standards **1:29** [a]Lit *flesh* **1:30** [a]Lit *of Him* [b]Or *both*

**NLT**

nothing what the world considers
important. 29 As a result, no one can
ever boast in the presence of God.
30 God has united you with Christ
Jesus. For our benefit God made him
to be wisdom itself. Christ made us
right with God; he made us pure
and holy, and he freed us from sin.
31 Therefore, as the Scriptures say, "If
you want to boast, boast only about
the LORD."*

**1:19** Isa 29:14. **1:24** Greek *and Greeks.* **1:26** Or *high born.* **1:28** Or *God chose those who are low born.* **1:31** Jer 9:24.

Serious football fans will remember the name "Roy Riegels." If you've never heard of him, a simple Internet search will detail his claim to fame—if you can call it that. He had his moment in the spotlight during the 1929 Rose Bowl, in which he played for the University of California, Berkeley. In the middle of a rather complicated play, he wound up with a fumbled ball. He snatched it up and ran 65 yards, until being stopped just short of the goal line. Fans came unglued—screaming and cheering in utter disbelief. You see, Roy Riegels had a problem: *He ran the ball to the wrong goal line.* The wrong fans cheered, and in the end the wrong team won. Until his death in 1993, Roy would be known as "Wrong Way Riegels."

The same thing can happen to a church. It can also happen to a Christian. We can inadvertently spend an incredible amount of energy helping the wrong side without realizing it. The first-century church in Corinth fell into this category. We might call them "Wrong Way Corinth," because without realizing it, those muddled, misguided Christians were helping the wrong side. So like a master coach, Paul opened God's playbook and explained His truth as something they never would have invented: a crucified Messiah and a crucified self as the way to life everlasting.

After Paul planted the church in Corinth, that congregation gradually deteriorated into an arrogant, wrongheaded, squabbling community on the verge of losing its testimony as a God-glorifying local body of Christ. They tucked their thumbs under their suspenders and bragged about incidental things like who had baptized them (1:12-15). Pride led them to elevate human rhetoric and cleverness over the good news about Jesus' death and resurrection. In short, the gospel's heart was being trampled by the feet of humanistic pseudo-intellectualism. This fleshly viewpoint needed to come face-to-face with the true meaning of the cross of Jesus Christ.

## — 1:18-19 —

In 1:18 Paul begins to explain why he did not preach the gospel to the Corinthians by resorting to clever speech (1:17). To have done so would have required him to jettison the cross from the gospel. Why? Because the message concerning the crucifixion of Christ and its saving benefits to believers is frankly ludicrous by the world's standards. To those who had not received the forgiveness of sins through faith in Christ's debt-cancelling death, the cross was pure folly. The notion that one perfect man could die in place of innumerable sinners—and that this sacrifice was sufficient payment, applied freely to all who believed—was about as bizarre a message as anybody in the first century would have heard.

For believers, however, Christ's death on the cross takes center stage; it is crucial for every aspect of salvation: past, present, and future. Paul's use of the present participle "being saved" (1:18) suggests that he has at the forefront of his mind the present progress of sanctification, in which believers are delivered from sin's power through the life of cross-bearing. In Luke 9:22-24, Jesus tells us what this aspect of present salvation from a life of disobedience and sin looks like: "The Son of Man must suffer many things and be rejected by the elders and chief priests and scribes, and be killed and be raised up on the third day. . . . If anyone wishes to come after Me, he must deny himself, and take up his cross daily and follow Me. For whoever wishes to save his life will lose it, but whoever loses his life for My sake, he is the one who will save it."

I doubt that most people today understand what Jesus meant when He talked about taking up our cross daily, because we don't see the cross used as a means of execution. In the Roman Empire, however, people sentenced to die by crucifixion had to carry at least a section of their crosses through the city to their appointed place of public execution. This practice demonstrated to all observers that the condemned rebels had finally submitted to the state—in death![3] So Jesus meant, "If you want to follow My path, and if you want to be a genuine disciple of Mine, you must be willing—*every day*—to put to death your stubborn will and personal desires. And you must readily accept the Father's will—as I have—over your own."

Now to unbelievers, that message of the cross sounds absolutely foolish—both the idea that the Son of God would voluntarily die for sinners and the notion that saved sinners should voluntarily die to themselves for the sake of discipleship. The word Paul uses for "foolishness" (1 Cor.1:18) is *mōria* [3472], related to *mōros* [3474], from which we get our English word "moron." From the world's perspective, only a moron would believe the message of the cross and live a life of self-sacrifice in light of the cross. But for believers who are being delivered from a life of hopeless bondage to sin by taking up their crosses and following Christ, the cross is "the power of God" (1:18).

Talk about countercultural! I love the fact that God's message of salvation and sanctification flies in the face of all man-made religious, social, and psychological expectations. Paul knew how contrary this theology of the cross must have sounded to his readers in Corinth; he knew that the last thing they wanted to do was to take up their crosses by surrendering their rights, privileges, and benefits. Drawing from Isaiah 29:14, Paul wisely backs up his "foolish" message of the cross with an important Old Testament truth.

The context of Isaiah 29:14 found the struggling northern kingdom of Israel caught in a trap. The general of the Assyrian army was poised like a coiled rattlesnake ready to strike. Convinced that a merciless enemy was about to destroy them, the people of Israel felt stuck in a dilemma—to follow human wisdom or God's calling through His prophet. Rather than respond to God's call to repent and turn to Him for supernatural deliverance, Israel followed the human wisdom of politicians who said, "We need to align ourselves with Egypt—the only nearby superpower with enough military might to defend us against Assyria. Forget this radical religious obsession with repentance and holiness." Relying on human force, human wisdom, and human power, Israel compromised her standard of separation from the pagan nations. Absolute tragedy resulted. Israel looked for wisdom in the intellect of man, and she paid dearly for it (2 Kgs. 17).

By alluding to this passage from Isaiah, Paul reminded the Corinthians that God's plans and methods "destroy the wisdom of the wise" and set aside "the cleverness of the clever" (1 Cor. 1:19). Even though the message of the cross may seem "moronic," it's the power of God for salvation and the only key to an abundant life.

## — 1:20-25 —

As if pointing his finger across the crowd of squabbling believers in Corinth, Paul probes that congregation: "Where is the wise man? Where is the scribe? Where is the debater of this age?" (1:20). In light of God's act in trumping human reason with the message of the cross, none of the Gentile geniuses, Jewish scholars, or Greek eggheads amounted to anything. Not only could the greatest sources of wisdom in the world contribute *nothing* beneficial to the cross, but their attempts at refining, intellectualizing, or rationalizing the message only undermined it. So thoroughly has God turned the tables on the wisdom (*sophia* [4678]) of the world, it is rendered "foolish" (1:20)!

Paul pushes it farther. The greatest pursuits of worldly wisdom inevitably fail to lead to the one true God of the Bible—"The world through its wisdom did not come to know God" (1:21). Even in our own day, many brilliant astronomers peer into space with the most powerful telescopes ever invented, yet their intensive scouring of the universe never leads them beyond the created realm to the Creator Himself. On the other extreme, many scientists focus their powerful microscopes on the smallest particles of matter, seeking some kind of explanation for the order, the complexity, and the beauty of the physical universe, yet they also fail to find the all-powerful and all-wise Orderer Himself.

Only through the "foolishness of the message" can we come to know God as He truly is (1:21). When Paul calls the message of the gospel "foolish," he writes from the world's perspective. From God's perspective and from that of the believer, the gospel is true and ultimate wisdom. Paul amplifies his point, describing the reasons both Jews and Greeks find themselves confused by the simple message and dumbfounded by the obvious truth (1:22). Jews demanded proof in the form of signs and wonders that would validate the authenticity of the message. Greeks pursued rationalistic explanations—intellectual and logical proofs that any thinking person could compute on their own. Both of these responses to the gospel appear reasonable from the human perspective. Yet they fail to lead people to Christ.

The Jews looked for a victorious warrior Messiah, who would usher in the kingdom by miraculously vanquishing the Roman Empire and restoring the glories of the Davidic kingdom (Matt. 27:42; Luke 1:68-75; 24:21; Acts 1:6).[4] Instead, Jesus had performed his miracles among smaller groups of the disenfranchised, despised, and rejected. He preached a message of repentance, righteousness, and peace. He called for self-sacrificial surrender to the will of God, following in His footsteps —even to the cross, if necessary. He refused to perform miracles on demand (Matt. 12:38-41), alienating the religious zealots who were eager to overturn the political establishment for their own vindication. How could the Jews believe that this Jesus was their long-awaited Savior? This peasant preacher of Nazareth was a "letdown" in their eyes, and so they stumbled because of misguided expectations (1 Cor. 1:23).

The Greeks' search for wisdom took a different path, but ended up at the same dead end. They looked for either an illustrious philosopher-king or a wise seer-sage who could tap into the loftiest thoughts of the realm of the mind and soul and who would satisfy the human longing for a utopian society (Acts 17:18-21). Instead, they learned about a divine ruler who humbled Himself to be born a poor Jew, grew into manhood in obscurity, and spent three years speaking parables about a kingdom characterized by irrational altruistic virtues. Instead of founding a school of philosophy, this would-be sage ended His ministry betrayed by His own people and abandoned by most of His disciples—hardly good PR for a budding academic with His sights set on global influence! In short, a heroic religious figure like Jesus, the crucified Messiah, scandalized the Greek mind (1 Cor. 1:23).

Paul concludes his thoughts on the "wise folly" of the cross (1:24-25). In the world's eyes, the gospel of Jesus Christ is foolishness; but for us who believe, Christ is power and wisdom personified (1:24). In fact, "the foolishness of God is wiser than men, and the weakness of God is stronger than men."

## — 1:26-31 —

Paul then personalizes the contrast between the "wisdom" of the world and the "folly" of the gospel (1:26). The nature of the gospel's power through what the world perceives as "foolishness" should have been evident to them in the humble backgrounds of the believers themselves. He reminds the Corinthians that few of them were considered wise, mighty, or noble "according to the flesh," that is, according to merely human standards. Yes, Corinth had its share of intellectual superstars, such as Apollos, but for the most part, the Corinthian Christians couldn't boast in their worldly wisdom, riches, or pedigrees.

Yet in light of the message of the gospel, Paul reminds his readers that without God all human beings—from the cultural "crème de la crème" to the bottom of the social barrel—are tramps living in the dumps of human depravity. Neither the upper echelons of society nor the lowest rungs of the ladder can boast in any merit before God, who calls us by His own grace and mercy, not based on our own worthiness. Despite our filthy condition, God mercifully reaches down, plucks us from the garbage heap, and begins His process of transforming us into valuable pieces of art.

By choosing to save people from among the dregs of society, God shames the wise and the powerful (1:27). By building up His kingdom from the despised and rejected—the political, social, cultural, religious, and intellectual "have-nots" (1:28)—God sends the world a game-changing message: "No man may boast before God" (1:29). In fact, the cross levels the playing field, sealing all under guilt before a just and holy God (Rom. 3:23). So what's the solution to the universal condemnation of all? Grace. Paul says, "For by grace you have been saved through faith; and that not of yourselves, it is the gift of God; not as a result of works, so that no one may boast" (Eph. 2:8-9).

Such grace should remind us that the Master, not the masterpiece, should always receive the praise and the glory. God has no tolerance for the proud, the arrogant, the self-sufficient—those who view themselves as minigods, usurping the one true God's place as the all-powerful, all-wise King of creation. By debasing the arrogant, He humbles them, making them acknowledge their poverty and enabling them to receive His great riches (see Dan. 4:28-37).

Paul then contrasts the Corinthians' spiritual deficiencies with the all-sufficiency of Christ. Everything humans lack because of their depravity and finitude has been provided for them through Jesus Christ. He is "wisdom from God, and righteousness and sanctification, and redemption" (1 Cor. 1:30).

The world looks for heroes, but God seeks the humble. The world praises power, prestige, and wealth; God turns our attention to Christ, the gentlest, humblest person who ever lived. People love to rise through the ranks, to be exalted by society, to be rewarded with riches, but God has given His Son preeminence over all creation and promises us a place with Christ in the heavenly places, enjoying the same exaltation and riches through Christ alone (Eph. 2:6-7). Left to ourselves, we are nothing, but in Christ, we are invaluable. The difference lies in Him, not in us. Thus we should never boast in our own merit before God (1 Cor. 1:29). Rather, if we boast at all, we can only "boast in the LORD" (1:31).

Paul's final exhortation to boast in no thing and no one but the Lord echoes a powerful passage from Jeremiah 9:23-24.

> Thus says the LORD, "Let not a wise man boast of his wisdom, and let not the mighty man boast of his might, let not a rich man boast of his riches; but let him who boasts boast of this, that he understands and knows Me, that I am the LORD who exercises lovingkindness, justice and righteousness on earth; for I delight in these things," declares the LORD.

# APPLICATION: 1 CORINTHIANS 1:18-31

## The Wisdom of God's Folly

"The foolishness of God is wiser than men" (1:25). Paul's words remind me of a meeting I had a number of years ago, when I sat across the table from a brilliant physician. We talked at length about a phase of his work before I found an opportunity to steer our conversation to the gospel of Jesus Christ.

I opened the paper napkin and I drew on one side a steep cliff and on another side another cliff, leaving a big gap in between. This "bridge" illustration has often been used to communicate the reconciling work of Christ. Simple. To the point. On one side of the gulf I put "man"; on the other side, "God." Then I built a little ladder at the bottom, showing how humans try to get across on their own: good works, charity, church attendance, morality, philosophy, spirituality—all humanistic attempts

to bridge the gap between God and man. Then I put in the middle a large cross as the bridge and showed a man on one side walking across by faith in the Lord Jesus' death and resurrection (15:1-5). I finished after about four minutes, turned it around, slid it across the table and asked, "What do you think?"

Without much thought, that physician blinked then blurted out, "In a million years I could never believe something so illogical and simplistic!"

That's the response of a man who couldn't fit the simplicity of the gospel into his sophisticated philosophical framework. In a sense, I feel sorry for the intellectual whose own mental acumen, hardened by stubborn pride, becomes a stumbling block to salvation.

Let's admit it. Dismissive reactions to the gospel from highbrow skeptics and cynical critics can tempt us to shy away from sharing the good news of Christ's life-changing death and resurrection. In fact, a "that's stupid!" or a "how could you believe something like that?" response can feel like a kick in the gut and make us ask ourselves the same question. *Is* the gospel too simplistic and ridiculous to believe?

Not at all!

We need to remember that cultured criticisms of Christian claims have been around since the early days of the church. In fact, around the year AD 210, the Christian apologist Tertullian of Carthage engaged in a fierce defense of the faith against heretics who believed the biblical gospel was too unsophisticated to accept "as is." They attempted to soften its rough edges, modify its offensive elements, and transform Christianity into something more philosophically pleasing to the elite thinkers of the day.

In response to the charge that the message of incarnation, death, and resurrection of the God-man was utter folly, Tertullian wrote, "It *is* of course foolish, if we are to judge God by our own conceptions. But . . . consider well this Scripture, if indeed you have not erased it: 'God hath chosen the foolish things of the world, to confound the wise.'"[5] Quite appropriately, Tertullian was quoting 1 Corinthians 1:27, reminding his readers that the world's standards of intellectual respectability are irrelevant when it comes to the truth of God. In fact, Tertullian turned the tables on the skeptics and critics. He said we should believe the claims of the gospel not in spite of their intellectual absurdity, *but because of it.* He argued that no reasoning human would ever make up something like the crucified God-man and try to preach it around the world, *unless it were true.* If humans simply invented the gospel, they would have concocted something much more philosophically respectable—something like the perversions of the faith spouted by the heretics. Tertullian famously wrote: "The Son of God was crucified; I am not ashamed because men must needs be ashamed of it. And the Son of God died; it is by all means to be believed, because it is absurd. And He was buried, and rose again; the fact is certain, because it is impossible."[6] I *love* that statement!

I'm convinced that each of us needs to recommit to standing tall and proud on the "absurdity" of the gospel. We shouldn't be ashamed of it. All of us who have experienced reconciliation know that it is the power of God for salvation (Rom. 1:16). So what if worldly-minded unbelievers scoff at it? Let them scoff! Critics will mock us for believing it. So be it! Instead of backing down and cowering in fear, let's renew our commitment to embrace the "ridiculous," knowing that "the foolishness of God is wiser than men" (1 Cor. 1:25). Before you read on, take a moment to ask God to grant you boldness and confidence to live and proclaim the message of the cross (Eph. 6:19).

# The Hidden Depths of God . . . Revealed!

## 1 CORINTHIANS 2:1-16

**NASB**

1 And when I came to you, brethren, I did not come with superiority of speech or of wisdom, proclaiming to you the [a]testimony of God. 2 For I determined to know nothing among you except Jesus Christ, and Him crucified. 3 I was with you in weakness and in fear and in much trembling, 4 and my [a]message and my preaching were not in persuasive words of wisdom, but in demonstration of the Spirit and of power, 5 so that your faith would not [a]rest on the wisdom of men, but on the power of God.

6 Yet we do speak wisdom among those who are mature; a wisdom, however, not of this age nor of the

**NLT**

1 When I first came to you, dear brothers and sisters,* I didn't use lofty words and impressive wisdom to tell you God's secret plan.* 2 For I decided that while I was with you I would forget everything except Jesus Christ, the one who was crucified. 3 I came to you in weakness—timid and trembling. 4 And my message and my preaching were very plain. Rather than using clever and persuasive speeches, I relied only on the power of the Holy Spirit. 5 I did this so you would trust not in human wisdom but in the power of God.

6 Yet when I am among mature believers, I do speak with words of wisdom, but not the kind of wisdom that

rulers of this age, who are passing
away; 7 but we speak God's wisdom
in a mystery, the hidden *wisdom*
which God predestined before the
ages to our glory; 8 *the wisdom* which
none of the rulers of this age has
understood; for if they had under-
stood it they would not have cruci-
fied the Lord of glory; 9 but just as it
is written,

"THINGS WHICH EYE HAS NOT
SEEN AND EAR HAS NOT
HEARD,
AND *which* HAVE NOT ENTERED
THE HEART OF MAN,
ALL THAT GOD HAS PREPARED FOR
THOSE WHO LOVE HIM."

10 [a]For to us God revealed *them*
through the Spirit; for the Spirit
searches all things, even the depths
of God. 11 For who among men knows
the *thoughts* of a man except the
spirit of the man which is in him?
Even so the *thoughts* of God no one
knows except the Spirit of God.
12 Now we have received, not the
spirit of the world, but the Spirit who
is from God, so that we may know
the things freely given to us by God,
13 which things we also speak, not in
words taught by human wisdom, but
in those taught by the Spirit, [a]com-
bining spiritual *thoughts* with spiri-
tual *words*.

14 But [a]a natural man does not ac-
cept the things of the Spirit of God,
for they are foolishness to him;
and he cannot understand them,
because they are spiritually [b]ap-
praised. 15 But he who is spiritual ap-
praises all things, yet he himself is
appraised by no one. 16 FOR WHO HAS
KNOWN THE MIND OF THE LORD, THAT

belongs to this world or to the rulers
of this world, who are soon forgot-
ten. 7 No, the wisdom we speak of is
the mystery of God*—his plan that
was previously hidden, even though
he made it for our ultimate glory be-
fore the world began. 8 But the rulers
of this world have not understood
it; if they had, they would not have
crucified our glorious Lord. 9 That
is what the Scriptures mean when
they say,

"No eye has seen, no ear has
heard,
and no mind has imagined
what God has prepared
for those who love him."*

10 But* it was to us that God re-
vealed these things by his Spirit.
For his Spirit searches out every-
thing and shows us God's deep se-
crets. 11 No one can know a person's
thoughts except that person's own
spirit, and no one can know God's
thoughts except God's own Spirit.
12 And we have received God's Spirit
(not the world's spirit), so we can
know the wonderful things God has
freely given us.

13 When we tell you these things,
we do not use words that come from
human wisdom. Instead, we speak
words given to us by the Spirit,
using the Spirit's words to explain
spiritual truths.* 14 But people who
aren't spiritual* can't receive these
truths from God's Spirit. It all sounds
foolish to them and they can't under-
stand it, for only those who are spiri-
tual can understand what the Spirit
means. 15 Those who are spiritual
can evaluate all things, but they
themselves cannot be evaluated by
others. 16 For,

"Who can know the LORD's
thoughts?
Who knows enough to teach
him?"*

NASB

HE WILL INSTRUCT HIM? But we have the mind of Christ.

**2:1** [a]One early ms reads *mystery* **2:4** [a]Lit *word* **2:5** [a]Lit *be* **2:10** [a]One early ms reads *But* **2:13** [a]Or *interpreting spiritual* things *for spiritual* men **2:14** [a]Or *an unspiritual* [b]Or *examined*

NLT

But we understand these things, for we have the mind of Christ.

**2:1a** Greek *brothers.* **2:1b** Greek *God's mystery;* other manuscripts read *God's testimony.* **2:7** Greek *But we speak God's wisdom in a mystery.* **2:9** Isa 64:4. **2:10** Some manuscripts read *For.* **2:13** Or *explaining spiritual truths in spiritual language,* or *explaining spiritual truths to spiritual people.* **2:14** Or *who don't have the Spirit;* or *who have only physical life.* **2:16** Isa 40:13 (Greek version).

In our age, few things seem more convincing than a personal example. We might teach a truth from the Scriptures, properly interpret a text, draw out its unchanging theology, and apply it to the lives of our listeners. We may even point to others who have lived the truth themselves. Yet when a teacher's or preacher's own personal life is used to show how the truth of God's Word works, people tend to listen more attentively, believe more readily, and apply the Word more eagerly. Paul's life was a testimony to God's truth at work.

After pointing out the contrast between the eloquence of worldly wisdom with its polished rhetoric and the humble, simple truth of the Christian faith, Paul reminds the Corinthians about the nature of his own apostolic ministry among them. He doesn't do this to point out his own strengths or to turn the spotlight on himself. To the contrary! He refers to his own ministry as an example of how God uses simple means to reveal His hidden depths, and how it is the work of God's own Spirit and not mere human intellect that reveals God's wisdom.

## — 2:1-5 —

To understand Paul's description of his ministry, we need to remember that he lacked nothing in educational and intellectual ability. He had been a disciple of Gamaliel, a famous rabbi of the first century (Acts 5:34; 22:3). Beyond that, Paul could hold his own in a debate with detractors (Acts 19:8-10; 26:24-29). So it's not that Paul *could not* have come to the Corinthians with "superiority of speech or of wisdom" (1 Cor. 2:1). Rather, Paul *chose* not to. Why? Because he determined to remove himself from the equation and let the Spirit of God do the work of persuading. Instead of pummeling the Corinthians with premises, syllogisms, and logical constructs, Paul presented them with "Jesus Christ, and Him crucified" (2:2). Everything else was either superfluous or worse: a distraction from the gospel itself.

When Paul served the Corinthians, he did so "in weakness and in fear and in much trembling" (2:3). This image doesn't match the mental picture many of us have of that courageous, "go-for-broke" apostle. Some believe that Paul was not cowering in fear of the Corinthians, but exhibiting genuine "fear and trembling" in the face of his awesome duty to conscientiously communicate the gospel of Christ to unbelievers.[7] Others suggest that Paul referred to his inability to measure up to cultural expectations of spellbinding delivery by those presenting an argument to a public audience (2 Cor. 10:10).[8] It may even be that Paul was simply not "up to par" when he arrived in Corinth, perhaps suffering from his "thorn in the flesh" that had impacted his normal capacity to communicate in strength (2 Cor. 12:7-9). Whatever the case, Paul embraced his calling to minister in humility and to depend on the Lord's strength more than ever (Phil. 2:12-13).

The results were staggering. What Paul failed to exhibit in courage and talent, God more than made up in supernatural power; His grace was abundantly sufficient. As Paul spoke with his wavering foreign accent, the gospel exploded throughout the streets of Corinth. The Holy Spirit moved into shops, homes, temples, synagogues, and narrow back alleys. People came and listened to Paul, not because he could entertain the crowd, but because they felt drawn by the substance of his message and the powerful testimony of the accompanying miracles.

Paul didn't try to mimic the rhetoric of the masters or formulate a clever argument like the logicians. He didn't strut. Instead, he relied entirely on "demonstration of the Spirit and of power" (1 Cor. 2:4). Only then could Paul ensure that the Corinthians' faith would rest on the power of God rather than on human wisdom (2:5). Paul was convinced of a vital spiritual truth of which we need a constant reminder: Human genius and oratorical ingenuity can't lure people into the kingdom. Only the simplicity of the gospel, applied to the heart by the Holy Spirit, can humble people and lead them to renounce worldly ways and to embrace the Way, the Truth, and the Life.

## — 2:6 —

Paul's appeal to the cross rather than to reason and his reliance on the Spirit rather than on rhetoric didn't go over well with most people in Corinth. Thus, the dividing line began to be drawn between those who were given eyes to see and ears to hear (see Matt. 13:13-17) and those who simply could not understand those things that are discerned by the Holy Spirit.

Paul clears up the misconception that the gospel is meaningless gobbledygook concocted by God simply to trip up those who can't bring themselves to make a blind leap of faith (1 Cor. 2:6). Like an iceberg that conceals its depth far beneath the surface, unbelievers cannot see the hidden depths of wisdom and truth inherent in the Christian faith. So, realizing that some may interpret his disparaging of worldly wisdom as an admission that accepting the gospel requires intellectual suicide, he tackles the age-old conflict between faith and reason, reconciling them in the hidden depths of God.

The wisdom spoken of in this verse is neither empirical fact-finding nor intuitive common sense, but *insight*—perception about people, problems, ourselves, life. Paul calls it "God's wisdom," "the thoughts of God," "the things of the Spirit," and "the mind of Christ" (2:7, 11, 14, 16). Only the mature in Christ can possess this wisdom, which should give spiritual babes the incentive to grow. For the deeper we grow in the truth of God—taught not by human wisdom, but by the Spirit—the more wisdom we'll have to grow toward spiritual maturity (Heb. 5:14–6:1).

## — 2:7-9 —

Paul delves more deeply into God's hidden wisdom (2:7-9), explaining why nonbelievers can see only the tip of the iceberg.

*The wisdom of the gospel is a mystery.* Paul explains that believers "speak God's wisdom in a mystery" (2:7). The Greek word for "mystery" is *mystērion* [3466], which refers to something previously hidden that now has been revealed. Like a secret to be shared among a select few, God has made the mystery of the gospel crystal clear to believers, the recipients of His revelation; but the gospel remains obscured to those who have not yet entered God's inner circle. Paul goes even deeper when he describes how the hidden wisdom of God had been "predestined before the ages to our glory." Paul uses the same imagery in Ephesians 1:4, when he says God "chose us in Him before the foundation of the world." Although the gospel of the incarnation, death, and resurrection of the Son of God came in a surprising way, God had intended it long before time began.

*The wisdom of the gospel is not understood without the Spirit.* The mystery of the gospel has been made clear to believers, but the wisdom of the gospel is not understood by unbelievers (1 Cor. 2:8). The Greek word Paul uses for "understand" is *ginōskō* [1097], which refers to a knowledge born of deep personal understanding.[9] This depth of understanding can come only as a gift by the assistance of the Holy Spirit. Second Corinthians 4:3-4 says, "And even if our gospel is veiled, it is veiled to those who are perishing, in whose case the god of this world has blinded the minds of the unbelieving so that they might not see the light of the gospel of the glory of Christ." Reminding his readers about the human rulers (both Roman and Jewish) who executed Jesus, Paul says, "If they had understood it [the mystery of God], they would not have crucified the Lord of glory" (1 Cor. 2:8). Even through the spiritual ignorance of the unbelieving political powers, God brought to light the profound mystery of the gospel.

*The wisdom of the gospel is not discoverable by humans.* Revealing a mystery and discovering a mystery are two different things. God revealed to humanity what humans through their own methods and pursuits could never have discovered. In our age, in which many regard the scientific method as the new equivalent to the Ten Commandments, the "seeing is believing" approach to reality makes little room for faith. A typical argument against the gospel often goes something like this: "We don't *observe* people rising from the dead, nor do we *hear* reliable reports of people rising from the dead. Therefore, the idea that anybody has ever risen from the dead is best understood as a myth or legend."

This "show me" philosophy of life isn't new to our age. In fact, Paul probably heard it from some skeptics in his day. Anticipating this kind of objection to the unbelievable nature of the gospel, Paul responds by paraphrasing Isaiah 64:4, describing the hidden mystery of the gospel as "things which eye has not seen and ear has not heard, and which have not entered the heart of man, all that God has prepared for those who love him" (1 Cor. 2:9). What God Himself reveals in His own time cannot be discovered through observation, investigation, direct intuition, or human logic. People can spend their whole lives studying at the most prestigious schools, adding a chain of letters after their names, traveling the world over, and experiencing all life has to offer. Yet these empirical means can never discover the depths of God's mystery, which can be revealed only by the Holy Spirit through faith.

## — 2:10-13 —

If humans can't discover the wisdom of God by human methods, understand it by human intellect, or believe it by human power, then how can anybody know and believe the gospel? Paul tackles this question next. We can understand Paul's explanation in terms of the *priority* (2:10), the *process* (2:10-11), and the *purpose* (2:12-13) of spiritual revelation.

The *priority*. God chose those who trust in Him to receive His wisdom, as Paul explains: "For *to us* God revealed them" (2:10, emphasis added). God reveals His wisdom not to the world's erudite scholars, influential leaders, or super wealthy (1:27-30). Instead, He chose to reveal himself to those who come to Him by God's undeserved grace through simple faith (Eph. 2:8-9).

The *process*. Besides the Spirit's work in guiding believers to the truth of the gospel (John 16:8-13), the Spirit also dwells within believers from the moment they place their faith in Christ, beginning His work of transforming us into Christ's image (John 14:17; 1 Cor. 12:13; 2 Cor. 3:18). Through the Spirit's indwelling (Rom. 8:9, 11), He searches for us the "depths of God" (1 Cor. 2:10), communicating His thoughts to us as we draw upon His resources (2:11-12; John 16:13-15; Eph. 4:14-19). Paul argues that just as the spirit of a human knows the hidden thoughts and attitudes of that individual, so the Spirit of God knows the hidden mysteries of God. The Spirit's role in the world, then, is to reveal to believers the content of these mysteries.

The *purpose*. God promises to give us the Spirit the moment we are saved. If we have trusted in Him, the Spirit communicates the divine wisdom of Christianity, because humans can never understand it on their own. The purpose of this revelation is twofold: "that we may know the things freely given to us by God" (1 Cor. 2:12) and that we may "speak" (2:13) these things to others, ministering the Holy Spirit through the very words He inspired (2 Tim. 3:16). These words of the Spirit—the words of Holy Scripture—are able to affect spiritual change because they are not merely human words, but words "taught by the Spirit" (1 Cor. 2:13). Both the thoughts and the words themselves are given by revelation from God (2 Pet. 1:21).

To recap: God revealed the truth of the gospel by the Holy Spirit. The Holy Spirit expressed these truths in "spiritual words," not merely human expression. Therefore, when we study the words of Scripture and pass them on to others, we become personally involved in God's process of proclaiming the mystery once hidden but now revealed through the church (Eph. 3:10).

## — 2:14-16 —

Though the believer taught by the Spirit can spend a lifetime exploring the depths of the hidden mysteries of God, not so for the unbeliever, whom Paul styles the "natural man" (2:14). Such a person does not accept the "things of the Spirit," that is, the mysteries of the gospel, the person and work of Christ, the meaning of Holy Scripture, and how all of these relate to the person's standing before God. So Paul uses the term "natural man" as a label for the kind of worldly-minded person he had been describing throughout 1 Corinthians 1–2—a person who functions in the realm of the world's wisdom, demanding empirical proof at every turn, and seeking logical explanations for everything. To such a person, the things of the Spirit are "foolishness."

Without the Holy Spirit's indwelling ministry, unbelievers will never fully grasp, truly believe, and personally experience the riches of the Spirit, for they are "spiritually appraised" (2:14). The word "appraised" means "discerned to be true." Only through the eyes of faith given by the Holy Spirit can a person even begin to delve beneath the surface of God's revealed Word to comprehend its hidden wisdom. An unbeliever may "understand" the words superficially, but to embrace them, love them, believe them, and live them—that requires the miraculous illuminating work of the Spirit.

The flip side of the unsaved person—the natural person—is the maturing Christian, whom Paul describes as "he who is spiritual" (2:15). Such a person, gifted and guided by the Holy Spirit, operates beyond the understanding of the world's wisdom. By saying that a believer "is appraised by no one," Paul is not saying that each Christian is beyond reproof or correction (see 5:1-5, 12-13; 10:15). Rather, those who align themselves to the Spirit's wisdom and submit themselves to the Christian worldview fall into the same category as the gospel: They become foolish to the eyes of the world and cannot be evaluated based on worldly reason, rhetoric, or philosophy.

To put it plainly, unbelievers will never quite "get" their believing friends and family members. They won't understand why they choose to live the way they do, why they sacrifice worldly pursuits, give selflessly, or serve faithfully. Unbelievers don't see the point of Christian virtue when there's so much more to gain from worldly vice. The "natural person" will never fully grasp the Spirit-led convictions of the "spiritual person."

The reason unbelievers cannot grasp the beliefs and decisions of believers rests on the fact that believers' lifestyles reflect the unfathomable mysteries of God—the self-denying life of the cross of Jesus Christ. What foolishness to the world! A "natural person" gazing at the life of a "spiritual person" encounters in small part "the mind of the Lord," which no mere human can know (2:16). Paul alludes to Isaiah 40:13, which communicates the absolute otherness of God's wisdom, knowledge, and counsel. So, when unbelievers encounter believers who have submitted to the Spirit-taught wisdom, knowledge, and counsel of God, they will stand dumbfounded. Because "we have the mind of Christ" (1 Cor. 2:16), those without the mind of Christ will never comprehend our ways.

# APPLICATION: 1 CORINTHIANS 2:1-16

## Delving into the Depths of God

"Been there, done that." In the 1980s, younger people (especially) used this phrase to indicate that they had already partaken of the experience in question and to imply that they no longer had any interest in it. When it comes to studying Scripture, I've found that many Christians feel the same way: "been there, done that." They won't admit it, of course. They might even still read the obligatory verse or two of the Bible to get their quick "fix" for the day. Yet many who once had engaged in methodical Bible study, had read through the entire Old and New Testaments, or had memorized many passages of Scripture, sometimes place the ongoing, deep study of Scripture low on their priority list. The reason? "Been there, done that."

Yet Paul's words concerning the revealed mystery of God in 1 Corinthians 2 tell us something vital about Scripture—His written revelation—that we should never forget. Because the words of Scripture are not mere human words but words "taught by the Spirit" (2:13), the richness of their relevance for our lives is inexhaustible. We finite humans could no more fully plumb the depths of Holy Scripture than we could fully comprehend the mind of God. Every time we return to the pure springs of God's infinite wisdom in Scripture, our finite cups overflow as the Holy Spirit, who is both the Author and the Teacher of Scripture, illumines our minds and applies to our lives just what He wants for us that hour, that day, or that year. This idea of both simplicity and depth is put beautifully by the words of Gregory the Great, a sixth-century church father:

> For as the word of God, by the mysteries which it contains, exercises the understanding of the wise, so usually by what presents

> itself on the outside, it nurses the simple-minded. It presents in open day that wherewith the little ones may be fed; it keeps in secret that whereby men of a loftier range may be held in suspense of admiration. It is, as it were, a kind of river, if I may so liken it, which is both shallow and deep, wherein both the lamb may find a footing, and the elephant float at large.[10]

Maybe you've read through the Bible once or twice. Maybe you've committed many verses or even a whole book to memory. Maybe you've studied through several books with commentaries, like the one you're reading now. Great! Keep it up! But don't be afraid to go deeper. How do you do that? By reviving the lost art of *meditation* on God's Word (Josh. 1:8). Meditation focuses our thoughts on a single verse or passage of Scripture for an extended period of time. In meditation, we ponder specific truths of Scripture slowly, piece by piece, allowing our minds to dig deeply into a word, phrase, idea, or principle from God's Word as the Spirit drills deep into our hearts and minds to deposit that truth permanently in our souls. Think of meditation as scriptural saturation.

How do you plumb the depths of God's mysteries by meditation on His Word? Let me suggest five practical steps to follow, using Proverbs 3:5-6 as an example.

1. *Emphasize different words and phrases.* In meditating on Proverbs 3:5-6, focus on specific terms: "*Trust* in the LORD" or "Trust in the LORD with *all* your heart." Think first about *trusting*. Later, ponder the vastness of that word *all*. When you read the warning, "do not lean on your *own* understanding," call to mind the many ways you plunge in and work things out for yourself.

2. *Paraphrase the verse, making it personal.* Rethink and restate the verse using your own words in the process. For example: "Lord, you are commanding me to lean on You—turn my life over to You completely—to stop my habit of worrying and working things out my way, as I frequently do." Realize that the Spirit is speaking to you through His inspired Word.

3. *Compare the verse with other Scripture.* Reflect on this in relation to two or three other passages that relate to your verse, using Bible cross-references, study notes, or search tools for help. Weave these other passages into your thoughts. For Proverbs 3:5-6, you'll discover that the Spirit's thoughts in Psalm 37:4-5, Philippians 4:6-7, or 1 Peter 5:7 provide additional insight and deeper perspective.

4. *Relate the verse to your present circumstance.* Let's suppose you feel worried, restless, and ill at ease. You know it's wrong, but you can't seem to stop. You come across Proverbs 3:5-6 and decide to meditate on these words. As you do, keep your ongoing habits and specific problems in mind. Ask for insight from the Lord. List your worries one by one. Identify them. Having identified them, look them over in the light of that passage. Then turn your discoveries into prayer as you release to the Lord your problems and worries.

5. *Use prayer as a follow-up.* Always remember to conclude with prayer. Ask Him not only to communicate His divine thoughts into your thoughts, but to apply those thoughts in your life. Ask for strength to trust Him without worrying. Thank Him in advance for the change He will bring when you understand and faithfully follow His Word.

No spiritual Christian could ever say "been there, done that" about meditating on God's Word. Why? Because if you have ever really experienced the depth of God's wisdom through meditation, you'd be saying "there now, doing it" and teaching others to do the same.

## Cure for Divisions

### 1 CORINTHIANS 3:1-23

**NASB**

1 And I, brethren, could not speak
to you as to spiritual men, but as to
men of flesh, as to infants in Christ.
2 I gave you milk to drink, not solid
food; for you were not yet able *to*
*receive it*. Indeed, even now you are
not yet able, 3 for you are still fleshly.
For since there is jealousy and strife
among you, are you not fleshly, and
are you not walking [a]like mere men?
4 For when one says, "I am of Paul,"
and another, "I am of Apollos," are
you not *mere* men?
5 What then is Apollos? And what

**NLT**

1 Dear brothers and sisters,* when I
was with you I couldn't talk to you
as I would to spiritual people.* I
had to talk as though you belonged
to this world or as though you were
infants in Christ. 2 I had to feed you
with milk, not with solid food, because you weren't ready for anything
stronger. And you still aren't ready,
3 for you are still controlled by your
sinful nature. You are jealous of one
another and quarrel with each other.
Doesn't that prove you are controlled
by your sinful nature? Aren't you living like people of the world? 4 When
one of you says, "I am a follower of
Paul," and another says, "I follow
Apollos," aren't you acting just like
people of the world?
5 After all, who is Apollos? Who

is Paul? Servants through whom you
believed, even as the Lord gave *op-*
*portunity* to each one. 6 I planted,
Apollos watered, but God was caus-
ing the growth. 7 So then neither the
one who plants nor the one who wa-
ters is anything, but God who causes
the growth. 8 Now he who plants and
he who waters are one; but each will
receive his own [a]reward according
to his own labor. 9 For we are God's
fellow workers; you are God's [a]field,
God's building.

10 According to the grace of God
which was given to me, like a wise
master builder I laid a foundation,
and another is building on it. But
each man must be careful how he
builds on it. 11 For no man can lay a
foundation other than the one which
is laid, which is Jesus Christ. 12 Now
if any man builds on the foundation
with gold, silver, [a]precious stones,
wood, hay, straw, 13 each man's work
will become evident; for the day will
show it because it is *to be* revealed
with fire, and the fire itself will test
[a]the quality of each man's work. 14 If
any man's work which he has built
on it remains, he will receive a re-
ward. 15 If any man's work is burned
up, he will suffer loss; but he himself
will be saved, yet so as through fire.

16 Do you not know that you are a
[a]temple of God and *that* the Spirit of
God dwells in you? 17 If any man de-
stroys the [a]temple of God, God will
destroy him, for the [a]temple of God is
holy, and [b]that is what you are.

18 Let no man deceive himself. If
any man among you thinks that he
is wise in this age, he must become
foolish, so that he may become wise.
19 For the wisdom of this world is fool
ishness before God. For it is written,

is Paul? We are only God's servants
through whom you believed the
Good News. Each of us did the work
the Lord gave us. 6 I planted the seed
in your hearts, and Apollos watered
it, but it was God who made it grow.
7 It's not important who does the
planting, or who does the watering.
What's important is that God makes
the seed grow. 8 The one who plants
and the one who waters work to-
gether with the same purpose. And
both will be rewarded for their own
hard work. 9 For we are both God's
workers. And you are God's field.
You are God's building.

10 Because of God's grace to me, I
have laid the foundation like an ex-
pert builder. Now others are build-
ing on it. But whoever is building on
this foundation must be very careful.
11 For no one can lay any foundation
other than the one we already have—
Jesus Christ.

12 Anyone who builds on that
foundation may use a variety of ma-
terials—gold, silver, jewels, wood,
hay, or straw. 13 But on the judg-
ment day, fire will reveal what kind
of work each builder has done. The
fire will show if a person's work has
any value. 14 If the work survives, that
builder will receive a reward. 15 But
if the work is burned up, the builder
will suffer great loss. The builder will
be saved, but like someone barely es-
caping through a wall of flames.

16 Don't you realize that all of you
together are the temple of God and
that the Spirit of God lives in* you?
17 God will destroy anyone who de-
stroys this temple. For God's temple
is holy, and you are that temple.

18 Stop deceiving yourselves. If you
think you are wise by this world's
standards, you need to become a fool
to be truly wise. 19 For the wisdom of
this world is foolishness to God. As
the Scriptures say,

NASB

"*He is* THE ONE WHO CATCHES THE WISE IN THEIR CRAFTINESS"; 20 and again, "THE LORD KNOWS THE REASONINGS of the wise, THAT THEY ARE USELESS." 21 So then let no one boast in men. For all things belong to you, 22 whether Paul or Apollos or Cephas or the world or life or death or things present or things to come; all things belong to you, 23 and you belong to Christ; and Christ belongs to God.

**3:3** [a]Lit *according to man* **3:8** [a]Or *wages* **3:9** [a]Or *cultivated land* **3:12** [a]Or *costly* **3:13** [a]Lit *of what sort each man's work is* **3:16** [a]Or *sanctuary* **3:17** [a]Or *sanctuary* [b]Lit *who you are*

NLT

"He traps the wise
in the snare of their own
cleverness."*

20 And again,

"The LORD knows the thoughts of
the wise;
he knows they are worthless."*

21 So don't boast about following a particular human leader. For everything belongs to you—22 whether Paul or Apollos or Peter,* or the world, or life and death, or the present and the future. Everything belongs to you, 23 and you belong to Christ, and Christ belongs to God.

**3:1a** Greek *Brothers.* **3:1b** Or *to people who have the Spirit.* **3:16** Or *among.* **3:19** Job 5:13. **3:20** Ps 94:11. **3:22** Greek *Cephas.*

Many of the Christians in Corinth were a mess. We might go so far as to call them "pigpen Christians." God had rescued them from the mire of their sinful lives, washed them clean by the blood of Christ, and illumined their minds by the Holy Spirit. Yet they still liked to hang out close to the pigpen, longing for the warm muck, dipping their feet in the gritty mud, poking their noses through the fence, and wishing they could take another roll in the sludge, just one more time.

After sharply contrasting the "spiritual" person (the saved) with the "natural" person (the unsaved) in 1 Corinthians 2:14-16, Paul now strongly rebukes the Corinthian Christians, suggesting that they could not be objectively described as "spiritual." Instead, their attitudes and actions placed them in a middle category: They no longer behaved like the unsaved, but neither did they behave like the saved. They were "carnal" Christians, pathetically immature. Paul supports the charge of spiritual immaturity (3:1-4) by pointing out the destructive divisions in the church. He then uses three powerful illustrations to describe the kind of attitudes and actions they should exhibit in the church (3:5-17). Finally, he calls his readers to reject their folly and embrace the wisdom of God, which can heal their divisions and unite them in Jesus Christ (3:18-23).

## — 3:1-5 —

Besides the unsaved "natural" (*psychikos* [5591]) person (2:14) and the thriving "spiritual" (*pneumatikos* [4152]) person (2:15), Paul introduces the Corinthians to a third kind of person, called "fleshly" (*sarkikos* [4559])—genuine believers who nevertheless root around in the pigpens of their old natures and resist the control of the Holy Spirit in their lives. They have been justified—declared "not guilty" because of their faith in the finished work of Jesus Christ. But they have failed to walk the path of sanctification—the progressive spiritual growth toward maturity experienced by believers who enjoy a vital fellowship with God, embracing the "mind of Christ" (2:16) and seeking to follow Him by the power of the Holy Spirit.

This in-between group of "carnal" or "fleshly" Christians—justified but not engaged in working out their sanctification—characterized a significant number of the believers in the Corinthian church. In fact, so dominant was the fleshly characteristic of the church that Paul openly charged the entire church with this trait: "And I, brethren, could not speak to you as to spiritual men, but as to men of flesh" (3:1). Note that Paul doesn't dump them into the category of the "natural" or unsaved (2:14). Yet because of their lack of spiritual maturity, neither can he address them fully as "spiritual," those whose lives reflect the vibrant, fruitful life of a believer.

Were the Corinthians saved? Yes.

Were they sanctified? No.

Paul gives three characteristics of those who are "of the flesh."

First, *they are genuine Christians who act like non-Christians* (3:1, 4). The Corinthians were truly saved—no doubt about that. Paul addresses the church as "saints" (1:2) and calls them "brethren" who are "in Christ" (3:1). These designations can refer only to fellow believers. Paul says, however, that he couldn't address them as "spiritual men" but only as "men of flesh." In fact, their behavior looked more like that of "mere men" than that of regenerated believers (3:4). So, it is clear that true, born-again believers can sometimes appear indistinguishable from unbelievers in the manifestation of (or the lack of) their good works.

Second, *carnal Christians lack spiritual growth* (3:2). Just as we would never expect an infant to eat a steak, we cannot expect new believers to digest the meatier doctrines of the Christian faith. Yet Paul expected that after some training and time, these Corinthian believers would grow out of their bottle-feeding days and be ready to handle the kind of deep teaching described in 1 Corinthians 2. The tragedy was that even after enough time for spiritual growth, the Corinthians remained as babes in Christ. They fit into the same category as those described in the letter to the Hebrews:

> For though by this time you ought to be teachers, you have need again for someone to teach you the elementary principles of the oracles of God, and you have come to need milk and not solid food. For everyone who partakes only of milk is not accustomed to the word of righteousness, for he is an infant. But solid food is for the mature, who because of practice have their senses trained to discern good and evil. (Heb. 5:12-14)

Paul says the Corinthians are "still fleshly" (1 Cor. 3:3), implying that they necessarily started their Christian lives as "fleshly" (like all new believers) but that God intended for them to grow out of that immature, fleshly state.

Third, *carnal Christians nurse unconfessed sin* (3:3-4). Paul begins to pinpoint the specific evidence of their carnality: They harbored jealousy and strife toward each other. Such wicked attitudes were unfitting for those who had "put on the Lord Jesus Christ" (Rom. 13:13-14). Paul even lists jealousy and strife as among the "deeds of the flesh" condemned in Galatians 5:20. The Corinthians should have known better than to tolerate these unrepentant sins in their midst. Their formation of schisms and parties in the church—"I am of Paul," "I am of Apollos" (1 Cor. 1:12)—demonstrated that their jealousy and strife had reached such a frenzied pitch that open conflict had actually broken out.

Paul challenged their whole perception of Christian leadership: Neither Paul nor Apollos—the imagined "leaders" of their denominational alliances—would have been even mildly impressed by their loyalties (3:4). In fact, Paul reminds the Corinthians that both men are simply "servants" (3:5) through whom they had believed. What a jolting revelation! Paul sounds a clear message: "How can the Paulites Party and the Apollos Fan Club stand at odds with each other in Corinth, when both Paul and Apollos are players on the same team?" Only spiritually infantile minds suffering from an acute case of carnal Christianity could turn these two fellow servants of the gospel against each other through jealousy and strife.

## — 3:6-17 —

To dispel the rising pressure between the schismatic groups in Corinth, Paul had to come up with a better way to explain the harmonious work of Paul and Apollos. In a church that had pitted those two co-laborers against each other, only by driving home the unity of their apostolic work could Paul hope to reconcile the warring factions in Corinth. This was no time for complex theological propositions and syllogistic subtleties. Paul needed to paint a persuasive picture quickly. To do so, he followed in the footsteps of the Master Teacher—Jesus Himself—and communicated the truth of the church-planting ministry in Corinth through a series of three images: plant, building, and temple.

*Plant* (3:6-9). When the Corinthian Christians followed after the teachers of the Word rather than the God of the Word, they proved to be weak saplings in the faith. Their immaturity became obvious when some took sides with Paul's ministry, others with Apollos (3:5). The Corinthian factions had made demigods out of those men, revering their own favorites such that they would follow one to the exclusion of the other. Paul challenges their error head-on when he makes a distinction between the sowers and the soil.

The sowers were those who planted, watered, fertilized, pruned, and harvested for Jesus. Paul describes them as "servants through whom you believed" (3:5). Just as it was in ancient Corinth, so every church today has those who labor at sowing the Word. None of them qualify to be rallied around and treated like celebrities. Rather, they are messengers—personal agents of Christ sent to bring the good Word of God to those who believe. Paul says the sowers of the good news are partners working together (3:6), not competing to out-plant the others. Paul planted the church in Corinth through his ministry of preaching. Apollos came afterwards to water the church through his teaching ministry. Yet God alone—neither Paul nor Apollos—causes the spiritual growth (3:7).

Though Paul and Apollos had *distinct* ministry callings, they did not have *separate* ministries. Their ministries of planting and watering were "one" (3:8). Preaching *and* teaching, evangelism *and* discipleship, gospel proclamation *and* spiritual formation, were simply different aspects of a unified ministry to "make disciples" (Matt. 28:19). Paul emphasized his essential unity with Apollos by describing the two of them as "God's fellow workers" (1 Cor. 3:9).

Though united under the common umbrella ministry of disciple-making, each individual servant is still personally responsible in ministry before the Lord, from whom "each will receive his own reward according to his own labor" (3:8). Paul never rejects the idea of our individual responsibility to be the best servant each of us can be. Yet neither does Paul forget the vital truth that these individual sowers are not *independent* of each other, but *interdependent* on each other and mutually *dependent* on God Himself, who alone can produce healthy fruit in the gospel ministry.

Paul calls the Corinthians "God's field." They are the soil worked by the laborers, Paul and Apollos. Instead of producing blossoming plants for which the sowers could be proud, however, the Corinthians produced useless weeds. Only by responding to all of the Spirit-enabled ministries of all of God's apostles, prophets, evangelists, pastors, and teachers (Eph. 4:11-16) would the church be able to produce abundant and long-lasting fruit. By picking and choosing whom they would follow, the Corinthians risked producing only thorns and thistles.

This is a great time to pause and ask ourselves some probing questions. Are we like the Corinthians, growing crabgrass, thorny weeds, and dandelions? Or are we like blooming, fragrant fruit trees displaying God's goodness and mercy? Just as Paul urged the Corinthians, so we also need to be urged to transplant the refreshing fruit of the Spirit where the rotten fruit of sin had once grown (Gal. 5:22-23).

*Building* (1 Cor. 3:10-15). After using the field and sower image to emphasize the Corinthians' desperate need for guided spiritual growth toward maturity, Paul suddenly changes metaphors and describes the Corinthian church as a building. This image stresses the quality they should strive for in constructing their spiritual structure. He escorts them through each stage, from laying the foundation, through the actual construction, and on to the final inspection.

Barry Beitzel

Paul likened ministry in Corinth to a building project. The foundation (the person and work of Jesus Christ) had already been laid by the apostles and prophets. Now the rest of the believers in Corinth were responsible for adding to the building.

As the original planter of the church in Corinth, Paul could regard himself as the foreman, the "wise master builder" (3:10). Yet just as Paul's general calling as an apostle was a gift of grace (Rom. 1:5), so the specific work he began at Corinth was "according to the grace of God" given to him (1 Cor. 3:10). Neither the wisdom nor the skill, neither the plan nor the resources—for building the foundation of the church—had come from Paul. *Everything* came from God Himself. This foundation upon which the ministers in Corinth could build is none other than Jesus Christ Himself—the message of His person and work, which constitutes the gospel of salvation (3:11).

After underscoring the importance of the foundation of Jesus Christ, Paul warns the Corinthians about the need for care in their part of the construction work (3:10), focusing on the quality of their work. He urges his readers to use only the best materials—long-lasting and priceless elements like gold, silver, and precious stones. They are to avoid altogether the flimsy and flammable cheap materials like wood, hay, and straw (3:12).

Paul warns that the quality of each builder's work will be tested by fire (3:13-15). In Paul's writings, "the day" most often refers to the coming day of judgment at the return of Christ (1 Thes. 5:4; 2 Thes. 2:2), when Christ Himself will take His seat and judge believers for their works—not as a basis for salvation, but as a basis for rewards (Rom. 14:10; 2 Cor. 5:10). Like the works of the Corinthians, our own works one day will be tested—not to decide who has merited salvation, but to determine the rewards a believer receives.

*Holy temple* (1 Cor. 3:16-17). Finally, moving quite naturally from the image of a building project, Paul introduces the image of the local church in Corinth as a holy temple of God. Ralph Earle notes, "In a sense it could be said that the Christians together constituted God's dwelling place in Corinth."[11] Paul describes the church corporately as a "temple" elsewhere (Eph. 2:21; 2 Cor. 6:16), though he also refers to each individual Christian as a temple of God (1 Cor. 6:19), and he sometimes refers to the literal, physical temple in Jerusalem (2 Thes. 2:4). Here, however, Paul tells the Corinthians that corporately as God's people they constitute a dwelling place for the Holy Spirit (1 Cor. 3:16). As a church body, they were to visibly represent the living God on earth.

Yet the church's honor of serving as God's unique representative in Corinth carried with it a harrowing responsibility: Those who contribute to the destruction of the temple of the local church, either through neglect or bad behavior, will be destroyed (3:17). This does not refer to believers who commit suicide, as the context here refers not to destroying an individual's human body (temple) but to the whole corporate body of the church in a particular place. The idea is that God values the ministry of the local church so highly that He threatens destruction against anybody who would soil His holy sanctuary on earth (3:17).

We see examples of God acting decisively for the holiness of His church in the New Testament. God struck dead Ananias and his wife Sapphira for financial dealings with the church that lacked full integrity (Acts 5:1-11). James, the brother of Jesus, mentions that some Christians may have become ill because of unrepentant sin (Jas. 5:15), and Paul similarly mentions some in Corinth who had become "weak and sick" and even died for improperly participating in the Lord's Supper (1 Cor. 11:28-30). So, those who defile God's holy temple—the local church—will be subject to divine discipline in order to maintain the purity of the church.

## — 3:18-23 —

In these last several verses Paul adds a capstone to the argument he has been building throughout the first few chapters. He adds nothing substantially new but summarizes what he had been urging all along, this time with a specific application of these truths to their situation. In light of the contrast between human and divine wisdom (1:18-25), Paul urges his readers to "become foolish" in the eyes of the world in order to "become wise" by God's standards (3:18). To do otherwise is to deceive oneself into thinking that the world's wisdom (*sophia* [4678]) has something authentic and permanent to offer. Paul counters this false notion by reiterating his main theme: "The wisdom of this world is foolishness before God" (3:19). To reinforce this maxim, Paul alludes to Job 5:13 and Psalm 94:11:

> He captures the wise by their own shrewdness,
> And the advice of the cunning is quickly thwarted. (Job 5:13)

> The Lord knows the thoughts of man,
> That they are a mere breath. (Ps. 94:11)

Paul then aims his practical exhortation specifically at the Corinthians' sin: exalting the status of one particular servant of God over another, something worldly-minded people would do, but not something expected of God's children. They must not "boast in men," who are only servants of God (1 Cor. 3:21). Exalting people perpetuates immaturity rather than humility. Idolizing people leads to disappointment, disillusionment, and ultimately, a precipitous crash. Any god but the Lord is sure to fall from its pedestal.

Paul's statement that "all things belong to you" (3:22) may be hard to understand at first glance. Craig Keener explains it this way: "God's servants are for the church, not the church for God's servants."[12] The worldly approach to leadership involves a popular, persuasive, or powerful leader whose followers are always at his beck and call. In other words, all things belong to the ruler, king, or guru. That may be the bylaws of the kingdom or the cult, but that's not the way God has structured His body, the church. Instead, the leaders of the church are to be servants of God, ministering as shepherds, guides, and examples for the flock. God has given several servants to each church, not just one, and as all of these servants are working together, the church will grow toward a healthy, wholesome, and balanced maturity.

William Barclay described Paul's words here as prose that "suddenly takes wings and becomes a lyric of passion and poetry."[13] Paul says that not only the ministries of Paul, Apollos, and Cephas have been given by God for the purpose of their spiritual growth, but, in fact, *everything* is useful for their journey heavenward—the world, life, death, things present and future—because *everything* ultimately belongs to Christ and God (3:22-23). This may seem like over-the-top exaggeration, but Paul says essentially the same thing in Romans 8:28: "And we know that God causes all things to work together for good to those who love God, to those who are called according to His purpose." Without qualification, all things are choreographed by the all-powerful, all-wise, all-knowing God for the good of His people.

That may seem like foolishness to the world. But to believers living by the Spirit, that represents the wisdom of God.

## APPLICATION: 1 CORINTHIANS 3:1-23

### Building Up . . . or Tearing Down?

Clearly, God takes His spiritual building project—the church—very seriously. So seriously, in fact, that Paul warns of dire consequences if anyone contributes to its *destruction* rather than to its *construction* (3:17).

But what about us? Do we care enough about the growth of fellow believers in our local churches to seriously evaluate our own contributions to its ministry? I'm not talking about financial contributions (though that's certainly important). I'm talking about the things Paul was writing about under the power of the Holy Spirit: building up the body of Christ through quality character and service toward our brothers and sisters in Christ.

Our building projects will one day be inspected by eyes that can see into every nook and cranny, crack and crevice, closet and attic of our lives. So we should resist taking shortcuts in the local church ministry set before us. We should follow God's blueprint exactly, building our lives on His foundation with materials that will withstand the blaze of His coming glory.

Surely, 1 Corinthians 3 should cause us to ask practical questions related to the quality of the materials we're using in the spiritual construction of our own local churches. Are we building up . . . or tearing down? To help us ponder this, let's ask ourselves a few probing questions. Don't rush through them. Ask them seriously, and answer them honestly.

- Am I building up my fellow believers in my local church with quality bricks of humility, contentment, patience, perseverance, love, and integrity?
- Or am I contributing poor-quality works in my church like pride, ambition, impatience, weakness, bitterness, or disharmony?
- Am I neglecting ministry opportunities that could be building up my local church members? What are they? How soon can I get involved?
- Have I failed to see my local church with the same love and priority that God sees it, as his "temple" (3:16)? What things in my life have I been consistently placing ahead of God's church?
- Am I truly giving my whole heart, soul, mind, and strength to the Lord's service? On what things am I focusing my greatest affections and attention?

In light of the emphasis in 1 Corinthians 3 that Paul places on each believer's ministry in the local church, it might be a good idea for us to run through this series of questions regularly.

# CORRECTING ILLS AND IMMORALITY (1 CORINTHIANS 4:1–6:20)

Nobody likes correction. From the five-year-old who's told she didn't wash up properly to the fifty-year-old whose employer criticizes his lackluster performance—people don't want to be told they've done something wrong. Some of us get defensive, trying to blame somebody else or striking back at the person correcting us. Even those who take it well would resonate with the admission of the author of Hebrews: "All discipline for the moment seems not to be joyful, but sorrowful" (Heb. 12:11).

Christians, however, should realize that correction by God through His Word, His works, and His workers is a necessary part of spiritual growth. Our heavenly Father disciplines us so we can "share His holiness" (Heb. 12:10). Unlike our earthly parents—who may have punished us wrongly at times by being too harsh or too lax—the Lord always chastens us for the right reasons, in the right way, at the right time, and to the right degree (Heb. 12:10-11).

So it is with authority and love that Paul uses his pen as a rod of correction to discipline the wayward Corinthian Christians for a variety of ills, including immorality. We've already seen in the previous section that Paul had to correct schisms, factions, parties, and divisions in Corinth. Now, he reasserts his unique apostolic authority (1 Cor. 4:1-21) and challenges the Corinthians on an issue of gross sexual immorality: "that someone has his father's wife" (5:1). Paul then describes the principles of church discipline, seeking to purge the church of wickedness and to purify its people (5:1-13). Besides this, the Corinthian Christians didn't hesitate to sue one another in secular court (6:1-8), and some failed to accompany their conversion to Christianity by a converted lifestyle of sexual purity (6:9-20). So Paul, as their father in the faith, turns his attention to the Corinthians' failure to live up to their reputation as followers of Jesus Christ.

Paul's strong words correcting community ills and personal immorality continue to speak to us in the twenty-first century. We would all do well to hear the words and heed the warnings, avoiding the unpleasant but necessary discipline God will use to restore His disobedient children.

### KEY TERMS IN 1 CORINTHIANS 4:1–6:20

***oikonomos* (οἰκονόμος)** [3623] "steward," "custodian," "caretaker"
In 1 Corinthians 4:1-2, Paul says he and his fellow apostles should be regarded as "stewards" (*oikonomos*) of the mysteries of God (4:1), entrusted with a great responsibility for which they must be found faithful (4:2). The word *oikonomos* literally means "rule of a house," and referred primarily to a manager or caretaker who worked under the authority of the lord of the house (Luke 12:42; 16:1). In Romans 16:23 the word refers to a "treasurer" of the city, entrusted with public funds. Church leaders, too, are regarded as "stewards" of the local assembly (Titus 1:7), as are all believers who have a responsibility toward each other in the church (1 Pet. 4:10).

***porneia* (πορνεία)** [4202] "immorality," "fornication"
A most general term for sexual immorality, *porneia* can include premarital or extramarital sexual relations, including prostitution and homosexuality. The specific term for adultery, *moicheia* [3430], can sometimes be used synonymously, as in Galatians 1:19 where many Greek manuscripts include *moicheia* instead of *porneia*, though the range of meaning for *porneia* is much broader. The root *porn-* still endures in modern English in the word "pornography" (*pornē* + *graphein*), which designates a graphic representation of immoral sexual behavior.

# Corrections from a Faithful Father
## 1 CORINTHIANS 4:1-21

NASB

1 Let a man regard us in this manner,
as servants of Christ and stewards of
the mysteries of God. 2 In this case,
moreover, it is required [a]of stewards that one be found trustworthy.
3 But to me it is a very small thing
that I may be examined by you, or
by *any* human [a]court; in fact, I do

NLT

1 So look at Apollos and me as mere
servants of Christ who have been put
in charge of explaining God's mysteries. 2 Now, a person who is put in
charge as a manager must be faithful. 3 As for me, it matters very little
how I might be evaluated by you
or by any human authority. I don't

not even examine myself. 4 For I am conscious of nothing against myself, yet I am not by this acquitted; but the one who examines me is the Lord. 5 Therefore do not go on [a]passing judgment before [b]the time, *but wait* until the Lord comes who will both bring to light the things hidden in the darkness and disclose the motives of *men's* hearts; and then each man's praise will come to him from God.

6 Now these things, brethren, I have figuratively applied to myself and Apollos for your sakes, so that in us you may learn not to exceed what is written, so that no one of you will become [a]arrogant in behalf of one against the other. 7 For who regards you as superior? What do you have that you did not receive? And if you did receive it, why do you boast as if you had not received it?

8 You are already filled, you have already become rich, you have become kings without us; and indeed, *I* wish that you had become kings so that we also might reign with you. 9 For, I think, God has exhibited us apostles last of all, as men condemned to death; because we have become a spectacle to the world, [a]both to angels and to men. 10 We are fools for Christ's sake, but you are prudent in Christ; we are weak, but you are strong; you are distinguished, but we are without honor. 11 To this present hour we are both hungry and thirsty, and are poorly clothed, and are roughly treated, and are homeless; 12 and we toil, working with our own hands; when we are reviled, we bless; when we are persecuted, we endure; 13 when we are slandered, we try to [a]conciliate;

even trust my own judgment on this point. 4 My conscience is clear, but that doesn't prove I'm right. It is the Lord himself who will examine me and decide.

5 So don't make judgments about anyone ahead of time—before the Lord returns. For he will bring our darkest secrets to light and will reveal our private motives. Then God will give to each one whatever praise is due.

6 Dear brothers and sisters,* I have used Apollos and myself to illustrate what I've been saying. If you pay attention to what I have quoted from the Scriptures,* you won't be proud of one of your leaders at the expense of another. 7 For what gives you the right to make such a judgment? What do you have that God hasn't given you? And if everything you have is from God, why boast as though it were not a gift?

8 You think you already have everything you need. You think you are already rich. You have begun to reign in God's kingdom without us! I wish you really were reigning already, for then we would be reigning with you. 9 Instead, I sometimes think God has put us apostles on display, like prisoners of war at the end of a victor's parade, condemned to die. We have become a spectacle to the entire world—to people and angels alike.

10 Our dedication to Christ makes us look like fools, but you claim to be so wise in Christ! We are weak, but you are so powerful! You are honored, but we are ridiculed. 11 Even now we go hungry and thirsty, and we don't have enough clothes to keep warm. We are often beaten and have no home. 12 We work wearily with our own hands to earn our living. We bless those who curse us. We are patient with those who abuse us. 13 We appeal gently when evil things are said about us. Yet we are treated

**NASB**

we have become as the scum of the
world, the dregs of all things, *even*
until now.

14 I do not write these things to
shame you, but to admonish you
as my beloved children. 15 For if you
were to have countless tutors in
Christ, yet *you would* not *have* many
fathers, for in Christ Jesus I became
your father through the gospel.
16 Therefore I exhort you, be imita-
tors of me. 17 For this reason I have
sent to you Timothy, who is my be-
loved and faithful child in the Lord,
and he will remind you of my ways
which are in Christ, just as I teach
everywhere in every church. 18 Now
some have become [a]arrogant, as
though I were not coming to you.
19 But I will come to you soon, if the
Lord wills, and I shall find out, not
the [a]words of those who are arrogant
but their power. 20 For the kingdom of
God does not consist in [a]words but in
power. 21 What do you desire? Shall I
come to you with a rod, or with love
and a spirit of gentleness?

**4:2** [a]Lit *in* **4:3** [a]Lit *day* **4:5** [a]Lit *judging anything* [b]I.e. the appointed time of judgment **4:6** [a]Lit *puffed up* **4:9** [a]Or *and to angels and to men* **4:13** [a]Or *console* **4:18** [a]Lit *puffed up* **4:19** [a]Lit *word* **4:20** [a]Lit *word*

**NLT**

like the world's garbage, like every-
body's trash—right up to the present
moment.

14 I am not writing these things to
shame you, but to warn you as my
beloved children. 15 For even if you
had ten thousand others to teach you
about Christ, you have only one spir-
itual father. For I became your father
in Christ Jesus when I preached the
Good News to you. 16 So I urge you to
imitate me.

17 That's why I have sent Timothy,
my beloved and faithful child in the
Lord. He will remind you of how I fol-
low Christ Jesus, just as I teach in all
the churches wherever I go.

18 Some of you have become ar-
rogant, thinking I will not visit you
again. 19 But I will come—and soon—
if the Lord lets me, and then I'll find
out whether these arrogant people
just give pretentious speeches or
whether they really have God's
power. 20 For the Kingdom of God
is not just a lot of talk; it is living
by God's power. 21 Which do you
choose? Should I come with a rod to
punish you, or should I come with
love and a gentle spirit?

**4:6a** Greek *Brothers.* **4:6b** Or *If you learn not to go beyond "what is written."*

No parent likes to see a son or daughter go astray. Over a life of ministry, I have seen this scenario up close and personal. Mothers and fathers who had given their all to rearing their sons or daughters in the faith watch helplessly as their children slip away and vanish into the fog of the world's alluring temptations. Sometimes, like the prodigal son, a child adrift eventually returns to safe harbors. I've seen it happen enough times to get a real sense of the joy that the father of the prodigal son felt when he saw that lost child shamefully shuffling up the walkway. But not all stories of rebellious kids end with a fatted-calf feast and a family celebration. I have also seen parents agonize over an apostate child during the balance of their lives, tearfully praying night and day for the one who fled the faith, having rushed headlong into the irreversible consequences of sin. These are heartbreaking scenes from the tragic reels of life.

When the apostle Paul heard the dreadful report about the Corinthians' immature, carnal beliefs and behavior, he responded like a desperate father would when hearing about the dangerous attitudes and actions of a wayward child. After all, he was their original apostolic witness and therefore their spiritual "father" in the faith. He felt a deep, personal obligation for their spiritual growth and health, as any decent father would feel for his child.

Yet Paul's approach to spiritual parenting looked nothing like the namby-pamby approach to parenting that coddles rather than corrects, pampers rather than reproves. Instead, Paul applied the heavenly Father's approach to discipline, knowing that eternal benefits far outweigh the momentary suffering: "All discipline for the moment seems not to be joyful, but sorrowful; yet to those who have been trained by it, afterwards it yields the peaceful fruit of righteousness" (Heb. 12:11).

With authority and love, Paul used his pen as a rod of correction to discipline the unruly Corinthians. Though we cannot hear the cries of these believers as they endured the pain of their reproof, we can read the stinging rebukes they received and see how they apply to us today.

## — 4:1-5 —

Paul eases into this section of strong reproof with a smooth transition from his previous warning against personality-centered schisms (3:21-23). He further characterizes the apostles and other teachers like Apollos as "servants of Christ and stewards of the mysteries of God" (4:1). The word translated "servants," *hypēretēs* [5257], refers to one who acts under the orders of another, specifically drawing on an image of submission to one of greater authority. The word "steward," *oikonomos* [3623], etymologically refers to one who is put in charge of a household or estate. With these terms Paul illustrates both his submission to the absolute authority of Christ as well as his God-given authority as a handpicked manager of the gospel. He therefore is responsible to be "found trustworthy" (4:2).

A glimpse of the situation in Corinth (4:3) reveals that many in the Corinthian church who had formed parties around Apollos or Peter or some other celebrity had turned up their noses at Paul's manner of ministry. They had passed judgment on his teaching and therefore rejected his apostolic authority as a chosen steward of the gospel. Paul reminds them that his gospel ministry was not subject to any human judgment, whether that came from the Corinthian Christians, the world, or even his own estimation of his value to the kingdom (4:3). Rather, as a servant of Christ and a steward of His mysteries, Paul was accountable directly to God Himself (4:4).

The phrase translated "human court" literally says, "human day," intentionally contrasted with the coming day of the Lord (3:13), in which all people will be held accountable for their faithfulness to their God-given tasks.[1] With this future evaluation by Christ looming on the horizon, Paul warns the Corinthians to withhold their own judgment of others' ministries (4:5). When Christ returns, He alone will "bring to light the things hidden in the darkness and disclose the motives of men's hearts" (4:5). With these words Paul refers to the future judgment seat of Christ (2 Cor. 5:10).

Paul's message to us today is straightforward: Let's have no judgment-seat-of-Christ rehearsals on earth! None of us qualifies for that. Let's forego judging other people based on what we think we see or hear. Instead, let's leave that to the Lord, because He's able to do two things that human beings can never do: First, He can bring to light the things hidden in the darkness. He alone knows the complete story. We get bits and pieces and can only touch the surface of each issue. Second, Christ has the ability to disclose the motives of the heart. He knows not only *what* somebody says or does, but *why* they say or do it. No mere human can ever do that.

All of this discussion positions Paul for his correction of the Corinthians' errors. Though he is a servant of Christ, Paul still holds a position of authority in relationship to the church in Corinth. As their father in the faith, Paul exhorts them to imitate him.

## — 4:6-13 —

Having established that he had both a right and a responsibility to discipline the church in Corinth as their spiritual father, Paul transitions into this disciplinary section (4:6). Paul notes that he had set up himself and Apollos "figuratively" as examples for the Corinthians to see the kind of attitudes needed to carry out the Corinthians' own self-sacrificial ministries with one another.

Paul warns the Corinthians "not to exceed what is written" (4:6). Commentators have long wrestled with the meaning of this statement. Did Paul mean to stick closely to the Scriptures? If so, this would be a strange place to suddenly warn his readers about being faithful to Scripture, because Paul does not quote any particular Scripture here, nor does he develop the idea of fidelity to Scripture in this context. Or does Paul mean that the Corinthians should not transgress what he himself had written to them? This might be the case, as Paul mentions a former letter (5:9). That letter, however, seems to have been written about avoiding sexual immorality, which is not Paul's theme here. Although the interpretation of this phrase is difficult to pin down with certainty, the context suggests that Paul is referring to those in Corinth who were exceeding their proper bounds as Christians through arrogance, perhaps boasting in their particular favorite teachers or even bragging about their own spiritual or physical accomplishments (4:6).

In response to their excessive and unbalanced attitudes and actions, Paul rebukes the Corinthians with three rhetorical questions designed to blister their egos (4:7). Then with sharp sarcasm he grabs them by the shoulders, looks them in the eye, and snaps them out of their self-absorbed fit (4:8).

First Paul asks, "Who regards you as superior?" (4:7). Answer: *no one*. The Corinthian church was on equal footing with all other churches. Second, "What do you have that you did not receive?" Answer: *nothing*. Originally they had heard the gospel from Paul, were saved by Christ, and were trained by Paul and Apollos. Everything had come from someone else. Third, "Why do you boast as if you had not received it?" This last question must have stung. As A. T. Robertson put it, Paul "punctures effectually the inflated bag of false pride."[2] In the final analysis, the Corinthians had no basis for boasting and bragging, only for thanking and praising. Like the Corinthians, we must shun delusions of grandeur, always remembering that "every good thing given and every perfect gift is from above, coming down from the Father of lights, with whom there is no variation or shifting shadow" (Jas. 1:17).

The Corinthians' sense of superiority so compromised their testimonies that Paul felt moved to deliver a piercing blow (1 Cor. 4:8-13). A little background to the Corinthian situation helps us understand why Paul resorts to this strong reproof that borders on scathing sarcasm. David Prior notes:

> At the heart of the boasting at Corinth was the conviction that they were really a very successful, lively, mature and effective church. The Christians were satisfied with their spirituality, their leadership, and the general quality of their life together. They had settled down into the illusion that they had become the best they could be. They thought they had "arrived."[3]

Like a skilled marksman shooting down a runaway hot-air balloon, Paul punctures the Corinthians' inflated egos with a barrage of piercing scorn. Their attitudes and actions were not those of humble servants dedicated to faithfully carrying out God's work, but those of lavishly fulfilled kings (4:8)—astute, mighty, and illustrious (4:10). Indeed, Paul acknowledges that part of the Christian hope is one day to reign with Christ at His return, but the Corinthians were divvying up their little fiefdoms as if the kingdom of heaven already had arrived—without either the apostles or Christ! Had they fully embraced the gospel of the death and resurrection of Christ, they would have realized there can be no crown without the cross, no ecstasy without agony, no exaltation without humiliation.

In contrast to the Corinthians' territorial travesty, Paul points out the lowly position of the genuine apostolic ministers, whom the world saw as weak, dishonored fools (4:10). He calls himself and other church leaders "men condemned to death" and "a spectacle to the world" (4:9). As evidence for their apparently inferior position in contrast to the Corinthians' noble outlook, Paul produces a litany of experiences he had endured "to this present hour" (4:11). Look at the long list of humiliating, debilitating, and potentially crushing sufferings he endured in his quest to follow in the footsteps of Jesus Christ (4:11-13):

- hunger
- thirst
- poor clothing
- rough treatment
- homelessness
- toil
- revilement
- persecution
- slander

In short, the apostles were treated like the scum of the earth and the dregs of society (4:13). Paul's powerful rhetoric reveals a vital point: Living for Christ often puts one at odds with society. The implication? The Corinthians' boastful and selfish attitudes and actions—driven by arrogance and pride—have no place in a life that imitates Christ.

## — 4:14-21 —

Emerging from his scathing criticism of the Corinthians' out-of-control haughtiness, Paul reaffirms his affectionate relationship with his spiritual children. He assures them that his purpose is not to shame them, but to admonish them as his "beloved children" (4:14). The Greek word for "shame" here is *entrepō* [1788], which conveys the idea of turning against oneself, while the word "admonish" (*noutheteō* [3560]) means to impress something upon the mind. Paul didn't wish to turn the Corinthians against themselves, but to encourage a change of heart. In other words, this isn't a guilt trip, but a call to repentance intended to straighten out their twisted thinking and to correct their erroneous behavior.

Though the Corinthians had enjoyed the blessings of many gifted teachers—such as Apollos—after Paul initially planted the church, Paul maintained a special relationship with, and therefore a responsibility for, them as their "father through the gospel" (4:15). Continuing with this analogy of fatherhood, Paul exhorts the Corinthians to look to him, their spiritual father, as an example to follow. As I reflect on Paul's words, I realize how few Christian leaders can say this. It is my observation that far too many believers in positions of authority and responsibility do not have the spiritual maturity needed to provide a trustworthy example to others. They may be gifted orators, efficient organizers, or visionary CEOs, but when it comes to the character qualities of humility, self-sacrifice, and earnest determination to fulfill one's calling regardless of the obstacles, not many modern Christian leaders come immediately to mind. Paul, however, could fit the profile of a Christian leader worthy of following.

Paul knew the value of authentic, in-the-flesh, hands-on examples to drive home the principles of Christian discipleship. Because Paul could not travel to Corinth himself, he sent Timothy as a model of a "faithful child" in the Lord. Evidently, Timothy had taken seriously the idea of discipleship as an imitation not only of beliefs but also of lifestyle. With his physical presence among the Corinthians, Timothy would provide an observable example of Paul's ways in Christ (4:17).

As an experienced minister, he knew that his letter, and even Timothy's visit, would engender feelings of animosity from some of the hard cases in Corinth (4:18). Because of this, Paul punctuates this section with a warning: "I will come to you soon, if the Lord wills, and I shall find out, not the words of those who are arrogant but their power" (4:19). That is, Paul would find out the substance behind the superficiality. Would these boasters be able to drum up the kind of authentic spiritual authority given to Paul as a handpicked apostle of the true kingdom of God (4:20)? Of course, the answer was "no." In the end, Paul knew, the brash claims of the self-proclaimed leaders were only the crows of defiant bigmouths attempting to build their own kingdoms on a sandy foundation of empty words.

Paul ends this section with a choice for the Corinthians (4:21): On the one hand, they could receive Paul as a stern, strict, harsh father with rod in hand to reprimand his wayward children—and for that, they needed only to continue in their headstrong ways. On the other hand, they could welcome him as a gentle, loving father ready to impart to them some spiritual blessing on his arrival—and for that, they needed to repent, turn from their selfish ways, and restore unity in the church through practicing humility.

In the end, the choice was theirs. We have the same choice today.

## APPLICATION: 1 CORINTHIANS 4:1-21

### Paul on Spiritual Parenting

So far as we know, the apostle Paul had no physical children.[4] He did, however, have many spiritual children—converts to the Christian faith. Because Paul took his responsibilities as a spiritual father very seriously, we find several practical reminders about how to shepherd as spiritual parents. We can apply these principles to those with whom we minister and with our own children.

First, *spiritual parenting requires selfless sacrifice on behalf of our spiritual children.* In 1 Thessalonians Paul wrote, "But we proved to be gentle among you, as a nursing mother tenderly cares for her own children. Having so fond an affection for you, we were well-pleased to impart to you not only the gospel of God but also our own lives, because you had become very dear to us" (1 Thes. 2:7-8). This was Paul's approach everywhere he went. The Corinthian Christians were no exception. Paul consistently poured out his life for those he led to faith in Christ, teaching us that ministry is not merely the transference of information. It means personal, deep, committed involvement in the lives of those to whom we minister. Think about your own ministry context. Do you merely impart information, or do you pour yourself into the lives of others?

Second, *spiritual parenting means exhorting and encouraging toward spiritual maturity and setting a worthy example.* This is the positive aspect of parenting. Paul wrote, "Just as you know how we were exhorting and encouraging and imploring each one of you as a father would his own children, so that you would walk in a manner worthy of the God who calls you" (1 Thes. 2:11-12). He also exhorted the Corinthian Christians to imitate him (1 Cor. 4:15-16). Paul had to maintain an exemplary life to exhort his readers to follow in his footsteps. This should make us wonder if we might be guilty of exhorting and encouraging our spiritual children hypocritically, trying to impart to them something we do not possess ourselves—spiritual maturity. If we don't have faith in and love for Christ, exhibited in a life of consistent good works, how can we expect to promote such godly qualities in the lives of others?

Third, *spiritual parenting means confronting and correcting when gentle encouragement isn't enough.* Paul called for immediate repentance, with severe consequences for remaining in disobedience. He referred to the possible need for him to come to Corinth "with a rod," that is, as an implement of parental correction (4:21). Sometimes spiritual leaders must do the hard thing in confronting and correcting their wayward spiritual children. I know most of us would rather live in an igloo than confront a fellow believer, but we should never lose sight of the noble goal of correction: restoration of the wandering child's fellowship with God and with others. If mature spiritual parents don't rebuke and correct believers when they need it, who will do it?

Our calling as spiritual parents for those we mentor, teach, disciple, or otherwise influence is just as important as our physical parenting. When we self-sacrificially give ourselves to this task through our words and example, mustering the strength to confront the wayward, we will have fulfilled our obligation as spiritual parents.

# How to Handle a Scandal
## 1 CORINTHIANS 5:1-13

**NASB**

1 It is actually reported that there is immorality among you, and immorality of such a kind as does not exist even among the Gentiles, that

**NLT**

1 I can hardly believe the report about the sexual immorality going on among you—something that even pagans don't do. I am told that a man in your church is living in sin

**NASB**

someone has his father's wife. 2[a]You
have become [b]arrogant and [a]have
not mourned instead, so that the
one who had done this deed would
be removed from your midst.
3For I, on my part, though absent
in body but present in spirit, have
already judged him who has so com-
mitted this, as though I were present.
4In the name of our Lord Jesus, when
you are assembled, and [a]I with you
in spirit, with the power of our Lord
Jesus, 5*I have decided* to deliver such
a one to Satan for the destruction of
his flesh, so that his spirit may be
saved in the day of the Lord [a]Jesus.
6Your boasting is not good. Do you
not know that a little leaven leavens
the whole lump *of dough?* 7Clean
out the old leaven so that you may
be a new lump, just as you are *in fact*
unleavened. For Christ our Passover
also has been sacrificed. 8Therefore
let us celebrate the feast, not with
old leaven, nor with the leaven of
malice and wickedness, but with the
unleavened bread of sincerity and
truth.
9I wrote you in my letter not to
associate with immoral people;
10I *did* not at all *mean* with the im-
moral people of this world, or with
the covetous and swindlers, or with
idolaters, for then you would have
to go out of the world. 11But [a]actu-
ally, I wrote to you not to associate
[b]with any so-called brother if he is
an immoral person, or covetous, or
an idolater, or a reviler, or a drunk-
ard, or a swindler—not even to eat
with such a one. 12For what have I
to do with judging outsiders? Do you
not judge those who are within *the*
*church?* 13But those who are outside,

**NLT**

with his stepmother.* 2You are so
proud of yourselves, but you should
be mourning in sorrow and shame.
And you should remove this man
from your fellowship.
3Even though I am not with you in
person, I am with you in the Spirit.*
And as though I were there, I have al-
ready passed judgment on this man
4in the name of the Lord Jesus. You
must call a meeting of the church.*
I will be present with you in spirit,
and so will the power of our Lord
Jesus. 5Then you must throw this
man out and hand him over to Sa-
tan so that his sinful nature will be
destroyed* and he himself* will be
saved on the day the Lord* returns.
6Your boasting about this is
terrible. Don't you realize that this
sin is like a little yeast that spreads
through the whole batch of dough?
7Get rid of the old "yeast" by remov-
ing this wicked person from among
you. Then you will be like a fresh
batch of dough made without yeast,
which is what you really are. Christ,
our Passover Lamb, has been sacri-
ficed for us.* 8So let us celebrate the
festival, not with the old bread* of
wickedness and evil, but with the
new bread* of sincerity and truth.
9When I wrote to you before, I told
you not to associate with people who
indulge in sexual sin. 10But I wasn't
talking about unbelievers who in-
dulge in sexual sin, or are greedy, or
cheat people, or worship idols. You
would have to leave this world to
avoid people like that. 11I meant that
you are not to associate with anyone
who claims to be a believer* yet in-
dulges in sexual sin, or is greedy, or
worships idols, or is abusive, or is
a drunkard, or cheats people. Don't
even eat with such people.
12It isn't my responsibility to judge
outsiders, but it certainly is your
responsibility to judge those inside
the church who are sinning. 13God

God [a]judges. REMOVE THE WICKED MAN FROM AMONG YOURSELVES.

**5:2** [a]Or *have you...?* [b]Lit *puffed up* **5:4** [a]Lit *my spirit, with the power* **5:5** [a]Two early mss do not contain *Jesus* **5:11** [a]Lit *now* [b]Lit *together if any man called a brother is* **5:13** [a]Or *will judge*

will judge those on the outside; but as the Scriptures say, "You must remove the evil person from among you."*

**5:1** Greek *his father's wife.* **5:3** Or *in spirit.* **5:4** Or *In the name of the Lord Jesus, you must call a meeting of the church.* **5:5a** Or *so that his body will be destroyed;* Greek reads *for the destruction of the flesh.* **5:5b** Greek *and the spirit.* **5:5c** Other manuscripts read *the Lord Jesus;* still others read *our Lord Jesus Christ.* **5:7** Greek *has been sacrificed.* **5:8a** Greek *not with old leaven.* **5:8b** Greek *but with unleavened [bread].* **5:11** Greek *a brother.* **5:13** Deut 17:7.

As Christians living in a lost and fallen world, we often act like we're living on tiny Christian islands surrounded by a polluted sea beating upon our shores. Or we feel like we dwell in airtight spiritual ecosystems inside a Bible bubble, shielded and protected from the outside world. Yet this kind of isolationist mentality presents a problem for biblical Christianity. Jesus called us to be "in the world" but not "of the world" (John 17:11, 14-16). In other words, we should be *insulated* from the morally corrupting influences of our times but not *isolated* from the people of the world.

All of us can appreciate the tension this creates as we feel ourselves stuck in the center of a tug-of-war between running from the world and falling into it. Yes, some believers relieve the tension by building social walls around their holy huddle to keep them and their communities safe. Too many believers, however, have given in to the other extreme. They have let go of the purity of life presented in Scripture and provided by the empowerment of the Holy Spirit, only to slide into the cesspool of moral depravity.

In 1 Corinthians 5, Paul addresses the problem of a member of the church who had done just that. He had surrendered to corruption's seductive call and steered his ship into the jagged rocks of scandalous sin. Yet it may initially strike us as odd that Paul rebukes not only the sinner's repugnant acts but also the church's tolerant attitude toward the sin. Like modern-day liberal Christians who carry about the name of Christ but tolerate lifestyles and behaviors in direct conflict with the Bible's standards, the Corinthian church was proud of its hands-off approach to the sins of others. Paul shows them the seriousness of this complacency and teaches them how churches are to handle a scandal through church discipline.

## — 5:1-3 —

Like poisonous pollution seeping into a city's water supply, moral pollution had crept into the Corinthian church and threatened to poison the entire congregation. Without cushioning his readers for the sudden impact of the subject at the forefront of his mind, Paul directs attention to the terribly destructive situation at Corinth. We can make three significant observations (5:1) regarding this sin.

First, *the sin was well known.* Paul says that the sin was "actually reported." We can almost hear the disgust in Paul's tone. Nobody should hear the kind of report he had heard about a church whose members professed to be followers of Christ. Yet the most troubling part of this sin was that it was being broadcast far and wide. This was no secret sin, concealed with a cover-up to keep people from discovering the truth. Rather, the news had come easily to Paul, perhaps through members of Chloe's household (1:11) or through other men who had come to him (16:17-18). Or maybe it was so scandalous that the bad news had swept like a raging forest fire from church to church until it reached the ears of Paul from a number of sources.

Second, *the sin was revolting.* This isn't to say that some sins are beautiful or acceptable, but in this particular case, Paul emphasizes that the kind of sin reported "does not exist even among the Gentiles" (5:1). In other words, even non-Christian pagans would be shocked at the type of sexual immorality (*porneia* [4202]) being tolerated by the Corinthian Christians. What was that sin? A believing member of their church—presumably a young man—was engaged in sexual immorality with his stepmother. Apparently his father was still married to her since Paul refers to the woman as "a wife," not a "widow." This was an incestuous relationship between what amounted to a son and his mother!

Third, *the sin was ongoing.* Paul wasn't merely expressing his surprise that some young adolescent had fallen head-over-heels for his father's new, younger bride and caused a bit of an embarrassing uproar in the church. Rather, Paul describes the sin as a permanent fixture among the church. It was a case of immorality "among" the church—in their midst, right before their eyes, under their noses. In other words, the church knew all about the relationship yet did nothing *at all* about it!

This last point brings the greatest rebuke from Paul. As John White and Ken Blue note, "Unless someone in the church decides to go lovingly to the person involved in the scandal with the object of establishing the truth, effecting righteousness and seeking to bring about reconciliation, *every single member in the church who is aware of the situation is sinning every moment—is in fact a participator in the sin of the 'identified sinner' in one way or another. The church is sinning by avoiding corrective church discipline.*"[5] Every church must deal with sin among its members. Therefore, no church should shirk its responsibility to confront it. But the Corinthians were doing just that.

## — 5:2-3 —

Surprisingly, not only did the Corinthians fail to confront the sin of incestuous immorality in the church, but they even went to the other extreme: They became arrogant about it, as if the grace of Christ made them exempt from obeying His commands. Put bluntly, they sinned that grace might abound (see Rom. 6:1-2). They had been wading in the stagnant waters of pride for so long that it blinded them to the filth of the situation. In response to their "I'm okay, you're okay" approach to sin, Paul confronts them for their passivity, corrects their attitude toward the sin, and then instructs them about the proper approach to the situation.

First, Paul rebukes the Corinthians with blunt honesty. He says, "You have become arrogant" (1 Cor. 5:2). The "you" here in Greek is in the plural, showing that Paul is holding the entire Corinthian congregation responsible for the individual engaged in the sin. The Greek word (*physioō* [5448]) translated "arrogant" literally means "puffed up." It's used seven times in the New Testament, six of them in 1 Corinthians alone.[6] They had been inflated with a destructive view of grace. Salvation in Christ, they thought, permitted believers to do whatever they wanted. Instead of this arrogant approach to sin, they should rather have "mourned," as one might mourn at a funeral over the death of a loved one. Here the loss is not of a person's life, but of the church's purity.

Sadly, the Corinthian church had succumbed to a false teaching about grace that is growing fast in our own day. Some believe that once a person is justified before God and saved freely apart from any good works, that person may then do whatever is desirable, because saving grace covers everything. Yet Romans 6:1 says, "Are we to continue in sin so that grace may increase?" Romans 6:2 answers it with as strong a negative as you can find anywhere in the Scriptures: "May it never be!" Salvation by grace through faith alone does not logically lead to an "anything goes" lifestyle. In fact, if we have a full understanding of the work of God in salvation, we'll remember that the Holy Spirit not only permanently seals us freely by His grace (Eph. 1:13; 2:8-9; 2 Cor. 1:22), but He also indwells us, moving us from the inside out to submit to His will and obey His commands. This means that the indwelling Spirit, by His grace alone, continues to work in us both to desire and to perform good works—not to earn salvation, but as an outworking of salvation (Eph. 2:10; Phil. 2:12-13). The result is a holy life.

The Corinthians, puffed up by an aberrant view of grace that gave license for immorality, tolerated even gross sin. They should have removed the perpetrator from the church (1 Cor. 5:2). This would have marked not only their abhorrence of the sinful acts, but also their concern for the purity of the church and their desire to move the sinner toward repentance and restoration (Gal. 6:1-2). Instead, the church remained polluted and the individual unrepentant.

Paul takes a bold stand against the majority opinion in Corinth (1 Cor. 5:3). In many ways, his disciplinary intervention from afar demonstrates just how low the Corinthian church had sunk. Whatever leadership was then present in Corinth, these leaders had neither the moral compass nor the skill to navigate what should have been a clear, open-and-shut case of church discipline. Paul realized that for the good of the sinning brother and the purity of the church, *someone* must take a stand. If the congregation and its leadership lacked the power to do so, Paul would have to pull rank and pass judgment himself. In fact, having sized up the situation from his remote location (he was with them only "in spirit," but absent "in body"), Paul pronounced his apostolic judgment against the sinner, an authoritative verdict binding on the local church.

## — 5:4-5 —

In the remainder of the chapter, Paul gives the Corinthians specific instructions for carrying out the judgment he issued as an apostle. By the same apostolic authority, Paul taught that God has vested the church with the authority to pass this kind of judgment, and he expected the church in Corinth to have already taken proper action against the unrepentant sinner. Only because they failed to carry out proper church discipline did Paul step in as an apostle. Today all churches, following biblical principles for church discipline, have both a responsibility and the authority to protect the purity of the church and to hold unrepentant sinners accountable with a view toward their restoration.

Paul touches on the results of the disciplinary action (5:4-5). We might describe this as Paul's instructions on how to carry out the verdict of his judgment. First, they were to pass judgment not with their own authority—the authority of the pastor, the elders, a bishop, or the words of a church's constitution or bylaws—but rather on the moral authority of "our Lord Jesus" (5:4). By gathering in the name of the Lord Jesus, they were to exercise His authority in obedience to His commands. Paul may very well have in mind the instructions concerning church discipline in Matthew 18. Having carried out the discipline by the proper principles, with firmness and humility, they could have full confidence that they had the Lord's approval and were functioning with His authority.

Second, they were to carry out the discipline when they were "assembled." The Greek verb is *synagō* [4863], from which the word "synagogue" is derived. It means "to gather together" and refers to the official gathering of the congregation. So, this judgment was not to take place secretly or behind closed doors. Remember, at this point the incestuous relationship had been broadcast far and wide, and from all accounts it appeared that the Corinthian congregation not only knew, but the members had approved of the immoral relationship. To reverse this perception and to communicate to the whole church the seriousness of the offense, church discipline needed to be public. This doesn't mean, of course, that every confrontation of sin should start as a public matter. Private sin should oftentimes be dealt with privately, but the principle seems to be that the more public, prominent, and unrepentant the sin, the more public and official the discipline (1 Tim. 5:20).

Third, they were to "deliver such a one to Satan" (1 Cor. 5:5). In other words, the Corinthian church was to excommunicate the sinning Christian from the fellowship of the church. In the first-century church, this involved not only an official removal from membership so one was no longer regarded as a brother or sister in Christ (1 Cor. 5:2), but it also involved removal from the blessings of the Lord's Table (10:16), receiving benevolent help from the church (Eph. 4:28; 1 Jn. 3:17), and the spiritual protection offered through the presence of the Holy Spirit in the congregation (2 Thes. 3:3). The excommunicated believer would be ejected into Satan's domain, the world, where he would be outside the spiritual protection of the church and unable to repel the attacks of Satan (1 Pet. 5:8).

One of two results would follow the official excommunication of this unrepentant believer. If he continued without repentance and restoration, he could suffer physical death, either as built-in consequences of a destructive, sinful lifestyle (Rom. 1:26-27), or as the result of God's own hand of discipline against unrepentant believers (Heb. 12:5-11; cf. 1 Cor. 11:30; 1 Jn. 5:16). But another way to understand Paul's statement concerning "the destruction of his flesh" (1 Cor. 5:5) is that the sinning believer's fleshly desires would be ultimately defeated after Satan pushed those passions to extremes and the sinner finally came to his senses, like the prodigal son after a fruitless and futile life of debauchery (Luke 15). In either case, the purpose of this discipline was not merely punitive, and it could not be the eternal damnation of this sinning believer. The goal of this harsh discipline was restoration, "that his spirit may be saved in the day of the Lord Jesus" (1 Cor. 5:5). William Barclay explains:

> Always at the back of punishment and discipline in the early Church there is the conviction that they must seek not to break but to make the man who has sinned. . . . Discipline should never be exercised for the satisfaction of the person who exercises it, but always for the mending of the person who has sinned and for the sake of the Church. Discipline must never be vengeful; it must always be curative.[7]

Paul commands churches to lovingly correct, not vindictively punish, members who persist in sinning (cf. Matt. 18:15-17). Once a change of mind and heart is gained, congregations should welcome prodigals home with open arms (Luke 15:20-24; 2 Cor. 2:6-8). In this way, ultimately, the sinner, either by the Lord's hand of discipline or by repentance before the church, would be saved from a sinful lifestyle (1 Cor. 3:15).

## — 5:6-8 —

Paul moves from the discipline of the sinner for the purpose of repentance and restoration to the purification of the church. Even if the perpetrator does not repent, the moral purity of the church requires the expulsion of the unrepentant from its midst. Because we are all representatives of the body of Christ, we directly affect each other for good or bad. Just as yeast invades every part of a lump of dough (5:6), so one Christian's unrepentant sin corrupts an entire congregation. Years ago a student of Greek at Dallas Seminary once tried to paraphrase this verse by reference to the old slogan for Brylcreem: "A little dab'll do ya!" I would modify his loose translation with one word to fit the context: "A little dab'll do ya *in*." Just a small amount of sin is enough to contaminate the whole congregation. One microscopic virus can infect and cripple the whole body. One hole in a tire can stop the entire car. One "F" on a test can lower your whole GPA.

The seriousness of the offense Paul cites, however, meant that they were dealing with more than just a "dab" of sin. So Paul firmly admonishes them, "Clean out the old leaven"—his analogy for their old lifestyles characterized by impurity and immorality. Instead, they were to be in their daily practice what they were in their position before God: pure and holy—figuratively, unleavened.

In this one verse we have all the ingredients of Paul's doctrines of justification and sanctification. As believers in Christ, the moment we believe we are "justified"—declared righteous by God, while still in our sinning state. Yet we also are called to a life of "sanctification"—becoming progressively more righteous in our daily experience, as we are gradually renewed and conformed to the image of Christ. So, when Paul tells the Corinthians that they "are in fact unleavened" (5:7), he refers to being *positionally* unleavened—their legal righteous standing before God (2 Cor. 5:17; Rom. 6:1-12). When he urges them to "clean out the old leaven so that you may be a new lump" (1 Cor. 5:7), he refers to being *progressively* unleavened—their practical transformation toward the spiritual reality (Rom. 12:1-2; 2 Cor. 3:18).

Neither their *positional* nor their *progressive* righteousness is of their own power, but because of the person and work of Jesus Christ. This is why Paul says, "For Christ our Passover also has been sacrificed" (1 Cor. 5:7). Christ's sacrifice for their sins—past, present, and future—purchased not only freedom from the penalty of sin (justification), but also freedom from the power of sin (sanctification). By embracing Christ as their Passover sacrifice, they could find forgiveness and cleansing.

Paul further develops the Passover analogy in light of the Jewish Passover practice of ridding their homes of all leaven in preparation for the Passover feast. On the day before the Passover began, the Law said that every Jewish family must light a candle and search high and low for any leavening agent (Exod. 12:15, 19; 13:7). Every bit must be cast out in order to keep the Passover feast in purity. Paul calls the believers to do as the Jews did: hunt down every sin that might infect the church and purge it from the community through genuine repentance (1 Cor. 5:7). The Corinthians were to rid themselves of the old leaven of malice and wickedness (their former practices as unrepentant pagans) and replace it with the pure, unleavened bread of "sincerity and truth" (5:8).

## — 5:9-13 —

Paul's instructions about church discipline in 5:9-13 come as a shock to many "judge not" advocates in our culture. But these words also seem to fly in the face of many "judge the world" Christians who tend to shake their fingers at sinners on the outside while graciously overlooking the gross sins of fellow believers in their midst.

In response to these erroneous views, Paul refers to a previous letter he had sent to Corinth, one which apparently was misunderstood or misapplied. In that letter he had instructed the Corinthians not to associate with "immoral people" (5:9). They had apparently taken this as an admonition to isolate themselves from the immoral people of the world—the non-Christian heathen. To do this, they would need to literally depart from the world (5:10). Paul clarifies his intention: "But actually, I wrote to you not to associate with any so-called brother if he is an immoral person, or covetous, or an idolater, or a reviler, or a drunkard, or a swindler—not even to eat with such a one" (5:11).

To many, those words sound ultra harsh, but Paul's point is as vital for us in the twenty-first century as it was for the Corinthians in the first. We are not called to force our biblical standards of righteousness on those outside the church who have never been taught and have never committed themselves to a life of discipleship. In fact, because they have never received the Spirit, they lack the ability to subject themselves to God's laws (Rom. 8:7). Instead, we are called to hold one another accountable, stimulating one another to love and good deeds (Heb. 10:24).

So, when it comes to defiant believers who habitually and unrepentantly engage in a worldly lifestyle of sin, we are told to remove them from fellowship (1 Cor. 5:11). This removal includes even withdrawing the most intimate form of fellowship in the ancient world—enjoying a meal together. Here the reference may be specifically to the Lord's Supper, which often was accompanied by a "charity meal" that provided intimate fellowship as well as provisions for the poor. In other words, believers under church discipline were removed from both the spiritual and physical sustenance the local body of believers offered to its members.

The authority and responsibility of the church to "remove the wicked man from among" the congregation (5:13) might seem brutal to our tolerance-sensitive ears. Such church discipline is necessary, though, and Paul asks a rhetorical question that grammatically, in Greek, implies an affirmative answer: "Do you not judge those who are within the church?" (5:12). In short, the church must leave the world of unbelieving sinners to the judgment of God and exercise discipline among its own members (5:12-13).

# APPLICATION: 1 CORINTHIANS 5:1-13

## Judge for Yourselves

Years ago, if you asked people to quote their favorite Bible verse, you might hear, "The LORD is my shepherd, I shall not want" (Ps. 23:1) or "For God so loved the world, that He gave His only begotten Son, that whoever believes in Him shall not perish, but have eternal life" (John 3:16). Nowadays, I think many people would respond with, "God is love" (1 Jn. 4:8) or "Do not judge so that you will not be judged" (Matt. 7:1). The biblical presentation of a God who is our Master and Shepherd and who saves believers from hell through the death of His Son used to be the common understanding of even the most nominal Christians. In the last two decades, however, the general perception of God has dramatically changed. Now He's seen as a gentle father figure who loves people so much that He would never think of judging anybody for anything. With this picture of God comes an ideal image of the loving, tolerant church that embraces all people regardless of their beliefs and practices. "Thou shalt tolerate everybody's lifestyle" has become the new unwritten commandment that trumps anything "negative" the Bible might say.

Paul's brief discussion of church discipline in 1 Corinthians 5 challenges head-on the notion of unchecked tolerance for sin. In response to these vital truths, I want to share four application points to help bring clarity and balance to our understanding of this important topic.

First, *overlooking serious sin is not loving but dangerous*. You often will hear people say, "Well, we don't care how the people in our fellowship live. That's between them and God. The main thing is that we all love Jesus and love each other." Paul's words in 5:1-13 refute this idea. Think about it. If you have a child who reaches for a drink of poison, you don't say, "That's dangerous, but I'm going to be loving and let my child decide. That's between the child and his Maker." Never! We snatch the poison away and risk hurting the child's feelings.

Paul said, "Remove the wicked man from among yourselves." In this day with our loose church culture, you'll be called a legalist if you apply this verse—I guarantee it! You could be slandered, persecuted, and sued, not only by the sinners involved, but by observers who just don't have the stomach for doing the right thing. Waiting in the wings of many grace-preaching churches are people ready to tag a person as a legalist whenever such a person takes a stand against serious, unrepentant sin. But we must commit ourselves to doing what is right, even when it's unpopular.

Second, *confronting serious sin is not optional but essential.* Of course, there are clear guidelines to follow that ensure this process conforms to God's standards. Read Matthew 18:15-17 very carefully. Study it. Meditate upon it. Then apply it cautiously. Notice that the text makes no room for backing down from confrontation or backing out of the process. For the sake of the church's health and the sinner's restoration, we must all engage in the process when wisdom dictates.

Third, *dealing with serious sin is not to be penal but remedial.* James wrote, "He who turns a sinner from the error of his way will save his soul from death and will cover a multitude of sins" (Jas. 5:20). Invariably, there are self-proclaimed Christian "bouncers" who feel like it's their mission to snatch sinners from churches, escort them to the door, and rough them up enough to guarantee they never show their faces in the sanctuary again. Even the Corinthians had such people, as we see in 2 Corinthians 2. Yet, the purpose of church discipline is not to humiliate, infuriate, or aggravate wandering saints. The purpose is to urge them to see the error of their ways and to shepherd them back to repentance and fellowship. Is your attitude that of a bouncer or a shepherd?

Finally, *correcting serious sin is not external but internal.* Church discipline is to be carried out *by* believers and *for* believers. Church correction would never even have to occur, however, if Christians kept their private worlds centered on the Lord Jesus Christ rather than themselves.

This is a perfect time to do an inventory in your life and determine if there are any secret sins that could potentially grow up or blow up into open scandals. Now is the time to turn away from those sins, repent, and save yourself from the humiliation of discipline, either from the Lord or from His people.

# To Sue or Not to Sue?

## 1 CORINTHIANS 6:1-11

**NASB**

1 Does any one of you, when he has a [a]case against his neighbor, dare to go to law before the unrighteous and

**NLT**

1 When one of you has a dispute with another believer, how dare you file a lawsuit and ask a secular court to decide the matter instead of taking

not before the [b]saints? 2 Or do you not
know that the [a]saints will judge the
world? If the world is judged by you,
are you not competent *to* [b]*constitute*
the smallest law courts? 3 Do you
not know that we will judge angels?
How much more matters of this life?
4 So if you have law courts dealing
with matters of this life, [a]do you ap-
point them as judges who are of no
account in the church? 5 I say *this* to
your shame. *Is it* so, *that* there is not
among you one wise man who will
be able to decide between his breth-
ren, 6 but brother goes to law with
brother, and that before unbelievers?
7 Actually, then, it is already a de-
feat for you, that you have lawsuits
with one another. Why not rather
be wronged? Why not rather be de-
frauded? 8 On the contrary, you your-
selves wrong and defraud. *You do*
this even to *your* brethren.
9 Or do you not know that the un-
righteous will not inherit the king-
dom of God? Do not be deceived;
neither fornicators, nor idolaters,
nor adulterers, nor [a]effeminate, nor
homosexuals, 10 nor thieves, nor *the*
covetous, nor drunkards, nor revil-
ers, nor swindlers, will inherit the
kingdom of God. 11 Such were some
of you; but you were washed, but you
were sanctified, but you were justi-
fied in the name of the Lord Jesus
Christ and in the Spirit of our God.

**6:1** [a]Lit *matter* [b]Or *holy ones* **6:2** [a]V 1, note a [b]Or try *the trivial cases?* **6:4** [a]Or *appoint them... church* **6:9** [a]I.e. effeminate by perversion

it to other believers*! 2 Don't you
realize that someday we believers
will judge the world? And since you
are going to judge the world, can't
you decide even these little things
among yourselves? 3 Don't you real-
ize that we will judge angels? So you
should surely be able to resolve or-
dinary disputes in this life. 4 If you
have legal disputes about such mat-
ters, why go to outside judges who
are not respected by the church? 5 I
am saying this to shame you. Isn't
there anyone in all the church who is
wise enough to decide these issues?
6 But instead, one believer* sues an-
other—right in front of unbelievers!
7 Even to have such lawsuits with
one another is a defeat for you. Why
not just accept the injustice and leave
it at that? Why not let yourselves be
cheated? 8 Instead, you yourselves
are the ones who do wrong and cheat
even your fellow believers.*
9 Don't you realize that those who
do wrong will not inherit the King-
dom of God? Don't fool yourselves.
Those who indulge in sexual sin, or
who worship idols, or commit adul-
tery, or are male prostitutes, or prac-
tice homosexuality, 10 or are thieves,
or greedy people, or drunkards, or
are abusive, or cheat people—none
of these will inherit the Kingdom of
God. 11 Some of you were once like
that. But you were cleansed; you
were made holy; you were made
right with God by calling on the
name of the Lord Jesus Christ and by
the Spirit of our God.

**6:1** Greek *God's holy people;* also in 6:2. **6:6** Greek *one brother.* **6:8** Greek *even the brothers.*

If they aren't luring us in with billboards, they're enticing us on television. If they aren't combing police reports for accident victims to solicit, they're mailing color pamphlets to our homes trying to stir up interest in their services. Lawyers. Admittedly, there are times we need these trained, skilled, and experienced professionals to help us work through

## LAWSUITS IN GRECO-ROMAN SOCIETY

### 1 CORINTHIANS 6:1

In ancient Greece, home of the world's first democracy, the courts bustled with activity. Barclay writes, "[The Greeks] were characteristically a litigious people. The law courts were one of their chief entertainments. . . . In a Greek city every man was more or less a lawyer and spent a very great part of his time either deciding or listening to law cases."[8]

The Greek city of Athens was especially notorious for its fondness of litigation. Because lawsuits often were won by those who presented not the best evidence but the most persuasive arguments, those with great oratorical skills were highly prized. One historian writes, "The fondness of the Athenians for litigation and their never failing abundance of lawsuits and also of political processes caused the art of forensic eloquence to flourish."[9]

Corinth, with its metropolitan atmosphere, international trade centers, and close proximity to Athens—the lawsuit capital of Greece—couldn't help but become polluted by the lawsuit mania. Keener notes, "Roman society was notoriously litigious, and Corinth, with its rising class of *nouveau riche*, was even more so. Many ancient lawsuits addressed property matters among the wealthy; some grievances were simply pretexts for avenging insults and pursuing enmity."[10]

Combine the Corinthian Christians' keenness for rhetorical skill with their adoption of the culture's fascination with litigation, and the sad result of believers suing other believers in civil court was bound to infect the church.

complicated contracts, business ventures, or serious cases in which our rights have been violated. But let me suggest that our world has become lawsuit-crazed, sometimes turning the legal profession into a market-driven industry.

What we see today is nothing new. In the Greco-Roman culture that enveloped the Corinthian church, lawsuits abounded. Sadly, as we have seen, the Christians in Corinth had been slow to abandon many of the vices of the secular culture; the rage over civil litigation was no exception. In 6:1-11 Paul identifies a major problem plaguing his readers: lawsuits among the brethren. He exposes its source and offers a solution fit not only for first-century believers but also for Christians in this generation.

### — 6:1 —

Like the pagans around them, the Corinthian Christians took their interpersonal disputes with other believers to the civil courts, where unbelievers judged their cases according to Roman civil law. Whether it related to family matters, property, inheritance, breach of contract, or slander, these civil suits had become common enough that Paul had heard about them and saw the need to address the problem head-on.

Paul's probing question in 6:1 drips with incredulity and disdain. It was more of a jab or a stab than a gentle inquiry, since Paul already knew that some had taken cases before unbelievers (6:6-8). So when we read this introduction to the topic of lawsuits among brethren (6:1), we probably ought to picture Paul with brows raised, stunned by the audacity of his children in the faith.

Paul's indignant reaction to the situation in Corinth is punctuated all the more when we remember that in the previous chapter Paul had to chastise the church for failing to pass moral judgment on sexual perversion in their midst. Not only did they not judge those who needed to be judged for the sake of the holiness of the church (1 Cor. 5:12), but when they *did* judge one another, they turned to unregenerate judges, further compromising their holiness!

### — 6:2-3 —

After catching the attention of the perpetrators, Paul develops his argument based on solid theological foundations: Christian identity and destiny. He begins by reminding them of who they are in Christ in light of the promises of what they will become: judges not only of the world (6:2) but also of angelic beings (6:3). One day, after the resurrection from the dead, the saints will reign with Christ as judges over both the spiritual and earthly realms (Jude 1:14-15; Rev. 2:26-27; 3:21; 20:4).

Based on this theological truth, Paul argues from the greater to the lesser. Because one day the saints will be entrusted with judging the weightiest matters of the future world, why are they having such trouble arbitrating the smallest issues of the present world (1 Cor. 6:2-3)? The language Paul uses to refer to lawsuits appropriate for "the smallest" courts (6:2) likely refers to trivial matters that never should have achieved such a pitch of fury.

This reference also indicates that Paul is specifically referring to what we call civil lawsuits as opposed to criminal cases. One commentator notes: "In speaking of Christians taking Christians to court, Paul does not specify any criminal cases because he teaches elsewhere that these must be handled by the state (Rom. 13:3, 4). In the expression *pragma echōn* ('having a lawsuit or dispute'), Paul means to include different kinds of property cases (1 Cor. 6:7)."[11] Paul does not attack human government as the God-ordained institution empowered to promote law and justice in the world.[12] In fact, Christians always have regarded criminal cases to be under the legitimate jurisdiction of the state. Paul's condemnation specifically applies to voluntary civil suits filed by individual believers against other individual believers.

Paul's point is that the matters under consideration were so minor that they didn't require the attention of legal experts. Once the believers really understood their position in Christ and they appropriated biblical principles, they had all the essentials necessary for arbitrating their own disputes among church members. They needed only to apply them.

## — 6:4-6 —

Without putting down the wisdom and authority of the civil magistrates, Paul puts the perspective of the unregenerate judge in its proper place. The values and virtues of the Christian faith, sourced in love and centered on grace, do not match the values and virtues of the civil courts—justice that follows the letter of the law. The difference between secular courts and sacred counsel is the difference between law and grace. The unbelieving legal experts don't understand the Christian life. They don't understand what it means to walk in the Spirit, to look at things from God's perspective, to weigh the temporal against the eternal, and to look out not only for our own interests, but also for the interests of others. We should recall that for the lost man, such spiritual things are "foolishness" (2:14). The opinions of such a judge should have no account in the church (6:4), which is governed by the law of Christ operating in unconditional love among the brethren.

From a mature, spiritually-minded Christian perspective, asking a worldly-minded non-Christian to settle disputes among believers who are to live according to Christ's otherworldly mandates is like entering a writing contest with judges who can't read. The idea isn't only absurd, but, as Paul says, it's shameful (6:5). In an outburst sharp with sarcasm, Paul marvels that the Corinthians apparently had failed to find even one wise man among them qualified to arbitrate disputes among believers in the church (6:5). His point particularly stings when we recall that the Corinthians were proud of their alleged wisdom (1 Cor. 1–2). Based on the fact that "brother goes to law with brother" before unbelieving judges (6:6), an outside observer might logically infer that the wisest of the Corinthian leaders were fools who couldn't handle even simple worldly matters.

## — 6:7-8 —

In any lawsuit the goal is to win big. Nobody files a case with the courts if they expect to lose. Yet according to Paul, the very fact that they resorted to civil litigation meant that, from God's perspective, they had lost already (6:7). As the world watched Christian "love" and "fellowship" disintegrate into hate and infighting, they sneered at the claims of the faith even more than usual. No wonder Paul said they were already defeated: Before the eyes of the world, they had lost their testimony as authentic disciples of Christ (John 13:35). Before the eyes of other Christian churches throughout the world, they had lost their holiness and unity. Regardless of the outcome of the civil lawsuit, the believers would come out behind with regard to their spiritual lives, and the church itself would be stained with yet another scandal.

Because the loss of personal testimony and corporate witness carries eternal weight, Paul looked at disputes over temporal matters in a different light. It would be better, he says, to be wronged and defrauded than to be known as someone who wrongs and defrauds others (1 Cor. 6:8). If fellow Christians wrong us, we should take it as an opportunity to follow Christ's clear admonitions: "But whoever slaps you on your right cheek, turn the other to him also. If anyone wants to sue you and take your shirt, let him have your coat also. Whoever forces you to go one mile, go with him two. Give to him who asks of you, and do not turn away from him who wants to borrow from you" (Matt. 5:39-42).

If we are to live as disciples of Christ, observing all that He commanded us (Matt. 28:20), a good place to start is in our interaction with fellow believers. Yet His countercultural teachings are tough to apply. Like the Corinthians, our tendency is to stand up for our rights and fight for our reputations and possessions. To return blow for blow and offense for offense, however, does not reflect the teachings of Christ, but rather the values of the world.

## — 6:9-11 —

In 6:9-11, Paul shifts his strategy to further contrast the values and lifestyles of unbelievers with that of the status and inheritance of believers. Many of the vices he lists are either sexual in nature (fornicators, adulterers, effeminate, and homosexuals) or have to do with ill-gotten gain (thieves, the covetous, swindlers). This further strengthens his case that Christians have no business taking their disputes before non-Christians. Note the stark contrast:

| BELIEVERS | UNBELIEVERS |
|---|---|
| Inheritors of the kingdom of God, washed, sanctified, justified in the name of the Lord Jesus Christ and in the Spirit of God (6:11) | Fornicators, idolaters, adulterers, effeminate, homosexuals, thieves, covetous, drunkards, revilers, swindlers (6:9-10) |

When Paul states that the wicked will not inherit the kingdom of God, he is not implying that the Corinthians might lose their salvation. Nowhere in this passage—unlike 5:1—does he accuse them of any of the vices listed in 1 Corinthians 6:9-10. On the contrary, he explicitly states that some of them used to practice those things prior to their salvation (6:11). His point is that the believers, indwelled by the Spirit and destined to act as judges (6:3) in the kingdom, have access to more than enough wisdom to judge civil disputes among themselves. The secular judges may have a high position in the earthly kingdom, either by inheritance or appointment, but they themselves are often guilty of sinful lifestyles that would cloud their judgment and disqualify them from settling matters among believers.

# APPLICATION: 1 CORINTHIANS 6:1-11

## Escaping the Legal Swamp

"I've got my rights!"

"I've got it coming to me!"

"I just want my fair share!"

"I don't have to take that from you!"

Those are the overused words of our sue-saturated generation. Children sue their parents. Pupils sue their teachers. Athletes sue their coaches. Wives sue husbands and employees sue employers. And it isn't limited to unbelievers. Christians are now waist deep in the legal swamp. Christian neighbors sue each other. Christian faculty members are filing suit against the administrations of schools, colleges, and seminaries. Churches not only sue one another, but congregations now sue their pastors—and vice versa. Parishioners who have complaints about the counseling they received from their ministers are turning to the courts to voice their anger and to seek a large financial settlement!

Yes, brothers and sisters in the family of God actually are dragging each other through the mucky mire of the legal swamp, often to the exclusion of any attempts at reconciling face to face. You would think 1 Corinthians 6:1-8 had somehow fallen out of their Bibles!

Don't think I'm naïve enough to believe that we Christians don't need laws or that we never have reason to complain, or that I'm blind to the fact that wolves in sheep's clothing still prey on and exploit flocks. We must be discerning, alert, and ever mindful that human depravity must be held in check and such wickedness in our churches must be exposed. Yet the way we go about it, the spirit with which we handle conflict, the attitudes we exhibit while working through the difficult process of reconciliation—*that's* where too often we abandon our Christian values and take up worldly vices like weapons. Instead of dealing with these things from a spiritual perspective, too often we press the issue from a strictly legal standpoint. Even if we win the case, we don't walk away humble and grateful. We walk away proud and emboldened, usually ready to strike the next person or group that crosses us.

It seems to me that Christians today need a reminder about how to resolve disputes in a thoroughly godly manner. Let me urge you to spend some time studying and meditating upon the following passages, jotting down some observations about what God is telling us about dispute resolution.

| PASSAGE | OBSERVATIONS |
|---|---|
| 1 Corinthians 6:1-8 | |
| Romans 12:14-19 | |
| Ephesians 4:31-32 | |

Don't stop with just a few observations. Go back and turn these into commands. How is God asking us to adjust our worldly attitudes and actions? How are we to respond to those who offend, harm, or betray us?

You'll discover, as I have, that God's approach is countercultural, radical, and almost unbelievable. It doesn't come naturally, nor can it be implemented with a stubborn will and a proud spirit. Unselfishness must prevail. A Christian approaching conflict resolution biblically must be willing to listen, to negotiate, to yield, to confess, to forgive, to submit, to release, and ultimately to forget.

But, you see, that's what brings about the joy of restoration, strengthened relationships, and authentic fellowship. Humility replaces pride. Thankfulness cancels out arrogance. Mercy flies in the face of resentment. Love conquers all.

## My Body and Me

### 1 CORINTHIANS 6:12-20

**NASB**

12 All things are lawful for me, but not
all things are profitable. All things
are lawful for me, but I will not be
mastered by anything. 13 Food is for
the [a]stomach and the [a]stomach is
for food, but God will do away with
both [b]of them. Yet the body is not
for immorality, but for the Lord, and
the Lord is for the body. 14 Now God
has not only raised the Lord, but will
also raise us up through His power.
15 Do you not know that your bodies
are members of Christ? Shall I then
take away the members of Christ
and make them members of a prostitute? May it never be! 16 Or do you not
know that the one who joins himself to a prostitute is one body *with
her?* For He says, "THE TWO SHALL
BECOME ONE FLESH." 17 But the one
who joins himself to the Lord is one
spirit *with Him.* 18 Flee immorality.
Every *other* sin that a man commits

**NLT**

12 You say, "I am allowed to do anything"—but not everything is good
for you. And even though "I am allowed to do anything," I must not
become a slave to anything. 13 You
say, "Food was made for the stomach, and the stomach for food."
(This is true, though someday God
will do away with both of them.) But
you can't say that our bodies were
made for sexual immorality. They
were made for the Lord, and the
Lord cares about our bodies. 14 And
God will raise us from the dead by
his power, just as he raised our Lord
from the dead.

15 Don't you realize that your
bodies are actually parts of Christ?
Should a man take his body, which
is part of Christ, and join it to a prostitute? Never! 16 And don't you realize
that if a man joins himself to a prostitute, he becomes one body with her?
For the Scriptures say, "The two are
united into one."* 17 But the person
who is joined to the Lord is one spirit
with him.

18 Run from sexual sin! No other
sin so clearly affects the body as this

is outside the body, but the [a]immoral
man sins against his own body. 19 Or
do you not know that your body is a
[a]temple of the Holy Spirit who is in
you, whom you have from [b]God, and
that you are not your own? 20 For you
have been bought with a price: there-
fore glorify God in your body.

**6:13** [a]Lit *belly* [b]Lit *it and them* **6:18** [a]Or *one who practices immorality* **6:19** [a]Or *sanctuary* [b]Or *God? And you...own*

one does. For sexual immorality is a
sin against your own body. 19 Don't
you realize that your body is the
temple of the Holy Spirit, who lives
in you and was given to you by God?
You do not belong to yourself, 20 for
God bought you with a high price. So
you must honor God with your body.

**6:16** Gen 2:24.

We live in an age infatuated with the human physique. Each year people spend billions of dollars on cosmetics, exercise equipment, fitness clubs, fashion, vitamins, diet programs, and plastic surgery. Beautiful, sculpted bodies parade before us in every form of media. The perfect body, we are told, is different than ours—whether curvier, sleeker, slimmer, or more toned and muscular.

Along with the body craze has come an obsession with sex that has reached insane proportions. Television, magazines, movies, and the Internet provide a smorgasbord of opportunities to poison the mind with greatly distorted and often perverse pictures of human sexuality. God-given sexual desires—perfectly healthy and holy in the context of faithful marriage—are exploited into opportunities for immoral images, attitudes, and actions.

These worldly distortions of the human body and human sexuality should concern us, but they should not surprise us. From time immemorial the world has been departing from a balanced, godly view of the physical body. Case in point: The next issue of Corinthian immorality that Paul seeks to correct involves a perversion of human bodily existence and sexual practice. In 1 Corinthians 6:12-20, Paul challenges the church's misconceptions and misdeeds, calling the believers to a life of physical purity to conform to their spiritual holiness.

## — 6:12 —

Without doubt, Paul was a preacher of Christian liberty. In one of his earliest letters, he wrote, "It was for freedom that Christ set us free" (Gal. 5:1). Ripping this verse from its context, however, a person could wield this slogan in defense of any kind of excessive lifestyle or wanton immorality. It is not hard to imagine that in the Corinthian culture, Paul's teaching on Christian liberty might have been taken as an endorsement for a hedonistic lifestyle among Christians.

The imbalanced Corinthians had fully embraced one side of Paul's doctrine of liberty without embracing the other. They shouted "Amen!" to the first part of Galatians 5:13—"For you were called to freedom, brethren"—but had forsaken the second part—"only do not turn your freedom into an opportunity for the flesh." They had so emphasized the theological truth that we are free from serving the old master, the Law of Moses, that they had utterly forgotten the equally important truth that we have been joined to Christ in order to bear righteous fruit for God (Rom. 7:4). Though they welcomed the idea that "all things are lawful for me" (1 Cor. 6:12), they wrongly took it for a banner to hang over their harmful justification of sexual immorality and other selfish desires (8:4-13; 10:23-33).

Obviously, what Paul said and what the Corinthians heard were two different things. This prompted Paul to clear up the misunderstanding by setting up two guardrails to keep Christian liberty within its proper bounds: *expediency* and *self-control.*

*Freedom is to be guided by expediency* (6:12). Christians are indeed free from the Mosaic Law as a covenant that once governed the Hebrews' special relationship with God. That old covenant granted blessing for obedience or cursing for disobedience (Gal. 3:10-14). But this freedom from the covenant of the Law as a way of life does not logically lead to the conclusion that believers now have a right to do anything they please, regardless of its effects on themselves or others. Rather, by the wisdom that comes from the Spirit, believers are to be guided by whether an act is "profitable" (*sympherō* [4851]), that is, whether it is advantageous, useful, or beneficial. The word implies a mutual edification—building up a group. As Paul says elsewhere, "So then we pursue the things which make for peace and the building up of one another. . . . Each of us is to please his neighbor for his good, to his edification" (Rom. 14:19; 15:2).

*Freedom is to be guided by self-control* (6:12). The Corinthians needed to learn that when they indulged their sinful desires, they actually were losing their freedom instead of gaining it. To engage in unbridled immorality is to trade in our freedom of righteousness for shackles of lust. Isn't it astounding how self-deceived we can be when it comes to the distinction between freedom and bondage? How frequently we say, "I'm going to have my own way!" We think that's liberty, when in reality we have simply bowed our heads to the very thing we couldn't possibly say "no" to: greed, gluttony, pornography, gossip, addictions, or any other gratification to which we surrender our freedom. When believers don't use their freedom to serve God, they unwittingly serve sin.

The 1960 Roger Corman film, *The Little Shop of Horrors*, tells the story of a struggling flower shop saved from bankruptcy when customers begin lining up from all over to see a strange new hybrid plant related to a Venus flytrap, named Audrey Jr. What customers don't realize, however, is that Audrey Jr. will feed only on human blood! As the celebrity plant grows, so does its appetite. In order to maintain the success of the flower shop, the out-of-control, carnivorous plant needs to be fed an increasingly large diet. Ultimately, rather than benefiting the business with financial success, Audrey Jr. controls the lives of the shop workers, reducing them to virtual slaves of its insatiable hunger.

This classic dark comedy illustrates the seductive nature of sin. At first it seems to grant freedom as we bask in its pleasures and enjoy its benefits. But we quickly lose control, finding ourselves enslaved to a feeding frenzy that grows increasingly ravenous as we continue to gratify its desires. That's not freedom. That's slavery.

## — 6:13-14 —

Having established the two guardrails that protect us against extremes of Christian liberty, Paul points his readers to the destination of freedom by explaining God's purpose for their bodies.

Paul begins by alluding to what was likely a common proverb in the decadent Greek party scene: "Food is for the stomach and the stomach is for food" (6:13). Keener notes that this statement "fits the common association of gluttony with intercourse; both were sometimes available in the banquets of the wealthy. This also represented the sort of logic by which some Greeks had justified promiscuity: as 'food was for the stomach,' so the body was designed for intercourse."[13] When Paul concludes that "God will do away with both of them" (6:13), it may be that he refers to the fact that someday in eternity God will put an end to the insatiable desires of the body for physical sustenance. It could also be that this was the "punch line" of the Greek hedonistic philosophy, similar to the proverb, "Let us eat and drink, for tomorrow we may die" (Isa. 22:13). In any case, the Corinthian Christians reasoned something like this: When your body is hungry, feed it. When it thirsts, quench it. When it lusts, indulge it. When it craves, satiate it. Before long the situation was out of control.

The weak mortal condition of the body in this world does not lead to the conclusion that we can simply treat it however we want, as if it is disposable rubbish. Paul corrects this false dualism of the hedonistically influenced Corinthians by emphasizing that not only our souls

## BODY AND SOUL

### 1 CORINTHIANS 6:15

The common secular Greek approach to body and soul in the first century was that the body was material, temporary, and merely a distraction from our true being—the soul. In this approach, what happened to the body was irrelevant to the soul. By contrast, the Bible and the early Christians taught that the physical body was part of God's original good creation (Gen. 2:7), and therefore the physical body was an essential part of humanity. Though the physical body is currently subject to corruption, suffering, sin, and death in this present life, God's plan is *not* to annihilate the body and free our souls in a bodiless existence for eternity. As remarkable as it may sound, God's plan is to restore and glorify the physical part of our humanity through bodily resurrection (1 Cor. 15:42-43).

The Corinthians struggled with a view of the human body that differed greatly from ours—the body was like a prison or tomb of the soul, merely a physical shell of the "real person." In light of this strong dualism that separated soul and body, the body could be understood to have no moral value, but because of its sensual, earthy appetites, it seduced the good soul to sin and dragged it down into the gutters of vice.

Two approaches to life emerged from this philosophy. One group became *ascetics*; those who, through harsh self-discipline and even self-mutilation, went to ridiculous extremes to curb the body's desires. Others became *hedonists*. They believed that, since only the soul would survive death, it didn't matter what was done through the body. They gave the body every opportunity to quench its lustful longings. Both approaches were to be found in Corinth (6:12-13; 7:5) and, unfortunately, had infected many of its Christian inhabitants. Paul therefore needed to teach them about the place of the human body in God's design.

but also our bodies are to be submitted to the service of the Lord, not to the service of immorality (1 Cor. 6:13). He also reminds us that our present mortal bodies will be in direct continuity with our future immortal bodies. God truly raised Jesus Christ from the dead. The very body that had been crucified and buried was not disposed of or annihilated, but glorified, transformed, and made immortal by the power of God. In the same way, believers' bodies also will be resurrected to live in an immortal, glorious, spiritual condition (6:14). Yes, our bodies will be qualitatively transformed, but they will be the very bodies that have existed on this earth (see 1 Cor. 15).

Because these same bodies are to be resurrected and glorified to reign as kings and rule as judges over heaven and earth, they should never be used for sexual immorality—whether premarital, extramarital, homosexual, bisexual, incestuous, or bestial. Christ has purchased not only our souls but also our bodies from the slave market of sin (1 Cor. 6:20; 7:22-23; Titus 2:14; 1 Pet. 1:18-19). Therefore, we should serve God through our bodies, worshiping Him by abstaining from any form of sexual immorality. Simply put, our physical bodies are to be fully incorporated in the process of sanctification (being made progressively holy in practice), just as our bodies are destined to be fully involved in future glorification (the ultimate perfection in holiness through resurrection).

## — 6:15-20 —

In 6:15-20, Paul continues to argue against the Corinthians' imbalanced views of the body and sexual immorality. He presents three facts about our bodies that further confirm their worth and our responsibility to use them in the service of God.

First, *our body is a physical extension of Christ in this world* (6:15). Just as the church is the body of Christ (Eph. 4:12), and since each one is a member of that body (Rom. 12:5), the "body of Christ" cannot be regarded as *only* spiritual and invisible; rather, it is manifested through a physical presence, just as Christ was both spiritual and physical. Each member of Christ's body is to represent the Lord on earth. Like ambassadors in a foreign land who act as their nation's eyes, ears, hands, and mouth, we are Christ's ambassadors in this world, carrying out His interests in His name. Only by consecrating our physical bodies to the service of God can we fulfill our calling to be not only Christ's heart and mind in the world, but also His hands and feet.

Second, *our body is to be a living picture of our relationship with Christ* (6:15-18). Because we are members of Christ's body—spiritually and physically—we should be just as appalled at sexual immorality in our personal lives and in the life of the church as we would be at the idea that Christ Himself would chase after prostitutes. So disgusting is the idea that Paul utters the strongest condemnation of such a thought: *mē genoito* [3361 + 1096], "May it never be!" . . . "God forbid!" . . . "Perish the thought!"

When we engage in the sin of sexual relations outside of marriage, we form an immoral union that mars our holy alliance with God through Christ. Why? Because the sexual union is a physical expression of the most intimate union two people can have. They become "one flesh" (6:16). Yet some of the Corinthians held the body in such low regard that they failed to see the spiritual implications of their physical actions. Those who joined themselves with the Lord, perhaps through the personal self-consecration pictured in the physical rite of baptism, became "one spirit with Him" (6:17). The physical act illustrated a spiritual reality. Therefore, by subsequently submitting their bodies to immorality, they contradicted their spiritual union with Christ.

Yet the Corinthians failed to understand the close relationship between the inner, spiritual reality and the outer expression. They held that whatever was done by or through the body was not *immoral* but *amoral*—that is, morally irrelevant. Paul refutes their claim, saying, "The immoral man sins against his own body" (6:18). Sex outside of marriage is wrong because it abuses the body with pleasures that don't last and that, ultimately, are vulgar sources of regret. So Paul commands the Corinthians to "flee immorality" (6:18).

Third, *our body is a living temple of the Holy Spirit* (6:19). In 1 Corinthians 3, Paul likened the church in Corinth to a temple of God in which the Holy Spirit dwells (3:16). There the emphasis was on the corporate body of believers as the temple, with the Spirit dwelling among the gathered community in a unique way. In 1 Corinthians 6, however, Paul draws out another important type of indwelling of the Spirit—His presence in the body of each individual believer (6:19). Just as God manifested His presence in Solomon's majestic temple, setting it apart from all other buildings for special use to glorify Him (2 Chr. 5:11–7:16), so the Spirit indwells each of us who has been bought with the priceless blood of Christ, setting us apart from all others for His glory alone (Rom. 8:9, 11; 1 Cor. 6:20).

God sent His Son to die in order to redeem us from sin. One day, God will raise us from the dead, as He did with Christ Jesus, so we can reign with Him forever (6:2-3). In the meantime, the Lord has called us to live according to His standards and by His indwelling power. He bought us at the highest price imaginable, His own life. He gave us the noblest vocation, representatives of the Lord Jesus Christ on earth. He prepared us for the most glorious end, eternal life in our resurrected, glorified bodies. How can we do less than honor Him through obedience, especially through our bodies? If we truly belong to Christ, how could we not consecrate our bodies to His service? How could we not flee from the slavery of immorality in all its forms and run back to the liberating arms of Jesus?

# APPLICATION: 1 CORINTHIANS 6:12-20

## My Goal? His Glory!

Our physical bodies are not disposable waste, fertilizer for flowers, or food for worms. This pagan notion of the flesh is an affront to God's handiwork. He created us with both immaterial and material aspects—both originally good—so we could serve as His image-bearers in creation. As His redeemed people, one day God will transform our mortal bodies into immortal bodies, but until that time our bodies are a physical extension of Christ, a moral illustration of the Lord, and a temple for the indwelling Spirit.

All of this leads to a compelling conclusion, which Paul underscored with a simple imperative: "Therefore glorify God in your body" (6:20).

God let His Son die to redeem our bodies from a lifestyle of sin and rebellion. One day, God will raise us from the dead and redeem our bodies from death and decay. In our glorified state, we will reign with Him forever (6:2-3). In the meantime, the Lord expects us to live in our mortal bodies according to His standards—reflecting the light of His truth. Physical mortality should never be an excuse for physical immorality.

Paul reminds us that we have been bought "with a price"—the precious blood of Christ (6:20). How can we do less than honor Him through an obedient, God-glorifying life? If we belong to Christ, we should serve Him faithfully and consistently. Not just in our thought life. Not merely with our feelings. But with our hands, our feet, our eyes, our ears, our tongues. What we say, what we do, where we go, what we watch, what we listen to—all these things are to be done for His glory.

How do we do this?

First, *we avoid the extreme of asceticism*. That is, we neither neglect our bodies as if they are irrelevant to our spiritual lives, nor do we reject our bodies as if they are distractions to God's service. Denying the needs of the body isn't spiritual. After all, we're embodied creatures designed with God-given needs and desires. Mature Christians don't deny these; they submit them to God's will and use them for His glory. We all need food, clothing, shelter, companionship, and intimacy. All of these, though, should be sought according to God's commands.

Second, *we avoid the extreme of hedonism*. We honor God with our bodies by keeping passions under control. We don't dive in to sexual immorality. We don't overindulge in food and drink. We don't focus on our physical appearance while our character and virtue suffer. And we don't build our physique while neglecting our spiritual health.

Because we were bought at a price, our goal for our bodies should be His glory.

# STRENGTHENING FAMILY AND FELLOWSHIP (1 CORINTHIANS 7:1–10:33)

Important issues + Differing opinions = Controversy.

That formula sums up the content of 1 Corinthians 7–10. I've named this section "Strengthening Family and Fellowship," but don't let that positive title fool you. The subjects Paul addresses in these four chapters touch a lot of sensitive nerves for many people—actually, *these topics are downright controversial*. They are controversial because they deal with intimate areas of people's lives and with public aspects of church life:

- Should I get married or remain single?
- How can I handle an unhappy marriage?
- Is it ever okay to pursue a divorce?
- Are there cultural taboos I need to acknowledge or avoid?
- Are there different roles for men and women in worship?
- What is the proper way to observe the Lord's Table?

A major transition in Paul's letter occurs at 1 Corinthians 7 as he moves away from urgent matters of conflicts and immorality in the church that had been brought to his attention by others (1:11; 5:1). Paul now turns to address important matters raised by the Corinthians themselves (7:1). He begins with issues that touch every believer of every generation: marriage, singleness, and divorce (7:1-40).

Then he moves on to questions regarding meat sacrificed to idols and Christian freedom as it relates to the faith of brothers and sisters in Christ who have a weaker conscience (8:1-13). Pointing to his own life of ministry as an example, Paul urges the Corinthians to surrender their personal rights for the sake of the gospel (9:1-27). Such attitudes and actions would go a long way in promoting peace and harmony in a church plagued with conflict and division.

Paul concludes this section by reminding the Corinthians of the incompatibility of worshiping the true God through Jesus while also worshiping idols (10:1-33). True worship involves authentic fellowship with Christ and others at the table of the Lord. Idolatry involves fellowship with demons!

### KEY TERMS IN 1 CORINTHIANS 7:1–10:33

***gameō* (γαμέω)** [1060] "to marry," "wed"
This word is used nine times in 1 Corinthians 7 alone, and an alternative form, *gamizō* (which is listed in Strong's as *ekgamizō* [1547]), is used twice in 7:38. Paul's discussion of principles governing marriage is the clearest and most detailed in the New Testament. Though attitudes toward the institution of marriage have changed over the centuries, the basic structure has remained intact—a man and a woman covenanting together for life with a view toward establishing a nurturing family. Yet for Paul, marriage is also more than a necessary social institution; Christian marriage is a picture of the relationship between Christ and the church (Eph. 5:25-32), a theological fact that helps explain the seriousness with which Paul treats the institution in 1 Corinthians 7.

***gnōsis* (γνῶσις)** [1108] "knowledge," "understanding"
Related to the verb *ginōskō* [1097], the kind of knowledge described by *gnōsis* is acquired knowledge, something achieved through experience or relationship. This kind of knowledge is not always apparent on the surface of things. The New Testament uses the term frequently for the kind of knowledge that comes from divine revelation (Eph. 1:17). Paul uses the term in 1 Corinthians to refer to knowledge as a God-given window into reality through which informed, mature believers can view life (1 Cor. 8:7). If such knowledge is not controlled by love, however, it can harm rather than heal (8:1).

# Advice on Marriage Matters
## 1 CORINTHIANS 7:1-16

NASB

1 Now concerning the things about
which you wrote, it is good for a
man not to touch a woman. 2 But be-
cause of immoralities, each man is to
have his own wife, and each woman
is to have her own husband. 3 The
husband must [a]fulfill his duty to his

NLT

1 Now regarding the questions you
asked in your letter. Yes, it is good to
abstain from sexual relations.* 2 But
because there is so much sexual im-
morality, each man should have his
own wife, and each woman should
have her own husband.
3 The husband should fulfill his

wife, and likewise also the wife to her
husband. 4 The wife does not have
authority over her own body, but the
husband *does;* and likewise also the
husband does not have authority
over his own body, but the wife *does.*
5 Stop depriving one another, except
by agreement for a time, so that you
may devote yourselves to prayer, and
[a]come together again so that Satan
will not tempt you because of your
lack of self-control. 6 But this I say by
way of concession, not of command.
7 [a]Yet I wish that all men were even
as I myself am. However, each man
has his own gift from God, one in this
manner, and another in that.

8 But I say to the unmarried and
to widows that it is good for them
if they remain even as I. 9 But if they
do not have self-control, let them
marry; for it is better to marry than
to burn *with passion.*

10 But to the married I give instruc-
tions, not I, but the Lord, that the wife
should not [a]leave her husband 11 (but
if she does leave, she must remain
unmarried, or else be reconciled to
her husband), and that the husband
should not [a]divorce his wife.

12 But to the rest I say, not the Lord,
that if any brother has a wife who is
an unbeliever, and she consents to
live with him, he must not [a]divorce
her. 13 And a woman who has an
unbelieving husband, and he con-
sents to live with her, she must not
[a]send her husband away. 14 For the
unbelieving husband is sanctified
through his wife, and the unbeliev-
ing wife is sanctified through [a]her
believing husband; for otherwise
your children are unclean, but now
they are holy. 15 Yet if the unbelieving
one leaves, let him leave; the brother

wife's sexual needs, and the wife
should fulfill her husband's needs.
4 The wife gives authority over her
body to her husband, and the hus-
band gives authority over his body
to his wife.

5 Do not deprive each other of
sexual relations, unless you both
agree to refrain from sexual inti-
macy for a limited time so you can
give yourselves more completely to
prayer. Afterward, you should come
together again so that Satan won't
be able to tempt you because of your
lack of self-control. 6 I say this as a
concession, not as a command. 7 But
I wish everyone were single, just as
I am. Yet each person has a special
gift from God, of one kind or another.

8 So I say to those who aren't mar-
ried and to widows—it's better to stay
unmarried, just as I am. 9 But if they
can't control themselves, they should
go ahead and marry. It's better to
marry than to burn with lust.

10 But for those who are married, I
have a command that comes not from
me, but from the Lord.* A wife must
not leave her husband. 11 But if she
does leave him, let her remain single
or else be reconciled to him. And the
husband must not leave his wife.

12 Now, I will speak to the rest of
you, though I do not have a direct
command from the Lord. If a fellow
believer* has a wife who is not a be-
liever and she is willing to continue
living with him, he must not leave
her. 13 And if a believing woman has
a husband who is not a believer and
he is willing to continue living with
her, she must not leave him. 14 For
the believing wife brings holiness
to her marriage, and the believing
husband* brings holiness to his
marriage. Otherwise, your children
would not be holy, but now they are
holy. 15 (But if the husband or wife
who isn't a believer insists on leav-
ing, let them go. In such cases the

NASB

or the sister is not under bondage in such *cases*, but God has called [a]us [b]to peace. 16 For how do you know, O wife, whether you will save your husband? Or how do you know, O husband, whether you will save your wife?

**7:3** [a]Lit *render* **7:5** [a]Lit *be* **7:7** [a]One early ms reads *For* **7:10** [a]Lit *depart from* **7:11** [a]Or *leave his wife* **7:12** [a]Or *leave her* **7:13** [a]Or *leave her husband* **7:14** [a]Lit *the brother* **7:15** [a]One early ms reads *you* [b]Lit *in*

NLT

believing husband or wife* is no longer bound to the other, for God has called you* to live in peace.) 16 Don't you wives realize that your husbands might be saved because of you? And don't you husbands realize that your wives might be saved because of you?

**7:1** Or *to live a celibate life;* Greek reads *It is good for a man not to touch a woman.* **7:10** See Matt 5:32; 19:9; Mark 10:11-12; Luke 16:18. **7:12** Greek *a brother.* **7:14** Greek *the brother.* **7:15a** Greek *the brother or sister.* **7:15b** Some manuscripts read *us.*

Countless dangers threaten both the sanctity and the survival of marriage in today's generation. From same-sex unions to cohabitation, from domestic abuse to no-fault divorce, from runaway mothers to deadbeat dads—marriage seems to be caught in the crossfire of modern controversies. Political activists, social radicals, religious liberals, and cultural critics all seem to have set their sights on the marriage relationship.

Yet these social, political, and religious forces don't come close to the number-one enemy of marriage in both the ancient world and in our own: *selfishness*. The unholy "trinity" of me, myself, and I leave no room for *him* or *her*—the "better half" of the marriage relationship. In our ego-driven culture, people have a difficult time grasping (much less valuing and modeling) biblical principles regarding marriage. Yet Scripture often addresses marriage matters, providing timeless wisdom applicable to marriage issues in every generation.

So, as the storm of contemporary controversy surrounds us, let's look beyond the horizon of dark, ominous clouds. Let's allow the light of God's Word to pierce the darkness, leading us to the safe shelter of holiness in the midst of the storm.

## — 7:1 —

Paul opens 1 Corinthians 7 with the words, "Now concerning the things about which you wrote." The Corinthians had written the apostle regarding issues about which there had been questions, controversies, or both. Similar phrases throughout the letter reveal that this chapter on marriage and singleness marks the beginning of his direct replies to matters that greatly concerned the church at Corinth (7:25; 8:1; 12:1; 16:1, 12). Although we don't have that original letter of correspondence from Corinth to Paul, we can guess what questions they had asked based on the apostle's responses. The first question had something to do with the value of the single versus the married life: Is it better to get married or to stay single, and how would one go about making such a decision? What an important, practical question!

Paul's answer in 7:1 is: "It is good for a man not to touch a woman." Here the word "good," *kalos* [2570], refers to that which is ideal or preferable, and the phrase translated "to touch a woman" was an ancient idiom for sexual relations.[1] Paul is not admonishing men to avoid sexual relations outside of marriage here. He already dealt with that issue in the previous section. Rather, Paul focuses on whether it is preferable for a man to get married or to remain single.

## EXCURSUS: MRS. APOSTLE PAUL?

### 1 CORINTHIANS 7:8

Several years back, the novel *The Da Vinci Code* caused a stir when its plotline suggested that Jesus Christ had been married to Mary Magdalene. In response, both liberal and conservative biblical scholars agreed that the idea was the stuff of unbridled (and, I would add, ungodly) imagination. It might have made intriguing fiction, but the idea of a "Mrs. Christ" was simply preposterous.

But what about a "Mrs. Apostle Paul"? Is it plausible (or at least possible) that Paul the apostle had ever been married? Neither the New Testament nor other early Christian literature answers this question conclusively. Scholars who think Paul was once married appeal to two main arguments. First, in Paul's day, marriage was expected among pious Jews when they reached the age of eighteen. Because Paul zealously upheld the traditions of his people (Acts 22:3; 26:5; Gal. 1:14), it follows that he must have been married earlier in his life. But Jewish bachelors were not unheard of in the first century, especially those who were single for the sake of ministry, like John the Baptizer and Jesus. Perhaps Paul, too, was an exception to the norm. Also, if Paul had been married, why didn't he mention this when he taught about marriage?

Second, Paul's power to vote in the Sanhedrin suggests he may have been part of this Jewish judicial body (Acts 26:10), and that position was open only to men who were married and had children. These rules of eligibility, however, weren't set until late in the first century or early in the second, many years after Paul's death. Paul's career, even if it included the Sanhedrin, didn't require marriage.

Ultimately, the jury is still out on the question of whether there ever was a "Mrs. Apostle Paul" earlier in his life. But one thing is certain: By the time he penned 1 Corinthians between AD 53 and 55, he was single (1 Cor. 7:7), and he remained so to his death.

In order to understand the thrust and context of Paul's argument, we need to jump ahead to 7:26: "I think then that this is good in view of the present distress, that it is good for a man to remain as he is." Note that his advice for a man to "remain as he is"—unmarried—applies to a specific time of distress in the life of the Corinthian church. The "present distress" probably refers to persecutions Christians were suffering at the hands of Roman officials. Paul advised that in times of physical hardship, upheaval, or crisis, it would be wiser to stay single to avoid the compounded struggles associated with the recently married life. So, as we step into Paul's discussion of marriage, we need to realize that he was not in any way disparaging the marriage relationship, nor was he promoting the lifestyle of monks and nuns!

### — 7:2-6 —

Although Paul began by granting that the single life might be preferable to the married life, as a realist he understood that not everybody had been called to a life of singleness. In fact, though single men and women may have more time to devote to undistracted ministry (7:35), they also must contend with temptations that lure them away from sexual purity. So, if the temptations toward sexual immorality are too great for a person to lead a pure single life, that individual should marry (7:2). In this counsel, Paul isn't conveying a low opinion of marriage, as if it is the last alternative after every other attempt at controlling sexual desire has failed.

We need to remember that Paul's admonition for people to remain as they are isn't a blanket statement that all single Christians must remain single indefinitely. Paul was answering a specific question in light of specific, distressing circumstances unique to the church in Corinth. However, even if that crisis were to lift, Paul clearly asserted that some Christians are called to a life of singleness, just as some are called to marriage. In essence, Paul was saying, "If you are single, that's a high, honorable calling. But it is no good trying to live the single life if you are spending every waking hour battling against your uncontrollable sexual desires. Instead, it is better to be married."

Far from being a puritanical prude, Paul taught that married couples had responsibilities for satisfying each other's sexual needs. In 1 Corinthians 7:3-5 he outlines the duties of husband and wife within marriage. The term translated "duty" (7:3) refers to a "debt" to be paid. The New Testament uses this word in other contexts when referring to settling a bill with an individual or the government (Matt. 18:23-32;

Rom. 13:7). Jesus uses the term "fulfill" in Matthew 22:21 when He says, "Render to Caesar the things that are Caesar's; and to God the things that are God's." Applying this imagery to marriage, Paul is saying that husbands and wives must faithfully render to each other what they had promised in their marriage covenants. What was behind this exhortation? Likely some contingent in Corinth reasoned this way: If the single, celibate life dedicated to God was especially virtuous, then perhaps married couples could still be especially spiritual if they lived as if they were not married. This ascetic impulse was misguided (see "Body and Soul," p. 98).

Since sexual intimacy is so essential in marriage, couples need to ensure that their mates' physical needs are met. Remembering that their bodies belong to their mates will help (1 Cor. 7:4). Paul says that husbands and wives have authority over each other's bodies. What a startling image of mutual submission and accountability! Imagine what a marriage would look like if each spouse was always looking out for the interests of the other, all of the time. When one spouse needs or desires the deepest intimacies of love, the other spouse should delight in fulfilling that need.

Paul gives only one exception to this rule: Husbands and wives are to deprive each other only "by agreement," that is, by mutual consent (7:5). This agreed abstinence for a temporary period of time is meant to have a spiritual purpose: for devoting themselves to prayer. Likely Paul has in mind something like fasting in conjunction with prayer, in which certain physical needs are denied for a set period of time in order to focus fully on consecration or petition to God. It is noteworthy that "fasting" from sexual intimacy is only to last "for a time," in order to keep Satan from tempting the weak flesh toward immorality outside of marriage. Simply put, we are asking for trouble in our marriages if we deprive our partner of sexual intimacy.

Paul notes that this principle of temporary abstinence as a spiritual discipline is a "concession" (7:6). The Greek word *syngnōmē* [4774] means "permission to do something."[2] Paul clarifies that regular sexual intimacy in marriage is to be regarded as the norm, the command. On the other hand, abstaining from sexual relations is only an exception for rare occasions of special seasons of prayer. Paul had to clear up this misunderstanding because those in Corinth, susceptible to misinterpreting Paul's words (5:10), might have mistaken his concession as the ideal rule to be followed.

## — 7:7-9 —

Next Paul returns to the question of whether singleness or marriage is preferable for any given individual. Paul admits that for the sake of the gospel, he would prefer that all people were single, like him. To paraphrase his thought here, it is as if Paul were saying, "If I had my druthers, I would call together a band of men and women who forsook the married life, committed themselves to single-minded devotion to the work of the gospel, and lived in celibate self-control for the rest of their lives." While Paul modeled that lifestyle, he realized that not all men and women are like him. Not all have the same "gift from God." Some are gifted with being single, others with marriage (7:7).

For those who have, however, found themselves in an unmarried state, Paul offers a bit of timely advice (7:8). For the "unmarried" condition Paul uses the Greek word *agamos* [22]. The word can refer to those who have never been married,[3] but elsewhere in 1 Corinthians 7 it refers to those who were formally married but are married no longer (7:11, 34). So, Paul's advice in these few verses applies to both the never-married and the formerly-married—anybody not in a permanent marriage relationship. This advice also includes "widows," women whose husbands had passed away. Paul exhorts those in this situation of singleness to remain single, as Paul had chosen to remain single (7:8).

Though the continued single life would be preferable for the sake of a life of undistracted devotion to the service of the Lord (7:32-35), Paul realizes that not all unmarried people have the gift of celibacy. So, for those singles who would be distracted from a life of ministry by the constant battle against burning passions of the flesh, "it is better to marry" (7:9). Not all people are able to dedicate themselves to an unmarried life.

## — 7:10-16 —

Paul turns from the unmarried to the married, offering vital advice concerning divorce and remarriage. Whereas the previous instructions addressed the homes of the unmarried, divorced, and widowed, Paul next applies his apostolic wisdom to the fragile and sometimes fractured homes of the unhappily married.

Up front, Paul states the Lord's ideal for marriage: "that the wife should not leave her husband . . . and that the husband should not divorce his wife" (7:10-11). Paul reminds his readers that this teaching is not his own, but a reiteration of Jesus' own teaching on the subject of divorce. We find a brief treatment of this teaching in Matthew 5:32, where Jesus said, "Everyone who divorces his wife, except for the reason of unchastity, makes her commit adultery; and whoever marries a divorced woman commits adultery." The word translated "unchastity" in Jesus' teaching is *porneia* [4202], a broad term for sexual immorality. Later, in Matthew 19, Jesus treated the issue of divorce and remarriage in greater detail: "Because of your hardness of heart Moses permitted you to divorce your wives; but from the beginning it has not been this way. And I say to you, whoever divorces his wife, except for immorality (*porneia*), and marries another woman commits adultery" (Matt. 19:8-9).

By referring to Jesus' teaching on this matter, Paul reaffirms the basic biblical principle of marriage: permanency. Mates are to cleave to each other, bond together, become one flesh, building a strong home upon the solid and sure foundation of a stable marriage. Christian couples should not give in to the destruction of divorce, but should do everything in their power to nurture and build their marriage on the ideal of permanency.

Without denying the seriousness of the ideal that marriage should be a lifelong commitment, Paul also acknowledges the reality of our sin-infested world. Even the healthiest marriages have been tainted by the effects of sin, making the ideal of permanency a challenging task. Some marriages become so twisted by the Fall that the ideal is not always upheld. Paul doesn't shy away from this reality. Instead, he faces it head-on, giving practical guidelines for handling painful and dysfunctional marriages God's way.

For Christians whose marital bonds have been severed by the sharp edge of sin or selfishness, Paul counsels that the divorced couple either remain unmarried or be reconciled with one another (1 Cor. 7:11). Paul doesn't indicate the cause of the separation. Perhaps there was abandonment or some other crisis that had led to separation. Perhaps it was simply a case of "irreconcilable differences." The language seems to suggest mild reasons for leaving, like common marital conflicts rather than serious matters such as unrepentant adultery or overt abuse. Jesus Himself allowed for Christians to marry people other than their former partners when their divorce was caused by sexual immorality (Matt. 19:9).

What about marriage in which only one mate is a believer? Should these unions continue, or should spiritual incompatibility allow for dissolution? Jesus never addressed this issue. Paul, however, provides us with spiritually sound advice based on his God-given apostolic authority. Paul's phrase "I say, not the Lord" (1 Cor. 7:12) doesn't mean that he is merely giving his own private opinion on the matter. Rather, he means that his instructions are not based on any former direct command from Christ. Here the Holy Spirit is speaking to new situations through the inspired, prophetic pen of the apostle. With regard to marriages in which one spouse is an unbeliever, Paul says that if the unbelieving spouse is willing to remain in union with the believing partner and accompanying Christian convictions and lifestyle, the believer should not seek separation (7:12-13).

Paul gives sound reasons for keeping such spiritually mixed marriages intact. First, the unsaved spouse is "sanctified," or placed in a unique relationship of blessing, because of being married to a Christian (7:14). Just as Laban's household was blessed because of Jacob (Gen. 30:27), and Potiphar's household was blessed because of Joseph (Gen. 39:5), so non-Christian mates are blessed because of their Christian spouses. One great blessing is the unbeliever's exposure to the person and message of Jesus Christ through the testimony of the believing spouse, keeping open the possibility of salvation (1 Cor. 7:16).

Second, when a Christian spouse stays with the willing non-Christian partner, the children also benefit. Children raised in a mixed home have greater opportunity to see the love of Christ exhibited in the believing parent's life than those who must live with the consequences of a broken home.

Clearly, Paul valued a believer's faithfulness to the marriage vow as the ideal, but Paul also knew that in our fallen world, unbelieving spouses don't always endure in that union. What happens when the non-Christian spouse divorces the Christian mate, contrary to the believer's wishes? Rather than fight the breakup, Paul instructs the innocent, believing spouse to "let him leave" (7:15). In such cases, the Christian is the victim of a willful desertion and is, therefore, "not under bondage." In other words, the child of God is no longer bound to that marriage relationship. That believer then falls into the category of the "unmarried" person (7:8)—free to marry a fellow believer "in the Lord" (7:39), but urged to remain single for the sake of an undistracted ministry.

# APPLICATION: 1 CORINTHIANS 7:1-16

## Working through Quittin' Time

In a departure from the traditional family values I grew up with decades ago, many in our modern culture would call it quits on jobs, churches, contracts and, yes, marriage, rather than work through the tough times and strive for the ideal: commitment through good times and bad. I could bore you with endless statistics, facts, and figures, but instead let me just state the reality of our times: What was once not even an option is now standard operating procedure. Retaining the option to "turn off" one's marital vows has now been in vogue for an entire generation, and we are witnessing its tragic effects on families, children, churches, and society.

In light of Paul's clear encouragement to remain married except for extreme circumstances, let's consider committing ourselves to the countercultural—but thoroughly Christian—response to marital problems. Let's commit to working through . . . regardless! Let me remind you that any achievement worth remembering is stained with the blood of diligence and determination while etched with the scars of disappointment. With few exceptions, to run, to quit, to escape, even to hide, will not solve what led to the conflict and separation.

So, are you facing seemingly insurmountable marriage difficulties today? Or enduring the long, slow simmer of a relationship that looks fine on the outside but is eroding within? Have you been tempted to drop out, give up, run away? Let me encourage you to give it a second or third thought. It's my observation that in many cases, couples call it quits long before they reach any sort of biblical grounds for separation or divorce. Irreconcilable differences, personal happiness, and "I just don't love you anymore" aren't biblical reasons for divorce. Yet these too often become the grounds for retreat when Scripture exhorts us to continue to fight the good fight.

If you're thinking about throwing in the towel, don't (unless, of course, there are abuses that endanger you and/or your children). Stand still. Refuse to retreat. Look at the situation as God looks at it and draw upon His power to hold up under the blast. For sure, this calls for determination and great patience. Nobody ever said the Christian life was easy. And marriage, even for Christians, can produce the most difficult challenges in one's life. Yet God promises His sustaining grace and powerful presence through the trials and troubles we encounter.

As you stop to take stock and recommit yourself to "working through quittin' time," turn to Scripture as your guide. Let it renew your mind, alter your attitudes, and light your path. Besides 1 Corinthians 7, the Bible provides at least five crucial passages on the vital issues of marriage, separation, divorce, and remarriage. Take time to dig into them so you can better understand God's mind on these matters. Note the things that God repeats, emphasizes, commands, and permits. Become an informed adult who has made a serious study of Holy Scripture. Then adjust your own thoughts, emotions, and actions accordingly.

Genesis 2:18-25
Deuteronomy 24:1-4
Matthew 19:3-12
Ephesians 5:22-33
1 Peter 3:1-7

# Getting the Most from Our Lot in Life

## 1 CORINTHIANS 7:17-40

**NASB**

17 Only, as the Lord has assigned to each one, as God has called each, in this manner let him walk. And so I direct in all the churches. 18 Was any man called *when he was already* circumcised? He is not to become uncircumcised. Has anyone been called in uncircumcision? He is not to be circumcised. 19 Circumcision is nothing, and uncircumcision is nothing, but *what matters is* the keeping of the commandments of God. 20 Each man must remain in that [a]condition in which he was called.

21 Were you called while a slave? [a]Do not worry about it; but if you are able also to become free, rather [b]do that. 22 For he who was called in

**NLT**

17 Each of you should continue to live in whatever situation the Lord has placed you, and remain as you were when God first called you. This is my rule for all the churches. 18 For instance, a man who was circumcised before he became a believer should not try to reverse it. And the man who was uncircumcised when he became a believer should not be circumcised now. 19 For it makes no difference whether or not a man has been circumcised. The important thing is to keep God's commandments.

20 Yes, each of you should remain as you were when God called you. 21 Are you a slave? Don't let that worry you—but if you get a chance to be free, take it. 22 And remember,

the Lord while a slave, is the Lord's
freedman; likewise he who was
called while free, is Christ's slave.
23 You were bought with a price; do
not become slaves of men. 24 Breth-
ren, each one is to remain with God
in that *condition* in which he was
called.

25 Now concerning virgins I have
no command of the Lord, but I give
an opinion as one who [a]by the mercy
of the Lord is trustworthy. 26 I think
then that this is good in view of the
[a]present distress, that it is good for
a man [b]to remain as he is. 27 Are you
bound to a wife? Do not seek to be
released. Are you released from a
wife? Do not seek a wife. 28 But if you
marry, you have not sinned; and if a
virgin marries, she has not sinned.
Yet such will have [a]trouble in this
life, and I am trying to spare you.
29 But this I say, brethren, the time
has been shortened, so that from
now on those who have wives should
be as though they had none; 30 and
those who weep, as though they did
not weep; and those who rejoice,
as though they did not rejoice; and
those who buy, as though they did
not possess; 31 and those who use
the world, as though they did not
make full use of it; for the form of
this world is passing away.

32 But I want you to be free from
concern. One who is unmarried is
concerned about the things of the
Lord, how he may please the Lord;
33 but one who is married is con-
cerned about the things of the world,
how he may please his wife, 34 and
*his interests* are divided. The woman
who is unmarried, and the virgin, is
concerned about the things of the

if you were a slave when the Lord
called you, you are now free in the
Lord. And if you were free when the
Lord called you, you are now a slave
of Christ. 23 God paid a high price
for you, so don't be enslaved by the
world.* 24 Each of you, dear brothers
and sisters,* should remain as you
were when God first called you.

25 Now regarding your question
about the young women who are
not yet married. I do not have a com-
mand from the Lord for them. But
the Lord in his mercy has given me
wisdom that can be trusted, and I
will share it with you. 26 Because of
the present crisis,* I think it is best
to remain as you are. 27 If you have
a wife, do not seek to end the mar-
riage. If you do not have a wife, do
not seek to get married. 28 But if you
do get married, it is not a sin. And if a
young woman gets married, it is not
a sin. However, those who get mar-
ried at this time will have troubles,
and I am trying to spare you those
problems.

29 But let me say this, dear brothers
and sisters: The time that remains is
very short. So from now on, those
with wives should not focus only on
their marriage. 30 Those who weep
or who rejoice or who buy things
should not be absorbed by their
weeping or their joy or their posses-
sions. 31 Those who use the things
of the world should not become at-
tached to them. For this world as we
know it will soon pass away.

32 I want you to be free from the
concerns of this life. An unmarried
man can spend his time doing the
Lord's work and thinking how to
please him. 33 But a married man
has to think about his earthly re-
sponsibilities and how to please his
wife. 34 His interests are divided. In
the same way, a woman who is no
longer married or has never been
married can be devoted to the Lord

**NASB**

Lord, that she may be holy both in
body and spirit; but one who is mar-
ried is concerned about the things of
the world, how she may please her
husband. 35 This I say for your own
benefit; not to put a restraint upon
you, but [a]to promote what is appro-
priate and *to secure* undistracted de-
votion to the Lord.

36 But if any man thinks that he
is acting unbecomingly toward his
virgin *daughter,* if she is past her
youth, and if it must be so, let him
do what he wishes, he does not sin;
let [a]her marry. 37 But he who stands
firm in his heart, [a]being under no
constraint, but has authority [b]over
his own will, and has decided this in
his own heart, to keep his own virgin
*daughter,* he will do well. 38 So then
both he who gives his own virgin
*daughter* in marriage does well, and
he who does not give her in marriage
will do better.

39 A wife is bound as long as her
husband lives; but if her husband
[a]is dead, she is free to be married to
whom she wishes, only in the Lord.
40 But in my opinion she is happier
if she remains as she is; and I think
that I also have the Spirit of God.

**7:20** [a]Lit *calling* **7:21** [a]Lit *Let it not be a care to you* [b]Lit *use* **7:25** [a]Lit *has had mercy shown on him by the Lord to be trustworthy* **7:26** [a]Or *impending* [b]Lit *so to be* **7:28** [a]Lit *tribulation in the flesh* **7:35** [a]Lit *for what is seemly* **7:36** [a]Lit *them* **7:37** [a]Lit *having no necessity* [b]Lit *pertaining to* **7:39** [a]Lit *falls asleep*

**NLT**

and holy in body and in spirit. But a
married woman has to think about
her earthly responsibilities and how
to please her husband. 35 I am say-
ing this for your benefit, not to place
restrictions on you. I want you to
do whatever will help you serve the
Lord best, with as few distractions as
possible.

36 But if a man thinks that he's
treating his fiancée improperly and
will inevitably give in to his passion,
let him marry her as he wishes. It
is not a sin. 37 But if he has decided
firmly not to marry and there is no
urgency and he can control his pas-
sion, he does well not to marry. 38 So
the person who marries his fian-
cée does well, and the person who
doesn't marry does even better.

39 A wife is bound to her husband
as long as he lives. If her husband
dies, she is free to marry anyone
she wishes, but only if he loves the
Lord.* 40 But in my opinion it would
be better for her to stay single, and I
think I am giving you counsel from
God's Spirit when I say this.

**7:23** Greek *don't become slaves of people.* **7:24** Greek *brothers;* also in 7:29. **7:26** Or *the pressures of life.* **7:39** Greek *but only in the Lord.*

The disease of discontentment is an overlooked ailment. Yet consider for a moment some of the effects on those infected by its silent yet destructive presence.

Discontentment leads to rash, foolish decisions that we may regret for years. Under its influence, men have abandoned their families, families have abandoned their churches, and churches have abandoned their Lord. It can empty our wallets, drain our bank accounts, and ruin our lines of credit. On top of all that, it can affect our reputations, marking us not as stable people others can count on, but as flighty, flaky, and indecisive. Discontentment is a devastating disorder that robs us of joy, peace, patience, faithfulness, and self-control.

Though Paul primarily was dealing with issues of married and single life in 1 Corinthians 7, the principle of contentment is foundational to questions about whether, when, and whom to marry. So, before Paul refocuses on issues related to the single versus the married life (7:25-40), he steps back to examine the life of contentment (7:17-24). Discontentment with the current circumstances of life is an issue that plagues modern-day men and women as much as it troubled those in the first century, and Paul's principles here can be applied to more than just the question of singleness versus marriage.

## — 7:17-24 —

Having just urged his believing readers to continue to live in marriage with their unbelieving spouses who are willing to stay married (7:12-13, 16), Paul takes a sudden step out of the specific issue of marriage to address a matter that underlies the entire discussion: getting the most out of our lot in life. Paul appeals to a universal principle, one which he shared with all the churches: to remain in the general condition in which a person was called as a Christian (7:17). Because God has called each person from a particular social realm and unique life situation, that person should continue in that same situation. Why? The answer: in order to continue as a light in that particular social sphere (7:16).

Because such a principle could be easily misunderstood and misapplied, Paul immediately offers several concrete examples of the kinds of social and cultural realms he had in mind:

- Jewish believers should not shed their Jewishness and act like Gentiles (7:18).
- Gentiles should not shed their unique culture and act like Jews (7:18).
- Slaves should not fret about being freed from their legal obligations of service (7:21).
- Those who are free should not seek to indenture themselves to new masters (7:21, 23).
- The engaged should not break off their engagements (7:27).
- The single should not rush into marriage (7:27).

In the midst of these basic instructions, Paul intends that each believer find contentment to remain in whatever condition that person was in when called (7:20, 24). Supporting this principle is both a theological reason and a practical reason.

*The theological reason.* The gospel of salvation by grace through faith in Jesus Christ does not prefer one social, economic, ethnic, racial, or cultural category over another. Elsewhere Paul wrote, "There is neither Jew nor Greek, there is neither slave nor free man, there is neither male nor female; for you are all one in Christ Jesus" (Gal. 3:28). This theological purpose of staying put guarantees that those on the outside will look through the windows into the Christian faith and see a space not occupied by people of the same color, status, and pay grade; but they will see a startlingly diverse community of various races, languages, and classes.

*The practical reason.* Imagine if everybody who became a Christian decided to take vows of celibacy, poverty, silence, and solitude, forsaking their careers, families, communities, and pastimes. The body of Christ would shrivel up and die as it morphed into a corporate recluse, turning its back on the world and retreating into obscurity. The church's strategic presence in the nooks and crannies of this world would silently vanish like water vaporizing on a sunny day. Or imagine if all new believers turned their calling as a Christian into a calling to full-time vocational ministry. That may sound like an answer to prayer, but in reality the distorted body of Christ would grow top-heavy and topple as it lost all of its faithful, generous lay people whose honest labor in the secular realm produces an abundance of wealth to support those in ministry. The practical truth is that God has called people from all paygrades, social strata, lifestyles, careers, cultures, and situations in order to create a community of diversity and harmony, not sameness and monotony. As we believers exercise contentment and remain in the circumstances in which we were called, we continue to be salt and light in our own communities. We continue to exercise an influence on our unsaved friends, relatives, colleagues, and acquaintances.

Yet we lambs like to wander! Like fielded sheep, we poke our heads past our fenced boundaries to graze in another's pasture—where the grass seems to taste so much better than ours. But if we were to stop and listen, we would hear others' chomping as they grazed on our grass, leaving *their* green fields for ours. You've seen it. Stressed-out parents knee-deep in Lego blocks and over their heads in extracurricular activities might look longingly at the wide-open schedules and freewheeling lifestyles of couples without children. At the same time, those same married couples not blessed with kids may look with envy at those with children, hoping and praying with tears that the Lord would bless them with a baby. Just down the street, a single woman, settled into a nine-to-five career of her dreams, might wish she had someone to eat dinner with besides her purring cat. Across the street, a married man may wonder if he made the right choice back when he tied the knot with his new bride, considering where he could have taken his career if it weren't for all the ongoing marital responsibilities.

Too many look at their life circumstances and see only the negatives. They don't see the God-glorifying ministry potential inherent in their callings. Paul's principles of contentment in 1 Corinthians 7 encourage us to look at our own life situations differently. He advises all God's people on both sides of the fence to defeat discontentment and to get the most out of their lot in life.

## — 7:25-35 —

With a final reiteration of the principle of being content with where God has placed us (7:24), Paul applies this principle to the question of whether it is right for single men and women to marry, thus drastically changing their circumstances. Paul's advice to singles, in a nutshell: "Staying unmarried is desirable but not demanded." He supports his point with two advantages singles have that married people don't. Though Paul's advice concerning singles is not drawn directly from Jesus' teaching, it was revealed to Paul by the Holy Spirit and is just as authoritative as Christ's teachings (7:25; 2 Pet. 1:21; 3:15-16).

First, *singles will experience less distress and personal difficulty in a hostile world* (1 Cor. 7:26-28). Although persecution had been sporadic and localized in Paul's day, based on Jesus' teaching (Matt. 23:34) and on reading the signs of the times, the apostle knew that full-blown persecution was just around the corner. In fact, about ten years after Paul wrote this letter, the Roman emperor Nero falsely blamed Christians for setting the imperial capital ablaze. He slaughtered believers of all ages; one rampage followed another, blowing past Rome's city limits into the rest of the empire like shock waves of a massive explosion. The horrible persecutions left a dreadful wound on the body of Christ that would take decades to heal. In light of this impending doom, Paul knew that those with spouses and children would find themselves tempted to deny the faith, or at least compromise their testimonies, in order to protect their families.

Many of us don't face these kinds of challenges to the marriage relationship. Most of us, though, deal with other kinds of hardships exacerbated by married life: the loss of a job, the death of a mate or child, the rebellion of teenagers, financial stress, and other daily trials and tribulations associated with family life. Because believers still face the brunt of the world's hostility toward Christ, Paul's advice to stay single still applies to some of us today. Watching a mate or child suffer can often feel unbearable. It can drive us to despair.

Those already bound to spouses, either by marriage or legal engagement, should fulfill their commitments, even though they will experience intense hardship (1 Cor. 7:27). But those who are released from either a marriage (by divorce) or engagement (by canceling of a marriage contract) should strongly consider remaining single—at least until the crises Paul expected would pass by.

Because Paul emphasized so strongly the value of staying single, the Corinthians might have begun to think that marriage itself was sinful. Because of that possibility, he clarifies that marrying is not a sin (7:28). Marriage itself is good. In fact, earlier he said it was far preferable than living in a state of burning lust (7:9). The goodness and wholesomeness of marriage, however, doesn't change the fact that those who marry in, or shortly before, times of social and economic crises brought on by persecution will experience greater hardship.

The same is true even without external persecution. Compared to the single life, the married life is hard. Over approximately fifty years of ministry, I estimate that for every single person who has come to me or my pastoral staff for counseling through challenging situations, we have had twenty-five married couples knocking on our doors. Those of us in ministry fully understand the value of premarital counseling. Truth be told, part of the strategy during this brief window of time prior to the wedding is to help some engaged couples recognize that they are not at all prepared to get married at that time. Why? Because far too many young couples rush passionately into a marriage commitment without fully understanding that the married life is hard.

The large number of divorces today is a telltale sign that marriage provides anything but an idyllic pasture of sweet clover. Yes, healthy marriages can bring love, joy, fulfillment, and excitement, all at a high cost of production. Marriage increases our responsibilities, readjusts our hopes and dreams, and consistently cuts into our "me-time." Author Mike Mason minces no words as he explains: "Angering, humiliating, melting, chastening, purifying, it touches us where we hurt most, in the place of our lovelessness. Dragging us into lifelong encounters which at times may be full of boredom, tension, unpleasantness or grief, marriage challenges us to abandon everything for the sake of love."[4]

Second, *singles can embrace spiritual matters with fewer secular distractions* (7:29-35). Paul begins by reminding his readers that the age in which they live is a temporary arrangement of things: "The time has been shortened" (7:29) and "the form of this world is passing away" (7:31). In other words, during the era between the first and second coming of Christ, people are living as if things will continue unabated forever (2 Pet. 3:4), but informed, mature Christians know better. Because we have insight into God's plans for this world, we know that the current systems making up the cultures, societies, economies, and systems of our world are temporary (see Luke 20:34-36). Thus, Paul wrote in Colossians 3:2, "Set your mind on the things above, not on the things that are on earth."

When we fully comprehend the temporary and tentative nature of the current age, wise Christians seek to invest time in eternal matters. Those with their time and energy wrapped up in family, leisure, and possessions tend to get drawn into the concerns of this world and can easily lose sight of spiritual priorities. So, with a heavenly-minded worldview, believers may be engaged in—but not enslaved to—marriage, mourning, merrymaking, marketing, and material things (1 Cor. 7:29-31).

Married couples are concerned about cultivating their marriages and satisfying their spouses' needs and desires, and there is everything right about that. It is a vital part of the marriage obligation. Because of this, Paul points out the obvious fact that those who are unmarried not only have more time and resources to devote to a life of Christian service, but they will also be undistracted by the essential commitments required of married men and women (7:32-35). Yes, married couples should be involved in ministry, but their time and energy are necessarily divided. Those of us who are married and involved in full-time ministry know the kind of tension and strain this can place on marriage and family. It is a balancing act many men and women have trouble carrying out. This is Paul's thought here. Let's not misunderstand his intentions. He is not forbidding marriage. He is engaging in premarital counseling, warning his readers of the sobering realities of the married life (7:35).

## — 7:36-40 —

In most of our Western cultures, in which men and women "hang out," date, court, woo, and somehow find their mates through a subjective, unpredictable process, Paul's advice (7:36-38) doesn't make a lot of sense. Many marriages in Paul's day were arranged beforehand, as the parents of young men and women worked out the details of the weddings like contractual agreements, often without the input or even the awareness of their sons or daughters—the ones who were getting married. We need to resist the temptation to pass judgment on such a cultural practice. There are many Christians in other cultures where the tradition of arranged marriages still prevails.

This idea of arranged marriages (or legal betrothal) stands in the background of Paul's advice (7:36-38); but another issue also needs to be resolved, which can be seen when comparing different translations (such as the NASB and the NLT) of these verses. Some translations understand the man referred to in 7:36-38 as the father of an unmarried daughter; others understand him as a young man betrothed (legally engaged) to a woman. It is not easy to decide which is being addressed here, but I side with those who hold that Paul is addressing a father's responsibility for his unmarried daughter.[5]

In a culture in which it was the father's responsibility to plan for the future of his daughter, which included finding a suitable husband and providing an appropriate dowry, his ears might have perked up when he heard Paul's advice concerning the benefits of singleness. This might have led him to call off betrothals he had already arranged or to volunteer his daughter to a life of singleness that didn't actually suit her. Paul, however, urges such fathers to honest reflection before making such decisions (7:37). In short, neither singleness nor marriage should be entered into casually or for self-serving reasons.

Finally, Paul shifts attention from the virgins to the widows (7:39-40). His advice is consistent with everything he has been urging throughout this chapter. As long as a wife's husband lives, the woman is legally bound to him as his wife. Upon his death, however, the marriage bond is severed, and she now has the freedom to marry another believing man (7:39). Yet guided by the Spirit's wisdom, Paul once again suggests that widows consider devoting their single years to the Lord's service (7:40).

In all of these circumstances, Paul's mind is guided by the general principle of contentment. Rather than seeking something else due to envy, discontent, or dissatisfaction, he desires men and women to be patient in their circumstances. They should recognize their top priority is serving the Lord in this temporary world, investing in eternity rather than involving themselves in a series of radical life changes that amount to spinning their wheels in a world going nowhere.

# APPLICATION: 1 CORINTHIANS 7:17-40

## Thoughts on Single-Mindedness

If you're single, Paul's words in this passage are especially addressed to you. While studying them, maybe you have realized that you haven't spent your time as you should. Maybe you have begun to see that the attention given to your career or finding a mate has been misdirected. If your response to singleness has been unbiblical, riddled with discontent, or driven by envy of someone else's life circumstances, you can turn it around and make it count for Christ by following three one-word exhortations.

*Rejoice!* Thank God for your singleness and enjoy it as His best for you at this time in your life. He is in control of your circumstances. If and when He wants them to change, He will bring it about in His own time. Be content with the place God has for you at this stage in your life and make the most of it.

*Reorient!* Redirect your focus and rechannel your energies. Instead of focusing on the horizontal plane of this temporary world, focus on the vertical—God's eternal calling. Reorient your priorities and your energy to devote yourself totally to God and His work. When you're seeking first His kingdom and His righteousness, whatever else you need will be added to you—from contentment in the single life to the right mate at the right time (Matt. 6:33).

*Relax!* Quit hungering for the grass on the other side of the fence. Stay in your pasture and feed on the many benefits God has for you there. The pasture of singleness can be a place of contentment and even fulfillment if you will rest in Him, wait on Him, and serve Him through trusting obedience.

It is my candid observation that many single Christians aren't interested in being fully devoted to the Lord. Perhaps that is true because they are following only the drives and desires of their lives, pursuits dictated to them by the prevailing cultural values and not by the priorities of Scripture. But in 1 Corinthians 7 Paul presents a different picture: a single man or woman, old or young, willing and able to be devoted to the Master's service. Some are called to that undistracted life for a season, others for a lifetime. Has God called you to singleness at this time? If so, rejoice, reorient, and relax—and get the most from your lot in life.

# "Meating" in the Middle
## 1 CORINTHIANS 8:1-13

**NASB**

1 Now concerning things sacrificed to idols, we know that we all have knowledge. Knowledge [a]makes arrogant, but love edifies. 2 If anyone supposes that he knows anything, he has not yet known as he ought to know; 3 but if anyone loves God, he is known by Him.

4 Therefore concerning the eating of things sacrificed to idols, we know that [a]there is no such thing as an idol in the world, and that there is no God but one. 5 For even if there are so-called gods whether in heaven or on earth, as indeed there are many gods and many lords, 6 yet for us there is *but* one God, the Father, from whom are all things and we *exist* for Him; and one Lord, Jesus Christ, by whom are all things, and we *exist* through Him.

7 However not all men have this knowledge; but some, being accustomed to the idol until now, eat *food* as if it were sacrificed to an idol; and their conscience being weak is defiled. 8 But food will not [a]commend us to God; we are neither [b]the worse if we do not eat, nor [c]the better if we do eat. 9 But take care that this [a]liberty of yours does not somehow become a stumbling block to the weak. 10 For if someone sees you, who have knowledge, dining in an idol's temple, will

**NLT**

1 Now regarding your question about food that has been offered to idols. Yes, we know that "we all have knowledge" about this issue. But while knowledge makes us feel important, it is love that strengthens the church. 2 Anyone who claims to know all the answers doesn't really know very much. 3 But the person who loves God is the one whom God recognizes.*

4 So, what about eating meat that has been offered to idols? Well, we all know that an idol is not really a god and that there is only one God. 5 There may be so-called gods both in heaven and on earth, and some people actually worship many gods and many lords. 6 But for us,

There is one God, the Father,
by whom all things were created,
and for whom we live.
And there is one Lord, Jesus Christ,
through whom all things were created,
and through whom we live.

7 However, not all believers know this. Some are accustomed to thinking of idols as being real, so when they eat food that has been offered to idols, they think of it as the worship of real gods, and their weak consciences are violated. 8 It's true that we can't win God's approval by what we eat. We don't lose anything if we don't eat it, and we don't gain anything if we do.

9 But you must be careful so that your freedom does not cause others with a weaker conscience to stumble. 10 For if others see you—with your "superior knowledge"—eating in the temple of an idol, won't

not his conscience, if he is weak, be
strengthened to eat things sacrificed
to idols? 11 For through your knowl-
edge he who is weak is ruined, the
brother for whose sake Christ died.
12 And so, by sinning against the
brethren and wounding their con-
science when it is weak, you sin
against Christ. 13 Therefore, if food
causes my brother to stumble, I will
never eat meat again, so that I will
not cause my brother to stumble.

**8:1** [a]Lit *puffs up* **8:4** [a]Lit *nothing is an idol in the world;* i.e. an idol has no real existence **8:8** [a]Or *present* [b]Lit *lacking* [c]Lit *abounding* **8:9** [a]Lit *right*

they be encouraged to violate their
conscience by eating food that has
been offered to an idol? 11 So be-
cause of your superior knowledge,
a weak believer* for whom Christ
died will be destroyed. 12 And when
you sin against other believers* by
encouraging them to do something
they believe is wrong, you are sin-
ning against Christ. 13 So if what I
eat causes another believer to sin, I
will never eat meat again as long as
I live—for I don't want to cause an-
other believer to stumble.

**8:3** Some manuscripts read *the person who loves has full knowledge.* **8:11** Greek *brother;* also in 8:13. **8:12** Greek *brothers.*

I've never completely understood vegetarians. I certainly have nothing against them. In fact, it looks like Adam, Eve, and the other people who lived prior to Noah's Flood ate only fruits, vegetables, and grains (Gen. 1:29-30; 9:3). If people want to go retro and leave the beef and chicken to me and other carnivores, I'm fine with that. But once in a while, I run into a hyperherbivore. Judgmental as any sour-faced legalist, those fanatics not only avoid all meat and animal products, but they also want to force their personal opinions on everybody they meet. Their opinions go beyond eschewing meat for health reasons; they believe it's morally wrong for *anybody* to eat meat. Period.

This question about whether we should eat meat may seem irrelevant to us today. Those who would judge us for biting into a big, juicy burger are few and far between. But what about those who judge us for drinking champagne at a New Year's Eve party? Or trick-or-treating on Halloween? Or going to a movie, dancing, playing Xbox, or listening to secular music? All of these things find their way onto different people's lists of Christian "no-nos."

The hot issue in the Corinthian church wasn't whether to go to movies, play video games, or drink sparkling champagne. Instead, they fretted about the appropriateness of eating meat that had been sacrificed to idols. I don't know of any Christian vegetarian who opposes eating meat because it might have been offered to a goddess of fertility or a god of wine. Yet the principle Paul employed to settle this question is just as applicable to the debated practices and "gray" areas of our day as it was to this issue in Corinth.

## CORINTHIAN IDOLS

### 1 CORINTHIANS 8:4

Corinth was one of many centers of idol worship in the ancient world. As a part of this worship, an animal was brought before a priest to be sacrificed. Only parts of the animal were burned—usually the legs, fat, and internal organs. The leftovers—usually the best pieces of meat—were often consumed among the participants at a festive meal, taken home to enjoy in private, or sold in public marketplaces.[6]

This posed a problem for believers, because when they ate as invited guests at a person's home or bought meat at the marketplace, chances were good that some of it came from an animal sacrificed in the worship of a false god. In that worship, consuming the meat sacrificed to the idol was the same as participating in the worship of the idol. One commentator explains this knotty dilemma:

> The believers of Corinth and the other Greek cities found themselves in a difficult position in regard to the heathen society around them. On the one hand, they could not absolutely give up their family and friendly relations; the interest of the gospel did not allow them to do so. On the other hand, these relations were full of temptations and might easily draw them into unfaithfulness, which would make them the scandal of the Church and the derision of the heathen.[7]

## — 8:1-6 —

In 1 Corinthians 8, Paul abruptly transitions to a completely new topic: "concerning things sacrificed to idols" (8:1). This issue presented a threefold dilemma for Christians because there were three ways a person might end up partaking of the offerings to idols. The first was by actually showing up at a pagan temple and eating of the fellowship

### Temple Sacrificed Meat

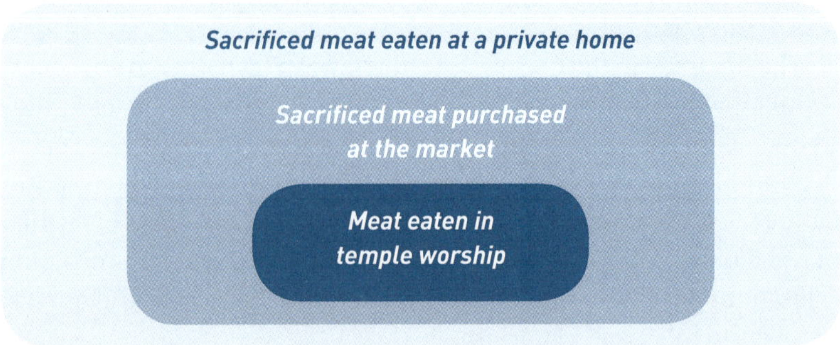

meal in honor of the pagan god. The second way a Christian might eat meat sacrificed to idols was by purchasing the meat in the marketplace for eating at home. A third way to partake of sacrificed animal meat was to be invited to a meal at a friend's home that included meat that came from a pagan temple. Therefore, as Paul begins to answer the Corinthians' inquiry regarding the appropriateness of eating meat sacrificed to idols, he must address all three layers of this problem.

At the start of his written instructions, Paul appeals to the believer's liberty in Christ. He has referred to this principle before. In 1 Corinthians 6:12 he writes, "All things are lawful for me, but not all things are profitable." The Corinthians had knowledge of their freedom in Christ, but this knowledge had led some to become arrogant rather than loving toward others (8:1). Their pride caused them to abuse their freedom, overstepping the bounds of wisdom and holiness into the mire of careless folly and sin. This had already occurred in the issue of sexual immorality (5:1-2).

Paul straightens them out by setting up a contrast between arrogant knowledge and edifying love (8:1). The Greek word for "edifies" is *oikodomeō* [3618], which originally meant "to build a house." The word for "makes arrogant" is *physioō* [5448], which means to blow something up with a bellows, to inflate.[8] A good rendering of the last part of the verse could be "knowledge blows up, but love builds up." Knowledge is a God-given window into reality through which we can view life, but if it is not controlled by edifying love (*agapē* [26]) it can become a dangerous weapon that destroys rather than builds. Rather than self-inflating knowledge (8:2), Paul argues for a love of God (8:3) that manifests itself in love for others (8:9).

Paul brings this principle to bear on the issue of eating meat sacrificed to idols. All Christians share knowledge of the one true God through their faith in the one Lord, Jesus Christ. Though the foolish pagans may believe that their statues of wood, gold, silver, and stone have divine powers, Christians know they are merely man-made relics of a depraved religious system (8:4-6). Based on this knowledge, the implication is clear: Since idols are merely human creations, and since there is only one true God, eating meat that has been sacrificed to a piece of carved wood or molded silver is really inconsequential. After all, how can meat, in and of itself, be made evil by gods that don't exist?

The Christian worldview should therefore drive out the superstitions that often surround us. Fear of bad luck over broken mirrors, walking under ladders, black cats, or certain numbers should be driven out by the knowledge believers have of the one true God and how His world works. Yet having this knowledge without love for God and one another can lead to all kinds of problems. Why? Because not all believers have a mature understanding of these things.

## — 8:7-13 —

Paul notes that not all people have the same knowledge (*gnōsis* [1108]) as the mature thinkers (8:7). That is, some new believers who once had been steeped in idolatrous religious cults may take longer to come to grips with a proper view of the world. We might extend this to modern-day examples to illustrate the point. New believers who had been heavily involved in the wild party scene with lots of booze and drugs may balk at Christians who see nothing wrong with meeting a group of friends at a "bar and grill." Believers who were saved from a life of sex addiction might raise their brows at a believer who has no problem going to see certain movies or visiting the beach. Or those who had been involved in eastern mysticism might believe that Christians who burn incense at home are unwittingly conjuring up demons. Knowledgeable Christians, however, know that in and of themselves, these places and things are harmless. But younger Christians, weak in the faith and early in their discipleship, may still associate these things with the wickedness in which they once participated.

This is why Paul appeals not merely to the Corinthians' proper knowledge of theology and logic, but also to their responsibility to love weaker believers—those who were saved but untaught and immature. Ignorant of a balanced Christian worldview, they may have been easily offended at others' exercise of their liberty. Being accustomed to the pagans' theology of the idol—that it had in and of itself a real mystical power—they still bought into the idea that the meat sacrificed to the idol was contaminated by association and therefore spiritually harmful to them (1 Cor. 8:7).

These believers didn't realize that the meat issue is *amoral*—morally neutral. Eating the meat would not affect their relationship with Christ one way or another (8:8). The one who eats is not harmed; the one who abstains is not blessed. In fact, the question of meat should be moot among those who have a mature understanding of the Christian worldview. But because many in Corinth still had a very sensitive conscience toward the issue of meat sacrificed to idols, Paul urges the mature in knowledge to exercise love by putting a lid on their liberty when dealing with the weaker brothers and sisters in Christ (8:9). Maturity includes self-restraint.

Paul reveals the folly that results from the arrogant application of knowledge (8:10). Those who were mature in knowledge felt so sure that the meat sacrificed to idols was nothing that they rushed straight into the temples to eat the meat hot off the altars (8:10). These bold but insensitive carnal believers had overstepped their liberty, failing to temper their decisions with love and self-control. As a result, they careened headlong into licentiousness and brought a number of weaker believers with them. Those weaker brothers had not yet come to a place where they could say, "This is just a piece of meat." For them, it was still a means of worshiping false gods, resulting in a violation of their conscience and a corruption of their simple faith (8:11).

Romans 14 treats this same issue, addressing how to wisely and lovingly adjust the application of our knowledge to the spiritual needs of weaker believers. There Paul writes words of mature wisdom: "I know and am convinced in the Lord Jesus that nothing is unclean in itself; but to him who thinks anything to be unclean, to him it is unclean. For if because of food your brother is hurt, you are no longer walking according to love. Do not destroy with your food him for whom Christ died" (Rom. 14:14-15). Returning to 1 Corinthians, the implications of causing fellow believers to stumble in their conscience is serious: "By sinning against the brethren and wounding their conscience when it is weak, you sin against Christ" (1 Cor. 8:12).

The heart of the problem is a failure of knowledgeable believers to look out not only for their own interests but also for the interests of others (Phil. 2:4). By imprudently flaunting their liberty in Christ to eat any kind of meat they wanted, whenever they pleased, those believers weakened the fellowship of the church. Paul attacks this foolish flaunting of freedom in the presence of a weaker believer with an extreme solution: "If food causes my brother to stumble, I will never eat meat again" (1 Cor. 8:13). The Greek text is even more explicit, using the phrase *ou mē* [3364]. . . *eis* [1519] *ton aiōna* [165], literally "never, ever . . . unto the age." That is, if enjoying a piece of meat meant causing a brother in Christ to be dragged back into a lifestyle he had just escaped, *Paul would rather abstain from eating meat forever*!

Paul isn't talking about tiptoeing around the legalistic scruples of sanctimonious believers—those who have made Christianity a meticulous system of dos and don'ts. Paul takes a strong stand against the religious legalism of self-proclaimed experts in the Law who, for theological reasons, want to drag every Christian under the yoke of Judaism (Gal. 5:1; 1 Tim. 1:7). This is not about that. Here, Paul is talking about protecting the tender conscience of a weak believer. In a nutshell, he's telling us that Christian love must wisely temper Christian liberty.

## APPLICATION: 1 CORINTHIANS 8:1-13

### Tempering Liberty with Love

You meet a younger Christian at church, you strike up a friendship, and suddenly you realize this person really looks up to you for spiritual guidance. You detect right away that this person has not been discipled well. They don't have the signs of mature knowledge.

You are a well-tuned marathon runner; your new friend is just getting into jogging. Paul refers to such a person as a weaker brother in the faith. Do you slow your pace to help this believer develop, or pass him off to somebody else more at that level? To use a different example: You're a concert pianist; she's in her first year of piano lessons. Do you reduce your tempo and skill level to play duets together, or pair her up with a teacher who has patience for novices?

Now, let's take this a step further. Let's assume this new believer is a recovering alcoholic, saved out of a twenty-year battle with alcohol and slowly learning how to live a life that doesn't revolve around bars and nightclubs. On the other hand, you come from a family that occasionally enjoyed a glass of wine with a nice meal, served champagne at special occasions, or used alcohol in cooking or desserts. In other words, alcohol has been just a neutral part of your world. What do you do when this new believer comes around? Do you cook the same recipes and serve the same beverages? Do you surrender your own freedom in Christ for the sake of the weaker believer? Or do you avoid the hassle and not invite that person into your life?

These types of situations reveal our real attitudes. Even though today we don't have to battle the issue of eating meat sacrificed to idols, our world is strewn with controversial gray areas that can trip up those who are not yet skilled enough to nimbly navigate them. When you face these issues, you need to quickly determine the proper priority. Do you exercise your Christian liberty or practice Jesus' love? Do you view weaker believers as nuisances or embrace them as those who need to be discipled in the faith?

Regardless of our differing stances on the gray issues of life, we all have been called to obey one black-and-white command in Scripture: "Love one another" (John 13:34). In each situation, we are to wisely apply love and self-control, not always seeking ways to live out our own freedom in Christ, but looking for opportunities to show patience and extend grace toward others.

# Sacrificing Rights for Rewards
## 1 CORINTHIANS 9:1-27

**NASB**

1 Am I not free? Am I not an apostle?
Have I not seen Jesus our Lord? Are
you not my work in the Lord? 2 If to
others I am not an apostle, at least I
am to you; for you are the seal of my
apostleship in the Lord.
3 My defense to those who examine
me is this: 4 [a]Do we not have a right
to eat and drink? 5 [a]Do we not have a
right to take along a [b]believing wife,
even as the rest of the apostles and
the brothers of the Lord and Cephas?
6 Or do only [a]Barnabas and I not
have a right to refrain from working?
7 Who at any time serves as a soldier
at his own expense? Who plants a
vineyard and does not eat the fruit
of it? Or who tends a flock and does
not [a]use the milk of the flock?
8 I am not speaking these things
according to [a]human judgment, am
I? Or does not the Law also say these
things? 9 For it is written in the Law of
Moses, "YOU SHALL NOT MUZZLE THE
OX WHILE HE IS THRESHING." God is
not concerned about oxen, is He?

**NLT**

1 Am I not as free as anyone else? Am
I not an apostle? Haven't I seen Jesus
our Lord with my own eyes? Isn't it
because of my work that you belong
to the Lord? 2 Even if others think I
am not an apostle, I certainly am to
you. You yourselves are proof that I
am the Lord's apostle.
3 This is my answer to those who
question my authority.* 4 Don't we
have the right to live in your homes
and share your meals? 5 Don't we
have the right to bring a believing
wife* with us as the other apostles
and the Lord's brothers do, and as
Peter* does? 6 Or is it only Barnabas
and I who have to work to support
ourselves?
7 What soldier has to pay his own
expenses? What farmer plants a
vineyard and doesn't have the right
to eat some of its fruit? What shep-
herd cares for a flock of sheep and
isn't allowed to drink some of the
milk? 8 Am I expressing merely a
human opinion, or does the law
say the same thing? 9 For the law of
Moses says, "You must not muzzle an
ox to keep it from eating as it treads
out the grain."* Was God thinking
only about oxen when he said this?

NASB

10 Or is He speaking altogether for our sake? Yes, for our sake it was written, because the plowman ought to plow in hope, and the thresher *to thresh* in hope of sharing *the crops.* 11 If we sowed spiritual things in you, is it too much if we reap material things from you? 12 If others share the right over you, do we not more? Nevertheless, we did not use this right, but we endure all things so that we will cause no hindrance to the gospel of Christ. 13 Do you not know that those who perform sacred services eat the *food* of the temple, *and* those who attend regularly to the altar have their share [a]from the altar? 14 So also the Lord directed those who proclaim the gospel to get their living from the gospel.

15 But I have used none of these things. And I am not writing these things so that it will be done so in my case; for it would be better for me to die than have any man make my boast an empty one. 16 For if I preach the gospel, I have nothing to boast of, for I am under compulsion; for woe is me if I do not preach the gospel. 17 For if I do this voluntarily, I have a reward; but if against my will, I have a stewardship entrusted to me. 18 What then is my reward? That, when I preach the gospel, I may offer the gospel without charge, so as not to make full use of my right in the gospel.

19 For though I am free from all *men,* I have made myself a slave to all, so that I may win more. 20 To the Jews I became as a Jew, so that I might win Jews; to those who are under [a]the Law, as under [a]the Law

NLT

10 Wasn't he actually speaking to us? Yes, it was written for us, so that the one who plows and the one who threshes the grain might both expect a share of the harvest.

11 Since we have planted spiritual seed among you, aren't we entitled to a harvest of physical food and drink? 12 If you support others who preach to you, shouldn't we have an even greater right to be supported? But we have never used this right. We would rather put up with anything than be an obstacle to the Good News about Christ.

13 Don't you realize that those who work in the temple get their meals from the offerings brought to the temple? And those who serve at the altar get a share of the sacrificial offerings. 14 In the same way, the Lord ordered that those who preach the Good News should be supported by those who benefit from it. 15 Yet I have never used any of these rights. And I am not writing this to suggest that I want to start now. In fact, I would rather die than lose my right to boast about preaching without charge. 16 Yet preaching the Good News is not something I can boast about. I am compelled by God to do it. How terrible for me if I didn't preach the Good News!

17 If I were doing this on my own initiative, I would deserve payment. But I have no choice, for God has given me this sacred trust. 18 What then is my pay? It is the opportunity to preach the Good News without charging anyone. That's why I never demand my rights when I preach the Good News.

19 Even though I am a free man with no master, I have become a slave to all people to bring many to Christ. 20 When I was with the Jews, I lived like a Jew to bring the Jews to Christ. When I was with those who follow the Jewish law, I too lived

though not being myself under [a]the
Law, so that I might win those who
are under [a]the Law; 21 to those who
are without law, as without law,
though not being without the law
of God but under the law of Christ,
so that I might win those who are
without law. 22 To the weak I became
weak, that I might win the weak; I
have become all things to all men, so
that I may by all means save some.
23 I do all things for the sake of the
gospel, so that I may become a fellow
partaker of it.

24 Do you not know that those who
run in a race all run, but *only* one re-
ceives the prize? Run in such a way
that you may win. 25 Everyone who
competes in the games exercises
self-control in all things. They then
*do it* to receive a perishable wreath,
but we an imperishable. 26 Therefore
I run in such a way, as not without
aim; I box in such a way, as not beat-
ing the air; 27 but I [a]discipline my
body and make it my slave, so that,
after I have preached to others, I my-
self will not be disqualified.

**9:4** [a]Lit *It is not that we have no right to eat and drink, is it?* **9:5** [a]Lit *It is not that we have no right to take along...Cephas, is it?* [b]Lit *sister, as wife* **9:6** [a]Lit *I and Barnabas* **9:7** [a]Lit *eat of* **9:8** [a]Lit *man* **9:13** [a]Lit *with* **9:20** [a]Or *law* **9:27** [a]Lit *bruise*

under that law. Even though I am
not subject to the law, I did this so
I could bring to Christ those who are
under the law. 21 When I am with the
Gentiles who do not follow the Jew-
ish law,* I too live apart from that
law so I can bring them to Christ. But
I do not ignore the law of God; I obey
the law of Christ.

22 When I am with those who are
weak, I share their weakness, for
I want to bring the weak to Christ.
Yes, I try to find common ground
with everyone, doing everything I
can to save some. 23 I do everything
to spread the Good News and share
in its blessings.

24 Don't you realize that in a race
everyone runs, but only one person
gets the prize? So run to win! 25 All
athletes are disciplined in their train-
ing. They do it to win a prize that will
fade away, but we do it for an eter-
nal prize. 26 So I run with purpose
in every step. I am not just shadow-
boxing. 27 I discipline my body like
an athlete, training it to do what it
should. Otherwise, I fear that after
preaching to others I myself might
be disqualified.

**9:3** Greek *those who examine me.* **9:5a** Greek *a sister a wife.* **9:5b** Greek *Cephas.* **9:9** Deut 25:4. **9:21** Greek *those without the law.*

Imagine this scene. You're a member of a baseball team playing its most important game of the season. It's the bottom of the ninth inning. The score is tied, the bases loaded, there are no outs, and you are up to bat.

Taking a few practice swings on your way to the batter's box, you look down at the third base coach for the signal. Expecting a "swing away" sign, you begin to churn inside when he dips his hat, wipes his nose, and then licks his thumb: the dreaded "sacrifice fly" signal.[9]

"What does the coach mean?" you think to yourself. "He expects me to fly out on purpose so the team can score? What about my .350 batting average? Give me a few swings and I can knock this ball out of the park. We'll win by four runs instead of one, and most of all, I'll end the game in a blaze of glory—just like Robert Redford in *The Natural*!"

So you're faced with a decision. Will you sacrifice your right to hit the ball wherever you please in order to let another teammate get a run? Or will you grab for the glory by attempting to hit it out of the park?

As we have already seen, the Corinthian team suffered from envy, selfishness, pride, and strife. Each member's viewpoint reflected a distinct, isolated player, giving little thought to how one player's actions would affect the rest of the team. In 1 Corinthians 9:1-18, Paul shows us the attitudes they practiced—their pep cheer was "I've got my rights!" Then, in a dugout talk, Paul exhorts the team to model his own strategy for victory: placing the needs of the body of Christ above personal rights. Only when they began to compete in the contest of life as members of a team rather than as independent players looking out only for themselves would they be eligible for eternal rewards.

## — 9:1-2 —

The Corinthians had been liberated by Christ to live in freedom from the Law (Gal. 5:1), and they were intent on exercising their newfound rights. But if there was an upside-down way of doing something, the Corinthians would find it. They had used their freedom to feed their egos and fleshly desires, spending their liberty on selfish pursuits. Rather than bolstering their team members in the body of Christ, they demanded their rights. So, Paul challenges their attitude by arguing from the greater to the lesser. If Paul himself sacrificed his rights as an apostle, then how is it that the church members at Corinth could insist on having their rights honored?

Paul begins by simply listing his credentials, the highlights of his résumé with which his readers were thoroughly familiar (1 Cor. 9:1-2). He was a believer freed from the Law, a handpicked apostle of God, an eyewitness of the resurrected Christ, and a laborer who had borne fruit for the kingdom.

Not one of the Corinthian believers could argue against his stats. If it hadn't been for Paul's ministry in their city, they would have remained lost. To return to our baseball analogy, it's as if Paul, the manager of the team, were to pick up a bat and approach the plate. He of all people had the right to do as he pleased on that playing field, far more than any of the members of the team who were not coaches or managers.

## — 9:3-14 —

In order to set an example, Paul offers what he calls a "defense," or *apologia* [627] for his practice, just in case some might judge him or criticize him for his methods of doing ministry (9:3). The term *apologia* basically

# A Biblical Basis for Paying Your Pastor

## 1 CORINTHIANS 9:9

*Occasionally one hears complaints about the "professionalization" of the ministry. This often comes from those who believe church leaders should minister free of charge. Some churches have even done away with what they style "the clergy class," opting for a plurality of lay leaders, no pastors, and definitely no paid leadership positions. Sometimes people even claim that the original churches were only house churches, small communities run by the older men of the church, and that the idea of a trained, ordained, and paid professional reflects a fall away from the original New Testament ideal.*

*Such views, however, don't stand up under biblical scrutiny. In 1 Corinthians 9:9-11, Paul makes the case that ministry workers were to be compensated with material things for their spiritual work (9:11). Only a fool would muzzle an ox to keep it from eating while plowing the fields (9:9). So only foolish churches would hold back a fair wage from those engaged in the work of the ministry. In fact, the wage was expected to be enough to free up a minister from having to work outside the ministry setting—and to provide for familial needs (9:4-6).*

*Paul also addresses the issue of paying church leaders when he spells out some of the basics of pastoral ministry in 1 Timothy 5:17-18. He writes, "The elders who rule well are to be considered worthy of double honor, especially those who work hard at preaching and teaching. For the Scripture says, 'You shall not muzzle the ox while he is threshing,' and 'The laborer is worthy of his wages.'" From this passage we see that the principle of paying laborers in church ministry extended beyond the apostles and itinerant missionaries. Local church leaders (the elders) who committed a significant amount of their time to teaching and preaching were also to be compensated materially.*

means "an answer" or "explanation," so Paul begins to explain himself, giving the logic of his perspective on self-sacrificial ministry. Just as Paul has listed his credentials, he also underlines the rights that go along with his high position: the right to sufficient food and drink (9:4); the right to bring a family along on ministry travel (9:5); and the right to draw ministry support from those to whom he ministers (9:6-11).

In other words, as an apostle, Paul had the right to expect full material and financial support for himself (and a family, if he had one). Other ministers of the gospel, such as James, Jude, and Cephas, had exercised this right to a living wage in their own apostolic ministries (9:5). Like the Old Testament priests who were granted the right to eat some of the sacrifice of the altar (9:13), the Lord desires those who preach the gospel to earn their living through the offerings of those to whom they minister (9:14).

Although Paul was fully entitled to exercise these rights, he voluntarily chose to sacrifice them. He opted to "endure all things" so that he would not cause any "hindrance to the gospel of Christ" (9:12). How would Paul's acceptance of his right to ministry support place an obstacle in the path of the Corinthians' acceptance of the gospel? William Barclay provides a possible answer: "Men judge a message by the life and character of the man who brings it; and Paul was determined that his hands would be clean. He would allow nothing in his life to contradict the message of his lips. Someone once said to a preacher, 'I cannot hear what you say for listening to what you are.' No one could ever say that to Paul."[10]

The world in which Paul ministered had been overrun by charlatans, opportunists, and soothsayers who were "in it for the money." The market was flooded with all kinds of philosophical and religious claims, each peddled by teachers who wanted to be paid for access to their enlightened ideas. If Paul had stepped into Corinth taking up a love offering every time he preached his message, the good news of Jesus Christ would have been immediately associated with the fakes.

## — 9:15-18 —

Even though Paul had the right to earn a living from the gospel ministry, he wisely chose to surrender this for a greater good. By doing so, Paul was able to prove through his lifestyle that he was completely sold out to the gospel. The gospel itself was enough to compel him to preach (9:16). He needed no laud and honor, no applause from his audience, and definitely no remuneration.

I'm often asked by young Christians wrestling with whether they are being called into a career of vocational Christian ministry, "How do I know if God's calling me to preach?" I often answer, "If you can imagine yourself being content doing anything else, do that instead." Paul said that if he didn't preach the gospel he would be miserable (9:16). For Paul, his ministry wasn't an unwanted burden, like somebody who had been drafted into the military to fight in a war not personally supported. Paul had voluntarily enlisted by his own free will, surrendering his life—and his rights—to full-time service of the gospel (9:17).

So willing and eager was Paul to preach the gospel that he saw this privilege as a reward in itself: "What then is my reward? That, when I preach the gospel, I may offer the gospel without charge, so as not to make full use of my right in the gospel" (9:18). These words were not intended to fill the Corinthians' eyes with awe as the people considered Paul's altruistic approach to life. They were meant to instill needed guilt in those who had been arrogantly asserting their rights over others. In a church renowned for its selfishness, Paul's contrasting example of *selflessness* would have shocked those who had the eyes to see.

## — 9:19-23 —

I am convinced that we haven't really begun to live the devoted Christian life until Paul's words in 1 Corinthians 9:19 can become our words: "For though I am free from all men, I have made myself a slave to all, so that I may win more." As Christians, we have the right to use our liberty and position in Christ to enjoy all God has for us. But we also have the responsibility and privilege of sharing the gospel and building up other Christians in the faith. This necessarily calls for humility, sacrifice, and teamwork (Eph. 4:1-16).

Paul develops this thought further, describing some specific ways he gave up his personal identity, preferences, and practices for the sake of others (1 Cor. 9:20-22). When he preached the gospel to Jews, he altered his lifestyle so as not to offend those to whom he was ministering (9:20). When he preached to Gentiles who had no interest in the Law and what they perceived as the "fussiness" of Jewish rules and regulations, Paul lived in a way that wouldn't distract them from the grace of God (9:21). To outcasts, sick, downtrodden, and poor, Paul determined to live with little so the focus would remain on Jesus Christ alone (9:22). Without compromising the truths of the gospel or the holy life of a follower of Jesus Christ, Paul altered his practice on neutral issues such as eating and drinking, cultural norms, or styles of worship, all "for the sake of the gospel," in order to "by all means save some" (9:22-23).

## THE ISTHMIAN GAMES

### 1 CORINTHIANS 9:24

In 1 Corinthians 9:24-27, Paul draws on Greek athletic imagery to illustrate the self-discipline he employs in order to gain the eternal prize. Corinth was within 10 miles of the site of the popular Isthmian Games, which were held both the year before and the year following the Olympic Games—twice every four years. Our modern Olympic games are modeled after these ancient athletic contests, which included competitions in chariot racing, wrestling, boxing, music, and poetry.[11] Although the participation was traditionally limited to Greeks, Romans were allowed to compete after 228 BC.[12]

Thus, by Paul's day, these games attracted both competitors and spectators from the entire Roman Empire, which only increased their popularity and profitability. According to the ancient historian Strabo, these games brought much commercial prosperity to the local economy.[13] Certainly, an athletic custom of such magnitude and importance could not fail to appeal to the Corinthians' imagination as an analogy for Paul's struggle for self-mastery.

www.HolyLandPhotos.org

Isthmian crown

One striking contrast Paul made had to do with the prize that so many athletes strove to win, versus the prize he sought. Ancient Greek athletes who won in the Isthmian Games were given a wreath made out of either celery or pine. But Paul sought to discipline himself in order to win an imperishable prize. His readers would have understood this argument from lesser to greater, as they were well aware of the self-denial and disciplined training athletes endured in order even to be eligible to enter the competitions.

## — 9:24-27 —

Paul describes here (9:24-27) in vivid imagery the life of a go-for-broke minister of the gospel, one who has not only given up creature comforts for the sake of the ministry but has given up all things for the sake of the call. He did this in view of eternal, not temporal, rewards. These verses drip with the sweat of athletes. You can almost hear their grunts and groans as you read these colorful words.

While reflecting on the Christian life, Paul used an illustration familiar to all of his readers: the renowned Isthmian Games held near Corinth every other year. Such imagery would have resonated with his Corinthian readers as Paul taught them to become spiritual victors focused on their heavenly rewards.

Throughout this passage, it's important to remember that Paul isn't talking about working hard to earn salvation. The whole context is selfless participation in ministry by those already saved. Paul uses an athletic illustration to explain that not all Christians will be rewarded equally for the way they lived and invested their time, energy, and resources. Paul already has informed the Corinthians (3:12-15) that some will appear before Christ's judgment seat expecting a pat on the back for a job well done, but when their works are tested with fire, they will all be burned to ashes. These believers will never receive crowns from the Lord for faithful service.

Other Christians, however, who serve selflessly, will be rewarded for the spiritual good they accomplished during their sacrificial earthly marathon (2 Cor. 5:9-10). So Paul encourages his readers to compete like dedicated athletes, saying, "Run in such a way that you may win" (1 Cor. 9:24). Anybody can receive a number, enter a race, and be included as part of the team. But only those who finish the race will receive recognition and reward.

Paul expressly contrasts the earthly reward expected in the Isthmian Games with the eternal, heavenly reward expected by faithful ministers of the gospel, those who have "self-control in all things" (9:25). He powerfully argues from the lesser to the greater, from the useless to the priceless: If those rewarded with a withering wreath disciplined their bodies until they hurt, how much more should believers discipline their lives for heavenly rewards?

In 9:26-27, Paul stops using the plural term "we" and speaks in the first-person singular, "I," using himself as a model. As he runs the spiritual race, he doesn't stop for anything. He keeps the goal in mind, which allows him to avoid unnecessary distractions and foolish pursuits, lest he become like a runner sprinting in the wrong direction or a boxer wildly swinging at the air (9:26). Paul knew that the potent temptations of the world threaten to draw our attention away from the greater calling. It takes discipline to avoid their allurements—the kind of self-control that allows us to cross the finish line victoriously or leave the boxing ring on our feet instead of on our backs (9:27).

# APPLICATION: 1 CORINTHIANS 9:1-27

## Batter Up!

A hush falls over the dugout. The fans in the stands have cut their chatter and all eyes focus on you. But only two eyes concern you—the third-base coach is staring through you, repeating the signal for "sacrifice" one last time.

The umpire breaks the silence: "Play ball!"

You have been here before. This time, what will you do? Will you yield your right to swing at any pitch however you want? Will you strive for a home run to impress all those fans holding up signs with your name on them? Or will you follow your coach's signal and sacrifice your run to first base so that somebody else can make the winning run and be cheered as the hero?

Paul's exhortation in 1 Corinthians 9 calls each of us not only to "take one for the team" but to give everything we have for it. We must always put the love of Christ and the love of His body, the church, above our own interests. At times, this means giving up virtually everything—our rights to exercise our Christian liberty, our rights to choose our own paths in life, our rights to convenience, to comfort, and to happiness. It always means pouring ourselves out on the spiritual altar as living sacrifices (Rom. 12:1), forsaking debilitating sins and foolish distractions for the sake of the kingdom.

Nobody wants to lose in the race of life. So, why do so many of us do things that are guaranteed to leave us empty-handed when Christ takes His seat and hands out heavenly rewards? Why do we fail to do the things we know we're called to do?

Simple: We forget our purpose. We run life's race haphazardly, forgetting the goal of self-surrendered Christlikeness set before us. Unprepared, fatigued, muscles taut, wearing our hiking boots, we run wherever *we* want, ignoring the path He has set before us, forgetting the prize He offers for faithfulness.

One commentator of a bygone era puts it eloquently:

> We go and take our place in the course as though the prize could be won without any running at all, or as if there were no prize worth running for. We dream and loiter and fold our arms; we turn aside to look at every object of passing interest; or if we did

> begin with some vigour, all the zest and warmth of the struggle grows feebler and fainter when it ought to become more animated, and . . . we care little what hindrances occur to stop our course, and to risk a dishonourable fall.[14]

Whether we relate best to the metaphor of the all-star batter or the marathon runner, Paul's exhortation to us today remains the same: Only when we sacrifice our personal, individual rights in this life will we be eligible for rewards in the next. What a hard thing to do—how rarely it occurs! Each day we have to choose how we will play in the game of the Christian life. Will we play as a star, making our own decisions, pursuing our own paths? Or will we throw ourselves into the game as a faithful member of a team, looking out for others? The decision is a tough one, and it is one that must be made daily.

To help turn our attitudes into actions, let's step into the dugout and hear the ninth-inning instructions from the coach. Study Romans 12; in the left box, note what Paul commands us to do. Then, in the right box, jot down at least three ideas about how you can take action in obedience to these commands.

| PAUL'S COMMANDS | YOUR RESPONSES |
|---|---|
| | |

# Careful Steps to Our Ultimate Objective

## 1 CORINTHIANS 10:1-33

**NASB**

1 For I do not want you to be unaware,
brethren, that our fathers were all
under the cloud and all passed

**NLT**

1 I don't want you to forget, dear
brothers and sisters,* about our an-
cestors in the wilderness long ago.
All of them were guided by a cloud

NASB

through the sea; 2 and all were bap-
tized into Moses in the cloud and
in the sea; 3 and all ate the same
spiritual food; 4 and all drank the
same spiritual drink, for they were
drinking from a spiritual rock which
followed them; and the rock was
[a]Christ. 5 Nevertheless, with most of
them God was not well-pleased; for
they were laid low in the wilderness.

6 Now these things happened as
examples for us, so that we would not
crave evil things as they also craved.
7 Do not be idolaters, as some of them
were; as it is written, "THE PEOPLE
SAT DOWN TO EAT AND DRINK, AND
STOOD UP TO PLAY." 8 Nor let us act
immorally, as some of them [a]did, and
twenty-three thousand fell in one
day. 9 Nor let us try the Lord, as some
of them [a]did, and were destroyed by
the serpents. 10 Nor grumble, as some
of them [a]did, and were destroyed by
the destroyer. 11 Now these things
happened to them as an example,
and they were written for our in-
struction, upon whom the ends of
the ages have come. 12 Therefore let
him who thinks he stands take heed
that he does not fall. 13 No tempta-
tion has overtaken you but such as is
common to man; and God is faithful,
who will not allow you to be tempted
beyond what you are able, but with
the temptation will provide the way
of escape also, so that you will be
able to endure it.

14 Therefore, my beloved, flee from
idolatry. 15 I speak as to wise men;
you judge what I say. 16 Is not the cup
of blessing which we bless a shar-
ing in the blood of Christ? Is not the
[a]bread which we break a sharing in

NLT

that moved ahead of them, and all
of them walked through the sea on
dry ground. 2 In the cloud and in the
sea, all of them were baptized as fol-
lowers of Moses. 3 All of them ate the
same spiritual food, 4 and all of them
drank the same spiritual water. For
they drank from the spiritual rock
that traveled with them, and that
rock was Christ. 5 Yet God was not
pleased with most of them, and
their bodies were scattered in the
wilderness.

6 These things happened as a
warning to us, so that we would
not crave evil things as they did, 7 or
worship idols as some of them did.
As the Scriptures say, "The people
celebrated with feasting and drink-
ing, and they indulged in pagan rev-
elry."* 8 And we must not engage in
sexual immorality as some of them
did, causing 23,000 of them to die in
one day.

9 Nor should we put Christ* to the
test, as some of them did and then
died from snakebites. 10 And don't
grumble as some of them did, and
then were destroyed by the angel of
death. 11 These things happened to
them as examples for us. They were
written down to warn us who live at
the end of the age.

12 If you think you are standing
strong, be careful not to fall. 13 The
temptations in your life are no dif-
ferent from what others experience.
And God is faithful. He will not allow
the temptation to be more than you
can stand. When you are tempted, he
will show you a way out so that you
can endure.

14 So, my dear friends, flee from
the worship of idols. 15 You are rea-
sonable people. Decide for your-
selves if what I am saying is true.
16 When we bless the cup at the
Lord's Table, aren't we sharing in
the blood of Christ? And when we
break the bread, aren't we sharing

the body of Christ? 17 Since there is one [a]bread, we who are many are one body; for we all partake of the one [a]bread. 18 Look at [a]the nation Israel; are not those who eat the sacrifices sharers in the altar? 19 What do I mean then? That a thing sacrificed to idols is anything, or that an idol is anything? 20 *No,* but *I say* that the things which the Gentiles sacrifice, they sacrifice to demons and not to God; and I do not want you to become sharers in demons. 21 You cannot drink the cup of the Lord and the cup of demons; you cannot partake of the table of the Lord and the table of demons. 22 Or do we provoke the Lord to jealousy? We are not stronger than He, are we?

23 All things are lawful, but not all things are profitable. All things are lawful, but not all things edify. 24 Let no one seek his own *good,* but that of his [a]neighbor. 25 Eat anything that is sold in the meat market without asking questions for conscience' sake; 26 FOR THE EARTH IS THE LORD'S, AND [a]ALL IT CONTAINS. 27 If one of the unbelievers invites you and you want to go, eat anything that is set before you without asking questions for conscience' sake. 28 But if anyone says to you, "This is meat sacrificed to idols," do not eat *it,* for the sake of the one who informed *you,* and for conscience' sake; 29 I mean not your own conscience, but the other *man's;* for why is my freedom judged by another's conscience? 30 If I partake with thankfulness, why am I slandered concerning that for which I give thanks?

31 Whether, then, you eat or drink

in the body of Christ? 17 And though we are many, we all eat from one loaf of bread, showing that we are one body. 18 Think about the people of Israel. Weren't they united by eating the sacrifices at the altar?

19 What am I trying to say? Am I saying that food offered to idols has some significance, or that idols are real gods? 20 No, not at all. I am saying that these sacrifices are offered to demons, not to God. And I don't want you to participate with demons. 21 You cannot drink from the cup of the Lord and from the cup of demons, too. You cannot eat at the Lord's Table and at the table of demons, too. 22 What? Do we dare to rouse the Lord's jealousy? Do you think we are stronger than he is?

23 You say, "I am allowed to do anything"*—but not everything is good for you. You say, "I am allowed to do anything"—but not everything is beneficial. 24 Don't be concerned for your own good but for the good of others.

25 So you may eat any meat that is sold in the marketplace without raising questions of conscience. 26 For "the earth is the LORD's, and everything in it."*

27 If someone who isn't a believer asks you home for dinner, accept the invitation if you want to. Eat whatever is offered to you without raising questions of conscience. 28 (But suppose someone tells you, "This meat was offered to an idol." Don't eat it, out of consideration for the conscience of the one who told you. 29 It might not be a matter of conscience for you, but it is for the other person.) For why should my freedom be limited by what someone else thinks? 30 If I can thank God for the food and enjoy it, why should I be condemned for eating it?

31 So whether you eat or drink, or

NASB

or whatever you do, do all to the glory of God. 32Give no offense either to Jews or to Greeks or to the church of God; 33just as I also please all men in all things, not seeking my own profit but the *profit* of the many, so that they may be saved.

**10:4** [a]I.e. the Messiah **10:8** [a]Lit *acted immorally* **10:9** [a]Lit *made trial* **10:10** [a]Lit *grumbled* **10:16** [a]Lit *loaf* **10:17** [a]Lit *loaf* **10:18** [a]Lit *Israel according to the flesh* **10:24** [a]Lit *the other* **10:26** [a]Lit *its fullness*

NLT

whatever you do, do it all for the glory of God. 32Don't give offense to Jews or Gentiles* or the church of God. 33I, too, try to please everyone in everything I do. I don't just do what is best for me; I do what is best for others so that many may be saved.

**10:1** Greek *brothers.* **10:7** Exod 32:6. **10:9** Some manuscripts read *the Lord.* **10:23** Greek *All things are lawful;* also in 10:23b. **10:26** Ps 24:1. **10:32** Greek *or Greeks.*

In one of his most significant works, *One Day in the Life of Ivan Denisovich,* Russian novelist Alexander Solzhenitsyn presents an unadorned and disturbing picture of life in a Siberian labor camp.

The protagonist in the story, Ivan Denisovich, has been unjustly sentenced to ten years of grueling labor. But Solzhenitsyn chooses not to unfold for us the long years that stretch before the prisoner; rather, he narrows our focus, letting us experience with Ivan the regime of just one day: "from the first clang of the rail to the last clang of the rail."[15]

Though our own context and that of Ivan Denisovich are worlds apart, many of the statements Solzhenitsyn makes in his classic novel strangely resonate with our own society. They deal with transcendent issues of personal loyalty, human dignity, and faith. These topics appear throughout the novel, creating a thematic thread running from page to page.

But amid the development of these major themes of human existence, the author has strewn a few minor motifs that can get obscured in the shadows and rarely catch the passive reader's eyes. One such theme is the purpose our lives can have if we live with a clear, ultimate objective set before us.

Persistently hungry, chilled to the core, and cursed with every reason to give in to despair, Ivan Denisovich had a job to do, a reason to face each morning. His task was to build a wall from brick and mortar. He took simple pride in just knowing he had made it through another day and was constructing a fine wall. Rather than fumbling through his daily existence wondering when his pointless life would end in Siberia's gray, subzero winter, Ivan approached each day with renewed resolve, determination, and purpose.

Just as Ivan Denisovich built his wall with barrows of brick and buckets of mortar, so Paul, "a wise master builder," laid the foundation of the church in Corinth (3:10), then charged the believers with the daily task of building upon it—brick by brick, one carefully placed piece at a time. Their job was simple: Build up the body of Christ. With this goal clearly in mind, Paul also gave them detailed instructions for daily construction.

The problem was that the Corinthian believers had each been building their own little dwellings for themselves with no regard for the glorious temple they were supposed to be constructing together. They had forsaken the authentic fellowship of the body for self-centered focuses that weaken and injure the body rather than heal and strengthen it. So, beginning with the example of the Hebrews in the wilderness, Paul urges the Corinthians to stick to the guidelines God had given them to live by (10:1-11). He then returns to the theme he introduced in 1 Corinthians 8—eating meat consecrated to the idolatrous worship of false gods, contrasting it with the proper worship and fellowship in the body of Christ (10:12-22). Finally, he leads them to refocus their efforts on the ultimate purpose of life: the glory of God (10:23-31).

## — 10:1-11 —

Paul urges that the way forward for the Corinthians begins by looking to the past. He points them specifically to the Hebrews' exodus from Egypt and their experiences as the people of God in the wilderness wanderings. He appealed to this history as an illustration because the believers in Corinth needed to learn the same lesson as the children of Israel: Neither the Israelites of old nor the Corinthians in Paul's day could blame their failure to follow God's guidelines on receiving unclear instructions. Both had been privileged to receive the latest and greatest revelations from God in their own days—revelations so astounding that they would become both the objects of unparalleled faith and of cynical disbelief for millennia.

Paul draws analogies between the Hebrews' exodus from slavery in Egypt and the Corinthians' conversion from a life of slavery to sin (10:1-4). Paul employs a common first-century Jewish rhetorical device called "typology," a term derived from the Greek word *typos* [5179], which Paul uses in 1 Corinthians 10:6, 11: "Now these things happened as examples [*typos*] for us . . . . Now these things happened to them as an example [*typos*], and they were written for our instruction, upon whom the ends of the ages have come." Grant Osborne distinguishes typology from prophecy and describes its use in the New Testament:

> Typology differs from direct prophecy in that the latter texts [prophecies] are forward-looking and directly predict the New Testament event, while typology is indirect and analogously

> relates the Old Testament event to the New Testament event. The early Christians (like the Jews) saw all of salvation history . . . as a single continuous event. Therefore events in the past are linked to those in the present, so that God's mighty deeds like the exodus or the return from exile foreshadow the experiences of God's present community, the church.[16]

By correlating New Testament truths with Old Testament events, Paul reminds the Corinthians of their own miraculous deliverance from their former slavery to sin and of their present life of deliverance. They naturally would have understood how these events foreshadowed their own initiation into the faith, including baptism and the celebration of the Lord's Supper.

| THE HEBREWS' DELIVERANCE FROM SLAVERY | THE CORINTHIANS' DELIVERANCE FROM SIN |
|---|---|
| Hebrews passed under the cloud, which symbolized the presence of the Holy Spirit among the Israelites (Exod. 13:21). | Corinthians entered into the presence of the Holy Spirit indwelling the church as the temple of God (1 Cor. 3:16). |
| Hebrews passed through the Red Sea by a miraculous deliverance from slavery (Exod. 14:21-22). | Corinthians passed through the waters of baptism, marking their deliverance from a life of sin (1 Cor. 1:13). |
| Hebrews were "baptized" into Moses in the cloud and the sea, that is, fully associated with Moses as their spiritual and physical head (Exod. 14:31). | Corinthians were baptized into Christ as head of the church by the baptism of the Holy Spirit (1 Cor. 12:13) and the baptism of water (1 Cor. 1:13). |
| Hebrews partook of the "spiritual" food, the manna from heaven, which sustained their physical lives (Exod. 16:4-36). | Corinthians partook of the Lord's Supper as a sign of intimate spiritual fellowship with Christ and one another, receiving spiritual blessings (1 Cor. 10:16-17). |

The idea of being "baptized into Moses" (10:2) might appear confusing at first, until we realize that Paul's analogy pulls together three distinct but inseparable ideas concerning baptism in the New Testament: baptism in water as an outward symbol of faith, baptism by the Holy Spirit as a spiritual reality that occurred at the time of belief (Acts 10:47), and the idea that both the spiritual and physical baptisms were baptisms or, literally, immersions "into Christ Jesus" (Rom. 6:3). That is, just as a garment immersed in dye emerges a different color, so also a person baptized into a particular teacher's worldview emerges a devoted convert to that new teaching and way of life. Moses did not perform any baptism ceremonies, but the circumstances of the Exodus were a picture of spiritual and physical baptism, as the people trusted Moses' God-given words and were delivered. With reference to this Old Testament baptism "into Moses" (1 Cor. 10:2), one commentator notes that this "simply means they were initiated and inaugurated under God into union with him and also with Moses and his leadership."[17]

God's presence among the people in the cloud, the deliverance via the Red Sea, the prophetic leadership of Moses, and heavenly food and drink: Every one of these privileges was much more than the provision of a physical need for the ancient Israelites. Each of them was also an act of divine grace. In our lives, too, there is no gift, blessing, or privilege we enjoy that meets only a physical need. With each kindness shown to us—even the seemingly small acts of provision—God shines forth His grace and mercy toward us. What was true of the Hebrews in the Old Testament is true of Christians in the New.

You'd think that a people as blessed as the Hebrews would have instantly and unquestioningly responded to God with thankfulness and obedience. But it didn't unfold that way in the wilderness of Sinai. After listing their many blessings, Paul explains that God was "not well-pleased" with most of them (10:5). Out of the hundreds of thousands of Israelites in that first generation that escaped Egypt, only Joshua and Caleb pleased God. The rest of the rebellious Israelites—bestowed with indescribable physical and spiritual blessings—were strewn across the wilderness over the next forty years. One commentator notes, "What a spectacle is that which is called up by the apostle before the eyes of the self-satisfied Corinthians: all those bodies, sated with miraculous food and drink, strewing the soil of the desert!"[18]

In what ways did the Hebrews fail to please the God who had delivered them, and how did their example of disobedience and judgment become a warning to the believers in Corinth? Paul points out the vices that the Hebrews and the Corinthians had in common.

*They craved evil things* (10:6). Paul starts off by identifying a deep-seated attitude of the heart—lusting after evil. Dissatisfied and ungrateful amid blessings, the Hebrews kept longing to go back to Egypt (Num. 11:4-6). The Corinthians, like many believers, struggled against their former lifestyles, tempted to "go back" to the evil of their past (1 Cor. 6:9-11).

*They engaged in idolatry* (10:7). After being delivered by the great "I AM," the Hebrews fashioned a golden calf and declared that idol to be the one responsible for their freedom (Exod. 32:4-6). Ultimately, an idol is anything that takes God's rightful place on the throne of our lives. The Corinthians, like many today, placed other people and other things above the appropriate and solitary lordship of Christ (1 Cor. 3:3-4).

*They became immoral* (10:8). The Israelites turned their idolatry into a drunken orgy (Exod. 32:6-7). The idolatry that began with an evil attitude and continued with a substitution of other things for God resulted in an immoral corruption of character and action. The Corinthians, too, had their share of impurity in attitude and practice (1 Cor. 5:1-2).

*They tested the Lord's faithfulness* (10:9). Questioning God's faithfulness in providing for them, the Hebrews asked Moses, "Why have you brought us up out of Egypt to die in the wilderness?" (Num. 21:5). God responded with judgment (Num. 21:6). Daring God to come through on His promises shows a lack of faith. As we will see in 1 Corinthians 15, some in Corinth failed to fully believe even the basic tenets of Christian doctrine (15:12).

*They grumbled against God's leaders* (10:10). When the Hebrews didn't get what they wanted, they complained bitterly and relentlessly against God's ordained leadership (Num. 16:41; 17:5, 10). In a context of self-seeking schism, the Corinthian Christians, too, tended to complain, grumble, and rebel against those who had been placed in authority over them.

## — 10:12-22 —

The point of Paul's typological application of the tragic events following the Hebrews' exodus rang loud and clear. The Corinthians were headed for a similar kind of judgment by the hand of God if they didn't repent of their own lust, idolatry, immorality, unfaithfulness, and grumbling. In the name of celebrating their liberty from the Law, forgiveness of past, present, and future sins, and their freedom of conscience in Christ, the Corinthians participated in idolatrous practices at the local temples. As Paul explains, this was just one curve on the downward spiral into the pit of demon worship.

Believing that their baptism in the Holy Spirit, seal of water baptism, and participation in the grace-giving life of the church provided them an infinite expense account to spend on sin, the Corinthians received a sobering warning from Paul to shock them out of their twisted theology: "Therefore let him who thinks he stands take heed that he does not fall" (1 Cor. 10:12). The word *heed* means "to look at something." Paul is saying, in essence, "If you think that you will avoid the disciplining hand of God's judgment because of your conversion to Christianity, take a closer look: Realize that you—yes, even you—are liable to the discipline of the holy God."

Yet with Paul's stern warning comes a positive encouragement. Though the Corinthians faced all kinds of trials and temptations, God promises that He will faithfully "provide the way of escape" from these temptations or tests of faith. The Greek word translated "temptation," *peirasmos* [3986], can refer to tests that challenge the integrity of one's faith (as in 1 Pet. 1:6). But it can also refer to "temptations," things that appeal to our sinful tendencies and challenge our moral integrity (Luke 4:13). In the context of 1 Corinthians 10:13, Paul seems to have in mind the everyday snares of sin, but he could also have in mind various trials of faith that come with everyday life. In any case, he says that up to this point they only had to deal with temptations "common to man." Because Paul is about to discuss the spiritual, demonic dimension of idolatry, he may be referring to the opportunity they have at this moment to turn away from their current, mundane course of spiritual decline before they find themselves in a "supernatural" situation from which it would be much harder to escape, though it would never be too late to turn around and begin to do the right thing (10:13).

The Corinthians desperately needed this encouragement, for they had chosen to live on the unraveling fringe of the Christian experience. Living dangerously close to the pagan world, they surrounded themselves with all its temptations. Paul warned that if they kept going in the same direction, what had begun as a celebration of liberty would end as a lamentation of bondage to sin, complete with demonic oppression. The express content of this warning is: "Flee from idolatry" (10:14).

Paul positions this warning like a flashing sign in front of the straying Corinthians because he understood the devastating implications of outright participation in idolatrous worship. To support this initial warning sign, he waves two more yellow flags to urge the Corinthians to slam on the brakes, put it in reverse, and leave their idolatrous practices in the rearview mirror (10:15).

First, *association with idolatry leads to participation in false religion.* Through two examples—the Lord's Table and the nation of Israel—Paul shows the Corinthians how this first step toward spiritual disaster occurs (10:16-18). Notice that the idea of *sharing/sharers* (*koinōnia* [2842]/ *koinōnos* [2844]) comes up three times in this passage. The word refers to intimate fellowship with one another. When believers properly partake of the bread and wine of communion, they participate in a confession of faith that they can see, taste, smell, touch, and hear. In the fullest physical sense, believers confess the incarnation of the God-man, who took on real flesh and blood (John 1:14), who died for our sins and rose from the dead to give us new life. With Christ presiding at the table as the host of His supper and by participating in the "cup of blessing" and the "one bread," believers are fellowshipping with Him through the Holy Spirit (John 14:16-17). They are also fellowshipping with one another as "one body," united in this solemn observance (1 Cor. 10:17).

The Israelites had also participated with God in fellowship and worship through the sacrifices of the Old Testament Law (Deut. 12:18). It was Jesus, the unseen host of the Lord's Supper, and God the Father, the unseen reason behind the sacrifices of Israel, who made these things meaningful and powerful.

Taking his readers back to the issue he introduced in 1 Corinthians 8, Paul clarifies his warning about the spiritual dangers of idolatry (10:19-20). He reaffirms that there is nothing inherently good or bad with the actual meat sacrificed to an idol (8:8), since idols are merely physical objects that have no power in and of themselves. But he clarifies that *there is* real danger in the demonic spirits that people have spiritual fellowship with when they engage in the idolatrous sacrificial worship in the pagan temples. Commentator R. C. H. Lenski puts it well:

> It is a great mistake to imagine that back of their idolatry and their idol sacrifices there is nothing but an empty vacuity. True enough, as 8:4 makes plain, the gods of the idols have no existence whatever; no being by the name of Jupiter exists, and this is true with respect to the other gods. But something does exist, something that is far more terrible than these pseudo-gods, namely an entire kingdom of darkness which is hostile to God, a host of demons or fallen angels who are ruled by the greatest of their number, namely, Satan.[19]

The heart of the problem with Corinthian Christians showing up at the pagan temples to partake of the best charbroiled steaks in town, hot off the grill, was that their presence and their actions were precisely the same as those engaged in the worship of demons. Like fire and water, Satan and Christ don't mix (10:21). God won't tolerate split loyalties. He never did in Israel's day (Deut. 32:21–25; 2 Kgs. 17:7-23; Ps. 78:54-64), and He didn't in the Corinthians' day. He doesn't in our day, either. When it comes to us splitting our loyalties between the one true God and demonic idols, our God is rightly a jealous God (1 Cor. 10:22). That is one fact we must never forget!

## — 10:23-33 —

Paul concludes this section regarding strengthening authentic fellowship in the body of Christ by reiterating a theme he first introduced in 1 Corinthians 6: "All things are lawful, but not all things are profitable" (6:12; 10:23). Putting the two principles together, we get both the negative and the positive boundaries for exercising Christian liberty.

### 1 Corinthians 6:12; 10:23

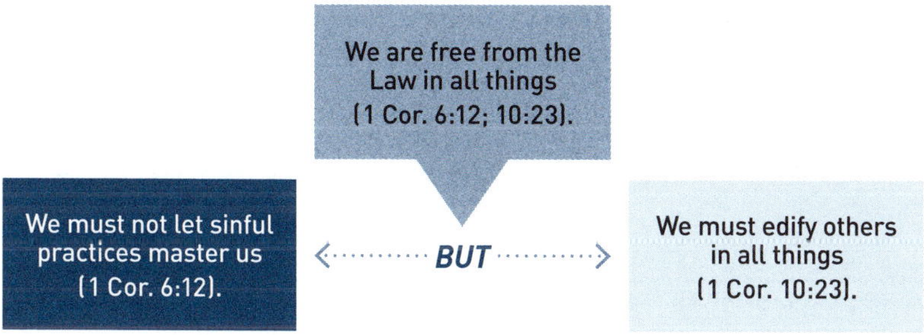


The basic guidelines for wisely determining whether we should or should not engage in any otherwise neutral practice can be summarized in three questions:

1. Does the practice avoid a wicked, immoral lifestyle (6:12–20)?
2. Does the practice seek the good of our brothers and sisters in Christ (10:23)?
3. Does the practice ultimately bring glory to God (6:20; 10:31)?

So, to sum up Paul's argument concerning meat sacrificed to idols, let's look again at our three-tiered diagram of the various kinds of meat a believer might acquire and consume, and ask our three questions.

### Temple Sacrificed Meat

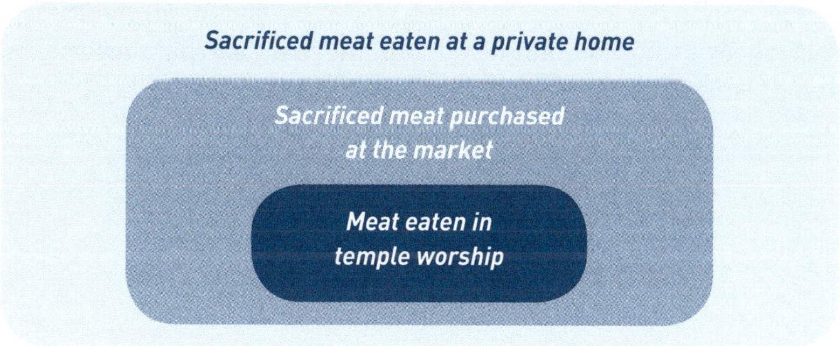

With regard to eating meat while involved in temple worship (the blue center of the diagram), to Paul this is a no-brainer. This practice engages in idolatry and spiritual immorality (question 1), it causes other brothers and sisters in Christ to follow into sin (question 2), and it dishonors God by worshiping demons (question 3).

Concerning sacrificed meat purchased at the meat market (the second, lighter blue circle), Paul gives the following advice: "Eat anything that is sold in the meat market without asking questions for conscience' sake" (10:25). In other words, if we treat the meat as simply a harmless creation of God purchased in a neutral environment (10:26), then it does not involve idolatry and immorality (question 1), it does not cause a weaker brother or sister to stumble (question 2), and it glorifies God when the food is received with thanksgiving (10:30) (question 3).

Finally, with regard to sacrificed meat eaten at an unbeliever's home (the outside, lightest blue circle), Paul says that if the unsaved host does not mention where the meat came from, believers may eat freely (10:25). If the one serving the guests makes a point that the meat was sacrificed to idols, however, then he is likely to be viewing the meal as an extension of his own devotion to the pagan god. In that case, for the sake of the Christian's testimony and the conscience of weaker believers, the Christian should quietly abstain from eating the food (10:27-29).

Ultimately, Christians should be willing to set aside their right to exercise Christian freedom for the sake of fellowship with God and with one another. The truth of the gospel of Christ is already offensive enough (1:17-18), and we must never surrender our stand on the non-negotiable truths of the person and work of Jesus Christ—even if it seems like foolishness to the world. When it comes to questionable, optional, or "gray" areas of our practice, however, we should eagerly heed Paul's command: "Give no offense either to Jews or to Greeks or to the church of God; just as I also please all men in all things, not seeking my own profit but the profit of the many, so that they may be saved" (10:32-33).

# APPLICATION: 1 CORINTHIANS 10:1-33

## Keeping the "Ps"

Every day Christians are faced with decisions—not simply between right and wrong, but between good, better, and best. God has given us a world filled with beauty for us to enjoy, but how do we determine where to draw the line between delighting in His gracious provision and overindulging in sinful desires? As we seek to put into practice Paul's teachings in 1 Corinthians 10, let's consider three basic principles that will equip us to make wise, healthy decisions and set us on a course for a God-honoring life: the *profit principle*, the *people principle*, and the *purpose principle*.

*The profit principle* (10:23). The profit principle reminds us that our freedom in otherwise neutral matters is not to be exercised at another's expense, but for another's profit. Note that the emphasis here is on the benefit to others, not simply for ourselves. As we consider everything from how we spend our time to how we spend our money, we should constantly ask ourselves some probing questions. Who will benefit from this? How will they benefit? Would other actions be more profitable? This kind of thinking will work against our natural tendency toward self-centeredness.

Romans 14:19-20 makes the same point in stark terms. Let me challenge you to memorize this passage: "So then we pursue the things which make for peace and the building up of one another. Do not tear down the work of God for the sake of food. All things indeed are clean, but they are evil for the man who eats and gives offense." While in theory, Christians are free to participate in all sorts of activities that are not immoral in themselves, we are also called to focus on those things that will benefit others.

*The people principle* (1 Cor. 10:24, 33). Closely tied to the profit principle is the people principle. As we seek to engage in activities and make decisions that are more profitable for others, we need to be careful that we truly have the good of others in mind. This means getting to know people. Not just their names. Not just their résumés. It means getting to know their needs, their hurts, their pains, their strengths and weaknesses. Only then can we actually answer the question, "Is this in their best interests?"

Giving people what they want or fulfilling their immediate desires isn't always what will benefit them most. This is especially true in parenting. Sometimes the greatest profit for a child comes from withholding what the child desires. Sometimes it means giving our children what they don't want. Philippians 2:3-4 underscores this same point. These are verses worth memorizing: "Do nothing from selfishness or empty conceit, but with humility of mind regard one another as more important than yourselves; do not merely look out for your own personal interests, but also for the interests of others."

*The purpose principle* (1 Cor. 10:31). Do you eat or drink? Do it to the glory of God. Do you play baseball or hockey? Do it to the glory of God. Do you preach or teach? Do it to the glory of God. Whether you fix tires, serve fast food, study algebra, clean homes, run for president, or raise children—all of these things should be done with one purpose: God's glory.

We shouldn't just think about big career choices, either. The little things in life that tend to be done with reluctance should be done with God's glory as our focus—pleasing Him, as if in His service. I mean things like loading the dishwasher, doing the laundry, cleaning the bathroom, making the bed, moving chairs at church, taking care of a sick child, even living out your retirement. Whatever you do, consider it a service to your one Lord God. He owns it all anyway: your life, your time, your energy. It's all on loan from Him.

Why don't you take a moment to memorize 1 Corinthians 10:31? What a great way to begin to place the purpose principle center stage in your everyday life! "Whether, then, you eat or drink or whatever you do, do all to the glory of God."

# ORDERING CHURCH AND WORSHIP (1 CORINTHIANS 11:1–14:40)

I can recall the experience as if it happened this morning. The place: the northeastern edge of what was then called Formosa, near Taipei. The year: 1958. Our ship had stopped at the mouth of the harbor, unable to proceed. Straight ahead, less than a mile, we could see the ship's dock. If we would just press on and stay the course, it appeared we would be safely ashore in no time. Instead, we awaited the arrival of the harbor pilot. Once he came aboard, rather than cutting a straight path through the calm waters, we felt the ship slowly steer to port, then to starboard, as he began a long, meandering route back and forth through the waters, as if intentionally prolonging the voyage.

To many, this zigzagging route seemed unnecessary, even ridiculous. But as we peered over the ship's rail into the clear harbor waters below, we suddenly understood. Strategically scattered beneath the surface of the water we could see the menacing spikes of highly charged mines, ready to explode at the slightest nudge of our ship's hull. The harbor pilot, who knew the location and depth of every mine, steered the ship along an invisible path that avoided a disastrous encounter in the deep.

Later, we had the same experience in the Yokohama harbor as we slowly made our way to the pier. Those waters were neither difficult nor turbulent. But they were delicate and potentially explosive!

Like the waters of that harbor, 1 Corinthians 11–14, deep with powerful truths and wide with practical application, also conceals some potential mines of controversy that could easily explode into conflict. Even today those highly charged issues can (and often do) ignite into fiery disagreements between Christians, not only within a single church but between churches and denominations:

- The relationship between men and women in the church, especially regarding headship and submission (11:1-16)
- The proper understanding and practice of the Lord's Supper (11:17-34)

- The right view and practice of spiritual gifts (12:1-31)
- The question of the cessation of certain gifts (13:1–14:25)
- The proper elements of corporate worship (14:26-40)

You don't have to have been a pastor for five decades to learn that when these issues are addressed carelessly, the situation can backfire on you. In fact, over several decades of pastoral ministry, I've seen many churches and parachurch ministries dealt crippling blows when pastors and teachers failed to navigate these waters with care.

My own strategy in steering a path through this section will not be to ignore, dodge, or downplay the controversial details. I intend to tackle these issues directly and frankly, but also wisely and respectfully. Not every detail here is completely clear, so we'll set our minds on the big picture and keep our hearts focused on the practical applications.

Beginning in 1 Corinthians 11:1, Paul exhorts his readers to apply the teachings they had received from him for proper order in the churches. No doubt, the Corinthians had failed to exhibit proper order through

## KEY TERMS IN 1 CORINTHIANS 11:1–14:40

***oikodomeō* (οἰκοδομέω)** [3618] "to edify," "to build"
***oikodomē* (οἰκοδομή)** [3619] "edification," "building"

In its original, literal sense, *oikodomeō* and its noun form, *oikodomē*, referred to the construction of a house (*oikos* "house" + *demos* "to build"). This literal sense is used metaphorically by Paul in reference to various means used to promote the development of Christian growth in knowledge, wisdom, and virtue. In 1 Corinthians Paul argues that the primary function of the gathered church is to edify, or build up, believers. This excludes aberrant, self-serving uses of spiritual gifts (14:12, 26). Christians are to always seek to edify others, not to merely build up themselves.

***charisma* (χάρισμα)** [5486] "free gift," "gift of grace"

Derived from the verb *charizomai* [5483], "to give generously," and related to the word for "grace" (*charis* [5485]), *charisma* is a verbal noun that emphasizes that which has been given. The word highlights the utterly gracious nature of the gift rather than focusing on the gift itself. We might translate it "benevolence" or "bestowed favor." In this sense, the gracious gift should never be regarded as the independent property of the recipient apart from the purpose of its bestowal. Paul uses the term in 1 Corinthians 12 to refer to supernatural abilities (spiritual gifts) bestowed by the Holy Spirit to be used for building up the church (12:4). The "charismatic" movement today is characterized by an emphasis on these spiritual gifts.

submission to Christ and to one another (11:1-16). This resulted in self-centered divisions and offensive conflicts even in the observance of the Lord's Supper (11:17-34)—a celebration meant to display the church's unity. In keeping with this factious spirit, the Corinthians also exercised spiritual gifts in ways that highlighted their selfish ambition, though their demonstrations of the gifts of the Spirit should have displayed humility and deference for one another (12:1–14:40). In the midst of these chapters, Paul points out that only an attitude of authentic, selfless, unconditional *agape* [26] love could cure the Corinthians' self-centered and divisive approach to the Christian life (1 Cor. 13).

# Of Hair and Hats

## 1 CORINTHIANS 11:1-16

**NASB**

1 Be imitators of me, just as I also am
of Christ.

2 Now I praise you because you
remember me in everything and
hold firmly to the traditions, just as
I delivered them to you. 3 But I want
you to understand that [a]Christ is the
head of every man, and the man is
the head of a woman, and God is the
head of [a]Christ. 4 Every man who has
*something* on his head while praying
or prophesying disgraces his head.
5 But every woman who has her head
uncovered while praying or proph-
esying disgraces her head, for she
is one and the same as the woman
[a]whose head is shaved. 6 For if a
woman does not cover [a]her head, let
her also [b]have her hair cut off; but if
it is disgraceful for a woman to [b]have
her hair cut off or [a]her head shaved,
let her cover [a]her head. 7 For a man
ought not to have his head covered,
since he is the image and glory of
God; but the woman is the glory of
man. 8 For man [a]does not originate
from woman, but woman from man;
9 for indeed man was not created
for the woman's sake, but woman

**NLT**

1 And you should imitate me, just as
I imitate Christ.

2 I am so glad that you always keep
me in your thoughts, and that you
are following the teachings I passed
on to you. 3 But there is one thing I
want you to know: The head of every
man is Christ, the head of woman is
man, and the head of Christ is God.*
4 A man dishonors his head* if he
covers his head while praying or
prophesying. 5 But a woman dishon-
ors her head* if she prays or prophe-
sies without a covering on her head,
for this is the same as shaving her
head. 6 Yes, if she refuses to wear a
head covering, she should cut off
all her hair! But since it is shameful
for a woman to have her hair cut or
her head shaved, she should wear a
covering.*

7 A man should not wear anything
on his head when worshiping, for
man is made in God's image and
reflects God's glory. And woman re-
flects man's glory. 8 For the first man
didn't come from woman, but the
first woman came from man. 9 And
man was not made for woman, but

**NASB**

for the man's sake. 10 Therefore the
woman ought to have *a symbol of*
authority on her head, because of
the angels. 11 However, in the Lord,
neither is woman [a]independent of
man, nor is man [a]independent of
woman. 12 For as the woman [a]origi-
nates from the man, so also the man
*has his birth* through the woman;
and all things [b]originate from God.
13 Judge [a]for yourselves: is it proper
for a woman to pray to God *with her*
*head* uncovered? 14 Does not even
nature itself teach you that if a man
has long hair, it is a dishonor to him,
15 but if a woman has long hair, it is
a glory to her? For her hair is given
to her for a covering. 16 But if one is
inclined to be contentious, we have
no [a]other practice, nor have the
churches of God.

**11:3** [a]I.e. the Messiah **11:5** [a]Lit *who is shaved* **11:6** [a]Lit *herself* [b]Lit *shear herself* **11:8** [a]Lit *is not from* **11:11** [a]Lit *without* **11:12** [a]Lit *is* [b]Lit *are* **11:13** [a]Lit *in* **11:16** [a]Lit *such*

**NLT**

woman was made for man. 10 For this
reason, and because the angels are
watching, a woman should wear a
covering on her head to show she is
under authority.*

11 But among the Lord's people,
women are not independent of
men, and men are not independent
of women. 12 For although the first
woman came from man, every other
man was born from a woman, and
everything comes from God.

13 Judge for yourselves. Is it right
for a woman to pray to God in public
without covering her head? 14 Isn't
it obvious that it's disgraceful for a
man to have long hair? 15 And isn't
long hair a woman's pride and joy?
For it has been given to her as a cov-
ering. 16 But if anyone wants to argue
about this, I simply say that we have
no other custom than this, and nei-
ther do God's other churches.

**11:3** Or *to know: The source of every man is Christ, the source of woman is man, and the source of Christ is God.* Or *to know: Every man is responsible to Christ, a woman is responsible to her husband, and Christ is responsible to God.* **11:4** Or *dishonors Christ.* **11:5** Or *dishonors her husband.* **11:6** Or *should have long hair.* **11:10** Greek *should have an authority on her head.*

There was a time in America when every man who wanted to be taken seriously wore a hat in public. That was simply the cultural expectation in the 1940s and 1950s. Leave the house, grab your hat. Step indoors, remove it. There was an entire unspoken, unwritten "hat etiquette" that governed the "whos, wheres, and whens" of hat-wearing. I don't remember the "whys" ever really being explained. Men just did it. Everybody who was anybody (or who wanted to be anybody) wore a hat. In fact, in the 1960s, when hat-wearing began to wane, some squint-eyed traditionalists felt it was scandalous for John F. Kennedy to appear in public with his hair blowing in the wind!

The truth is, wearing a hat didn't make you respectable. Nor did wearing a suit and tie make you a professional. Combing your hair back or parting it didn't make a person either a conservative or a liberal. Fashions change, styles flux, and what was considered modest in one generation may be considered stuffy in another. Nevertheless, without denying the reality that customs and manners constantly change in our culture, we also have to admit that what we wear and how we present ourselves on the outside often sends a message to others about what they can expect of us on the inside.

Be honest. When you see a teen with dyed hair, countless piercings, tattoos, and a T-shirt with a picture of Charles Manson, do you think "class president" or "future criminal"? Now, we may be completely wrong in our judgment. For all we know, that kid could be a godly young person. But thinking people know that in every culture, what we wear on the outside communicates something about our allegiances, values, identity, and beliefs. A man who wears a kilt is usually identifying with his Scottish ancestry. A woman in an apron presents the image of a homemaker. Again, our interpretation of the person may be wrong, but that doesn't change the fact that these cultural conventions intentionally or unintentionally convey character. If we falsely conclude that a respectable young man in the Manson T-shirt is a lawless rebel, part of the blame lies with the kid who chose that day's wardrobe without thinking about the message he was sending to those who don't know him.

This brings us to the situation Paul addresses in 1 Corinthians 11:1-16. In essence, Paul asks his readers to consider what their own style of dress might be communicating in their own cultural settings. This question is of paramount importance for Paul's readers, because believers are to represent Jesus Christ to the world, and the world will form its opinions about the Savior based on the visual image reflected in the lives of His followers.

## — 11:1-2 —

Paul begins 1 Corinthians 11 by echoing a statement he made earlier (4:16): "Be imitators of me, just as I also am of Christ" (11:1). Many commentators regard this as a summary statement that concludes 1 Corinthians 10.[1] In that case, Paul exhorts the Corinthians to follow his example of surrendering his own rights and privileges for the sake of others (10:33), just as Christ did for our sakes. Yet the verse also serves as a perfect hinge, transitioning to his next discussion. He praises the Corinthians for following the teaching he had given while living with them. They remembered him, following his example, taking hold of the traditions he taught to them (11:2).

Paul's words demonstrate that not everything the church had been doing was wrong. There were praiseworthy elements as well as areas of concern. All churches, in fact, could be described this way. Even in the healthiest churches we can find pockets of discord, conflict, or shameless sin. Likewise, in declining churches we find signs of life, glimpses of hope, and those who have remained faithful even in the darkest times. Paul is fair to give credit where credit is due (1:4-9).

Yet as his discussion reveals, not everybody in Corinth had taken Paul's words to heart, following his Christlike example of selfless humility. Some had drifted from Paul's instruction, creating divisions and cliques in the body (11:18). So Paul straightens their course, steering them back to the doctrinal foundation, ultimately looking to Christ Himself as their example.

## — 11:3-6 —

Before Paul begins prescribing principles that govern proper attire, he gives a lesson from theology. The Bible doesn't arbitrarily toss around dos and don'ts. Rather, our attitudes and actions are to conform to God's character, plan, purpose, and order. This is why Paul lays a firm doctrinal foundation prior to drawing a few practical conclusions. He starts with a reminder about God's order of headship and humility.

Theologically, the plan and purpose of creation and redemption begin with God the Father, who sent God the Son (Gal. 4:4; 1 Cor. 8:6). The Son humbly submitted to the will of the Father in coming to the earth to become incarnate, to live in perfect obedience to His will, and to die for the sins of the world (Luke 22:42; John 5:36; 8:28; 12:49; 1 Cor. 15:3). Though the Father and Son are equal in their divinity (John 1:1; 5:18; 10:30), glory (John 17:5), and eternality (John 8:58), the Father functions as the "head" of the Son as the triune God works out the Father's plan of redemption (Phil. 2:6-8). This is why Paul can say that "God is the head of Christ" (1 Cor. 11:3).

The Greek word *kephalē* [2776] refers literally to the physical head of a person's body (Matt. 10:30), but it is also used in a figurative sense, referring to a "chief" or "authority" in a chain of command (Eph. 1:22; Col. 1:18). In 1 Corinthians 11:3-10, Paul uses the word *kephalē* nine times, switching between the figurative and the literal senses. In 1 Corinthians 11:3, all of his uses are figurative. God the Father is the "authority" over Christ, who submitted to His Father's will throughout His life. Likewise, Christ is the head of "every man"—that is, all people are subject to Christ—whether rich or poor, powerful or weak, free or slave. Christ is the chief authority in the lives of men and women. Then, in the realm of the family, the husband is the head of the home (Eph. 5:22-23), leading his wife and children as their protector and provider (Eph. 5:25).

From the first link to the last, the chain of authority starts with God the Father and moves to God the Son, man, and finally, to the woman. This order isn't established to enforce relationships of superiority or inferiority. Rather, the order is meant to promote harmony and peace in the family relationship. (Please read those two sentences again.) This concept of order is consistent with God's pattern of establishing order throughout His creation. He ordered the heavenly bodies to function in harmony, ruling over day and night (Psalm 136:8-9). He established church authority resting in the faithful preachers and teachers of God's Word (Heb. 13:7). In the realm of human government, He assigned political authority to promote good and punish wickedness (Rom. 13:1-7; 1 Pet. 2:13-14). Without these structures of headship, all of these institutions would collapse into chaos.

With this foundational truth of divine orderliness firmly established, Paul builds his practical application in 1 Corinthians 11:4. In light of the theological principle of headship, "every man who has something on his head while praying or prophesying disgraces his head." The word *disgrace* means "to bring shame upon" (cf. 1:27), and here, the man's "head" is Christ. In the Corinthians' culture, a woman covered her head as an indication of sexual modesty and submission to her husband's authority. For a man to wear a head covering would have symbolically communicated to the culture a blurring of the gender roles, thus reflecting badly on the man's "head," Jesus Christ. The reference to "praying or prophesying" tells us that Paul was specifically referring to men who were speaking publicly and prominently in the church meeting, where they would be viewed by many as a representative of Jesus Christ.

Paul then turns to the woman's appropriate attire when praying or prophesying in the worship service (11:5-6). In contrast to the men, who were to have their heads uncovered, their wives were to maintain the appropriate cultural symbol and keep their heads covered. To uncover their heads would have sent the message that they were no longer regarding their husbands as head of the home. Gender roles would have again been blurred, bringing shame on the husband (her "head," 11:5) and confusion to the congregation. Paul likens women with their heads uncovered to those with shaved heads—in their culture a shocking image! Paul's rhetoric is sharp. It's as if he's saying, "If you're going to publicly communicate that the God-ordained order in the family is no longer relevant to you, why not go all the way and style your hair like a man!"

Let me explain this with a modern analogy. Imagine if a woman comes to church and declares to her friends, "As of last Friday, I'm no longer Mrs. Smith. I've changed my name back to Ms. Jones." What's the first thing you'd think? You would probably assume Ms. Jones and Mr. Smith were either separated or having serious marital problems. Why? Because in our culture the common practice of a wife taking her husband's last name (or at least a hyphenated name) indicates the oneness of the marriage relationship and traditionally reflects the deference of the wife to her husband's headship in the family. It might be that the marriage of Mr. Smith and Ms. Jones is, in reality, perfectly fine, but Ms. Jones's words and actions are sending the wrong message. A similar blurring of family order and gender roles would have been communicated in Paul's day by a woman tossing aside her head covering or a man covering his head in public worship.

## — 11:7-10 —

Paul switches gears in 11:7-10, moving from the theological and cultural argument for appropriate attire to the scriptural argument. A man must seek to bring honor rather than shame to his authority—Jesus Christ—because in the order of creation he is called to function as "the image and glory of God" (11:7). Remember, to cover his head would draw confusion and ridicule on the man, which would reflect poorly on the reputation of the Savior. As the "image of God," human beings are to serve as God's representatives in this world, exercising God's rule on His behalf over the created order: "Then God said, 'Let Us make man in Our image, according to Our likeness; and let them rule over the fish of the sea and over the birds of the sky and over the cattle and over all the earth, and over every creeping thing that creeps on the earth'" (Gen. 1:26).

The Genesis narrative tells us that God created the male human first—Adam (Gen. 2:7). After tasking Adam with promoting God's rule and furthering His creative work by cultivating and keeping the garden (Gen. 2:15), God fashioned Eve from Adam's rib as a suitable helper (Gen. 2:18). She, too, would participate in the work to which humans were called, not as the head of the family, but alongside her husband.

The word *helper* is the first descriptive term in the Bible used for woman (Gen. 2:18). Scripture doesn't describe her as "slave," "doormat," or "pet." "Helper" is not a term of inferiority, but of equality. In fact, it implies that left to himself, Adam alone was insufficient to accomplish everything God wanted humans to accomplish. Eve was a necessary partner in projecting God's glory through her husband into the created realm. In logical order, God made woman for the man, not the other way around. Man was created first, and the woman was derived from him to assist and complete him (1 Cor. 11:8-9). She reflected Adam's glory, mirroring his character—just as Adam reflected God's glory, mirroring his character in the pre-Fall condition (11:7).

Paul explains that in light of the biblical order of creation and the distinct but inseparable roles of men and women as image-bearers of God, wives in Paul's culture should have, literally, "authority" on their heads (11:10). The word "symbol" is not in the original Greek text. Here, Paul points beyond the head covering (a mere cultural symbol) to that which it represents—an attitude of submission to God-ordained authority. The focus is on a wife's attitude toward her husband's authority, specifically her public display of this godly attitude. There should be no contradiction between her inward attitude and her outward appearance.

In mentioning the presence of angels as a motivating factor for proper attire in worship, Paul seems to go off on a brief tangent. Commentators wrestle with how to interpret the words in Greek translated, "because of the angels." After suggesting that the presence of angels as spectators in the church's worship is the most likely interpretation, one commentator sums up several other interpretations:

> Other (but less acceptable) explanations have been suggested for the words "because of the angels": (a) evil angels lusted after the women in the Corinthian congregation; (b) angels are messengers, that is, pastors; (c) good angels learn from women; (d) good angels are an example of subordination; (e) good angels would be tempted by a woman's insubordination.[2]

Whatever our interpretation of "angels," Paul's point is clear: Wives with an attitude of submission ought to reflect that attitude in a culturallyappropriate manner in the worshiping community. To do otherwise would be to bring shame upon their husbands and promote disorder in the church.

## — 11:11-16 —

So far, Paul has impressed upon his readers the necessity for women to exhibit their godly attitude of submission in the family relationship and in prayer. This biblical truth, however, can sometimes become an excuse for downgrading the status of women in the marriage relationship. Rather than seeing her as an equal partner with a distinct role under the headship of the husband, some have taken submission to an unhealthy and unbiblical extreme. So, to avoid presenting only one side of the issue, Paul wisely gives us a look at the flip side.

Showing the equality and mutual dependence of men and women, Paul tells us that neither the husband nor the wife is independent in the marriage relationship. Yes, Eve originally came from Adam, so males originally were the source of females. But ever since the initial creation, all men were born from women (11:11-12). Both men and women are absolutely essential to reflect God's image and glory, to exercise His dominion over the world on His behalf, and to "be fruitful and multiply, and fill the earth, and subdue it" (Gen. 1:28). The woman is an essential, invaluable part of God's plan. In His plan, men and women are spiritual equals—possessing differing roles in the marriage relationship, but equal nonetheless.

Finally Paul appeals to what we might call today "common sense," not from a humanistic, secular perspective, but from a wise, Spirit-filled perspective. In light of his arguments from theology and Scripture, he urges the Corinthians to judge for themselves whether it is proper in their cultural context for a woman to pray in church with her head uncovered (1 Cor. 11:13). The obvious answer is: "No, that would send the wrong message."

Paul then offers a bit of corroborative evidence: the natural physical differences between women and men (11:14-15). Naturally, women have long, flowing hair covering their heads. In most cultures throughout history a woman's hair has been her glory, regarded as a feature of beauty. Men, on the other hand, have grown beards, and as a general rule they have been more susceptible to hair loss in their adult years than have women. While many men may lose their hair with age, women rarely do so. Paul uses these observations to argue that even nature demonstrates a clear distinction between men and women.[3]

In Paul's closing argument, he appeals to authority. A woman covering her head in public meetings of the church was, according to Paul, a practice common to all the churches. Keener notes, "He appeals to the practices of the churches in the eastern Mediterranean, . . . a culture in which most respectable women covered their hair in public."[4] So widespread was the cultural symbol of the head covering as a sign of decency, modesty, and submission to headship that Paul could confidently say that those who would seek to reject the practice would be going against a broad consensus of godly, wise Christians throughout the world.

# APPLICATION: 1 CORINTHIANS 11:1-16

## The Orthodoxy of Hair-esy

To many of us reading Paul's arguments and instructions on whether a woman should wear head coverings, the issue sounds strange. I have tried to emphasize that in Paul's day, the head covering communicated a woman's propriety, modesty, and respect for order and headship. In many Western cultures, head coverings no longer carry this meaning. If a woman wears a hat in today's church, some might even come to an opposite conclusion: She's showing off, trying to stand out, or imposing her worldly fashions onto the church!

As you can probably tell, I am not in favor of applying Paul's specific instructions concerning head coverings in his unique cultural context to our own culture today. I am, however, convinced that we need to apply the principles underlying Paul's instructions. We should ask ourselves, "If Paul were to step into our churches today, what visible signs of order and submission would he see?" As we seek to apply Paul's underlying doctrines to our own context, we should keep three principles in mind.

First, *we need to remember that matters of fashion and style are culturally conditioned and personally applied.* I have seen fashion trends come and go, and then come back again. Bell bottoms, straight jeans, rolled jeans, torn jeans, long dresses, short skirts, hats, toupees, long hair, short hair, wide ties, short ties, thin ties, bow ties—the list goes on and on. There is such a thing as "indecency," but the standards of "modesty" and "propriety" vary from culture to culture. Search the whole Bible and you won't find a scissor length for haircuts, a "knee rule" for skirts, or a dress code for Sunday worship. Whatever decisions we make about how we dress in our own culture, we should strive to communicate to others on the outside what is true of us on the inside.

Second, *we need to keep in mind that our style should reflect our Christian identity as well as our sexual identity.* When it comes to our physical appearance—hairstyle, jewelry, clothing, cosmetics, or body art—do we make decisions based on the goal of glorifying God (1 Cor. 10:31)? Do we seek to point people to Him or attract people to us? Are we trying to display our own individual independence and personality or reflect His character and values? At the same time, are we dressing in ways that highlight our distinct sexuality and gender role, as defined by Scripture? As a woman, have you embraced your femininity as a gift from God? As a man, have you accepted the roles and responsibilities that accompany your own masculinity as assigned by Him? Are these gender roles reflected in the ways you conduct yourself externally toward others? By your dress, your speech, and your conduct around members of the opposite sex? If you're married, do your actions in these areas shame or honor your spouse?

Finally, *we should willingly adapt our styles to glorify God*. This is where Paul's principles can get delicate. Be painfully honest as you answer the following questions:

- Have you made a conscious decision to let go of your own image for His image?
- Are there specific fashion trends you need to avoid because they may not be regarded as holy, clean, and modest?
- Are your decisions in clothing culturally appropriate for your gender role, or are you intentionally pushing the envelope?
- Have you checked your motives about your decisions? Why do you dress the way you do—from shoes to hairstyles to cosmetics and fancy watches? Is it ever an attempt to hide something lacking inside or to call attention to yourself?

Take this opportunity now to make an important decision about this delicate issue, since others are watching and forming opinions. Make certain you are adapting your style to reflect God's glory, not your own.

## The Lord's Supper Now and Then
### 1 CORINTHIANS 11:17-34

NASB

17 But in giving this instruction, I do
not praise you, because you come
together not for the better but for the
worse. 18 For, in the first place, when
you come together [a]as a church, I
hear that [b]divisions exist among
you; and in part I believe it. 19 For
there must also be factions among
you, so that those who are approved
may become [a]evident among you.

NLT

17 But in the following instructions, I
cannot praise you. For it sounds as if
more harm than good is done when
you meet together. 18 First, I hear that
there are divisions among you when
you meet as a church, and to some
extent I believe it. 19 But, of course,
there must be divisions among you
so that you who have God's approval
will be recognized!

20 Therefore when you meet together,
it is not to eat the Lord's Supper, 21 for
in your eating each one takes his
own supper first; and one is hungry
and another is drunk. 22 What! Do
you not have houses in which to eat
and drink? Or do you despise the
church of God and shame those who
have nothing? What shall I say to
you? Shall I praise you? In this I will
not praise you.

23 For I received from the Lord that
which I also delivered to you, that
the Lord Jesus in the night in which
He was betrayed took bread; 24 and
when He had given thanks, He broke
it and said, "This is My body, which
is for you; do this in remembrance of
Me." 25 In the same way *He took* the
cup also after supper, saying, "This
cup is the new covenant in My blood;
do this, as often as you drink *it*, in
remembrance of Me." 26 For as often
as you eat this bread and drink the
cup, you proclaim the Lord's death
until He comes.

27 Therefore whoever eats the
bread or drinks the cup of the Lord
in an unworthy manner, shall be
guilty of the body and the blood of
the Lord. 28 But a man must examine
himself, and in so doing he is to eat
of the bread and drink of the cup.
29 For he who eats and drinks, eats
and drinks judgment to himself if he
does not judge the body rightly. 30 For
this reason many among you are
weak and sick, and a number [a]sleep.
31 But if we judged ourselves rightly,
we would not be judged. 32 But when
we are judged, we are disciplined by
the Lord so that we will not be condemned along with the world.

20 When you meet together, you
are not really interested in the Lord's
Supper. 21 For some of you hurry to
eat your own meal without sharing with others. As a result, some
go hungry while others get drunk.
22 What? Don't you have your own
homes for eating and drinking? Or
do you really want to disgrace God's
church and shame the poor? What
am I supposed to say? Do you want
me to praise you? Well, I certainly
will not praise you for this!

23 For I pass on to you what I received from the Lord himself. On
the night when he was betrayed, the
Lord Jesus took some bread 24 and
gave thanks to God for it. Then he
broke it in pieces and said, "This is
my body, which is given for you.* Do
this in remembrance of me." 25 In the
same way, he took the cup of wine
after supper, saying, "This cup is the
new covenant between God and his
people—an agreement confirmed
with my blood. Do this in remembrance of me as often as you drink
it." 26 For every time you eat this
bread and drink this cup, you are
announcing the Lord's death until
he comes again.

27 So anyone who eats this bread
or drinks this cup of the Lord unworthily is guilty of sinning against* the
body and blood of the Lord. 28 That
is why you should examine yourself
before eating the bread and drinking
the cup. 29 For if you eat the bread or
drink the cup without honoring the
body of Christ,* you are eating and
drinking God's judgment upon yourself. 30 That is why many of you are
weak and sick and some have even
died.

31 But if we would examine ourselves, we would not be judged by
God in this way. 32 Yet when we are
judged by the Lord, we are being disciplined so that we will not be condemned along with the world.

NASB

33 So then, my brethren, when you come together to eat, wait for one another. 34 If anyone is hungry, let him eat at home, so that you will not come together for judgment. The remaining matters I will arrange when I come.

**11:18** [a]Lit *in church* [b]Lit *schisms* **11:19** [a]Or *manifest* **11:30** [a]I.e. are dead

NLT

33 So, my dear brothers and sisters,* when you gather for the Lord's Supper, wait for each other. 34 If you are really hungry, eat at home so you won't bring judgment upon yourselves when you meet together. I'll give you instructions about the other matters after I arrive.

**11:24** Greek *which is for you;* other manuscripts read *which is broken for you.* **11:27** Or *is responsible for.* **11:29** Greek *the body;* other manuscripts read *the Lord's body.* **11:33** Greek *brothers.*

A family reunion is almost a thing of the past. I suppose some people would be hard-pressed to name all their cousins, second cousins, great-uncles and great-aunts, much less recall where they all live. The "extended family" has shrunk over the years, so getting together as a group usually occurs only at weddings and funerals.

I was born in the 1930s and raised in the South where family reunions were big. Year after year—sometimes for a whole week—the extended family on my mother's side would gather for what might just as well have been called a convention or a lengthy powwow. We congregated at my granddad's bay cottage, and we spent about 75 percent of the time laughing, singing, and having fun and 25 percent of the time eating!

The food would have put any barbeque or all-you-can-eat buffet to absolute shame. My granddad would hire a fellow to come and dig a barbeque pit. One of the uncles who owned a ranch brought the beef and pork and chickens. We caught fish and seafood from the gulf and we would all eat together for five or six solid days. Those were some of the best days of my life, as we renewed relationships that had faded over the course of the year, strengthened family commitments that had waned, and reconciled with those with whom we may have had some minor spats. Each member of the family contributed something to the whole family at our annual reunions.

Family reunions didn't start in the 1930s, however. Back in the AD 30s, as He celebrated the Passover feast with His disciples the night before His crucifixion (Matt. 26:26-30), Jesus Christ instituted what could be called a Christian family reunion, in which God's family gets together frequently for sharing, caring, reflecting, reconciling, singing, praying, fellowshipping, recommitting, and commemorating the person and work of Jesus Christ. It has come to be known as the Lord's

## THE LOVE FEAST AND THE LORD'S SUPPER

### 1 CORINTHIANS 11:20

The love feast, or "*agapē* [26] meal" (Jude 1:12), in the early church looked a lot like a potluck meal today, but it functioned more like an offering on behalf of the poor. The wealthy would either host or provide food and drink from their abundance while those with little or nothing would bring what they could afford. The destitute would come empty-handed and leave with filled stomachs and hands full of provisions to get their families through the week.[5] So, the "love feast" functioned as more than just a fellowship meal. It included family fellowship, but it also involved charity and provision for the needy.

In addition to that "charity meal," the church also observed the "Lord's Supper," which is sometimes called the Eucharist, from the Greek word for "thanksgiving" (*eucharistia* [2169]). This probably originated as a reference to prayers of thanksgiving offered in conjunction with a special observance of bread and wine in commemoration of Christ's incarnation and saving death on the cross. As part of the fellowship of the church community, the leader of the service would call attention to the bread and wine, using these elements as a visible, tangible representation of the real, physical, bodily incarnation, death, and resurrection of Jesus Christ.

Through the observance of the Lord's Supper, the early church realized intimate spiritual and physical fellowship with one another as the body of Christ, reconciling before God and one another, and consecrating itself anew to God. More than just a memorial, it was a real expression of genuine fellowship as believers lingered to share, sing, and enjoy their time together with all barriers down, all status ignored, and all bonds strengthened.

So, these two distinct but inseparable aspects of early Christian worship—the love feast and the Lord's Supper—emphasized authentic unity in the body of Christ. This unity was evident not only through words but through actions. As believers came to the meeting of the church physically hungry and spiritually thirsty, they departed physically and spiritually satisfied, having had meaningful fellowship with Jesus Christ through intimate fellowship with His body, the church.

Supper. In this celebration of the heart of the Christian message, believers participate together in the most meaningful, most intimate form of worship, which includes partaking together of a common loaf and drinking from a common cup.

## — 11:17-22 —

Like many things they touched, the Corinthians managed to twist and distort the Lord's Supper. The one element of worship intended to reflect the unity and harmony of the body of Christ had become a mark of disunity and contention. How tragically ironic! The observance meant to bring spiritual strength and health to the church was instead bringing physical weakness and death. The Corinthians had turned what God intended to be a celebration of charity and remembrance into a gluttonous orgy of pride and selfishness. Small wonder Paul refused to praise them for their behavior! Their assembly left people not improved, but divided and discouraged (11:17). Far from edifying their local body, they were destroying it. They had so perverted the Lord's Supper that Paul wished they had never observed it at all.

These severe words set Paul's tone for the remainder of the chapter, as he describes the shameful behavior of some of the believers in Corinth. They were supposed to "come together as a church" (11:18) to "eat the Lord's Supper" (11:20) as a sign of their mutual love and support for one another as members of the body of Christ. Instead, divisions, cliques, and parties developed among them (11:18). Paul acknowledges the impossibility of perfect unity in any local body, because not everybody will exhibit the same level of maturity (11:19). Divisions caused by sinful, carnal, or rebellious members of the church would spotlight the holy, spiritual, and humble, thereby demonstrating who should be followed and imitated. But the degree of divisiveness in Corinth that Paul mentions (1:10-12) indicates that these schisms went far beyond those necessary for highlighting holiness. The whole congregation seems to have been threatened with fracture, disorder, and chaos.

Though the Corinthians were supposed to gather to celebrate their unity in Christ, various factions and cliques huddled into their own exclusive groups. One of the purposes of the charity meal (or "love feast") was to provide for the needy families of the congregation suffering from hunger. Instead, this opportunity for genuine, unconditional love expressed through the gracious benevolence of the wealthy on behalf of the poor turned into a "Dutch treat" approach in which the rich got fatter and the poor went hungry (11:21). It seems that the classes divided. The wealthy hung out with their own kind, living high on the hog, the middle class shared their bread, vegetables, water, and wine, and the destitute were kept at arm's length, ignored and abandoned to hunger at a time when they needed the church's love the most. How insensitive! How pathetic!

Paul completely challenges their carnal attitude and actions at the meal. He bluntly says that what they were doing was *not* the Lord's Supper (11:20). It bore no resemblance to what Jesus had instituted and intended to be carried out in their meetings together as a church family. During the Last Supper, Jesus demonstrated the kind of selfless humility they were supposed to exhibit toward one another:

> Jesus, knowing that the Father had given all things into His hands, and that He had come forth from God and was going back to God, got up from supper, and laid aside His garments; and taking a towel, He girded Himself. Then He poured water into the basin, and began to wash the disciples' feet and to wipe them with the towel with which He was girded. . . . So when He had washed their feet, and taken His garments and reclined at the table again, He said to them, "Do you know what I have done to you? You call Me Teacher and Lord; and you are right, for so I am. If I then, the Lord and the Teacher, washed your feet, you also ought to wash one another's feet. For I gave you an example that you also should do as I did to you. Truly, truly, I say to you, a slave is not greater than his master, nor is one who is sent greater than the one who sent him. If you know these things, you are blessed if you do them." (John 13:3-5, 12-17)

The selfless attitude and actions Jesus expressed during the original last supper looked nothing at all like those demonstrated in the Corinthians' meetings. So far removed was the Corinthians' twisted version of the Lord's Supper from an exhibit of mutual love and humility that Paul could legitimately say, "it is not . . . the Lord's Supper" (1 Cor. 11:20). The wealthy who always had enough to eat should have followed the example of Christ by eating their fill at home, then joining the church in order to provide for the poor and needy from their abundance. Instead, their gluttonous and self-centered actions suggested that they despised the church and brought embarrassment to those who had nothing to eat (11:22).

Likely speaking in hyperbole—exaggeration for rhetorical effect—Paul contrasts the logical results of such a practice: "one is hungry and another is drunk" (11:21). Like a group of whining two-year-olds, they clung to what they could call "Mine!" Drunken and gorged on their own food and wine, they had not yet learned to share. They had not learned the lesson of Christ's selfless humiliation at the Last Supper. When I read 1 Corinthians 11:20-21, I picture a father who has rebuked his older son repeatedly for not sharing with his younger siblings. At his wits' end, Paul exclaims, "What shall I say to you? Shall I praise you? In this I will not praise you" (11:22).

## — 11:23-26 —

In order to repair the Corinthian church's self-centered and splintered fellowship meals, Paul dug into the depths of the faith to lay some serious theological groundwork. He doesn't appeal to common sense, reason, or regulations. Instead, he returns to the very words and actions of Jesus, reminding the Corinthians of the practice he had received from the Lord to be repeated in the churches from that moment on.

Paul says that he received his instructions concerning the Lord's Supper directly from the Lord Himself (11:23). When did he receive this teaching? In Paul's initial encounter with the resurrected and glorified Jesus on the road to Damascus (Acts 9), the Lord Jesus articulated the basics of the gospel message of forgiveness of sins by faith in Christ (see Acts 26:18). He also mentioned that He would appear to Paul in the future (Acts 26:16). We are told about some of these visits and interactions between Jesus and Paul (Acts 18:9-10; 2 Cor. 12:8-9). So when Paul told the Corinthians that he had received instructions concerning the Lord's Supper directly from Jesus, he likely referred to one of the revelations he received during the years leading up to his first missionary journey, perhaps during his three years in Arabia (Gal. 1:17-18). Unlike a middleman who was passing on mere hearsay, Paul's teaching concerning the Lord's Supper came from Jesus Himself.

Paul describes in summary fashion the highlights of the events at the Last Supper, although he himself had not been present (1 Cor. 11:23-25). That dark night when Judas would betray Him, Jesus gathered His disciples to celebrate the traditional Jewish Passover meal. At that meal the Son of God did something unexpected, something that completely broke from centuries of tradition surrounding the Passover observance. After He took the bread and gave thanks, He broke it and said, "This is My body, which is for you; do this in remembrance of Me" (11:23-24; see Matt. 26:26; Mark 14:22; Luke 22:19). While His disciples still pondered this sudden change in practice, Jesus took another new turn after the meal, when he picked up a cup of wine and said, "This cup is the new covenant in My blood; do this, as often as you drink it, in remembrance of Me" (1 Cor. 11:25; see Matt. 26:27-28; Mark 14:23-24; Luke 22:20).

Through His alteration of the Passover tradition, Jesus initiated something new. In fact, He explicitly distinguished this new observance of the bread and wine by calling it a "new covenant" (11:25). The word "covenant" refers to a promise or pact between two parties in which there is mutual agreement. The old covenant was based on

## XCURSUS: THE LORD'S SUPPER OR THE LORD *AS* SUPPER?

### 1 CORINTHIANS 11:24

Many people throughout history have taken the words "This is My body" and "This is My blood" (11:24-25) quite literally. Since medieval times, the Roman Catholic Church has held to the dogma of transubstantiation—that the bread and wine are miraculously and literally transformed into the actual physical body and blood of Jesus, so participants mysteriously consume the flesh and blood of the Savior.[6] Though the Protestant Reformers rejected transubstantiation, they had such a difficult time agreeing on the nature and purpose of the bread and wine that the first Protestant Reformers split into two parties—the Lutherans and the Zwinglians. Luther insisted that the words "This is My body" must be taken literally. Zwingli preferred a more metaphorical or symbolic interpretation. The Calvinist or Reformed tradition took a mediating position. To this day, some Protestant traditions hold to a "real presence" or "real spiritual presence" of Christ in the bread and wine. Others believe the bread and wine are visible symbols of an invisible reality, that Christ's "presence" at the Supper is mediated through the power of the Holy Spirit, just as He is present where believers are gathered in His name (Matt 18:20).

I think the problem with all of these views is not so much that they are providing wrong answers, but that they're starting with the wrong questions. Nowhere in the New Testament do we see Jesus or Paul or Peter or any other inspired author interpreting Jesus' words either literally or figuratively. In fact, the New Testament doesn't seem concerned with questions about what the bread and wine *are*. Rather, it seems more concerned with how the proper observance of the Lord's Supper is meant to affect the participants, the manner in which they are to partake, and the meaning of the celebration.

That being said, my own view is that the bread and wine (or, more often in our culture, the bread and juice) were never meant to be taken as anything more than bread and wine. They are symbols of Christ's body and blood. We receive them as from the Lord's hands; we do not receive them as if we were literally and mysteriously consuming the Lord's flesh and blood. This was the earliest view of the church, as one Roman Catholic historian himself admits: "According to a concept proper to Judaism, this meal was first seen as 'eating with Christ,' recognized as present through faith. . . . An evolution occurred in the direction of 'eating Christ' according to the concept of Jewish sacrifices . . . and pagan sacred meals, in which the oblations offered to the deity and accepted by it were regarded as bearers of its presence."[7]

In no way, however, should my view of the bread and wine as symbols be understood as belittling the observance of the Lord's Supper. They are not *mere* symbols in the sense that they are therefore *insignificant*. The proper observance of the Lord's Supper as described by Paul in 1 Corinthians 11 brings real spiritual benefit to believers who unite around this all-important celebration, demonstrating unity with one another, the remembrance of the Savior's death, and an attitude of praise and thanksgiving toward God.

the Law of Moses, but the new covenant is based on Jesus' blood—His sacrifice in our place to pay the complete penalty of sin. While those under the Law were condemned, those covered by the blood of the new covenant are free from all condemnation (see Rom. 8:1-2).

The original Lord's Supper was a touching moment in the lives of the disciples, but at the same time, the men reclining around this table felt disturbed and confused as Jesus spoke of His death and atoning sacrifice. They had been looking forward to a deliverer. They had seen His miracles and had become convinced of His identity as the eternal Son of God incarnate. Jesus, however, spoke not of conquest and victory, but of suffering, death, and departure. Clearly they had not yet come to terms with Christ's prediction of His humiliation, in which He would empty Himself of all divine glory, as Paul wrote, "Being found in appearance as a man, He humbled Himself by becoming obedient to the point of death, even death on a cross" (Phil. 2:8).

Jesus made the purpose of the Lord's Supper clear by repeating the phrase "in remembrance of Me" (1 Cor. 11:24-25). Paul explains the significance of this when he writes, "For as often as you eat this bread and drink the cup, you proclaim the Lord's death until He comes" (11:26). The Lord's Supper is a time for the family of God to reunite around His Table and commemorate His death. The bread and wine take on sacred significance because they represent His body sacrificed for us and His blood shed for us. It is a confession of faith without words—faith in the incarnation of the Son of God and His atoning sacrifice for our sins. It is the gospel of Christ's person and work that addresses not only the heart and mind, but all five senses, reminding us in the most tangible way of the intimate fellowship we enjoy with our Lord Jesus Christ.

## — 11:27-34 —

After presenting the ideal for this church family reunion around the Table of the Lord, Paul returns to the mess the Corinthians had made of it. One of the house rules about the Lord's Supper is that we are to dress for the occasion—inwardly, that is—casting off the rags of pride, selfishness, gluttony, and drunkenness. Paul spells out the seriousness of disobedience (11:27). To eat the bread and drink of the cup in an "unworthy manner" brings guilt punishable by physical judgment (11:29-30). When believers come to the table in a sinful condition, failing to be cleansed of their sin by the sacrificed body and shed blood of Christ, they bring shame upon Christ's suffering and death. Coming to the Lord's Table with unclean souls, with known sin in our lives, brings reproach upon the Savior. The discipline Paul mentions isn't purely punitive but is also fatherly, intended to bring offenders to repentance and restoration to a holy life and fellowship in the body (11:32; cf. Heb. 12:5-7).

How does Paul say the Corinthians can partake of the Lord's Supper in a worthy manner and thereby avoid such discipline from God? First, a person must "examine himself" (1 Cor. 11:28), pleading with the Lord as David did:

> Search me, O God, and know my heart;
> Try me and know my anxious thoughts;
> And see if there be any hurtful way in me,
> And lead me in the everlasting way. (Ps. 139:23-24)

Second, a person must "judge the body rightly" (1 Cor. 11:29). Some have taken this as a reference to judging whether the bread and wine are the literal body and blood of Christ or merely a symbol, but the context suggests that Paul is referring to treating the corporate "body of Christ," *the church*, in a respectful and dignified manner. Paul's chief complaint is that in celebrating the Lord's Supper, certain believers in the church in Corinth were completely denying the self-sacrificial humility exemplified in Christ's incarnation and atonement. Instead of working toward building up the body of Christ, their failure to provide for the poor and needy among them was actually tearing it down.

Third, the observers must "wait for one another" (11:33). Each member of the church must look out for the interests of others. Paul reiterates his advice that those who are hungry and have means of satisfying their appetites at home should do so (11:34), because when they gather around the table, they must see to the needs of others instead of themselves. They should strive for unity through humility, offering themselves as living sacrifices to God (Rom. 12:1-2).

In closing, Paul accompanies his strong warning with a comforting promise. If the wayward, selfish gluttons at Corinth realign their faulty practices with Christ's attitudes and actions, judging themselves rightly, they will escape judgment (1 Cor. 11:31). Instead of becoming weak and sick or dying, they will experience the blessing of the cup as they fellowship with God and one another around this sacred Table (10:16).

# APPLICATION: 1 CORINTHIANS 11:17-34

## Affirming the Family Reunion

Something happened in the Swindoll family when we stopped having family reunions. We began to drift apart. The smaller, nuclear families became tiny islands, eventually losing contact with the other islands of aunts, uncles, cousins, nieces, and nephews. By and by, it has come to the point that today I can hardly tell you where most of my extended family is located. Why? Because we stopped having a family reunion.

Chances are that in your church you have a regular "church family reunion" around the Lord's Table. Some churches celebrate it weekly, some monthly, some quarterly. Some churches partake of the Lord's Supper in Sunday morning worship, some in an evening service, others in smaller groups in a less centralized and less formal venue. Whatever your particular church's practice, let me encourage you to take every opportunity to participate in your church's family reunion.

Not only are you invited, but Paul commands you to eat and drink of the bread and cup—to keep on proclaiming the Lord's death until He comes. Something unhealthy happens when Christians become dissociated from the family of God around the Lord's Table. Something occurs in their spiritual walk and relationship with others over the passing of time. They lose their sense of belonging to the family, which lessens their feeling of unity with the body. As time passes, a significant part of their spiritual development slows. Why? Because the Lord's Supper calls all of us to reconsider Christ's person and work on our behalf. It urges us to rededicate ourselves to living the gospel in our everyday walk and talk. It asks us to reconcile with others as we approach the Table as one body. It requires that we confess and repent of unconfessed sin prior to partaking.

When celebrating the Lord's Supper, how are your table manners? Do you eat with unwashed hands? Do you share the meal grudgingly? Remember what this family reunion represents. Enjoy it with wholehearted thanksgiving and observe it with appropriate reverence. Most of all, enjoy it together, having sought forgiveness and secured reconciliation with those in the body of Christ you may have wronged.

# One Body, Many Members
## 1 CORINTHIANS 12:1-31

NASB

1 Now concerning spiritual *gifts*, brethren, I do not want you to be unaware. 2 You know that when you were pagans, *you were* led astray to the mute idols, however you were led. 3 Therefore I make known to you that no one speaking [a]by the Spirit of God says, "Jesus is [b]accursed"; and no one can say, "Jesus is Lord," except [a]by the Holy Spirit.

4 Now there are varieties of gifts, but the same Spirit. 5 And there are varieties of ministries, and the same Lord. 6 There are varieties of effects, but the same God who works all things in all *persons.* 7 But to each one is given the manifestation of the Spirit for the common good. 8 For to one is given the word of wisdom through the Spirit, and to another the word of knowledge according to the same Spirit; 9 to another faith [a]by the same Spirit, and to another gifts of [b]healing [a]by the one Spirit, 10 and to another the [a]effecting of [b]miracles, and to another prophecy, and to another the [c]distinguishing of spirits, to another *various* kinds of tongues, and to another the interpretation of tongues. 11 But one and the same Spirit works all these things, distributing to each one individually just as He wills.

12 For even as the body is one and *yet* has many members, and all the members of the body, though they are many, are one body, so also is Christ. 13 For [a]by one Spirit we were all baptized into one body, whether

NLT

1 Now, dear brothers and sisters,* regarding your question about the special abilities the Spirit gives us. I don't want you to misunderstand this. 2 You know that when you were still pagans, you were led astray and swept along in worshiping speechless idols. 3 So I want you to know that no one speaking by the Spirit of God will curse Jesus, and no one can say Jesus is Lord, except by the Holy Spirit.

4 There are different kinds of spiritual gifts, but the same Spirit is the source of them all. 5 There are different kinds of service, but we serve the same Lord. 6 God works in different ways, but it is the same God who does the work in all of us.

7 A spiritual gift is given to each of us so we can help each other. 8 To one person the Spirit gives the ability to give wise advice*; to another the same Spirit gives a message of special knowledge.* 9 The same Spirit gives great faith to another, and to someone else the one Spirit gives the gift of healing. 10 He gives one person the power to perform miracles, and another the ability to prophesy. He gives someone else the ability to discern whether a message is from the Spirit of God or from another spirit. Still another person is given the ability to speak in unknown languages,* while another is given the ability to interpret what is being said. 11 It is the one and only Spirit who distributes all these gifts. He alone decides which gift each person should have.

12 The human body has many parts, but the many parts make up one whole body. So it is with the body of Christ. 13 Some of us are Jews, some are Gentiles,* some are slaves, and some are free. But we have all

**NASB**

Jews or Greeks, whether slaves or free, and we were all made to drink of one Spirit.

14 For the body is not one member, but many. 15 If the foot says, "Because I am not a hand, I am not *a part* of the body," it is not for this reason [a]any the less *a part* of the body. 16 And if the ear says, "Because I am not an eye, I am not *a part* of the body," it is not for this reason [a]any the less *a part* of the body. 17 If the whole body were an eye, where would the hearing be? If the whole were hearing, where would the sense of smell be? 18 But now God has placed the members, each one of them, in the body, just as He desired. 19 If they were all one member, where would the body be? 20 But now there are many members, but one body. 21 And the eye cannot say to the hand, "I have no need of you"; or again the head to the feet, "I have no need of you." 22 On the contrary, [a]it is much truer that the members of the body which seem to be weaker are necessary; 23 and those *members* of the body which we [a]deem less honorable, [b]on these we bestow more abundant honor, and our less presentable members become much more presentable, 24 whereas our more presentable members have no need *of it*. But God has *so* composed the body, giving more abundant honor to that *member* which lacked, 25 so that there may be no [a]division in the body, but *that* the members may have the same care for one another. 26 And if one member suffers, all the members suffer with it; if *one* member is [a]honored, all the members rejoice with it.

27 Now you are Christ's body, and individually members of it. 28 And God has [a]appointed in the church, first apostles, second prophets,

**NLT**

been baptized into one body by one Spirit, and we all share the same Spirit.*

14 Yes, the body has many different parts, not just one part. 15 If the foot says, "I am not a part of the body because I am not a hand," that does not make it any less a part of the body. 16 And if the ear says, "I am not part of the body because I am not an eye," would that make it any less a part of the body? 17 If the whole body were an eye, how would you hear? Or if your whole body were an ear, how would you smell anything?

18 But our bodies have many parts, and God has put each part just where he wants it. 19 How strange a body would be if it had only one part! 20 Yes, there are many parts, but only one body. 21 The eye can never say to the hand, "I don't need you." The head can't say to the feet, "I don't need you."

22 In fact, some parts of the body that seem weakest and least important are actually the most necessary. 23 And the parts we regard as less honorable are those we clothe with the greatest care. So we carefully protect those parts that should not be seen, 24 while the more honorable parts do not require this special care. So God has put the body together such that extra honor and care are given to those parts that have less dignity. 25 This makes for harmony among the members, so that all the members care for each other. 26 If one part suffers, all the parts suffer with it, and if one part is honored, all the parts are glad.

27 All of you together are Christ's body, and each of you is a part of it. 28 Here are some of the parts God has appointed for the church:

first are apostles,
second are prophets,
third are teachers,

third teachers, then [b]miracles, then gifts of healings, helps, administrations, *various* kinds of tongues.
29 All are not apostles, are they? All are not prophets, are they? All are not teachers, are they? All are not *workers of* [a]miracles, are they?
30 All do not have gifts of healings, do they? All do not speak with tongues, do they? All do not interpret, do they?
31 But earnestly desire the greater gifts.

And I show you a still more excellent way.

12:3 [a]Or *in* [b]Gr *anathema* 12:9 [a]Or *in* [b]Lit *healings* 12:10 [a]Lit *effects* [b]Or *works of power* [c]Lit *distinguishings* 12:13 [a]Or *in* 12:15 [a]Lit *not* a part 12:16 [a]Lit *not* a part 12:22 [a]Lit *to a much greater degree the members* 12:23 [a]Or *think to be* [b]Or *these we clothe with* 12:25 [a]Lit *schism* 12:26 [a]Lit *glorified* 12:28 [a]Lit *set some in* [b]Or *works of power* 12:29 [a]Or *works of power*

then those who do miracles,
those who have the gift of healing,
those who can help others,
those who have the gift of leadership,
those who speak in unknown languages.

29 Are we all apostles? Are we all prophets? Are we all teachers? Do we all have the power to do miracles?
30 Do we all have the gift of healing? Do we all have the ability to speak in unknown languages? Do we all have the ability to interpret unknown languages? Of course not!
31 So you should earnestly desire the most helpful gifts.

But now let me show you a way of life that is best of all.

**12:1** Greek *brothers.* **12:8a** Or *gives a word of wisdom.* **12:8b** Or *gives a word of knowledge.* **12:10** Or *in various tongues;* also in 12:28, 30. **12:13a** Greek *some are Greeks.* **12:13b** Greek *we were all given one Spirit to drink.*

Have you ever experienced a performance of Bach's *Brandenburg Concertos*, Beethoven's *Ninth Symphony*, or Handel's *Messiah*? I don't mean having Bach's intricate notes tickle your ears through tiny white ear buds, or Beethoven's bold crescendos rattle the windows of your den, or Handel's moving "Hallelujah Chorus" sanctify your car stereo. That would be *listening* to the music; I mean *experiencing* it.

There is a major difference between listening to a recording of Mozart on your home stereo and experiencing it live at the symphony hall. The notes may be the same, but our awareness of the conductor, the members of the orchestra, and the distinct movements and sounds of various instruments is completely lost when we passively hear a recording of the sounds. There is something about seeing the music happen that creates a sense of wonder and exhilaration. Rather than thinking of the music as a technically satisfying product, we experience it as a profoundly human work of art.

At the symphony, you witness the entire orchestra assembled as a whole. When you gaze at the black-tied conductor, it appears as though he is conjuring up the music from another world, like a magician in *The Sorcerer's Apprentice*. Yet when you pan across the stage and see the passionate labor of the individual and gifted musicians, you realize that whatever inspiration may appear to be summoned by that "magic wand" of the conductor, the perspiration of the artists creates the beautiful sounds that fill the concert hall. Though the individual musician plays a vital role in the symphony, only when they all perform together as a harmonious body can we fully experience the scope, breadth, and depth of the symphonic music.

Similarly, understanding how spiritual gifts work melodiously in a church body takes more than just listening to the harmony the members make when tuned in to their gifts. It takes seeing each member of the church as an essential individual instrument, vital to the whole body. And it takes an appreciation for the work of the Great Conductor—the Holy Spirit—who gifts and guides each individual and the body according to His will and according to His purpose: the building up of the body of Christ.

In 1 Corinthians 12, Paul provides a solid understanding of spiritual gifts. He focuses not so much on the details of each gift, but on how and why the gifts together produce a full, real-life sound. When believers practice the gifts properly, the rich, harmonious sound that results glorifies God as the Lord's people build up one another in love.

## — 12:1-3 —

Paul ends his instructions concerning the proper observance of the Lord's Supper with the words, "The remaining matters I will arrange when I come" (11:34). He gave them just enough details to answer their questions and solve their current crisis, and he anticipated offering further instruction in person during a future visit. Paul now moves on to the next area of controversy and conflict in Corinth: the proper attitude toward and practice of spiritual gifts. He begins with a phrase he uses repeatedly for a sharp transition to a completely new topic: "Now concerning" (12:1).[8]

Regarding the subject of spiritual gifts, Paul didn't want anybody in Corinth to shrug their shoulders and say, "I don't really know much about that, and I don't really care." Paul marks the importance of the issue by saying he doesn't want the believers to be "unaware" or ignorant. Paul believed it is vital for Christians to have the right knowledge of spiritual gifts, understanding how they are to function in the lives of each believer and, more importantly, in the life of the church community.

Paul then contrasts the dimness of the Corinthians' former understanding as pagans with the light of the Spirit they have experienced as believers in Christ (12:2-3). Before they were saved, they were without the Spirit, who is the solution to our ignorance and the source of true knowledge. In their former lost condition, they served dumb, powerless idols out of ignorance—the depraved spiritual capacity of all men and women who lack the eye-opening grace of the Holy Spirit's regenerating power. But now, as believers who have been enabled by the indwelling Spirit to confess Jesus as "Lord" (12:3), they no longer reject Christ, but accept Him for Who He really is: the Savior and Lord.

## — 12:4-11 —

Having urged the Corinthians to continue to grow in knowledge, Paul begins to instruct them concerning the theory behind the practice of spiritual gifts (*charisma* [5486]). The problem in Corinth was not that they were ignorant of the presence of spiritual gifts, but that they were unspiritual and extreme in their application. They knew that they had been given spiritual gifts, but they did not know how to properly utilize them.

To illustrate the specific problem in Corinth, let me use an analogy. Like a dozen musicians each having mastered a different instrument, the Corinthians gathered not to perform a harmonious symphony, but to outperform one another and argue about which instrument was the best. They showed up to show off! But anybody who has ever tried to play in an orchestra or sing in a choir knows that making beautiful, melodious music takes more than just gathering in a crowd and strumming, blowing, beating, or clanging our own instruments—or breaking out in a vocal solo—in ways that please only ourselves. It takes an understanding of the theory behind the notes and a willingness to play our parts with others for the sake of something bigger than our own individual and self-serving performance.

To correct the Corinthians' charismatic confusion, Paul goes back to the fundamentals. He explains the source of spiritual gifts (12:4-6), the purpose of the gifts (12:7), the identity of the gifts (12:8-10), and the distribution of the gifts (12:11).

*The source of spiritual gifts* (12:4-6). Spiritual gifts come to believers from the triune God—Father, Son, and Holy Spirit—who, working in perfect harmony, give members of the church a "variety" of gifts and ministries.

Paul describes the diversity of spiritual gifts with the word *diairesis* [1243], a Greek term that implies distinctions and differences.[9] The root of this word is related to the word *hairesis* [139], which we translate as "heresy" or "faction." Whereas *hairesis* implies a destructive faction (1 Cor. 11:19; Gal. 5:20; 2 Pet. 2:1), *diairesis*, in contrast, connotes a constructive variety. The Corinthians' problem was that they were turning *diairesis* into *hairesis*—turning healthy diversity given as a gift from God into unhealthy conflict caused by the selfishness of humans. Chaos resulted.

All believers of every age must remain united on the central core of orthodox theology and practice, standing shoulder to shoulder against dangerous heresies and uniting under the essential truths of the Christian faith.[10] Christianity, however, was never meant to produce an army of clones or a franchise of copycat churches. Paul says that the one triune God creates a healthy variety of gifts, leading to a diversity of ministries, producing a panorama of results (1 Cor. 12:4-6). Notice that the entire Godhead is involved in the gift-giving. Paul likely refers to this unity and diversity of the Godhead as an example for the intended unity and diversity of the believers in Corinth.

*The purpose of spiritual gifts* (12:7). God has spiritually gifted each one of us. In the same way that each member of an orchestra plays a specific instrument, each member of God's family has been given specific gifts that manifest the active presence of the Holy Spirit. The word "manifestation" means "making something evident or obvious." When believers exercise their gifts, God's people become tangible, evident, meaningful expressions of God's active presence on earth.

The purpose of this diversity of gifts is to serve "the common good" (12:7). "Common good" is a translation of a word derived from the Greek verb *sympherō* [4851], which means "to bring together." God never intended for us to practice and perform our spiritual instruments in insulated, soundproof rooms. He wants us to take our seats in the orchestra and, under the direction of the Spirit, make beautiful, harmonious music that builds others up.

*The identity of spiritual gifts* (12:8-10). Paul names several spiritual gifts present in the early church. The Corinthian church had been generously blessed with a great variety of gifts (1:7), but this list, though extensive, is not exhaustive. With merely a sampling of the kinds of gifts the Spirit bestows upon believers, Paul emphasizes repeatedly that it is the "same Spirit" who provides all of the gifts.

Based on this passage as well as a few others (Rom. 12:6-8; Eph. 4:11; 1 Pet. 4:10-11), we can observe the great diversity of gifts given to the church for its edification. These could be categorized into "support

## CURSUS: GIFT, GIFTS, AND FRUIT

### 1 CORINTHIANS 12:7

An important biblical distinction often becomes muddled in our minds as we try to sort out what the Bible teaches about spiritual gifts. Before plunging too deeply into the topic, we need to understand the distinctions between *the gift of the Spirit*, *the gifts from the Spirit*, and *the fruit of the Spirit*.

*The Gift of the Holy Spirit*. Some passages of Scripture describe the Holy Spirit Himself as a gift to believers (e.g., Acts 2:38). Given at the moment a believing sinner places faith in Christ, the Holy Spirit comes to permanently indwell that person, uniting the believer with Christ forever. Jesus foretold the coming of the Holy Spirit this way: "I will ask the Father, and He will give you another Helper, that He may be with you forever; that is the Spirit of truth, whom the world cannot receive, because it does not see Him or know Him, but you know Him because He abides with you and will be in you" (John 14:16-17). That day came fifty days after Christ's resurrection when the gathered believers were all "baptized with the Holy Spirit" (Acts 2:1-4; 10:47; 11:16). This one-time, unrepeatable baptism of the Holy Spirit is the moment that the Holy Spirit Himself takes up residence within each believer. This gift can never be taken away.

*The Gifts from the Holy Spirit*. All believers, baptized by the Holy Spirit, have also been given spiritual gifts from the Holy Spirit. These are skills and abilities, supernatural enablement or assistance, given to benefit the body of Christ. As gifts, they cannot be earned. Paul wrote: "Since we have gifts that differ according to the grace given to us, each of us is to exercise them accordingly" (Rom. 12:6). They can't be sought after or prayed for, and they're not awarded for faithfulness. They are distributed "to each one individually just as He [the Holy Spirit] wills" (1 Cor. 12:11).[11] Our responsibility and privilege is to exercise these gifts for the benefit of the church. Gifts from the Holy Spirit are therefore ministry-oriented and unique to each individual. Put simply, a gift from the Holy Spirit is a special skill or ability which enables each believer to contribute to the whole body of Christ with ease, joy, and effectiveness.

*The Fruit of the Holy Spirit*. The fruit of the Spirit manifests itself in character qualities—virtues produced from within us by the power of the indwelling Spirit. Galatians 5:22-23 gives a sampling of the kinds of qualities the Spirit nurtures: "But the fruit of the Spirit is love, joy, peace, patience, kindness, goodness, faithfulness, gentleness, self-control." Through His Spirit, God works in all believers to accomplish those things that please Him (Phil. 2:13).

To sum up, all believers in Jesus Christ have been baptized with the Holy Spirit and therefore have received the gift of the abiding Spirit Himself. The indwelling Spirit of God then bestows upon each individual unique spiritual gifts to exercise for the building up of the body of Christ, the church. The Spirit also nurtures within us the manifestations of His spiritual character, producing the fruit of the Spirit, which enable us to live godly, virtuous lives.

gifts" (apostleship, prophecy, evangelism, pastoring, teaching), "service gifts" (administrations, exhortation, faith, giving, helps, mercy), and "sign gifts" (discerning spirits, miracles, healings, tongues, interpretation of tongues). Paul emphasizes how these various gifts are meant to function together harmoniously for the common good.

| SPIRITUAL GIFTS LISTED IN SCRIPTURE | | | |
|---|---|---|---|
| Romans 12:6-8 | 1 Corinthians 12:4-11, 28 | Ephesians 4:11 | 1 Peter 4:10-11 |
| Prophecy | Word of wisdom | Apostles | Speaking |
| Service | Word of knowledge | Prophets | Serving |
| Teaching | Faith | Evangelists | |
| Exhorting | Healing | Pastors | |
| Giving | Miracles | Teachers | |
| Leading | Prophecy | | |
| Mercy | Distinguishing of spirits | | |
| | Speaking in languages | | |
| | Interpreting languages | | |

*The distribution of spiritual gifts* (1 Cor. 12:11). Like a conductor who hands out the right parts of an orchestral score to the right musicians, the Holy Spirit distributes His gifts to all believers "just as He wills" (12:11). It is not true that a believer can only have one gift. Nor is it true that a believer must plead for, seek after, or earn any gift. As a matter of fact, the Holy Spirit individually distributes the gifts according to His plan and pleasure. He selects our gifts for us personally, tailoring them to our personalities and skills to be used for His glory and purposes.

## — 12:12-14 —

To drive home the need for the church to be an interdependent community growing together rather than independent practitioners growing apart, Paul likens the unity and diversity of the body of Christ to the unity and diversity of the human body (12:12). From the tops of our heads to the soles of our feet, each part of our body, though often radically diverse, is united as a whole. Likewise, every member of Christ's church is part of the same organic, interdependent, diverse-yet-united body.

The truth of the unity of the body of Christ isn't comparable to the unity of a man-made society like a club or human organization. Rather, a profound spiritual reality underlies the principle of unity in diversity. The Holy Spirit baptizes each individual believer into spiritual union with Christ (12:13), joining us all into one spiritual body, united to Christ as our head. According to one commentator, by referring to this common experience of the baptism of the Holy Spirit, "Paul seems . . . to be saying both that Christians are in the Holy Spirit, and that the Holy Spirit is in Christians, parallel to our being in Christ and Christ being in us."[12]

Unfortunately, in the church today the teaching of the baptism of the Holy Spirit has become a battleground of confusion and division rather than a basis for clarity and unity. We are commanded to be filled with the Holy Spirit (Eph. 5:18), but being baptized by the Holy Spirit is not our responsibility. When we put our trust in Christ, the Holy Spirit baptizes us, permanently changing our membership from Satan's family (John 8:44; 1 Jn. 3:8-10) to the family of God.[13]

## — 12:15-27 —

Next Paul builds on his analogy, and with wit and humor he paints a ludicrous picture of the parts of the human body rebelling against each other. The Corinthian readers immediately would have realized that Paul was indirectly ridiculing their own behavior. Paul basically argues that if our feet and ears could speak, and if they behaved the way the Corinthian believers were behaving in the church, they would say the most outlandish things. They would feel self-conscious about their apparently insignificant roles in the body and wish they could have a more prominent function (12:15-16).

Yet Paul clarifies that just as diversity in the human body is essential to proper functioning, so also diversity in the body of Christ is essential (12:17). A creature made up of one huge ear, a single giant nose, or a bulbous floating eyeball would be absurdly useless compared to the composite body of organs with its senses of taste, touch, sight, smell, and hearing. A body cannot be comprised of one single member (12:19-20).

God didn't create bodies that have only one function. That would make us grotesque beasts unworthy of the all-wise and all-powerful God who creates beauty, symmetry, and harmony in His creation.

Similarly, God didn't design the church to have all its members possess the same spiritual gifts, but He "placed the members, each one of them, in the body, just as He desired" (12:18). Being the head, that is His prerogative.

Only in its functional diversity can a unified body have ongoing health and genuine growth. In a healthy body of believers, all the members depend on each other and help each other function at their best. In our physical bodies, an eye may be able to see a piece of nourishing fruit, but it requires an arm to extend its reach to pluck the fruit from the tree with the fingers. Then the body requires a mouth with teeth to eat it, along with a whole host of unseen internal organs to digest the fruit so it can nourish the body. In the same way, some members of the body of Christ may seem insignificant on the surface. Consider the tiny hammer, anvil, and stirrup bones of the ear. Though tiny, they hold part of the secret to the world of hearing and balance, and the other members desperately need them. So it is in the church (12:21-24).

In 12:25-26, Paul explains why God has created us to be interdependent parts of a whole rather than independent entities. By overcoming our natural tendency toward division through mutual love and concern for one another (12:25), we exhibit God's supernatural power and grace for the whole world to see. Jesus said, "By this all men will know that you are My disciples, if you have love for one another" (John 13:35). It's easy to love those who are like us, to spend time with the honored, to befriend those who benefit us. It's far more difficult to overcome our carnal contempt for the weak, our fleshly envy of the strong, and our selfish neglect of the suffering. By the work of the Holy Spirit, an otherwise disunited gathering of selfish human beings can overcome their fleshly desires and unite through humility and love.

In short, by overcoming self and embracing others through acknowledging our own neediness in the body of Christ and through contributing to the needs of others, we demonstrate to all that we are "Christ's body, and individually members of it" (1 Cor. 12:27).

## — 12:28-31 —

Finally, Paul emphasizes the spiritual side of his analogy, explaining that there is no such thing as an exclusive gift in the body of Christ. Perhaps because it was a miraculous gift that easily attracted personal attention, the gift of speaking in tongues had been overemphasized by the Corinthians. They had made it a mark of acute spirituality, without which a person's spiritual walk was questioned. To counter this imbalance, Paul acknowledges that God has set order within the church, with the offices of the apostles, prophets, and teachers having a place of particular authority because of their role in proclaiming God's Word (12:28). After these roles, other gifted individuals—workers of miracles and healings, helpers and administrators, and speakers of various tongues—take their place as part of a harmonious whole.

Paul points out that not all Christians are called to be apostles, prophets, and teachers, just as not all have been given the ability to work miracles, effect healings, and speak in tongues (12:29-30). Any insistence that the evidence of a person's salvation, baptism of the Holy Spirit, or spiritual maturity requires that the individual speak in tongues flatly contradicts Paul's rhetorical questions here. They are phrased in such a way in the Greek language that they demand a negative answer. Simply put, *not all people are expected to speak in tongues*.

In closing, Paul urges the Corinthians as a corporate body—and all of us today—to "earnestly desire the greater gifts" (12:31). The greater gifts, such as prophecy and teaching, effectively and directly build up the whole body of Christ. The lesser gifts, such as tongues, build up only a small part, and do so only through the indirect process of interpretation (14:1-5). In light of the fact that the purpose of all the gifts is the building up of the body, we should follow a "more excellent way" (12:31)—the way of self-sacrificial love for one another (13:1-13).

## APPLICATION: 1 CORINTHIANS 12:1-31

### Giving Your Gift and Glorifying the Giver

Learning music theory is never an end in itself. The goal is that it be used with a musical instrument or a voice—practiced and perfected. In response to Paul's general principles of spiritual-gift theology, we should be both eager and equipped to put our gifts to good use. Let me share three responses to these truths regarding spiritual gifts.

First, *being aware of your spiritual gifts pleases God.* God wants you to know the areas in which you have been gifted. How do you discover these gifts? Your church likely has resources to help you uncover your spiritual gifts, and thankfully, you can find numerous in-print and online "spiritual gift inventories" as well. The very best way to discover spiritual gifts, however, is to get involved in ministry and see where the Spirit leads and equips. As an example, for someone who possesses the gift of mercy, showing compassion to another person is almost as natural as breathing. Likewise, gifted teachers can't imagine themselves doing anything other than facing a group of eager learners and opening God's Word to them. And those with a gift of giving always seek opportunities to share with others because of their generosity.

When you exercise your spiritual gift, you find yourself freed, liberated, and blessed. Rather than a chore that drains you, it's a privilege that energizes you. Ray Stedman emphasizes this point in his book *Body Life*: "The exercise of a spiritual gift is always a satisfying, enjoyable experience. . . . Jesus said it was his constant delight to do the will of the one who sent him. The Father's gift awakened his own desire and he went about doing what he intensely enjoyed doing."[14]

Second, *being willing to use your gift benefits the whole body of Christ*. Knowing your gift and faithfully using that gift are two completely different things. When you use your gift, everyone is blessed. It's true, we may sometimes feel like our contribution is insignificant, but Paul explains in 1 Corinthians 12 that this is simply wrong. Just remember, there is no part too small. You may not carry the melody or set the rhythm for the rest of the orchestra, but without your part, the sound wouldn't be as full and harmonious. Without your part, the sounds will always be less than complete. So identify your areas of giftedness and get involved!

Third, *being satisfied with your gift honors its Giver*. You will never bring as much glory to God as when you are doing what He created and gifted you to do. Don't waste time longing for gifts you don't have or yearning for opportunities that aren't available. Exercise the gifts you have been given and take hold of the opportunities for ministry that have been placed before you.

Yes, you could join the mass of pew-fillers who sit in their seats, fold their arms, and watch like spectators, as just 20 percent of church members actually exercise their spiritual gifts and do the work of the ministry. But when you do, you must realize that you are squandering the gifts God has given you for the purpose of building up your fellow believers. There is a part to play in the ministry that only you can play. If you refuse to use your gift, your brothers and sisters in Christ miss out on an important means of spiritual growth, and worse, your Creator is robbed of the glory He rightly deserves.

# Love: The Greatest of All
## 1 CORINTHIANS 13:1-13

NASB

1 If I speak with the tongues of men
and of angels, but do not have love,
I have become a noisy gong or a
clanging cymbal. 2 If I have *the gift*
*of* prophecy, and know all mysteries
and all knowledge; and if I have all
faith, so as to remove mountains, but
do not have love, I am nothing. 3 And
if I give all my possessions to feed *the*
*poor,* and if I surrender my body [a]to
be burned, but do not have love, it
profits me nothing.

4 Love is patient, love is kind *and*
is not jealous; love does not brag
*and* is not arrogant, 5 does not act
unbecomingly; it does not seek its
own, is not provoked, does not take
into account a wrong *suffered,* 6 does
not rejoice in unrighteousness, but
rejoices with the truth; 7 [a]bears all
things, believes all things, hopes all
things, endures all things.

8 Love never fails; but if *there are*
*gifts of* [a]prophecy, they will be done
away; if *there are* tongues, they
will cease; if *there is* knowledge, it
will be done away. 9 For we know
in part and we prophesy in part;
10 but when the perfect comes, the
partial will be done away. 11 When
I was a child, I used to speak like
a child, think like a child, reason
like a child; when I [a]became a man,
I did away with childish things.
12 For now we see in a mirror [a]dimly,
but then face to face; now I know
in part, but then I will know fully
just as I also have been fully known.

NLT

1 If I could speak all the languages of
earth and of angels, but didn't love
others, I would only be a noisy gong
or a clanging cymbal. 2 If I had the
gift of prophecy, and if I understood
all of God's secret plans and pos-
sessed all knowledge, and if I had
such faith that I could move moun-
tains, but didn't love others, I would
be nothing. 3 If I gave everything I
have to the poor and even sacrificed
my body, I could boast about it;* but
if I didn't love others, I would have
gained nothing.

4 Love is patient and kind. Love is
not jealous or boastful or proud 5 or
rude. It does not demand its own
way. It is not irritable, and it keeps
no record of being wronged. 6 It does
not rejoice about injustice but re-
joices whenever the truth wins out.
7 Love never gives up, never loses
faith, is always hopeful, and endures
through every circumstance.

8 Prophecy and speaking in un-
known languages* and special
knowledge will become useless.
But love will last forever! 9 Now our
knowledge is partial and incom-
plete, and even the gift of prophecy
reveals only part of the whole pic-
ture! 10 But when the time of perfec-
tion comes, these partial things will
become useless.

11 When I was a child, I spoke and
thought and reasoned as a child. But
when I grew up, I put away childish
things. 12 Now we see things imper-
fectly, like puzzling reflections in a
mirror, but then we will see every-
thing with perfect clarity.* All that I
know now is partial and incomplete,
but then I will know everything com-
pletely, just as God now knows me
completely.

NASB

13 But now faith, hope, love, abide these three; but the [a]greatest of these is love.

13:3 [a]Early mss read *that I may boast* 13:7 [a]Or *covers* 13:8 [a]Lit *prophecies* 13:11 [a]Lit *have become...have done away with* 13:12 [a]Lit *in a riddle* 13:13 [a]Lit *greater*

NLT

13 Three things will last forever—faith, hope, and love—and the greatest of these is love.

13:3 Some manuscripts read *sacrificed my body to be burned.* 13:8 Or *in tongues.* 13:12 Greek *see face to face.*

"Love is a many-splendored thing." . . . "Love is all you need." . . . "Love conquers all." . . . "Love lifts us up where we belong." . . . "Love is in the air." . . . "Love changes everything." . . . "What the world needs now is love, sweet love." . . . "Love is all around."

This mosaic of love-song clichés reminds us that our world is filled with the language of "love." The word gets thrown around constantly and carelessly. "Love" is used to describe our feelings for everything from God to chocolate, from cars to pets, from football to family. Sadly, the kind of love implied by the world's popular poems and platitudes bears little resemblance to the meaning of love described throughout the Bible, and particularly epitomized and memorialized in 1 Corinthians 13.

Although it occurs as we approach the end of the book, 1 Corinthians 13 can be regarded as the "thematic center" of 1 Corinthians. In this passage Paul contrasts unconditional *agapē* [26] love—the ultimate Christian virtue—with the kinds of character vices that had marred the Corinthians' interactions with one another. The "love chapter," as it has often been called, convicts us and inspires us. It is doctrinally dense yet practically rich. A. T. Robertson rightly comments:

> Plato . . . and many others have written on love, but Paul has here surpassed them all in this marvelous prose-poem. It comes like a sweet bell right between the jangling noise of the gifts in chapters 12 and 14. It is a pity to dissect this gem or to pull to pieces this fragrant rose, petal by petal. Fortunately Paul's language here calls for little comment, for it is the language of the heart.[15]

Let's explore this "love chapter" with the understanding that we aren't seeking merely to be inspired and informed, but to be challenged and changed.

## — 13:1-3 —

Though it would be easy to snip 1 Corinthians 13 from its page, frame it, and hang it on our walls as a constant reminder of authentic love, we must never forget the context from which this beautiful passage emerges. Standing in the center of Paul's correction of the Corinthians' self-seeking exercise of spiritual gifts is 1 Corinthians 13. They were strutting their own giftedness out of selfish ambition rather than using their gifts for the benefit of the whole body. Through this love chapter, Paul argues that only those things done from a heart of love (*agapē* [26]) are virtuous.

The impressive acts Paul lists in 13:1-3 form a hyperbole to argue from the greater to the lesser. The idea is this: Even if we do works that are by all appearances miraculous, astonishing, and extreme, they ultimately amount to nothing without the key ingredient of *agapē* love. Without the motivating presence of this kind of love, the most eloquent, impressive speech—even of angels—would sound like a cacophonous clang. Without love, our prophecies, revelations, knowledge, faith, and charity are worthless, empty shells, unworthy of praise and reward.

Some have misunderstood Paul's use of the rhetorical device of

## THE THREE LOVES

### 1 CORINTHIANS 13:4

The Greek language of Paul's day had at least three common words that can be translated by the English word "love": *erōs* (this term does not appear in the New Testament), *philia* [5373], and *agapē* [26]. The word *erōs* very often referred to a self-pleasing, passionate love, from which we get our English term "erotic." All too often, this is the level of love implied by our pop songs and glorified in trashy romance novels, risqué primetime dramas, and feel-good movies that inevitably end when the dashing guy gets the perfect girl.

The word *philia* refers to the affection and closeness one feels in friendships, partnerships, or other intimate kinships. It's "brotherly love," a strong emotional, psychological, and social bond of camaraderie between two people.

Even though we find deep emotions in these two words, neither *erōs* nor *philia* match the kind of love that imitates the love of God.

In 1 Corinthians 13, Paul refers to *agapē* love—the kind of love that seeks the highest good of the other person, even at the price of one's own comfort, safety, and benefit. The word *agapē* was not used frequently outside Jewish and Christian literature. Unlike the short-lived *erōs* or the two-way *philia*, *agapē* implies permanence, unconditional charity, a decision more than a feeling, a commitment more than a relationship. *Agapē* means loving not for one's own benefit, but for the benefit of others.[16]

hyperbole in this passage, understanding 1 Corinthians 13:1 to make a distinction between a kind of speaking in tongues as a human language (Acts 2:6) and a type of speaking in tongues as a heavenly, angelic, or prayer language. The Greek construction, however, suggests that Paul added the reference to angelic languages to push his example to the highest conceivable extreme: "If I were to speak in the languages of men—and even of angels—but didn't have love, I would be a noisy gong or a clanging cymbal" (1 Cor. 13:1).[17] The context demonstrates that Paul was presenting hypothetical examples of the most extreme and excessive acts possible. Note the repeated use of the word "all": "If . . . I know *all* mysteries and *all* knowledge. . . if I have *all* faith. . . if I give *all* my possessions. . ." (13:2-3).

Of course, Paul knew that nobody could speak all the languages of humanity and heaven, any more than people could know everything, reveal everything, and give everything. Yet Paul's argument is even more compelling, given these exaggerated hypothetical feats: Without love, the most eloquent speech, insightful knowledge, and sacrificial acts are useless.

Paul wants to impress upon his readers a vital formula (13:1-3):

EVERYTHING – LOVE = NOTHING

## — 13:4-7 —

After explaining the matchless value of love as the essential ingredient in a fruitful Christian life, Paul gives a clear, poetic description of *agapē* love. He includes several positive aspects (what love *is*) and several negative contrasts (what love *is not*).

| POSITIVE ASPECTS | NEGATIVE CONTRASTS |
|---|---|
| is patient | is not jealous |
| is kind | does not brag |
| rejoices with the truth | is not arrogant |
| bears all things | does not act unbecomingly |
| believes all things | does not seek its own |
| hopes all things | is not provoked |
| endures all things | does not take into account a wrong |
| | does not rejoice in unrighteousness |

When we scan this list, we quickly realize that the negative elements precisely describe some of the problems the Corinthian church had been facing. Love is not jealous, but the Corinthians were marred by "jealousy and strife" (3:3). Love does not brag, but the Corinthians boasted (4:7; 5:6). Love is not arrogant, but the Corinthians had allowed arrogance to flourish (4:18-19; 5:2). Love does not act unbecomingly, but the Corinthian church tolerated shameful and disgraceful intrusions (6:5; 11:4, 22). Love does not seek its own, but the Corinthians had spiraled into selfish egotism (10:24). The contrasts could go on. In short, even though the Corinthian church had plenty of money, an enviable location, countless spiritual gifts, and a legacy of celebrity teachers, they lacked the one thing they most needed, in fact, the greatest thing—love.

The Corinthians were infatuated with the things they had—the trappings of religion, the incidentals of life, the external forms. Instead, they should have striven for love. That powerful fruit of the Spirit would have transformed even the trappings into treasures of transformation and the incidentals into tools to build up the body of Christ.

## — 13:8-13 —

Paul adds one final characteristic of love to his list: "Love never fails" (13:8). At first glance, this might suggest that love itself can be trusted never to let us down. In the context, however, Paul contrasts the ever-abiding, never-terminating permanence of love with the temporary nature of some of the gifts and experiences with which the Corinthians were so enamored. Love never collapses, never fades, never loses hope, and never ends. In fact, *agapē* love, because it is an essential part of God's own nature (1 Jn. 4:8), will continue forever.

Against the permanence of love Paul juxtaposes three gifts that will fade away with time: prophecy, tongues, and knowledge (1 Cor. 13:8). Prophecy—the ability to pronounce the revelations of God with divine prophetic authority—"will be done away" (*katargeō* [2673]). This suggests that the gift of prophecy will be done away by some external force or condition that renders it obsolete.

Paul also points out that one of the Corinthians' favorite gifts, tongues, "will cease" (13:8). The Greek word is *pauō* [3973], found here in the middle voice, indicating that its function will come to a stop in and of itself. How sobering this must have sounded to the ears of those puffed-up tongues-speakers in Corinth who had thought themselves so grand. One day the very experience they used to set themselves up above the rest would simply peter out.

Finally, Paul mentions that knowledge "will be done away," using the same verb as he used of prophecy (13:8). Paul doesn't mean that awareness of information would be done away, for then we would all be mindless entities for eternity. The word "knowledge" likely refers to the acquisition of knowledge, either by diligent study or more likely through God's special revelation of the "word of knowledge" (12:8).

Currently the content of our prophetic utterances and supernatural knowledge is "in part" (13:9). That is, even prophets, given special authoritative messages from God, never had the complete picture (1 Pet. 1:10-11). And those of us who diligently search the Scriptures will forever have unanswered questions. Until Christ returns, our present world will always be characterized by partial knowledge and partial prophecies—sufficient to live a life of faith, hope, and love, but far from perfect and complete. The apostle John contrasted our current condition of partial knowledge with that of future clarity: "Beloved, now we are children of God, and it has not appeared as yet what we will be. We know that when He appears, we will be like Him, because we will see Him just as He is" (1 Jn. 3:2).

When Paul refers to the coming of "the perfect," when "the partial" (that is, prophecy and knowledge) will be "done away" (1 Cor. 13:10), he likely has in mind that condition of perfect knowledge and maturity we will experience when Christ returns and establishes His rule. At that time, "the earth will be full of the knowledge of the LORD as the waters cover the sea" (Isa. 11:9). Concerning this future time, God spoke through the prophet Jeremiah, "'They will not teach again, each man his neighbor and each man his brother, saying, "Know the LORD," for they will all know Me, from the least of them to the greatest of them,' declares the LORD" (Jer. 31:34).

It is worth noting that despite mentioning that tongues "will cease" (1 Cor. 13:8), Paul doesn't refer to them in 13:9-10. He doesn't say that we speak in tongues "in part," nor does he say the tongues will be "done away" by an outside force, as will occur with prophecy and knowledge (13:8). Rather, this passage does not explicitly answer the question concerning *when* tongues will cease in and of themselves. Paul tells us that when the "perfect" comes—perhaps the condition of the world at the return of Christ, or, as some suggest, the completion of the New Testament—then those things that are "in part" (prophecy and knowledge) "will be done away" (*katargeō*). From this passage alone, we can't

## When the Perfect Comes

| **PROPHECY** (partial) "will be done away" (1 Cor. 13:8) | **TONGUES** "will cease" (1 Cor. 13:8) | **KNOWLEDGE** (partial) "will be done away" (1 Cor. 13:8) |
|---|---|---|
| *When?* *When the Perfect Comes* | *When?* *(unanswered)* | *When?* *When the Perfect Comes* |

be sure if Paul meant that tongues, too, would continue until that perfect condition, or if he meant that they would have already ceased on their own prior to this.

Paul illustrates the truth of the mature condition of humanity with two examples. As little children, our speaking, thinking, and reasoning are immature. When we look back as adults on our childhood, we reflect on the ignorant and naïve ways we thought and talked about the world. When we were children, however, we were not even aware of our immature condition. As we grew and became mature men and women, we outgrew our temporary, childish ways. In the same way, when Christ presents His bride perfect and complete, resurrected and glorified, without spot or blemish (Eph. 5:27), we will look back on our days in our mortal flesh as a temporary period of ignorance and immaturity. The opinions we held, the things we fought about, the issues on which we were once so dogmatic—these things will be replaced with a full knowledge and understanding that can come only when Christ returns (1 Cor. 13:11).

Second, Paul likens our present understanding of spiritual things to a person looking "in a mirror dimly" (13:12). In the ancient world through most of the medieval period, mirrors were made of burnished bronze, poor reflectors of reality.[18] The word "dimly" is the Greek term *ainigma* [135], from which we derive our English word "enigma." God's speaking to Moses openly "mouth to mouth" was contrasted with speaking "in dark sayings" (Num. 12:8, in the Greek translation, *ainigma*). Keener notes, "Christians presently see a mere reflection, only a little beyond what Moses and the prophets saw."[19]

Yes, the New Testament brings a much fuller revelation of Christ and God's work of redemption than the Old Testament; but compared to the

Mirrors in the ancient world—often made from polished copper or bronze—presented a dim, distorted, and imperfect picture of reality.

glory that will be revealed to us, our understanding is still partial (Rom. 8:18-19; 1 Cor. 2:9). When Christ returns, the distorted images of reality, the mysteries of life, the doctrinal enigmas, and the riddles of suffering all will be gone. When we see the Savior face-to-face, all our question marks will be changed to exclamation points!

Paul declares that love is not the only thing that will endure beyond this world: "But now faith, hope, love, abide these three" (13:13). These cardinal virtues of the Christian life will not only "abide"—Paul's term for an ever-present endurance—but they are "now" present. The implication is clear: Instead of obsessing over the current gifts of the Spirit that will vanish in the future, we should invest our time and energy in nurturing faith, hope, and love, as these benefit us not only in the present age, but throughout time and for all eternity.

Among these three virtues, however, Paul draws a distinction: "But the greatest of these is love" (13:13). Why? Because, as Barclay says, "Faith without love is cold, and hope without love is grim. Love is the fire which kindles faith and it is the light which turns hope into certainty."[20] Also, when Christ returns, faith and hope will be diminished while love will be intensified. Though our perfect trust in God will always endure, our faith in the promises of God and our belief in things that cannot be seen will be satisfied by the fulfillment of all His promises. Similarly, though believers will live for eternity with the expectation of continued growth in relationship with God and others, the hope of glory we have today will be fulfilled when Christ returns. So, while faith and hope diminish and fade with the blessed face-to-face vision of God, our love for Him will only grow with each passing moment—forever and ever.

# APPLICATION: 1 CORINTHIANS 13:1-13

## Putting Love to Work

Far too often we have turned 1 Corinthians 13 into little more than a sentimental, framed piece of poetry, something to hang on our wall or wear on a keychain—pretty words to admire. But Paul meant for us to take these words to heart, to cherish them, to meditate upon them, and ultimately, to allow them to transform our lives from the inside out. As I think about this magnificent chapter of the Bible, I realize the applications are almost countless. To help us begin putting love to work, let's consider several self-evaluating questions that arise from our study of this chapter. Let me encourage you to not be satisfied by simply answering these questions. Dwell on them. Meditate on them.

First, do you consider love absolutely essential in your ministry? Is love the single most important aspect in your relationships with others? Or have you become enamored with the mission and the methods? The Corinthians loved to point at their many spiritual achievements—the impressive résumés of their accomplishments. Have you fallen into the same trap? If the members of your family were questioned privately, would they describe you as somebody motivated by authentic love? Or as someone driven by accomplishments, activities, and projects?

Second, do you demonstrate your love? Does it show through the ways you treat others? It is difficult for many of us to show our love to others, especially when we have been burned in the past when we expressed our love without reservation. Love is risky—especially the quality of love described in 1 Corinthians 13. Even though it may require us to lay it all on the line, we should strive for the kind of self-sacrificial, other-centered love that reflects the character of God. Review the positive aspects and negative contrasts of love in 1 Corinthians 13:4-7, then ask yourself, "How well do I measure up to this standard?" Use these verses to identify and admit the unloving areas in your life and begin to correct them by the power of the Holy Spirit. Ask Him to enable you to change each of these specific long-standing habits.

Third, does your love fade in and out? Is it fickle—hot and cold? Even though loving isn't safe or easy, it must be unconditional and consistent. Does your love fluctuate because you depend on the responses of others? Is it really *agapē* love? Or have you been operating in your marriage, family, church, or ministry at the level of *philia* love? (See the feature "The Three Loves," p. 191.) Think about how you respond to others when they act in unloving ways toward you. Do you have opportunities in your life to minister with unconditional grace and mercy toward the unlovely? Or do you reserve your love for those who "deserve" it?

Finally, does love come to the surface of your life more than any other virtue? In Paul's description of the fruit of the Spirit, love comes first (Gal. 5:22). James says the "royal law" is to "love your neighbor as yourself" (Jas. 2:8). Paul writes elsewhere that love "is the fulfillment of the law" (Rom. 13:10). If those around you were to identify one virtue to describe you, would it be love? Or would they see the great zeal and conviction with which you hold and defend the articles of the Christian faith? Would they say you are a person who has become preoccupied with the return of Christ, living in great hope and anticipation? Would they characterize you as somebody dedicated to the work of the ministry? All of these things are good—even great—but without unconditional love expressed through specific, hands-on demonstrations of grace, mercy, and charity toward others, "the greatest of these" Christian virtues is diminished.

The ability to love can come only from love's divine Source. So as we try to bridge the loveless canyon in our hearts, let's recall afresh the great love God has shown us through the Lord Jesus. Let's depend on the inner working of His Holy Spirit to produce in us a genuine and consistent *agapē* love for others.

# An Answer to Charismatic Confusion

## 1 CORINTHIANS 14:1-40

**NASB**

1 Pursue love, yet desire earnestly
spiritual *gifts*, but especially that you
may prophesy. 2 For one who speaks
in a tongue does not speak to men
but to God; for no one [a]understands,

**NLT**

1 Let love be your highest goal! But
you should also desire the special
abilities the Spirit gives—especially
the ability to prophesy. 2 For if you
have the ability to speak in tongues,*
you will be talking only to God, since
people won't be able to understand
you. You will be speaking by the

but [b]in *his* spirit he speaks mysteries.
3 But one who prophesies speaks to
men for edification and exhortation
and consolation. 4 One who speaks
in a tongue edifies himself; but one
who prophesies edifies the church.
5 Now I wish that you all spoke in
tongues, but *even* more that you
would prophesy; and greater is
one who prophesies than one who
speaks in tongues, unless he inter-
prets, so that the church may receive
edifying.
6 But now, brethren, if I come
to you speaking in tongues, what
will I profit you unless I speak to
you either by way of revelation or
of knowledge or of prophecy or of
teaching? 7 Yet *even* lifeless things,
either flute or harp, in producing a
sound, if they do not produce a dis-
tinction in the tones, how will it be
known what is played on the flute or
on the harp? 8 For if the [a]bugle pro-
duces an indistinct sound, who will
prepare himself for battle? 9 So also
you, unless you utter by the tongue
speech that is clear, how will it be
known what is spoken? For you will
be speaking into the air. 10 There are,
perhaps, a great many kinds of [a]lan-
guages in the world, and no *kind* is
without meaning. 11 If then I do not
know the meaning of the language, I
will be to the one who speaks a [a]bar-
barian, and the one who speaks will
be a [a]barbarian [b]to me. 12 So also you,
since you are zealous of [a]spiritual
*gifts*, seek to abound for the edifica-
tion of the church.
13 Therefore let one who speaks in
a tongue pray that he may interpret.
14 For if I pray in a tongue, my spirit
prays, but my mind is unfruitful.

power of the Spirit,* but it will all
be mysterious. 3 But one who proph-
esies strengthens others, encourages
them, and comforts them. 4 A person
who speaks in tongues is strength-
ened personally, but one who speaks
a word of prophecy strengthens the
entire church.
5 I wish you could all speak in
tongues, but even more I wish you
could all prophesy. For prophecy is
greater than speaking in tongues,
unless someone interprets what you
are saying so that the whole church
will be strengthened.
6 Dear brothers and sisters,* if I
should come to you speaking in an
unknown language,* how would
that help you? But if I bring you a
revelation or some special knowl-
edge or prophecy or teaching, that
will be helpful. 7 Even lifeless instru-
ments like the flute or the harp must
play the notes clearly, or no one will
recognize the melody. 8 And if the bu-
gler doesn't sound a clear call, how
will the soldiers know they are being
called to battle?
9 It's the same for you. If you speak
to people in words they don't under-
stand, how will they know what you
are saying? You might as well be
talking into empty space.
10 There are many different lan-
guages in the world, and every lan-
guage has meaning. 11 But if I don't
understand a language, I will be a
foreigner to someone who speaks it,
and the one who speaks it will be a
foreigner to me. 12 And the same is
true for you. Since you are so eager
to have the special abilities the Spirit
gives, seek those that will strengthen
the whole church.
13 So anyone who speaks in
tongues should pray also for the abil-
ity to interpret what has been said.
14 For if I pray in tongues, my spirit is
praying, but I don't understand what
I am saying.

**NASB**

15 What is *the outcome* then? I will pray with the spirit and I will pray with the mind also; I will sing with the spirit and I will sing with the mind also. 16 Otherwise if you bless [a]in the spirit *only,* how will the one who fills the place of the [b]ungifted say the "Amen" at your giving of thanks, since he does not know what you are saying? 17 For you are giving thanks well enough, but the other person is not edified. 18 I thank God, I speak in tongues more than you all; 19 however, in the church I desire to speak five words with my mind so that I may instruct others also, rather than ten thousand words in a tongue.

20 Brethren, do not be children in your thinking; yet in evil be infants, but in your thinking be mature. 21 In the Law it is written, "BY MEN OF STRANGE TONGUES AND BY THE LIPS OF STRANGERS I WILL SPEAK TO THIS PEOPLE, AND EVEN SO THEY WILL NOT LISTEN TO ME," says the Lord. 22 So then tongues are for a sign, not to those who believe but to unbelievers; but prophecy *is for a sign,* not to unbelievers but to those who believe. 23 Therefore if the whole church assembles together and all speak in tongues, and [a]ungifted men or unbelievers enter, will they not say that you are mad? 24 But if all prophesy, and an unbeliever or an [a]ungifted man enters, he is convicted by all, he is called to account by all; 25 the secrets of his heart are

**NLT**

15 Well then, what shall I do? I will pray in the spirit,* and I will also pray in words I understand. I will sing in the spirit, and I will also sing in words I understand. 16 For if you praise God only in the spirit, how can those who don't understand you praise God along with you? How can they join you in giving thanks when they don't understand what you are saying? 17 You will be giving thanks very well, but it won't strengthen the people who hear you.

18 I thank God that I speak in tongues more than any of you. 19 But in a church meeting I would rather speak five understandable words to help others than ten thousand words in an unknown language.

20 Dear brothers and sisters, don't be childish in your understanding of these things. Be innocent as babies when it comes to evil, but be mature in understanding matters of this kind. 21 It is written in the Scriptures*:

"I will speak to my own people
through strange languages
and through the lips of
foreigners.
But even then, they will not listen
to me,"*
says the LORD.

22 So you see that speaking in tongues is a sign, not for believers, but for unbelievers. Prophecy, however, is for the benefit of believers, not unbelievers. 23 Even so, if unbelievers or people who don't understand these things come into your church meeting and hear everyone speaking in an unknown language, they will think you are crazy. 24 But if all of you are prophesying, and unbelievers or people who don't understand these things come into your meeting, they will be convicted of sin and judged by what you say. 25 As they listen, their secret thoughts

disclosed; and so he will fall on his
face and worship God, declaring that
God is certainly among you.
26 What is *the outcome* then, breth-
ren? When you assemble, each one
has a psalm, has a teaching, has a
revelation, has a tongue, has an in-
terpretation. Let all things be done
for edification. 27 If anyone speaks
in a tongue, *it should be* by two or at
the most three, and *each* in turn, and
one must interpret; 28 but if there is
no interpreter, he must keep silent
in the church; and let him speak to
himself and to God. 29 Let two or three
prophets speak, and let the others
pass judgment. 30 But if a revelation
is made to another who is seated,
the first one must keep silent. 31 For
you can all prophesy one by one, so
that all may learn and all may be ex-
horted; 32 and the spirits of prophets
are subject to prophets; 33 for God is
not *a God* of confusion but of [a]peace,
as in all the churches of the saints.
34 The women are to keep silent
in the churches; for they are not
permitted to speak, but are to sub-
ject themselves, just as the Law also
says. 35 If they desire to learn any-
thing, let them ask their own hus-
bands at home; for it is [a]improper
for a woman to speak in church.
36 [a]Was it from you that the word of
God *first* went forth? Or has it come
to you only?
37 If anyone thinks he is a prophet
or spiritual, let him recognize
that the things which I write to
you are the Lord's commandment.

will be exposed, and they will fall to
their knees and worship God, declar-
ing, "God is truly here among you."
26 Well, my brothers and sisters,
let's summarize. When you meet
together, one will sing, another will
teach, another will tell some special
revelation God has given, one will
speak in tongues, and another will
interpret what is said. But every-
thing that is done must strengthen
all of you.
27 No more than two or three
should speak in tongues. They must
speak one at a time, and someone
must interpret what they say. 28 But if
no one is present who can interpret,
they must be silent in your church
meeting and speak in tongues to God
privately.
29 Let two or three people proph-
esy, and let the others evaluate what
is said. 30 But if someone is proph-
esying and another person receives
a revelation from the Lord, the one
who is speaking must stop. 31 In this
way, all who prophesy will have a
turn to speak, one after the other, so
that everyone will learn and be en-
couraged. 32 Remember that people
who prophesy are in control of their
spirit and can take turns. 33 For God
is not a God of disorder but of peace,
as in all the meetings of God's holy
people.*
34 Women should be silent during
the church meetings. It is not proper
for them to speak. They should be
submissive, just as the law says. 35 If
they have any questions, they should
ask their husbands at home, for it
is improper for women to speak in
church meetings.*
36 Or do you think God's word orig-
inated with you Corinthians? Are you
the only ones to whom it was given?
37 If you claim to be a prophet or
think you are spiritual, you should
recognize that what I am saying is
a command from the Lord himself.

**NASB**

38 But if anyone does not recognize
*this,* he [a]is not recognized.
39 Therefore, my brethren, desire
earnestly to prophesy, and do not
forbid to speak in tongues. 40 But all
things must be done properly and in
an orderly manner.

**14:2** [a]Lit *hears* [b]Or *by the Spirit* **14:8** [a]Lit *trumpet* **14:10** [a]Lit *voices* **14:11** [a]Or *foreigner* [b]Or *in my estimation* **14:12** [a]Lit *spirits* **14:16** [a]Or *with the* [b]I.e. unversed in spiritual gifts **14:23** [a]V 16, note 2 **14:24** [a]V 16, note 2 **14:33** [a]Or *peace. As in all...saints, let* **14:35** [a]Or *disgraceful* **14:36** [a]Lit *Or was* **14:38** [a]Two early mss read *is not to be recognized*

**NLT**

38 But if you do not recognize this,
you yourself will not be recognized.*
39 So, my dear brothers and sisters,
be eager to prophesy, and don't for-
bid speaking in tongues. 40 But be
sure that everything is done properly
and in order.

**14:2a** Or *in unknown languages;* also in 14:4, 5, 13, 14, 18, 22, 26, 27, 28, 39. **14:2b** Or *speaking in your spirit.* **14:6a** Greek *brothers;* also in 14:20, 26, 39. **14:6b** Or *in tongues;* also in 14:19, 23. **14:15** Or *in the Spirit;* also in 14:15b, 16. **14:21a** Greek *in the law.* **14:21b** Isa 28:11-12. **14:33** The phrase *as in all the meetings of God's holy people* could instead be joined to the beginning of 14:34. **14:35** Some manuscripts place verses 34-35 after 14:40. **14:38** Some manuscripts read *If you are ignorant of this, stay in your ignorance.*

It was six men of Indostan
To learning much inclined,
Who went to see the Elephant
(Though all of them were blind),
That each by observation
Might satisfy his mind.[21]

So begins the familiar poem by nineteenth-century poet John Godfrey Saxe titled, "The Blind Men and the Elephant," a humorous retelling of an ancient Hindu folk tale. In this story, six blind men, having never heard of an elephant before, approach the massive creature at different points, examine their small part of the beast, and then draw their conclusions about the animal based on their limited observation.

The first blind man falls against the animal's broad and sturdy side, concluding that the elephant is like a wall. The second, feeling the smooth, sharp tusk, determines that the elephant is like a spear. The third, grasping the squirming trunk, pictures an animal much like a snake. The fourth blind man, feeling around a massive, rough-skinned leg, deduces that the elephant actually resembles a tree. The fifth, examining the elephant's floppy ear, compares the animal to a waving fan. The sixth blind man, seizing the creature's swinging tail, concludes that the elephant is like a rope.

The poem concludes this comical portrayal of their failed investigations with these words:

And so these men of Indostan
Disputed loud and long,
Each in his own opinion
Exceeding stiff and strong,
Though each was partly in the right,
And all were in the wrong![22]

As we prepare to wade through Paul's argument concerning the proper function of spiritual gifts—and especially the question of the gift of tongues—we need to understand its individual parts in light of the whole. This is always true of our interpretation of Scripture, but it becomes especially vital when we tackle a controversial issue for which numerous voices dispute "loud and long," all holding their opinions "exceeding stiff and strong."

Some commentators on Scripture avoid the controversy by simply ignoring the "elephant in the room." Paul, however, spilled much ink sorting through the Corinthian problem of charismatic confusion, so we need to address the issues he raised with honesty, objectivity, fairness, and balance.

Sincerely seeking the truth, Christians today ask questions like:

- How important is the gift of speaking in tongues?
- Should we strive to speak in tongues?
- Does the gift of tongues belong in our churches?
- Is it really a spiritual gift, or simply an ecstatic emotional high?

Curious and confused, the church at Corinth plied Paul with similar questions almost two thousand years ago. In 1 Corinthians 14, Paul provides several helpful principles and guidelines on the value and role of the gift of speaking in tongues in the first century. My goal is to understand the parts in light of the whole, so we will quickly walk through all forty verses in one broad sweep. This way we can avoid the common error of taking individual verses out of context and wrongly concluding that our "elephant" is actually a snake, a spear, or a rope.

Before plunging into the details of this passage, let me make two brief introductory remarks to help us consider the whole picture. First, we're studying 1 Corinthians 14, not tongues. We need to let Paul's words put this issue into the proper perspective. Whole books can be (and have been) written trying to untangle this knotty topic of tongues,[23] but this book isn't one of them.

Second, the main subject of 1 Corinthians 12–14 is spiritual gifts as a whole; it is not restricted to the single subject of speaking in tongues. Paul emphasizes the gift of tongues in 1 Corinthians 14 not because of its special importance among the spiritual gifts, but because the Corinthians had taken it to improper extremes. Knowing that the Corinthians had been abusing this gift in particular, Paul spends time on this subject not to exalt it, but to show its relative unimportance in relation to other gifts.[24]

With this proper perspective on the proverbial "elephant in the room," let's begin working our way through these verses carefully and cautiously, understanding what Paul wrote, not what we wish he had written.

## — 14:1-19 —

Gently transitioning from his eloquent chapter on love, Paul applies the standard of selfless, other-centered *agapē* [26] love to the Corinthians' extreme and erroneous practice of spiritual gifts. If anything in the church is meant to reflect deference for one another, it is spiritual gifts. Yet the very things that had been given to promote edification, mutual support, and unity in the church had become a point of major contention. This is why Paul narrows the full weight of 1 Corinthians 13 into a sharp, pointed command: "Pursue love" (14:1).

The verb "to pursue" indicates an all-out, go-for-broke chase, as police might pursue a most-wanted criminal or a hunter might track down the prey. With the die-hard pursuit of self-sacrificial love, we should see a proper prioritizing of those activities that most directly and quickly achieve that goal. This is why Paul says that among the spiritual gifts that are properly desired, the gift of prophecy should be held as paramount above all others (14:1).

We tend to think of prophecy as predicting the future, but prophecy is not always predictive. True prophecy, however, is always a direct word from God. Before the Scriptures were complete, God's inspired, authoritative message was communicated to the early church through the lips of recognized prophets. Authentic prophets had to have "a message from God in the form of special revelation, . . . guidance regarding its declaration so that it would be given forth accurately, and the message itself had to have the authority of God."[25]

The prophet was much needed in the first century because the New Testament was not yet complete. So the prophets, together with the apostles, formed the foundational ministries of the church of the first generation (Eph. 2:20). Today the authoritative, prophetic teachings of

## XCURSUS: ARE THERE APOSTLES AND PROPHETS TODAY?

### 1 CORINTHIANS 14:3

Occasionally, I come across preachers or teachers who claim to be "apostles" or "prophets." Most often they use those titles in their most general senses. Missionaries may use the term *apostle* as "one who is sent" or preachers may use *prophet* as either "one who proclaims a message" or "one who stands alone and firm," as most of the ancient prophets did. Aside from being confused about the Bible's own definitions of these terms, such "apostles" and "prophets" are harmless. On occasion, however, we find a self-styled "apostle" or "prophet" who claims to be the same kind of apostle or prophet we see in the New Testament, upon which the church itself is built (Eph. 2:20). That is, this person claims to have precisely the same kind of authority as Peter, Paul, or John—authority to provide inspired, authoritative, and direct messages from God Himself.

Is this possible? Can there be genuine apostles and prophets today?

When we submit our understanding to the Word of God and the testimony of the early church, it becomes clear that the answer is no. The foundational offices of apostles and prophets were only for the first-century church period. According to Scripture, "God has appointed in the church, first apostles, second prophets" (1 Cor. 12:28), indicating first in sequence as the foundational offices of the church. Also, Paul noted that the marks of an authentic apostle included having "seen Jesus our Lord" (9:1). In 1 Corinthians 15:7, when Paul lists the eyewitnesses of the resurrected Jesus, he indicates that Christ appeared to James and "then to all the apostles," he himself being "last of all," who, having seen Christ as the last apostle, was "untimely born" (15:8).

Another essential sign of "a true apostle" was the ability to perform authenticating "signs and wonders and miracles" (2 Cor. 12:12). This function of signs and wonders as confirming the original apostles' message is discussed in Hebrews 2:3-4, where the author writes, "After it [the gospel] was at the first spoken through the Lord, it was confirmed to us by those who heard, God also testifying with them, both by signs and wonders and by various miracles and by gifts of the Holy Spirit according to His own will." Likewise, Mark 16:20 agrees that the disciples of the Lord "went out and preached everywhere, while the Lord worked with them, and confirmed the word by the signs that followed."[26] The miraculous gift of speaking in tongues would have been included in this category of sign gifts intended to authenticate the unique ministry of the Spirit in the apostolic and prophetic age.

Is it possible that God continued the foundational apostolic ministry beyond the first century? Wouldn't it make sense for God to continue calling apostles and prophets, confirming His message with signs and wonders, and broadening the foundation of the church in future generations? Interestingly, when we turn to the earliest generation of Christians after the original apostles and prophets, we see that those original disciples of the apostles and prophets referred to those offices as foundational ministries that had ceased.[27] This is especially important when we consider how the early church determined whether a particular Christian writing should be regarded as Scripture. The mid-second-century Muratorian Canon wisely rejected the inspiration of a book entitled *Shepherd of Hermas* based on the fact that it was written *after* the time of apostles and prophets:

*(continued on next page)*

"It cannot be read publicly to the people in church either among the Prophets *whose number is complete*, or among the Apostles, *for it is after their time*."[28]

So, both the Bible and the records of the earliest church after the apostles demonstrate that the New Testament apostles and prophets were a fixed number in the first generation of the church. Their teachings concerning the crucified and risen Lord, as well as their writings, were foundational for the church. When their lives on earth came to an end, so did their offices. Today their doctrines are preserved in Scripture and taught by their living disciples—the evangelists, pastors, and teachers (Eph. 4:11). Therefore, it is safe to say that no one can legitimately claim to be an authoritative apostle or authentic prophet in the church today. It would also make sense, then, that the signs, wonders, and miracles that had been given to confirm the unique authority of apostles and prophets would have also come to an end at the close of the apostolic age. This would have included prophesying and speaking in tongues.

the apostles and prophets are preserved for every believer and every church through their writings contained in the Bible, making the need for living apostles and prophets unnecessary. So, when Paul elevates the teaching of the prophets in 1 Corinthians 14, the parallel in our modern church is the faithful proclamation of Scripture by the church's preachers and teachers.

As Paul tries to steer the wayward Corinthians away from their narrow obsession with the miracle of speaking in tongues, he first argues that prophecy is superior to tongues for both believers (1 Cor. 14:1-19) and for unbelievers (14:20-25). He gives three reasons for his statement regarding the superiority and priority of the gift of prophecy over the gift of tongues.

First, *speaking in tongues without interpretation does not edify the church, but prophecy does* (14:2-4). When we read Paul's words without the whole context, we can easily forget that Paul is not prescribing proper behaviors, but describing the Corinthians' improper attitudes and actions in order to correct them. Paul refers to the hypothetical person who is engaged in speaking in a tongue that is not understood by anybody—not even by the speaker (14:2). In such a case the only one who understands is God. The prepositional phrase "in his spirit" reflects one Greek word, *pneumati* (from *pneuma* [4151]), meaning "in/by spirit" that, in fact, lacks the pronoun "his." It therefore may mean "in the spirit realm," as opposed to the physical, audible realm (see 1 Pet. 3:18; Rev. 1:10), emphasizing the fact that the one speaking in a tongue is understood only by God, not others. Or it could simply mean "by [means of] the Holy Spirit" (1 Pet. 1:12).

In contrast to speaking in tongues, which is not understood by people in the church, prophesying is addressed to those who can understand the message (1 Cor. 14:3). With this understanding comes "exhortation and consolation," which leads to "edification"—"building up"—(*oikodomē* [3619]). Paul passes judgment against the one who improperly exercises the gift of tongues for selfish reasons: "One who speaks in a tongue edifies himself; but one who prophesies edifies the church" (14:4). Some have read this as suggesting that speaking in tongues is a gift for self-edification, while prophecy is for corporate edification. It rather seems, however, that Paul is correcting an error of some in the church in Corinth who were using the gift of tongues selfishly rather than selflessly—seeking to build themselves up through pride or arrogance rather than seeking to exercise the gift in a way that builds others up. Thus, we might paraphrase 1 Corinthians 14:4 this way: "The one who insists on speaking in a tongue in church without interpretation is selfishly trying to edify himself, but the one who prophesies is properly edifying the church." Considering that all spiritual gifts are given "for the common good," including tongues (12:7, 10), Paul must mean in 1 Corinthians 14:4 that speaking in tongues for the purpose of self-edification is an illegitimate abuse of the gift.

Second, *speaking in tongues does not benefit the hearer without an interpreter, but prophecy benefits everyone* (14:5-15). Again Paul stresses the purpose of spiritual gifts as "edification" of the church. The only way for the miraculous utterance of unknown languages to have its intended benefit for the body is for the words to be interpreted. Though Paul would wish that everybody could experience the miraculous enablement to speak the "mighty deeds of God" in an unknown language (Acts 2:11), without interpretation for those who do not understand the language, the church will not be edified. Therefore, without interpretation, prophecy is a far greater and more beneficial gift than speaking in tongues (1 Cor. 14:5).

To illustrate the importance of interpretation for the proper use of tongues in the church, Paul uses three analogies: musical instruments, the battle cry of the bugle, and language itself (14:7-9). If notes played on the flute and harp are not distinguished by tone, pitch, and proper rhythm, they are only noises, not music—like the cacophony of sounds one hears as an orchestra tunes up prior to a performance (14:7). If the bugler just blows random notes, troops won't know whether to attack or retreat (14:8). Language must be clear and distinct for a message to be understood (14:9). Without people present who understand the language—or without a miraculous ability to interpret the language—the meaning of the utterances will not be communicated, and the church will not be edified (14:10-12).

The only solution to this unacceptable practice into which the Corinthians had fallen was to pray for the interpretation of the tongue (14:13), because although real words were being spoken mysteriously by the power of the Spirit, not even the speaker of the words understood them (14:14). Such a scenario fails to abide by Paul's repeated exhortation throughout this passage and the entire letter of 1 Corinthians: "seek to abound for the edification of the church" (14:12).

Third, *speaking in tongues without an interpreter does not instruct the assembly, but prophecy does* (14:16-19). Some have taken Paul's words contrasting praying "with the spirit" and praying "with the mind" (14:15) as two different practices—praying in tongues and normal prayer. It seems more likely, however, that Paul is talking about a single practice of spirit-enabled prayer in a person's known language. That is, Paul is saying, "Because the person speaking in tongues doesn't understand the meaning, it is better to pray in your normal language (with the mind)—relying on the power of the Holy Spirit—and in Jesus' name (in the Spirit), rather than simply praying only by the power of the spirit without the mind." This idea of praying at the same time with the mind and the spirit suggests that for Paul all heartfelt, sincere, humble prayer is "spiritual," not just the kind that comes by a miraculous enabling of the Spirit to speak in other languages. Intelligible prayers, blessings, and thanksgivings are understood not just by God, but also by the speaker and those who are present (14:16-17).

Though Paul admits that he speaks in tongues more than everybody else (14:18), he sets himself up as an example of how to keep the practice of this gift in proper perspective. He says, "In the church I desire to speak five words with my mind so that I may instruct others also, rather than ten thousand words in a tongue" (14:19). Paul is saying that normal, spirit-filled proclamation of the truth in simple language everybody can understand is hundreds of times more desirable than speaking in tongues.

## — 14:20-25 —

Not only is prophecy a better teaching tool for believers, it is more helpful for unbelievers and church visitors, too. Paul moves from the relatively weak benefit of tongues for edifying believers (14:1-19) to the inferior use of tongues for the benefit of unbelievers (14:20-25).

Paul begins by exhorting the Corinthians to grow up, to be mature in their thinking about speaking in tongues (14:20). Here he transitions from describing the Corinthians' self-centered, incomplete, and ultimately unacceptable practice of tongues to describing the real, God-ordained purpose of tongues in the early church. To do so, he reflects on the words of the prophet Isaiah, paraphrasing from Isaiah 28:11-12. There Isaiah warned unbelieving Israel that God's judgment was approaching. One sign of the coming judgment was that the foreign tongues of the Assyrians would perk up their ears—Israel would know that they had been unfaithful to God's covenant as foreigners began to tread upon the land promised to Israel.

This fits perfectly with the Pentecost account in Acts 2:1-13, where the foreign languages uttered by the apostles were a sign to some of Jerusalem's unbelieving Jews. Because they had rejected Jesus as their Messiah and were rejecting the apostles' own proclamation of Christ's resurrection, the tongues of foreign people in the land of Israel were sending a double message to those unbelieving Jews present: Unless they repented and accepted Jesus as their Messiah, God would send the blessing of the gospel to the nations, and judgment would come to the nation of Israel. Paul argues in 1 Corinthians 14:20-22 that the gift of tongues continues to function "for a sign" to unbelieving Jews that their rejection of the Messiah was a critical error, and that they could expect only judgment as a result.

How was the miracle of tongues a sign for unbelieving Jews? Imagine this scene. You are a faithful Jew living in Corinth. You hear of the commotion caused by one apostle named Paul and his subsequent followers—how they had led astray a number of once-faithful Jews and many God-fearing Gentiles. This band of Christians had convinced numerous people that some peasant carpenter from Nazareth was actually the Messiah, even though he had been crucified as a criminal by the Roman government. Not only were they claiming Jesus was the Messiah, but they said He had risen from the dead and sent His chosen apostles throughout the world to preach salvation not only for the Jews but also for uncircumcised Gentiles. The story couldn't get more preposterous to your pious Jewish ears. Because of the pitch of controversy, however, you decide to sneak into their assembly and see for yourself what kinds of blasphemies these charlatans are confessing. As you enter and hear the Gentile believers praying, you suddenly hear your own Hebrew tongue being spoken perfectly by Gentiles who couldn't possibly have known your language. They're speaking about the magnificent works of God through Jesus Christ, the risen Lord. Now you have proof that God indeed is among this group of Gentiles, which doesn't bode well for the local synagogue that has officially marked them as heretics. Now you have a decision to make: join the Christians and embrace Jesus as your Messiah, or stay true to the synagogue in the face of the miraculous proof of God's presence in the church.

So, Paul teaches that the gift of tongues in Corinth was the same sign-gift of speaking in tongues seen throughout the book of Acts, where God was giving a sign to the Jews that He was turning his blessing away from Israel to the Gentiles.[29] This sign should have been taken as a warning that if Israel did not repent and accept Jesus as their Messiah, judgment would come. Thus, speaking in tongues—even the tongues used in Corinth—was meant to be a sign to unbelieving Jews that the Spirit was truly present among Gentile Christians, a sign that harkened back to the warning of judgment in Isaiah 28:11-12 and beckoned His people to repent. When judgment finally came upon the nation of Israel (about AD 70) in the form of the Roman siege and destruction of Jerusalem, that purpose of the sign of speaking in tongues would have expired. The gift of prophecy, however, was given to edify the body of Christ (1 Cor. 14:22). Both of these—prophecy and tongues—would have eventually become obsolete toward the end of the first-century period of the apostles.

Paul continues to compare and contrast the most directly edifying gift, prophecy, with the least body-building gift, tongues (14:23-25). Imagine the scene: Someone stands up and speaks words unintelligible to the vast majority—if not all—of those in the assembly. Then another. And another. No interpretation is given. Instead, those who speak in the unknown languages accomplish only one thing: They stand out in the crowd. An unbeliever or visitor, completely unfamiliar with the miracle of tongues, hears nothing but gibberish. He leaves the church in confusion, concluding that the people are crazy.

In contrast, prophecy not only instructs believers, but it also convicts unbelievers because they can actually understand the words in their own language. This understanding begins a process involving conviction, disclosure, worship, and finally acknowledgement of God's presence (14:24-25). This applies equally to today's unbeliever who hears the preaching of God's Word from the pulpit during a Sunday service.

## — 14:26-35 —

Having contrasted the least gift (tongues) with the greatest (prophecy), Paul then draws some vital practical conclusions intended to solve the charismatic crisis in Corinth. He returns to the principle of mutual edification—each person bringing something to contribute in the assembly that will be beneficial to the whole body. If tongues are practiced in the church, they must be accompanied by a public interpretation, so that all things will be done "for edification" (14:26).

Paul's comment tells us something of the way the early church worshiped. In the first-century church, worship appears to have been spontaneous, but orderly. They didn't have a completed Bible, but they had competent and gifted preachers and teachers, apostles and prophets. As the Spirit swept through the church, He gifted each person to contribute something for the common good: psalms, lessons, revelations, interpreted tongues—a variety of gifts given for the good of the whole body.

Because unbelieving Jews were still being called upon to repent, embrace Jesus as Messiah, and avoid the looming judgment and destruction of Jerusalem (which ultimately occurred in AD 70), the miraculous sign of speaking in tongues was still in full operation in Corinth. Paul knew, however, that this charismatic experience had gotten out of control, so he wisely advised the church concerning the orderly practice of the gift in the assembly. First, Paul explains that tongues should never be spoken by more than three people during a worship service—and never by more than one person at a time (14:27). Second, tongues may be practiced in public worship only if there is an interpreter—either somebody who happens to know the language spoken or somebody miraculously gifted to understand and interpret the message. If this qualification cannot be met, then the tongues-speaker must keep silent in the church (14:27-28). Again, the principle of corporate edification must govern everything we do in our worship services.

Yet speaking in tongues was not the only element of the church's assembly that needed to be properly ordered. The same principle of "two or three" also related to the practice of prophesying. This was to be done in order, so that the leaders of the churches could discern whether these were the genuine utterances of prophets or the dangerous declarations of false teachers (14:29). Because God is not a God of confusion, but of order (14:33), prophets must speak in turn, demonstrating the kind of dignity, solemnity, and seriousness expected of the work of God (14:30-32). Neither tongues nor prophecy should produce confusion and chaos. Contrary to how some practice the gifts today, authentic gifts of the Holy Spirit are marked by self-control (14:32)—one of the fruits of the Spirit (Gal. 5:23). In light of this principle, David Prior contrasts the biblical picture of the proper use of spiritual gifts with the chaotic phenomenon we often hear about today:

> The person with the gift can choose either to use it or not to use it. . . . For this reason it is very misleading to use such language as "ecstasy" . . . to describe any of the Spirit's gifts, but particularly speaking in tongues. Such terminology re-introduces pagan concepts and experiences into the arena of God's operations. His Spirit does not override the wills and minds of human beings.[30]

In furthering his discussion of orderly and appropriate conduct in public worship, Paul provides instruction concerning the authoritative proclamation of the prophetic word with regard to women. We must read Paul's instructions in 1 Corinthians 14:34-35 in light of several facts about the early church: First, men and women are created as equal heirs to the promises of salvation (Gal. 3:28). Second, women had significant ministry roles in the early church (Rom. 16:1-7). Third, the early church also had prophetesses who obviously engaged in the prophetic ministry (Acts 21:9). Fourth, women were permitted to pray and prophesy under the proper authority of their husbands (1 Cor. 11:5). Fifth, for His own purposes God has appointed men to serve in the authoritative role of elders—those primarily responsible for leading, teaching, and preaching (1 Tim. 3:1-7; 5:17). Sixth, women were not to "teach or exercise authority over a man," but to remain quiet during the time of public address (1 Tim. 2:12). This prohibition from speaking does not apply to all public address in church, but to what we might today call the "pulpit ministry"—the official function of a preaching pastor.

Taken together, it appears best to read Paul's strong language instructing women to "keep silent in the churches" (1 Cor. 14:34) as referring to official speaking in the capacity of the teaching and preaching elders (or "pastors"). What appears to be in view, given the context, is a role of dialogue and discussion that would take place among the plurality of elders, likely among those given the authority to "pass judgment" among the leadership (14:29). Though women could pray and prophesy, only the ordained male elders as the leaders of the church were to teach and preach from an authoritative position.

To our modern ears, Paul's words that limit women from functioning in elder or pastor roles may sound out-of-date or chauvinistic. In light of the Jewish culture from which the church originally emerged, however, we see that Paul's words are actually quite liberating. In Jewish culture, women were not allowed to learn the Law at all. Both teaching *and* learning the Scriptures were the privilege of men only. Yet Paul clearly challenges this position without abandoning the principle of male headship among the leadership of the church. He notes: "And if they desire to learn anything, let them ask their own husbands at home" (14:35).

## — 14:36-40 —

Like many edgy, trendy, and flashy churches today, the Corinthians appear to have viewed themselves as pacesetters, those who flippantly threw off order, tradition, and conventions—even those established by Christ and the apostles. Claiming to have a higher spirituality than all others, and likely appealing to the authority of their own so-called prophetic gifts, the Corinthians created a "do-it-yourself" form of Christian worship characterized by disorder, division, and chaos.

Paul responds to their elitist and innovative spirit with a bite of sarcasm: "Was it from you that the word of God first went forth? Or has it come to you only?" (14:36). Clearly, the answer was "no." Paul saw fit to put the Corinthians in their place. They were no more important than any of the other churches planted by Paul and the rest of the apostles. Like all the other churches throughout the world, they were subject to the same orthodoxy and order.

Many in Corinth had claimed to be "a prophet or spiritual," believing that this meant they were freed from the principles and procedures regulated by the apostles. Paul notes, however, that a mark of authentic prophets and the truly spiritual is their recognition of apostolic authority (14:37). If the Corinthians ignored the fact that his apostolic teaching was from the Lord, they, in turn, would be ignored (14:38). This gentle threat indicates a severing of official recognition, essentially a disavowing of one's Christian character and authority.

After giving this warning, Paul provides one final comparison between prophesying and speaking in tongues. Because of the beneficial and immediate edification that can come through prophesying, the Corinthians were to "desire earnestly to prophesy" (14:39). This did not mean speaking in tongues was ruled out, however, provided that it was interpreted for the sake of edification (14:26). Yet Paul's primary concern was that "all things be done properly and in an orderly manner" (14:40).

A worship service should be a beautiful, meaningful, and edifying experience for all. It should be open to the appropriate contributions of all, under the oversight of properly ordained leadership, and all of this without a trace of disorder, chaos, or confusion. Most of all, all things must be done with one goal in mind: the mutual edification of the body of Christ.

## APPLICATION: 1 CORINTHIANS 14:1-40

### Prophecy and Tongues Today?

I've never been one to fight with fellow believers over nonessentials of the faith. I do have positions on disputed doctrines like the order of end-times events and the meaning of Genesis 1. And I have preferences regarding less-central practices like the right observance of baptism and the Lord's Supper and appropriate worship music. But I would never condemn believers with different views or split churches over these and other noncentral matters. This is especially true in the case of spiritual gifts. I have seen churches ripped apart over these issues. The saddest thing about this is that spiritual gifts were given to the church for the purpose of building it up, not tearing it down!

But are the gifts of prophecy and speaking in tongues available today? I've already hinted at my own answer to this question in the comments on 1 Corinthians 14, but let me state it more clearly before we ask how we should respond to these practices in many churches today.

Back in Paul's day, the New Testament had not been completed. Apostles and prophets with unique abilities to hear and convey revelations from God had been given to the church as its historical foundation. During that period, God's word came through such men and women—apostles, prophets, and prophetesses. The means by which these special revelations came were visions, dreams, prophesying, and speaking in tongues. And in that apostolic and prophetic era, the authenticity and authority of these men and women were confirmed by miracles. Remember, any charlatan or demoniac could put on a show and make wild claims. But God made sure to confirm His message in ways that ruled out the possibility of deception.

By the end of the first century, numerous churches had been planted by the apostles and built up by the prophets. These foundational teachers left behind the New Testament Scriptures, which continued to serve as the church's doctrinal and practical foundation. This is why we hold to *sola Scriptura*—"Scripture alone" is the final authority in all matters of faith and practice. With this firm foundation in place, revelatory gifts like prophecy and tongues would no longer be needed (see 13:8-10). While God could certainly do miraculous things in the church throughout history, first-century revelations would have faded with the twilight of the apostles and prophets and the arrival of the New Testament.

So what about prophecies and tongues today? Many believe they are genuinely new revelations from God's Spirit. If so, they would necessarily be of the same authority as Scripture, and our belief in *sola Scriptura* would be just as threatened as it was when the pope claimed to have equal authority with the Bible. Others say prophecies and tongues are not additional revelations, but merely reassertions of what the Bible already teaches—more like applications rather than revelations. But then why would they even be necessary? This would threaten the doctrine of the sufficiency of Scripture.

A former charismatic pastor wrestled with these questions and came to the following conclusion:

> The inescapable dilemma is this: if the mystery of Christ has been fully revealed, then prophetic revelations can add nothing to it. If, however, tongues and prophecy are confined to the boundaries of canonical Scripture (as many assert), then they are not, properly speaking, revelations—they are repetitions and as such are superfluous. Furthermore, since these gifts functioned to confirm the giving of new revelation, then their purpose has been entirely fulfilled.[31]

So, what do we do if we believe we have the gift of tongues today? Or what do we say to others who claim to have this special gift? Let me give us two important reminders to help us evaluate these experiences.

First, *any authentic gift of the Spirit must conform to the Bible's prescription for its use*. Without dispute, every gift of the Spirit—whether the gift of helps or the gift of healing—was given for building up the church, not puffing up the one with the gift (14:12). The edification of the church is to result in unity and love, not disunity and conflict (Eph. 4:11-16). If a person's practice of a spiritual gift does not build up the church, does not lead to unity, and does not promote love, then we have ample reason to doubt that such a gift is the work of the Spirit of God.

Second, *we don't all need to agree on the issue of spiritual gifts*. Some believe God regularly heals today in response to prayers. Others believe healings are rare. Some believe God can speak through visions and dreams, even to unbelievers on the mission field. Others believe these experiences were limited to the first century. Some believe speaking in tongues today is a valuable prayer language. Others think it passed away in the first century. Nevertheless, Christians can still enjoy unity and fellowship over the essentials of the faith without agreeing on all the details of disputed issues. All true Christians embrace core doctrines like the Trinity, the deity and humanity of Christ, His atoning death and miraculous resurrection, and salvation by grace alone through faith alone in Christ alone. Sometimes, in the midst of controversial issues, we all need to step back, take a deep breath, and remind ourselves that we are all united around vital doctrines that mark us as true Christians. We don't need to see eye-to-eye on every nonessential matter.

# CONCERNING DEATH AND RESURRECTION (1 CORINTHIANS 15:1-58)

Since the earliest days of the apostles, two categories of errors have weaseled their way into the Christian faith: errors that challenge orthodoxy (right belief) and errors that challenge orthopraxy (right practice). Though both of these serious errors must be sternly resisted, there is a clear distinction in severity between these two. The following chart compares errors of orthopraxy and errors of orthodoxy.

| ERRORS OF ORTHODOXY | ERRORS OF ORTHOPRAXY |
|---|---|
| Failure to believe the central doctrines of the Christian faith. | Failure to live up to the standards of Christian virtue. |
| An error that marks a person as a false brother. | An error that occurs within a community of true believers. |
| Persistence in errors of orthodoxy *clearly* indicates lack of salvation. | Persistence in errors of orthopraxy *might* indicate a lack of salvation. |
| Thankfully, a rare occurrence among churches that preach the truth. | Unfortunately, a common problem, even among churches that preach the truth. |
| Destructive to a church's health, potentially deadly to its life as an authentic local church. | Damaging to Christian witness, a church's effectiveness, and believers' growth. |
| **Correct Response** | **Correct Response** |
| Conversion to Christ and saving faith in the essential truths of the gospel. | Repentance from sin and consecration to right living by the power of the Holy Spirit. |

So far in his first letter to the Corinthians, Paul has primarily addressed the church's errors of *orthopraxy*. They had failed to live up to the Christian virtues of love, unity, peace, morality, and humility that should have characterized growing, Spirit-filled believers. At times, the heinousness of moral failure may have led Paul to question the genuineness of a few of the believers' conversions (5:11-13; 6:9-10); yet as a whole, Paul regarded the people in the church at Corinth to be genuine Christians struggling with immaturity and carnality (1:4-9; 6:11).

In light of the challenges to orthopraxy in Corinth, 1 Corinthians 13 can be regarded as the "practical pinnacle" of the treatise. In 1 Corinthians 15, however, Paul makes a sudden transition from serious issues of orthopraxy to a severe issue of *orthodoxy*, making this chapter the theological summit of Paul's grand letter. He begins with a reiteration of that which is "of first importance"—the message of the gospel of the person and work of Jesus Christ (15:1-11). From this center and source of the Christian faith—the atoning death and life-giving resurrection of Jesus Christ—Paul details the doctrine of our own future resurrection at the return of Christ (15:12-58).

## KEY TERMS IN 1 CORINTHIANS 15:1-58

***anastasis* (ἀνάστασις)** [386] "resurrection," "rising up"
In the ancient world, the vast majority of people believed in some kind of conscious existence after death—either in heaven, hell, or some other uncertain place. Jews and Christians were unique in their expectation of a physical, bodily resurrection at the final judgment, in which the righteous would be rewarded in their restored but glorified bodies while the wicked would be punished in their resurrection bodies. In the Bible, ultimate salvation involves more than "life after death." It includes *anastasis*—resurrected physical life *after* "life after death."

***euangelion* (εὐαγγέλιον)** [2098] "good news, gospel"
The English term "gospel" comes from the Middle English compound "good-spell," where "spell" means "tale." The gospel is therefore the "good story." The Greek term *euangelion* described the favorable report of a messenger from the battlefield or the official proclamation that an heir to the king had been born. The good news that Paul proclaimed concerned Jesus Christ's death for sin and His resurrection as well as salvation by grace alone through faith alone in Christ alone. Paul's brief "review" of the gospel essentials in 1 Corinthians 15:1-5 is regarded by scholars as the *sedes doctrinae*, or "seat of doctrine," for the gospel. Here Paul intended to define the gospel for his readers. In clear, simple terms, 1 Corinthians 15:3-4 answers the question, "What is the gospel?"

# The Most Important Point of All

## 1 CORINTHIANS 15:1-11

**NASB**

1 Now I make known to you, brethren, the gospel which I preached to you, which also you received, in which also you stand, 2 by which also you are saved, if you hold fast [a]the word which I preached to you, unless you believed in vain.

3 For I delivered to you [a]as of first importance what I also received, that Christ died for our sins according to the Scriptures, 4 and that He was buried, and that He was raised on the third day according to the Scriptures, 5 and that He appeared to Cephas, then to the twelve. 6 After that He appeared to more than five hundred brethren at one time, most of whom remain until now, but some have fallen asleep; 7 then He appeared to [a]James, then to all the apostles; 8 and last of all, as [a]to one untimely born, He appeared to me also. 9 For I am the least of the apostles, [a]and not fit to be called an apostle, because I persecuted the church of God. 10 But by the grace of God I am what I am, and His grace toward me did not prove vain; but I labored even more than all of them, yet not I, but the grace of God with me. 11 Whether then *it was* I or they, so we preach and so you believed

**15:2** [a]Lit *to what word I* **15:3** [a]Lit *among the first* **15:7** [a]Or *Jacob* **15:8** [a]Lit *to an untimely birth* **15:9** [a]Lit *who am*

**NLT**

1 Let me now remind you, dear brothers and sisters,* of the Good News I preached to you before. You welcomed it then, and you still stand firm in it. 2 It is this Good News that saves you if you continue to believe the message I told you—unless, of course, you believed something that was never true in the first place.*

3 I passed on to you what was most important and what had also been passed on to me. Christ died for our sins, just as the Scriptures said. 4 He was buried, and he was raised from the dead on the third day, just as the Scriptures said. 5 He was seen by Peter* and then by the Twelve. 6 After that, he was seen by more than 500 of his followers* at one time, most of whom are still alive, though some have died. 7 Then he was seen by James and later by all the apostles. 8 Last of all, as though I had been born at the wrong time, I also saw him. 9 For I am the least of all the apostles. In fact, I'm not even worthy to be called an apostle after the way I persecuted God's church.

10 But whatever I am now, it is all because God poured out his special favor on me—and not without results. For I have worked harder than any of the other apostles; yet it was not I but God who was working through me by his grace. 11 So it makes no difference whether I preach or they preach, for we all preach the same message you have already believed.

**15:1** Greek *brothers;* also in 15:31, 50, 58.
**15:2** Or *unless you never believed it in the first place.* **15:5** Greek *Cephas.* **15:6** Greek *the brothers.*

Whenever people travel to Greece for the first time, most have one major destination in mind: the famed city of Athens. To this day, the name "Athens" is synonymous with "philosophy," "culture," and "civilization." For centuries, Athens could stake its claim as the ancient crossroads of the intelligentsia. Though the world was owned and operated by Rome, the most learned men of the Empire got their philosophical concepts from a hill in the city of Athens called the Areopagus, or "Mars Hill." It was there that the greatest Greek thinkers formulated and popularized views on politics, religion, culture, and philosophy that would endure for millennia. In fact, if you travel to Athens today, you can see the timeworn stones and benches on which sat some of the world's greatest thinkers.

There Paul had both the privilege and challenge of presenting Christ to the intelligentsia of the Greek-speaking world. His preaching was characterized by unwavering truth and tactful diplomacy. Meeting them on their own soil, establishing common ground, and even quoting from their own Greek poets, Paul could engage the Greek thinkers in ways that captured their hearts and their minds, until a very specific part of the Christian truth turned them off: "Now when they heard of the resurrection of the dead, some began to sneer" (Acts 17:32). The resurrection of the dead is for many the great Continental Divide between faith and unbelief. (See "Body and Soul" on p. 98.)

Located near Athens, Corinth was greatly influenced by this Greek mind-set. Being a city that valued pleasure above learning, Corinth left the thinking to her Athenian neighbors, adopting without question their attitudes toward the resurrection of the body. The eagerness to appear "wise" by the world's standards had been a constant objective among the Corinthians (1 Cor. 1:18-25). In 1 Corinthians 15:1-11, we discover that some felt tempted to succumb to the pressure of philosophical respectability by denying one of the make-or-break doctrines of the Christian faith: the bodily resurrection (*anastasis* [386]) of Jesus Christ. Perhaps they started by reinterpreting the promise of a believer's own bodily resurrection, arguing that it was a "spiritual" resurrection rather than a "physical" rising from the dead. Yet this doctrinal error took a dangerous step toward the rejection of Christ's resurrection. When we read Paul's thorough and passionate treatment of His resurrection in 1 Corinthians 15, it is easy to surmise that a few in Corinth already were softening this philosophically offensive claim of the Christian faith, that on the third day Jesus miraculously and bodily arose from the dead. Clearly, the very heart of orthodoxy was at stake—and *it still is.*

Let me put this plainly: Christ's miraculous, bodily resurrection from the dead is not up for grabs. It never has been and it never will be. That Christ had been raised from the dead was not the controversy in Corinth. Yes, there were a few doubters—men and women who did not yet believe—who hung out among the Corinthian Christians. They may have raised their brows like Athenian sophists when Christ's resurrection was proclaimed. Paul acknowledged that such unbelievers would occasionally visit the church in Corinth (14:23-24). But the church as a whole had no problem accepting both the death *and* resurrection of Jesus.

Yet some believers in Corinth had likely capitulated to the Greek philosophers' disdain for the material body to such a degree that they were denying their own physical resurrections. They were clear on the resurrection of Jesus, but confused about the destinies of their own bodies. That should not surprise us. Even today, many Christians are quite confused about the order of our redemption and resurrection and how our bodies are involved in God's ultimate plan for salvation. Some believers have a foggy picture of what the people of God experience when they die, where they go, and what happens next. Too often people say, "When we die and go to heaven, we will finally be whole." Not so. Or they claim, "Once we escape from our earthly bodies, we will finally enjoy perfect bliss in heaven forever." Not true. Both of these ideas incorporate only half the story, failing to tell the rest of God's plan for our full redemption of both soul *and* body, immaterial *and* material, spiritual *and* physical.

To challenge the incomplete picture of the believers' redemption, Paul begins with the epicenter of all things Christian—the miraculous resurrection of Jesus Christ from the dead. The heartbeat of Christianity is the good news of Christ's atoning death and glorious resurrection. Understanding these essential gospel truths about the person and work of Jesus Christ will regulate both doctrine and practice. So Paul turns to this core of orthodoxy in order to set the Corinthians straight on the vital concern over the nature of our own resurrection bodies.

### — 15:1-5 —

The message of the gospel (*euangelion* [2098]) is both simple and profound. It can be expressed in five words—"Jesus died and rose again"—or it can be expounded in sixteen chapters (Romans 1–16). We can describe what we mean by "Jesus" (the person of Christ), we can detail the saving significance of Christ's death (the substitutionary atonement), and we can defend the historicity of the bodily resurrection of Jesus (apologetics). Even young children, however, can learn the basic content of the gospel message: "Jesus died and rose again."

Because of the Corinthians' specific problems, the apostle focuses his review of the gospel on the resurrection of Christ. As he makes the gospel known to his readers, however, he doesn't leave the other crucial issues unmentioned. For the sake of simplicity and clarity, Paul describes the *process* of passing on the gospel (1 Cor. 15:1), the *objective* of the gospel (15:2), and the *content* of the gospel (15:3-5).

Paul reminds the Corinthians of the *process* by which they had originally received the gospel message (15:1). He leads their minds back to the time that he had been personally present among them, having just arrived at Corinth from Athens, preaching Jesus Christ to them (Acts 18:1-4). The Corinthian Christians "received" this gospel, a synonym for "believing" and "accepting" (John 1:12; 1 Thes. 2:13). Not only did they receive it by faith, but they also continued to "stand" in it. Paul uses this term to indicate his confidence that the Corinthians were "standing firm" in the gospel (cf. 2 Cor. 1:24), reminding us that if there were any who had utterly rejected the essential content of the gospel at Corinth, they were only a very small minority of weeds among a vast majority of genuine plants.

The *objective* of the gospel becomes clear: "by which also you are saved" (1 Cor. 15:2). Note that Paul doesn't refer to their salvation as a past event, as he does in Ephesians 2:8—"By grace you have been saved through faith." Nor does he use the future aspect of salvation as entrance into eternal reward after the Last Judgment, as in 1 Corinthians 3:15—"He himself will be saved." Rather, Paul emphasizes the present aspect of salvation by using the present tense: "you are [being] saved" (15:2). Paul refers to what we call "sanctification salvation"—an ongoing process by which believers are conformed more and more to the image of Christ by putting to death the deeds of the flesh and making alive the deeds of the Spirit (Rom. 8:12-13; Gal. 5:16). In this context, the "word" Paul preached to the Corinthians refers to the daily denial of self, taking up one's cross, and following the Lord (Luke 9:23). Paul is saying that if our practical lives are not reflecting the truth of the gospel which we accepted, then we have believed in vain—that is, to no practical result. In other words, Paul exhorts the Corinthians to *apply* their orthodoxy so as to arrive at orthopraxy—right living conformed to right belief.

Beginning in 1 Corinthians 15:3-4, Paul reminds the Corinthians of the *content* of the gospel message. Here we have, in as compact and simple language as possible, a reminder of the essence of the gospel, including two facts and two irrefutable evidences for each fact.

| **FACTS** | Christ died for our sins | | Christ rose from the dead | |
|---|---|---|---|---|
| **PROOFS** | Scriptures | Burial | Scriptures | Witnesses |

The fact that Christ died has always been undeniable. Even a skeptical critic of Christianity will acknowledge that Jesus of Nazareth died. It takes no faith to believe this irrefutable fact of history. That Christ died *for our sins*, however, is a matter of faith not directly evident in the events of Christ's death and burial. Therefore, God's special revelation of the significance of the Messiah's death must interpret the meaning of the historical fact. We find this proof in an Old Testament prophecy of the coming Messiah written about seven hundred years prior to the advent of Jesus (Isa. 53:5-9):

> But He was pierced through for our transgressions,
> He was crushed for our iniquities;
> The chastening for our well-being fell upon Him,
> And by His scourging we are healed.
> All of us like sheep have gone astray,
> Each of us has turned to his own way;
> But the LORD has caused the iniquity of us all
> To fall on Him.
>
> He was oppressed and He was afflicted,
> Yet He did not open His mouth;
> Like a lamb that is led to slaughter,
> And like a sheep that is silent before its shearers,
> So He did not open His mouth.
> By oppression and judgment He was taken away;
> And as for His generation, who considered
> That He was cut off out of the land of the living
> For the transgression of my people, to whom the stroke
> was due?
> His grave was assigned with wicked men,
> Yet He was with a rich man in His death,
> Because He had done no violence,
> Nor was there any deceit in His mouth.

Jesus' burial proved the historical fact of His death. Scripture proved the saving significance of His death as a substitutionary atonement for our sin: He died in our place so we could be eternally freed from the penalty of death.

In 1 Corinthians 15:4-5, Paul reviews the second essential tenet of the gospel: that Christ rose from the dead. Again, he presents this as a fact, verified by a long list of eyewitnesses—including Paul himself—most of whom were still alive when Paul wrote his words to the Corinthians (15:6). Yet even the resurrection of Christ had been predicted in the Old Testament. Quoting Isaiah again (53:10-12):

> But the LORD was pleased
> To crush Him,
> putting Him to grief;
> If He would render Himself as a guilt offering,
> He will see His offspring,
> He will prolong His days,
> And the good pleasure of the LORD will prosper in His hand.
> As a result of the anguish of His soul,
> He will see it and be satisfied;
> By His knowledge the Righteous One,
> My Servant, will justify the many,
> As He will bear their iniquities.
> Therefore, I will allot Him a portion with the great,
> And He will divide the booty with the strong.

That this prophecy of the Resurrection had been fulfilled by none other than Jesus of Nazareth was confirmed to Paul and hundreds of other eyewitnesses through a variety of appearances.

## — 15:5-8 —

It doesn't take faith to believe Jesus died, but to believe in the miraculous, bodily resurrection of Jesus takes great faith. People don't just come to life again after being dead for thirty-six hours! Resurrection wasn't any more believable in the first century than it is in the twenty-first century. This is why Jesus appeared repeatedly, not only to his closest disciples but also to doubters.

In the book of Acts, Luke describes the numerous encounters with the risen Christ this way: "To these [apostles] He also presented Himself alive after His suffering, by many convincing proofs, appearing to them over a period of forty days and speaking of the things concerning the kingdom of God" (Acts 1:3). Luke was no fifth-generation historian rummaging through a growing collection of rumors and legends. He was himself a personal companion of Paul and other firsthand witnesses of the life, death, and resurrection of Jesus (Luke 1:1-2). Luke emphasizes the fact that the appearances of Jesus were real. They were not just momentary glimpses out of the corners of their eyes, but prolonged visits with their Master and Lord. Rather than being subjective visions and dreams, they were real group experiences with the risen Savior—walking with Him, eating with Him, touching Him, and talking with Him.

In 1 Corinthians Paul mentions no fewer than six different episodes of Christ's appearance (15:5-8), and even this brief survey is not exhaustive:

- To Cephas (Peter)
- To the Twelve
- To more than five hundred at one time
- To James, the brother of Jesus
- To all the apostles
- To Paul himself

With both the prophetic Scriptures and the numerous eyewitnesses of the risen Lord pointing to the resurrection of the crucified Messiah, there could be no doubt in the minds of hundreds of original disciples that Jesus of Nazareth had miraculously risen from the dead. Physically—in the same body that had been crucified and buried—Jesus was both restored and glorified, His body transformed into a perfect, immortal condition, no longer susceptible to suffering and death. Fit for glory, Jesus Christ conquered death not only for Himself but also for all who would believe on Him for eternal life.

## — 15:8-11 —

In 1 Corinthians 15:8-11, Paul gets personal, telling us what the Resurrection means in his own life and adding his own unimpeachable firsthand testimony to the authenticity of the Resurrection. Yet as one "untimely born," his witness to the risen Lord was unique. The description refers to a child born too early—a "premature birth."[1]

In using this imagery to describe himself, Paul contrasts his background to that of the other apostles—the infants who had been chosen, handpicked, trained, and developed at the feet of Jesus. When they were born into apostleship, they were ideal examples of the kind of apostles Christ wanted to raise. Then "Paul the preemie" came along. He had been a vile, hateful persecutor of the church (15:9), nowhere near willing or ready to accept Jesus as Lord and Savior; yet, the Lord appeared to him and saved him in the very midst of his aggressively rebellious activities. From that moment on, Paul's sudden, dramatic, and otherwise inexplicable transformation from Saul the anti-Christian persecutor to Paul the go-for-broke apostle would become a testimony to the truthfulness of the resurrection of Jesus that baffles historians to this day. No reasonable explanation can be found for Paul's conversion to Christ other than the fact of the resurrection of Jesus Christ.

The reality of the Resurrection radically and permanently changed the course of Paul's life. Because he had once viciously persecuted the church, he knew that he was unfit for salvation, much less for a ministry as an apostle (15:9). Because of the great extent of his rebellion against Christ, Paul understood far more than most the miracle of God's grace (15:10). In light of his former severe antagonism toward Christians, Paul rightly attributed his calling and his ministry to the unmerited grace of God (15:10). In thankful response to this calling, Paul determined to put the grace of God to good work—not to earn or to secure his salvation, but to show his love toward the One who had rescued him.

Empowered by the miraculous grace of God, Paul kicked it into high gear as he determined to live the rest of his life in the Master's service. He points out what was by this time obvious to everybody: "I labored even more than all of them," referring to all the other eyewitnesses of the resurrected Jesus (15:10). He quickly acknowledges, however, that his missionary accomplishments did not result from his own efforts, but only because of the grace of God working through him. In light of this fact, Paul could step back and remind his readers that he and the other apostles were all part of the same team (15:11). Like a harmonious chorus, the apostles sang in unison the anthem of Christ, preaching His atoning death and life-giving resurrection. The person and work of Jesus Christ alone—not the preacher who delivers the message—is all that can save the undeserving sinner.

# APPLICATION: 1 CORINTHIANS 15:1-11

## Signs of Our Own Resurrection Life

Paul's encounter with the resurrected Savior on the road to Damascus (Acts 9:1-8) marked an irreversible turning point in his life. There the spiritually dead, depraved, condemned sinner—bent on destroying the church of Christ—was spiritually raised from the dead, forgiven of his sins, and recruited into the service of the King. Grace on parade!

Like Paul, all of us who have believed in Christ have been plucked from our rebellious, wayward paths. We may not have persecuted Christ's cause in the same way that Paul did, but we all denied the saving power of His death and the reality of His victorious resurrection in our own ways (Isa. 53:6). Just as He did with Paul, so Jesus has brought salvation even to us! As a result of His unmerited grace, God has not only given us eternal life through faith in the death and resurrection of His Son, but He has given us the presence of His Holy Spirit—the Lord and Life-giver—to put to death our sinful lifestyles and raise us in newness of life.

As we review Paul's reflection on his miraculous encounter with God's resurrection life (1 Cor. 15:9-11), we can glean at least four signs that prove we have not believed in vain, that we are daily dying to our sinful selves, and that we are being raised to a life of obedience in Christ (Rom. 6:1-11).

First, *Paul exhibited no pride* (1 Cor. 15:9). He openly admitted his unworthiness, refused to compete with his peers, and recognized his own weaknesses. What about you? Do you have an inflated view of your own significance? How important is it to you that you be noticed, commended, rewarded, and recognized for your work in the church? Reflect on the sinful lifestyle or state of rebellion from which God has saved you, and then banish pride and any spirit of entitlement from your thinking.

Second, *Paul had a genuine appreciation for grace* (15:10). Paul attributed everything valuable in his life to God's grace: "But by the grace of God I am what I am." Does your life reflect these words? Do you recognize that without Him you can do nothing? Do you attribute your successes to His grace? Equally important, do you demonstrate this grace toward others through generosity, affirmation, patience, and forgiveness?

Third, *Paul expressed a humble admission of his accomplishments* (15:10). Paul didn't deny the fact that he had accomplished much for the Lord. His record was open to all. Yet he approached this fact with genuine humility, being quick to point any admirers to the Source of his accomplishments. Do you hide your accomplishments in a show of false humility? Or do you share them but fail to point to Christ as your example and to the Spirit as your enabler?

Fourth, *Paul emphasized his honest appreciation for others* (15:11). Although Paul admitted that he had "labored even more than all of them," he never felt concerned about who got the credit. If you have not lost your competitive spirit, if you are always concerned about being number one, ask God right now to change you, to break that habit, to give you a genuine appreciation for others. Only then will you be delivered from your critical, narrow mind-set toward others and be transformed by a loving relationship with the resurrected Lord.

# Living in the Light of the Resurrection

## 1 CORINTHIANS 15:12-34

**NASB**

12 Now if Christ is preached, that He has been raised from the dead, how do some among you say that there is no resurrection of the dead? 13 But if there is no resurrection of the dead, not even Christ has been raised; 14 and if Christ has not been raised, then our preaching is vain, your faith also is vain. 15 Moreover we are even found *to be* false witnesses of God, because we testified [a]against God that He raised [b]Christ, whom He did not raise, if in fact the dead are not raised. 16 For if the dead are not raised, not even Christ has been raised; 17 and if Christ has not been raised, your faith is worthless; you are still in your sins. 18 Then those also who have fallen asleep in Christ have perished. 19 If we have hoped in

**NLT**

12 But tell me this—since we preach that Christ rose from the dead, why are some of you saying there will be no resurrection of the dead? 13 For if there is no resurrection of the dead, then Christ has not been raised either. 14 And if Christ has not been raised, then all our preaching is useless, and your faith is useless. 15 And we apostles would all be lying about God—for we have said that God raised Christ from the grave. But that can't be true if there is no resurrection of the dead. 16 And if there is no resurrection of the dead, then Christ has not been raised. 17 And if Christ has not been raised, then your faith is useless and you are still guilty of your sins. 18 In that case, all who have died believing in Christ are lost! 19 And if our hope in Christ is only

Christ in this life only, we are of all
men most to be pitied.
20 But now Christ has been raised
from the dead, the first fruits of those
who are asleep. 21 For since by a man
*came* death, by a man also *came* the
resurrection of the dead. 22 For as in
Adam all die, so also in [a]Christ all will
be made alive. 23 But each in his own
order: Christ the first fruits, after that
those who are Christ's at His com-
ing, 24 then *comes* the end, when He
hands over the kingdom to the God
and Father, when He has abolished
all rule and all authority and power.
25 For He must reign until He has put
all His enemies under His feet. 26 The
last enemy that will be abolished is
death. 27 For HE HAS PUT ALL THINGS
IN SUBJECTION UNDER HIS FEET. But
when He says, "All things are put in
subjection," it is evident that He is
excepted who put all things in sub-
jection to Him. 28 When all things are
subjected to Him, then the Son Him-
self also will be subjected to the One
who subjected all things to Him, so
that God may be all in all.
29 Otherwise, what will those do
who are baptized for the dead? If the
dead are not raised at all, why then
are they baptized for them? 30 Why
are we also in danger every hour?
31 I affirm, brethren, by the boast-
ing in you which I have in Christ
Jesus our Lord, I die daily. 32 If [a]from
human motives I fought with wild
beasts at Ephesus, what does it profit

for this life, we are more to be pitied
than anyone in the world.
20 But in fact, Christ has been
raised from the dead. He is the first of
a great harvest of all who have died.
21 So you see, just as death came
into the world through a man, now
the resurrection from the dead has
begun through another man. 22 Just
as everyone dies because we all be-
long to Adam, everyone who belongs
to Christ will be given new life. 23 But
there is an order to this resurrection:
Christ was raised as the first of the
harvest; then all who belong to Christ
will be raised when he comes back.
24 After that the end will come,
when he will turn the Kingdom over
to God the Father, having destroyed
every ruler and authority and power.
25 For Christ must reign until he
humbles all his enemies beneath his
feet. 26 And the last enemy to be de-
stroyed is death. 27 For the Scriptures
say, "God has put all things under
his authority."* (Of course, when it
says "all things are under his author-
ity," that does not include God him-
self, who gave Christ his authority.)
28 Then, when all things are under his
authority, the Son will put himself
under God's authority, so that God,
who gave his Son authority over all
things, will be utterly supreme over
everything everywhere.
29 If the dead will not be raised,
what point is there in people being
baptized for those who are dead?
Why do it unless the dead will some-
day rise again?
30 And why should we ourselves
risk our lives hour by hour? 31 For I
swear, dear brothers and sisters, that
I face death daily. This is as certain
as my pride in what Christ Jesus our
Lord has done in you. 32 And what
value was there in fighting wild
beasts—those people of Ephesus*—
if there will be no resurrection from

**NASB**

me? If the dead are not raised, LET
US EAT AND DRINK, FOR TOMORROW
WE DIE. 33 Do not be deceived: "Bad
company corrupts good morals."
34 Become sober-minded [a]as you
ought, and stop sinning; for some
have no knowledge of God. I speak
*this* to your shame.

**15:15** [a]Or *concerning* [b]I.e. the Messiah **15:22** [a]I.e. the Messiah **15:32** [a]Lit *according to man* **15:34** [a]Lit *righteously*

**NLT**

the dead? And if there is no resur-
rection, "Let's feast and drink, for
tomorrow we die!"* 33 Don't be fooled
by those who say such things, for
"bad company corrupts good char-
acter." 34 Think carefully about what
is right, and stop sinning. For to your
shame I say that some of you don't
know God at all.

**15:27** Ps 8:6. **15:32a** Greek *fighting wild beasts in Ephesus.* **15:32b** Isa 22:13.

As you doze after hitting the snooze alarm, the phone rings, forcing you to stumble out of bed in the gray predawn light. You fumble clumsily for the phone as it rings again. You pick it up, press "talk," and listen to a wavering, grief-stricken voice trying to get the words out. The news shocks you.

Suddenly, unexpectedly, the grim reaper has struck again.

Maybe this time it is a parent or grandparent, your brother or sister, or a close friend. In any case, when news of the death of a loved one reaches us, we feel stunned. Disbelief, confusion, and grief lead to lingering remorse. Wave upon wave of choking sorrows well up within us as we do our best to believe what we've heard.

Death. We've all felt its sting. But for those of us who believe in Christ, there is a soothing comfort in the midst of otherwise excruciating, unbearable pain: *the resurrection.*

The resurrection is all we have to cling to when death has snatched a loved one from our arms. The resurrection of Christ is the promise of ultimate perfection, the hope of glory, the reward of faith, the basis of eternal life. Our own resurrection is the personal expectation of a breaking dawn, the rays of the Son transforming us and our dark world with the coming of a new and glorious day. Stop and think. Without the resurrection, our lives would have no hope, no meaning. The realm of darkness would endure victoriously, and death would perpetually sit enthroned as king.

Yet the apostle Paul shines the coming glorious light of the resurrection into our present lives when he discusses the central place of Christ's miraculous resurrection. It is, in fact, the guarantee of our own eternal life and future bodily resurrection. Paul asserted these basic Christian truths in a cultural context unsympathetic toward the idea of the redemption of the human body. Some of the Corinthians had

# Waiting for Dad

## 1 CORINTHIANS 15:16-20

*I'll never forget the night I stroked the hair from my father's forehead and kissed him goodbye for the last time. At that moment, a hundred boyhood memories played around in my head.*

- *When I learned to ride a bike, he was there.*
- *When I wrestled with multiplication tables, his quick and clever wit erased the hassle.*
- *When I discovered the adventure of driving a car, he was near, encouraging me.*
- *When I got my first job (delivering newspapers), he coached me on how to increase my subscriptions and win the prize. It worked!*
- *When I mentioned a young woman I had fallen in love with, he pulled me aside and talked straight about being a responsible husband . . . loving and caring for her.*
- *When I did a hitch in the Marine Corps, the discipline I had learned from him made the transition much easier.*

*To this day, certain smells and sounds still remind me of my dad. Oyster stew. The ocean breeze. Smoke from an expensive cigar. The nostalgic whine of a harmonica. A camping lantern. Car polish. Fun songs from the thirties and forties. Freshly mowed grass. A shrill whistle from a father to his kids around supper time. And, of course, Old Spice aftershave.*

*All of those things were once trademarks of my dad's physical presence in my life. Now they are lingering reminders of his absence. He left this world like he lived in it: quietly, graciously, with dignity, without demands or harsh words or even a frown. He surrendered himself to the cursed enemy of life. Death—selfish, insatiable, vicious—but conquered and temporary.*

*I knew without a tiny thought of doubt that my father had been received with open arms into the presence of his Lord and Savior. Absent from the body, he was present with the Lord. But I also know*

(continued on next page)

*that every day of my own life on this earth brings me closer to a glorious reunion—not only with my father, but with my mother and with all those fellow believers who preceded me in death. Now I await with eager anticipation the moment when heaven's door opens and the Lord Jesus steps out, bringing with Him the souls of all those who have fallen asleep. I'm waiting for that moment of resurrection, of reunion.*

*Yes, I'm awaiting the sharp, piercing blast of the last trumpet to raise the dead, the transformation of the living into glorious, immortal bodies. I'm awaiting the worshipful strum of the harps and lyres (and, I hope, a massive pipe organ!) in the unfathomable heavenly worship. But I'm also awaiting the nostalgic whine of a harmonica held in the glorified hands of the man who left so much for me when he left this earth so many years ago.*

*I'm waiting for Dad.*

scoffed at the idea of a literal bodily resurrection. Many had embraced the Greek philosophy that the body was the perishable, contaminated, and disposable seat of all humanity's problems—not just the sin that had taken control of it, but the physical body itself (see "Body and Soul," p. 98). Because of this intrusion of philosophy, they had failed to come to terms with the Christian hope of the future bodily resurrection. So, in 1 Corinthians 15:12-34, Paul puts the Corinthians' errant opinions to death and raises in them a renewed hope for eternal life in their immortal, glorious, resurrection bodies.

## — 15:12-19 —

Having established Christ's miraculous, bodily resurrection from the dead as an essential part of the gospel message (15:1-11), Paul asks a perplexing question: "Now if Christ is preached, that He has been raised from the dead, how do some among you say that there is no resurrection of the dead?" (15:12). Note that not everybody was leaning in this direction; only "some among" the Corinthians were denying the future resurrection from the dead.

Paul skillfully argues against this minority view within the Corinthian congregation by taking the errant opinion to seven logical conclusions. With each successive point, he casts brighter light on the Corinthians' doubts about the meaning and significance of the resurrection from the dead.

First, *if the resurrection is false, then Christ Himself was not raised* (15:12-13, 16). Denying the resurrection of our bodies also requires that we deny the Lord's resurrection, for they are intimately linked (6:14). When Christ returns, "we will be like Him" (1 Jn. 3:2), for God will "transform the body of our humble state into conformity with the body of His glory" (Phil. 3:21). In fact, Christ is the "firstborn from the dead" (Col. 1:18), indicating that our resurrection is inseparably connected to Christ's. So, logically, if our own future resurrection is to be understood only metaphorically or spiritually, then we must also understand Christ's resurrection in the same way.

Second, *if the resurrection is false, our message is empty* (1 Cor. 15:14). Like dominoes, Paul's second argument joins the force of the first to topple the Corinthians' flawed theological reasoning. If resurrection itself is false, then Christ's resurrection is false, and if Christ's resurrection is false, then the message of the gospel itself is "vain" (15:14). The word "vain" comes from the Greek word *kenos* [2756], meaning "empty," "hollow," "devoid of content." Without the resurrection, the good news of Christ is no news at all. John Stott put it well: "The person and work of Christ are the rock upon which the Christian religion is built. If he is not who he said he was, and if he did not do what he said he had come to do, the foundation is undermined and the whole superstructure will collapse."[2]

Third, *if the resurrection is false, our faith is vain* (15:14). With the collapse of the objective fact of the resurrection comes the loss of the heart and soul of the gospel message itself; as a result, our faith in that message is also empty and worthless (15:14, 17). Without His resurrection, our faith will never change lives. In light of the promise of our own resurrection, our faith is strengthened by hope, hope is motivated by promise, and promise is sealed by Christ's own resurrection from the dead.

Fourth, *if the resurrection is false, we are all liars* (15:15-16). If there is no such thing as a literal resurrection from the dead, then everyone who claimed to have seen the resurrected Lord is quite obviously a liar: Paul, Peter, the apostles, James, the five hundred. Although they did not claim to have seen the risen Lord in person, one might even say that every Christian thinker and leader who has defended the faith has therefore lied—Augustine, Aquinas, Martin Luther, John Calvin, John Wesley, Charles Spurgeon, C. S. Lewis, Billy Graham. Even Christ Himself, who predicted His own resurrection and the resurrection of all of us (John 2:18-22; 5:25-29), has lied to us. All the martyrs who died believing in Christ's resurrection and hoping for their own resurrection have died for a lie.

Fifth, *if the resurrection is false, then we are lost in our sins* (1 Cor. 15:17). If Christ had remained dead in His tomb, we would still be dead in our sins. His death and resurrection provided payment of our infinite debt to God and the power of eternal life. Good news—we aren't left to ourselves to earn any part of our salvation! From beginning to end, Christ's work of death and His resurrection have provided everything we need for salvation and eternal life.

### If the Resurrection Is False . . .

Sixth, *if the resurrection is false, then the dead are lost* (15:18). If there is no resurrection, then those believers who have gone before us in death have perished. Following his overarching principle of "as with Christ, so with His body, the church," Paul argues convincingly that if Christ Himself has not been raised, but has been destined to an eternal ghostly existence without a resurrection body, then all those "in Christ" will also perish in the same way—flittering about as bodiless wisps of vapor, unable to enjoy the blessings of the new heaven and the new earth, unable to embrace their loved ones, unable to enjoy the new creation that will be fashioned for them. Yet because Christ Himself has been raised, all those "in Him" will be raised as well.

Seventh, *if the resurrection is false, then we are to be pitied* (15:19). Paul puts it bluntly: "If we have hoped in Christ in this life only, we are of all men most to be pitied," because they had sacrificed and suffered so much for the gospel and had placed all their hopes on the risen Savior. David Prior captures Paul's reasoning:

> Paul sees this attitude to Jesus as pitiable and pathetic: if there is no such thing as resurrection, much of Jesus' teaching falls to the ground and he is revealed to be a liar. Yet the Corinthian Christians had set their hope on Christ as Lord of life, death and eternity. If he was not raised from the dead, he is not Lord of anything. If life here on this earth is all there is, it makes no sense to base our hope on the groundless promises of one who made empty assertions about eternity.[3]

## — 15:20-28 —

In 1 Corinthians 15:12-19, Paul gives the tragic answer to the question, "What if there were no resurrection?" Then he does an about-face. With two words, "but now" (15:20), he shifts from the hypothetical to the factual, from the "what if" to the "what is." He writes, "But now Christ has been raised from the dead, the first fruits of those who are asleep" (15:20).

"Those who are asleep" is Paul's favorite euphemism for believers who have died. It is not our souls that sleep—once we die, our immaterial parts are absent from the body and the earthly realm and immediately taken into the presence of the Lord in a place of peace and paradise (Luke 23:43; Phil. 1:21, 23; 2 Cor. 5:6, 8; 12:4). We will be fully conscious, pleasantly content, but yet incomplete. Why? Because our bodies will be "sleeping" in the grave, awaiting resurrection. Our salvation will be complete only when both our immaterial and material parts are reunited—the long-awaited redemption of our bodies (Rom. 8:23).

The "first fruit" of our resurrection is the resurrection of Jesus Christ. William Barclay explains the background of this image from the Old Testament Law in Leviticus 23:10-11.

> When the barley was cut it was brought to the Temple. There it was threshed with soft canes so as not to bruise it. It was then parched over the fire in a perforated pan so that every grain was touched by the fire. It was then exposed to the wind so that the chaff was blown away. It was then ground in a barley mill, and the flour of it was offered to God. That was the first-fruits. And it is very significant to note that not until after that was done could the new barley be bought and sold in the shops and bread be made from the new flour. The first-fruits were a sign of the

harvest to come; and the Resurrection of Jesus was a sign of the resurrection of all believers which was to come.[4]

The outcome of Jesus' resurrection is described in 1 Corinthians 15:21-22. The death that entered the world through the sin of Adam was reversed by Christ's resurrection from the dead. All those humans who are born "in Adam" (15:22)—that is, the entire physical human race—are born in a state of mortality, destined to die. All those who are born again "in Christ," however—the spiritual family of believers incorporated into Christ by the baptism of the Holy Spirit (12:13)—will likewise follow suit in Christ's resurrection. Like a Hebrew worshiper who took his first fruits to the temple, Jesus' resurrection points to the full harvest to come—the resurrection of the saints.

The emphasis now shifts from the past to the future—from Christ's resurrection to ours (15:23). Paul explains our resurrection in relation to some upcoming end-times events. He gives few details and focuses on the ultimate destiny of believers. Paul presents a general outline of a three-stage resurrection process, with a clear order of events but no specific timetable for fulfillment.

*First stage: Christ the first fruits* (15:23). This already has occurred, when Jesus Christ rose from the dead (Matt. 28:1-20). Jesus became the firstborn from the dead (Col. 1:18; Rev. 1:5), indicating that He is the first "among many brethren" (Rom. 8:29). Since Christ's resurrection, we who believe in Him and are spiritually united to Him by the Holy Spirit are associated with His resurrection as a guarantee of our own (Eph. 1:13-14).

*Second stage: those who are Christ's* (1 Cor. 15:23). This resurrection will occur after an undefined period of time "at His coming." Those who have died believing in Him will be raised as part of the harvest that follows the first fruits. Describing this miraculous event, Paul writes in 1 Thessalonians 4:16-17: "For the Lord Himself will descend from heaven with a shout, with the voice of the archangel and with the trumpet of God, and the dead in Christ will rise first. Then we who are alive and remain will be caught up together with them in the clouds to meet the Lord in the air, and so we shall always be with the Lord."

*Third stage: the unsaved dead* (1 Cor. 15:24-27). The ultimate end to all of God's enemies, including death itself, will occur sometime after the resurrection of believers. We know that the span of time between the first and second stages of the resurrection process already has lasted nearly two thousand years. Though Paul doesn't explicitly predict here the time that will elapse between the second and third stages,

Revelation 20:4-5 tells us that there will be a reign of Christ and His resurrected saints for one thousand years on the earth. During this earthly reign, Christ will have destroyed all ungodly dominion, authority, and power. He will then put all enemies under His feet (1 Cor. 15:24-25). At the end of this thousand-year reign, death itself will be destroyed, as all unbelieving souls are raised up to face the judgment of God, and death itself will be thrown into the "lake of fire"—also known as "the second death" (Rev. 20:7-15). At that point, everything in the universe will have been submitted to the lordship of Christ, functioning under the submission of God the Father (1 Cor. 15:27-28). The transfer of the kingdom back to God the Father (15:27-28) indicates that the earthly kingdom of Christ during the thousand-year reign will come to an end, and all the redeemed will continue to live in the eternal state under the direct kingship of the Father and the Son. This will occur in what the Bible describes as the new heaven and the new earth (Rev. 21:1–22:5). Then and only then will the triune God be universally confessed, praised, worshiped, and served as "all in all" (1 Cor. 15:28)—that is, recognized by all as the sovereign Lord with supreme power in the universe.

## The Three-Stage Resurrection Process

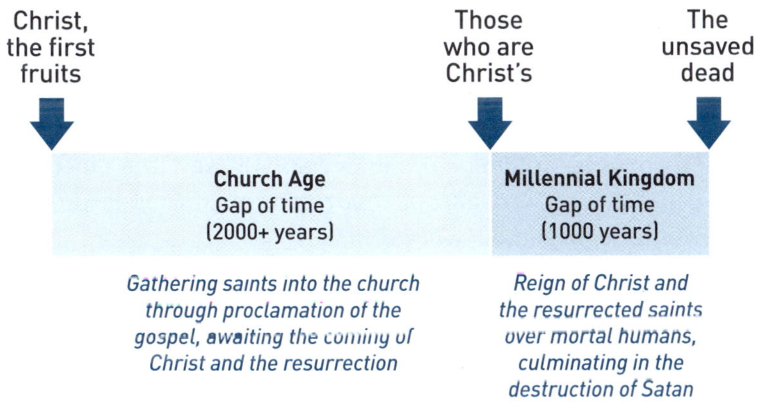


## — 15:29-34 —

Paul has thus far pointed to the past (the resurrection of Christ) and to the future (our coming resurrection). In the next few verses, he brings his readers back to the present to discuss our practical response to these central theological truths.

He begins by appealing to the Corinthians' practice of baptizing "for the dead" (15:29). If the dead are not raised, why, he asks, are people baptized for them? This passage has prompted many suggestions about what Paul is referring to by this baptism for the dead.[5] Some include:

- Baptizing living believers on behalf of loved ones or ancestors who have died
- An aberrant practice of baptism among the Corinthians that adopted pagan rituals of baptizing for the dead
- Washing corpses in preparation for burial to demonstrate the honor of the physical body, which will be resurrected
- Honorary, posthumous baptism for believers who had died prior to being baptized
- Baptism of living converts to take the place of those who had gone on ahead, in anticipation of a reunion of all believers of every age after the resurrection
- Baptism in honor of a martyr who had impacted a believer in a special way

We can rule out the practice of baptizing living believers for the benefit of loved ones or ancestors who died without being baptized (first option above). This has never been a belief or practice of orthodox Christians from the first century on. Only Mormons have opted for this position. Deciding which of the remaining explanations makes the best sense in the context, however, is not easy. Keener comments, "Probably Paul's theological shorthand here made clearer sense to the Corinthians than it does to us."[6] Regardless of the correct interpretation of this verse, Paul's main point is clear. If there were no resurrection, such a practice would be nothing more than empty liturgy. The practice of being baptized into the death *and resurrection* of Christ is absurd if we confess only death without resurrection.

Yet wholehearted belief in the resurrection has more profound, practical implications. Paul points out that belief in the resurrection ought to affect our attitudes toward this present life (15:30-31). Motivated by the rewards of immortality in our glorified, resurrected condition, believers are "in danger every hour" (15:30). In fact, they "die daily" (15:31), giving up their rights, comforts, privileges, and earthly goals. This Christian philosophy of life affects even our willingness to risk our physical lives for Christ (15:32). Weighed against the priceless gift of eternal life, the present earthly treats and treasures become corruptible trinkets of no value. As the missionary martyr Jim Elliot famously wrote in his journal, "He is no fool who gives what he cannot keep to gain that which he cannot lose."[7]

## THE WILD BEASTS OF EPHESUS?

### 1 CORINTHIANS 15:32

In 1 Corinthians 15:32, Paul mentions having "fought with wild beasts at Ephesus." This line has puzzled theologians and historians who have questioned whether Paul meant these words to be taken literally, in reference to some kind of attempt at feeding him to the animals in the arena, or to some other kind of danger he faced during his missionary journeys.

Though it is possible that Paul referred to some literal experience with wild animals known to the Corinthians, several points support a metaphorical rather than a literal interpretation of Paul's intention (see 16:8-9).

First, as a Roman citizen, Paul wouldn't have been thrown into the arena to fight with beasts, since this practice was reserved mainly for heathens, savages, or slaves. Under Roman law, noncitizens like Jesus or Peter could be executed publicly as a spectacle and even for "entertainment" purposes. Citizens of Rome, however, were granted a private, more dignified execution by beheading outside the city, which was Paul's fate.

Second, in his extensive autobiography in 2 Corinthians 11:22-33, Paul never mentions wild beasts, but instead talks about dangers from his countrymen, "dangers in the city," and "dangers among false brethren" (2 Cor. 11:26). It seems that if Paul had had a literal encounter with wild beasts, he would have mentioned it in that litany of his previous sufferings.

Third, in his record of Paul's daring missionary exploits, the meticulous chronicler, Luke, doesn't mention wild beasts in Ephesus or anywhere else. He mentions stoning, trials, ill-treatment, and suffering, but no wild beasts.

Fourth, other early Christian writers such as Ignatius of Antioch also used the imagery of wild animals metaphorically in reference to false brethren and opponents of the Christian faith.[8] This suggests that such language and imagery would have been understood as metaphorical by Paul's original audience.

Besides this revaluing of our earthly life, Paul also notes that the resurrection should affect our moral behavior. If we are living only for this life, the indulgent, hedonistic philosophy makes sense: "Let us eat and drink, for tomorrow we die" (15:32). If there is no reward in eternity, then why not live it up? Why not say yes to any and all cravings of the flesh? Why not hang out with the restless and rebellious crowd, party until dawn, and live a life of fun-filled debauchery, flushing all virtues and morals down the toilet (15:33)? If the rejection of the resurrection, eternal life, and future rewards leads to immorality and sin, then belief in the resurrection should lead to a life characterized by sober-minded judgment and holiness (15:34).

## APPLICATION: 1 CORINTHIANS 15:12-34

### Raised to Newness of Life

After arguing from an if-there-were-no-resurrection perspective, (15:12-32), Paul switches his premise and gives us three commands to obey in light of the truth of the resurrection. These three exhortations provide us with clear, direct applications for our lives today.

First, quoting a proverb from Greek literature—"Bad company corrupts good morals" (15:33)—Paul urges us to listen discerningly, distinguishing right doctrine and practice from the false opinions of the crowd and the depraved culture around us. If we become enmeshed with ungodly people, their philosophies will become our own. As we are increasingly "baptized" by the culture's values, beliefs, and practices, our own baptism into the death and resurrection of Christ will become less and less a part of our character. Are you aware of the dangers of the world's deceptive philosophies? Do you surround yourself with godly people to imitate? Consider the various worldly influences that bombard you with their deceptive messages: television, radio, Internet, schools, co-workers, advertisements, etc. Then consider the number of positive Christian influences in your life. How can you help balance these, putting to death the philosophies of the world and breathing new life into a Christian worldview?

Second, we must become sober-minded. Paul sounds a clear wake-up call: "Become sober-minded as you ought" (15:34). We must be aware of how easy it is to slip into a clueless slumber or stumble into a passive stupor. With each poisonous dose of the world's intoxicating brew of temptations, we increasingly find ourselves obsessed with its tune of "Eat, drink, and be merry, for tomorrow we shall die." We have got to wake up to the fact that our society devours personal identity, encouraging mechanistic living and groupthink philosophies. To do so, we need to renew our minds (Rom. 12:2). We need to take our thoughts captive to the obedience of Christ (2 Cor. 10:5). We need to dwell on things that are true, honorable, right, pure, lovely, reputable, excellent, and worthy of praise (Phil. 4:8). Living like that results in putting to death the deeds of the flesh and walking in newness of life (Rom. 6:4).

Third, we must simply "stop sinning" (1 Cor. 15:34). In light of our claim to know God intimately and to have a personal relationship with Him through Jesus Christ, we must listen with a sensitive heart to the voice of the indwelling Spirit who convicts us of our sin. We should keep short accounts, confessing our sin and being cleansed from all unrighteousness (1 Jn. 1:8-10; 1 Pet. 1:14-16). Nothing is as exciting, satisfying, or rewarding as turning away from the deeds of the flesh through the enabling power of the Holy Spirit (Rom. 8:13).

In short, as we await the resurrection and transformation of our mortal bodies at the return of Christ, let's deliberately put to death the attitudes and actions of the flesh. With equal vigor, let's renew our minds, modeling the resurrection life by the power of the Holy Spirit.

# Our Future Bodies
## 1 CORINTHIANS 15:35-49

NASB

35 But someone will say, "How are the
dead raised? And with what kind of
body do they come?" 36 You fool! That
which you sow does not come to life
unless it dies; 37 and that which you
sow, you do not sow the body which
is to be, but a bare grain, perhaps of
wheat or of [a]something else. 38 But
God gives it a body just as He wished,
and to each of the seeds a body of
its own. 39 All flesh is not the same
flesh, but there is one *flesh* of men,
and another flesh of beasts, and another flesh of birds, and another of
fish. 40 There are also heavenly bodies and earthly bodies, but the glory
of the heavenly is one, and the *glory*
of the earthly is another. 41 There is
one glory of the sun, and another
glory of the moon, and another glory
of the stars; for star differs from star
in glory.

NLT

35 But someone may ask, "How will
the dead be raised? What kind of
bodies will they have?" 36 What a
foolish question! When you put a
seed into the ground, it doesn't grow
into a plant unless it dies first. 37 And
what you put in the ground is not the
plant that will grow, but only a bare
seed of wheat or whatever you are
planting. 38 Then God gives it the new
body he wants it to have. A different
plant grows from each kind of seed.
39 Similarly there are different kinds
of flesh—one kind for humans, another for animals, another for birds,
and another for fish.

40 There are also bodies in the
heavens and bodies on the earth. The
glory of the heavenly bodies is different from the glory of the earthly bodies. 41 The sun has one kind of glory,
while the moon and stars each have
another kind. And even the stars differ from each other in their glory.

**NASB**

42 So also is the resurrection of the dead. It is sown [a]a perishable *body,* it is raised [b]an imperishable *body;* 43 it is sown in dishonor, it is raised in glory; it is sown in weakness, it is raised in power; 44 it is sown a natural body, it is raised a spiritual body. If there is a natural body, there is also a spiritual *body.* 45 So also it is written, "The first MAN, Adam, BECAME A LIVING SOUL." The last Adam *became* a life-giving spirit. 46 However, the spiritual is not first, but the natural; then the spiritual. 47 The first man is from the earth, [a]earthy; the second man is from heaven. 48 As is the earthy, so also are those who are earthy; and as is the heavenly, so also are those who are heavenly. 49 Just as we have borne the image of the earthy, [a]we will also bear the image of the heavenly.

**15:37** [a]Lit *some of the rest* **15:42** [a]Lit *in corruption* [b]Lit *in incorruption* **15:47** [a]Lit *made of dust* **15:49** [a]Two early mss read *let us also*

**NLT**

42 It is the same way with the resurrection of the dead. Our earthly bodies are planted in the ground when we die, but they will be raised to live forever. 43 Our bodies are buried in brokenness, but they will be raised in glory. They are buried in weakness, but they will be raised in strength. 44 They are buried as natural human bodies, but they will be raised as spiritual bodies. For just as there are natural bodies, there are also spiritual bodies.

45 The Scriptures tell us, "The first man, Adam, became a living person."* But the last Adam—that is, Christ—is a life-giving Spirit. 46 What comes first is the natural body, then the spiritual body comes later. 47 Adam, the first man, was made from the dust of the earth, while Christ, the second man, came from heaven. 48 Earthly people are like the earthly man, and heavenly people are like the heavenly man. 49 Just as we are now like the earthly man, we will someday be like* the heavenly man.

**15:45** Gen 2:7. **15:49** Some manuscripts read *let us be like.*

For some things we have more questions than answers. And then even our answers can lead to new questions. The biblical teaching concerning the resurrection of our bodies is one of those issues with more ellipses than periods, more question marks than exclamation points. For example, what about infants? Will they be resurrected as babies or as adults? What happens to the bodies of those who have been cremated, dismembered by an explosion, or lost at sea? This can lead to possibilities even more outlandish. What about transplant recipients? What happens to their new organs at the resurrection? What about those who died millennia ago, for whom not even a trace of their physical bodies remains? This can lead to the ridiculous. What happens if I'm standing on somebody's grave when the resurrection occurs? What if we are at an open-casket funeral?

If we let it happen, the chain of questions can go on endlessly.

Most of these questions stem from a lack of knowledge about the biblical doctrine of resurrection. Scripture lays before the reader in simple yet profound ways answers to the most important questions concerning life, death, and resurrection. It doesn't attempt to respond to all of our "yeah, buts," our far-fetched hypotheticals, or the speculative conjuring of inquisitive minds. And Scripture certainly doesn't go out of its way to satisfy the snide scoffing of a skeptical critic, whose goal is not understanding but ridicule.

Though Scripture provides no complete treatise on the resurrection, Paul's prolonged discourse in 1 Corinthians 15:35-49 does point us to a better understanding of the nature of the resurrection body. Although his replies don't give us all the specifics, they do give us general principles about our future bodies and a deeper understanding of the value of our present ones.

## — 15:35-41 —

Some in the church at Corinth had accepted the gospel of Jesus Christ's death and resurrection, but when it came to their own resurrection, their confidence teetered. After all, Jesus is the unique God-man; we are mere humans. Maybe the Corinthians thought He fit into a completely different category from us. Or maybe they viewed even Christ's resurrection not as an actual redemption and perfection of His physical body, but as a "rising" of His spirit from the earth to heaven. Or perhaps they redefined the nature of Christ's resurrection body to make it far more spiritual than physical. Whatever logic they followed that led them to denying and downplaying the reality of the resurrection of believers, it had gained enough of a following for Paul to address their confusion by answering two of their nagging questions: "How are the dead raised? And with what kind of body do they come?" (15:35).

Paul dismisses the first question with one sharp rebuke: "You fool!" (15:36). When it comes to the miracle of the resurrection of the dead, asking how God is able to do something reveals either a lack of understanding of or a complete absence of faith in God's omnipotence. God can do whatever He pleases! Jesus clearly taught, "With God all things are possible" (Matt. 19:26).

The second question is more reasonable, as it deals with an understandable curiosity about the nature of our resurrected bodies. Using analogies and contrasts, Paul invites his readers to look ahead with faith and hope at their own resurrection bodies. He doesn't give a comprehensive explanation of the resurrection, but he does provide sufficient detail to put the Corinthians' questions to rest.

Paul first sketches three word pictures that illustrate what our future bodies will be like. The analogies he uses are seeds, flesh, and celestial bodies.

*Seeds* (1 Cor. 15:36-38). The first analogy illustrates both the personal continuity as well as the qualitative discontinuity between the corpse that had been buried and the body that will be raised. Paul doesn't deny a relationship between the two, but the relationship is not simply a reconstitution of the dead parts of the decomposed body. The resurrection isn't simply mortal life resuscitated, nor is it a weird scene from the latest zombie movie. God forbid! The continuity between the mortal body and the resurrection body, however, is *real*, just as the relationship between a seed and the plant that sprouts from the ground is real. Yet the seed itself vanishes, absorbed into the new reality of the plant which looks completely different from the seed.

## From Seed to Plant

Yet between the seed and the plant we observe a clear continuity of species. When you plant wheat, you get wheat, not watermelons. When you plant an orange tree, you get oranges, not mangoes. The specific identity of the seed determines the identity of the plant. Likewise, between our body that dies and is buried and the body that rises from the grave, we will see continuity of personhood. We will rise from the dead in a form that is distinctly and uniquely us. Also, the diversity in which God delights will continue to mark even resurrected humanity. What a great thought! You will still be you, and I will still be me, but the resurrection will make you a *better* you and me a *better* me. To understand this continuity, we must look to Christ. Yes, the body that was buried on Friday stepped forth from the tomb on Sunday morning—but the mortal had been "swallowed up by life" (2 Cor. 5:4). Was Jesus'

resurrection body the same as the body that was buried? Yes and no. It was completely the same in personal identity, but completely different in physical quality. In other words, Jesus rose in *His* body, not in somebody else's. The body that was buried was transformed into the body that was raised, not destroyed and replaced.

*Flesh* (1 Cor. 15:39). Paul's second analogy emphasizes the distinctiveness of our future bodies. In creation, God has carefully marked each species of animal with distinctions all its own. We, too, will continue to bear the distinguishing features of our present bodies for the purpose of identity and diversity. Jesus' disciples were able to recognize their resurrected Lord (John 20:19-20). That assures us that we will be recognizable to others and also be able to identify our loved ones. The idea that we will be indefinite, luminous beings has no foundation in Scripture. Just as humans were created in Eden to live in distinct bodies unique to each of us, so in the restoration of Eden, humans will experience perfect community in diversity.

*Celestial bodies* (1 Cor. 15:40-41). In his last analogy, Paul pictures the diversity of our future bodies, noting the differences in glory among heavenly bodies—the sun, the moon, and the various stars—and the difference between them and earthly bodies. By analogy, our future bodies will be different from our present earthly bodies, and in the same way no two stars shine with the same brightness, so each of us will have a distinct "glory" of our own. All of us who one day will be glorified in our "heavenly" bodies will experience a quality and condition of life far superior in glory to what we experienced in our earthly bodies.

## — 15:42-49 —

Having drawn a general picture of our resurrection bodies through everyday analogies, Paul adds color to his sketch with a series of contrasts. Without denying personal continuity between the body that died and the body that will be raised, Paul emphasizes the qualitative discontinuity between the two (15:42-49).

| PRESENT BODY | RESURRECTION BODY |
|---|---|
| Perishable | Imperishable |
| Dishonorable | Glorious |
| Weak | Powerful |
| Natural | Spiritual |
| Earthly | Heavenly |

*Perishable versus imperishable* (15:42). Aging leaves its marks on all of us—dimming our eyes, shutting the doors of our hearing, causing our lips to tremble, turning our spirit of adventure into one of fear (Eccl. 12:1-7). Slowly but surely our bodies wear down, deteriorate, die. All humans have a "shelf life" that is less than what we wish we had. Yet when we are raised in our new bodies, we will be imperishable. Instead of winding down, we will be revving up. Instead of deteriorating, we will be thriving. Instead of dying, we will be eternally growing in our ageless relationships with God and others.

*Dishonorable versus glorious* (1 Cor. 15:43). Because of their mortal, perishable, and sinful condition, our present bodies can be deemed "dishonorable" compared to the glorious condition of our resurrection bodies. The Greek word *atimia* [819], "dishonor," indicates shame or disgrace, and may imply the detestable practices associated with the fallen human condition. Yet Paul also may have in mind the condition of the body after its death, when it is "sown" (that is, buried) in dishonor, hidden away under the earth or in a tomb because of the intolerable stench of death and the unbearable decay that ensues within days. In any case, neither moral nor physical dishonor will characterize the resurrection body, only glory and honor.

*Weak versus powerful* (15:43). Though in this life some of us are much stronger than others physically, mentally, or emotionally, all of us have weaknesses. We all are susceptible to sickness, to injury, to errors of reason, or to moral failures. Faulty, frail, and declining in strength—that's the present human condition. Yet these weaknesses will be utterly vanquished by the powerful condition of our resurrection bodies. William Barclay captures Paul's thought:

> It is nowadays fashionable to talk of man's power, but the really remarkable thing is his weakness. A draught of air or a drop of water can kill him. We are limited in this life so often simply because of the necessary limitations of the body. Time and time again our physical constitution says to our visions and our plans, "Thus far and no farther." We are so often frustrated because we are what we are. But in the life to come the limitations will be gone. Here we are compassed about with weakness; there we will be clad with power.[9]

*Natural versus spiritual* (15:44-46). The word translated "natural" is the Greek word *psychikos* [5591], which means "pertaining to being material or physical."[10] It usually implies a person dominated by the desires of the natural person rather than the promptings of the Spirit (2:14; Jas. 3:15). In this "natural" life, we must constantly restrain the desires of the flesh (Rom. 7:14-25). But in our future resurrected bodies, we will encounter no temptations—we will be dominated by the power of the Holy Spirit and therefore we will live as Christ lives—in complete holiness and submission to the Father. By calling the resurrection body "spiritual," Paul was not implying that it will be "ghostly" or "immaterial." In fact, we will be like Christ physically (1 Jn. 3:2)—able to do everything He did in His resurrected body (John 20:19-29; Luke 24:33-43). Yet we will be completely free from the weight of earthiness, the gravity of sin, and the downward pull of our fallen condition (Rev. 21:4).

As further clarification of the natural–spiritual distinction, Paul contrasts the first man, Adam, with the perfect Man, Christ (1 Cor. 15:44-49). Adam and Christ had at least two things in common: Their beginnings were both unique and sinless. But what they accomplished was altogether different. Formed from the dust of the ground, the first man, Adam, became a "living soul" when the Lord God stooped down from heaven and breathed into him the "breath of life" (15:45; Gen. 2:7). The word translated "soul" (*psychē* [5590]) shares the same root as *psychikos*, "natural," which Paul uses in 1 Corinthians 15:44 to describe our present earthly bodies. It relates not to the highest quality of being—"spirit" (*pneuma* [4151])—but to the animating principle of the physical world. Paul thus contrasts Adam's earthly origins as a "soul" with Christ's heavenly origins as a "spirit" (1 Cor. 15:45, 47).

Christ, who came from heaven, had existed eternally in the same power and glory as the Father (John 1:1-3; 17:5; Phil. 2:6). When He took on humanity at the Incarnation, Christ did not lose His heavenly status, but added full humanity to His fully divine nature (John 1:14; Phil. 2:7). So the eternal Son of God, without diminishing His deity, took on the flesh and soul of humanity, becoming exactly like us in all respects, except for our fallen sin nature (Heb. 4:15). Having taken on humanity, suffering, and dying as payment for sin, Christ was raised up to new life. This involved a glorification of the Adamic nature He had assumed—what Paul calls in shorthand becoming "a life-giving spirit" (1 Cor. 15:45). Having been raised above the highest earthly plane, Christ took His resurrected humanity into the heavenly realm, becoming the source of spiritual life to all who believe (1 Jn. 4:9; 5:11; Rom. 8:2, 10).

*Earthly versus heavenly* (1 Cor. 15:47-49). Paul's theologically dense discourse in 1 Corinthians 15:44-46 leads to his main point regarding the nature of our future resurrection bodies. We naturally born humans bear the same physical, earthly nature as Adam, including his sinful disposition (15:48-49). When we are resurrected, however, we will bear the same spiritual, heavenly nature as Christ—free from the domain of sin and able to dwell forever with Him in both the heavenly and earthly realms (15:48-49). The following chart sums up Paul's contrast between our current "in Adam" condition and our future "in Christ" destination. Though our bodies were born earthly and destined to perish, this condition is temporary. One day our spirits will be reunited with our earthly bodies, which will have been miraculously resurrected, transformed, and glorified—fit for heaven. Then our bodies will share the heavenly destination of Christ's resurrected body.

### Adam and Christ

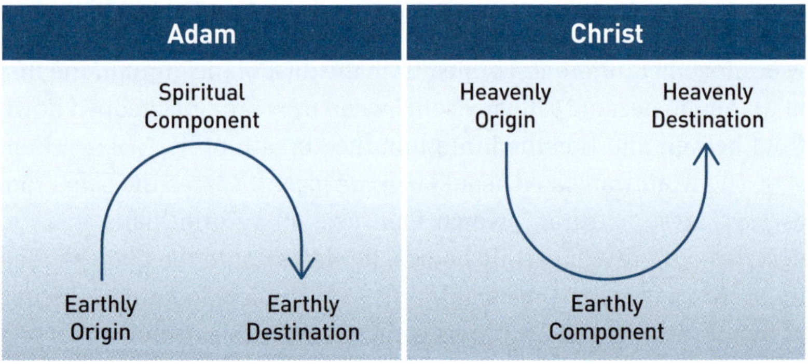


## APPLICATION: 1 CORINTHIANS 15:35-49

### Body Matters

The promise of the resurrection tells us that God has planned a glorious future for His physical creation. He has placed His seal of approval not on the sin we commit in this world, but on the physical creation itself. God originally created all things "good"—including humans (Gen. 1:31). By becoming truly human, Christ demonstrated that nothing is inherently wrong with the material world or the physical body, for He could be fully divine and fully human—spiritual *and physical*—without compromising His holiness (John 6:69). By resurrecting Christ's body from the grave, God demonstrates that not only our spiritual aspects but even our physical component is part of His plan of redemption (Rom. 8:23).

God has an interest in His physical creation and especially in our physical bodies. We were never meant to disparage or neglect our physical bodies but to love, respect, and care for them, using them to bring glory to God (Rom. 12:1; 1 Cor. 6:15, 20; Eph. 5:28).

So, in light of Paul's discussion, let's consider the value of our present bodies—something we all need to be reminded of in a world that tends either to idolize the human physique or to denigrate it as a worthless distraction. Maintaining a healthy, spiritual balance between these extremes can be difficult, but by focusing on a few key principles, we can walk a straight and wholesome path between indulgence and indifference.

First, *remember that God designed your body for you, so accept it as it is*. In accepting the body God has given you, you can embrace His sovereignty and grace in your life. You say "yes" to part of His plan for you, and you begin to value what He values (Matt. 6:25-32; Ps. 139:13-15; Luke 12:6-7). If He gives each tiny seed a body suited especially for it (1 Cor. 15:38), think about how much more skill He used in creating each one of our bodies. Of course, nobody is perfect. We all have blemishes, weaknesses, malformations, or irreversible injuries of some sort. But God uniquely created each of us, and we must use our bodies for His glory in spite of their limitations.

Second, *remember that God planned the distinctions between you and others, so don't compare yourself to someone else*. Even in our resurrected state, God will see fit to maintain diversity among human beings. So why would comparisons make sense now? Comparing occupations, grades, appearance, and giftedness will result in envy, jealousy, strife, and conflict. Instead, we should embrace our uniqueness. Relax. Be content with how He has made you. Appreciate the differences in others, too, extending grace to be different to our co-workers, spouses, pastors, teachers, children, siblings, and friends. A good principle to follow is this: Accept and enjoy yourself exactly as you are. Remember that God has made you different so you can make a difference for Him.

Third, *remember that God determined that your body would have certain limitations, so stop condemning yourself*. Since we all bear an earthly image, it is unrealistic to expect perfection. Until our resurrection, we all bear the image of the first man, Adam, in his fallen condition—finite, frail, faulty, and flawed. Therefore, unless you're toting around a resurrection body ahead of everybody else, you will never be able to live a perfect life. But don't fret! Stop condemning yourself because of nagging sin. Confess it, claim God's gracious forgiveness, and move on (1 Jn. 1:9). Continue to struggle against it, knowing that help is on the way. One day we will be removed from the domain of sin, having been reforged into the image of the sinless, victorious Christ. Then, at last, we will never sin, suffer, or die again. Until then, "press on toward the goal for the prize of the upward call of God in Christ Jesus" (Phil. 3:14).

## The Greatest Mystery Ever Told
### 1 CORINTHIANS 15:50-58

NASB

50 Now I say this, brethren, that flesh
and blood cannot inherit the king-
dom of God; nor does [a]the perishable
inherit [b]the imperishable. 51 Behold,
I tell you a mystery; we will not all
sleep, but we will all be changed,
52 in a moment, in the twinkling of
an eye, at the last trumpet; for the
trumpet will sound, and the dead
will be raised [a]imperishable, and we
will be changed. 53 For this [a]perish-
able must put on [b]the imperishable,
and this mortal must put on immor-
tality. 54 But when this [a]perishable
will have put on [b]the imperishable,
and this mortal will have put on im-
mortality, then will come about the
saying that is written, "DEATH IS
SWALLOWED UP in victory. 55 O DEATH,
WHERE IS YOUR VICTORY? O DEATH,
WHERE IS YOUR STING?" 56 The sting
of death is sin, and the power of sin
is the law; 57 but thanks be to God,
who gives us the victory through our
Lord Jesus Christ.

NLT

50 What I am saying, dear brothers
and sisters, is that our physical bod-
ies cannot inherit the Kingdom of
God. These dying bodies cannot in-
herit what will last forever.
51 But let me reveal to you a
wonderful secret. We will not all
die, but we will all be transformed!
52 It will happen in a moment, in the
blink of an eye, when the last trum-
pet is blown. For when the trumpet
sounds, those who have died will be
raised to live forever. And we who
are living will also be transformed.
53 For our dying bodies must be trans-
formed into bodies that will never
die; our mortal bodies must be trans-
formed into immortal bodies.
54 Then, when our dying bodies
have been transformed into bodies
that will never die,* this Scripture
will be fulfilled:

"Death is swallowed up in
victory.*
55 O death, where is your victory?
O death, where is your sting?*"

56 For sin is the sting that results
in death, and the law gives sin its
power. 57 But thank God! He gives us
victory over sin and death through
our Lord Jesus Christ.

[58]Therefore, my beloved brethren, be steadfast, immovable, always abounding in the work of the Lord, knowing that your toil is not *in* vain in the Lord.

**15:50** [a]Lit *corruption* [b]Lit *incorruption* **15:52** [a]Lit *incorruptible* **15:53** [a]Lit *corruptible* [b]Lit *incorruption* **15:54** [a]V 53, note 1 [b]V 53, note 2

[58]So, my dear brothers and sisters, be strong and immovable. Always work enthusiastically for the Lord, for you know that nothing you do for the Lord is ever useless.

**15:54a** Some manuscripts add *and our mortal bodies have been transformed into immortal bodies.* **15:54b** Isa 25:8. **15:55** Hos 13:14 (Greek version).

Everybody loves a mystery, but nobody likes being left in the dark. Who among us would be content watching a Sherlock Holmes mystery that cuts off ten minutes before the ending, leaving us wondering how that great detective ingeniously pieced together the seemingly indecipherable clues? Or who could tolerate a clever riddle with no solution? Who relishes problems without answers? Or a locked room without a key? Or even jokes with no punch line? We all want to be "in on the secret," kept in the loop, privy to insider information.

The Christian faith answers a lot of nagging questions about life: What is God like? Where did we come from? What's wrong with us? Will it ever get fixed? What happens after death? What must I do to be saved? At the same time, the claims of the Christian faith can lead to deeper questions: How can I be sure of my salvation? How does prayer work with an all-knowing, sovereign God? How does God raise us up from the dead? Why would He do such a thing?

In the previous passage, Paul began answering some of the Corinthians' questions regarding the doctrine of the believers' future bodily resurrection (15:35-49). He describes the nature of the resurrection body, but another nagging question remains: If all the dead in Christ are to be raised upon His return, what about those believers in Christ who have not yet died? Will they miss out on this transformation and glorification? Will they get stuck in their mortal bodies, having to die before experiencing the glories of eternal life? To this last question, Paul responds with a resounding "No." In 1 Corinthians 15:50-58 he addresses the destiny of those believers who are still living when Christ descends from heaven at His coming.

## — 15:50 —

Paul begins addressing the question of the resurrection of believers who are still alive at the return of Christ by setting forth a principle: "Flesh and blood cannot inherit the kingdom of God; nor does the perishable inherit the imperishable." This statement about flesh and blood might seem contrary to Paul's teaching earlier in this chapter that we will inherit the kingdom of heaven in new bodies. But note that Paul doesn't say, "A *body* cannot inherit the kingdom of God." We know that a body can inherit the kingdom of God, because Jesus himself ascended to heaven in a body, having been raised in bodily form (Acts 1:9). It should be remembered that when Jesus was resurrected, he did, in fact, have "flesh and bones" (Luke 24:39), that is, a real physical body, though it had become perfect and immortal. So we would misread Paul's words if we were to conclude that only immaterial spirits are fit for heaven. What then is the solution to this puzzle? Paul's parallelism helps us understand.

| | | |
|---|---|---|
| Flesh and blood cannot | inherit | the kingdom of God |
| The perishable [cannot] | inherit | the imperishable |

In his thinking, "the kingdom of God" and "the imperishable" stand in parallel to each other. The quality of the coming kingdom of God, in contrast with the present kingdom of earth, will be "imperishable." Likewise, the bodies of believers dwelling in that kingdom of God will conform to this imperishable, incorruptible quality. Paul says that in the resurrection of the dead, the body that died was "perishable," but it will be raised "imperishable" (1 Cor. 15:42). So, when Paul refers to "flesh and blood" that cannot inherit the kingdom of heaven, he is not referring to physical bodies *per se*, but to bodies that share the same fallen and physically corruptible nature of Adam.[11] By extension he is also referring to humanity's fallen, mortal, perishable condition in this world, not unlike the way this idiom is used in Hebrews 2:14. All this stands in contrast to the existence in the spirit realm (Eph. 6:12).

So Paul assures his readers that the kind of bodies we have on earth—perishable and susceptible to pain, suffering, and death—cannot inherit the kingdom of God. That kingdom will be characterized by immortality and eternal life, excluding things that deteriorate and die. But will those who are alive in their mortal, "flesh and blood" bodies at the return of Christ be kept out of the kingdom of God? Will they have to die first and then be raised? Will they be part of a lower-quality kingdom, missing out on the infinite glories of heaven? Paul answers this question with what theologians call the doctrine of the Rapture.

## — 15:51-53 —

Paul reveals the "mystery" that solves the problem of what will happen to living saints when Christ returns. Not all believers will "sleep," that is, not everybody will die physically prior to entering the kingdom of God. Yet all believers will be "changed" (15:51)—transformed from their "flesh and blood" existence into an immortal form that can dwell throughout eternity in heaven. Not all believers will enter this new condition through resurrection; those who are still alive on earth when Christ returns to raise the church from the dead will simply be transformed without ever having died. So quick will be this transformation from mortal to immortality for the living believers that it will be like the scarcely noticeable blink of an eye (15:52).

This transformation will be heralded by the resonant sound of the "last trumpet" and immediately preceded by the resurrection of dead believers in the new, imperishable bodies that Paul describes (15:35-49). In the Bible, trumpets are used for various purposes. The trumpet blast gathered the people of Israel to meet their God (Exod. 19:16-19; Isa. 27:13). It also was to herald the coming of the Day of the Lord—a time of fierce wrath and judgment on the earth (Joel 2:1). By referring to the "last trumpet," Paul looks forward to the end times, the final gathering of the rescued saints prior to the judgments of the Great Tribulation (Rev. 3:10).

This same event of the resurrection of dead saints and the transformation of the living is described in 1 Thessalonians 4:15-17.

> For this we say to you by the word of the Lord, that we who are alive and remain until the coming of the Lord, will not precede those who have fallen asleep. For the Lord Himself will descend from heaven with a shout, with the voice of the archangel and with the trumpet of God, and the dead in Christ will rise first. Then we who are alive and remain will be caught up together with them in the clouds to meet the Lord in the air, and so we shall always be with the Lord.

At that time, when those living in their perishable flesh and blood bodies will put on imperishable bodies, clothed in immortality instead of corruption (1 Cor. 15:53), then they will be caught up with the resurrected saints in the clouds. So, one way or another—either by resurrection or by transformation—the result will be the same. All believers in Christ will be changed and raptured—"caught up" in the sky to be with the Lord (1 Thes. 4:17). Then Christ will fulfill His promise recorded in

John 14:2-3: "In My Father's house are many dwelling places; if it were not so, I would have told you; for I go to prepare a place for you. If I go and prepare a place for you, I will come again and receive you to Myself, that where I am, there you may be also."

## — 15:54-58 —

Having revealed the mystery of what will happen to living believers when Christ returns, Paul immediately sounds the signal of victory over the greatest enemies of humanity: sin and death. That damnable duo of destruction currently reigns over our mortal lives of "flesh and blood." But on that day, when the trumpet sounds, God will deal a fatal blow to sin and death when our perishable, mortal bodies are transformed into imperishable, immortal bodies incapable of sin, suffering, or corruption (15:54).

Ever since the day when Adam and Eve abdicated their dominion over this world by succumbing to Satan's temptation (Gen. 1:28-30; 3:17-19), death has reigned over all humanity. Yet on that day when death itself is reversed and God's plan of cosmic redemption is put into motion (Rom. 8:18-23), death's apparent victory will be undone. Paul says that on that day death itself will be conquered, its deadly stinger finally removed, its power forever crushed (1 Cor. 15:55).[12]

After the resurrection and rapture of believers, never again will we grieve the loss of a loved one. *Never again* will we worry about terminal diseases. *Never again* will we cope with the frailties of old age. *Never again* will we plan funerals, execute wills, and worry about the loved ones we leave behind. *Never again* will we need to nurse the lingering emptiness and grief we feel when a spouse, a child, or a parent is taken from us by the enemy. On that day, death's sting will be permanently gone. What a magnificent promise!

Paul explains that death gains its authority over man through sin (1 Cor. 15:56). By the Law, sin is strengthened, as it condemns us before a holy and righteous God, reminding us that the "wages of sin is death" (Rom. 6:23). When we are raised up from the grave or transformed and caught up from this earth, the impulse to sin will be eradicated. *Never again* will we suffer as victims of robberies or violent crimes. *Never again* will people devastate families through incurable addictions. *Never again* will marriages be broken, children abused, families abandoned. *Never again* will we watch helplessly as society deteriorates around us. Instead, sin itself will be vanquished by life, immortality,

## CURSUS: IS PAUL'S "LAST TRUMPET" THE SEVENTH UMPET OF REVELATION?

### 1 CORINTHIANS 15:53

At this point I need to clarify a common misunderstanding about the "last trumpet" described by Paul in 1 Corinthians 15:51-52. He writes, "Behold, I tell you a mystery; we will not all sleep, but we will all be changed, in a moment, in the twinkling of an eye, at the last trumpet; for the trumpet will sound, and the dead will be raised imperishable, and we will be changed." Referring to the same event, Paul writes in 1 Thessalonians 4:16–17, "For the Lord Himself will descend from heaven with a shout, with the voice of the archangel and with the trumpet of God, and the dead in Christ will rise first. Then we who are alive and remain will be caught up together with them in the clouds to meet the Lord in the air, and so we shall always be with the Lord."

Some scholars equate the "last trumpet" in 1 Corinthians 15:52 and "the trumpet of God" in 1 Thessalonians 4:16 announcing the rapture of the church with the seventh trumpet of Revelation 11:15. On the surface this may seem like a reasonable assumption, given that the seventh trumpet in Revelation appears to be the last trumpet of a series. A close examination, however, reveals that these two trumpets refer to separate prophetic events.

The seventh trumpet of Revelation 11:15 clearly announces the final phase of the wrath of God during the future Tribulation, the beginning of Christ's reign, and the praises of the heavenly chorus in response to this epochal change of power. In contrast, Paul's end-times trumpet refers to

*(continued on next page)*

| 1 CORINTHIANS 15:51-52 | 1 THESSALONIANS 4:14-17 | REVELATION 11:15-18 |
|---|---|---|
| Last trumpet sounds | Christ descends from heaven | Seventh angel sounds |
| | Voice of archangel is heard | |
| | Trumpet of God sounds | |
| Dead saints raised | Dead saints raised | |
| Living saints changed | | |
| | Living saints caught up | |
| | Resurrected and raptured saints meet Christ in the air | |
| | | World kingdom becomes Christ's kingdom |
| | | God takes His power and begins to reign |
| | | God's wrath comes |
| | | Dead judged |
| | | Prophets and saints rewarded |

the bodily resurrection and the "catching up" of believing saints from the earth. When we place all these accounts side by side, we observe that the only thing these passages have in common is the mention of a trumpet. So, is it still possible that Paul's "last trumpet" and John's seventh trumpet are the same?

To answer this question, we must keep in mind that Paul wrote 1 Thessalonians around AD 50 and 1 Corinthians around AD 55. Because John had his visions and wrote Revelation around AD 96, Paul would not have been aware of the series of seven trumpet judgments recorded in the book of Revelation. So, we can confidently conclude that Paul himself was not referring to the seventh trumpet of Revelation when he mentioned the "last trumpet." But could John have been referring back to Paul's final trumpet when he mentions the angel sounding the seventh trumpet in Revelation 11:15? Had it been John's intention to make this connection, he probably would have used the term "last trumpet" to erase any doubt. Or he would have at least made a specific reference to the saints' resurrection and rapture, or to the descent of Christ—events announced by Paul's "last trumpet."

In light of this, it appears that these two trumpet blasts refer to separate prophetic events. Paul's "last trumpet" announces the resurrection, rapture, and rescue of the church from the earth prior to the beginning of the seven-year tribulation period. The seventh trumpet blast of Revelation 11 brings the series of trumpet judgments to a close, previews both the wrath and reign of Christ, and makes way for the visions leading up to the seven bowls of wrath (Rev. 12–16).

and eternal righteousness—a victory over sin and death that can come only "through our Lord Jesus Christ" (1 Cor. 15:57).

These profound promises are already enough to fuel our hope for a lifetime. That abiding hunger for a world set right will one day be satisfied with the resurrection and the world to come. But Paul concludes this discussion on our future hope not with another look forward but with a hard look inward and outward. In light of the hope of our resurrection—made sure by Christ's resurrection—we are to be "steadfast, immovable," abounding in God's work with full assurance that there will be a reward for our labors (15:58). Because all Scripture is given by God "so that the man of God may be adequate, equipped for every good work" (2 Tim. 3:17), it should come as no surprise that these prophetic truths would lead to practical applications. God didn't reveal details of the end times so we could get our prophecy charts right. He gave them so we could get our lives right.

# APPLICATION: 1 CORINTHIANS 15:50-58

## Our Response to the Mystery

Paul's teaching about our resurrection and rapture, and its implications for the Christian's victory over sin and death, leads to a practical response. It isn't just "sweet by-and-by" truth to ponder during quiet moments when we have time to theorize about the ephemeral. This is life-changing truth meant to affect the decisions we make Monday through Sunday.

Paul doesn't urge that believers set dates for the Rapture, quit their jobs, and sell their possessions to wait for the loud blast of the last trumpet. Indeed, Jesus told us that no one except the Father knows the season, day, or hour of His return (Matt. 24:36, 42; Acts 1:6-7). From the human perspective, Christ could return at any moment. Accordingly, Paul encourages believers to live in light of the Lord's imminent return, to "be steadfast, immovable, always abounding in the work of the Lord, knowing that your toil is not in vain in the Lord" (1 Cor. 15:58).

Did you catch that? In response to the doctrine of our any-moment resurrection, transformation, and catching up to be with Christ, we should remain firm in our faith, immovable in our convictions, and abounding in our Christian lives. We should live with the Lord's reward to us in view, fulfilling God's unique calling in our lives.

We can't wait until the trumpet sounds to give attention to our spiritual lives. By then it will be too late. We will have squandered countless opportunities in this life to render service to the Lord out of gratitude not only for what He has done for us, but for what He will do. Do we live as if today could be our last chance to invest time in life's most significant things? What would our daily schedules look like if we knew Christ was returning at eleven o'clock tonight? Well, the secret's out. He is coming back! We'll be transformed into immortal bodies to spend eternity with Him wherever He goes. When He does come, will He find us abounding in His work? Standing steadfast? Unable to be swayed? In short, are we living today in light of His return?

# CONCLUDING INSTRUCTIONS AND WARNINGS (1 CORINTHIANS 16:1-24)

Have you ever been on a hike deep in the wilderness? I don't mean a walk through the park or a jaunt through the local arboretum. I mean *deep*—when what you were calling the "woods" is now called a "forest," and the sun you had relied on to tell directions can be seen only occasionally peeking through a rare break in the canopy of trees above. The path you're on winds back and forth, and if you weren't following a map that insists you're getting closer to the trailhead, you'd swear you were going in circles. Birds, crickets, frogs, and owls improvise a soundtrack for your journey. You're no longer on a hike. You're on an adventure. But as you begin to approach the trailhead where rugged paths meet paved roads, and fellow explorers park their cars and don their hiking gear, the forest slowly transitions to woods. Underbrush gives way to mowed grass. Soon you can see the sky again. The birds' intense symphony turns into a charming lullaby.

Paul's letter to the Corinthians can sometimes feel like that. His original readers may have anticipated a straight journey through a pleasant valley of spiritual truths and practical principles, but instead they found themselves surrounded by controversy and strong reproof. Thankfully, the apostle Paul was a faithful guide. He wasn't trying to lead his readers deep into a jungle of issues in order to abandon them to confusion but to rescue them from their delusions and restore them to a place of peace and light.

As we emerge from the tangled forest of controversy that characterized the first fifteen chapters of 1 Corinthians, we enter a peaceful clearing. Paul's tone lightens from harsh rebuke to practical exhortations and straightforward warnings as he concludes with a few minor matters, chief of which is the proper collection for the saints (16:1-4). With some personal remarks, Paul speaks of Timothy's coming to the church in Corinth, emphasizing the value Paul placed on personal presence and face-to-face interaction in addition to his authoritative letter (16:5-12). He concludes this great epistle of strong reproofs with an exhortation to stand firm in the faith with love for the Lord and hope for His coming (16:13-24).

## KEY TERMS IN 1 CORINTHIANS 16:1-24

***logeia* (λογεία)** [3048] "collection," "voluntary contribution"
In Greek literature *logeia* is used to designate occasional contributions to a particular cause rather than regular, systematic taxes. Such contributions may sometimes be related to needs arising from crises or the support of religious orders. In Paul's two uses of the term in 1 Corinthians 16:1-2, he draws on this cultural understanding that the "collection" was a voluntary offering for the sake of the desperately needy believers in the Jerusalem church. It would be regarded as giving that is distinct from the regular giving to the needs of their own local church.

***marana tha* (μαράνα θά)** [3134] "Lord, come!"
After calling down a curse of judgment upon those who fail to love the Lord (*anathema* [331]), Paul calls down the Savior Himself with the exclamation *marana tha* (1 Cor. 16:22), "Our Lord, come!" This Aramaic phrase probably had its roots in the original Jewish church in Jerusalem. At the close of his letter, Paul called on the Lord Jesus, praying that He would come soon to act as Judge and King.

# Antidotes to the Poison of Parochialism

## 1 CORINTHIANS 16:1-12

**NASB**

1 Now concerning the collection for
the saints, as I directed the churches
of Galatia, so do you also. 2 On the
first day of every week each one of
you is to [a]put aside and save, as he
may prosper, so that no collections
be made when I come. 3 When I ar-
rive, whomever you may approve, I
will send them with letters to carry
your gift to Jerusalem; 4 and if it is

**NLT**

1 Now regarding your question about
the money being collected for God's
people in Jerusalem. You should fol-
low the same procedure I gave to the
churches in Galatia. 2 On the first day
of each week, you should each put
aside a portion of the money you
have earned. Don't wait until I get
there and then try to collect it all at
once. 3 When I come, I will write let-
ters of recommendation for the mes-
sengers you choose to deliver your
gift to Jerusalem. 4 And if it seems

NASB

fitting for me to go also, they will go with me.

5 But I will come to you after I go through Macedonia, for I am going through Macedonia; 6 and perhaps I will stay with you, or even spend the winter, so that you may send me on my way wherever I may go. 7 For I do not wish to see you now *just* in passing; for I hope to remain with you for some time, if the Lord permits. 8 But I will remain in Ephesus until Pentecost; 9 for a wide door [a]for effective *service* has opened to me, and there are many adversaries.

10 Now if Timothy comes, see that he is with you without [a]cause to be afraid, for he is doing the Lord's work, as I also am. 11 So let no one despise him. But send him on his way in peace, so that he may come to me; for I expect him with the brethren.

12 But concerning Apollos our brother, I encouraged him greatly to come to you with the brethren; and it was not at all *his* desire to come now, but he will come when he has opportunity.

**16:2** [a]Lit *put by himself* **16:9** [a]Lit *and* **16:10** [a]Lit *fear; for*

NLT

appropriate for me to go along, they can travel with me.

5 I am coming to visit you after I have been to Macedonia,* for I am planning to travel through Macedonia. 6 Perhaps I will stay awhile with you, possibly all winter, and then you can send me on my way to my next destination. 7 This time I don't want to make just a short visit and then go right on. I want to come and stay awhile, if the Lord will let me. 8 In the meantime, I will be staying here at Ephesus until the Festival of Pentecost. 9 There is a wide-open door for a great work here, although many oppose me.

10 When Timothy comes, don't intimidate him. He is doing the Lord's work, just as I am. 11 Don't let anyone treat him with contempt. Send him on his way with your blessing when he returns to me. I expect him to come with the other believers.*

12 Now about our brother Apollos—I urged him to visit you with the other believers, but he was not willing to go right now. He will see you later when he has the opportunity.

**16:5** *Macedonia* was in the northern region of Greece. **16:11** Greek *with the brothers;* also in 16:12.

It doesn't take days of around-the-clock observation to recognize that the Corinthian church suffered from acute selfishness and sectarianism. Rather than loving unconditionally even to the point of personal sacrifice, they pursued their own interests (10:24, 33; 13:5). Instead of banding together as fellow soldiers on the spiritual battlefield, they huddled in their self-designated squadrons and skirmished with each other (1:12; 3:4; 11:18).

I have seen these same conditions plague numerous churches during my life of ministry. As congregations become inwardly focused, they lose sight of their outward mission. This leads to a narrow ministry scope. The problems and concerns of that individual local church take center stage. Because nobody sees eye to eye on everything, special interests form and conflict ensues. Before you know it, hostility replaces harmony as open warfare mars that tiny island of a congregation—believer against believer over some of the most ridiculous things imaginable.

Yet the poison of parochialism can be countered with a few simple antidotes. When the members of a church begin looking up from their provincial problems to see the great needs in the world around them, they gain some perspective on their own pettiness. As the dire and urgent needs of those outside their church walls become the focus of attention rather than their own selfish concerns, they will begin to see that the church is bigger than their own congregation and that the mission transcends their own ministries.

Having chastised the Corinthians for their sectarianism, Paul begins to turn their attention from their own problems to the church beyond their borders. He reminds them of a major financial need among their brothers and sisters in Jerusalem—the grandmother congregation of all the churches (16:1-4). He then reminds them that Corinth itself is merely one small dot in a constellation of ministries among which their own apostolic founders are working. By lifting their heads out of their narrow sectarian focus, they would discover the part they could play in helping others overcome trials and hardships. In short, the Corinthians needed a dose of global awareness to cure their obsession with local problems.

## — 16:1-4 —

Before we look at the opening words of 1 Corinthians 16, we should return briefly to Paul's closing words of chapter 15. Though chapter breaks weren't part of the Greek text penned by the original writers of Scripture, the editors who later divided it at this point had good reason to do so. Paul begins with a Greek construction that indicates a moderate contrast: *peri de* [4012 + 1161], "Now concerning." He already has used the phrase several times to indicate either a complete change of topic (7:1; 8:1; 12:1) or at least a transition to a different issue within a larger topic (7:25).

Although Paul clearly moves on to a different subject—"the collection for the saints" (16:1)—his previous exhortation sets the context: "Therefore, my beloved brethren, be steadfast, immovable, always abounding in the work of the Lord, knowing that your toil is not in vain in the Lord" (15:58). The Corinthians were to thrive in doing the Lord's work, persevering in whatever they set their hearts and minds to, because their efforts would not go unnoticed by a just and all-knowing

God who will one day reward their faithfulness. Their attitudes and actions toward contributing to "the collection" (16:1) were to be no different: steadfast, immovable, always abounding.

In referring to "*the* collection for *the* saints" (16:1, italics mine), Paul has in mind not simply the regular giving to the church's normal ministry funds, but to a special collection (*logeia* [3048]) designed for a particular purpose. In the case of this collection, we know that numerous churches were involved in the project, including the various "churches of Galatia" (16:1). The money was to go to the body of believers in Jerusalem, to aid the saints who were suffering financial hardship (16:3). Because this was "above and beyond" their normal regular giving, Paul reminds them that they are to contribute to the special offering "as [each] may prosper" (16:2)—that is, according to their ability. Understandably, some could give more, some less. Finally, Paul made special arrangements for the transport of this offering to those in need (16:3-4), indicating the uniqueness of this opportunity to bless others.

In these brief verses, Paul touches on a number of important principles regarding giving—principles that will get more thoroughly fleshed out in 2 Corinthians 8–9. Let's highlight just a few of these.

First, *giving should be systematic*. Paul urges the Corinthians to set aside money for this offering each week (1 Cor. 16:2). This may refer to the weekly gathering for Sunday worship (Acts 20:7), but it also indicates thoughtful planning—setting aside the "firstfruits" of one's earnings at the beginning of the week.[1] This was not supposed to be a "spare change," last-minute offering when Paul arrived. He urges careful, conscious, and deliberate giving. This is why Paul tells them to systematically "put aside and save" (1 Cor. 16:2).

Second, *giving should be an individual matter according to one's ability*. Paul says, "every week *each one*" should support the Jerusalem relief fund (16:2, italics mine), not just the particularly wealthy or the overly sacrificial. Not just people with personal connections with the brothers and sisters in Jerusalem. *Everybody* was to get involved in giving a portion of their offering to that need far away. Yet this didn't mean that each member of the Corinthian congregation was expected to give the same amount. Instead, Paul says that each should give "as he may prosper" (16:2). The amount of their weekly wages might differ drastically, but all of them should have the same attitude toward giving: as an expression of thankfulness for whatever the amount of the Lord's blessing.

Third, *giving should be a private matter, not a public spectacle*. Paul did not want to employ marketing gimmicks, tacky fundraising stunts, or strong-arm tactics. He did not do anything that would compromise each believer's personal decision about giving. In fact, he made it a point that "no collections be made" when he arrived in Corinth (16:2). The envelope containing each believer's offering should be sealed, so to speak. Paul was particularly discreet when it came to handling the Corinthian church's pooled offering. He wanted no personal part in collecting it, counting it, or delivering it. He would, however, put his seal of approval on whomever they chose to deliver it, accompanying them himself if the gift were large enough (16:3-4).

Paul just scratches the surface on giving in this letter. His detailed treatment of money matters will come in his next letter to the Corinthian church. As we might expect from a church that seems to be hard of hearing and slow to obey, the Corinthians did not exactly heed his soft and gentle exhortation to fulfill their promise to give (2 Cor. 8–9). Nevertheless, by turning the Corinthians' attention toward the desperate needs of the church in Jerusalem and by calling on them to contribute to the cooperative efforts of other churches in the larger body of Christ, Paul seeks to correct their long-standing habit of selfishness.

## — 16:5-12 —

Having urged the Corinthians to prepare their special financial assistance prior to his arrival (1 Cor. 16:2-3), Paul smoothly transitions into a brief discussion of his anticipated itinerary. In 1 Corinthians 16:5-12, he exhibits the high value he places on personal, one-on-one discipleship. With his own anticipated visit, Timothy's on-the-ground work among them, and the hoped-for arrival of Apollos, Paul highlights the preference for personal presence as a means of authentic discipleship.

First, he shares his travel plans. He had planned to visit Macedonia first (16:5), then travel on to Corinth to visit them in person. Earlier Paul had noted that some of his opponents in Corinth had doubted he would ever show his face in the city again (4:18). Now the intention to come becomes part of his set itinerary (4:19).

Yet for Paul, the church in Corinth wasn't just a layover. He hoped to roll up his sleeves and to get involved in their lives for an extended period of time, "if the Lord permits" (16:6-7). Paul's day-to-day plans were always subject to the Lord's will, but he still exhibited a firm resolve to engage in face-to-face ministry with his spiritual children in Corinth. For the time being, however, Paul had to complete his ministry in Ephesus "until Pentecost" (16:8). A door of great opportunity had opened there, even though his ministry was fraught with opposition (16:9).

While Paul completed his work in Ephesus, he sent his close ministry associate Timothy to Corinth (16:10). He encourages his readers to accept Timothy just as they would accept him, showing proper respect and hospitality to that fellow worker in the gospel. Because of the conflicts in Corinth over Paul's apostolic authority, he had grounds to worry that Timothy's reception might be marred with awkward discomfort or even outright rejection (16:10-11). Paul therefore goes out of his way to urge them to "send him on his way in peace," that is, with the blessing of the church both spiritually and financially. Not only were they to provide for his temporal needs while he visited them in Corinth, but they were expected to provide assistance for Timothy's trip to Ephesus.

Finally, Paul mentions Apollos again—one of the Corinthians' favorite teachers from the early days of their founding (1:12). Though Paul had "greatly" urged Apollos to visit Corinth, he had declined until a more opportune moment (16:12). By mentioning this interaction with his "brother" Apollos over strategic ministry matters, Paul indicates the essential unity between Paul and Apollos. These men saw each other as ministry partners, not competitors, so their disciples should see them in the same light (3:4-6).

By recognizing that the ministry transcends their own city limits, the Corinthians would overcome their sectarianism and see themselves as one small part of a much larger global body of Christ. They would see that Paul had fruitful ministry in Ephesus; Apollos's love for the brethren extended beyond his fans in Corinth; and Timothy, relatively unknown to the Corinthians, deserved as much respect as Paul because of his labors for the gospel far and wide. Once the Corinthians could see their place in a larger worldwide church, they would be able to become partners for ministry to others rather than parasites of ministry from others.

# APPLICATION: 1 CORINTHIANS 16:1-12

## Putting Money to Work for Ministry

It has been said that money can buy us anything but happiness and take us everywhere but heaven. It is both a cause of evil, for those pursuing it with passion, and an effect of evil for those who acquire it by unlawful means. In the coffers of the wicked it can lead to great destruction, but in the hands of the righteous it can bring great good for many. In our money-crazed world, where people sit glued to the stock market report as though it were a sporting event, the importance of money can be greatly exaggerated. The truth is, there are many things in this world money simply can't buy.

- Money can't buy intelligence, just an education.
- Money can't buy wisdom, just experiences.
- Money can't buy health, just medicine.
- Money can't buy a family, just a house.
- Money can't buy friendship, just companionship.
- Money can't buy love, just sex.

That is not to say money has no role to play in life. Like air itself, nobody can live in our modern world without money. And, as Paul points out in 1 Corinthians 16:1-4, without reliable financial support, Christian ministries would peter out. Churches would close their doors. Mission fields would grow over. Bibles would not be printed. Christian organizations would be abandoned. While money can't buy the blessing of God, money itself can be a blessing—both to the giver and to the recipient.

Near the end of 1 Corinthians, Paul gently touched on the importance of financial giving. Giving is not simply for our local churches, where we see direct benefits for ourselves and our families. Rather, the kind of giving Paul describes in 1 Corinthians 16:1-4 is part of a larger context of an awareness of, and involvement in, the ministry beyond our narrow edge of the global body of Christ. The church in Corinth was called to contribute to meeting the needs of many people whom they would never meet and to show hospitality toward ministers they hardly knew (16:10-11). Neither of these contributions would result in tangible benefits for the church in Corinth itself—or for its members.

Paul makes it clear, however, that our giving should reach beyond our own churches and into the lives of believers around the world.

So, how about you? Have you unwittingly succumbed to limiting your giving to ministries that benefit only you, your family, or your church? Would Paul be pleased with your giving patterns, or would he exhort you to engage in a broader ministry beyond the walls of your church and your own immediate concerns?

One of the best ways to critically examine your giving is to review your charitable donations. Go through your checkbook, your electronic debit statements, or your bank accounts. Jesus said, "Where your treasure is, there your heart will be also" (Matt. 6:21), so take some time to evaluate where your treasure is actually going. Where do you invest your finances? What percent of your monthly income goes to necessities? What percent toward luxuries? Toward frivolities? Are you giving regularly to your local church's ministry or withholding even that? Beyond your local church, do you give to other God-honoring ministries? Carefully think through these questions and, if necessary, make some changes in your giving patterns.

Admittedly, you may not be able to see, hear, or feel the direct benefits of your giving when you choose to bless believers and ministries beyond your own horizons. But do not forget the words of the Lord Jesus: "It is more blessed to give than to receive" (Acts 20:35).

# Standing Firm to the End
## 1 CORINTHIANS 16:13-24

**NASB**

13 Be on the alert, stand firm in the
faith, act like men, be strong. 14 Let
all that you do be done in love.
15 Now I urge you, brethren (you
know the household of Stephanas, that [a]they were the first fruits
of Achaia, and that they have devoted themselves for ministry to the
saints), 16 that you also be in subjection to such men and to everyone
who helps in the work and labors. 17 I
rejoice over the [a]coming of Stephanas and Fortunatus and Achaicus,
because they have [b]supplied what

**NLT**

13 Be on guard. Stand firm in the
faith. Be courageous.* Be strong.
14 And do everything with love.
15 You know that Stephanas and
his household were the first of the harvest of believers in Greece,* and
they are spending their lives in service to God's people. I urge you, dear
brothers and sisters,* 16 to submit to
them and others like them who serve
with such devotion. 17 I am very glad
that Stephanas, Fortunatus, and Achaicus have come here. They have
been providing the help you weren't

was lacking on your part. 18 For they
have refreshed my spirit and yours.
Therefore acknowledge such men.
19 The churches of Asia greet you.
Aquila and Prisca greet you heartily
in the Lord, with the church that is in
their house. 20 All the brethren greet
you. Greet one another with a holy
kiss.
21 The greeting is in my own hand—
[a]Paul. 22 If anyone does not love the
Lord, he is to be [a]accursed. [b]Mara-
natha. 23 The grace of the Lord Jesus
be with you. 24 My love be with you all
in Christ Jesus. Amen.

**16:15** [a]Lit *it was* **16:17** [a]Or *presence* [b]Or *made up for your absence* **16:21** [a]Lit *Paul's* **16:22** [a]Gr *anathema* [b]I.e. O [our] Lord come!

here to give me. 18 They have been
a wonderful encouragement to me,
as they have been to you. You must
show your appreciation to all who
serve so well.
19 The churches here in the prov-
ince of Asia* send greetings in the
Lord, as do Aquila and Priscilla*
and all the others who gather in their
home for church meetings. 20 All the
brothers and sisters here send greet-
ings to you. Greet each other with a
sacred kiss.
21 HERE IS MY GREETING IN MY OWN
HANDWRITING—PAUL.
22 If anyone does not love the Lord,
that person is cursed. Our Lord,
come!*
23 May the grace of the Lord Jesus
be with you.
24 My love to all of you in Christ
Jesus.*

**16:13** Greek *Be men.* **16:15a** Greek *in Achaia,* the southern region of the Greek peninsula. **16:15b** Greek *brothers;* also in 16:20. **16:19a** *Asia* was a Roman province in what is now western Turkey. **16:19b** Greek *Prisca.* **16:22** From Aramaic, *Marana tha.* Some manuscripts read *Maran atha,* "Our Lord has come." **16:24** Some manuscripts add *Amen.*

I see it all the time when I fly:

- A young couple in love parting ways, wondering if their budding romance will survive the hardships of a long-distance relationship
- A soldier embracing his wife and children before boarding the plane, unsure of what his tour of duty might bring
- Grandparents heading home after a far-too-brief visit with grandchildren who live too far away for them to see frequently

I know you've witnessed scenes like these—touching, heart-wrenching, sometimes downright agonizing. Most of us have lived moments like these.

At times of parting, some people drape the experience in a shroud of somber silence, knowing that too much chatter will cheapen their final embrace and that words will fail to express the depth of their sadness. Others, however, try to get in as many last words as possible: short, succinct, desperate farewells; blessings, promises, reminders; bits of advice before their loved ones are out of sight: "Take care!" "Text me when you arrive!" "Be sure to call us!" "Send our love to Aunt Rita!" "We'll be praying for you!" "Don't forget us!"

As the apostle Paul approaches the end of his letter of "tough love," he begins to rattle off a similar series of final words as part of his emotional farewell. For all he knew, these could have been his final words to the Corinthians. Though he planned on visiting them in person (16:2-7), there were no guarantees that his plans fit God's mysterious itinerary. As he wraps up this message to a messy church, Paul presents a rapid-fire series of exhortations (16:13-20), followed by a curse and a blessing—an appropriate finale for a bittersweet letter like 1 Corinthians.

## — 16:13-20 —

Paul's seven commands to his friends in Corinth at the conclusion of this letter address two topics. First, Paul gives some general instructions about how Christians should act toward the world (16:13-14). Second, he transitions to discuss how believers should treat one another in the church (16:15-20). For a worldly-minded church such as Corinth, beset with self-centered problems affecting their peace and unity, these final principles would be quite appropriate.

Paul's commands for responding to unbelievers (16:13-14) were not merely to be memorized or written down—they were meant to be put into practice immediately and lived out continually. As we read Paul's words to the Corinthians, let's listen to them as if he were writing directly to us today.

First, "*Be on the alert*" (16:13). This phrase means to be "awake" or "watchful." It implies having discernment. Paul similarly urged the elders of Ephesus to "be on the alert" (Acts 20:31). Jesus gave this imperative several times (Matt. 24:42-43; 25:13), and Peter used it to warn his readers of the wiles of the devil: "Be of sober spirit, be on the alert" (1 Pet. 5:8). Clearly, the Bible helps us to be consistently aware of what is going on around us.

I have heard it said that the world can be divided into three categories of people:

1. The few who make things happen
2. The many who watch things happen
3. The vast majority who have no idea what's happening

Paul warns us not to be part of the ignorant masses who have their heads either in the clouds or in the sand. Rather, we are always to be aware. How aware are you of the realities of the world around you? Do you keep a keen eye on the subtle and obvious dangers, distractions, and desperate needs of the world? Or, like the vast majority who have no idea what's happening, do you fall asleep at your Christ-appointed post? *Be on the alert!*

Second, *"Stand firm in the faith"* (1 Cor. 16:13). It is one thing to hear the truth of the gospel, but quite another to receive it. The Corinthians had believed the truth of Christ's death for their sins and resurrection from the dead (15:1-4). Yet Paul takes the personal absorption of the faith to a deeper level: standing firm in it. Believers live in a twisted, turbulent world—a world inspired by Satan to snatch the faith from our grasp and delude our minds with poisonous doctrines of demons. In this kind of environment, standing firm can be a challenge. We must counter Satan's great challenges with our faith, rebuke his scoffing criticisms, resist his tantalizing doubts, and endure his alluring temptations.

Without doubt, the attacks will come. Suddenly. Unexpectedly. Aimed straight for the weakest chinks in our spiritual armor (Eph. 6:11-17). When they do, will you be able to repel Satan's assault against your faith? Or will you waver and retreat at the first volley of flaming arrows? Understand this: The time to commit to standing strong is before the great battle.

Third, *"Act like men"* (1 Cor. 16:13). No, Paul is not a sexist, trying to urge tender men to man up and get in touch with their macho side, or implying that women are too weak to resist the devil. The original Greek word means "to conduct one's self in a manly or courageous way."[2] Essentially, it means to grow up, start acting like an adult rather than like a child, push toward spiritual maturity rather than wallow in your preschool mantra of "me, me, me." Recalling that the struggle against spiritual immaturity ran deep in the Corinthian church (3:1-3), we can see that this exhortation is best understood in relation to the nonbelieving world around them. They needed to set aside their fussiness, whining, and complaining and instead progress toward maturity in Christ, but they had failed to shed their dependence on the blankies, bottles, and binkies that had soothed them in their baby Christian days. These "props" of comfort were closely connected to the secular world around them. How easy it was for them to slip back into the secular crib of their infancy rather than learn to walk on their own two feet by the grace of God and through the power of the Spirit!

What about you? Do you find yourself more "at home" with the world around you than with the family of God? Are you easily offended? Do you cling to your personal rights and privacy? Maybe it is time to grow up—to leave the nursery of the world and enter the school of higher spiritual learning.

Fourth, *"Be strong"* (16:13). Paul is not interested in physical strength for the Christians in Corinth. He could not have cared less about how they might perform in the Isthmian Games, how heavy a burden they could schlep, or whether they could hold their own in a fistfight. Rather, as he explains to the Ephesians, he wanted them "to be strengthened with power through His Spirit in the inner man" (Eph. 3:16).

The strength to obey the Lord is not connected to an Olympian physique. It comes by the power of God to the inner person—the unseen character, attitudes, affections, and passions that drive us toward the good and away from the bad. In Philippians 2:13, Paul lets us in on a secret about the inner power that transforms our outer lifestyle: "It is God who is at work in you, both to will and to work for His good pleasure." Our responsibility is to take on the world's challenges with strength, but we must do so knowing that our strength comes from the Lord, not from ourselves.

Fifth, *"Let all that you do be done in love"* (1 Cor. 16:14). The first four commands (16:13) sound like abrupt orders shouted by a platoon commander on a battlefield: Wake up! Stand firm! Be a man! Be strong! If we stopped reading there, we might think Paul was urging us to grit our teeth, square our jaws, puff out our chests, and take on the world with a militant, combative demeanor. The next imperative, however, puts everything in perspective: *Do everything in love.*

We should not forget that the brilliant "love chapter" (1 Cor. 13) is also nested amid the hard exhortations and tangled problem-solving of most of 1 Corinthians. Love is meant to hold the whole argument together. Without love, you will not be alert and discerning, but rather narrow and suspicious. If you stand firm without love, you will be an isolated fanatic, ugly in temperament and intolerant toward the lost. Without love to balance your maturity, you will be critical, judgmental, and harsh. And if you are strong yet have no love, you will lack the tenderness that will attract others to your bridled strength. Notice the one characteristic Jesus said would identify His disciples: "By this all men will know that you are My disciples, if you have love for one another" (John 13:35).

Sixth, *"Be in subjection to . . . acknowledge such men"* (1 Cor. 16:15-18). Paul now changes his focus from our responses to non-Christians to our treatment of fellow believers (16:15). Along with the change in his point of view, he also changes his tone of voice—from terse commanding to earnest pleading.

Paul introduces a man and his family who were well-known to the Corinthian Christians. Stephanas had been among the earliest converts to the faith when Paul first arrived in Corinth (1:16; 16:15). He also had visited Paul in Ephesus along with two other representatives from Corinth, Fortunatus and Achaicus (16:17).[3] Paul urges his readers to "be in subjection to such men" as Stephanas, as well as "to everyone who helps in the work and labors" (16:16). In this way, they would "acknowledge" these men (16:18). The Greek term for "acknowledge" (*epiginōskō* [1921]) means "to respect"—the kind of respect that leads to submission. Paul therefore exhorts the Corinthians to submit to the leadership of Stephanas, Fortunatus, and Achaicus out of respect for their office as leaders in the church and because of their obvious faithfulness in serving in their ministries.

Paul's words should cause each of us to reevaluate our approach to selecting church leaders. David Prior writes: "We tend to give leadership to those who have received one particular kind of education, who have a measure of articulacy and general ability to think and speak on their feet, who measure up to worldly criteria for leadership. . . . [But what Paul says] indicates that the authentic, solid leadership of a local church will come from people who give themselves to serving the saints."[4]

Once leadership is in place in a local church, church members are expected to respect and submit to that leadership. Such a concept of submission to appointed church leaders may fall on unsympathetic ears in our world of rebellion, independence, and over-the-top individuality. But Paul is not alone in his exhortation to be subject to properly appointed local church leaders. The author of Hebrews writes, "Obey your leaders and submit to them, for they keep watch over your souls as those who will give an account. Let them do this with joy and not with grief, for this would be unprofitable for you" (Heb. 13:17).

Seventh, *Greet one another with a holy kiss* (1 Cor. 16:19-20). In these two verses, Paul uses the Greek word for "welcome" or "greet" (*aspazomai* [782]) four times. These greetings reinforce the notion of the larger body of Christ that extends beyond the local church in Corinth—a fact that the self-absorbed, immature believers in Corinth may have forgotten. But the need for close fellowship within their own church ran even deeper than interchurch formalities between congregations separated by rivers, mountains, and seas. In fact, Paul had to exhort the Corinthians themselves to "greet one another"! Their own local church, marred with schisms, desperately needed to foster an environment of acceptance and forgiveness.

Even today, in our stiff, hands-off society, in which real personal relationships and life-on-life intimacy are cheapened by online networks, many of us feel afraid to literally reach out and embrace somebody. We would just as soon text them, email them, or leave a voice message. But we need to freely give and receive tangible signs of affection—the squeeze of a hand, a friendly embrace, a genuine expression of affirmation. One of the best ways to truly communicate our love to others is through personal presence and tangible contact.

## — 16:21-24 —

If you had been reading the original letter written to the church in Corinth, you would have noticed a sudden change between verses 20 and 21. At that point the penmanship changes from the neat, tidy, and stylish script of a secretary to the large, heavy scratches from Paul's own hand (see Gal. 6:11). In his own words scribbled with his own distinctive handwriting, Paul brings his long, winding letter to a close with words that first shine like sunlight, then rumble like thunder, and finally refresh like cool rain. What a fitting conclusion for an epistle filled with both high praise and profound disappointment, comforting words and scolding rebukes.

The first words from Paul's own hand are of warm greetings (1 Cor. 16:21). Though Paul had hurled some stern words at the Corinthians for their sinful behavior, he now reassures them that they are bona fide members of his family. With his very own hand he extends a "greeting" to the church in Corinth. He does not, however, leave the rabble-rousers and heretics in Corinth without a final warning. He puts his harsh condemnation in what Greek grammars call a "first class condition"—"If anyone does not love the Lord, he is to be accursed" (16:22). The grammar does not imply that Paul suspects any particular Corinthian readers of this sin; rather, it makes a general warning to anybody who might be listening in about the consequences of failing to love Christ. The word for "love" in this statement is *phileō* [5368], the love of friendship, dedication, and affection, not the unconditional, supernatural love expressed with *agapaō* [25]. Therefore, I conclude that Paul didn't expect a miraculous devotion to Christ, but a genuine affection for Him. Those whose hearts refused even this? *Anathema!*

The Greek word *anathema* was used to translate the Hebrew word *herem* [H2764] (cf. Lev. 27:28-29; Josh. 6:17-18) in the ancient Greek translation of the Old Testament. Here it means that the person who did not love the Lord was reckoned as standing under condemnation—the eternal wrath of God. It is roughly equivalent to saying "let them be damned" without making a vulgar curse. At minimum, it meant for the Corinthians that such people should be put out of the loving fellowship of the church and rejected as unbelievers. Yes, Paul wanted the Corinthians to love one another, greet one another affectionately, show their unconditional affection for the true brethren—but godly love has its limits. Christian love has no place for tolerating outright rebellion against the authentic person and work of Jesus Christ. Remember Jesus' command: "Do not give what is holy to dogs, and do not throw your pearls before swine, or they will trample them under their feet, and turn and tear you to pieces" (Matt. 7:6). The truth is, not everyone who wants our Christian attention and affection is a true brother or sister in the Lord.

After calling down the curse of God's judgment upon those who despise the Savior, Paul calls down the Savior Himself with the Aramaic phrase *marana tha* [3134] (1 Cor. 16:22), which means, "Our Lord, come!" Paul didn't translate this for his Greek-speaking readers, who knew what it meant because it had likely been used in songs and hymns that had originated in the earliest Christian communities in Aramaic-speaking Judea.[5] In the same way, we understand the Hebrew word *hallelujah* [H1984/H3050] as a universal word of joyful praise. For those who love the Lord, the coming of Christ means blessing and reward; but for those who despise him, it means judgment and cursing.

At this point in his letter, Paul has exhorted, refuted, corrected, encouraged, reminded, counseled, and rebuked. When he finally comes to his farewell, he opens his arms to give the believers in Corinth—his beloved children in the faith—two gifts that will comfort them: grace and love (16:23-24). Nothing less than the grace of the Lord Jesus Christ could heal their divisions (16:23). Nothing could encourage their hearts more than to hear that despite their shortcomings, Paul's love was with them (16:24). How those final words must have soothed sore consciences! They were accepted, faults and all, by their Savior and by their teacher.

# APPLICATION: 1 CORINTHIANS 16:13-24

## Keep Your Kisses! How about a Holy Hug?

Most of us live in a no-touch, keep-your-distance society. If we brush up against somebody, we apologize, and if a man puts his hand on a woman, he'd better be married to her! It's even true in our families. A father who embraces a son embarrasses him: "Aw, Dad, don't do that." In our culture, showing affection for one another has been reduced to a cautious pat on the back, a brisk handshake, or an awkward, one-armed, side hug.

But this "don't touch me" attitude wasn't part of the early church. Five New Testament epistles mention the "holy kiss" as an appropriate expression of love for brothers and sisters in Christ (Rom. 16:16; 1 Cor. 16:20; 2 Cor. 13:12; 1 Thes. 5:26; 1 Pet. 5:14). In the first century, this was a common form of greeting between family members as a sign of affection.[6] Applying this same gesture toward the members of one's spiritual family made sense. After all, Christians referred to one another as brothers, sisters, and children of the same heavenly Father.[7]

Like the celebration of the Lord's Supper and the "love feast," the "holy kiss" was meant to reinforce visibly the unity of the brethren. The great fourth-century preacher John Chrysostom said, "Having then knit them together by his exhortation, he naturally bids them use the holy kiss also as a means of union: for this unites, and produces one body. This is holy, when free from deceit and hypocrisy."[8]

In some Middle Eastern and European cultures, people still greet loved ones with a gentle kiss on the lips or on the cheek. In most Western cultures, however, this kind of greeting has been replaced by a "holy handshake" or "holy hug." Either way, the message is the same: "I love you like a brother or sister."

Think of some other obvious expressions of genuine love you could exhibit among your brothers and sisters in Christ. What kinds of actions would communicate as plainly as a brotherly kiss or a warm embrace? How about providing a meal to a family in need or a car ride for a person who has lost the use of a vehicle? What about encouraging your church leaders with cards and gifts rather than tearing them down with complaining and gossip? How about spending time with loved ones beyond your immediate family?

In our fast-paced world, it's so easy to get away with a nod and a wave when we walk by people we know in our churches. But we're called to a greater degree of affection and a greater commitment to love. We're called to get up close and personal with our brothers and sisters in Christ. Anything we can do to strengthen these relationships in our churches will move us closer to the depth of love and fellowship enjoyed in the first century.

# INSIGHTS ON 2 CORINTHIANS

*We can describe Paul's letter as a treatise on the stuff of authentic ministry—in all its earthiness and harsh, human realities. This vivid picture of raw but real ministry sheds a stark light on the inferior motives, methods, and messages of false ministers. For those engaged in the nuts and bolts of ministry today, this is one remarkable letter.*

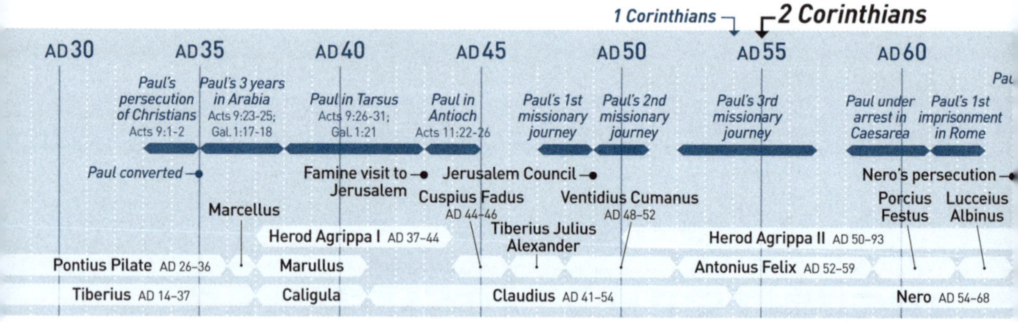


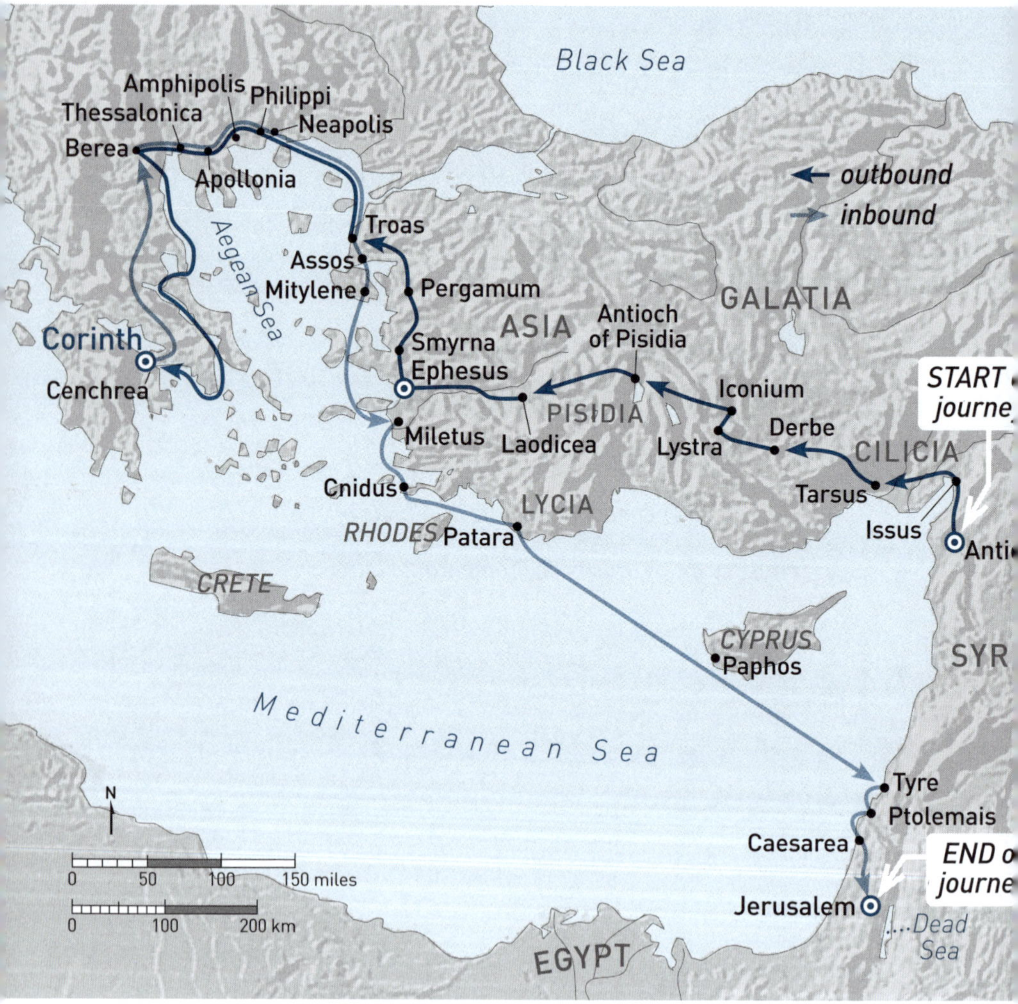


**Paul's Third Missionary Journey.** Paul and his companions set out once again from Antioch and journeyed across Asia and Greece to Corinth. In Luke's account of this journey in Acts 18:23–20:2, Paul concentrates his time in Ephesus, but it seems that he also made a trip to Corinth (2 Cor. 12:14; 13:1).

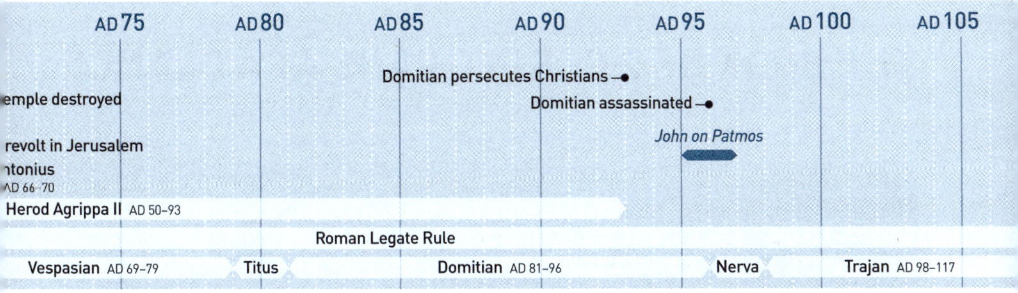


# 2 CORINTHIANS

## INTRODUCTION

All of us could name some famous person we've never met, but whom we greatly respect, admire, or even adore. At times, the admiration people have for great men and women can approach the level of worship, especially when we forget a basic rule of our doctrine of humanity: with only One extraordinary exception, every person who has ever lived has suffered from the frailties and failings of fallenness—even the martyrs who took a stand for Christ or contributed significantly to building up His church.

Let your mind wind backwards with me as we recall several of the people from our Christian past whose lofty peaks loom large on the broad plains and rolling hills of history: Billy Graham . . . Jonathan Edwards . . . John Wesley . . . John Calvin . . . Martin Luther . . . Thomas Aquinas . . . Anselm . . . Augustine . . . Athanasius, to name only a few. Yet, like snow-capped mountains that in the distance appear like majestic jewels touching the heavens, the closer we get to those spiritual giants of the past, the more we realize they, like us, are made of dirt.

## HEAVENLY TREASURE IN AN EARTHEN VESSEL

The truth is that depravity is universal. Every great man or woman of God bears the marks of imperfect humanity. In some, those marks are more obvious than in others. Without fail, our too-high estimations of godly saints get cut down to size by reality.

I've thought often of the greatness of the apostle Paul. What a stunning résumé he had:

- Planted countless churches from east to west
- Penned over a dozen New Testament letters
- Formulated the basic doctrines of the faith

# THE BOOK OF 2 CORINTHIANS AT A GLANCE

| SECTION | THE CRUCIAL CONCERNS OF MINISTRY | THE MINISTRY OF RECONCILIATION |
|---|---|---|
| PASSAGE | 1:1–3:18 | 4:1–5:21 |
| THEMES | The Mystery of Suffering<br>Authentic Forgiveness<br>The New Covenant Ministry | Treasure in Earthen Ves<br>Ambassadors for Chri<br>Effective Ministry |
| KEY TERMS | Ministry | Boasting |
| | Comfort<br>Affliction | Glory<br>Reconciliation |

| E REALISTIC RTRAIT OF MINISTRY | THE SELF-SACRIFICIAL MINISTRY | THE TRUE APOSTOLIC MINISTRY |
|---|---|---|
| 6:1–7:16 | 8:1–9:15 | 10:1–13:14 |
| ood and Bad elationships<br>he Joy of a ood Report<br>l-Life Ministry | Examples of Generosity<br>Joyful Giving<br>Ministry of Giving | Exposing the Fakes<br>Boasting in Weakness<br>Sufficiency of Grace |
| Foolish | | |
| ncourage<br>alvation | Grace<br>Thankfulness | Disguise<br>Weakness |

- Poured out all he had for his Savior and Lord
- Died a martyr at the hands of the Romans

Perhaps none but Christ has left a greater impact on the Christian faith than this seemingly bigger-than-life figure, with his unparalleled gospel vision, missionary zeal, and passionate pursuit of holiness. But thanks to his second letter to the Corinthians, we can resist the temptation to elevate Paul to some deified status.

## KEY TERMS IN 2 CORINTHIANS

***aphrōn* (ἄφρων)** [878] "foolish," "senseless," "ridiculous"
Our English word "moron" derives from the Greek *mōros* [3474], "fool," which always carries a negative connotation. *Aphrōn* is a milder term for "foolishness," with the sense of "ridiculous" or "inane," and is a closer equivalent to the mildness of our English "fool." Paul applies this term to himself in 2 Corinthians as he fights folly with folly (11:16), foolishly bragging after the manner of his opponents. Paul's boasting, however, was not completely "ridiculous," because in contrast with his opponents, his claims were actually true (12:6).

***diakonia* (διακονία)** [1248] "service, ministry"
***diakonos* (διάκονος)** [1249] "servant, minister"
The words "servant" and "service" both come from a Greek root that, in its most literal sense, refers to a table waiter. By extension, this family of terms carries the idea of serving obediently, willingly, and submissively from a heart of humility. In the New Testament, *diakonos* can mean a servant with a certain mission (Rom. 15:8); a personal assistant (Matt. 22:13); or a person in the office of "minister" in a local church (Phil. 1:1). Acts 6:1-6 recounts the appointment of the first deacons in the church. Paul uses these terms for "minister" and "ministry" in the general sense of a self-sacrificing servant in the kingdom of Christ.

***kauchēsis* (καύχησις)** [2746] "a boasting"
***kauchaomai* (καυχάομαι)** [2744] "to boast, brag"
Depending on the context, the verb "to boast" can have either a positive or negative connotation. Most positively, we might render it "to glory in" things pertaining to God (so Rom. 15:17, NIV). In the natural realm, it could refer to a person who "takes pride in" the good of another (2 Cor. 7:4). In the most negative sense, boasting "according to the flesh" involves a self-centered pride resulting in exaggerated bragging (Rom. 3:27; 2 Cor. 11:18). In 2 Corinthians Paul is forced to "boast" of his own ministry accomplishments to put his bragging opponents in their places, though this negative use of boasting was intended for a positive rhetorical effect (11:18; 12:5).

Yes, Paul was an invaluable treasure to the Christian church, but like every other believer of every era, Paul was 100 percent human. He faced human challenges. He suffered human defeats. He experienced human temptations, and he battled his own human weaknesses. Thankfully, he also had a very human estimation of himself, acknowledging that he was "least of the apostles" (1 Cor. 15:9), "least of all saints," (Eph. 3:8), and "foremost of all [sinners]" (1Tim. 1:15).

The apostle Paul was indeed a great man, but he was only a man.

As a human minister of the gospel, Paul faced the kinds of struggles and frustrations that every missionary or pastor has faced since. In 2 Corinthians—the most emotionally transparent of all his letters—Paul opens the doors of his personal life, freely expressing his feelings about himself and his ministry. The first chapter of 2 Corinthians gives us a sample of this transparency: "For we do not want you to be unaware, brethren, of our affliction which came to us in Asia, that we were burdened excessively, beyond our strength, so that we despaired even of life" (1:8). Think about that! As a weak and fragile human, Paul coped with real-life emotions—anxiety, affliction, stress, and even the black hole of despair.

Yet because of God's grace, Paul never lost himself in the perplexing events of life. He never reached a point when he felt devoid of hope or separated from God's sustaining mercy. In the very midst of his struggles, he found strength in the presence of Christ:

> But we have this treasure in earthen vessels, so that the surpassing greatness of the power will be of God and not from ourselves; we are afflicted in every way, but not crushed; perplexed, but not despairing; persecuted, but not forsaken; struck down, but not destroyed; always carrying about in the body the dying of Jesus, so that the life of Jesus also may be manifested in our body. For we who live are constantly being delivered over to death for Jesus' sake, so that the life of Jesus also may be manifested in our mortal flesh. (4:7-11)

In the midst of his struggles, Paul could see beyond them and rest his abiding hope on his Savior. When Paul was at his weakest, Christ could shine forth His greatest strength (12:10).

## HEAVEN'S TREASURES IN AN EARTHY EPISTLE

Paul's second letter to the Corinthians is the least structured of all his letters. In it, Paul meanders even more than in the first letter he had sent to Corinth. That letter, addressing healthy church life, had been delivered, read, and taken by many as a slap in the face. In fact, so many disliked the corrections in 1 Corinthians that some began employing the age-old rhetorical strategy of ad hominem attack—that is, challenging the credibility, motives, and character of the author to avoid dealing with the writer's confrontations. It became a classic case of mud-slinging in an attempt to diminish Paul's reputation and heighten their own.

We can reconstruct the events that transpired after 1 Corinthians by piecing together clues from the book of Acts and from 2 Corinthians. After ministering in Corinth, Paul traveled to Ephesus, where he left Priscilla and Aquila when he returned to his home church in Antioch (Acts 18:21-22). After a time in Antioch, Paul slowly made his way back to Ephesus, encouraging the churches along the way—this was the beginning of his third missionary journey. Some time after he arrived again in Ephesus (AD 53–55), Paul wrote 1 Corinthians. His stay there, which included daily teaching in the "school of Tyrannus" (Acts 19:9), is described in Acts 19:1-20. At the end of his time in Ephesus, he determined in his heart to travel north through Macedonia, then to Achaia—the region of Corinth—and finally, to sail on to Jerusalem (Acts 19:21). He shared his plans to visit them (1 Cor. 4:19). And again, "But I will come to you after I go through Macedonia, for I am going through Macedonia" (1 Cor. 16:5). During this circuit he intended to visit several churches to collect the money they had pledged for support of the church in Jerusalem (1 Cor. 16:1-4). Prior to starting his itinerary, however, he sent Timothy and Erastus ahead through Macedonia (Acts 19:22). Paul likely referred to this sending of Timothy in 1 Corinthians 4:17; 16:10-11.

Before departing from Ephesus, Paul seems to have gotten wind of the Corinthians' cool response to his first letter. Perhaps Timothy himself had returned and reported that the Corinthian chaos was spiraling toward a Corinthian catastrophe, despite Paul's pleading. Delaying his departure to Achaia until things cooled down in Corinth, Paul wrote an interim letter mentioned in 2 Corinthians 2:3. This letter pulled no punches and seems to have dealt specifically with a single issue: their tolerance of sexual immorality.[1] Paul's fellow worker Titus probably bore this interim letter to Corinth on the apostle's behalf. This "tearful letter," as it is often called, seems finally to have prodded the church to action.[2]

Paul himself stayed in Ephesus until a riot occurred over his controversial teachings (Acts 19:23-41). Paul then departed for Macedonia, as earlier planned, passing through the port city of Troas. Upon arriving in Troas on his way from Ephesus to Macedonia, Paul hoped to find Titus and hear about the state of the Corinthian church. But he was disappointed: "I had no rest for my spirit, not finding Titus my brother; but taking my leave of them, I went on to Macedonia" (2 Cor. 2:13). There he labored amongst conflicts and hardships (7:5), exhorting the churches (Acts 20:1-2). While he was in Macedonia, Titus finally arrived from his visit to Corinth, after which Paul wrote 2 Corinthians (AD 55–56). Paul writes: "But God, who comforts the depressed, comforted us by the coming of Titus; and not only by his coming, but also by the comfort with which he was comforted in you, as he reported to us your longing, your mourning, your zeal for me; so that I rejoiced even more" (2 Cor. 7:6-7).

Upon his arrival, Titus shared with Paul a new twist in the Corinthian quagmire: under the spell of Paul's opponents, who claimed to be apostles and who challenged Paul's apostolic authority, a minority of rebels had fortified their positions and refused to leave. Instead, they were working to soften the Corinthians' allegiance to Paul and sever ties with him. As Paul wrote his response to this new turn of events in the drama of the Corinthian church, he unleashed his emotions like never before, finding himself in an awkward position. He had to further defend his authority as an authentic apostle against an influential faction of Judaizers who were still attempting to undermine his ministry and hijack the Christian community in Corinth for themselves. In response to this mutiny in progress, Paul launched 2 Corinthians. We can describe Paul's letter as a treatise on the stuff of authentic ministry—in all its earthiness and harsh, human realities. This vivid picture of raw but real ministry sheds a stark light on the inferior motives, methods, and messages of false ministers. For those engaged in the nuts and bolts of ministry today, this is one remarkable letter.

## OVERVIEW OF 2 CORINTHIANS

I've divided 2 Corinthians into five basic sections that relate to various facets of authentic Christian ministry.

*The Crucial Concerns of Ministry* (1:1–3:18). Paul begins his letter with a strong affirmation of God's comfort even in the midst of great affliction (1:1-11). Yet Paul immediately moves into a defensive mode, defending the integrity of his ministry and explaining the reasons for his strategic ministry decisions (1:12–2:4). He then addresses a few urgent issues facing the Corinthians: the need to forgive a repentant brother in Christ (2:5-11), the need to preach the Word with sincerity regardless of the hearers' responses (2:12-17), and the need to stand boldly for the ministry of glory found in the gospel of Jesus Christ (3:1-18).

*The Ministry of Reconciliation* (4:1–5:21). Like earthen vessels fashioned from clay but used to hold priceless treasures (4:7-12), frail humans can be filled with the eternal Spirit of God to carry out the glorious ministry of reconciliation (4:13-18). Because of our heavenly ministry, we also look forward to an eternal—not temporal—reward. We labor hard while in our mortal bodies as we anticipate with hope our immortal dwellings (5:1-10). Therefore, regardless of the personal cost, God's authentic minister strives to persuade others to reconcile with God (5:11-21).

*The Realistic Picture of Ministry* (6:1–7:16). Beginning with a realistic description of the hardships of Christian ministry (6:1-11), Paul urges the Corinthians to a life of personal and corporate holiness (6:12–7:1). He recounts the anguish he felt on the Corinthians' behalf when he heard of their difficult reception of his earlier letter, which turned to comfort when he learned that they had repented (7:2-13). The fact of their willingness to turn from wickedness and wrongdoing continues to give Paul confidence that they will persist on the path of righteousness (7:13-16).

*The Self-Sacrificial Ministry* (8:1–9:15). Part of the path of righteousness expected of the Corinthians was the fulfillment of their pledge to provide material assistance for their suffering brothers and sisters in Jerusalem (8:1-15). This leads to a rich discussion on the principles of giving, in which Paul emphasizes the need to be a "cheerful giver" (9:7), sacrificially giving resources —financial and otherwise—for ministry to others (9:1-15).

*The True Apostolic Ministry* (10:1–13:14). Finally, Paul defends the authenticity of his ministry as an apostle against those in the midst of the Corinthian church who had doubted and ridiculed his God-given authority (10:1-18). Fearful that they had fallen to deception by false teachers (11:1-6), Paul challenges the teaching and motives of his opponents (11:7-15). He "boasts" in the manner of his adversaries, setting forth his superior qualifications as an apostle of God (11:16–12:21), concluding that his authority comes just as much from his suffering in weakness as from his astonishing revelations and miracles. Warning that he will be coming to visit them soon, Paul's letter serves as a final call to offer their allegiances to the authentic ministers of the gospel and to return to a path of purity and righteousness (13:1-14).

# THE CRUCIAL CONCERNS OF MINISTRY (2 CORINTHIANS 1:1–3:18)

*What are we doing here?* This is a question that those with a passion for ministry need to ask constantly. Yet in our activity-oriented, "just do it" culture, too many involved in Christian ministry fail to ask and answer this basic question of purpose. In a world of countless options and opportunities, having a clear understanding of the crucial concerns of the ministry will help us decide what to do with our resources, who should be involved, and where we should concentrate our efforts.

*Who* should be involved in the ministry? What kind of experience, qualifications, and character should we bring to the mission? What qualifies us to be ministers of the gospel? Does physical and emotional suffering disqualify us for ministry . . . or make us even more qualified?

*What* should we be doing? How should we be going about the work of the ministry? Should we do something different or continue in the way we've been laboring for years? Should our ministry emphasize original proclamation (evangelism) or continual teaching (discipleship)?

*Where* should we be ministering? How do we know the Spirit is moving us somewhere else? Does an open door to other ministry opportunities necessarily mean that is where we belong? Does a closed door suggest we need to move on or stay put?

Today's pastors, evangelists, missionaries, preachers, teachers, and volunteer workers should constantly be asking such evaluative questions, and ours is not the first generation to cope with a variety of crucial ministry concerns. The apostle Paul and his ministry partners constantly had to ask the question, "What are we doing here?"

In Paul's day, false teachers—usually those promoting a mixture of Christianity and Judaism—were challenging his authority, his integrity, his teaching, and his methods. They questioned *what* he was doing, *who* he and his associates really were, and *where* and *when* they had chosen to minister. They especially pointed to Paul's uncertainties about God's ministry direction as signs of fickleness.

As an answer to these criticisms and challenges from dangerous false teachers who had poisoned the hearts and minds of many in Corinth, Paul responds throughout the book of 2 Corinthians by explaining the who, what, where, when, why, and how of his apostolic ministry. In the course of his exposition, he turns the question "What are we doing here?" back around to the Corinthians themselves: "What are *you* doing *there*?" In the process Paul ends up setting forth a blueprint for authentic ministry—a ministry anyone could trust.

In 2 Corinthians 1:1–3:18, Paul addresses the crucial concerns of ministry. He begins with a strong affirmation of God's comfort even in the midst of great affliction, suggesting that suffering actually qualifies a person for greater ministry impact rather than rendering the person ineffective (1:1-11). He then transitions to an explicitly defensive mode, defending his own integrity in ministry in light of strategic ministry decisions that prevented him from being able to follow through on his original plan to visit the Corinthians (1:12–2:4).

Paul then launches into a discussion of a few urgent issues facing the Corinthians: the need to forgive a repentant brother in Christ

## KEY TERMS IN 2 CORINTHIANS 1:1–3:18

### *thlipsis* (θλῖψις) [2347] "affliction," "tribulation"

The Greek word *thlipsis*, "tribulation," can refer to the coming Great Tribulation of the end times leading up to Christ's physical return (Matt. 24:21, 29), but more commonly it refers to general trials and afflictions experienced by Christians of every age (Matt. 13:21; 24:9; John 16:33; Rom. 5:3). Paul describes various afflictions or "tribulations" he had to endure in the course of his ministry (2 Cor. 1:8), some caused by external hardships, others by his concern for the churches (2:4). Whatever their source, we can have confidence that the "God of all comfort" will comfort us "in all our affliction" (1:3-4).

### *paraklēsis* (παράκλησις) [3874] "comfort," "encouragement"

In 2 Corinthians, "comfort" (*paraklēsis*) provides insight into the mystery of why God allows suffering. Ten times in 1:3-7, Paul uses words that share this same Greek root! If rendered literally, the word means "coming alongside of" for the purpose of giving aid or assistance to one in need. Authentic *paraklēsis* is given when we reach out and help others personally and selflessly. The God of all *paraklēsis* (1:3) allows His children to endure suffering so they will be equipped to extend *paraklēsis* toward others who are suffering (1:4).

(2:5-11), the need to preach the Word with sincerity regardless of the hearers' responses (2:12-17), and the need to stand boldly for the ministry of glory found in the gospel of Jesus Christ, depending on Christ alone for one's sufficiency (3:1-18).

What are we doing here? Paul's answer is simple. We're not here to proclaim our own merits, but to preach Christ Jesus as Lord (4:5).

# Unraveling the Mystery of Suffering
## 2 CORINTHIANS 1:1-11

**NASB**

1 Paul, an apostle of Christ Jesus by
the will of God, and Timothy *our*
brother,
To the church of God which is at
Corinth with all the [a]saints who are
throughout Achaia:
2 Grace to you and peace from God
our Father and the Lord Jesus Christ.
3 Blessed *be* the God and Father
of our Lord Jesus Christ, the Father
of mercies and God of all comfort,
4 who comforts us in all our afflic-
tion so that we will be able to com-
fort those who are in [a]any affliction
with the comfort with which we
ourselves are comforted by God.
5 For just as the sufferings of Christ
are [a]ours in abundance, so also our
comfort is abundant through Christ.
6 But if we are afflicted, it is for your
comfort and salvation; or if we are
comforted, it is for your comfort,
which is effective in the patient en-
during of the same sufferings which
we also suffer; 7 and our hope for you
is firmly grounded, knowing that as
you are sharers of our sufferings, so
also you are *sharers* of our comfort.
8 For we do not want you to be
unaware, brethren, of our affliction
which came *to us* in [a]Asia, that we

**NLT**

1 This letter is from Paul, chosen by
the will of God to be an apostle of
Christ Jesus, and from our brother
Timothy.
I am writing to God's church in
Corinth and to all of his holy people
throughout Greece.*
2 May God our Father and the
Lord Jesus Christ give you grace and
peace.
3 All praise to God, the Father of
our Lord Jesus Christ. God is our
merciful Father and the source of
all comfort. 4 He comforts us in all
our troubles so that we can comfort
others. When they are troubled, we
will be able to give them the same
comfort God has given us. 5 For the
more we suffer for Christ, the more
God will shower us with his comfort
through Christ. 6 Even when we are
weighed down with troubles, it is
for your comfort and salvation! For
when we ourselves are comforted,
we will certainly comfort you. Then
you can patiently endure the same
things we suffer. 7 We are confident
that as you share in our sufferings,
you will also share in the comfort
God gives us.
8 We think you ought to know,
dear brothers and sisters,* about
the trouble we went through in the

**NASB**

were burdened excessively, beyond
our strength, so that we despaired
even of life; 9[a]indeed, we had the
sentence of death within ourselves
so that we would not trust in our-
selves, but in God who raises the
dead; 10 who delivered us from so
great a *peril of* death, and will de-
liver *us,* [a]He on whom we have set
our hope. And He will yet deliver
us, 11 you also joining in helping us
through your prayers, so that thanks
may be given by many persons on
our behalf for the favor bestowed on
us through *the prayers of* many.

**1:1** [a]Or *holy ones* **1:4** [a]Lit *every* **1:5** [a]Lit *to us* **1:8** [a]I.e. west coast province of Asia Minor **1:9** [a]Lit *but we ourselves* **1:10** [a]One early ms reads *on whom we have set our hope that He will also*

**NLT**

province of Asia. We were crushed
and overwhelmed beyond our abil-
ity to endure, and we thought we
would never live through it. 9 In fact,
we expected to die. But as a result,
we stopped relying on ourselves and
learned to rely only on God, who
raises the dead. 10 And he did res-
cue us from mortal danger, and he
will rescue us again. We have placed
our confidence in him, and he will
continue to rescue us. 11 And you are
helping us by praying for us. Then
many people will give thanks be-
cause God has graciously answered
so many prayers for our safety.

**1:1** Greek *Achaia,* the southern region of the Greek peninsula. **1:8** Greek *brothers.*

Poets and hymn writers have a wonderful way of piercing the darkness of despair with brilliant rays of hope. But sometimes when we are over our heads in suffering or sorrow, words meant to comfort and console only frustrate and irritate.

> When through fiery trials thy pathways shall lie,
> My grace, all sufficient, shall be thy supply;
> The flame shall not hurt thee; I only design
> Thy dross to consume, and thy gold to refine.[1]

Beautiful words. True words. Comforting words. Yet chances are you and I never have those words in our hearts or on our lips when the fiery trials threaten to reduce our lives to ashes. Those great Sunday morning words of worship don't always make it out of the church and into the challenges of our lives.

I'll be the first to admit it. When I minister to families who have lost a mother to cancer, or a child to a drunk driver, or a son to an overdose, or a daughter's innocence to a sexual predator, somehow I don't think of telling them about the gold being refined or the dross being consumed. That poor family is drowning in the pain of their loss. Their pain is so potent it is physical. If the words of "How Firm a Foundation" have not sunk deeply into their hearts before that point in their Christian lives, a quick and desperate act of foundation repair on my part will not suddenly help them to unravel the mystery of suffering.

Illness, marital struggles, worry over children, stress about finances, anxiety over the future: These things can tie our hearts and minds in knots as we feel like life is interrogating us with a series of unanswerable questions—*Why, God? Why me? Why now? Why this?* The loud, dissonant sounds of suffering make it almost impossible to hear God's comforting anthem that could help us make sense of the seemingly senseless.

Second Corinthians was composed by a man who was no stranger to heartache. His body bore the marks of shipwreck, stoning, and a thorn in the flesh that wouldn't leave; his soul knew the pain of false rumors, misunderstanding, and loss. He lived with suffering, regularly facing it head on. These opening words state in simple terms his position, as best as he can explain it, regarding the pain, heartache, and suffering of life.

## — 1:1-3 —

Knowing that his authority has been pummeled by critics from both outside the church and within, Paul uses his opening words for this letter to Corinth to remind his readers of his credentials. He is "an apostle of Christ Jesus," not by his own choice but "by the will of God" (1:1). How sad that within just a few years of his founding the church with a ministry confirmed by signs, wonders, and miracles (12:12), the fickle Corinthians doubted the authenticity of his ministry. Paul's defense of his credentials as an authoritative spokesperson of Jesus Christ will run as a subtheme throughout this letter.

He mentions Timothy as his "brother" (1:1). Timothy had recently returned to Paul after visiting Corinth, relaying additional information about their less-than-ideal condition. Timothy himself was not an apostle in the official sense of the term, but he was an apostolic delegate, an evangelist and pastor who often served as Paul's representative—his hands, feet, eyes, and ears when Paul could not personally travel to, or remain in, various locations.

Interestingly, Paul addresses the letter not only to the church at Corinth, but beyond that to "all the saints who are throughout Achaia" (1:1). He may have extended its scope because the positive exhortations and negative corrections applied broadly to issues and problems throughout the region. Or he may have feared that the party of apostolic pretenders meddling in Corinth would spread their cancer throughout the region. Perhaps some already had done so. When it comes to false teaching, an ounce of prevention is worth a pound of cure.

With the formalities aside, Paul greets his beloved children in the faith warmly, employing his standard epistolary greeting: "Grace to you and peace from God our Father and the Lord Jesus Christ" (1:2). Though Paul begins the body of his letter with the word "blessed," his praise to the Father and Jesus Christ quickly transitions to a discussion of pain, suffering, and heartache. He praises God for both His mercies and His comfort (1:3). God shows mercy when He withholds deserved judgment or wrath from a person. In highlighting mercy, Paul reminds us that God protects us from the full brunt of pain and suffering we should expect from life. Because we are totally depraved sinners, in whom there is nothing good (Rom. 3:10-18), a God who metes out only justice (giving us what we deserve) should be pouring out wrath upon us every moment of our lives (Rom. 1:18). Yet nobody experiences such hellish horror. Instead, God is "the Father of mercies," not merely for believers but even for unbelievers, many of whom experience even less suffering than believers.

God is also the source of "all comfort," a positive dimension of God's ministry to us for grace and peace. God comforts us (2 Cor. 1:3-4) in every "affliction" (*thlipsis* [2347]). The word "comfort" is the key that unlocks Paul's explanation of the mystery of suffering. In these verses and the three that follow (1:3-7), the same Greek root, related to the verb *parakaleō* [3870], is used ten times. The idea is one of bringing help, consolation, or comfort. Like a nurse called to a patient's bedside or a companion who puts an arm around a friend to provide strength in weakness, *paraklēsis* [3874], "comfort," is given by those who care enough to reach out and help in times of need. It is one of the words Jesus uses for the Holy Spirit: "I will ask the Father, and He will give you another Helper [Comforter], that He may be with you forever" (John 14:16).

How does the Holy Spirit comfort the suffering? Many of us imagine that He does so mystically, immediately, and directly—and occasionally this happens. At times in the midst of a tragedy, crisis, or catastrophe, a sudden, inexplicable peace passes over us. From that moment on, we know, we believe, and we even feel that God is in control and we can rest in Him regardless of what comes (Phil. 4:7). More frequently, however, the Spirit works through Spirit-indwelled believers and the Spirit-filled community to minister to those who suffer. Through an encouraging word, a heart-felt embrace, a kind note, a loving presence, a side-by-side walk through death's valley—the Spirit works through His people to comfort those downtrodden by the pain and turmoil of life.

Now that we know that God comforts us, and how the Spirit ministers comfort in our lives, we can begin to look more closely at the reasons why God allows suffering in the first place. Paul touches on a few of them in the next several verses of this section, but the Bible gives no quick and easy solutions to the problem of suffering. Although I will point to three ways God uses our suffering in this world for our good and His glory, I don't want you to get the wrong impression that these three things will answer the ultimate question of "Why?"

Also, the reasons Paul gives for enduring hardship do not mean that the suffering, pain, and death we experience in this life are themselves good. We must deliberately resist thinking of death as a friend. Death is the enemy—the last great enemy the Lord Himself will destroy (1 Cor. 15:26). Yes, sometimes death ends pain and suffering, but that does not make it a friend. In those cases death is a dreadful result of the pain and suffering, which one day will be cured (Rev. 21:4). True, God does frustrate the wicked intentions of evil men who cause our suffering when He brings about a good that never would have happened otherwise (Gen. 50:20). That does not mean, however, that the wickedness, pain, and suffering were in and of themselves good. In those cases God is the good redeemer of the bad situation. To deny the essential badness of pain, suffering and death is to deny the clear teachings of His Word.

In light of these facts, the following three reasons for suffering, each introduced with "so that" (2 Cor. 1:4, 9, 11), must be understood as the redemptive work of an all-good, all-wise, all-powerful God who graciously and mercifully brings good effects from even the worst situations (Rom. 8:28). They are not reasons why the bad things should be thought of as "good."

## — 1:4-7 —

*Suffering prepares us to comfort others* (1:4-7). God's grace and power enable us to endure suffering through various means. When His comfort has done its work in our lives, then we in turn become the Holy Spirit's comforters for others who must endure similar situations.

A perfect contemporary example of this is Joni Eareckson Tada. When a diving accident in 1967 instantly transformed Joni from an energetic girl to a woman confined for life to a wheelchair, some no doubt thought her productive life had ended. Surely, countless people around her asked the haunting question, "Why?"[2] But the Lord used her horrible experience to minister to countless lives with the hope-filled, healing message of Christ.[3]

The comfort of God through a tragic experience can explode into a chain reaction of comfort for countless others. The parent who has lost a child can best comfort another grieving parent. The businessman who suffered bankruptcy can comfort others in the throes of financial disaster. Men and women who have endured the pain of chronic illness can best support those facing the same kinds of suffering. Those who have overcome the debilitating effects of depression can minister comfort to others who have been crippled by this insidious black hole in the soul.

Paul points out an important theological truth we would do well to keep at the forefront of our minds: Suffering is not a punishment, but a sharing in the "sufferings of Christ" (1:5). Just as our Lord Jesus suffered in this world, so we who have committed to following in His footsteps should not expect to escape the same kinds of suffering as our Master (Matt. 10:24). Just as Christ conquered suffering and death through resurrection, so also we will conquer, being raised by the same Spirit—a great hope and comfort (Rom. 8:11). Yes, we have been called to a life of much suffering, but God's comfort will assuage that suffering.

Paul points out that he and his apostolic associates such as Timothy and Titus provide examples of those who, like Christ, are called to suffer for the benefit of others. They have been afflicted with trials, persecution, imprisonment, and hardships for the sake of the Corinthian Christians (2 Cor. 1:6). As the Corinthians themselves faced uncomfortable pressure from false teachers, Paul and the other authentic teachers were in a position to encourage them to persevere through suffering (1:7).

## — 1:8-9 —

*Suffering keeps us from trusting ourselves* (1:8-9). Paul's experiences of suffering were not merely theoretical. Rather, the excessive persecutions that he and his companions faced in Asia exceeded their strength, pushing them even to despair of life itself (1:8). We do not know what specific "affliction" Paul faced in Asia, but clearly it was extreme. The Greek word for "despaired" is *exaporeō* [1820], which implies "the total unavailability of an exit."[4] Think about that! The great apostle Paul found himself cornered by catastrophe, unable to extricate himself, with nowhere in this world to turn and nobody in this world to turn to. From his limited perspective, when he saw himself teetering on the brink of mortal demise, he discovered a second purpose in suffering: "that we would not trust in ourselves, but in God who raises the dead" (1:9).

Intense suffering reminds us of our utter helplessness—something we often forget when everything seems to be going well. Proverbs 3:5-6 expresses this truth beautifully: "Trust in the Lord with all your heart And do not lean on your own understanding. In all your ways acknowledge Him, And He will make your paths straight."

The world's wisdom challenges this biblical truth. Secular psychologists, self-help gurus, and feel-good life coaches urge us to follow our hearts, trust in ourselves, and find our own inner strength. When the dire circumstances of life push us to the very edge of ourselves, however, we realize that we simply lack the knowledge, strength, and even the desire to go on. When worldly wisdom deceives us and personal resources run dry, God's strength and wisdom provide us with everything we need to be comforted in our suffering.

Thankfully, suffering is not God's final plan for His children. Through the pen of Jeremiah—called the "weeping prophet" because of his experiences of severe persecution, rejection, suffering, and pain—we read one of the greatest promises in the Bible: "'For I know the plans that I have for you,' declares the LORD, 'plans for welfare and not for calamity to give you a future and a hope'" (Jer. 29:11).

## — 1:10-11 —

*Suffering teaches us to give thanks in everything* (1:10-11). When He delivers us from hardship as a result of the faithful prayers of the saints, those prayer partners return praise and thanksgiving to God. This in turn builds hope and trust in the God who has delivered us. So, as we encounter suffering and then conquer it through answered prayer, we respond to Him with thanksgiving.

Paul's meditation on the mystery of suffering moves him from an attitude of morbid despair (1:8) to a confession of faith and hope in God, his deliverer (1:10-11). Because of God's pattern of faithfulness to us and to all the saints who have gone before us, we can have a spirit of gratitude *even in the midst of suffering.*

I know many people struggle with thanking and praising God in the midst of hardship, trials, or suffering. I have noticed that those who resist this practice are often struggling with bitterness, disappointment with God, and even doubts about His goodness. We might think that if they only knew how this fit into God's plan, they would be able to offer Him a token of thanks. But God never promises to explain the purpose of the suffering. Rather, He promises only that perseverance will be worth it in the end and that He can always be trusted to do what is right.

# APPLICATION: 2 CORINTHIANS 1:1-11

## Handling the Perplexities of Suffering

Three simple principles shed light on the mystery of suffering:

- Suffering prepares us to comfort others.
- Suffering keeps us from trusting ourselves.
- Suffering teaches us to give thanks in everything.

Easy to understand. A cinch to remember. Simple to teach.

But easy to embrace in the midst of a trial? *Not so fast!* Some of the simplest truths are almost impossible to recall and apply to the realities of everyday life. In the same way, some of the simplest commandments in Scripture are the most difficult to obey—love your neighbor as yourself; love the Lord your God with all that you are. So, how do we live out the principles in 2 Corinthians 1:1-11? I understand Paul's statements, but how do we put these into action? Let me share a few thoughts.

First, when suffering hits you and doesn't seem to let up, let me suggest something unnatural that might even offend your sensibilities: Instead of focusing on your present situation, think of how you can help others later. This will sound a note of hope. Consider the compassion you will gain and the comfort you can give to others who will face the same kind of trial. Broken people understand other people who are being broken. By pondering how your current pain might be able to minister to others in the future, you will gain both a perspective on the present and hope for the future. With this hope, offer your experience of suffering to God to use in His kingdom as He sees fit.

Second, rather than fighting, surrender; rather than resisting, release. This will increase your faith. Remember, life is bigger than you can handle. Give it to God. Stop trying to overcome your physical or emotional pain on your own. As you open yourself up to the Lord's comforting touch, He will flow into the dry, barren crevices of your life with the cool, sustaining, refreshing water of life. With faith, surrender your self-sufficiency to God so that you may experience His supernatural comfort and concern.

Third, although becoming bitter and depressed will come most naturally, give thanks instead. This will bring a note of peace. Even though getting angry makes better sense, promoting a spirit of thanksgiving will bring healing to your soul. By focusing on the blessings you have rather than the hardships you must endure, your attitude of thankfulness will become infectious, providing a tremendous testimony for those who want to experience the same kind of divine peace you enjoy.

Hope, faith, and peace: These three notes turn the otherwise discordant sounds of suffering into a harmonious chord. They may not answer all of the problems or unravel the mystery of pain in every respect, but they equip us with a new perspective from which to handle the perplexities of suffering.

# In Defense of Integrity
## 2 CORINTHIANS 1:12–2:4

**NASB**

12 For our [a]proud confidence is this:
the testimony of our conscience, that
in holiness and godly sincerity, not
in fleshly wisdom but in the grace of
God, we have conducted ourselves
in the world, and especially toward
you. 13 For we write nothing else to
you than what you read and under-
stand, and I hope you will under-
stand until the end; 14 just as you also
partially did understand us, that we
are your reason to be proud as you
also are ours, in the day of our Lord
Jesus.
15 In this confidence I intended at
first to come to you, so that you might
[a]twice receive a [b]blessing; 16 [a]that is,
to pass [b]your way into Macedonia,
and again from Macedonia to come
to you, and by you to be helped on
my journey to Judea. 17 Therefore, I
was not vacillating when I intended
to do this, was I? Or what I purpose,
do I purpose according to the flesh,
so that with me there will be yes,
yes and no, no *at the same time?*
18 But as God is faithful, our word

**NLT**

12 We can say with confidence and a
clear conscience that we have lived
with a God-given holiness* and sin-
cerity in all our dealings. We have
depended on God's grace, not on our
own human wisdom. That is how we
have conducted ourselves before the
world, and especially toward you.
13 Our letters have been straightfor-
ward, and there is nothing written
between the lines and nothing you
can't understand. I hope someday
you will fully understand us, 14 even
if you don't understand us now. Then
on the day when the Lord Jesus* re-
turns, you will be proud of us in the
same way we are proud of you.
15 Since I was so sure of your under-
standing and trust, I wanted to give
you a double blessing by visiting you
twice—16 first on my way to Macedo-
nia and again when I returned from
Macedonia.* Then you could send
me on my way to Judea.
17 You may be asking why I
changed my plan. Do you think I
make my plans carelessly? Do you
think I am like people of the world
who say "Yes" when they really
mean "No"? 18 As surely as God is

**NASB**

to you is not yes and no. 19 For the Son of God, Christ Jesus, who was preached among you by us—by me and Silvanus and Timothy—was not yes and no, but is yes in Him. 20 For as many as are the promises of God, in Him they are yes; therefore also through Him is our Amen to the glory of God through us. 21 Now He who establishes us with you in Christ and anointed us is God, 22 who also sealed us and gave *us* the Spirit in our hearts as a [a]pledge.

23 But I call God as witness [a]to my soul, that to spare you I did not come again to Corinth. 24 Not that we lord it over your faith, but are workers with you for your joy; for in your faith you are standing firm.

**NLT**

faithful, our word to you does not waver between "Yes" and "No." 19 For Jesus Christ, the Son of God, does not waver between "Yes" and "No." He is the one whom Silas,* Timothy, and I preached to you, and as God's ultimate "Yes," he always does what he says. 20 For all of God's promises have been fulfilled in Christ with a resounding "Yes!" And through Christ, our "Amen" (which means "Yes") ascends to God for his glory.

21 It is God who enables us, along with you, to stand firm for Christ. He has commissioned us, 22 and he has identified us as his own by placing the Holy Spirit in our hearts as the first installment that guarantees everything he has promised us.

23 Now I call upon God as my witness that I am telling the truth. The reason I didn't return to Corinth was to spare you from a severe rebuke. 24 But that does not mean we want to dominate you by telling you how to put your faith into practice. We want to work together with you so you will be full of joy, for it is by your own faith that you stand firm.

**NASB**

2:1 But I determined this [a]for my own sake, that I would not come to you in sorrow again. 2 For if I cause you sorrow, who then makes me glad but the one whom I made sorrowful? 3 This is the very thing I wrote you, so that when I came, I would not have sorrow from those who ought to make me rejoice; having confidence in you all that my joy would be *the joy* of you all. 4 For out of much affliction and anguish of heart I wrote to you with many tears; not so that you would be made sorrowful, but that you might know the love which I have especially for you.

**1:12** [a]Lit *boasting* **1:15** [a]Lit *have a second grace* [b]One early ms reads *joy* **1:16** [a]Lit *and* [b]Lit *through you into* **1:22** [a]Or *down payment* **1:23** [a]Lit *upon* **2:1** [a]Or *as far as I am concerned*

**NLT**

2:1 So I decided that I would not bring you grief with another painful visit. 2 For if I cause you grief, who will make me glad? Certainly not someone I have grieved. 3 That is why I wrote to you as I did, so that when I do come, I won't be grieved by the very ones who ought to give me the greatest joy. Surely you all know that my joy comes from your being joyful. 4 I wrote that letter in great anguish, with a troubled heart and many tears. I didn't want to grieve you, but I wanted to let you know how much love I have for you.

**1:12** Some manuscripts read *honesty.*
**1:14** Some manuscripts read *our Lord Jesus.*
**1:16** *Macedonia* was in the northern region of Greece. **1:19** Greek *Silvanus.*

Each one of us carries a deadly weapon. It can ruin a reputation, annihilate self-esteem, and destroy a person's dignity. Its poison causes embarrassment and shame. Though sometimes concealed, when brandished this weapon can injure everyone in sight, even the one who wields it. But more often than not it does its worst damage behind the scenes, cloaked in stealth, stabbing its victim in the back. What is this treacherous weapon? *The tongue.*

Washington Irving once wrote, "A sharp tongue is the only edged tool that grows keener with constant use."[5] In spite of the obvious pain that results from the assassination of a person's reputation and integrity, acts of verbal violence are continually committed in full light for everybody to see! Somehow our culture tolerates brutal acts of senseless slander as we mercilessly tear each other apart.

Sadly, in the blink of an eye the same tongue can switch from the most soothing salve of sweet syllables to the most venomous verbal poison. James, the brother of Jesus, has this to say about that double-edged stiletto: "It is a restless evil and full of deadly poison. With it we bless our Lord and Father, and with it we curse men, who have been made in the likeness of God; from the same mouth come both blessing and cursing" (Jas. 3:8-10).

I have said throughout my ministry that the tongue is the main reason for congregational conflicts. Show me a church that has split, and chances are that if you dissect that dissension, you will find that the tongue provided the fuel that fed the flames of destruction—not simply doctrinal disagreements, personality clashes, or differences of ministry vision. Most of the time, the uncontrollable, volcanic eruptions in our churches can be traced back to uncontrollable tongues—just as James said: "The tongue is a fire, the very world of iniquity; the tongue is set among our members as that which defiles the entire body, and sets on fire the course of our life, and is set on fire by hell" (Jas. 3:6).

Somehow politicians survive the booby traps of the campaign trail. Businesses survive the flaming arrows of bad press. Even Hollywood blockbusters and Broadway hits can rake in millions despite scathing reviews. But whole churches and ministries can be taken down by just one strategically placed rumor. Why? Because when it comes to Christian ministry, everything depends on the integrity of the messenger. You can take away my business, my money, and my possessions. But slash at my integrity and you have assaulted the heart of my life.

As children, we all chanted those words that were meant to strengthen us in the face of ridicule: "Sticks and stones may break my bones, but words will never hurt me." Hogwash! Words do hurt. Their harmful effects long outlast any physical blow. Among the many trials we face in our Christian life and ministry, few are more devastating than unfounded statements made against us—especially behind our backs with no opportunity to clear the air or defend ourselves. Such false assertions can be made against our conduct—things we did not do; against our words—things we did not say; or against our motives—things we did not mean.

In 2 Corinthians 1, we see that Paul himself received all three kinds of attacks from the false teachers lurking in the shadows of the Corinthian congregation, feeding false information to the confused members of that church. The goal? To alienate them from their founding apostle and align them with their own sinister party. In 2 Corinthians 1:12–2:4 we will expose the strategies of these terrorizers of integrity and examine Paul's rebuttal.

## — 1:12-14 —

The confused church in Corinth may not have fully realized how hurtful they had been to Paul, who had poured his energy into their conversion and spiritual growth. Writing several letters to that church, sending delegates ahead and leaving teachers behind, traveling there himself to exhort and strengthen them—no other church in the New Testament caused Paul as much grief or took as much of his time and energy. In fact, following on the heels of a paragraph concerning reasons for suffering (1:3-11), Paul immediately transitions into a defense of his true character in response to the harmful false accusations slung at him from across the Aegean Sea.

Here is our first glimpse into the situation in Corinth that was causing conflict between Paul and the church. It appears that Paul's conduct and sincerity had been called into question. Paul refuted the accusation with directness and clarity: "In holiness and godly sincerity, not in fleshly wisdom but in the grace of God, we have conducted ourselves in the world, and especially toward you" (1:12). For Paul to point to the consistent holiness and sincerity of himself and those working with him as the foundation for his defense means he was confident that nobody in Corinth would have been able to refute him. In fact, he was able to exhibit "proud confidence" in their own unimpeachable conduct. He merely *reminded* the Corinthians of their irreproachable lifestyle; he did not have to *convince* them of it.

How many of us could claim that we are consistently holy and sincere, full of wisdom and grace? Few of us would invite an investigation into our private lives, but Paul welcomed it: "Come on in, look around. I have nothing to hide." He points out that his letters conform to his blameless conduct (1:13-14). As one commentator notes, "Simple, sincere, not in man-made wisdom but in God's grace. Paul had no hidden meanings or ulterior motives in his correspondence with the Corinthians. He was aboveboard and straightforward in person; and he was the same way in his letters."[6]

Paul hoped that the words of this latest letter (2 Corinthians) would pierce through the misconceptions or deceptions that had been clouding their understanding, so that they would see things clearly (1:13). He hoped his words would dispel the seeds of distrust that had been planted by his opponents and that one day they would take as much pride in him and his ministry as he took in them and their conversion (1:14).

## — 1:15-22 —

The blatantly false accusations of carnal, improper conduct were relatively easy for Paul to overcome. He simply reminded his readers of the blameless conduct he had exhibited among them, principles matched in his writings. A more sinister verbal cancer was being spread, however, and this one had apparent (though not real) evidence to support it. Some were saying that Paul made promises he did not keep, that he said one thing but did another, that he was guilty of fickle vacillation and could not be trusted.

The allegations were persuasive because Paul had hoped to visit the Corinthians for a lengthy period of time but had not been able to come. In 1 Corinthians 16:5-7 he expresses his desire to see them after going through Macedonia, using contingent and tentative language like "perhaps I will stay with you" (1 Cor. 16:6) and "I hope to remain with you for some time" (1 Cor. 16:7), ending his desire to come with a key phrase: "if the Lord permits" (1 Cor. 16:7). Nowhere did Paul *promise* he would come according to a specific timetable, and in the sovereignty of God, things didn't turn out as he had hoped.

In 2 Corinthians 1:15-16, Paul admits he had planned on visiting the Corinthians twice during his trip to and from Macedonia. Evidently, the Corinthians mistook Paul's genuine intentions for a firm promise. So when he did not show up as hoped, they concluded, "If we can't trust Paul to keep a simple promise, how can we trust him to communicate to us the promises of God?" No doubt, these trumped-up charges were trumpeted by Paul's critics, always eager to find some way to tear down his credibility to build up their own. Paul counters with several rapid-fire responses phrased as questions, which in the original Greek expected negative answers (1:17):

- He wasn't vacillating in his intentions.
- He didn't make plans according to the flesh.
- He didn't say yes and no at the same time.

As Christians, our word ought to be our bond. When we say we will do something, we should do it. We should not require signed contracts, handshakes, or "pinky swears." When we say yes, it ought to mean yes. And if we can't follow through because of something beyond our control, we need to explain, apologize, and satisfy our obligation in some other way. I say this especially to parents rearing children. I have never seen a child lose respect for a parent when the parent had to apologize. But I have seen respect lost when the parent failed to follow through on a promise and was too proud to ask forgiveness and find a way to make things right with the child.

The apostle Paul was smart enough not to promise that he would visit the Corinthians. He had hoped. He had yearned. He had intended. And he had planned in the presence of God while submitting to His will. But he had not set forth a hard-and-fast promise. This provides us with another piece of veiled advice: Be careful about making promises you are not sure you will be able to keep. It is better to keep things undecided or up in the air than to promise and later disappoint.

To clear up any confusion, however, Paul made a distinction between his uncertain plans about the future and the word of God spoken authoritatively through the apostles, which was always trustworthy and unalterable (1:18-22). That is, the promise of salvation through Jesus Christ, preached by Paul, Silvanus, and Timothy, could be relied upon with all confidence. Though Paul's tentative plans—submitted to the will of God—did not always turn out as intended (1:15-16), the plans of God always

A **signet** was used throughout the ancient world and across the centuries to "mark" authenticity and ownership. The one pictured here is from the ninth century BC and was possibly used by Jeroboam II, a king of the northern kingdom of Israel (2 Kgs. 14:23-29).

reach the goal He intends. In fact, God gave believers the Holy Spirit as a pledge, permanently sealing them as a down payment.

The Greek word for "sealed" is *sphragizō* [4972]. The middle voice of the verb, used here, carries the sense that the Holy Spirit sealed us for Himself. Commentator C. K. Barrett gives us a little background on the meaning of the "seal" in the ancient world: "The seal, given and preserved intact, was proof that a document had not been falsified, or goods tampered with in transit. It was also a mark of ownership; and the Christian, sealed . . . with the Spirit, was both visibly marked out as God's property, and secured ready to meet examination at the day of judgment."[7]

Though the promises of God were set in stone and irrevocable, the Corinthians should have held Paul's own hoped-for plans as tentative, subject entirely to the will of God. Instead they had misunderstood his intention as a promise, an error that opened the door to the unfounded charge of fickle vacillation.

## — 1:23–2:4 —

Paul moves from clarifying that his plans and intentions were not the same as God's purposes and promises (1:15-22) to a brief explanation of why he did not travel to Corinth as he had originally hoped. Here Paul's words become a bit uncomfortable for his readers. The fault, he says, was not his but theirs. He delayed his journey in order to spare them a painful visit that would have cast a dark shadow on what should have been a joyous reunion (1:23; 2:1-2).

Because of the turmoil in Corinth caused by the schisms, insubordination, and tolerance of immorality, Paul had written 1 Corinthians. Their response to that letter had been partly positive, but not completely. Pockets of resistance still remained. After receiving news that the church still had not fully repented of their disorder and disobedience, Paul had written an additional letter (2:4)—a blistering one, probably following up on the incestuous relationship denounced in 1 Corinthians 5:1-8. In any case, Paul wanted to wait for their reaction to that letter rather than arrive on its heels as if he were reinforcing his mandates with a personal visit to "crack heads" like a harsh and vengeful taskmaster. He wanted to wait until the matter was resolved and the church was restored to love, joy, and peace. His words are those of a loving shepherd, not an angry, self-serving tyrant.

From 2 Corinthians 1:24, we can infer that some in Corinth—likely the false teachers who wanted to boost their own perceived authority—were also charging Paul with wanting to throw his spiritual weight around like some sort of domineering dictator lording it over their faith. Paul had to remind the Corinthians that even as an apostle, his role was one of a fellow worker (1:24) and servant (4:5).

True servanthood is a rare quality today. Our problem is a simple yet sad one: There are so few examples of it. Leaders in the church often lord their position over the flock. Often, employers breathe down the necks of their employees, impatient and demanding, and spouses try to push each other around and rule their children with a heavy hand. But Paul, who followed the pattern of Christ's self-sacrificial leadership (Mark 10:45), approached his apostolic role as a shepherd to be loved and respected, not as a tyrant to be feared and worshiped.

The accusations against Paul were either flat-out false, exaggerated beyond recognition, or simple misunderstandings. Yet in the hands of his adversaries, the rumor mill used these accusations to try to grind his reputation to a pulp. They accused him of carnal conduct (2 Cor. 1:12-14). He responded with facts. They accused him of fickle vacillation (1:15-22). He replied with clarification. They accused him of domineering dictatorship. He answered with cool constraint. Paul's critics targeted his conduct, words, and motives; he responded with facts, clarification, and constraint. What admirable wisdom and restraint!

# APPLICATION: 2 CORINTHIANS 1:12–2:4

## Time to Take a Stand

Most of us respond to false accusations in one of two ways. We either bite our tongues, hoping the matter will blow over, or we explode in rage, responding with our own exaggerated accusations. Both are understandable, but neither is profitable. The first response leaves the lie unanswered, but the smoldering coals of ruinous scandal don't quickly burn themselves out. At any moment they can flare up and explode into open controversy. Those fiery lies must be doused with a flood of truth. The second response only compounds the problem, fanning the flames of slander and spreading the fires of falsehood far and wide. The apostle Paul shows us a better way to respond to the hurtful false accusations of the opposition: firmly, calmly, and armed with the truth.

Of course, Paul was not the first person ever to face false accusations, and we all know he was not the last. Sooner or later, all of us will find ourselves on the pointed end of a sharp tongue. When we do, there are a few principles that will help us defend ourselves from its hurtful gash.

First, *there are times when defending one's integrity calls for strong action.* How do we do this? Number one: Go directly to the accuser (Matt. 18:15). Don't go to other people ahead of time or afterward to "get advice" or "gather prayer support." Those are often code words for "gossip" or "slander." Instead, go directly to the accuser, as Paul went directly to the Corinthians, first by letter, then eventually in person. Number two: Stay completely with the facts. Stay away from emotions, from sarcasm, and from the temptation to exact revenge. Stick with the "who, what, where, when, and why." Number three: Speak openly, firmly, and lovingly. There are times when you must defend your integrity with an accuser, but this should never be an occasion to forsake your integrity as a Christian witness.

Second, *there are times when the best response is silence.* In a few cases, absolute, sustained silence may be the best defense. For example, if you do not know who your accuser is, it is probably best to wait in silence. Or if the accuser is unavailable or inaccessible, back off and be still. At times, the more you defend yourself, the more you appear guilty. You should hold your peace. This, however, brings up an important question. How do we know when to speak up and when to be silent? The answer is *wisdom.* Proverbs 26:4-5 places both scenarios beside each other, demonstrating the complexities of wise living:

| PROVERBS 26:4 | PROVERBS 26:5 |
|---|---|
| Do not answer a fool according to his folly,<br>Or you will also be like him. | Answer a fool as his folly deserves,<br>That he not be wise in his own eyes. |

The wisest way to respond to a fool is determined on a case-by-case basis. Sometimes it's wise to answer; sometimes it's wise to be silent. In every case, then, we need to call on God for the wisdom needed to navigate these situations (Jas. 1:5). Plead to your heavenly Defender for vindication. Then step out of the way and let Him fight your battle (Ps. 26).

Finally, *whether with assertiveness or silence, never take revenge.* Whichever approach you use, leave the paybacks out of it. Paul's powerful words to the Romans ring loud and clear:

> Never take your own revenge, beloved, but leave room for the wrath of God, for it is written, "VENGEANCE IS MINE, I WILL REPAY," says the Lord. "BUT IF YOUR ENEMY IS HUNGRY, FEED HIM, AND IF HE IS THIRSTY, GIVE HIM A DRINK; FOR IN SO DOING YOU WILL HEAP BURNING COALS ON HIS HEAD." Do not be overcome by evil, but overcome evil with good. (Rom. 12:19-21)

If justice is to be meted out, God is perfectly capable—and willing—to handle that for us. Maybe one of the reasons we don't see God step in and handle many of our agonizing and painful problems with false accusers and adversaries is that we fail to give Him opportunity to do so. Step out of the way and let God fight for you!

# Confusing Pardon with Probation
## 2 CORINTHIANS 2:5-11

**NASB**

5 But if any has caused sorrow, he
has caused sorrow not to me, but in
some degree—[a]in order not to say too
much—to all of you. 6 Sufficient for
such a one is this punishment which
*was inflicted* by the majority, 7 so that
on the contrary you should rather
forgive and comfort *him,* otherwise
such a one might be overwhelmed by
excessive sorrow. 8 Wherefore I urge
you to reaffirm *your* love for him.
9 For to this end also I wrote, so that
I might [a]put you to the test, whether
you are obedient in all things. 10 But
one whom you forgive anything, I
*forgive* also; for indeed what I have
forgiven, if I have forgiven anything,
*I did it* for your sakes in the presence
of Christ, 11 so that no advantage
would be taken of us by Satan, for
we are not ignorant of his schemes.

2:5 [a]Lit *so that I not be burdensome* 2:9 [a]Lit *know the proof of you*

**NLT**

5 I am not overstating it when I say
that the man who caused all the
trouble hurt all of you more than he
hurt me. 6 Most of you opposed him,
and that was punishment enough.
7 Now, however, it is time to forgive
and comfort him. Otherwise he may
be overcome by discouragement. 8 So
I urge you now to reaffirm your love
for him.

9 I wrote to you as I did to test you
and see if you would fully comply
with my instructions. 10 When you
forgive this man, I forgive him, too.
And when I forgive whatever needs
to be forgiven, I do so with Christ's
authority for your benefit, 11 so that
Satan will not outsmart us. For we
are familiar with his evil schemes.

Several years ago I was thumbing through a thick section of want ads in the *Los Angeles Times*. That was before Google and Craigslist. Back then the closest thing to browsing the Internet was channel surfing or flipping through the newspaper, hoping something might catch your eye. So I glanced through the personal section of the want ads, hoping to find something interesting, informative, or intriguing. You'd find all sorts of odds and ends in that section: general announcements, personal messages, desperate pleas. Today, we scroll through electronic social network pages of random people we don't know.

I came across a few lines at the bottom of a page that dripped with emotion. The words were buried in the sea of black and white, but somehow they floated from the page, catching my attention. In a little, bordered, rectangular space, these nine words appeared: "Danny, please come home. Mom and Dad forgive you."

I read those words several times. I tried to imagine the background of Danny's life. I pictured myself in Danny's shoes in some distant region of that vast metropolis, discovering the words from his mom and dad that said, "We forgive you." I imagined the heartache those anguished parents were feeling—as a parent myself, it wasn't difficult to track their struggle. What did it take to get them to swallow their pride, their judgmental spirit, their anger and bitterness, and to say, "We forgive you"?

We have all known the joy of hearing those three words, "I forgive you." There is nothing quite as liberating as having a full pardon granted from a parent you've wronged, a spouse you've betrayed, a friend you've let down . . . or the Savior you've disobeyed. What a cool wave of relief washes over our painful, sweltering souls when we hear those words, "I forgive you."

So long as they are said with sincerity, that is. Sometimes people say, "I forgive you," but they really mean, "I'll let you back into my life under the following conditions . . ." In other words, for them, "pardon" actually means "parole." Instead of leaving you feeling liberated, it makes you feel unsettled, watched, and distrusted.

Sadly, failure to grant forgiveness to a genuinely repentant person can lead to deep wounding, permanent scarring, and an irreparable relationship between two people. Harmonious fellowship is left hanging. This is true for interpersonal relationships, including those among believers in a church. In fact, the Christians in Corinth struggled with this very issue, as one of their festering, unresolved conflicts was leading to painful schism in the body of Christ.

## — 2:5-6 —

The background to the lingering problem behind Paul's admonitions in 2 Corinthians 2:5-11 is most likely found in 1 Corinthians 5, where Paul confronted the Christians in Corinth about a very specific form of sexual immorality they were condoning under the banner of "grace." One of the members of the church was engaged in an ongoing incestuous relationship with his stepmother (1 Cor. 5:1)—a sin not even their pagan neighbors would have tolerated! Because they had refused to take disciplinary action against this infectious disease of immorality, Paul instructed them to clean house (1 Cor. 5:6-7), removing the immoral man from their midst as an act of discipline (1 Cor. 5:11-13).

Somewhere between 1 Corinthians and 2 Corinthians, however, perhaps in response to Paul's second "tearful letter" (2 Cor. 2:4), some in the church must have taken Paul's firm instructions as a warrant not only for immediate and decisive action against the perpetrator, but as permission for strong, even humiliating treatment. The Corinthians had first erred on one extreme by proudly condoning the immorality with a complete lack of remorse. Now the pendulum seems to have swung to the opposite error: an arrogant condemnation of the immoral person, *even though he had sincerely repented and sought reconciliation!*

Even if Paul has in mind a destructive sinner other than the man referenced in 1 Corinthians 5:1-13, the key element of the situation that the apostle addresses is clear: A sinning man had been severely and sufficiently disciplined by the church, resulting in his repentance. Instead of forgiving him, however, they kept him at arm's length. Instead of extending him gracious pardon, they put him on graceless probation. Paul acknowledges that the sinner had caused sorrow not only to Paul, but also to the whole congregation (2 Cor. 2:5). Yet Paul suggests the punishment he had already endured from the majority in the church is "sufficient" for his particular actions (2:6).

## — 2:7-9 —

How hard it is for some believers to accept the repentance of a fellow believer who has caused them harm, even after that person has endured the discipline that was due the sin and has been restored to spiritual health and fellowship. The memories of that sin can continue to prompt unwarranted distrust, unreasonable fear, and a lingering bitterness. But these things—contrary to love and grace—have nothing to do with authentic forgiveness.

Admittedly, some serious offenses and addictions require the body of Christ to suspend some repentant believers from full participation in church ministry and service. In fact, criminal offenses could very well lead to further consequences well beyond the control of the church. Nevertheless, when the church approaches each case with the goal of forgiveness and reconciliation, hope for recovery can be found in even the most bleak of circumstances. In every case, wisdom and prudence—along with love and grace—are needed.

However, the man in Corinth who had caused such trouble no longer needed discipline; he needed forgiveness. Notice the process that had already played out, up to the time when Paul wrote this letter:

- The man had engaged in obvious sin that harmed the reputation of the congregation. (2:5)
- With painful prodding, the church reprimanded the sinner and instituted a severe punishment—probably putting him out of the church and withdrawing spiritual and material protection. (2:6)
- This action brought about genuine repentance that led to "excessive sorrow" on the part of the sinner. (2:5-7)

Such signs of authentic remorse and contrition should have inspired the church's forgiveness, comfort, and love (2:7-8). Yet at this crucial stage, the process of reconciliation broke down.

Whereas in his previous letter Paul virtually had to force the church to act against the sinner, in this letter he finds himself in the ironic position of serving as the sinner's advocate. How baffling the Corinthian church must have been! That chaotic church had pushed Paul from executing the prosecution to coming to the sinner's defense. To prevent the repentant brother in Christ from being "overwhelmed by excessive sorrow" (2:7), Paul exhorted the Corinthians to "forgive and comfort him" (2:7) and to "reaffirm [their] love for him" (2:8).

I'm sure Paul was aware of the surprising nature of this new admonition. In one letter he ordered that the sinner be removed from their midst, posthaste. Now he was commanding them to readmit him without delay or reservation. The circumstances had clearly changed, requiring a change in response that the Corinthians seemed reluctant to make. Paul's new apostolic decree may not have made sense to those wielding the exacting gavel of judgment in Corinth. In fact, it may even have come as an embarrassment to them. I can imagine some in the church saying, "Okay, I think we've punished him enough. He's sincerely sorry and wants to be restored. I'm sure Paul would have wanted to bring about reconciliation." On the other hand, those overzealous for church purity may have responded, "No! Paul told us to clean out the leaven, so that's what we're doing! The decision is final. This guilty sinner had his chance. If Paul were here, he'd agree with us!"

Then 2 Corinthians arrives, and to some in Corinth, Paul's instructions may have appeared to reveal a flip-flop in his attitude, even though it was completely consistent with his principles of church discipline as a means toward reconciliation, not condemnation. Paul's new instruction, then, becomes itself a test to see if the Corinthians will be "obedient in all things" (2:9)—even in commands that don't seem to make a lot of sense to the church and may even appear on the surface to contradict his earlier policy of discipline.

## — 2:10-11 —

Paul then presents his own forgiving attitude and actions as an example to emulate (2:10). As their father in the faith, Paul assures them that his own policy of forgiveness for the truly repentant should give them confidence that when they act with the same spirit of grace and mercy, he will have their back. Forgiveness, like discipline, is not self-seeking. In fact, it can be downright difficult. Nevertheless, Paul tells the Corinthians that his pattern of forgiveness is "for your sakes in the presence of Christ," not for his own personal gain.

Why is full and prompt forgiveness so important? Why not make the repentant sinner squirm a little to show how much others have suffered because of the sin? Why not let the repentant individual wallow just a little longer in uncertainty and experience anguish in alienation as a deterrent from ever making that same mistake again? Because withholding forgiveness gives Satan an opportunity to take advantage of us (2:11).

This is one of the strongest warnings in all of Paul's letters. The phrase "by Satan" suggests that the devil slithers his way into a situation in which an individual or church refuses to extend full pardon to truly repentant sinners. If the process of reconciliation breaks down, then the insidious demon finds his way in to further sabotage the machine. But when the process of reconciliation is oiled by mercy and grace, neither the devil nor his demons will have opportunity to stir up resentment, anguish, sorrow, bitterness, rebellion, and schism.

Satan's evil "schemes" and conniving plans involve deception and destruction. In the case of the Corinthians, the adversary had deceived them into thinking that church discipline is all judgment and no mercy, all punishment and no grace. God's goal is not ridding the church of sinners, but reconciling sinners back to the church. When we forget that, we are no longer pursuing the Lord's will, but rather the devil's wiles.

## APPLICATION: 2 CORINTHIANS 2:5-11

### *Pardon*, not Parole

Paul's correction of the pendulum-swinging Corinthians can be summed up in one simple sentence that we would all do well to memorize: "Our forgiveness should be as swift as our discipline was severe." This applies to forgiveness among friendships, marriage-and-family relationships, and church membership. As we glance back at Paul's admonition to the believers in Corinth, we can see three practical principles regarding Christlike forgiveness that we all must take to heart and never forget.

First, *true repentance calls for immediate and full forgiveness.* I'm not talking about hasty forgiveness based on cheap repentance in the form of a flippant "Hey, I'm sorry!" or a coerced confession. I'm talking about *true* repentance—the kind you can see in their eyes, hear in their tone of voice, sense in their personal brokenness. When a person's heart is pierced by genuine conviction, the sense of shame and unworthiness can be almost overwhelming. It is also obvious. The prodigal son wanted to come back home as a servant rather than as a son (Luke 15:18-19). Those of us who have been injured or offended by the sinner's actions might be tempted to take the penitent individual up on the offer, but we need to resist this. The body of Christ has no probation period for genuinely repentant sinners. True repentance—heartfelt, not a shallow imitation—calls for restoration and celebration.

Second, *full forgiveness is demonstrative, not theoretical.* It is not something we think or feel, but something we do. Remember the commands in 2 Corinthians 2:7-8? They were to "forgive," "comfort," and "reaffirm." We forgive when we speak words of liberation to the offending party: "I forgive you. We are putting this behind us and moving on." We comfort when we come alongside those who offended us, not only forgiving them for their wrongs, but offering to help them rebuild and strengthen areas of weakness. We reaffirm when we restore them to their former level of relationship, inviting and involving them in our lives, trusting them with the rights and privileges they had before. Of course, every time we forgive like this, we risk. They may fail us again. We may place our trust on an unreliable soul. But that's grace. Grace is risky.

Third, *to hold back forgiveness invites trouble from the adversary.* When you refuse to forgive a genuinely repentant sinner, that person can stumble onto a downward spiral: Overwhelming sorrow leads to confusion, fruitlessness, and doubts about their standing before God. This can lead to unbiblical approaches to the Christian life: "What must I do to redeem myself from this? How can I improve myself to be acceptable to others and to the Lord?" Ultimately, frustration and bitterness set in. If that's not a path paved by the adversary, I don't know what is.

Are you holding a grudge? Are you holding something over somebody who has harmed you in the past, but who has genuinely repented? If so, you need to cancel the debt immediately, express your unconditional forgiveness, and begin restoring that relationship.

Is there somebody today who needs to hear and feel your forgiveness, comfort, and reaffirmation? What is preventing you from reaching out and touching that person with healing mercy and grace?

Are your unforgiving attitudes toward somebody resulting in their exasperation or desperation? Are they obsessed with gaining your approval? This may be a child, a spouse, or even a parent. You need to release them so they will not become a target for Satan's twisted temptations.

# What's That Smell?

## 2 CORINTHIANS 2:12-17

**NASB**

12 Now when I came to Troas for the
gospel of Christ and when a door was
opened for me in the Lord, 13 I had no
rest for my spirit, not finding Titus
my brother; but taking my leave of
them, I went on to Macedonia.
14 But thanks be to God, who al-
ways leads us in triumph in Christ,

**NLT**

12 When I came to the city of Troas to
preach the Good News of Christ, the
Lord opened a door of opportunity
for me. 13 But I had no peace of mind
because my dear brother Titus hadn't
yet arrived with a report from you. So
I said good-bye and went on to Mace-
donia to find him.
14 But thank God! He has made us
his captives and continues to lead

and manifests through us the sweet
aroma of the knowledge of Him in
every place. 15 For we are a fragrance
of Christ to God among those who
are being saved and among those
who are perishing; 16 to the one an
aroma from death to death, to the
other an aroma from life to life. And
who is adequate for these things?
17 For we are not like many, [a]ped-
dling the word of God, but as from
sincerity, but as from God, we speak
in Christ in the sight of God.

**2:17** [a]Or *corrupting*

us along in Christ's triumphal pro-
cession. Now he uses us to spread
the knowledge of Christ everywhere,
like a sweet perfume. 15 Our lives are
a Christ-like fragrance rising up to
God. But this fragrance is perceived
differently by those who are being
saved and by those who are perish-
ing. 16 To those who are perishing,
we are a dreadful smell of death and
doom. But to those who are being
saved, we are a life-giving perfume.
And who is adequate for such a task
as this?

17 You see, we are not like the many
hucksters* who preach for personal
profit. We preach the word of God
with sincerity and with Christ's au-
thority, knowing that God is watch-
ing us.

**2:17** Some manuscripts read *the rest of the hucksters.*

Paul's writings swell with profound and practical theology. Deep and rich, fascinating and transforming—the doctrinal length, breadth, height, and depth of his writings can capture and keep the attention of devoted Bible scholars for decades. When I read Paul's writings, however, I see more than weighty theology. I see authentic humanity.

When I read Paul's words, I see not only vehicles of divine revelation and epic truths, but I also see words wrought in conflict, hardship, and struggle. I see tear-stained pages, drops of blood, and beads of sweat. I guess that is why I am so deeply drawn into 2 Corinthians. This letter reveals Paul like an open book. Here, on page after page, Paul exudes authenticity. Built upon his steely frame, we see parts of him that are still papier-mâché. Among his rough edges and sharp points, we feel the soft terry cloth heart of a person whose compassion matches his exuberant passion.

In this spirit of vulnerability, Paul shared with the Corinthians a recent personal struggle, one he faced as he ministered at Troas. As he reflected on this, he took comfort in Christ's eternal victory, envisioning the believers' place in Christ's victory procession, marked with the fragrance of victory for those who are in Christ.

## — 2:12-13 —

Troas stood on the northwestern tip of Asia Minor (modern-day Turkey; see map of Paul's third missionary journey on page 278), far from Ephesus, where Paul had been ministering. It had been a long, difficult journey, but when he arrived, he found people eager to hear his message. The door had been opened wide for the gospel (2:12). Their spiritual hunger would have made any ambitious, numbers-driven preacher salivate with delight. Yet Paul found himself distracted, eaten away on the inside by emotional turmoil. He had "no rest" for his spirit (2:13).

The word translated "rest" (*anesis* [425]) can also be interpreted as "a loosening" or "a relaxing." It is the same word used in Acts 24:23 for "freedom" and in 2 Corinthians 8:13 for "ease." The idea seems to be that although Paul stood before an open gate leading to a garden of spiritual fruit almost falling from the trees, he felt distracted, disquieted, and dismayed. Some anxiety gripped his spirit and prevented him from focusing on his task of ministry. What should have been a relaxing ministry of ease became a trial and a chore.

It seems improbable that this could have happened to Paul, doesn't it? What kind of dried-up preacher stands before a great crowd of spiritual sponges and walks away without even a light sprinkling? Yet the great apostle Paul himself, self-proclaimed "apostle to the Gentiles" (Galatians 2:8), took his leave from Troas and went on to Macedonia. What would drive a man of Paul's endurance and determination to forgo this ministry opportunity?

He could not find Titus, his dear friend and brother in the Lord. Apparently, Titus was supposed to meet Paul in Troas to update him on the Corinthian situation and to help him in his ministry there. Yet when Paul arrived in Troas and failed to find Titus, his mind reeled, and his imagination fed him images of the worst kind. Had he been arrested? Betrayed by Jewish or Gentile opponents? Executed? Assassinated? Was he delayed by accident or illness? The possibilities were endless.

We all have been in situations like this, when our intense worry and fears of the unknown consume us, distracting us from tasks at hand. All of us who preach and teach the Word can relate to this. I have lost count of the times I found myself in the pulpit delivering a message with as much passion as I could muster, desperately desiring to be back home dealing with a marriage matter, or addressing a lingering breach in my relationship with my kids. Present in body, absent in mind—this all-too-common reality of public ministry hounds every minister of the gospel. And it pursued Paul during his brief stay at Troas like a rabid dog trying to nip at his heels.

David Lowery helps us understand Paul's specific concern more deeply:

> Despairing at his own inability to concentrate on the great potential for ministry in Troas (cf. 2 Cor. 7:5-6) Paul said good-by to the church there and pushed on to Macedonia. The door would remain open for him and on his return (cf. Acts 20:5-11) God used him mightily in their midst, but for the moment Paul departed, unable to rise to the occasion, no doubt feeling like a beaten man.[8]

## — 2:14-17 —

Instead of lingering on his feelings of defeat, Paul pressed on. He moved from his own weaknesses in ministry to Christ, who triumphs over every circumstance. Beginning in 2 Corinthians 2:14 and continuing through 2 Corinthians 6:10, Paul discusses the earthy realities of authentic ministry in greater depth than he does anywhere else in the New Testament. He begins this aside (2:14-17) by peering through a microscope, zooming in on three essentials of effective, Christ-centered, gospel-empowered ministry:

- Authentic ministers follow the Leader rather than take the lead. (2:14)
- Authentic ministers display God's grace regardless of human response. (2:14-16)
- Authentic ministers preach the Word despite their inadequacies. (2:16-17)

On the heels of describing his early departure from Troas to go on to Macedonia, Paul wrote, "But thanks be to God" (2:14). What an attitude! From the pits of uncertainty, desperation, and despair, Paul was able to praise God for His glorious deliverance. After a long discussion of the ministry, Paul will later return to the question of what happened to Titus, letting his readers in on the reason behind his praise to God: "But God, who comforts the depressed, comforted us by the coming of Titus; and not only by his coming, but also by the comfort with which he was comforted in you, as he reported to us your longing, your mourning, your zeal for me; so that I rejoiced even more" (7:6-7).

After Paul's exuberant thanksgiving (2:14), however, he doesn't immediately reveal the cause of his praise. It is as though Paul were trying to tell his readers that we ought to rejoice in the character of God as the powerful and trustworthy victor over all of our circumstances, even if we cannot see the triumph set immediately before our eyes. So, instead of sharing the news about Titus, he drew on a common image from their day that would communicate an important principle concerning the ministry.

William Barclay helps us see the picture in the mind of Paul and his readers when he used the word "triumph" for the kind of continual victory believers have in Jesus Christ (2:14):

> In a Triumph, the procession of the victorious general marched through the streets of Rome to the Capitol in the following order. First came the state officials and the senate. Then came the trumpeters. Behind them came those carrying the spoils taken from the conquered land. . . . Walking behind all these were the captive princes, leaders and generals in chains. . . . Then came the officers who attended the magistrates, the lictors bearing their rods, followed by the musicians with their lyres; then the priests swinging their censers with the sweet-smelling incense burning in them. After that came the general himself. He stood in a chariot drawn by four horses. . . . After him rode his family, and finally came the army wearing all their decorations and shouting *Io triumphe!*, their cry of triumph.[9]

Without getting too bogged down in the details of a Roman parade of triumph, we should note the first essential for authentic ministry: *authentic ministers follow the Leader rather than take the lead* (2:14). Christ, our Conquering King, leads us into battle. Paul says, "Thanks be to God, who always leads us in triumph in Christ" (2:14). Effective ministry occurs when we are in the train of Christ's triumph, not pursuing our own triumph. Christ chooses the battles. He claims the victory. Remember that at the cross Christ undertook a battle not rightly His in order that we might share in a triumph not rightly ours.

If we were to keep this principle in the center of our focus, we would see fewer names on ministries, projects, buildings, and churches. People would give anonymously, lead from among the ranks, and seek their reward from Christ in the future rather than recognition from Christians in the present. Don't get me wrong. There is nothing wrong with showing people appreciation when it is due. Sometimes, however, we adopt the world's ways and our culture's conditioning, seeking praise, glory, and laud for "our" victories rather than following Christ in His victory.

Relief of Roman **triumphal procession** on the Arch of Titus in Rome, Italy, depicting Titus's siege of Jerusalem in AD 70

Paul's image of the Roman processional points to a second essential of effective Christ-centered ministry: *authentic ministers display God's grace regardless of human response* (2:14-16). These ancient processionals were marked by an aroma, as giant censers of smoking incense were carried by the priests. The smell would flow equally over those exulting in triumph and those hanging their heads in defeat. To the former, the incense reinforced their victory over the enemy. To the latter, the smoke stung their nostrils with the incessant reminder of military defeat and imminent death.

Did you know that as Christians we give off an aroma? I'm not saying we emit a foul odor. I'm saying that our message, our morals, and our lifestyle either encourage people to believe and live like us, or they anger people who reject our beliefs and despise our lifestyles. I see this different response to the message most distinctly at funerals. When I speak of the resurrection before the casket of a loved one, I always get two very different responses from people in the gathering. Though all of them grieve the loss of their friend, loved one, or family member, only some rejoice in the hope of eternal life and reunion at the resurrection (1 Thes. 4:13-18). Those who have eternal life in Christ receive the message of resurrection as a sweet-smelling aroma of life. Others in the crowd, however, reject the message of the resurrection, regarding it as superstitious soothsaying—a useless crutch to get us through the unpleasant, hard realities of life. To them, the message of salvation in

Christ is a dead message—not of hope, but of death. The very same message of salvation in Jesus Christ can be received as the smell of life or of death, depending on whether people approach it in faith or unbelief.

Finally, Paul points out that *authentic ministers preach the Word despite their inadequacies* (2 Cor. 2:16-17). He refers to those who were "peddling the word of God" as ministers of insincerity, self-sufficiency, and personal promotion. They were in it for the fame, honor, and financial benefits. The image is one of street salesmen hawking their wares, interested only in making the sale and increasing their numbers. Just as there were money changers in the temple courtyard trying to make a killing on the religious devotion of others, there will always be street salesmen in the church peddling prophetic pills, cure-all tonics, positive thinking, health and wealth, legalism, and cynicism. In short, they will peddle whatever sells, whatever the public is gullible enough to purchase.

The truth is, however, that nobody is qualified for the job Paul and his fellow apostles and ministers were doing. His question, "Who is adequate for these things?" (2:16), implies a negative response: *nobody*! Nobody is self-sufficient; nobody can do it on their own. Paul himself was quite transparent and sincere about his weaknesses in ministering in Troas, desperate as he was to meet with and hear from Titus. Charlatans don't take off their masks and let people see the real, flawed individuals behind them.

Paul assured the Corinthians that he was no salesman. He represented the Lord, not himself. His adequacy was not in his persuasive words but in the authority of the One who sent him and the content of his message—Jesus Christ. Only when serving authentically, selflessly, and sacrificially can one be sure that one's ministry is being performed "in the sight of God" (2:17).

## APPLICATION: 2 CORINTHIANS 2:12-17

### An Honest Evaluation of Our Own Ministries

Now that we have looked into the open book of Paul's life—including some of his ministry struggles, fears, worries, concerns, and failings—it's time to read a page or two from our own lives. We will do this self-exam by focusing on four crucial categories and questions. This is an open-book exam; you can dig as deeply into the chapters and pages of your own heart as you are willing to go. Ask the Spirit to guide you in the process.

*Our dependence on God.* Are you really depending on God? Are you waiting on Him or rushing Him? When He doesn't seem to come through, do you take matters into your own hands and run ahead of Him? Sometimes God tests our dependence on Him in order to strengthen and deepen that virtue in our lives. This might mean impressing His will upon your heart to test your go-for-broke obedience. Or it may mean letting you wait for His guidance for what may seem like a long time. Both the voice of God and the silence of God can teach us to depend on Him.

*Our victory in Christ.* If you were to watch an exposé of your life, would it describe somebody victorious over doubt, fear, hypocrisy, pride, and sin? Or would it portray a despondent, defeated, less-than-effective Christian who wavers between activity and passivity? If Christ's power "always leads us in triumph" (2:14), could it be that you've been either following somebody else's parade or trying to lead your own? Have you ever committed yourself to God as a living sacrifice, voluntarily surrendering your body, your mind, your heart, and your will to Him (Rom. 12:1-2)? If not, what is keeping you from doing that right now?

*Our witness to the world.* How do you smell to those around you? I'm not talking about your cologne or perfume. I mean, are you exuding the scent of sin or the aroma of the Savior? Christlike character has an unmistakable fragrance. It will attract those God has prepared to hear and receive His good news, but it will drive away those whose hearts have been hardened. Their response is not your concern; that is up to the Lord. No believer, however, wants to be responsible for driving unbelievers away from Christ because of a hypocritical testimony in which we say or believe one thing and put off a putrid odor that points to something else. Richard Baxter once said, "Take heed to yourselves . . . lest you may unsay that with your lives which you say with your tongues."[10]

*Our authentic ministry.* People can spot charlatans and fakes pretty well. They are used to politicians grinning while lying through their teeth. They have seen TV preachers rail against immorality, right up until they got busted for engaging prostitutes. They have learned how to resist the barrage of high-pressure pitches from salesmen bent on taking their money. Only by modeling sincere authenticity can Christians counter this culture of posers and wannabes. Is being real one of your priorities? Do you let people in on your weaknesses as well as your strengths? Do you exhibit your vulnerabilities or do you conceal them with showmanship? Authenticity means coming to grips with who you are and being transparent about what your life is like beneath its polished exterior. It is painful to be real, but that's the way we impact others most deeply (1 Thes. 2:8).

As you reflect on and answer the questions above, ask yourself if your relationship with the Lord might have bottomed out at a superficial level. Thankfully, God always leads in triumph, so he always leads His children into a deeper relationship with him. If you want to have a deeper, more meaningful spiritual life, take some time to pray about that. The Lord is seeking humble, sincere, and authentic servants to advance His kingdom into the future. Will you answer the call?

## A New Covenant Kind of Ministry
### 2 CORINTHIANS 3:1-18

**NASB**

1 Are we beginning to commend
ourselves again? Or do we need, as
some, letters of commendation to
you or from you? 2 You are our letter,
written in our hearts, known and
read by all men; 3 being manifested
that you are a letter of Christ, [a]cared
for by us, written not with ink but
with the Spirit of the living God, not
on tablets of stone but on tablets of
[b]human hearts.

4 Such confidence we have through
Christ toward God. 5 Not that we are
adequate in ourselves to consider
anything as *coming* from ourselves,
but our adequacy is from God, 6 who
also made us adequate *as* servants of
a new covenant, not of the letter but
of the Spirit; for the letter kills, but
the Spirit gives life.

**NLT**

1 Are we beginning to praise ourselves
again? Are we like others, who need
to bring you letters of recommenda-
tion, or who ask you to write such
letters on their behalf? Surely not!
2 The only letter of recommendation
we need is you yourselves. Your lives
are a letter written in our* hearts;
everyone can read it and recognize
our good work among you. 3 Clearly,
you are a letter from Christ showing
the result of our ministry among you.
This "letter" is written not with pen
and ink, but with the Spirit of the liv-
ing God. It is carved not on tablets of
stone, but on human hearts.

4 We are confident of all this be-
cause of our great trust in God
through Christ. 5 It is not that we
think we are qualified to do anything
on our own. Our qualification comes
from God. 6 He has enabled us to be
ministers of his new covenant. This
is a covenant not of written laws, but
of the Spirit. The old written cov-
enant ends in death; but under the
new covenant, the Spirit gives life.

7 But if the ministry of death, in letters engraved on stones, came [a]with glory, so that the sons of Israel could not look intently at the face of Moses because of the glory of his face, fading *as* it was, 8 how will the ministry of the Spirit fail to be even more with glory? 9 For if the ministry of condemnation has glory, much more does the ministry of righteousness abound in glory. 10 For indeed what had glory, in this case has no glory because of the glory that surpasses *it*. 11 For if that which fades away *was* [a]with glory, much more that which remains *is* in glory.

12 Therefore having such a hope, we use great boldness in *our* speech, 13 and *are* not like Moses, *who* used to put a veil over his face so that the sons of Israel would not look intently at the end of what was fading away. 14 But their minds were hardened; for until this very day at the reading of the old covenant the same veil [a]remains unlifted, because it is removed in Christ. 15 But to this day whenever Moses is read, a veil lies over their heart; 16 but whenever a person turns to the Lord, the veil is taken away. 17 Now the Lord is the Spirit, and where the Spirit of the Lord is, *there* is liberty. 18 But we all, with unveiled face, beholding as in a mirror the glory of the Lord, are being transformed into the same image from glory to glory, just as from the Lord, the Spirit.

**3:3** [a]Lit *served* [b]Lit *hearts of flesh* **3:7** [a]Or *in glory* **3:11** [a]Lit *through* **3:14** [a]Or *remains, it not being revealed that it is done away in Christ*

7 The old way,* with laws etched in stone, led to death, though it began with such glory that the people of Israel could not bear to look at Moses' face. For his face shone with the glory of God, even though the brightness was already fading away. 8 Shouldn't we expect far greater glory under the new way, now that the Holy Spirit is giving life? 9 If the old way, which brings condemnation, was glorious, how much more glorious is the new way, which makes us right with God! 10 In fact, that first glory was not glorious at all compared with the overwhelming glory of the new way. 11 So if the old way, which has been replaced, was glorious, how much more glorious is the new, which remains forever!

12 Since this new way gives us such confidence, we can be very bold. 13 We are not like Moses, who put a veil over his face so the people of Israel would not see the glory, even though it was destined to fade away. 14 But the people's minds were hardened, and to this day whenever the old covenant is being read, the same veil covers their minds so they cannot understand the truth. And this veil can be removed only by believing in Christ. 15 Yes, even today when they read Moses' writings, their hearts are covered with that veil, and they do not understand.

16 But whenever someone turns to the Lord, the veil is taken away. 17 For the Lord is the Spirit, and wherever the Spirit of the Lord is, there is freedom. 18 So all of us who have had that veil removed can see and reflect the glory of the Lord. And the Lord—who is the Spirit—makes us more and more like him as we are changed into his glorious image.

**3:2** Some manuscripts read *your.* **3:7** Or *ministry;* also in 3:8, 9, 10, 11, 12.

*Success.* Just the sound of the word in our modern world works like a powerful stimulant. It brings to mind images of money, power, and prestige. Goals achieved, dreams fulfilled, obstacles overcome, enemies vanquished: Everybody loves a dose of success. And we know the recipe for success, don't we? Successful people are well educated, fashionably dressed, impeccably groomed, and socially savvy. They look the part. They sail through challenges on a vessel of self-confidence propelled by unswerving determination—no distraction can get in their way. These things draw crowds and cameras, and before you know it, their names and pictures are pasted all over the media. In turn, the fame factor then drives both them and their business or organization's marketing machine, generating more attention, more opportunities, more revenue—*more success.*

As difficult as it may be to accept, those are not the things that spell success in God's eyes. A person's outward appearance or social panache? God's not swayed an inch by them. Scripture says, "God sees not as man sees, for man looks at the outward appearance, but the LORD looks at the heart" (1 Sam. 16:7). Self-confidence that plows forward with goals and plans despite every obstacle? Only if the Lord wills. James wrote, "Instead, you ought to say, 'If the Lord wills, we will live and also do this or that'" (Jas. 4:15). Shameless self-promotion that sells a slick "public image" to a ready consumer culture? The Lord's not impressed. Paul wrote, "For it is not he who commends himself that is approved, but he whom the Lord commends" (2 Cor. 10:18). The world may be infatuated with glamour, guts, and glory, but God has a completely different standard of success.

Sadly, these worldly elements of success have worked their way into our churches and ministries. Nowadays a successful ministry is measured by how many thousands attend or tune in to your services, by the level of fame and influence of your preacher, or by the state-of-the-art amenities on your physical campus. During my life of ministry, I have pastored and ministered in small churches, medium-sized churches, and large churches, in congregations ignored by the surrounding community and in churches with a global impact. I have personally experienced the struggles and blessings inherent in different ministry scopes and scales. Let me tell you: Small churches that appear to be unsuccessful by the world's standards can be far more successful in God's eyes than giant churches with budgets that allow them to do anything they imagine. Powerful ministries with global celebrities at the helm can be bilking members and ruining lives rather than preaching the gospel and building up the body of Christ.

It is easy to get into the worldly mindset that the greater our qualifications, influence, and financial resources, the more God can use us. Paul, however, regarded all of his own human achievement apart from Christ as "rubbish" compared to knowing Jesus Christ (Phil. 3:4-9). Now, in 2 Corinthians 3, Paul completes the picture of an authentic new covenant ministry that God deems successful by *His* standards. Here we discover where our adequacy for service really comes from. Though Paul's teachings may surprise the world's masters of success and the worldly-minded Christian entrepreneurs, we should expect that our sufficiency comes not from ourselves, but from God alone.

## — 3:1-5 —

In 2 Corinthians 2:14-17, Paul says that he basks in the triumphal procession of Christ, in the fragrance of Christ's victory celebration, and in sincerity of heart. A critic of his ministry could read those words and think Paul was boasting about his stunning accomplishments to draw attention to himself. Indeed, we have already seen that Paul could have bragged about the miraculous deeds the Lord had performed by his hands. But here (3:1) Paul anticipates and addresses the potential charge of self-commendation.

In Paul's day, itinerant evangelists would often travel with letters of endorsements and recommendation, which functioned as authentication. Even before Jesus and the disciples, traveling wonder-working wannabes journeyed from city to city, trying to drum up excitement and reap a harvest of cash and commitment from unsuspecting crowds. When the gospel began to spread from Jerusalem to Judea and Samaria and then to the Gentile nations (Acts 1:8), the cadre of quacks didn't let up. In fact, Satan used the spread of the church to mobilize his own army of charlatans. These people went out of their way to distinguish themselves from Christ's authentic ambassadors of the new covenant by pointing out the apostles' apparent flaws and promoting their own accomplishments.

In light of these competitors, Paul reemphasized his own "letter" of commendation—the Corinthian Christians themselves (2 Cor. 3:2-3). Paul did not need a letter of approval. If anyone wanted to see whether he was a valid minister of the gospel, there was no need to look any farther than the members of the churches Paul had planted across Asia

Minor and Achaia—including the church in Corinth. Their changed hearts, affected by the "Spirit of the living God," were all the commendation he needed. Their authentic conversion demonstrated Paul's work as an authentic apostle.

Paul acknowledged, however, that his successful ministry was due not to his own work, but to Christ's work through him (3:4). In fact, he confessed his inadequacy, "Not that we are adequate in ourselves to consider anything as coming from ourselves, but our adequacy is from God" (3:5). How many ministers do you know who model that? How many Christians exhibit this kind of self-surrender? Paul's words stand in sharp contrast to a worldview that glorifies rags-to-riches stories of people pulling themselves up by their own bootstraps, taking extreme measures to be "discovered," or expending large amounts of time, money, and energy to toot their own horns. From Paul's perspective, it was not important that anybody see us, but that they see Him. The more we promote ourselves, the more we obscure the person and work of Christ.

## — 3:6-11 —

Beginning in 2 Corinthians 3:5, Paul illustrates the uniqueness of the new covenant kind of ministry entrusted to the apostles. So revolutionary is this gospel ministry that it not only stands in sharp contrast with what the world expects a successful enterprise to look like, but it also differs profoundly from the ministry of the old covenant. Under the old covenant—the Mosaic Law—God's truth was carved in stone and inscribed on paper. The commandments served as external standards that objectively judged a person as a sinner. In this way, the "letter" of the Law, though good and holy in itself (Rom. 7:12), served to "kill," that is, condemn us to judgment before a good and holy God (2 Cor. 3:6-7). It could not give life, because nobody was ever able to live up to its exacting standards (Rom. 3:10).

Enter Jesus of Nazareth. He stepped into this world as our representative—taking our place in perfectly fulfilling the Law. Then He took our place when He died on the cross, accepting our punishment on Himself for the world's sins and canceling the condemning power of the Law (Eph. 2:14-15). Finally, He rose again from the dead and ascended to heaven, sending the life-giving Spirit of God into the hearts of believers. Since then, God's righteous standards have been written on the hearts of believers (Jer. 31:33), so as they read God's revealed Word, they don't respond in shame and guilt as a result of condemnation. Instead, they respond in faith to Christ's saving work, giving thanks for their salvation, and living a good and holy life by the power of the indwelling Spirit. The Law served to show us our inability to meet God's standards, but His Spirit in us makes us adequate to meet any requirement.

Paul uses the image of "glory" to further advance his contrasts (2 Cor. 3:9-11). Think of glory as light. If you live in a part of the country relatively free from light pollution, you can exult in the twinkling glory of the stars and the soft luminescence of the moon. On a dark night, far from human light, a full moon can almost light your path. But as soon as the sun rises, the stars vanish, the moon pales, and all you can see is the brilliant dome of the sky illuminated by a blazing yellow sun. Where did the stars go? They are still in the sky, but now the intense glory of the sun far outshines anything else in the heavens.

Similarly, the old covenant with all its glory paled with the dawn of Christ. Yes, the Old Testament Law was good, righteous, and holy. It had been given by God through a miraculous series of events. Yet the glory of its "ministry of condemnation" (3:9) dims into obscurity in the light of the gospel's "ministry of righteousness" (3:9). In fact, so vast is the difference between the glory of the old covenant and the glory of the new that the contrast makes it appear as if the old had "no glory because of the glory that surpasses it" (3:10). Although the old covenant was full of glory, the new covenant's glory is far greater (3:11).

## — 3:12-16 —

The age of the new covenant also ushered in a fresh and radiant confidence. Paul wrote, "Therefore, having such a hope, we use great boldness in our speech" (3:12). Paul's boldness does not come from a confidence in his own ideas, abilities, or giftedness, but from the fact that the new covenant ministry entrusted to him far outshines even the good, holy, righteous old covenant ministry of Moses.

When Moses received the Ten Commandments on Mount Sinai, his face glowed as a visible, residual effect of having been in the presence of God. Imagine that! Coming down from that mountain, Moses had to veil his face to keep from blinding those who looked upon him (Exod. 34:29-35). Yet 2 Corinthians 3:13 says that Moses kept the veil over his face to cover up the fact that the glory was fading, indicating that outside the very presence of God, our own finite, sinful inadequacy cannot maintain the glory of God. After all, it was *God's* glory, which He shared with Moses, not Moses' self-generated glory.

For Paul, the veil represents an attempt to protect and preserve one's reputation—something we all do from time to time. If we remember that our sufficiency is found in Christ alone, however, this kind of "cover-up" is unnecessary. In Christ, the masks we wear to hide our inadequacies and weaknesses can be taken off and shattered—permanently. In fact, the sooner we do this, the better, because our masks and veils only obscure our own ability to see Christ clearly. They also distract others from seeing Christ in us.

Paul taught that a figurative veil of spiritual blindness overshadowed the minds and hearts of the majority of the Jewish people—their minds were "hardened" (3:14), so they could not discern Christ foreshadowed in the Old Testament (3:14-16). When the Spirit graciously invades their lives, however, He enlightens their minds, and the veil is taken away, revealing Christ in all His glory and also enabling the person to reflect Christ to others (3:16).

## — 3:17-18 —

When we come to Jesus, the power of the Holy Spirit transforms our lives. We come to the cross confessing our own inadequacy and claiming only His adequacy. But how quickly we believers seem to forget that the life of discipleship is a life of denying ourselves! It is a life of taking up the cross to follow Christ daily (Matt. 16:24). Instead, as we leave the shadow of the cross, we forget that our adequacy *still* comes from Christ alone. Like the hymnist said, "Nothing in my hand I bring, Simply to Thy cross I cling."[11]

Paul gives the secret of our confidence in 2 Corinthians 3:17-18. The source of our confidence is not found in ourselves, our riches, our gifts, positions, power, prestige, or accomplishments. Instead, the liberating source of our sufficiency is His Spirit (3:17). No longer do we need to live imprisoned in fear, shame, guilt, or a constant need to impress anybody—especially God. No longer do we need to feel concerned about transforming ourselves in our own power. Instead, we simply remove the veil of self-deception from our hearts, setting aside our own desire for recognition and accomplishment, and allow Christ to shine through us: "But we all, with unveiled face, beholding as in a mirror the glory of the Lord, are being transformed into the same image from glory to glory, just as from the Lord, the Spirit" (3:18).

# APPLICATION: 2 CORINTHIANS 3:1-18

## Two Essential Ingredients for Transformation

Recipes can be finicky things. Give the mixing bowl too much of one ingredient and it pays you back with a cake that's either too dry or too moist, too sweet or too eggy. Fail to add an ingredient or two and you may end up with fudge brownies that chew like cardboard or disintegrate into a pile of sawdust.

The same principle holds true for the transformed life. God has "granted to us everything pertaining to life and godliness" (2 Pet. 1:3). These things include the Father's love, the Son's sacrificial death and empowering resurrection, and the Spirit's presence within individual believers as well as the church. He has given us His inspired, inerrant Word as a perfect guide through the labyrinth of life. Yet believers often overlook two essential ingredients for a transformed life: God and time.

First, *God*. Yes, in our accomplishment-driven, reward-oriented culture, we tend to believe that we are saved by God's grace but transformed by our own works. We need to remember that *true spirituality comes from God; it doesn't come from us*. We can make ourselves available. We can take away the veil of false piety. We can yield to the Spirit's will and power instead of giving ourselves over to the flesh. But, in the end, only God has the power to energize our walk and bring true transformation to our lives. Consider memorizing these two important passages to help keep God's enabling power central in your pursuit of holiness:

> It is God who is at work in you, both to will and to work for His good pleasure. (Phil. 2:13)

> I have been crucified with Christ; and it is no longer I who live, but Christ lives in me. (Gal. 2:20)

Second, *time*. From fast-food joints, to ten-minute oil changes, to news headlines in thirty seconds, our twenty-first-century culture has grown accustomed to getting instant results. We used to be called the "microwave generation." Now people stare at the microwave and tap their feet impatiently for a hot beverage that used to take ten minutes to brew!

In this kind of instant-access, on-demand world, it's too easy to expect God to act on our truncated timeline. This is especially true with spiritual growth. When it comes to temptation and sin, we expect Him to just "zap it." When it comes to pain and suffering, we want Him to "take it away." When it comes to nurturing virtues, we want God to instantly infuse us with a new character. How easy it is to behave as if the God who performed all those great miracles of the Bible will miraculously make us into mature disciples. But God is not a magician waving a magic wand. From our perspective, God takes His time, but He does so with good reason—in order to lead us through a life of experiences designed to grow us. Let me suggest two more passages worth memorizing and meditating on. Both relate to the need for practice and a lifetime of experiences—in essence, time—in order for us to be transformed into the image of His Son.

> Solid food is for the mature, who because of practice have their senses trained to discern good and evil. (Heb. 5:14)

> Applying all diligence, in your faith supply moral excellence, and in your moral excellence, knowledge, and in your knowledge, self-control, and in your self-control, perseverance, and in your perseverance, godliness, and in your godliness, brotherly kindness, and in your brotherly kindness, love. (2 Pet. 1:5-7)

These two ingredients of a transformed life, God and time, should never be neglected. Without them, we will be trying to do the impossible on our own, always frustrated because the Christian life doesn't seem to be working out. With these two, we will slowly but surely be transformed "from glory to glory" (2 Cor. 3:18).

# THE MINISTRY OF RECONCILIATION (2 CORINTHIANS 4:1–5:21)

Can you imagine being Rip Van Winkle, having slept away a hundred years in some distant forest, aroused one Sunday to stumble into a modern church? Imagine the shock you would experience if you were transported from the nineteeth to the twenty-first century! Somewhere along the line, pews were replaced with folding chairs, sanctuaries and pulpits gave way to storefronts and stages, and the words to worship songs began to be projected on screens at the front of the church. I think some of our contemporary trends would take some getting used to.

Now imagine if the apostle Paul were to be transported from his first-century Greco-Roman world into our twenty-first-century modern culture. He would stumble around in amazement, rubbing his eyes in disbelief at the startling changes in architecture, art, transportation, communication, population, and medicine. If he could find his way around a modern town, I wonder if Paul would even be able to identify a Christian church for what it was. And if he did make his way into a typical evangelical church on a Sunday morning, would he join in the worship or scratch his head in disbelief?

The contemporary condition of the church would shock that founding apostle. As one of its original "fathers," the apostle Paul nursed the church in its infancy, helping it grow into its toddler years before passing it on to the next generation of believers, whom he and the other apostles had handpicked for the task. Theirs was a ministry by which sinful people could be reconciled to a holy God in Jesus the Messiah a ministry characterized by new creation in Christ (5:17). How do you think he would feel about today's ministers of the gospel—the direct heirs of the Christian faith, passed down from generation to generation? Would he be proud? Embarrassed? Confused? Approving? Angry?

Something tells me that many aspects of our ecclesiastical cultural capitulation would fall short of Paul's ideal ministry of reconciliation. We lack moral purity; Paul emphasized it. We are losing fidelity to in-depth biblical teaching; Paul exhorted it. We overemphasize emotional persuasion; Paul relied on the Spirit's work. Many churches have no idea who they are or what they are supposed to be doing; Paul had a strong sense of Christian conviction and a clear model of ministry as an ambassador of Christ, pleading with the world on behalf of Christ, "Be reconciled to God" (5:20). When we lose sight of that paramount calling, we drift further and further from the ideal into models and methods of ministry that look nothing like those of the New Testament.

We in the twenty-first century want to embrace an authentic Christianity and encourage authentic ministry. To do this, we need to know exactly what we are called and equipped to do. I've titled 2 Corinthians 4:1–5:21 "The Ministry of Reconciliation." Like earthen vessels fashioned from clay but used to hold priceless treasures (4:7-12), we frail and fallible human ministers are filled with the Spirit of God for the glorious ministry of reconciliation between God and humanity (4:13-18). Because of our heavenly mandate to reach unbelievers for Christ and train them as disciples, we look forward to an eternal—not temporal—reward. We should care little what our surrounding culture makes of us. Instead, we must labor hard in our mortal bodies as we anticipate, with hope and longing, our immortal dwellings (5:1-10). Therefore,

## KEY TERMS IN 2 CORINTHIANS 4:1–5:21

### *doxa* (δόξα) [1391] "glory," "honor"

In the ancient Greek translation of the Old Testament (called the Septuagint), God's *doxa* is usually a physical manifestation of His holy, righteous, transcendent essence (Exod. 16:7). The prophet Isaiah described a vision of God's glory filling the whole world (Isa. 6:3)—that is, His awesome attributes reflected in the greatness of His creation. For Paul, God's glory is the ultimate goal and end of all things (Eph. 3:21). In 2 Corinthians 4:1-7, Paul contrasts the greatness and glory of God with the fragile human vessels commissioned to communicate that glory to the world through the proclamation of the gospel of Jesus Christ.

### *katallagē* (καταλλαγή) [2643] "reconciliation"

The word "reconciliation" was an accounting or financial term which literally meant "an exchange" or "trade." Paul uses the term (and its verb form *katallassō* [2644]) in Romans 5:10-11; 11:15 and 2 Corinthians 5:18-20 to refer to a change in relationship because of the substitutionary work of Jesus Christ on the cross. Our sin and death have been reckoned to His account, while His life and righteousness have been transferred to ours. Therefore, the relationship between God and believers has been restored.

God's authentic minister strives to persuade others to reconciliation with God, regardless of the personal cost (5:11-21).

This ministry of reconciliation may not line up well with the contemporary ministry models prevalent in our churches, but if we would be true to Paul's vision of a fruitful ministry, we must strive for just such a ministry of reconciliation.

# Powerful Preaching in Pitiful Pots

## 2 CORINTHIANS 4:1-12

**NASB**

1 Therefore, since we have this minis-
try, as we received mercy, we do not
lose heart, 2 but we have renounced
the things hidden because of shame,
not walking in craftiness or adulter-
ating the word of God, but by the
manifestation of truth commending
ourselves to every man's conscience
in the sight of God. 3 And even if our
gospel is veiled, it is veiled [a]to those
who are perishing, 4 in whose case
the god of this [a]world has blinded
the minds of the unbelieving [b]so
that they might not see the light of
the gospel of the glory of Christ, who
is the image of God. 5 For we do not
preach ourselves but Christ Jesus as
Lord, and ourselves as your bond-
servants [a]for Jesus' sake. 6 For God,
who said, "Light shall shine out of
darkness," is the One who has shone
in our hearts to give the Light of the
knowledge of the glory of God in the
face of Christ.

7 But we have this treasure in
earthen vessels, so that the surpass-
ing greatness of the power will be
of God and not from ourselves; 8 *we
are* afflicted in every way, but not

**NLT**

1 Therefore, since God in his mercy
has given us this new way,* we never
give up. 2 We reject all shameful
deeds and underhanded methods.
We don't try to trick anyone or dis-
tort the word of God. We tell the truth
before God, and all who are honest
know this.

3 If the Good News we preach is
hidden behind a veil, it is hidden
only from people who are perishing.
4 Satan, who is the god of this world,
has blinded the minds of those who
don't believe. They are unable to see
the glorious light of the Good News.
They don't understand this message
about the glory of Christ, who is the
exact likeness of God.

5 You see, we don't go around
preaching about ourselves. We
preach that Jesus Christ is Lord, and
we ourselves are your servants for
Jesus' sake. 6 For God, who said, "Let
there be light in the darkness," has
made this light shine in our hearts so
we could know the glory of God that
is seen in the face of Jesus Christ.

7 We now have this light shining
in our hearts, but we ourselves are
like fragile clay jars containing this
great treasure.* This makes it clear
that our great power is from God, not
from ourselves.

8 We are pressed on every side by

NASB

crushed; perplexed, but not despair-
ing; 9 persecuted, but not forsaken;
struck down, but not destroyed;
10 always carrying about in the body
the dying of Jesus, so that the life
of Jesus also may be manifested in
our body. 11 For we who live are con-
stantly being delivered over to death
for Jesus' sake, so that the life of
Jesus also may be manifested in our
mortal flesh. 12 So death works in us,
but life in you.

**4:3** [a]Lit *in* **4:4** [a]Lit *age* [b]Or *that the light...image of God, would not dawn* upon them **4:5** [a]Two early mss read *through Jesus*

NLT

troubles, but we are not crushed.
We are perplexed, but not driven to
despair. 9 We are hunted down, but
never abandoned by God. We get
knocked down, but we are not de-
stroyed. 10 Through suffering, our
bodies continue to share in the death
of Jesus so that the life of Jesus may
also be seen in our bodies.

11 Yes, we live under constant dan-
ger of death because we serve Jesus,
so that the life of Jesus will be evi-
dent in our dying bodies. 12 So we live
in the face of death, but this has re-
sulted in eternal life for you.

**4:1** Or *ministry.* **4:7** Greek *We now have this treasure in clay jars.*

Power-mad people do not know what to do with Christ and the cross. Somehow, the idea of the omnipotent God of the universe handing Himself over to death on a cross does not fit into any of the world's categories. When we think of power, we think of strength. When nations want to display their power, they goose-step their soldiers up and down Main Street and follow them around with rumbling tanks and huge missiles capable of blowing holes in anything. Or they launch those missiles into the air and test massive bombs, rattling their sabers and flexing their military muscles so everybody around them will consider them a force to be reckoned with. In the minds of the political world, that is power.

On a personal level, we build up our biceps and get ourselves into shape. We wear "muscle shirts" to show off our mighty physiques so nobody will mess with us. On the other hand, when we cannot make ourselves look like the Incredible Hulk, we seek to find power in our positions. We look for the careers that will make us the most money or allow us to handle people with the greatest control. We flex our metaphorical muscles by manipulating circumstances, calling the shots, and influencing people's lives with our smallest decisions.

That kind of power bears no resemblance to the power of God displayed through Jesus Christ. The most significant paradox in the history of time occurred about two thousand years ago when God in the flesh *died.* Omnipotence surrendered to impotence. The Lord, who had the power to call down angels from heaven and wipe all of those evildoers from the face of the earth, in fact, *did not*. Instead, He became a lifeless corpse, dragged down from a cross and placed in a borrowed tomb.

With this "power paradox," in which strength is made perfect in weakness and the foolishness of the world becomes the wisdom of God, none of us should be surprised that the ministry by which God reconciles the world to Himself is also characterized by paradox. In fact, in 2 Corinthians 4:1-12, Paul highlights the great paradox of God's chosen messengers: The less these frail and fragile earthen vessels attract people to themselves, the more they display the glory of God.

## — 4:1-6 —

Continuing to build on the argument of 2 Corinthians 3 regarding the new covenant ministry of the Spirit, Paul builds a framework for his picture of effective, authentic ministry: "Therefore, since we have this ministry, as we received mercy, we do not lose heart" (4:1). Just as we have received mercy from Christ, we in turn show mercy toward others. When we floundered without help, neck-deep in misery, God stooped down through Christ and rescued us from our helpless predicament. Though we were muddied, soiled, and battered, He cleaned us and healed us by His great mercy.

When we come to terms with God's amazing love for us, expressed through His mercy toward us, we will have consistent stability. Paul says, "We do not lose heart" (4:1). Instead of returning to the mire of our old life, alienated from the mercy of God, we stand on our own two feet, enabled by His Spirit to walk strong and tall. God's mercy should lift our spirits, turn our attention outward toward others, and motivate us to share this mercy far and wide.

Though a correct mentality of mercy and stability sets us on the right path, it must translate into action. Paul delineates how our lives, once useless and ineffective, can be used by God to accomplish great things (4:2-4). He uses himself as an example of the purposeful possibilities for cleansed vessels prepared for the Master's service.

Paul modeled for us how to reject deceit, having renounced "things hidden"—secretive and underhanded deception. This stands in contrast to the charge of Paul's accusers in Corinth, who suggested he had been fickle and misleading in his ministry. Paul turns the tables, subtly indicating that his accusers, not he and his associates, had been walking in "craftiness" and "adulterating the word of God" (4:2). Paul remained the same person in public as in private. He did not tolerate duplicity in his life or in the lives of those who would seek to be ministers of the gospel.

Unlike many popular preachers and teachers today, Paul refused to rely on cleverness, wit, and charm to woo people into the kingdom. He had no place for gimmicks and tricks in order to get results. He refused to play on people's emotions. He knew that when you appeal to emotion to draw people in, you need to keep giving them an emotional fix to keep them coming. Rather, Paul relied upon the unadulterated word of God to do its work (4:2). Paul's strategy might appear quaint compared to that of the glitz and glamour preachers we have today. He simply presented the plain, unvarnished truth of the gospel, depending on the Spirit of God to do His work through His word.

True, Paul's plain preaching of the truth did not always result in massive numbers of converts or impressive emotional responses from his listeners. Often, such an approach to ministry feels like communicating with people who have no ability to hear, no way to see, and no disposition to believe (4:3). The gospel, indeed, is "veiled" to those who are perishing, who remain on the fence or who run from the truth.

Even though the hearts and minds of unbelievers are blinded by Satan (4:4), authentic ministers of the gospel need to continue to display the truth, steering clear of manipulation and guilt-inducing tactics that do not produce real, permanent results. Only the conviction of the Holy Spirit through the Word of God can bring about a change of heart:

> For the word of God is living and active and sharper than any two-edged sword, and piercing as far as the division of soul and spirit, of both joints and marrow, and able to judge the thoughts and intentions of the heart. And there is no creature hidden from His sight, but all things are open and laid bare to the eyes of Him with whom we have to do. (Heb. 4:12-13)

It is not our job to do spiritual heart surgery; only God can accomplish that. Therefore, manipulative methods and tactics should never be part of our ministry method. Rather, we should let the Spirit do His work through the Word, leaving us only one foolproof method for removing the veil (2 Cor. 3:14–4:6) and piercing the dark cloud of deception that shrouds the hearts of unbelievers. We must preach the Word, even in our frailty. We must not preach ourselves—drawing attention to our talents, gifts, resources, and abilities. We must rather preach "Christ Jesus as Lord," to whom we are merely bond-servants upon whom God has shown mercy (4:5).

Any leader, spiritual or otherwise, can easily become a celebrity in the eyes of those being led. When pastors build their egos on every word of praise, when they begin experiencing the phenomenon of fame, or when they start promoting themselves excessively, we have a real problem brewing. If your church's website mentions your pastor's name more than Jesus' name, that's a problem. When a popular preacher's name and image are pasted all over the church, there are serious issues with pride and priorities. Paul continually pointed to Jesus Christ as Lord, never allowing those he taught to view him as anything more than an earthen vessel carrying a priceless treasure.

How do you know when you have let pride creep into your ministry? When you frequently talk about yourself and your accomplishments. When you expect special treatment and flaunt your privileges. When you pursue promotion, bigger job titles, and higher pay. When you convince yourself that you must have a private jet to travel here and there. When you expect others to submit to your every word while allowing nobody to hold you accountable. When these attitudes and actions crop up in your life, you are headed for trouble. You need to step down until the Lord regains firm authority. Also, when you see these attitudes in other leaders, it is time to distance yourself from them. Those are the makings of a cult of personality, not a Christ-exalting church.

## — 4:7-12 —

In 2 Corinthians 4:7 Paul introduces the heart of the matter—something he has been touching upon lightly in the previous verses. Every believer is the recipient of a priceless treasure: the message of the gospel (4:7). This saving message brings the light of knowledge to our darkened minds and empowers us to overcome our pride as we preach Christ alone by the power of the Holy Spirit. Because of the indwelling Spirit, we have power to preach the gospel in purity—yet this powerful preaching is contained in pitiful pots. The NIV translation describes the containers of this blessing as "jars of clay." By this, Paul means saved, sealed, born-again human believers—himself included. We are the bearers of "the light of the gospel of the glory (*doxa* [1391]) of Christ, who is the image of God" (4:4).

In our "earthen vessels"—that is, our physical bodies (Gen. 2:7)—we carry about the presence of the Creator God who said, "Light shall shine out of darkness" (2 Cor. 4:6). Yet Paul's emphasis is not strictly on the presence of God through the indwelling Holy Spirit, true as this is and essential as it is for carrying out the work of the ministry. Rather, Paul primarily has in mind here the gospel message itself. He likens this powerful message to a treasure proclaimed through pitiful and brittle pots.

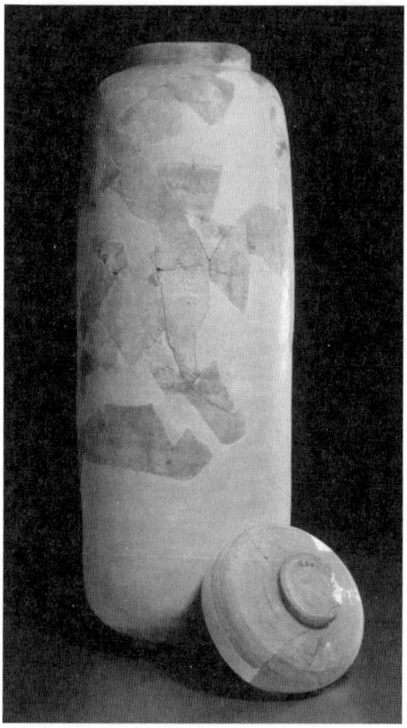

© Walters Art Museum

Paul likens authentic gospel ministers to ordinary earthen vessels—fragile clay pots that nevertheless contain the priceless treasure of the gospel.

God could have displayed His light through angelic beings, direct visions and dreams, or even through personal divine revelations to each individual. He could have, because God is bound by nothing but His own plans and promises. Yet God, for His own purposes, has decided to reveal the treasure through us. *Us!* Some days I wake up and wonder, "Why, God? Why us? Why me?" Considering our frailties, fallenness, and outright folly, it's a fair question. Let's face it: When Paul likens us to "earthen vessels," in some ways he is being optimistic! Some days we are just unshaped and unattractive lumps of clay (Rom. 9:21), or wispy clouds of dust (Gen. 3:19), or stony hearts (Prov. 28:14), or withering grass (1 Pet. 1:24).

We should be honored and humbled in the extreme to be included in God's plan to preserve and proclaim His priceless message. Yet somehow in the process we often forget the "clay pot" reality. Even in our churches, we work hard to impress each other, especially visitors. We try to handle the Scriptures with ease and finesse. We polish our performances to perfection. We downplay our flaws and patch up the cracks in our finish. We place our most treasured pots on display for all to see, failing to actually reveal the invaluable treasure inside. Yes, we're motivated to minister with excellence, to offer service to God with our whole heart. God is not pleased with a "just wing it" attitude or a hapless, shoot-from-the-hip approach to ministry. That kind of attitude does not honor the treasure. God delights in thoroughness, hard work, and excellence (Col. 3:23). But a noble offering to God can easily cross the line into shameless showmanship. Though we must do and give our best in service to our Savior, we must never shine the spotlight on ourselves. Rather, we are to let His light shine through us, just as 2 Corinthians 4:7 concludes: "that the surpassing greatness of the power will be of God and not from ourselves."

The next two verses reveal not only what Paul felt but how we often feel as fragile earthen vessels: afflicted, perplexed, persecuted, struck down (4:8-9). The adjectives in these verses present powerful images. "Afflicted" carries the idea of pressure, as when grapes get squeezed dry by a winepress. The Greek root is related to our word for "tribulation," an especially intense and usually prolonged trial. But while the extreme pressure may squeeze us, it will not crush us (4:8). The word "perplexed" means "to be at a loss," unable to explain things, disoriented by the barrage of problems, mishaps, tragedies, and challenges. We are sometimes, as William Barclay puts it, "at our wit's end but never at our hope's end."[1] This confusion does not lead to ultimate despair as if we had no hope (4:8). Both the external tribulations and internal consternation come as a result of being persecuted and beaten up, either physically, mentally, or emotionally. Yet these attacks leave us neither undefended nor destroyed. God will fight for us (4:9). We are, so to speak, "knocked down but not knocked out."[2]

Christ is never more visible in us than when others can find no other explanation for our hope and endurance through trials than His sustaining, strengthening inner work. When the clay pots are worn, chipped, or cracked, then the glorious treasure can shine through. When the minister of the gospel reveals his own struggles, hardships, and weaknesses, it becomes much easier to see the truth that it is God who is at work in us, both to will and to work for His good pleasure (Phil. 2:13).

Powerful preaching in pitiful pots: That is the paradox of the Christian life in general and Christian ministry in particular. In these temporary jars of clay, we are "always carrying about in the body the dying of Jesus, so that the life of Jesus also may be manifested in our body" (2 Cor. 4:10). As we are delivered over to the pain, suffering, and even death of this world, then the world can see the life of faith, hope, and love that comes only through the power of Jesus living in and through us (4:11). Paul himself—and his other apostolic companions—carried the physical scars of suffering on behalf of Christ. These constant, visible reminders authenticated Paul's ministry, backing up his words with wounds.

When Paul refers to being "delivered over to death" (4:11), he does not mean a literal death, although he would eventually be martyred. He means the cracking of our pots, the affliction and persecution inherent in authentic ministry (4:8-9). When we die to self, Jesus lives in us. When we lose, He wins. When we are weak, He is strong. When we are last, He is first. When we are dependent, He is dependable. When our weaknesses show, people realize it is not the pot that is significant, but

God's power within that matters most. When others see this "death" in us, it changes them.

When Paul reminded the Corinthians of the marks of suffering and lifestyle of self-surrender displayed in him and his fellow workers, it should have challenged and changed them, too. Or, as Paul put it, "death works in us, but life in you" (4:12). As an authentic minister of reconciliation, Paul was willing to "spend and be expended" for the Corinthians (12:15).

## APPLICATION: 2 CORINTHIANS 4:1-12

### Hide It under a Bushel? No!

The last time I checked, children still like to sing "This Little Light of Mine" in Sunday school—hand motions and all. What a great way to instill in the hearts and minds of our little ones the passion to let the light of the gospel shine through our lives: "Hide it under a bushel? No! I'm gonna let it shine!" . . . "Won't let Satan blow it out, I'm gonna let it shine!" . . . "Let it shine till Jesus comes, I'm gonna let it shine!"

The same idea stands behind Paul's principles for Spirit-empowered, Christ-centered ministry in 2 Corinthians 4:1-12. The light of the message of salvation shines from the pitiful pots of our mortal lives. We don't hide those pots under a bushel. We let the light shine out of them. We don't let Satan hijack the pot and paint it with his worldly designs to distract people from its glorious content. We let the glory of the gospel shine through. We don't let our trials and tribulations drive us to despair and cause us to surrender the battle. We let the light shine until Jesus comes.

To better understand and apply the principle of powerful preaching in pitiful pots, take some time to answer these ministry questions that must be asked. Let me give you two warnings, though. First, don't rush through them. If you think hard enough about them, the Spirit will use them to transform you. So think carefully. Second, don't use these principles to judge the ministries of others, such as your pastors, teachers, professors, or friends. Instead, apply them to your own Christian walk and ministry first.

First set of questions: How do you live up to Paul's example of a faithful, effective minister of the gospel? Do you exhibit an abundance of mercy? A consistent stability? A rejection of deceit? An unwillingness to resort to manipulative gimmicks? A refusal to mishandle Scripture? A steadfast submission to Christ's lordship? A devotion to keeping the focus on the person and work of Christ and not on yourself? Are the leaders and mentors in your life exhibiting these qualities, too, or have they adorned their earthen vessels so much that the message is being obscured?

Second set of questions: How brightly does your light shine before others? Do you avoid spiritual topics for fear of your own inadequacies? Do you change the subject when your personal faith and convictions come up? Does your lifestyle reflect the purity of the gospel or the filthiness of the world? In short, how brightly does your light shine from the earthen vessel to which it has been entrusted?

Third set of questions: Have you let the cracks, chips, and scratches on your earthen vessel distract you from keeping your own focus on the message? Nobody's perfect. In fact, through our imperfections Christ is seen most clearly. Think of your own particular imperfections, scars, and challenges. How can they be used to point to Christ's grace, mercy, and power? Think about times in your life during which you were most broken. How has God used these things to influence others?

Do you want to let your light shine before others? Make an impact in your work? Reach your school? Touch your neighbors? Heal your family? Then take the lid off your jar of clay and let the light of the glory of the gospel of Christ shine out of and through even the cracks of your broken life.

# The Right Focus
## 2 CORINTHIANS 4:13-18

NASB

13 But having the same spirit of
faith, according to what is written,
"I BELIEVED, THEREFORE I SPOKE,"
we also believe, therefore we also
speak, 14 knowing that He who raised
the Lord Jesus will raise us also with
Jesus and will present us with you.
15 For all things *are* for your sakes, so

NLT

13 But we continue to preach because
we have the same kind of faith the
psalmist had when he said, "I be-
lieved in God, so I spoke."* 14 We
know that God, who raised the Lord
Jesus,* will also raise us with Jesus
and present us to himself together
with you. 15 All of this is for your

NASB

that the grace which is [a]spreading to more and more people may cause the giving of thanks to abound to the glory of God.

[16]Therefore we do not lose heart, but though our outer man is decaying, yet our inner man is being renewed day by day. [17]For momentary, light affliction is producing for us an eternal weight of glory far beyond all comparison, [18]while we look not at the things which are seen, but at the things which are not seen; for the things which are seen are temporal, but the things which are not seen are eternal.

**4:15** [a]Lit *being multiplied through the many*

NLT

benefit. And as God's grace reaches more and more people, there will be great thanksgiving, and God will receive more and more glory.

[16]That is why we never give up. Though our bodies are dying, our spirits are* being renewed every day. [17]For our present troubles are small and won't last very long. Yet they produce for us a glory that vastly outweighs them and will last forever! [18]So we don't look at the troubles we can see now; rather, we fix our gaze on things that cannot be seen. For the things we see now will soon be gone, but the things we cannot see will last forever.

**4:13** Ps 116:10. **4:14** Some manuscripts read *who raised Jesus.* **4:16** Greek *our inner being is.*

"The day of one's death is better than the day of one's birth" (Eccl. 7:1). King Solomon, the erstwhile cynic sage who devoured the best this world had to offer, came to this startling conclusion in the midst of his wilderness wanderings through human wisdom and experience. If read out of context, his pessimistic words might seem like the musings of somebody who had given up on life entirely. The line that follows, however, puts things into perspective: "It is better to go to a house of mourning than to go to a house of feasting, because that is the end of every man, and the living takes it to heart" (Eccl. 7:2).

In other words, unlike the frivolity of a birthday party in which any miserable soul can pass as a "jolly good fellow," a person's entire life is seen for what it really was at a funeral (the house of mourning). There we hear what people really thought of the deceased, witness the person's life legacy, size up accomplishments and set-backs, and sum up victories and defeats. Only at the end of one's life can we see whether a person actually "fought the good fight . . . finished the course . . . kept the faith" (2 Tim. 4:7).

I think all of us would like to be remembered as people who didn't quit, who stayed at the task. If I were to choose something for my own epitaph, it would have to do with consistency and faithfulness, not merely starting well but finishing well. At my funeral, I would want people to say that even in the midst of temptations, he chose the narrow path of righteousness. In the face of stiff opposition, he persevered. In the presence of countless distractions, he kept the right focus.

This is the kind of legacy left to us by the ministry of the apostle Paul. From his blinding start on the road to Damascus to his binding shackles in a Roman dungeon, Paul remained faithful to the end. Even during a ministry that got him beaten, imprisoned, shipwrecked, and left for dead, he picked himself up and carried on. He truly fought the good fight. He completely finished the course. He consistently kept the faith.

Wouldn't you love to hear that commendation spoken about you? That kind of resolve does not result from a one-off New Year's resolution. Rather, a life lived with the right focus can be maintained only when we think about each of our moment-by-moment decisions from the vantage point of the end.

Finishing the course isn't easy. The lanes are narrow and littered with obstacles that rise up from nowhere. Pain, disappointment, heartache, and loss jog alongside us, drawing close enough to trip us up and make us stumble. It requires a great amount of self-sacrifice and discipline to keep from dropping out of the race. To finish the course well requires the right focus. It is not accomplished by self-hypnosis or a positive self-image. Rather, it requires enthusiastic determination and authentic vision, both of which Paul addresses in 2 Corinthians 4:13-18.

## — 4:13-15 —

One can hardly overestimate the ministry task before us. Think about it. Christ handed off a responsibility to "make disciples of all the nations" (Matt. 28:19) to a struggling band of scraggly, ragamuffin disciples—most of them social outcasts, blue-collar laborers, and unskilled in rhetoric. These were the men chosen to carry out an impossible work: the conversion of the world. Yet Paul exemplified a spirit of enthusiastic determination when he wrote, "Having the same spirit of faith, according to what is written, 'I believed, therefore I spoke,' we also believe, therefore we also speak" (2 Cor. 4:13).

The phrase "what is written" indicates that Paul was quoting an Old Testament passage of Scripture, upon which authority he rested his own argument. In this case, Paul incorporates a brief snippet from the Septuagint (the Greek translation of the Hebrew Scriptures) from Psalm 116:10. Yet he uses the excerpt to point to the entire psalm, which describes the author's experience of great pain and suffering to the brink of death. Craig Keener gives us an idea of how Paul is applying this text to his situation: "Because Jews and Christians sang or recited psalms, perhaps both he and his audience recognized that the verse's context was a psalm about the righteous sufferer's afflictions, offered to praise God for deliverance."[3]

Like that psalmist, Paul had experienced God's faithfulness even in his time of suffering. And like the psalmist, he proclaimed it far and wide. He continued on the path with determination and enthusiasm. But how can we hope to follow Paul's example? I see three specific thoughts on enthusiastic determination in the face of such an enormous task as serving Christ in the midst of hardship, suffering, and turmoil.

First, *enthusiastic determination grows out of being delivered by the Lord* (2 Cor. 4:13). When we come to an impasse in life, in which we feel weighed down by the burdens or bogged down by the difficulties, we should recall the way God has delivered us from these things in the past. Unfortunately, we quickly forget the Lord's deliverance when we are on safe ground again, or we view it as a onetime event. It is often difficult to believe God will deliver us again when we are in the center of the storm. That's why we should read about the ways God miraculously delivered His people in both the Old and the New Testaments, remembering that we serve that very same God. Consider this brief sampling of our Savior-God's glorious deeds of deliverance:

- Lot delivered from Sodom (Gen. 19:1-29)
- Joseph delivered from prison (Gen. 40–41)
- Israel delivered out of Egypt (Exod. 1–15)
- Daniel delivered from the lions' den (Dan. 6:1-28)
- Jonah delivered from the sea (Jon. 1:7–2:10)
- Jesus delivered from the grave (Matt. 27:32–28:10)
- Peter delivered from jail (Acts 12:1-11)

To maintain enthusiastic determination, remember that you serve a God who can deliver you from your troubles. Speak often about His works of deliverance in your life, and let His deliverance of others speak often to your own heart (2 Cor. 4:13). I have observed that when Christians get delivered, they often go on to new heights of motivation and enthusiasm because God saw them through a most difficult time. This is a major reason why we should share our testimonies, not only of our original salvation but also of God's answers to our prayers for deliverance. Don't keep them to yourself! Publish them abroad. Make them known to a world that doesn't believe God is living and active in the world today. Tell your Christian friends about God's answers to prayer. What it does to stimulate enthusiastic determination in *their* lives is amazing.

Second, *enthusiastic determination grows when we focus on our future resurrection* (2 Cor. 4:14). As Bible-believing Christians, we anticipate that day when we will all be changed in a moment, in the twinkling of an eye (1 Cor. 15:52). Then we will be given new, immortal, glorified bodies conformed to Christ's resurrection body. Those new bodies will neither age nor be subject to sickness, disease, suffering, or pain. Not even death can stop the work of God.

With this focus on our bodily resurrection, Paul is doing what lawyers call "pleading in the alternative." He just mentioned God's pattern of delivering His people from death as a motivator for enthusiastic determination (2 Cor. 4:13). Yet even if God's plan allows us to die, death is only a temporary victor. It may win this particular skirmish, but when Christ returns, death itself will be defeated. Paul wrote in 1 Corinthians 15:54, "When this perishable [body] will have put on the imperishable [body], and this mortal will have put on immortality, then will come about the saying that is written, 'Death is swallowed up in victory.'"

Third, *enthusiastic determination grows when we invest in the lives of others* (2 Cor. 4:15). When we take seriously the temporary nature of our present life and the glories of our future resurrection life, it should motivate us to "die" to ourselves and "live" for others. When this happens, teachers are resurrected in the lives of their students, parents in the lives of their children, pastors in the lives of their congregations. Paul says as much: "For all things are for your sakes" (4:15). Paul and his co-laborers spent their very lives investing in the Corinthians in order to reap a great harvest of thanksgiving and glory when the gospel spread through them (4:15).

If you've lost an enthusiastic determination for ministry, take a look at your life. Are you living with an inward focus rather than an outward focus on others and an upward focus on Christ? Have you begun to cloister yourself away from others? The life that reflects Christ's life exists to serve others, not ourselves (Phil. 2:3-11). So serve with self-sacrificial abandon! God promises that investing in others will be worth it. The soccer games are worth it. The out-of-pocket expenses are worth it. Those hours when nobody seems to appreciate your efforts are worth it. Keep affirming. Keep loving. Keep giving yourself. The worst thing you can do to destroy enthusiastic determination is to live a life completely unto yourself. I will guarantee you will languish and die a downhearted, cranky, and negative old person if you live only for yourself. People who give what they have for others have a remarkable ability to maintain contagious enthusiasm because they do not lose heart.

## — 4:16-18 —

It's happening. You can minimize its obvious effects, but you can't stop it. To some of us, it's happening worse than others. More wrinkles. More gray. More stooped shoulders. Less speed. Less vigor. Less energy. Maybe you are young enough to have not yet noticed, but it is nevertheless true: your "outer man" is decaying!

Every day we are getting older. And every day we are nearing the end of our earthly lives. From the world's point of view, this is not only frustrating and discouraging but downright tragic and depressing. But not so for believers in Jesus Christ, the resurrected God-man, who is "the resurrection and the life" (John 11:25). Without Christ, the outer person and this present mortal life are all we have; to lose them is to lose everything. But with Christ, our inner person is being renewed, restored, refreshed, awakened, and strengthened by the Holy Spirit every day (2 Cor. 4:16).

Our experience of this renewed vision for ministry while here in our earthly bodies will put our "momentary, light" afflictions into perspective (4:17). As we endure these hardships, reaping their benefits of character growth (Jas. 1:2-4; 1 Pet. 1:6-7), we know that God is not forgetting our labors and hardships but that He will reward us (1 Cor. 3:8; Heb. 6:10). If we could stack up all of the experiences that make our present lives painful and then compare this pile to the infinite weight of glory that is awaiting us at our resurrection, the "big stuff" of this world would vanish into insignificance.

This is the secret to a Christian's motivation for authentic ministry vision: We refuse to be discouraged because of the present circumstances. Let's face it: "The things which are seen" in this world disturb us. They will drag us down, distract us, steal our focus away from Christ, cause us to spend our time on frivolous things instead of the things of the kingdom, and blind us to a clear ministry vision. When our focus shifts to the things that are unseen, however—the glorious future we have in the restoration of the world under the eternal rule of Christ—then everything else gets placed in its proper perspective.

# Making Every Hour Our Finest

## 2 CORINTHIANS 4:16

*I was just shy of six years old, but I can remember my mother and father sitting silently before the family radio, listening past the intermittent crackling of the interference to the broadcast magically delivered from across the ocean. The old radio receiver made the voice of the famous statesman sound like he was speaking through a tin can, and I was too young to understand the importance of what he articulated, but I recall my parents attentively glued to the radio, holding on to every word.*

*It would be many years before I finally understood why.*

*June 18, 1940. I was five going on six; he was sixty-five going on sixty-six. On that day in hushed living rooms like ours across the world, British Prime Minister Winston Churchill stood before a captivated global audience and took his stand against a malevolent dictator, the likes of which the modern world had never known. From a tiny island nation separated from the enemy of humanity by a narrow channel of water, that great statesman, historian, and orator faced an enormous task with boldness. Though I was too young to comprehend his rousing speech at the time, since then his historic words have spoken to me a thousand times:*

> *The battle of France is over. I expect that the battle of Britain is about to begin. Upon this battle depends the survival of Christian civilization. Upon it depends our own British life, and the long continuity of our institutions and our Empire. The whole fury and might of the enemy must very soon be turned on us.*
>
> *Hitler knows that he will have to break us on this island or lose the war. If we can stand up to him, all Europe may be free and the life of the world may move forward into broad, sunlit uplands. But if we fail, then the whole world, including the United States, including all that we have known and cared for, will sink into the abyss of a new Dark Age made more sinister, and perhaps more protracted, by the lights of perverted science.*

(continued on next page)

*Let us therefore brace ourselves to our duties, and so bear ourselves that if the British Empire and its Commonwealth last for a thousand years, men will still say, "This was their finest hour."*

*How easy it is for an individual, a family, a church, and a nation to lose heart when they begin to lose focus. When I think about the enormity of the task of ministry before us in this generation, it is easy to feel overwhelmed. The increasingly bitter struggle for the souls of the lost, the growing hostility toward the Savior and His people, and the ominous clouds of pluralism and paganism—these things threaten the Christian church and its voice of truth in the world. Yet instead of growing fearful in the face of the dangers and surrendering to the armies of the enemy, the words of Winston Churchill motivate me to take a stand even in the face of an apparently impossible task. More than this, the repeated words of the apostle Paul in 2 Corinthians 4:1, 16 strengthen my resolve to face the enormity of the mission, come what may:*

> Therefore, since we have *this ministry, as we received mercy, we* do not lose heart. (4:1) (emphasis mine)

> We do not lose heart, *but though our outer man is decaying, yet our inner man is being renewed day by day.* (4:16) (emphasis mine)

# APPLICATION: 2 CORINTHIANS 4:13-18

## Wanted: Weavers, Investors, and Dreamers

Nowadays, weavers, investors, and dreamers get a bad rap. The term "basket weaving" is often used to connote a course of study that dodges anything academically challenging—a weaver is synonymous with a cop-out. Investors today are sometimes portrayed as heartless money-grubbers who will bend or even break financial rules to squeeze every last dividend out of the market. And although "dreamer" can be a positive designation for an innovator, people often use it in a derogatory sense for one whose head is in the clouds—so disconnected from real-world practicality as to be of no good to anybody, not even to oneself. But as we think about how to practically apply 2 Corinthians 4:13-18, I would exhort you: Keep on weaving, keep on investing, keep on dreaming!

First, *keep on weaving*. We keep the right focus on our ministry goals when we remember that today's deeds are individual threads in tomorrow's tapestry. That's easy to forget, isn't it? Every kindness, every thoughtful act, every encouraging word, every testimony shared, every forgiving response, even every smile—these are all seemingly insignificant deeds considered individually. If, however, you could catch a momentary glimpse of how all your threads fit into the full tapestry of God's plan, you would be even more motivated to keep on weaving those threads.

Second, *keep on investing*. We keep the right ministry focus when we realize that mortal people are immortals in the making. When we think of those around us as potential glorified saints—soon-to-be adopted sons and daughters of God—it will be hard for us to peter out in ministry. This idea isn't original with me. C. S. Lewis wrote:

> It is a serious thing to live in a society of possible gods and goddesses, to remember that the dullest and most uninteresting person you talk to may one day be a creature which, if you saw it now, you would be strongly tempted to worship. . . . There are no *ordinary* people. You have never talked to a mere mortal. Nations, cultures, arts, civilizations—these are mortal, and their life is to ours as the life of a gnat. But it is immortals whom we joke with, work with, marry, snub, and exploit.[4]

What an interesting twist on how we perceive the people around us. If that doesn't fuel your fire of enthusiasm for ministry, you are dealing with wet firewood! When we remember that every person we meet is immortal and that everything around us has the staying power of a puff of smoke, we'll be motivated to invest in the things that last. How do you invest? Open your mouth to tell the good news. Open your heart to share your story. Open your hands to help the hurting. Keep on investing.

Third, *keep on dreaming*. We can keep the right focus in life and ministry if we let our minds and imaginations rise above the temporalities of this world and touch the eternality of the next. Let yourself reflect on the unseen rather than the seen. I don't mean to detach yourself from the world, to withdraw from reality, or to pretend like the world around you isn't real. As Christians living in the time between the first and second comings of Christ, we need to hold on to both—living responsibly in this world while living responsively to the next. I challenge you to do that this very week. Dream about the world to come. Read about it in Revelation 21–22. Meditate on those future realities. You know what you'll discover? Joy. Peace. Courage. Perseverance. A new sense of priorities. Fulfillment. Contentment. The typical human dreams of material gain, financial success, and worldly achievements will fade into insignificance in the face of the world to come. Keep on dreaming.

Keep weaving. Keep investing. Keep dreaming. By doing that, you'll have the kind of focus you need to maintain an enthusiastic determination for ministry and an authentic vision to keep you going despite your dark and dreary circumstances.

## Hope beyond the Hearse
### 2 CORINTHIANS 5:1-10

**NASB**

1 For we know that if [a]the earthly tent
which is our house is torn down, we
have a building from God, a house
not made with hands, eternal in the
heavens. 2 For indeed in this *house* we
groan, longing to be clothed with our
dwelling from heaven, 3 inasmuch
as we, having put it on, will not be
found naked. 4 For indeed while we
are in this tent, we groan, being bur-
dened, because we do not want to be
unclothed but to be clothed, so that
what is mortal will be swallowed up
by life. 5 Now He who prepared us for
this very purpose is God, who gave to
us the Spirit as a [a]pledge.

6 Therefore, being always of good
courage, and knowing that while
we are at home in the body we are

**NLT**

1 For we know that when this earthly
tent we live in is taken down (that is,
when we die and leave this earthly
body), we will have a house in
heaven, an eternal body made for us
by God himself and not by human
hands. 2 We grow weary in our pres-
ent bodies, and we long to put on our
heavenly bodies like new clothing.
3 For we will put on heavenly bodies;
we will not be spirits without bod-
ies.* 4 While we live in these earthly
bodies, we groan and sigh, but it's
not that we want to die and get rid of
these bodies that clothe us. Rather,
we want to put on our new bodies so
that these dying bodies will be swal-
lowed up by life. 5 God himself has
prepared us for this, and as a guar-
antee he has given us his Holy Spirit.

6 So we are always confident, even
though we know that as long as we
live in these bodies we are not at

absent from the Lord— 7for we walk by faith, not by [a]sight— 8we are of good courage, I say, and prefer rather to be absent from the body and to be at home with the Lord. 9Therefore we also have as our ambition, whether at home or absent, to be pleasing to Him. 10For we must all appear before the judgment seat of Christ, so that each one may be recompensed for [a]his deeds in the body, according to what he has done, whether good or bad.

5:1 [a]Lit *our earthly house of the tent* 5:5 [a]Or *down payment* 5:7 [a]Or *appearance* 5:10 [a]Lit *the things through the body*

home with the Lord. 7For we live by believing and not by seeing. 8Yes, we are fully confident, and we would rather be away from these earthly bodies, for then we will be at home with the Lord. 9So whether we are here in this body or away from this body, our goal is to please him. 10For we must all stand before Christ to be judged. We will each receive whatever we deserve for the good or evil we have done in this earthly body.

5:3 Greek *we will not be naked.*

No matter what journey I take from here to there, I can't avoid it. No back road, no bypass, no alternate route can keep me from crossing its path. Thankfully, it doesn't intrude on my way every day, but it happens enough to remind me of some sobering realities none of us should ever forget.

I'll be driving my car from home to church, or from church to the seminary, or from a lunch meeting to a hospital. Suddenly a police car pulls into the intersection in front of me and slows to a stop, its light flashing but sirens silent. Another pulls up behind him and blocks the flow of traffic. Then another proceeds through the intersection. Just as I'm craning my neck to see what poor fellow had gotten into a fender bender, the truth hits me.

A long, black hearse escorted by another police car proceeds through the intersection. Behind it follows a limousine carrying a grieving family. Then the long train of vehicles trails behind, headlights shining in the noonday sun and all of the members of that mournful parade heading for the final resting place of a beloved sister, brother, father, mother, husband, co-worker, or friend. And as they file through the intersection, nobody honks. An unprecedented patience falls over the growing jam of traffic. We don't laugh. We don't groan. We watch in silence, knowing that one day all of us will be passengers at the head of a similar somber procession.

People often say only two things are certain in life: death and taxes. Well, you and I know people who have somehow weaseled their way out of the latter. But we know of nobody who has been able to cheat the former. Death is a certainty—not a question of *if*, but *when*. In fact, from a philosophical perspective, death is more certain than birth. Countless potential humans have never been born. Humans have devised numerous ways to prevent conception and birth, but they have never been able to prevent aging and death. *Not a single human being born into this world has escaped death apart from miraculous divine intervention.*[5] One astute writer puts the reality this way:

> This frustrates us, especially in a time of scientific breakthrough and exploding knowledge, that we should be able to break out of earth's environment and yet be stopped cold by death's unyielding mystery. Electroencephalogram may replace mirror held before the mouth, autopsies may become more sophisticated, cosmetic embalming may take the place of pennies on the eyelids and canvas shrouds, but death continues to confront us with its blank wall.[6]

As Solomon told us in Ecclesiastes, death is the great equalizer (Eccl. 2:14; 7:2; 9:2-3). It doesn't matter if you're a saint or a sinner, rich or poor, man, woman, or child, healthy or sickly, happy or sad—"it is the same for all" (Eccl. 9:2). So what is the difference between the believer and the unbeliever? What benefit has the Christian over the non-Christian if death ends the lives of both? Is there no hope beyond the hearse?

## — 5:1-5 —

When it comes to wrong ideas about what happens to us when we die, peddlers of falsehood take advantage of ignorance, uncertainty, fear, and disbelief. When people turn away from the sure knowledge revealed by God in Scripture, they become susceptible to all sorts of misconceptions. This is why Paul begins with an assertion that should instantly snare our attention: "We know" (5:1). When it comes to the vital questions of existence, we aren't left guessing, wondering, pondering, interpreting, or theorizing. The important things are *clear* in Scripture, for those who have the eyes of faith to see and believe them: "For we *know* . . ." Isn't that comforting? When we face our own inevitable mortality or the loss of our loved ones, we can *know with certainty* what the future holds. Isn't that amazing?

Paul then speaks of the earthly body by drawing on imagery familiar to him and his readers: tents. Don't forget that Paul himself was a tent-maker who had worked for a time in the very city of Corinth with Aquila and Priscilla, making and selling tents (Acts 18:1-3). Now allow me to explore this analogy a little, because I think this is what Paul has

## CURSUS: THEORIES OF DEATH IN "FOLK THEOLOGY"

### 2 CORINTHIANS 5:5-6

We are living in a world of soothsayers—people who willingly tell you what you like to hear simply because you like to hear it (and because they like your money). The apostle Paul put it this way: "For the time will come when they will not endure sound doctrine; but wanting to have their ears tickled, they will accumulate for themselves teachers in accordance to their own desires" (2 Tim. 4:3).

You will especially find this to be the case if you talk with people about their concept of death. Most people today do not want to accept "as is" the biblical teaching about death. Instead, they want to tweak it, tamper with it, or twist it into something more palatable. That is because the Bible's clear teaching about death requires us to make a decision in this life that will affect our eternity. Scripture clearly teaches that death is the ultimate result of sin (Gen. 2:17; 3:19; Rom. 6:23), and because all people are sinners (Rom. 3:23), nobody can escape its grasp (Eccl. 7:2). People are appointed to die but once; then our eternal destinies will be sealed (Heb. 9:27). If the chasm of sin that separates us from God is not spanned in this life by a relationship with our Savior, Jesus Christ, we will be lost for all eternity (Luke 16:19-31).

Because people today consider those facts too intolerant, dogmatic, or old-fashioned to be accepted without qualification, you will encounter other theories about death in what we might call "folk theology"—unbiblical myths about what happens when we die that serve to soften the harsh reality of death and avoid the biblical idea of judgment. I place these into three categories: *temporary transition*, *repeated reincarnation*, and *ultimate conclusion*.

*Temporary transition*. Many people today believe that death is simply a necessary passage that all people must go through before they reach their version of "heaven," "nirvana," or "paradise." Eventually, everybody will get there, though it may take longer for some. Some tie this to the Roman Catholic doctrine of purgatory, which comes from the root word for "purge." This refers to a place of spiritual purification for people who are not quite right with God in this life, but who will have a chance somehow to make atonement for their sins and imperfections prior to entering heaven. Purgatory is "an intermediate place between heaven and hell, where the unfinished business of earth is settled."[7] In folk theology, everybody eventually makes it through some such intermediate place to ultimately find their own way to God.

*Repeated reincarnation*. This eastern philosophy associated with Hinduism, Buddhism, and New Age religions holds that when humans die, their spirits depart their bodies only to be reborn into another earthly body. Recycling of the human spirit can go on indefinitely, bringing us to higher levels of happiness if we have lived a good life or to lower levels of misery if we have not. The notion of "karma" is connected to this concept—good or evil deeds in this life will determine the quality of life you will have in the next go-round.

*Ultimate conclusion*. Increasingly, people are buying into a nihilistic and materialistic view of death as simply a large period at the end of life's sentence. To them, death *is* the ultimate end. There is nothing beyond the grave: no heaven, no hell, no nirvana, no paradise, no reincarnation, no

*(continued on next page)*

consciousness, no existence. This belief often gives rise to a philosophy that says, "Eat, drink, and be merry, for tomorrow we die." This suggests that people should do whatever they want, when they want, with whom they want, all with no fear of divine punishment and no expectation of eternal reward. Life itself becomes empty and meaningless.

When people reject the revealed theology of the Bible, they open themselves up to "folk theology," turning away their ears from the truth and turning aside to myths (2 Tim. 4:4).

in mind as he compares our present earthly, mortal bodies (the current "tents") with our future heavenly, immortal bodies (the future permanent building from God).

I have spent enough time in a tent to know it is not the best place for a permanent dwelling (no offense to my Bedouin readers!). In fact, if you have ever been on a camping trip that lasted long enough to encounter cold or rainy weather, you will agree that tents are no match for a strong brick home built on a sure foundation. Tents are temporary dwellings—fun to sleep in with the kids in the woods or at the lake, but you and I know that it gets cold in the winter and it gets hot in the summer. Tents begin to sag. They start to leak. Tent pegs get loose. Holes form, critters invite themselves in, and a strong wind blows them away. Before very long, you are groaning for something more permanent.

Enter the "building" image. Paul says, "For we know that if the earthly tent which is our house is torn down, we have a building from God, a house not made with hands, eternal in the heavens" (2 Cor. 5:1). Here Paul refers to the marvelous transition from our present frail, fallen bodies to our future glorified, resurrected bodies. This is not the only time Paul mentions this miraculous transformation. In 1 Thessalonians 4:14-17, he wrote:

> For if we believe that Jesus died and rose again, even so God will bring with Him those who have fallen asleep in Jesus. For this we say to you by the word of the Lord, that we who are alive and remain until the coming of the Lord, will not precede those who have fallen asleep. For the Lord Himself will descend from heaven with a shout, with the voice of the archangel and with the trumpet of God, and the dead in Christ will rise first. Then we who are alive and remain will be caught up together with them in the clouds to meet the Lord in the air, and so we shall always be with the Lord.

When the Lord returns, those believers in Christ who had died in this life will be miraculously raised up in their restored, glorified bodies. Those believers who are still alive in their mortal bodies will experience a sudden transformation of their bodies as they get caught up in the air to meet the Lord and the resurrected believers from every generation. Paul mentions this very transformation from mortal bodies to immortal bodies in 1 Corinthians 15:52-53: "For the trumpet will sound, and the dead will be raised imperishable, and we will be changed. For this perishable must put on the imperishable, and this mortal must put on immortality."

In light of this expectation, Paul likens our present, corruptible bodies to a temporary "tent" in which we dwell; but our future, incorruptible resurrection bodies will be like a permanent building, not constructed of perishable materials from this world, but conformed to the building code for heavenly existence—untainted perfection, spiritual immortality, heavenly glory.

This fact brings up an interesting question. If Paul was waiting for the return of Christ, when the whole church would be resurrected and transformed into their new glorified bodies, why does he say we "have" (present tense) a body from heaven in 2 Corinthians 5:1? Had he changed his mind since writing 1 Thessalonians 4 or 1 Corinthians 15? Surely not! Rather, it seems best to interpret this present tense as indicating the certainty with which Paul holds the truth of the bodily resurrection.

The apostle John describes our salvation as a present reality, even though we have much more to come: "He who has the Son has the life; he who does not have the Son of God does not have the life. These things I have written to you who believe in the name of the Son of God, so that you may know that you have eternal life" (1 Jn. 5:12-13). Paul expresses a similar thought in 2 Timothy 4:8, "In the future there is laid up [present tense] for me the crown of righteousness, which the Lord, the righteous Judge, will award to me on that day; and not only to me, but also to all who have loved His appearing."

Therefore, from the perspective of a guaranteed promise of a future reality, John describes eternal life as something we *now* possess; and Paul refers to the reward believers will receive at the second coming of Christ as something that is *presently laid up* for him and for all who look forward to His appearance. In this way, too, Paul can speak of the heavenly, glorified, resurrection body as something that he *has*. We might paraphrase Paul this way: "If the earthly tent which is our present home is torn down, we have the guaranteed promise of a permanent structure from God, a sturdy building not built with human hands, but one that can dwell eternally in the heavenly realm."

Paul expresses his longing for the transformation from his mortal, earthly body to his immortal, heavenly body this way: "Indeed in this house we groan, longing to be clothed with our dwelling from heaven" (2 Cor. 5:2). Similarly, in Romans 8:23 he writes, "We ourselves groan within ourselves, waiting eagerly for our adoption as sons, the redemption of our body." In both passages, Paul says believers groan within themselves as they wait for the resurrection of the body.

Physicians make their living listening to these groaning tents. An orthopedic surgeon tries to keep the tent pegs from pulling loose. A dermatologist tries to keep the canvas in good shape. Surgeons cut and stitch, nip and tuck, trying to get just a little more life out of these flimsy, floppy tents we call our bodies. We groan because we are weary, rain-soaked campers longing for a permanent home (2 Cor. 5:2). But we do not desire to be free from a shelter—bodiless, ghost-like souls flittering about the heavens (5:3-4). The Christian's hope is not to be unclothed (5:4), but to be clothed with a new immortal body (5:4).

Many Christians get this wrong. They believe the Christian hope is simply dying so their souls may be free from their bodily existence. It is true that the Bible teaches the soul may be separated from the body for a stage in the process of our ultimate redemption, during which we are absent from our bodies but present with the Lord (5:8). But the full realization of salvation is not to be naked but to be clothed in new, immortal bodies at the time of the Resurrection. As Paul says in Philippians 3:20-21, "For our citizenship is [present tense] in heaven, from which also we eagerly wait for a Savior, the Lord Jesus Christ; who will transform the body of our humble state into conformity with the body of His glory, by the exertion of the power that He has even to subject all things to Himself."

We await the fulfillment of this promise because we know with certainty that it will one day come to pass. How? Because God gave us His Holy Spirit as a "pledge," a priceless deposit that guarantees what has been promised will come to pass (2 Cor. 5:5). Though our present, earthly body is wasting away, we can count on a new, glorious body to replace it one day.

## — 5:6-10 —

Along with most first-century Christians, Paul rightly expected that Jesus could have returned in his own lifetime. I say "rightly" because nobody knows when the Lord will come back (Matt. 24:36). His coming could literally be at any moment—perhaps today. This belief in the imminent return of Christ was just as true in the first century as it is in the twenty-first. Christ remains poised to step out of heaven as Judge and King as soon as the Father says, "Now!"

Because of this expectation, Paul speaks primarily in terms of anticipation—that his present earthly body would be "swallowed up by life" (2 Cor. 5:4), as though he would be among those who were still alive at the coming of the Lord and would experience, not death and resurrection, but instant transformation and rapture (1 Thes. 4:17; 1 Cor. 15:50-53). Paul also knew, however, that many Christians had already died since the founding of the church at Pentecost (Acts 2) and that it was possible that he and others would suffer physical death before the Lord returned. Therefore, in 2 Corinthians 5:6-10 Paul deals with two questions. First, what should we do while present in this mortal body, awaiting our future redemption? Second, what will happen to us if our earthly bodies die before Christ returns?

The first question is rather easy to answer. While we dwell on this earth, we are to be "of good courage" (5:6, 8). We "walk by faith, not by sight" (5:7), living in light of our future reward. In other words, we make the most of the time left to us here on earth, knowing that whatever we invest in the current ministry of reconciliation will reap eternal benefits when Christ returns. Therefore, our ambition in this life is "to be pleasing to Him" in all we do (5:9).

The answer to the second question is suggested in 5:6, 8. Paul says that to be "at home in the body"—referring to this present earthly body—means to be "absent from the Lord" (5:6). Likewise, the contrary is true: to be "absent from the body" means to be "at home with the Lord" (5:8). Paul expresses the same concept in Philippians 1:23-24, when in the midst of great trials and hardships, he writes, "But I am hard-pressed from both directions, having the desire to depart and be with Christ, for that is very much better; yet to remain on in the flesh is more necessary for your sake."

Yes, to be absent from this mortal body is to be present with the Lord, just as Jesus promised the thief on the cross, "Truly I say to you, today you shall be with Me in Paradise" (Luke 23:43). There is no hint of "soul sleep," an unconscious hiatus before resurrection in which we rest until Christ returns. Also, the idea of a purgatorial cleansing in some intermediate state does not fit this passage. To depart this earthly life through physical death—to be absent from the body—means to be present with the Lord. Paul is not suggesting, however, that this is the final experience of our resurrection. Those who die before Christ returns, then, will be with Him, awaiting the time of His return to resurrect their bodies and rapture the church, when all of us will be rewarded for our faithful service in the glories of His kingdom (Matt. 19:28-29; Rev. 3:21).

In fact, it may be that when Paul says God will "bring with Him [Jesus] those who have fallen asleep in Jesus" (1 Thes. 4:14), he is referring to Christ descending from heaven with the disembodied souls of the saints that had died prior to His second coming. These souls would then be reunited with their resurrected, glorified bodies (1 Thes. 4:16) and caught up with the transformed living saints (1 Thes. 4:17).

At this point in his description of what happens to believers when they die, Paul describes what will occur immediately after our resurrection and rapture: "For we must all appear before the judgment seat of Christ" (2 Cor. 5:10). The Corinthian believers well understood the concept of a "judgment seat," or *bēma* [968], in Greek. Paul himself had stood before the judgment seat of the Roman governor Gallio in Corinth years before, when hostile Jews accused him of violating their religious laws (Acts 18:12-17).

The judgment seat of Christ, however, will be different. Christ will not judge believers to determine innocence or guilt. That judgment of "not guilty" already was rendered when God declared us righteous at our conversion because of the saving death of Christ (2 Cor. 5:21). Because of the finished work of Christ, received as our own by faith in Him, our resurrection is guaranteed and our place in the kingdom of heaven is permanently assured (Eph. 1:13-14; 2 Cor. 1:22; 5:5). At the judgment seat of Christ, however, our future reward in the kingdom of God will be determined by the quality of our deeds and the motives behind them (see 1 Cor. 3:10-15; 4:4-5).

Interestingly, Paul does not describe the divine compensation for our faithful service in the present ministry of reconciliation. He states only that the reward will be in proportion to the deed itself, "whether good or bad" (2 Cor. 5:10). Some false teachers in Corinth may have been teaching a popular Greek philosophy that only the soul mattered and that sins of the body, such as sexual sins, were inconsequential (see feature on "Body and Soul" on page 98). Therefore, they reasoned, because we are saved by grace and because only our spirits matter, we can get away with any kind of carnal behavior in our bodies. But Paul completely annihilates this reasoning. In the

## What Happens to a Person after Death?

*"And inasmuch as it is appointed for men to die once and after this comes judgment . . ."* (Heb. 9:27)

| | At Death | Bodily Resurrection | Judgment | Eternal Destination |
|---|---|---|---|---|
| **Christian** | Christ's Presence<br>SOUL<br>BODY<br>The Grave | Resurrection at the Rapture<br>SOUL<br>BODY | Judgment Seat of Christ in Heaven for Rewards | Heaven |
| **Old Testament Believer** | Paradise/ Abraham's Bosom<br>SOUL<br>BODY<br>The Grave | Resurrection at Christ's Second Coming<br>SOUL<br>BODY | Judgment on Earth for Rewards | Heaven |
| **Tribulation Believer** | Christ's Presence<br>SOUL<br>BODY<br>The Grave | Resurrection at Christ's Second Coming<br>SOUL<br>BODY | Judgment on Earth for Rewards | Heaven |
| **Unbeliever** | Sheol/Hades Torment<br>SOUL<br>BODY<br>The Grave | Resurrection at the End of the Millennium<br>SOUL<br>BODY | Judgment at the Great White Throne for Sins | Hell/ Gehenna/ Lake of Fire |

very bodies in which we served the Lord, we will also be rewarded before Christ's throne. And therefore, in the very bodies in which we sinned, we will lose rewards. Paul Barnett sums up the thrust of Paul's message:

> The sure prospect of the judgment seat reminds the Corinthians—and all believers—that while they are righteous in Christ by faith alone, the faith that justifies is to be expressed by love and obedience (Gal. 5:6, Rom. 1:5) and by pleasing the Lord (2 Cor. 5:9). Our "confidence" that we will be "with the Lord" (v. 8) is to be held in tension with the "fear of the Lord" (v. 11), from which we serve Him.[8]

We must all appear before the judgment seat of Christ. There He will appraise our deeds and will look deeper than the action. He will see the motives behind them. He will look further than the quantity of deeds to examine the quality. And on the basis of His perfect knowledge, He will grant rewards or withhold them. Our response to this truth? Whether we are at home in the body or absent, our number one ambition should be "to be pleasing to Him" (2 Cor. 5:9).

## APPLICATION: 2 CORINTHIANS 5:1-10

### Is It Well with Your Soul?

> And Lord, haste the day when my faith shall be sight,
> The clouds be rolled back as a scroll;
> The trump shall resound, and the Lord shall descend,
> Even so, it is well with my soul.

In 1873, a Chicago businessman, Horatio Spafford, composed these lyrics following the tragic loss of four daughters in a shipwreck. In the midst of the storm of earthly trials, he was able to experience divine peace because, despite his loss, it was well with his soul.

Not many people today have this underlying confidence in the condition of their own souls before a righteous, holy God. Will it be well with your soul when the Lord descends as Judge and King? When God examines the thoughts, attitudes, motives, and deeds of your life? Or will it turn out to be a disappointing discovery?

I can't speak for you because I have no idea. But I do know "we must all appear before the judgment seat of Christ, so that each one may be recompensed for his deeds in the body, according to what he has done, whether good or bad" (5:10). Is that going to be a disappointing discovery, or will it be well with your soul? It is a probing thought indeed, which is why Scripture repeatedly urges us to give these questions serious consideration.

Here is what I want you to think about first: When you die, *where* will you live again? Will it be with the Lord or away from His presence forever? Will it be well with your soul in eternity? Have you come to terms with your own guilt before God, confessed your desperate need for forgiveness, turned away from trusting in yourself to be "good enough," and embraced Christ alone as your Savior? Only by grace alone through faith alone can you receive the free gift of reconciliation and eternal life. Then and only then will it be "well with your soul." The choices are heaven or hell. No in-between. No nirvana. No purgatory. No second chance. No reincarnation. No "holding tank" while you decide. No nothingness. Will it be eternal bliss filled with joy and relief and the rewards awaiting God's people? Or eternal judgment, away from God and all those things you hold dear? Only you can determine which.

Second, if you are already a believer and have passed from the threat of eternal death to the irrevocable promise of eternal life, is it well with your soul in a temporal sense? That is, are you making the most of your opportunities in this temporary life so that when you appear before the judgment seat of Christ to give an account of how you spent your days in service of the Savior, you will be honored rather than shamed? Though life is short, it is eternally significant. Have the incessant pressures and distractions of this world lured you away from those things that are most important? If it's already well with your soul, how well is it?[9]

# Crazies for Christ
## 2 CORINTHIANS 5:11-21

NASB

11 Therefore, knowing the fear of the
Lord, we persuade men, but we are
made manifest to God; and I hope
that we are made manifest also
in your consciences. 12 We are not
again commending ourselves to you
but *are* giving you an occasion to be
proud of us, so that you will have
*an answer* for those who take pride

NLT

11 Because we understand our fearful
responsibility to the Lord, we work
hard to persuade others. God knows
we are sincere, and I hope you know
this, too. 12 Are we commending our-
selves to you again? No, we are giv-
ing you a reason to be proud of us,*
so you can answer those who brag
about having a spectacular ministry

**NASB**

in appearance and not in heart.
13 For if we [a]are beside ourselves, it
is for God; if we are of sound mind,
it is for you. 14 For the love of Christ
controls us, having concluded this,
that one died for all, therefore all
died; 15 and He died for all, so that
they who live might no longer live
for themselves, but for Him who died
and rose again on their behalf.

16 Therefore from now on we recog-
nize no one [a]according to the flesh;
even though we have known Christ
[a]according to the flesh, yet now we
know *Him in this way* no longer.
17 Therefore if anyone is in Christ,
[a]*he is* a new creature; the old things
passed away; behold, new things
have come. 18 Now all *these* things are
from God, who reconciled us to Him-
self through Christ and gave us the
ministry of reconciliation, 19 namely,
that God was in Christ reconciling
the world to Himself, not counting
their trespasses against them, and
[a]He has [b]committed to us the word
of reconciliation.

20 Therefore, we are ambassadors
for Christ, as though God were mak-
ing an appeal through us; we beg you
on behalf of Christ, be reconciled to
God. 21 He made Him who knew no
sin *to be* sin on our behalf, so that
we might become the righteousness
of God in Him.

**5:13** [a]Lit *were* **5:16** [a]I.e. by what he is in the flesh
**5:17** [a]Or there is *a new creation* **5:19** [a]Lit *having*
[b]Lit *placed in us*

**NLT**

rather than having a sincere heart.
13 If it seems we are crazy, it is to bring
glory to God. And if we are in our right
minds, it is for your benefit. 14 Either
way, Christ's love controls us.* Since
we believe that Christ died for all, we
also believe that we have all died to
our old life.* 15 He died for everyone
so that those who receive his new life
will no longer live for themselves.
Instead, they will live for Christ, who
died and was raised for them.

16 So we have stopped evaluating
others from a human point of view.
At one time we thought of Christ
merely from a human point of view.
How differently we know him now!
17 This means that anyone who be-
longs to Christ has become a new
person. The old life is gone; a new
life has begun!

18 And all of this is a gift from God,
who brought us back to himself
through Christ. And God has given
us this task of reconciling people to
him. 19 For God was in Christ, recon-
ciling the world to himself, no longer
counting people's sins against them.
And he gave us this wonderful mes-
sage of reconciliation. 20 So we are
Christ's ambassadors; God is making
his appeal through us. We speak for
Christ when we plead, "Come back
to God!" 21 For God made Christ, who
never sinned, to be the offering for
our sin,* so that we could be made
right with God through Christ.

**5:12** Some manuscripts read *proud of yourselves.*
**5:14a** Or *urges us on.* **5:14b** Greek *Since one died for all, then all died.* **5:21** Or *to become sin itself.*

I'll admit it. Sometimes we Christians get a little crazy, at least from the perspective of outsiders. Frankly, if I were outside the faith, I'd think Christians are completely off their rockers too. If you live in a "Bible bubble," you may have forgotten how other people view us. But all you have to do is turn on the morning news during a political segment to be reminded. We are not reasonable, according to secular standards. We are too conservative, too dogmatic, and too intolerant. We believe strange things, speak a strange lingo, and have strange practices. Though our beliefs and practices used to be regarded as mainstream in Western society, now we are considered to be barely hanging on to the fringes.

The great A. W. Tozer put his finger on it when he wrote:

> A real Christian is an odd number anyway. He feels supreme love for One whom he has never seen, talks familiarly every day to Someone he cannot see, expects to go to heaven on the virtue of Another, empties himself in order to be full, admits he is wrong so he can be declared right, goes down in order to get up, is strongest when he is weakest, richest when he is poorest, and happiest when he feels worst. He dies so he can live, forsakes in order to have, gives away so he can keep, sees the invisible, hears the inaudible, and knows that which passeth knowledge.[10]

I repeat, we may appear to be a little strange. But that's not only the mark of a good Christian; that's the mark of a strong Christian. In my experience, the more mature you grow in an all-out commitment to serve Christ, the stranger you appear to the person disinterested in the things of Christ. In fact, we "crazy Christians" are in good company. Even Christianity's founder was considered insane by those around Him. The multitudes said that Jesus had "lost His senses" and was "possessed" (Mark 3:21-22). Many said He had "a demon" and was "insane" (John 10:20). So we shouldn't feel surprised if we, His followers, are regarded with the same contempt. For example, after hearing Paul's testimony concerning his conversion to Christ and his Christian convictions as an ambassador of Christ, King Agrippa told the apostle he was "out of [his] mind" (Acts 26:24). Hebrews 11 tells of the reaction other radical servants of the Lord God received:

> Others experienced mockings and scourgings, yes, also chains and imprisonment. They were stoned, they were sawn in two, they were tempted, they were put to death with the sword; they went about in sheepskins, in goatskins, being destitute, afflicted, ill-treated (men of whom the world was not worthy), wandering in deserts and mountains and caves and holes in the ground. (Heb. 11:36-38)

The world thinks we're crazy. That's okay! In fact, if nobody thinks you are a little out of step with the culture because of your Christian faith, then something's wrong with your walk. Your faith ought to raise eyebrows at times. People in your shop ought to look over their machine and say, "You said *what*?" Your students should do a double take. Your professors should frown. Your colleagues should ask you, "What did you say?" And your neighbors may very well ask if you are serious. When unbelievers notice the stark contrast between what they believe and what you believe, this becomes a platform for your testimony.

This is exactly what the apostle Paul did in 2 Corinthians 5:11-21. Written in the context of the preceding verse about the believers' judgment (2 Cor. 5:10), Paul explains how we are to live as believers by explaining his own behavior. His explanation, however, makes clear just why we tend to look so outlandish to the rest of the world. From this passage we can see four reasons why Christians are so misunderstood by those outside the faith:

- *Our mission is unique. (5:11-13)*
- *Our approach is different. (5:14-16)*
- *Our life is transformed. (5:17-19)*
- *Our role is unusual. (5:20-21)*

## — 5:11-13 —

We live in an age where personal choice reigns supreme. Most people think each individual has every right to choose to live any way desired: married or divorced, homosexual or heterosexual, religious or secular. So long as they do not harm anybody physically and directly, we are told we should accept people as God made them, tolerate their decisions, and stop trying to make them feel guilty or change their minds.

Paul, however, had a different take on the believers' responsibility. Whereas everybody else in the world has the prerogative to leave people to the errors of their ways, *our mission is unique*. We have a responsibility to share the truth with others. Instead of tacitly accepting others' beliefs and actions in an "I'm okay, you're okay" fashion, the looming reality of the judgment seat of Christ motivates us to "persuade men" to accept Christ (2 Cor. 5:11).

Note the word "persuade" used here. It is the Greek word *peithō* [3982], meaning "to convince," "to prevail upon," or "to win over." Paul's means of persuasion were not through force, shame, deception, or theatrics, but by intelligent reasoning from the Scriptures (Acts 18:4; 28:23). In other words, our fervent belief that Jesus alone is the Way, the Truth, and the Life (John 14:6) motivates us to a ministry of persuasion—trying to reason with people, convincing them through biblical revelation that Jesus is the Christ and their only hope of eternal

# "You Guys Are Weird!"

## 2 CORINTHIANS 5:13

*Because of my ministries at Stonebriar Church, Dallas Seminary, and Insight for Living, most of my day-to-day interactions are with other believers. Yes, I get out and interact with unbelievers when I travel, shop, and run errands, but my particular ministry calling confines me to a Christian community most of the time. This has not always been the case, however. At different periods in my life I had various kinds of interaction with unbelievers—and to this day I still remember how weird they thought we Christians are.*

*I remember one episode back when I was in the Marine Corps. There aren't too many sold-out Christians in the Marine Corps, and those who are stand out like a sore thumb. I remember a bunkmate of mine in Okinawa named Eddie who made it very clear to me as soon as his seabag hit the floor that he didn't want me to lay my religious trip on him. He made it unmistakably clear that my Christianity and his life were never to so much as brush up against each other by accident. So, in a weak moment, I reluctantly agreed.*

*Later I felt haunted that I agreed not to talk to him about Christ, so I began to live for Christ, hoping to communicate His grace and love through actions rather than words. After some time, I realized that I wasn't talking to him at all about my faith. So after pondering that reality, I worked out a way to make that happen.*

*At the time, I was in a rather intense Scripture memory program with The Navigators, so I asked Eddie one day, "Why don't you help me memorize these verses?"*

*In a weak moment he said, "Sure. Why not?"*

*So he'd lie on his bunk below, and I'd lie on my bunk above, and I'd spout all these verses. And he'd go through them and correct me: "No. That's not the word. You missed such and such."*

*And sometimes I'd miss a word or two on purpose to emphasize it. "God so . . ."*

(continued on next page)

*"Loved . . . loved."*

*"Right. God so loved . . ."*

*"The world."*

*"Right. God so loved the world . . ."*

*I'd work through these delightfully convicting verses, and Eddie would labor with me through them, one agonizing verse at a time.*

*When I got to 1 Peter 2:9, I'll never forget a comment he made. I was trying to memorize most of that chapter in the King James Version, and when I got to verse 9, I recited the following: "Ye are a chosen generation, a royal priesthood, an holy nation, a peculiar people."*

*Although I got it word perfect, Eddie interrupted me with a choice comment—when I got to "peculiar people," he said, "That guy Peter was right on. You guys are weird."*

life. This does not mean becoming obnoxious in the process. But, like Paul, we may go to great lengths to win a hearing with people from all walks of life (1 Cor. 9:19-22).

Paul clarifies that he was not trying to impress the Corinthians by his radical evangelistic lifestyle (2 Cor. 5:12). Rather, he wanted to simply present the facts so when his adversaries in Corinth bad-mouthed him and his fellow apostles, his defenders could speak on his behalf. His opponents took pride in "appearance" rather than in sincerity of heart. Paul, on the other hand, didn't seek the approval of the masses. He says, "If we are beside ourselves, it is for God" (5:13). The word "beside ourselves" is the same as the one used in Mark 3:21 when Jesus' own family feared He had lost His mind. Yet the Corinthians should have known that Paul wasn't crazy, but "of sound mind." After all, Paul had used reason and persuasion to convince them of the soundness of the gospel. The charge of lunacy came not from fellow believers but from outsiders and false teachers.

## — 5:14-16 —

A second reason we believers are so misunderstood in this world is that *our approach is different* (5:14-16). We have an internalized, compelling force that "controls us"—the love of Christ (5:14). Most people have nothing of the kind, no driving passion in life, no overarching purpose or plan for the decisions they make and the priorities they set. They do whatever seems expedient or pleasurable, living for their momentary, self-serving interests.

Christ's love for us and ours for Him now defines our lives. In the grip of this love, our outlook on the world changes. Three themes determine our choices and our paths: first, that Jesus Christ died for all (5:14). Second, that since all people are dead spiritually, they all need someone—Jesus—to give them new life. Third, that once we have given Him our lives, we no longer desire to live for ourselves but for Him (5:15). When we align our trajectory with these three markers, our approach to life will differ completely from the world. Unlike the world's positive "we're all good people" approach, we view all people—including ourselves—as essentially bad *apart from* divine grace. At the same time, we view all people as potentially "saveable" *because of* divine grace.

This is what Paul means when he says, "We recognize no one according to the flesh" (5:16). Just as we all once regarded Jesus as any other man, "according to the flesh," once we have accepted that He is the God-man who "died and rose again" on our behalf (5:15), our whole outlook changes and we view people as sinners who can be saved by the gospel of Jesus. This radically alters our perspective: we now view our own purpose in life as Christ-centered *in response to* divine grace.

## — 5:17-19 —

A third reason the world regards us as a little loony is because *our life is transformed* (5:17-19). Believers in Christ have not just turned over a new leaf. They have not simply managed to carry out a New Year's resolution past February. Nor have they been brainwashed into some kind of cultish lifestyle in which their every move is determined by some guru on high. Rather, they are truly changed from within—transformed!

"Therefore if anyone is in Christ, he is a new creature; the old things passed away; behold, new things have come" (5:17). Most people do not realize that Paul is alluding to a very important Old Testament passage, Isaiah 65:17: "For behold, I create new heavens and a new earth; and the former things will not be remembered or come to mind." The Isaiah text refers specifically to the renewal of creation that will come about after Christ returns and perfects this world, cleansing it from its wickedness and radically restoring and surpassing its original intention. Peter writes, "According to His promise [in the Old Testament Scriptures] we are looking for new heavens and a new earth, in which righteousness dwells" (2 Pet. 3:13). In Revelation 21–22, we catch a marvelous glimpse of this new condition.

In 2 Corinthians 5:17, Paul applies this imagery to the redeemed believer, indicating the stunning, radical, dramatic transformation that God designed to take place when a believer says "I do" to Jesus Christ. When Christ invades a life, He performs a miraculous act of re-creation, analogous to the extreme overhaul of creation itself that He will perform at the Second Coming. He brings into being something new. When this new life is born in us by the work of the Holy Spirit, not by human works (Gal. 6:15), we will be transformed from the inside out, changing our priorities, our relationships, and our actions. Only God can do this work in us, but once He has done it, we participate in living out the inner working (Phil. 2:12-13).

The first obvious sign of our transformed life is to fulfill our ministries of reconciliation (*katallagē* [2643]; 2 Cor. 5:18-19). God has commissioned each of us to show others that Jesus' death on the cross paid for our sin, appeasing God's wrath and bringing about forgiveness. His resurrection from the dead opened us up to a new life in relationship with Him through the powerful indwelling of the Spirit of resurrection (Rom. 8:11). To us, then, who have personally experienced this reconciliation with God, Christ has committed the message of reconciliation—the gospel of the person and work of Jesus Christ (2 Cor. 5:19).

## — 5:20-21 —

A fourth reason unbelievers think Christians are crazy is that *our role is unusual* (5:20-21). As representatives of Christ's righteous rule, we speak a different language, we have different customs and lifestyles, and we appear a bit like foreigners in a foreign land. We are ambassadors for a nation without borders, an invisible kingdom without currency, a King whose throne is in heaven and who reigns spiritually through the hearts of His people. One day, of course, He will establish His kingdom on this earth, and what was unseen will be made visible; but until that day, we have an unusual role to play as ambassadors of an invisible empire (5:20).

Ambassadors represent their homeland and its messages, promoting its policies to the people among whom they live. Their country is often judged by their actions as their deeds are watched and their words scrutinized. The same is true for us. Our true home is in heaven; our true sovereign is the Lord Jesus Christ. As His ambassadors, we represent King Jesus to those around us, even though they do not acknowledge Him as their own sovereign Lord. R. V. G. Tasker gives a succinct description of our unusual role as ambassadors for Christ:

> Ambassadors engaged upon human affairs are chosen especially for their tact, their dignity and their courtesy, and because they are gifted with persuasive powers. The ambassadors for Christ should show the same characteristics. They must never try to bludgeon men and women into the kingdom of God, but must speak the truth in love . . . by the gentleness and meekness of Christ.[11]

Our task as ambassadors is simple: to "beg" others on behalf of Christ to "be reconciled to God" (5:20). The simple content of this message of reconciliation is succinctly stated: "He made Him who knew no sin to be sin on our behalf, so that we might become the righteousness of God in Him" (5:21). This verse is the heart and soul of the saving power of the gospel. Jesus, the perfect God-man, the spotless Lamb of God, was made a sin offering in our place, just as Isaiah had prophesied centuries earlier, "But the LORD was pleased to crush Him, putting Him to grief, if he would render Himself as a guilt offering" (Isa. 53:10).

Through faith alone in the person and work of Jesus Christ, we become the righteousness of God. A real transfer occurs at the Cross: We trade our guilt for His innocence. Having been declared righteous (justified), we are completely free of guilt and shame and have become full heirs of a glorious promise.

Is that crazy talk? Maybe. But I would rather be a fool for Christ's coming kingdom than a wise man in a world that is passing away.

## APPLICATION: 2 CORINTHIANS 5:11-21

### How Can "Crazies" like Us Be Effective?

Unless you've been hiding in the wilderness for the last couple of decades, you've probably noticed that the world's gone crazy. Off-the-deep-end crazy. I know that if you turn on the television or surf the web, many of our politicians and media moguls make it look like Christians are the ones who have lost their minds because we refuse to call good evil and evil good. This leads to an important question. In a world that's lost its way, can we "crazies" be effective in representing Christ in word and deed? Let me share three things we can do to continue to be effective.

First, *we maintain our mission.* As 2 Corinthians 5:11 says, because the fear of the Lord guides our steps, we need to keep on pleading with this world that is off its rocker. We need to persuade them to consider the claims of Christ as Savior and Lord. We need to appeal to them to be reconciled to the creator God they've shut out or shunned. We can't afford to lose sight of our mission.

Second, *we keep our perspective.* Now that's a hard one. It's so easy to look at our message concerning Christ's death and resurrection and believe it has no relevance to the world today. In the cacophony of entertainment, politics, and business, it may feel like our little voice telling the "old, old story" just can't be heard. Nonsense! As ambassadors of Christ, we need to remember that God's booming voice speaks through our most timid whispers. It's God's Word that does the work. As 2 Corinthians 5:16 says, we should no longer regard anyone according to outward appearances. Remember, the flashiest rock star, the crookedest politician, and the worldliest tycoon will one day bow to the crucified and risen Lord. Our message has the power to bring them to their knees today, before it's too late.

Finally, *we fulfill our role as ambassadors.* We don't speak on our own behalf, but on Christ's. It isn't our message that we convey, but His gospel. We don't invite people to our church, but into His body. We don't build up our little kingdom, but His. Ambassadors who represent rulers of this world speak with their authority. If they had to stand on their own power and authority, they would collapse. In the same way, God is making His appeal to the world through us as ambassadors of Christ (2 Cor. 5:20). Therefore, we can stand in bold confidence when we open our mouths to share His good news and live our lives in a way that flies in the face of this world.

When people look at you funny for holding "quaint" or even "crazy" ideas about God, Christ, and holy living, don't fret. Maintain your mission. Keep your perspective. Fulfill your role as an ambassador of Christ.

# THE REALISTIC PORTRAIT OF MINISTRY (2 CORINTHIANS 6:1–7:16)

I've occasionally heard fellow pastors joke, "Ministry would be great if it weren't for all the people." Sometimes those are little more than throwaway words of a frustrated pastor blowing off steam—nothing meant by them, really, just some light-hearted jesting. On other occasions, however, these words get blurted out by a jaded minister who's ready to hang it up because of an ongoing personality conflict, pastoral power play, or congregational upheaval. How easy it is for the stresses of ministry to turn an optimistic idealist into a pessimistic cynic!

Much of this disappointment and disillusionment stems from an inaccurate portrait of the ministry. False expectations frequently come from the new pastor, fresh out of seminary, who rushes into ministry situations for which he is emotionally and spiritually unprepared. Other times the unrealistic expectations come from a congregation that expects their pastor to be "all things to all men" (1 Cor. 9:22), equipped with limitless energy and free of imperfections. Both of these preconceptions pose severe problems in ministry as expectations get dashed and failures get exaggerated.

To inoculate both the pastoral novice and the unrealistic congregation, Paul now paints a fair and balanced picture of what a life of ministry entails (2 Cor. 6:1–7:16). So far in this letter, Paul has addressed questions about his concerns in ministry (1:1–3:18) and described the purpose of his ministry of reconciliation (4:1–5:21). Here, he begins with a candid description of the brutal hardships of Christian ministry (6:1-10). He then urges the Corinthians to a life of personal and corporate holiness, for as the holy temple of God and dwelling place of the Holy Spirit, the church must be separate from the grubbiness of the world (6:11-18). Paul then discusses the very personal, emotional dimension of ministry hardship (7:1-7) and recounts the anguish he felt when he heard of the Corinthians' difficult reception of his earlier letter, though this reproof resulted in their repentance (7:8-16). In the midst of the ups and downs of ministry, Paul still chooses optimism over pessimism, trusting that the Corinthians will continue on the path of righteousness.

Second Corinthians 6:1–7:16 should be "required reading" for all who have been called into vocational Christian service.

## KEY TERMS IN 2 CORINTHIANS 6:1–7:16

***parakaleō* (παρακαλέω)** [3870] "to comfort," "exhort," "implore"

This verb often indicates an act of comfort, an expression of encouragement, or a word of exhortation. It can also be used when a person urges a hearer to an action in the hearer's own best interest (6:1). In 2 Corinthians 6–7, Paul gives insight into how God comforts His children through tangible means. For example, the coming of Titus "comforted" Paul, who had been depressed (7:6). He was also comforted by good news about the church (7:7). "To comfort" in this biblical sense involves personal presence and tangible actions, not merely well-wishing.

***sōtēria* (σωτηρία)** [4991] "salvation," "deliverance," "protection," "preservation"

The common rendering of *sōtēria* as "salvation" often leads the modern reader to assume it refers to the opposite of damnation—saved in a spiritual and heavenly sense. Its meaning in the New Testament, however, is much broader, including rescue from danger, preservation from harm, or deliverance from an imminent threat. In 2 Corinthians 7:10, for example, Paul uses *sōtēria* to refer to deliverance from the destructive practice of sin through repentance and restoration, not salvation of a person's soul from damnation.

# The Brutal Realities of Ministry

## 2 CORINTHIANS 6:1–10

NASB

1 And working together *with Him,* we
also urge you not to receive the grace
of God in vain— 2 for He says,

"AT THE ACCEPTABLE TIME
I LISTENED TO YOU,
AND ON THE DAY OF SALVATION
I HELPED YOU."

Behold, now is "THE ACCEPTABLE
TIME," behold, now is "THE DAY OF
SALVATION"— 3 giving no cause for
offense in anything, so that the min-
istry will not be discredited, 4 but in
everything commending ourselves

NLT

1 As God's partners,* we beg you not
to accept this marvelous gift of God's
kindness and then ignore it. 2 For
God says,

"At just the right time, I heard
you.
On the day of salvation,
I helped you."*

Indeed, the "right time" is now.
Today is the day of salvation.
3 We live in such a way that no one
will stumble because of us, and no
one will find fault with our ministry.
4 In everything we do, we show that

as [a]servants of God, in much endur-
ance, in afflictions, in hardships, in
distresses, 5 in beatings, in impris-
onments, in tumults, in labors, in
sleeplessness, in hunger, 6 in purity,
in knowledge, in patience, in kind-
ness, in the Holy Spirit, in genuine
love, 7 in the word of truth, in the
power of God; by the weapons of
righteousness for the right hand
and the left, 8 by glory and dishonor,
by evil report and good report; *re-*
*garded* as deceivers and yet true; 9 as
unknown [a]yet well-known, as dying
[a]yet behold, we live; as [b]punished
[a]yet not put to death, 10 as sorrow-
ful yet always rejoicing, as poor yet
making many rich, as having noth-
ing [a]yet possessing all things.

**6:4** [a]Or *ministers* **6:9** [a]Lit *and* [b]Or *disciplined*
**6:10** [a]Lit *and*

we are true ministers of God. We
patiently endure troubles and hard-
ships and calamities of every kind.
5 We have been beaten, been put in
prison, faced angry mobs, worked
to exhaustion, endured sleepless
nights, and gone without food. 6 We
prove ourselves by our purity, our
understanding, our patience, our
kindness, by the Holy Spirit within
us,* and by our sincere love. 7 We
faithfully preach the truth. God's
power is working in us. We use the
weapons of righteousness in the
right hand for attack and the left
hand for defense. 8 We serve God
whether people honor us or despise
us, whether they slander us or praise
us. We are honest, but they call us
impostors. 9 We are ignored, even
though we are well known. We live
close to death, but we are still alive.
We have been beaten, but we have
not been killed. 10 Our hearts ache,
but we always have joy. We are poor,
but we give spiritual riches to others.
We own nothing, and yet we have
everything.

**6:1** Or *As we work together.* **6:2** Isa 49:8 (Greek version). **6:6** Or *by our holiness of spirit.*

Most people have strange ideas about ministry and what goes on in ministers' lives. My heart goes out to the bewildered churchgoer who said on one exasperating occasion, "My problem is that God is a lot like our preacher. I don't see Him through the week, and I don't understand Him on Sunday." I think people wonder about their preachers during the week. If they don't see them on a Wednesday night or don't run into them shopping in the supermarket or attending a local sports event, people might have all kinds of unusual ideas about what a minister's life must be like. "What does that pastor *do* all week?"

Some think ministry is an ivory-tower affair. They picture a place of stained-glass solitude where pastors pore over the Scriptures in a study, surrounded by endless shelves of books. They see ministry as a virtual monastic life of solitude and study—except for a few hours on a Sunday morning. Others think ministry is for the superspiritual models of perfection: mature saints whose lives are all together and who get paid to live the way nobody else in the congregation can. On the negative side, others might think a minister is simply a well-polished charlatan, skilled in emotional manipulation and slick exploitation. Some especially harsh cynics look at pastors not as pious monks, but as powerful moguls—cultish gurus who like to tell people what to do.

None of these estimations are true, at least not among the pastors I've known over my lifetime of ministry. People in the ministry are neither perfect nor fiendish. Admittedly, all of us have weaknesses, problems, imperfections, and blemishes. We aren't always loving or patient, unselfish or forgiving. We can succumb to temptations and suffer from trials, just like anybody else. Ministers are imperfect people living in an imperfect world, called to a seemingly insurmountable task.

Nevertheless, God continues to call and set apart an army of ministers for every generation—pastors, professors, evangelists, and missionaries; Sunday school teachers, children's pastors, and youth volunteers; mentoring moms, small group facilitators, counselors, musicians, and worship leaders—all imperfect people called with a holy calling. In 2 Corinthians 5, Paul states that if we have been reconciled to God, then we have been given a ministry of reconciliation (5:18). God Himself has therefore committed some kind of ministry to each of us, not merely to a select elite (5:19). *All* believers are called to be His ambassadors (5:20).

Therefore, each of us, regardless of our particular role in ministry, should be prepared to handle its brutal realities—realities Paul addresses in 2 Corinthians 6:1-10.

## — 6:1-3 —

Paul begins his description of the realities of ministry with two exhortations that will help us keep it together when we face the inevitable trials, temptations, hardships, and frustrations of ministry: *do not receive the grace of God in vain* (6:1-2) and *cultivate credibility in ministry* (6:3-4).

On the heels of his call to take seriously the ministry of reconciliation as ambassadors of Christ, Paul exhorts the Corinthians to receive the grace of God with sincerity and urgency. The "grace of God" ( 6:1) could refer to the saving work of Jesus Christ (5:21)—the reconciliation that occurs through the Savior's substitutionary death for us. It could also refer to the ministry of reconciliation granted not only to the apostles, but to all believers in Christ (5:18-21). This does not have to be an either/or interpretation. Paul mentions both:

> Now all these things are from God [*that's grace in general*], who reconciled us to Himself through Christ [*that's saving grace*] and gave us the ministry of reconciliation [*that's the grace of ministry*]. (5:18)

In this context, the danger of receiving the grace of God "in vain" (6:1) refers to the tragedy of a fruitless ministry. The word "vain" in Greek is *kenos* [2756], which means "empty, without content, without result, useless."[1] A person's ministry can be fruitless in at least two ways. First, it might embrace a graceless Christian lifestyle that depends on self rather than on the Spirit, reducing the Christian faith to a religion of works-related righteousness rather than the righteousness that comes only by grace. When a person fails to live by grace, their ministries will be law-oriented rather than grace-oriented. In short, it will not be a ministry of reconciliation to God but alienation from God (Eph. 2:13-19). The Judaizers had this kind of works-based "ministry" down to a fine art; the message of the atoning work of Christ ricocheted off their hearts like arrows off a plate of steel.

Second, a person's ministry can be fruitless when it fails to take advantage of present ministry opportunities. Paul alludes to Isaiah 49:8 to support his assertion—"Thus says the LORD, 'In a favorable time I have answered You, and in a day of salvation I have helped You; and I will keep You and give You for a covenant of the people, to restore the land, to make them inherit the desolate heritages." The NASB translation capitalizes the "You" because the translators rightly understood this passage as a prophetic reference to the Messiah, called to be a Covenant to the people of Israel. When we examine the context of this messianic "Servant Song," we discover additional themes similar to Paul's discussion in 2 Corinthians 6, making it a fitting passage for Paul to quote.

The song in Isaiah 49 begins with a call for the "peoples from afar" (the Gentiles) to hear the word of the Lord (Isa. 49:1). As the person of the Messiah speaks, He recounts that the Lord had called Him from the womb (Isa. 49:1), making His mouth like a sword (Isa. 49:2; see also Rev. 1:16; 2:16; 19:15, 21) and hiding the Messiah in His quiver like a secret weapon (1 Cor. 2:6-8), ready to be fired in the fullness of time (Gal. 4:4). The prophetic voice of the Messiah then recounts the words of the Father: "You are My Servant, Israel, in Whom I will show My glory" (Isa. 49:3). Whereas national Israel, named after their patriarch, Jacob (Israel), utterly failed to reflect God's glory among the nations, Jesus Christ would succeed in this mission as the embodiment and epitome of Israel and heir of the covenant promises.

The voice of the Messiah in Isaiah 49:4 cries out as if he had "toiled in vain" and spent His strength "for nothing and vanity." That is, even though He labored to the utmost, fulfilling the will of the Father and paying the price for Israel's redemption, the nation refused to accept Him and instead rejected His lordship. This "failure" of the Messiah's mission, however, actually results in a greater plan of redemption when the "arrow" in God's quiver is pulled and fired into salvation history (Rom. 11:12, 15). He describes this expanded mission in Isaiah 49:5-6:

> And now says the LORD, who formed Me from the womb to be His Servant, to bring Jacob back to Him, so that Israel might be gathered to Him (For I am honored in the sight of the LORD, and My God is My strength),
> He says, "It is too small a thing that You should be My Servant to raise up the tribes of Jacob and to restore the preserved ones of Israel; I will also make You a light of the nations so that My salvation may reach to the end of the earth."

When Paul alludes to Isaiah 49:8, then, he extends the Messiah's new covenant ministry of reconciliation to the church, whose role it is to carry on Christ's proclamation of salvation not only to Israel, but also to all the nations. Why? Because now is "the acceptable time" and "the day of salvation" (2 Cor. 6:2). Christ has come. Israel has rejected Him. Yet their rejection has led to the preaching of the gospel of reconciliation throughout the world: "Their rejection is the reconciliation of the world" (Rom. 11:15). This means that so long as we have breath in our lungs, we should act as Christ's covenant ambassadors, "working together with Him" (2 Cor. 6:1) to make disciples of all the nations (Matt. 28:19).

Having warned the Corinthians about receiving the grace of God in vain (2 Cor. 6:1-2), Paul continues to help believers face the brutal realities of ministry with an additional exhortation: *Cultivate credibility in ministry* (6:3-4). How do we, as imperfect ministers of the gospel, keep the new covenant ministry from getting discredited? By not giving any cause for offense (6:3) and by being faithful servants, just as Christ is the faithful Servant par excellence (6:4; see Isa. 49:3-7).

The Greek term for "discredited" (*mōmaomai* [3469]) is used only here and in 2 Cor. 8:20. It means "to find fault or blame." The Hebrew equivalent (*qalown* [H7036]) is used in Proverbs 9:7, translated as "dishonor." Just imagine for a moment all the ways our ministry can be discredited. We could:

- break promises
- exploit disciples
- live hypocritically
- betray confidences
- compromise principles
- sacrifice integrity
- indulge greed
- live opulently
- behave lustfully
- lead selfishly

Sadly, we could all add to this already harrowing list. Any one of these could topple our ministries and bring dishonor to the gospel.

## — 6:4-10 —

As he sets out to paint a brutally honest picture of authentic Christian ministry, Paul lays aside the pastel palette that would naturally attract people to ministry. Instead, he reaches for darker hues that shock the senses and present a realistic picture of the life of those who have commended themselves as servants of God.

The word "servant" here is not the term for "slave" or "bond-servant," *doulos* [1401] (Rom. 1:1; Titus 1:1). Rather, Paul uses the term *diakonos* [1249]. This Greek word has a fairly broad range of meanings: "a generic servant," "a food server," "an agent with a special mission," or "an official minister in a church." In the New Testament, *diakonos* is used to mean a servant with a certain mission or task (Rom. 15:8; 1 Cor. 3:5; Eph. 3:7); an assistant of a particular person (Matt. 22:13; 2 Cor. 6:4; Col. 1:7); or an official appointment, office, or position as a "minister" in a local church (Phil. 1:1; 1 Tim. 3:8-12). Paul's usage in 2 Corinthians 6:4 relates mostly to the first two meanings: he and his companions, all of them sold out for the gospel ministry, viewed themselves as conscripted servants of God Himself, assigned with the specific task of proclaiming the Word far and wide.

This ministry, however, did not come with competitive compensation, a great benefits package, or a comfortable retirement plan. Paul's description demolishes every false image of Christian ministry. Under its weight, the ivory-tower image collapses, the perfect-saint portrayal fades, and the in-it-for-the-money idea loses credibility. Look at how Paul describes the brutal reality of Christian ministry: He served the Lord "in much endurance, in afflictions, in hardships, in distresses, in beatings, in imprisonments, in tumults, in labors, in sleeplessness, in hunger" (6:4-5).

That's not exactly the description you would expect to find in a seminary brochure, hear from those recruiting volunteers for ministry, or read in a missionary's quarterly report. Granted, not all ministers encounter extreme hardships like those Paul described. But ministers must prepare themselves for both pleasant and unpleasant times. In a word, they must "endure" (6:4). The Greek word for endurance is *hypomonē* [5281]. William Barclay explains its meaning:

> It is not easy to capture the richness or depth of this expression with a single word in English. It does not describe the frame of mind which can sit down with folded hands and bowed head and let a torrent of troubles sweep over it in passive resignation. It describes the ability to bear things in such a triumphant way that it transfigures them.[2]

If anyone ever endured hardships for the sake of ministry, it was Paul. But because he set up his life as a model for others, we can learn from the various trials he endured (6:4-5) as well as the vital attitudes he exhibited in the midst of those trials (6:6-7).

*Various trials endured* (6:4-5). First, Paul battled inner struggles—afflictions, hardships, and distresses. His "afflictions," or "pressures" as the Greek root *thlipsis* [2347] indicates, included concerns that pressed in and weighed him down. His "hardships" required that he do without those things that make life comfortable and secure. His "distresses" pushed him into tight spots, where he felt cornered and trapped. We get the picture of a minister who had become stressed out, mentally and emotionally drained.

Second, Paul experienced external troubles—beatings, imprisonments, and tumults. His "beatings" were physically painful, even torturous. He had been imprisoned many times, and his tumultuous situations landed him in the midst of violence, public outcries, and assaults. In short, Paul was severely persecuted, physically brutalized by his enemies.

Third, Paul endured the private disciplines of commitment to the cause—labor, sleeplessness, and hunger. Whatever it took to advance the cause of the gospel, he did it with little regard for his own well-being. He worked tirelessly and without ceasing to spread the gospel throughout the world. Yet he counted it all expedient for the joy of the Cross (11:23-28).

*Vital attitudes maintained* (6:6-7). Paul then fills in the dark tones of his painting with nine beams of light, reminding us that even in the midst of the gloom, God is present to see us through. Paul served the gospel ministry "in purity, in knowledge, in patience, in kindness, in the Holy Spirit, in genuine love, in the word of truth, in the power of God; by the weapons of righteousness for the right hand and the left" (6:6-7). Four of these attributes are external attitudes visible to other people: purity, knowledge, patience, and kindness. The remaining five wield their power in the hidden places of the heart: the Holy Spirit, a genuine love for others, the word of truth, the power of God, and the weapons of righteousness.

What is Paul's point in listing these vital attitudes? It is that even in the midst of internal and external pressures, a believer can be sheltered, shielded, and strengthened by the fruit of the Spirit (Gal. 5:22-23), the gifts of the Spirit (1 Cor. 12:4-7), and the spiritual armor of God (Eph. 6:10-17). What is the result of this "mixed bag" of horrendous ministry experiences endured by means of God's strengthening presence and providence? As one might expect, our entire ministries will be characterized by extreme ups and downs and even confusing contradictions:

| DOWNS | UPS |
|---|---|
| by dishonor | and glory |
| by evil report | and good report |
| regarded as deceivers | and yet true |
| as unknown | yet well-known |
| as dying | yet behold, we live |
| as punished | yet not put to death |
| as sorrowful | yet always rejoicing |
| as poor | yet making many rich |
| as having nothing | yet possessing all things |

Considering the light and dark sides of ministry, it is sometimes hard to know which image we project to others as Christians, especially those of us who have chosen ministry as our vocation—or rather, have been chosen for ministry. In light of the brutal realities of ministry, the vital attitudes described in 2 Corinthians 6:6-7 become all the more important to maintain, so that even if we are experiencing more downs than ups, we can keep our heads above water and breathe the refreshing air of the Spirit's sustaining grace.

# APPLICATION: 2 CORINTHIANS 6:1-10

## Reflecting, Risking, and Leaving a Legacy

A large group of people over the age of ninety-five were asked the question, "If you could live your life over again, what would you do differently?"[3] Their answers fell into three general categories. They said they would 1) *reflect more*, 2) *risk more*, and 3) *do more things that would live on after their death.*

Those are revealing answers, aren't they? They are filled with a wise understanding of the basics of a fruitful, abundant life—reflecting on what is most important, taking chances instead of shying away from the unknown, and leaving a legacy for the future. And yet those responses also reveal a tinge of regret.

I'll be honest. I am thrilled by the work the Lord has given me to do. Every day I thank God for the ministry He has given me—and the ability to press on even through the storms of conflict, the dark clouds of hardship, and the raging winds of controversy. Yes, I acknowledge the brutal realities of ministry, but by the grace of God I have been able to tread water when the floods of adversity pummeled my life—not by my own wisdom and strength, but by the purity, knowledge, patience, kindness, love, truth, power, and righteousness that have come by His Holy Spirit (2 Cor. 6:6-7). I can testify without hesitation: I love the ministry with my heart and soul.

That said, I know that not everyone is called to full-time Christian work as a lifelong career. Yet all believers are called to do the work of ministry (Eph. 4:12). *All believers.* Sadly, I fear too many perfectly capable believers live in such a way that they are headed for a retirement of regrets: "I wish I would have reflected more, risked more, and left more of a legacy."

Don't let this be you!

Have you *reflected* on your present involvement in ministry versus what you are actually capable of doing? Are there opportunities at your local church which you have dismissed without even reflecting on whether you should get involved? Take time to reflect on the ministry needs in your church or with those around you and determine specific ways you might contribute. Not next year. Not next semester. Not next month. Do it today!

Second, are you playing it safe with your life, refusing to take *risks*? For example, are you sitting on a heap of cash for a rainy day that may never come when you could be using it for strategic ministry opportunities? Or are you avoiding outreach opportunities because of the risks involved to your pride, reputation, schedule, or comfort? Take a hard look at your travel, ministry, work, and leisure plans over the coming year and ask yourself whether you are playing it too safe.

Third, will anything you are doing now live on after you die? Are you throwing yourself into your career to the neglect of your family and church? When you get to the end of your life, what will be the legacy of eternal significance you leave behind? Are you discouraging children or grandchildren from engaging in vocational ministry for the sake of more lucrative, but less eternally significant, careers? Ministering to others is a noble calling. Not the only one, but a noble one. It doesn't have to be vocational, paid ministry. Any positive impact you can have on other believers or unbelievers will echo into eternity.

Yes, ministry is hard. It can be mentally draining, emotionally painful, and physically demanding. When not balanced by consistent, prevailing prayer, mixed with vital attitudes to keep us afloat, we can sink under the stress and surrender to its incessant demands and deadlines. When we endure the tough times, however, ministry is the most rewarding and satisfying life anybody can live.

# Good Relationships and Bad Partnerships

## 2 CORINTHIANS 6:11-18

**NASB**

11 Our mouth [a]has spoken freely
to you, O Corinthians, our heart
is opened wide. 12 You are not re-
strained [a]by us, but you are re-
strained in your own [b]affections.
13 Now in a like exchange—I speak
as to children—open wide *to us* also.
14 Do not be [a]bound together with
unbelievers; for what partnership
have righteousness and lawless-
ness, or what fellowship has light
with darkness? 15 Or what harmony

**NLT**

11 Oh, dear Corinthian friends! We
have spoken honestly with you, and
our hearts are open to you. 12 There
is no lack of love on our part, but
you have withheld your love from
us. 13 I am asking you to respond as
if you were my own children. Open
your hearts to us!
14 Don't team up with those who
are unbelievers. How can righteous-
ness be a partner with wickedness?
How can light live with darkness?
15 What harmony can there be

**NASB**

has Christ with [a]Belial, or [b]what has
a believer in common with an un-
believer? 16 Or what agreement has
the temple of God with idols? For we
are the temple of the living God; just
as God said,

"I WILL DWELL IN THEM AND WALK
AMONG THEM;
AND I WILL BE THEIR GOD, AND
THEY SHALL BE MY PEOPLE.
17 "Therefore, COME OUT FROM
THEIR MIDST AND BE
SEPARATE," says the Lord.
"AND DO NOT TOUCH WHAT IS
UNCLEAN;
And I will welcome you.
18 "And I will be a father to you,
And you shall be sons and
daughters to Me,"
Says the Lord Almighty.

**6:11** [a]Lit *is open to you* **6:12** [a]Or *in us* [b]Lit *inward parts* **6:14** [a]Lit *unequally yoked* **6:15** [a]Gr *Beliar* [b]Lit *what part has a believer with an unbeliever*

**NLT**

between Christ and the devil*? How
can a believer be a partner with an
unbeliever? 16 And what union can
there be between God's temple and
idols? For we are the temple of the
living God. As God said:

"I will live in them
and walk among them.
I will be their God,
and they will be my people.*
17 Therefore, come out from among
unbelievers,
and separate yourselves from
them, says the LORD.
Don't touch their filthy things,
and I will welcome you.*
18 And I will be your Father,
and you will be my sons and
daughters,
says the LORD Almighty.*"

**6:15** Greek *Beliar;* various other manuscripts render this proper name of the devil as *Belian, Beliab,* or *Belial.* **6:16** Lev 26:12; Ezek 37:27. **6:17** Isa 52:11; Ezek 20:34 (Greek version). **6:18** 2 Sam 7:14.

It doesn't take people long to realize that this world runs on relationships. Each individual came into existence because of a relationship between a mother and a father. As we grow up, we have either good or poor relationships with our parents and family. Throughout our childhood and adult years, we make relationships, cultivate relationships, ruin relationships, start relationships, and end relationships. Humans are relational beings.

This should come as no surprise to Christians because of the truth that God exists in a trinity. Of all the religions in this world, Christianity is the only one with a God who, in and of Himself, exists in eternal relationship: Father, Son, and Holy Spirit. As creatures uniquely created according to the image and likeness of God (Gen. 1:26-27), we naturally reflect the unity and distinction of the Triune Godhead. We were created to live in relationship with God and with one another.

God's Word, the Bible, is also filled with accounts of relationships between people: people loving, people fighting, people planning, people praying, people laughing and singing, people grieving and sorrowing, people relating for good or ill. The Old Testament Law managed the Israelites' relationships with God and with others. In fact, Jesus summed up the whole Law in terms of relationship: "Love the LORD your God with all your heart, and with all your soul, and with all your mind. . . . Love your neighbor as yourself" (Matt. 22:37, 39).

Our lives are formed and transformed through a series of relationships. Bad company can corrupt us (1 Cor. 15:33), but good friends can strengthen us (Prov. 18:24). Close relationships with other believers must be mended and strengthened in order for the whole church to grow. At the same time, close relationships with unbelievers who have a completely different worldview and an opposite set of priorities than we do must be maintained with caution. Paul addresses both of these issues—good relationships and bad partnerships—in 2 Corinthians 6:11-18.

## — 6:11-13 —

It is easy to get lost in the meandering details of a letter like 2 Corinthians, so occasionally we need to pause, step back, and look at the big picture. In the opening of his letter, Paul reiterated his commitment to the Corinthian Christians, then went on to clear up some misunderstandings in their perception of him and his authority as an apostle. Some people were upset with him because they believed Paul had not followed through on his desire to visit them when he had hoped. They had taken his intended itinerary as an ironclad promise, so when circumstances prevented him from keeping to his original plan, the Corinthians mistakenly took that for fickleness.

It did not help things that these charges were exaggerated by Paul's opponents in Corinth, who were Judaizing Christians trying to steer the church away from Paul's teaching. The Judaizers themselves were trying to live with one foot in the new covenant and one foot in the old—the church and the synagogue, Christianity and Judaism. This kind of syncretism demanded compromises in Christian doctrine and practice, compromises that destroyed the essence of the gospel of salvation by grace through faith.

Between 2 Corinthians 2:14 and 6:10, Paul digressed from his original discussion concerning his relationship with the Corinthians. He wrote on a related, though subordinate, issue: the makings of an effective ministry. After all, ministry is about people. Evangelism and discipleship involve working with people. By definition, ministry means helping, serving, encouraging, exhorting, confronting, and relating to people. Paul's discussion of the ups and downs of authentic ministry provides an important background to the value he placed on relationships with people in the churches he helped establish. Now, in 2 Corinthians 6:11, Paul returns to his original train of thought and the purpose of his letter—the restoration of the relationship between Paul and the Corinthian Christians, which will allow him to continue ministering to them effectively.

In 6:11 Paul reminds the Corinthians about how freely he had given himself to them and how candid and honest he had been. Literally, the end of this verse says, "our heart is enlarged" (*platynō* [4115]). Both internally, in their feelings for them, as well as externally, through their words, Paul and his ministry partners felt and expressed deep love and care for the Corinthians. Paul reveals the depth of his emotion by directly calling on the Corinthians as a group in the midst of his sentence. New Testament scholar David Lowery explains it this way:

> Only rarely did he name his readers in the midst of a letter. When, for example, he was greatly exercised about the declension in the Galatian churches, he sharply rebuked them by name (Gal. 3:1). On the other hand when he recalled the Philippian church's faithful support of him in the early days of his ministry and in his prison experience, he called them by name (Phil. 4:15). Blending frustration and affection, Paul similarly hailed the Corinthians and called for them to respond with unrestrained love.[4]

The Corinthians, however, did not respond in kind—at least, not with the same level of intensity or the same outward manifestation. Instead, they were restrained in their affections (2 Cor. 6:12). The term "affections," from the almost impossible-to-pronounce Greek word *splanchnon* [4698], literally means "bowels"—the internal organs of heart, liver, and lungs. In the ancient world, it was believed that human emotions emanated from these organs because when a person would feel happy, sad, frightened, or courageous, the individual would feel a physical sensation churning in this part of the anatomy. Therefore, the term "bowels" came to refer metaphorically to deep, sincere, heartfelt feelings. With this word Paul implies that his relationship with the Corinthians had been one-sided. To play on Paul's imagery, he had "spilled his guts" to them, but they had guarded their hearts. This is why Paul speaks to them in the same way a loving father, yearning for a tender relationship with his children, might plead with them: "Now in a like exchange . . . open wide to us also" (6:13).

Have you ever tried to hug a child who did not hug back? Or converse with a moody teenager who grunts single-syllable answers in return? It is impossible to establish or build a healthy relationship like that, isn't it? In order for relationships to work, both parties have to freely share their feelings and open up in conversation. Yet the Corinthians had refused to make an emotional connection with the apostle.

## — 6:14-18 —

Oh, the irony! Though the Corinthians had been reserved in their relationship with Paul (their spiritual father in the faith), they had eagerly entered into intimate personal and professional relationships with unbelievers. What a lack of discernment! They locked out the people who cared about them most, who sacrificed and suffered for them, and then locked arms with those who would harm their walk with Christ.

Paul does not beat around the bush when he bluntly confronts their error: "Do not be bound together with unbelievers" (6:14). The term "bound together" comes from the word for yoking animals together as they plow a field. Paul may be drawing on an Old Testament principle in Deuteronomy 22:10, "You shall not plow with an ox and a donkey together." Oxen and donkeys pulled differently, so plowing a straight line would have been nearly impossible. Drawing a spiritual principle from the literal command, Paul argues that it is a mistake to hitch together a believer and an unbeliever in a close relationship that requires pulling together in a unified direction—whether marriage, business, or any other formal, longer-term contractual or covenant relationship. Why? Because believers and unbelievers have different goals, different worldviews, different methods, and different rules.

Many Christians take this verse to mean more than Paul intended and so choose to associate only with other believers all the time: shunning secular schools or colleges, using only Christian businesses, employing only Christian tradespeople, going only to restaurants owned and operated by Christians, and maintaining friendships only with Christian friends. But a glance at 1 Corinthians 5:9-10 assures us that this extreme application is not what Paul had in mind: "I wrote you in my letter not to associate with immoral people; I did not at all mean with the immoral people of this world, or with the covetous and swindlers, or with idolaters, for then you would have to go out of the world." If we refuse to associate with the lost, how will they ever come to know Christ? Paul's thought in 2 Corinthians 6 involves permanent, day-to-day kinds of formal relationships, not casual friendships and social interaction. We might use the term "partnership" to describe the kind of "bound together" relationship he has in mind.

What kind of "partnership" is this? How close is too close? Where do we draw the line? Helping us answer those questions Paul contrasts the completely opposite natures and conditions between Christians and non-Christians (6:14-16), using black-and-white examples:

| | | |
|---|---|---|
| Righteousness | VERSUS | Lawlessness |
| Light | | Darkness |
| Christ | | Belial |
| Believer | | Unbeliever |
| Temple of God | | Idols |

Underscore the words *partnership*, *fellowship*, *harmony*, *common*, and *agreement*. Together these words describe close, intimate, interdependent, shared, and single-minded relationships that take time to develop and are difficult to end. Believers and unbelievers should never enter into these kinds of relationships. *Never.* Why not? Because certain things are essentially distinct and fundamentally incompatible. The saved cannot have spiritually intimate relationships with the lost. They should not form relationships with unbelievers that would either lead to a compromise of Christian standards or jeopardize the consistency of their Christian witness.

You may be thinking ahead here: *What if I'm already married to an unbeliever?* Maybe you, too, were a non-Christian when you married, or you have only recently begun to take your faith seriously. Maybe you entered into a marriage with a person you thought was a believer but who has since proven to be either an unbeliever or a very immature Christian unwilling to grow. Or perhaps you entered into your relationship without knowing that believers and unbelievers were not to walk that path of intimacy. Does that mean you should seek to be unhitched—divorced?

No. Although Paul's exhortation in 2 Corinthians 6:14 warns us against entering into the relationship, once such a marriage is instituted, the principle of 1 Corinthians 7:13 kicks in. There Paul says that if your unsaved partner is willing to stay with you, you are to stay in the relationship and become a live-in witness for Christ. That will not be an easy calling. Like when an ox and a donkey plow together, conflicts will inevitably arise and will add an increased tension as you try to plow a straight path for Christ. It will not be easy, but it need not be considered impossible.

You might be thinking, *What if I have entered into a contractual or business partnership with an unbeliever? Should I get out of it?* No. Paul clearly held that even human covenants or contracts cannot be simply set aside or annulled (Gal. 3:15); we must let our "yes" be "yes" and our "no" be "no" (Matt. 5:37). If you can be released from a contract legally and ethically, that is one thing; but following through on obligations—even foolish ones—is a Christian virtue not easily bent.

The underlying reason for the prohibition against being bound together with unbelievers is found in 2 Corinthians 6:16-18. There Paul calls the corporate body of the church "the temple of the living God."[5] He weaves together Old Testament verses to emphasize the intimate relationship God Himself has with His people: "I will dwell in them" . . . "[I will] walk among them" . . . "I will be their God" . . . "They shall be My people" . . . "I will welcome you" . . . "I will be a father to you" . . . "And you shall be sons and daughters to Me" (6:16-18).[6] Because of our intimate relationship with the holy God, we should keep ourselves separate from unholy relationships. Because God is in our midst, we should "come out from their midst" (6:17). Because God has cleansed us by His sanctifying presence, we should "not touch what is unclean" (6:17).

Our relationship with God places us in an intimate, corporate relationship with other believers. This relationship involves spiritual harmony (6:16), personal purity (6:17), and familial intimacy (6:18). We are God's temple, and we should not bring into His temple anything or any relationship that dishonors Him or destroys the harmony, purity, and intimacy we are meant to experience in the body of Christ, the church.

## APPLICATION: 2 CORINTHIANS 6:11-18

### Safe Guidelines for Relationships

How can we stay on the straight and narrow path when it comes to relationships? Let me offer two rules of thumb that will help you decide how close to get to people in your life. The first is positive: an exhortation based on 2 Corinthians 6:11-13, which will strengthen our relationships with other believers in the church. The second is negative: a warning against being unequally yoked with unbelievers (6:14-16).

First, *unless there is an emotional bond, we cannot experience authenticity in a relationship.* All of us are called to closer, more intimate and interdependent relationships with our fellow believers. Yet the kind of intimacy we are called to experience can't happen without wholehearted transparency. This means honesty. It means open communication. It means sharing from our heart and caring through our actions.

Paul, by contrast, had a lopsided relationship with the Corinthians. He flooded them with affection; they responded with dryness (6:11-13). He poured into them; they drained him out. He embraced them with unconditional love; they gave him a cold shoulder and a formal handshake. Are you in that kind of relationship? Which side of the uneven relationship are you on? If you are cold to another's warmth—whether in church, in your family, or in your marriage—that kind of relationship can't continue without causing severe problems. Likewise, if you are pouring into a relationship and the other person or persons are not reciprocating your affections, you may need to ask yourself whether it is an authentic relationship based on mutual love and trust, or a shallow substitute. In either case, pray for the Lord's wisdom concerning how you can mend this inequality and bring the relationship to a place of health and stability.

Second, *unless there is spiritual equality, we dare not be bound in a partnership.* Unless your spiritual values and goals strongly agree with those of the potential partner—whether in marriage, business, or some other partnership—getting involved in a deep and permanent relationship will be like yoking a donkey to an ox. You will always be out of step with each other. One will be doing the heavy pulling while dragging the other along. And you will never be able to plow in a straight line. If you have found yourself cozying up too close to an unbeliever in a friendship, romantic relationship, or business partnership, ask yourself a few questions: Why am I drawn to this person? Have I seen myself compromise my biblical principles as a result of this relationship? How? Is this relationship affecting my current relationships with believers? Before God and with His help, do I need to put on the brakes in this relationship before it gets too intimate or becomes permanent?

God has designed us for close relationships, but He means for them to be healthy, wholesome, pure, supportive, and balanced. When they become unhealthy, destructive, or lopsided, it's time to address the problem. Our relationships ultimately exist for God's glory—either to shine as lights in a darkened world or to deepen intimacy in the church. Don't let the darkness dim your light, and don't let shallow relationships with other believers weaken the body of Christ.

# Reverence for God, Respect for Others, Relief from Distress

## 2 CORINTHIANS 7:1-7

**NASB**

1 Therefore, having these promises,
beloved, let us cleanse ourselves
from all defilement of flesh and
spirit, perfecting holiness in the fear
of God.
2 Make room for us *in your hearts;*
we wronged no one, we corrupted no
one, we took advantage of no one.
3 I do not speak to condemn you, for
I have said before that you are in our
hearts to die together and to live to-
gether. 4 Great is my confidence [a]in
you; great is my boasting on your
behalf. I am filled with comfort; I
am overflowing with joy in all our
affliction.
5 For even when we came into
Macedonia our flesh had no rest,
but we were afflicted on every side:
conflicts without, fears within. 6 But
God, who comforts the [a]depressed,
comforted us by the coming of Titus;
7 and not only by his coming, but
also by the comfort with which he
was comforted in you, as he reported
to us your longing, your mourning,
your zeal for me; so that I rejoiced
even more.

**7:4** [a]Lit *toward* **7:6** [a]Or *humble*

**NLT**

1 Because we have these promises,
dear friends, let us cleanse ourselves
from everything that can defile our
body or spirit. And let us work to-
ward complete holiness because we
fear God.
2 Please open your hearts to us. We
have not done wrong to anyone, nor
led anyone astray, nor taken advan-
tage of anyone. 3 I'm not saying this
to condemn you. I said before that
you are in our hearts, and we live
or die together with you. 4 I have the
highest confidence in you, and I take
great pride in you. You have greatly
encouraged me and made me happy
despite all our troubles.
5 When we arrived in Macedonia,
there was no rest for us. We faced
conflict from every direction, with
battles on the outside and fear on
the inside. 6 But God, who encour-
ages those who are discouraged, en-
couraged us by the arrival of Titus.
7 His presence was a joy, but so was
the news he brought of the encour-
agement he received from you. When
he told us how much you long to see
me, and how sorry you are for what
happened, and how loyal you are to
me, I was filled with joy!

One of the best-known television interviewers in the heyday of prime-time television was Barbara Walters. She wrote a book at the height of her journalism career titled *How to Talk with Practically Anybody about Practically Anything*. Though not written from a Christian perspective, it contains some gems of insight gained from experience in conducting interviews with many of the most fascinating people around the world. In that book she described the characteristic that virtually everyone finds most appealing:

> The most consistently endearing human trait is warmth. *Everybody* responds to the person who radiates friendliness from a serene core. Such people are lovely to be around because they don't reject or belittle and, best of all, they bring out the best, most generous qualities in the people they encounter.[7]

Isn't that true? In a world as big and as busy as ours, coldness seems to rule the day. People on the street don't respond to polite greetings. Baristas at the coffee shop barely make eye contact. Even friends and family members sometimes respond to our attempts at engaging in meaningful conversation with "Text me." No matter how sunny it may seem outside, the world feels like a pretty icy place. And as warm-blooded beings, we all continue to crave the warmth of relationships like we crave the warmth of a fire after a day in the snow. When we don't get this kind of warmth and acceptance from our families, friends, and fellow believers, we will seek it elsewhere.

This desire for acceptance and respect from others drives some young people to engage in sexual intimacy before marriage. It makes teens adopt dress styles and behaviors that identify them with a group or gang. It lures men away from their hectic families toward a responsibility-free adulterous relationship. Don't get me wrong: the need for acceptance and respect doesn't excuse these behaviors, but it does help us make sense of them. People long for someone to notice them, to drop what they're doing and pay attention, to care about them, to love them. They want authentic relationships more than anything on earth. All of us do.

As the 1980s country song goes, however, too many people are "lookin' for love in all the wrong places."[8] As a result, they find themselves in a pit of despair and distress out of which they can't seem to climb. Only when we find our acceptance in a reverent relationship with God will we discover a true respect for others that can develop into warm, growing, and healthy relationships. When that happens, we will have vertical and horizontal stability to find relief in the midst of distress.

## — 7:1 —

In the last chapter, Paul gave some guidelines for choosing our relationships—encouraging deep, open-hearted, transparent relationships among believers (6:11-13) and discouraging close, intimate partnerships with nonbelievers (6:14-18).

At this point we trip over a poorly placed chapter break. Remember, the chapter and verse numbers are not original to Paul. Those were added much later for our convenience to help us refer to specific passages. Paul begins 2 Corinthians 7:1 with words that immediately point us back to the previous discussion: "Therefore, having these promises . . ."

What promises? The promises that Paul described in 2 Corinthians 6:16-18:

- God will dwell in our midst and walk among us.
- He will be our God and we will be His people.
- God will welcome us as friends.
- He will be like a Father to us, and we will be like sons and daughters to Him.

In light of these promises of an enduring, intimate relationship with the eternal God of the universe, 7:1 emphasizes our response to God, echoing the idea of repentance and holiness mentioned in 6:17. In calling us to be separate from the world, God promises to comfort us with His presence. If we open our hearts to Him, He will fill our need for authentic, intimate, and permanent acceptance.

But to experience this kind of acceptance, we must have a vertical reverence (7:1). We must put Him first. This means your primary goal as a young adult is not to find a mate for life; it is to revere God in your life. Your goal as a businessperson is not to make a great name for yourself; it is to revere His holy Name. Your goal as a pastor or minister of the church is not to grow your church so it will be a force to be reckoned with; it is to help your congregation revere the Lord God Almighty and reckon with His holiness.

How do we demonstrate our fear and reverence for God? By making a clean break with defilement. By refusing to participate in anything unsavory to the Lord—any activity, attitude, relationship, or pattern of thinking (7:1). In fact, Paul says we should be "perfecting holiness in the fear of God." Now, "perfecting" is a word that could scare the daylights out of us, but we need to realize that God isn't asking us to become perfect before He'll associate with us. The word "perfecting" (*epiteleō* [2005]) in this context means "moving toward maturity." Paul uses the same word in Philippians 1:6—"He who began a good work in you will perfect it until the day of Christ Jesus." This doesn't mean we will be in a state of sinless perfection until Christ returns, but that God will continue to work in us in a forward trajectory of spiritual maturity throughout our lives. Our holiness is always a work in progress, an ongoing growth that comes when we reverence God in light of His great promises to us.

## — 7:2-4 —

Having our permanent relationship with the living God firmly in place, being recipients of His promises and responding to that vertical relationship with reverence that results in continuous purifying, we are then called to address our horizontal relationships. Paul thus transitions from our relationship with God to our relationships with other people (7:2-4). He uses his own relationship with the Corinthians as an example, returning to an idea he introduced in 2 Corinthians 6:11-13. There he had reached out to the Corinthians, but they had not reached back to him. Instead of opening their hearts, they had closed themselves off to him. Paul now returns to that issue, making three statements about how we are to relate to one another with mutual respect.

First, *when we respect someone, we make room for them in our hearts* (7:2). Real respect is necessary to lay the groundwork to become kindred spirits "to die together and to live together" (7:3). Sometimes this kind of relationship in which two hearts beat as one can come quite naturally. The world calls it "love at first sight." Most of the time, however, making room for others in our hearts takes a great amount of effort. We need to rearrange some of the furniture in our hearts to create a place for them. This kind of respect for others can be inconvenient, but if we are going to have a thriving ministry with others, we need to "make room."

Second, *when we respect someone, we don't condemn them* (7:3). Some of the Corinthians had done some pretty awful things. Many others had condoned them, and some even celebrated and encouraged them. Furthermore, many harbored negative attitudes toward Paul, and the faction of the Judaizers—Paul's arch-nemeses—still held sway over a part of the congregation. Paul could have shunned the Corinthians, saving himself time, energy, and expensive paper by simply writing them off until they repented. The "silent treatment" would have been understandable in this situation. Yet Paul respected the Corinthians enough to restrain himself from condemnatory words and actions that would have slammed the door shut on their relationship. Though he confronted them for their sin, Paul went to great lengths to couch his criticism in love and respect.

Third, *when we respect someone, we have confidence in them* (7:4). The Corinthians had made more than a few mistakes in their Christian walk. They had stumbled, fallen, gotten up, and stumbled again. How easy it would have been for Paul to diagnose the situation pessimistically and assign a bleak prognosis: Spiritually Terminal—Do Not Resuscitate!

# The Value of Confidence

## 2 CORINTHIANS 7:4

*When I began high school, I stuttered so badly I could hardly finish a sentence. With that speech impediment came a very low self-esteem. I learned to keep my mouth shut and maintain a low profile. The last place I wanted to be was in front of an audience! I lacked confidence in myself and with that lack of confidence came self-condemnation and a loss of relationships with others.*

*I banked that lack of confidence in a vault of my heart until a high school teacher named Dick Nieme cracked the combination and set me free: "Chuck, I want you on my debate team."*

*"Who, m-m-m-m-me?" I looked over my shoulder at the guy standing behind me. I thought for sure Mr. Nieme was talking to him. "Y-y-y-y-y-you want hi-him. You d-d-don't want m-me."*

*"No, I know who I want. I want you. You've got the right stuff, Chuck. We just need to tap into it." Starting the very next week, Dr. Dick Nieme met with me from 7:15 to 7:45 each morning before school for speech-therapy sessions—very common now, virtually unheard of back then. He helped me understand that my mind was running ahead of my ability to form the words in my mouth properly. (I have the exact opposite problem now!) He taught me to slow down, pace my thoughts, and concentrate on starting the words I wanted to say. He gave me exercises to hone my enunciation and to give a rhythm for each syllable to follow.*

*I joined the debate team, and ultimately, I loved it! That led to my participating in high school plays. Our drama team went on to enter the finals of the one-act play competition in the state of Texas. Dick Nieme was there all the way. When I failed, he coached and encouraged. At each triumph, he applauded louder than anyone else. He challenged me and inspired me, and we continued to set goals just beyond my reach. Finally, I auditioned for the lead role in the senior play and landed it!*

*When the curtain rose that night, Dick Nieme sat front row, center balcony. When I came out for my bow, he was the first to stand—he*

(continued on next page)

*whistled and cheered the loudest. He really embarrassed me, but I loved it.*

*Today, over fifty-five years later, I look back and realize how much I owe that man. He believed in me. He made room for me in his heart. He didn't condemn me. He had confidence in me. He even respected me. Because of that, he started me down the path to becoming the man—the preacher—that God intended. I'm glad I was able to express my deep gratitude to him before he died. I'm glad he knew the impact he had on at least one life.*[9]

Paul, however, treated his spiritual children with respect not for what they had done, but for what they could do; not for what they were, but for what they could become. Paul, being the greathearted man he was, believed in them, even when they failed. He stuck with them, encouraging them and spurring them toward greatness. He poured his life into them even when he saw no return on his investment, knowing that they were worth every moment of time and every ounce of energy he spent on them. Thankfully, by the time he wrote 2 Corinthians, he had begun to see signs of renewal and repentance. His confidence had begun to pay off; he could even boast on their behalf (7:4).

### — 7:5-7 —

The closing words of 2 Corinthians 7:4 mention two benefits that flow from Paul's prescription for relationships. When we respect others by making room for them in our hearts, refusing to condemn them, and holding out confident expectations for their growth and maturity, we can experience great comfort and joy in the midst of our affliction. Paul continues to develop the effects of the vertical reverence we have for God (7:1) and the horizontal respect we have for others (7:2-4) as he describes the relief from distress we can experience in the [illegible]t of our circumstances (7:5-7).

Paul faced numerous trials in ministry, including beatings, imprisonment, sleeplessness, and hunger (6:5). In 2 Corinthians 7:5-7 he adds to such external factors the internal struggle he endured as a minister of the gospel. When he arrived in Macedonia, not surprisingly, he suffered from severe exhaustion. Not only did he suffer conflicts from without, but also "fears within" (7:5). The word "fears" comes from the Greek word *phobos* [5401], from which we get our English word "phobia." It carries the idea of dread and panic, a shrinking from courage, and the desire to run for cover. Paul and his fellow workers struggled against distressing fears.

Nevertheless, in the midst of this emotional turmoil, God provided relief. How? *Through a relationship*: "But God, who comforts the depressed, comforted us by the coming of Titus" (7:6). Let me emphasize this point again. The ultimate source of relief from distress is God: "But *God* . . . comforted us." In this world, however, God usually uses natural means to accomplish His purposes, so He ministers to us through people—in Paul's case, through Titus. After Paul sank waist-deep in fears and neck-deep in depression, God drove away the floodwaters of distress and provided comfort.

Not only did Paul find comfort in seeing his ministry partner again, but Titus also bore great news concerning the Corinthian church. Titus reported their longing to see Paul, their mourning for their sins, and their zeal to realign themselves with their father in the faith (7:7). For this reason, Paul said, "I rejoiced even more." His encouragement knew no bounds.

## APPLICATION: 2 CORINTHIANS 7:1-7

### Singin' in the Rain

Remember that line from the Carpenters' old song? "Rainy days and Mondays always get me down"? Sometimes it seems like life has a lot more rainy days and Mondays than sunny days and Saturdays, doesn't it? There is another, even older song I want you to note: "Singin' in the Rain," sung by Gene Kelly in that classic musical of the same name from 1952. How do we go from "rainy days and Mondays" to "singin' in the rain"? Is it even possible? Yes it is!

In 2 Corinthians 7:1-7, we read Paul's account of going from moping on his rainy days (7:5-6) to singing in the rain (7:4, 7). How did he do it? We saw that Paul had already established the essential ingredients for finding relief from his distress. He cultivated a reverent relationship with God (7:1), and he maintained a respectful relationship with others (7:2-4). By means of these things, the God of the universe, who promises to abide with His people (6:11-18), provided comfort through Paul's interpersonal relationships with Titus and the Corinthians (7:5-7). What a simple yet significant prescription for relief!

Yet between the lines of these verses, I see two more principles at work that can enable us to face discouraging days, like Paul did, and still find ourselves singing during the rainy days of our lives.

First, *denying difficulties complicates our lives.* I hear and see a lot of denial among Christians, as if honestly admitting our faults and frailty were sinful. But admission is healthy, and denial complicates things. If it's raining, it's raining. If you're cold, you're cold. If you're sad, you're sad. There's nothing spiritual about denying depression if you're depressed. Scripture never says we are not to grieve. It says we are not to grieve *as those who have no hope* (1 Thes. 4:13). There is room for a lot of tears in that kind of grief, but they aren't hopeless tears. Denial of difficulties will complicate our problems. It prevents us from dealing with them, from bringing them to the Lord, and from being comforted by others around us.

Are you harboring internal grief all alone? Deep-seated fear or worry, veiled depression? Let it out! Bring it to your pastor, your spouse, your counselor, teacher, friend, or physician. If we deny the rain, we also deny the warmth and comfort God wants to give us through others.

Second, *resenting the rain stunts our growth.* James said, "Consider it all joy, my brethren, when you encounter various trials" (Jas. 1:2). The storms of life can teach us lessons, exercise our patience, drive us to depend on God's strengthening grace, and deliver us from a wrong course of sin. When life rains cats and dogs, we should stop, look, and listen. We should *stop* feeling sorry for ourselves or blaming someone else. It is noteworthy that the apostle Paul blamed no one. We need to put our blame to bed and put our resentment to rest.

*Look* for lessons to be learned in the rain. This can get tricky. Sometimes we won't know the lessons until it's sunny again. Sometimes we may never know exactly why God allowed a particularly difficult storm. We can look to God, however, and trust that His good and perfect will was accomplished through the difficulty. Looking for lessons in the rain can keep us from focusing only on the rain.

We also need to *listen*. In the noise of the rain, the Spirit of God sings silent lyrics with a distinct rhythm, discernible only to our souls through the ears of faith. I don't think we have any idea how many great songs were planted in the soil of pain and sorrow, how many great thoughts grew out of rainy days. Many of the great hymns were birthed from wombs of woe. Listen to what the Lord is teaching you about yourself, about life, about others, and about Him in the midst of the rain.

The next time it rains, consider the great lyrics of David in Psalm 40:1-3. Meditate on them. Memorize them.

> I waited patiently for the LORD;
> And He inclined to me and heard my cry.
> He brought me up out of the pit of destruction, out of the
>     miry clay,
> And He set my feet upon a rock making my footsteps firm.
> He put a new song in my mouth, a song of praise to our God;
> Many will see and fear
> And will trust in the LORD.

# Reproofs unto Repentance
## 2 CORINTHIANS 7:8-16

**NASB**

8 For though I caused you sorrow by
my letter, I do not regret it; though I
did regret it—*for* I see that that letter
caused you sorrow, though only for a
while— 9 I now rejoice, not that you
were made sorrowful, but that you
were made sorrowful to *the point of*
repentance; for you were made sor-
rowful according to *the will of* God,
so that you might not suffer loss in
anything [a]through us. 10 For the sor-
row that is according to *the will of*
God produces a repentance [a]without
regret, *leading* to salvation, but the
sorrow of the world produces death.
11 For behold what earnestness this

**NLT**

8 I am not sorry that I sent that severe
letter to you, though I was sorry at
first, for I know it was painful to you
for a little while. 9 Now I am glad I
sent it, not because it hurt you, but
because the pain caused you to re-
pent and change your ways. It was
the kind of sorrow God wants his
people to have, so you were not
harmed by us in any way. 10 For the
kind of sorrow God wants us to ex-
perience leads us away from sin and
results in salvation. There's no regret
for that kind of sorrow. But worldly
sorrow, which lacks repentance, re-
sults in spiritual death.
11 Just see what this godly sorrow

NASB

very thing, this [a]godly sorrow, has produced in you: what vindication of yourselves, what indignation, what fear, what longing, what zeal, what avenging of wrong! In everything you demonstrated yourselves to be innocent in the matter. [12]So although I wrote to you, *it was* not for the sake of the offender nor for the sake of the one offended, but that your earnestness on our behalf might be made known to you in the sight of God. [13]For this reason we have been comforted.

And besides our comfort, we rejoiced even much more for the joy of Titus, because his spirit has been refreshed by you all. [14]For if in anything I have boasted to him about you, I was not put to shame; but as we spoke all things to you in truth, so also our boasting before Titus proved to be *the* truth. [15]His [a]affection abounds all the more toward you, as he remembers the obedience of you all, how you received him with fear and trembling. [16]I rejoice that in everything I have confidence in you.

**7:9** [a]Lit *from* **7:10** [a]Or leading *to a salvation without regret* **7:11** [a]Lit *sorrow according to God* **7:15** [a]Lit *inward parts*

NLT

produced in you! Such earnestness, such concern to clear yourselves, such indignation, such alarm, such longing to see me, such zeal, and such a readiness to punish wrong. You showed that you have done everything necessary to make things right. [12]My purpose, then, was not to write about who did the wrong or who was wronged. I wrote to you so that in the sight of God you could see for yourselves how loyal you are to us. [13]We have been greatly encouraged by this.

In addition to our own encouragement, we were especially delighted to see how happy Titus was about the way all of you welcomed him and set his mind* at ease. [14]I had told him how proud I was of you—and you didn't disappoint me. I have always told you the truth, and now my boasting to Titus has also proved true! [15]Now he cares for you more than ever when he remembers the way all of you obeyed him and welcomed him with such fear and deep respect. [16]I am very happy now because I have complete confidence in you.

**7:13** Greek *his spirit.*

*Wisdom.* I'm no scholarly linguist, but in my experience, "wisdom" seems to be one of the most difficult concepts to grasp for people growing up and building a vocabulary. It often gets confused with intelligence, smarts, knowledge, common sense, experience, or even general information. For so many people, "wisdom" is an abstract idea rather than a concrete reality. I think one reason we have trouble defining this term is because we have so few examples of genuinely wise people. Another reason is because wisdom naturally draws on other forms of knowledge but must be distinguished from them.

Wisdom is not the same as intelligence or "book smarts" or academic education. I have met extremely smart people over the years, from astronauts to professional philosophers, from world-renowned scholars to greatly admired teachers. Not all of them were people I would describe as "wise." Nor is wisdom the same as experience, knowledge, or common sense that comes with age and maturity. If a person eventually learns by making the same mistake in life over and over again, he is no wiser than a trained house pet. Not every silver-haired man or woman wears that gray as a mark of wisdom.

The kind of true wisdom I'm thinking about is *divine perception*, the ability to see life from God's point of view, drawing on His knowledge, discernment, insight, diagnosis, and prognosis. People aren't born with that kind of wisdom. It comes from God, not from men. James affirmed: "But if any of you lacks wisdom, let him ask of God, who gives to all generously and without reproach, and it will be given to him" (Jas. 1:5).

Who needs this wisdom? In Proverbs 1:20-22, the personification of wisdom addresses three kinds of people: the naive (or simple-minded), the scoffers (or rebelliously cynical), and the fools (or intentionally ignorant). These people shrug off wisdom's tap on their shoulder and refuse to listen for her voice. They want to look at things from their own narrow, selfish, prejudiced, and worldly perspective rather than from God's point of view. Proverbs goes on to tell those of us who desire wisdom where to find it: "Turn to my reproof, behold, I will pour out my spirit on you; I will make my words known to you" (Prov. 1:23).

*Reproof*. Few of us associate wisdom and reproof. We often couple reproof and shame. Reproof and embarrassment. Reproof and punishment. Reproof and anger. But not reproof and wisdom! Reproof, another term for "rebuke," occurs when somebody points out a fault or flaw. It's not comfortable. It's sometimes extremely painful. But when we listen, it becomes a path toward wisdom.

In 2 Corinthians 7:8-16, we are able to listen in on a conversation between Paul and the Corinthians in which Paul refers to a reproof he gave them in an earlier letter. The Corinthians, enamored with worldly wisdom, needed to be set on the right path of divine wisdom. Paul intended his reproof to accomplish just that.

## — 7:8-12 —

Paul refers to a letter he sent during the interval between 1 Corinthians and 2 Corinthians, one that has been lost. This missing epistle is sometimes referred to as the "severe letter" or the "tearful letter" (2 Cor. 2:1-5), because in that tiny epistle he rebuked the Corinthians for tolerating a sinning member in their congregation, who I think was the same man mentioned in 1 Corinthians 5:1-13 because of his shameful and ongoing sexual immorality (see my comments on 2 Cor. 2:5-6). After sending it, Paul had second thoughts about the pain it was sure to inflict—much like a person might wish to click an "unsend" button after sending a harsh email that could potentially backfire and lead to more anger rather than constructive communication. Thankfully, however, after delivering the severe letter, Titus returned to report the Corinthians' repentant spirit, which brought great relief to Paul. Paul's sharp note of rebuke, though painful even for him to write, led to a change of heart among the Corinthians.

The difference between sorrow inflicted by God and sorrow inflicted by the world is that one is purposeful while the other is pointless. Sorrow "according to God" produces repentance; worldly sorrow produces death (7:9-10). From a spiritual perspective, the feelings of guilt, shame, and sadness that accompany a stern rebuke are not meant as a punishment, but as a call to repentance. By receiving the reproof, one opens the inner door of the soul to wisdom. By contrast, an angry reaction of resentment will bolt the door against an opportunity to learn from the experience.

When Paul says that godly sorrow produces "repentance" that leads to "salvation" (7:10), we need to ask ourselves, "What kind of salvation?" Not every instance of the word "salvation" (*sōtēria* [4991]) refers to the destiny of our soul when we die or where we'll spend eternity after our bodily resurrection. In 2 Corinthians 7, the "salvation" Paul refers to relates to being rescued from the consequences of sin. When a person starts down a path of rebellion and refuses correction, they begin to experience the effects of alienation from God's people, God's principles, and God's power. The result? That person loses the safety of the church, the wisdom of God's Word, and the benefits of spiritual nourishment and inner strength. The final outcome of this can be actual physical death (1 Jn. 5:16).

How do we know a person has responded with God-given wisdom to the correction? Paul provides something like a "checklist" to recognize true repentance (2 Cor. 7:11). He saw it in the lives of the Corinthians:

- Earnestness—a sincerity of heart
- Godly sorrow—an emotional response
- Vindication—an external verification of internal reality
- Indignation—a repugnant attitude toward the sin
- Fear—a renewed reverence for God
- Longing—a desire for righteousness
- Zeal—an enthusiasm for doing what's right
- Avenging of wrong—a payback for any damages or losses

Paul had no doubts that the Corinthians' response to his severe letter was genuine. Their words and actions demonstrated that they were "innocent in the matter" (7:11). Paul reminds the Corinthians that their mistake had done more than just the obvious damage limited to the sexual immorality itself. It had also created a rift between them and Paul. Their repentance, however, had not only corrected the initial problem of the man's sexual relations with his father's wife (1 Cor. 5:1-13), but it had also healed their relationship with God and with Paul (2 Cor. 7:12-13).

## — 7:13-16 —

Adding a personal touch, Paul exults in the Corinthians' victory over sin. Not only did it save the congregation itself from their damaged relationship with God and others, but it restored their reputation far and wide. Paul had apparently shared with Titus the confidence he had in the Corinthians to do what was right—a confidence that could have easily turned to a shattering disappointment. When Titus returned from his visit to Corinth, having carried the "severe letter" with its harsh rebuke, Paul's praise of the Corinthians proved to be well-placed. One commentator explains the situation this way:

> Despite Paul's affirmed confidence in the Corinthians, Titus might have been understandably hesitant to undertake this mission. . . . But any trepidation Titus may have felt proved groundless. Actually the Corinthians responded to him with deference, receiving him with fear and trembling. They zealously sought to carry out Paul's directives (2 Cor. 7:7, 11).[10]

Recall the emotional roller coaster we've ridden with Paul over the last two chapters. The ups and downs of ministry can feel nauseating at times, can't they? Yet at the end of it all, Paul lands in a place of comfort, rejoicing, and refreshment (7:13). What a change from the tension that existed before! Sin, anger, and distrust clouded everything. Without the strong reproof and the wise response to correction, none of this would have been possible.

Remember where we started? If we want to be wise, we need to heed God's reproofs—especially when they come from friends who love us, who care about us enough to rebuke us in ways that may seem harsh at the time. From the other angle, if we are going to have a fruitful ministry, we need to be willing to call unrepentant sinners to repentance, not out of spite but out of love (Eph. 4:15).

# APPLICATION: 2 CORINTHIANS 7:8-16

## Calling Each Other to Account

Clearly, the Corinthians were blessed to have a friend like Paul who didn't fear to wound them with the truth—a friend who loved them enough to point out their failings. Proverbs 27:6 states, "Faithful are the wounds of a friend." Most of us have friends with whom we can discuss spiritual things. But with how many of those friends do we really get personal? Ask yourself: If your close friend were going astray, would you feel comfortable stepping in to confront the sin? Or would you regard it as a "private matter" between your friend and God? On the other hand, do you have anybody in your life who would step on your toes or block your path to prevent you from heading toward death? Or have you gathered around yourself a group of "yes" friends, who tell you only what you want to hear?

It's not just for the believer's personal spiritual benefit, but for the good of the whole church body, that such quality relationships in which we can examine our integrity together prove indispensable. Although we like to think that our sins don't hurt anybody but ourselves, we're wrong. Sin causes collateral damage. We can easily forget about the emotional damage done to those who love and care about us. We can also overlook the damage done to the ministry. When one part of the body suffers, the whole body suffers with it (1 Cor. 12:26). We even forget about the offense to God, who won't sit back and watch as His beloved children run headlong into destruction (Heb. 12:5-11). God's discipline of His children can seem harsh, severe, and painful. But in the end "it yields the peaceful fruit of righteousness" (Heb. 12:11).

In 2 Corinthians 7, Paul reminded the Corinthians that their mistake had done more than just the obvious damage limited to the sexual immorality itself. It had also created a rift between them and Paul. But Paul faithfully called them to account, and their repentance healed their relationship with God and with Paul (7:12-13). Like Paul, faithful pastors must consistently engage in holding others accountable and giving biblical reproof as needed.

I'll be honest. I wish that confrontation, reproof, and discipline were not a part of ministry, but they are. In fact, Paul said to Timothy, his pastor-in-training: "All Scripture is inspired by God and profitable for teaching, *for reproof, for correction*, for training in righteousness; so that the man of God may be adequate, equipped for every good work" (2 Tim. 3:16-17, emphases mine). A central part of Timothy's pastoral ministry in Ephesus included preaching the Word in such a way that he would reprove and rebuke, not just exhort and teach.

Conflict within a congregation leads to anxiety (2 Cor. 2:4). It can be demoralizing for ministers and destructive to ministries. Reproof that leads to repentance, however, can resolve conflict and bring peace. This will lead to a flood of blessings that will renew relationships and revitalize ministries. True and faithful shepherds do not hesitate to bring required rebukes or administer necessary reproofs. Hirelings do neither.

# THE SELF-SACRIFICIAL MINISTRY (2 CORINTHIANS 8:1–9:15)

An old story tells of a man who, after twenty-five years of marriage, decided to divorce his wife—and sadly, she did not resist the idea. While working through the potential division of property for the impending financial settlement, the husband stumbled upon a box of old canceled checks written over the previous couple of decades. There he sat, hunched over the box, thumbing through one canceled check after another until he came across a faded, yellow check made out to the hotel where he and his bride had spent their honeymoon. After remembering the hope of that moment in his life, the husband set the check aside and continued through the box.

He didn't get far before something stopped him again. He grabbed another old check used as an installment on their first car. His pace slowed considerably as one canceled check after another continued to stir up emotionally charged memories of a long-forgotten past—a check paid to the hospital at the birth of their daughter, and another for the $2,000 down payment on their first small home.

Misty-eyed, the man pushed the box of checks aside and reached for the phone. He dialed his wife. He told her that they had too much invested in those twenty-five years together to just throw them away in the midst of their current hard times. He asked if she would be willing to start over afresh and anew. She agreed, and they began again.

If you and I could go through a family's checkbook or bank statements, we would read the story of their lives. We would find out what that family considers valuable—what they live for. I'm convinced that the lines in our account ledgers reveal a lot more about our walk with God than the underlines in our Bibles. They reveal the actual priorities in our lives, the treasures we value most. If a family spends 20 percent of its money on entertainment and recreation but only 5 percent on supporting its church and missions, that tells me something about what they value most. If I saw weekly greens fees for the local country club but only monthly contributions to the local church, I'd be curious about what those family members were doing the other three Sundays out of the month.

I can imagine some reading this might be feeling a little uncomfortable. To many, discussing money seems borderline unspiritual. After all, Scripture calls money "mammon" and "filthy lucre." Since greed consumes so many, it's easy to think that every time the subject comes up, it implies a malicious motive. It doesn't help to have to endure the manipulation and countless money-making gimmicks and slick techniques that flood the religious market and televangelists' programs today. When we see these "name it and claim it" prosperity gospel preachers on TV or hear them on the radio, it can make even legitimate discussions of finances from a biblical perspective feel dirty and disingenuous.

The fact is, money is *not* unscriptural *or* unspiritual. Even though money can be abused in unspiritual ways, material possessions themselves are neutral. When handled correctly, as God's Word instructs us to do, money can become one of the most important means of expressing our love for the Lord Jesus Christ and our commitment to His eternal work. It can be an objective gauge of the depth of our devotion to Christ. So important is a proper understanding of finances and giving, Paul devotes two whole chapters in this letter to money's relationship to the ministry.

Money is one of the most tangible ways we can give sacrificially, and self-sacrificial ministry is the theme that Paul draws on in 2 Corinthians 8:1–9:15, perhaps as he reflects on the hardships in ministry that he has just discussed (6:1–7:16). In the historical context of this letter, the Corinthians had already made a pledge to provide material assistance to their suffering brothers and sisters in Jerusalem. Paul reminds them of their financial commitment and calls them to fulfill their intention (8:1-15). This specific case leads to a rich discussion on the overarching principles of giving applicable to us today. In his exposition on handling finances biblically and wisely, Paul emphasizes the need to be a "cheerful giver" (9:7), one who gives generously and sacrificially of one's resources, financial and otherwise, for ministry to others (9:1-15).

### KEY TERMS IN 2 CORINTHIANS 8:1–9:15

***eucharistia*** **(εὐχαριστία)** [2169] "thankfulness," "giving of thanks"

The word *eucharistia* simply means "thanksgiving." Part of the church's regular worship included prayers and hymns of thanksgiving to God, thanking Him for both material and spiritual blessings. These prayers often were in conjunction with a special observance of the memorial meal of bread and wine, during which the church expressed its thankfulness for Christ's incarnation and saving death on the cross. The church also expressed "thanksgiving" in response to ongoing blessings. The ultimate purpose of God's liberal provision to His people is to bring glory to Himself by "producing thanksgiving to God" (9:11).

***charis*** **(χάρις)** [5485] "grace," "undeserved or unmerited favor," "cause of delight"

Though *charis* often refers to that which brings pleasure or delight, Paul frequently used *charis* as a special term for the undeserved and superabundant blessings that God bestows upon His people, especially unto salvation. In 2 Corinthians 8–9, Paul also uses the term in reference to a voluntary financial contribution given for the benefit of the suffering saints in Jerusalem (8:1). This horizontal, tangible manifestation of grace among believers reflects the vertical grace believers receive through Jesus Christ (8:9).

# Making Good Sense with Our Dollars

## 2 CORINTHIANS 8:1-9

NASB

1 Now, brethren, we *wish to* make
known to you the grace of God which
has been given in the churches of
Macedonia, 2 that in a great ordeal
of affliction their abundance of joy
and their deep poverty overflowed in
the wealth of their liberality. 3 For I
testify that according to their ability,
and beyond their ability, *they gave* of
their own accord, 4 begging us with

NLT

1 Now I want you to know, dear
brothers and sisters,* what God in
his kindness has done through the
churches in Macedonia. 2 They are
being tested by many troubles, and
they are very poor. But they are also
filled with abundant joy, which has
overflowed in rich generosity.
3 For I can testify that they gave not
only what they could afford, but far
more. And they did it of their own
free will. 4 They begged us again and

much urging for the favor [a]of partici-
pation in the [b]support of the [c]saints,
5 and *this,* not as we had [a]expected,
but they first gave themselves to the
Lord and to us by the will of God. 6 So
we urged Titus that as he had previ-
ously made a beginning, so he would
also complete in you this gracious
work as well.
7 But just as you abound in every-
thing, in faith and utterance and
knowledge and in all earnestness
and in the [a]love we inspired in you,
*see* that you abound in this gra-
cious work also. 8 I am not speaking
*this* as a command, but as proving
through the earnestness of others
the sincerity of your love also. 9 For
you know the grace of our Lord Jesus
Christ, that though He was rich, yet
for your sake He became poor, so
that you through His poverty might
become rich.

**8:4** [a]Lit *and* [b]Lit *service to the saints* [c]Or *holy ones*
**8:5** [a]Lit *hoped* **8:7** [a]Lit *love from us in you;* one
early ms reads *your love for us*

again for the privilege of sharing in
the gift for the believers in Jerusa-
lem.* 5 They even did more than we
had hoped, for their first action was
to give themselves to the Lord and to
us, just as God wanted them to do.
6 So we have urged Titus, who
encouraged your giving in the first
place, to return to you and encourage
you to finish this ministry of giving.
7 Since you excel in so many ways—
in your faith, your gifted speakers,
your knowledge, your enthusiasm,
and your love from us*—I want you
to excel also in this gracious act of
giving.
8 I am not commanding you to do
this. But I am testing how genuine
your love is by comparing it with the
eagerness of the other churches.
9 You know the generous grace of
our Lord Jesus Christ. Though he was
rich, yet for your sakes he became
poor, so that by his poverty he could
make you rich.

**8:1** Greek *brothers.* **8:4** Greek *for God's holy people.* **8:7** Some manuscripts read *your love for us.*

The church in Jerusalem was in serious trouble, its very existence in doubt. By the time Paul wrote 2 Corinthians, the Jewish church in Jerusalem had already passed its twentieth birthday. During those two decades, the Jewish believers in Jesus had been increasingly ostracized, persecuted, arrested, tried, and shunned. Some were even boycotted, exiled, and executed. Their own countrymen, family members, and friends had turned against them. The prophecy Jesus had uttered prior to His death and resurrection was coming to pass before their very eyes:

> Do not think that I came to bring peace on the earth; I did not come to bring peace, but a sword. For I came to SET A MAN AGAINST HIS FATHER, AND A DAUGHTER AGAINST HER MOTHER, AND A DAUGHTER-IN-LAW AGAINST HER MOTHER-IN-LAW; and A MAN'S ENEMIES WILL BE THE MEMBERS OF HIS HOUSEHOLD. (Matt. 10:34-36)

In Jerusalem and Judea, most of the same Jewish authorities and institutions that had sent Jesus of Nazareth to the cross still held power. To be a follower of Jesus under that regime had moved from uncomfortable to excruciating. As a result of the persecution, many Jewish Christians had no work. Who would hire or purchase goods from a "heretic" Christian? Without work, they had no money. Without money, they had no food. And considering the church in Jerusalem had burgeoned considerably in its early years (Acts 2:41; 4:4), they had reached the brink of financial ruin. One commentator puts it this way: "They must have become, in consequence of their conversion, the victims of social and economic ostracism. . . . Their business enterprises must in most cases have collapsed in ruins and family bonds been heart-breakingly severed."[1]

The Jerusalem church was hurting, and it broke Paul's heart to think that the church where it all began could be facing its end. At that point God gave him a seed thought: "As you travel through these areas, take up a collection for the needs of that church in Jerusalem." Paul mentions this "collection for the saints" of Jerusalem in 1 Corinthians 16:1, where he provided some general instructions on how the collection should be managed.

Now, in 2 Corinthians 8, Paul returns to that issue as the time for his arrival in Corinth draws near. Given the difficult bumps in the road in Paul's relationship with the Corinthian church over the preceding months, he understandably felt some concern about whether they would be willing to fulfill their financial commitment before the Lord. He sensed their enthusiasm for the project had begun to wane. Having been cut off from the apostles and temporarily severed from other Christian churches because of the internal strife and influence of Judaizing false teachers, the Corinthians' attention had been drawn inward. As a result, they had lost their outward focus. To help renew their faithfulness and encourage their outward vision, Paul sets before their minds' eye two examples of self-sacrificial giving: the Macedonians (8:1-5) and Jesus Christ (8:9). Between these two examples, Paul sandwiches his exhortation to the Corinthians (8:6-8).

## — 8:1-5 —

Paul begins by addressing the "brethren," that is, fellow Christians. This may seem insignificant, but we should keep in mind that the ministry of giving is a ministry of believers. God does not ask pagans to support His work; it is the responsibility of the family of God. Therefore,

Paul initially reminds them of their status as "brethren" who are to live as members of an extended family with bonds that extend beyond their local church.

Paul then draws attention away from their own affluent circumstances in Corinth to the financially destitute churches in Macedonia, likely the churches in Philippi, Thessalonica, and Berea (Acts 16:11–17:13). His purpose, however, was not to add more needy churches to the charity list, but to show that even in the midst of their "deep poverty," those churches "overflowed" in their joyful generosity (2 Cor. 8:1-2).

Generally speaking, we would assume that an outpouring of charitable giving would come from wealthy churches that could afford a generous philanthropic gesture. Yet Paul employs a common Jewish (as well as Greco-Roman) type of argument, called in Hebrew *qal wahomer* and in Latin *a minore ad maius*. We call it "from the lesser to the greater." His point is quite clear and compelling: If the poor and

In 2 Corinthians 8:1-5, Paul is probably referring to the churches in the Macedonian cities on this map. Paul encouraged the church in Corinth to give like these churches did, who gave in spite of very limited resources.

**GODLY GENEROSITY**
Paul never uses the word "money" in 2 Corinthians 8–9. Instead, he uses a number of other descriptive terms to refer to financial gifts or the act of giving:

- Grace of God (8:1)
- Wealth of liberality (8:2)
- Participation (8:4)
- Support (8:4)
- Gracious work (8:6, 7, 19)
- Generous gift (8:20)
- Ministry (9:1, 12, 13)
- Bountiful gift (9:5)
- Contribution (9:13)

destitute churches in the region of Macedonia can give above and beyond their means to fulfill their financial commitment (the lesser), *how much more* should the affluent church in Corinth be able to fulfill theirs (the greater).

We don't know all of the details of the Macedonians' financial plight, but we do know from ancient historical records that "poverty was a way of life in Macedonia generally."[2] In addition to this general economic malaise, "the Macedonian Christians had recently been subjected to considerable persecution which had tested their faith."[3] Nevertheless, in the midst of their poverty and affliction, they gave their financial contributions with an "abundance of joy" (2 Cor. 8:2).

Paul adds yet another dimension to their giving. They gave voluntarily: "of their own accord" (8:3). The Greek word for "accord" (*authairetos* [830]) is used in the entire New Testament only here and in 2 Corinthians 8:17. It comes from two Greek words for "self" and "choice," referring to a purely voluntary, free-will decision to commit oneself to a particular course of action. The Macedonians gave spontaneously, with no prompting or pressure. No compulsion. No guilt trips. In fact, they even pleaded with Paul and Titus to take their money (8:4).

What prompted such enthusiasm to meet the needs of people they had never met, even if it meant self-sacrifice? Simple: they saw this as a ministry opportunity, a "favor of participation" (8:4). The Greek word translated "favor" is *charis* [5485], which actually means "grace." The Macedonians didn't see helping needy believers as a laborious hardship but as a grace-based privilege. Because they had received the unmerited grace of God (8:1), this attitude of grace overflowed toward others, manifesting itself in a commitment to give graciously even when it hurt. This is grace-giving at its finest. Because they had first given themselves to the Lord in response to the grace of salvation received from Him, the decision to give sacrificially to the cause of supporting the suffering believers in Jerusalem came easily (8:5).

When we give ourselves without reluctance or reservation to the Lord, then giving our time, talents, or treasures comes naturally. We do not have to be convinced, manipulated, or coerced. We give freely, with an open heart and an open hand. On the other hand, when we find ourselves tightfisted and unwilling to give freely, the problem runs deeper than the balance in our checking account or our cash flow. The problem of selfishness is not financial but spiritual.

## — 8:6-8 —

In light of the startling example of the Macedonians' generosity, Paul turns to the Corinthians. Unlike the Macedonians, who were being ground under the heel of persecution and economic distress, the Corinthians flourished in financial freedom. They had the ability to complete the work they had started a year earlier. The question at hand was not ability, but willingness. Would they, like the Macedonians, fulfill the promise they had made and "complete . . . this gracious work as well" (8:6)?

Because the Corinthians already had made a pledge of participation (1 Cor. 16:1-2), Paul felt the freedom to hold them to it. They needed to be held responsible. He reminds them of their own abundance (in contrast to the Macedonian poverty). In fact, the Corinthians "abound in everything," not merely financial prosperity, but in faith, speech, knowledge, sincerity, and love (2 Cor. 8:7). They had it all! In his previous letter, Paul noted that they were "not lacking in any gift" (1 Cor. 1:7). Clearly Corinth had both the means and the spiritual motivation to accomplish the task before them. The question was whether they had the discipline and maturity to follow through on their commitment in the midst of their internal conflict.

Paul's reminder could be misconstrued as manipulation. He points out that this is not "a command," but merely an attempt to encourage them to hold up their end of the project, using the example of the Macedonians (2 Cor. 8:8). Paul didn't berate the church by barking orders. He never shamed them. Rather, he appealed to them to rekindle the dormant embers of their love. He graciously drew their attention away from their inward focus to the outward needs, from their self-centered nit-picking to other-centered ministry.

## — 8:9 —

We can find no better example of gracious giving than Jesus Christ. Paul calls this "the grace of our Lord," using the word "grace" for the fifth time in this section (8:1, 4, 6, 7). Paul's whole argument in favor of giving rests on a firm New Testament theology of grace. The implication is that all giving should come from a context of grace, not guilt; from love, not compulsion.

Don't miss the contrast between the illustration of the Macedonians and Christ. Though the Macedonians were poor, they gave as if they were rich. Though Jesus was rich, He lived like He was poor (8:9). Both of these acted out of grace—giving sacrificially of themselves for the sake of others. Acknowledging what the Macedonians had already done, Paul exhorts the Corinthians to follow the example of Jesus Christ, most beautifully illustrated in Philippians 2:5-8:

> Have this attitude in yourselves which was also in Christ Jesus, who, although He existed in the form of God, did not regard equality with God a thing to be grasped, but emptied Himself, taking the form of a bond-servant, and being made in the likeness of men. Being found in appearance as a man, He humbled Himself by becoming obedient to the point of death, even death on a cross.

## APPLICATION: 2 CORINTHIANS 8:1-9

### God Owns It All

An old farmer owned a cow that gave birth to twin calves. That afternoon at lunch, the farmer felt delighted to tell his wife, "Ol' Bessy had twins today. Twins! You know, honey, we only expected one calf, but the Lord blessed us with two. So we're gonna give one of those calves to the Lord and we're gonna keep one for ourselves. That's the way it ought to be."

So that farmer made a commitment to his wife that 50 percent of his blessing would go to feed the poor or be sold and the proceeds given to the church. How thrilled both of them were to be able to provide for others out of their abundance!

A couple of days later, however, the farmer's demeanor fell from joyful to somber. During lunch, he appeared deep in thought as he pushed his food around his plate and sighed heavily. After several minutes of silence, his wife finally asked him what was wrong.

"Well, I have some bad news. I was in the barn this morning and discovered that the Lord's calf died."

That poor old farmer meant well, I'm sure. But his choice was shortsighted. I wish I could step onto that fictional farm, sit down with that man and his wife, and share with him four simple, single-syllable words that could have turned a humorous anecdote of human nature into a moving illustration of Christlike giving. The four words aren't original with me,[4] and quite frankly they don't sound all that profound. But I have never come across four words in all my studies that can better put our possessions in perspective. Here they are: *God Owns It All.*

Look closely at the following verses. Memorize them. Meditate on them.

- "All the earth is Mine." (Exod. 19:5)
- "Behold, to the LORD your God belong heaven and the highest heavens, the earth and all that is in it." (Deut. 10:14)
- "Whatever is under the whole heaven is Mine." (Job 41:11)
- "The earth is the LORD's, and everything in it, the world, and all who live in it." (Ps. 24:1, NIV)
- "For every beast of the forest is Mine, the cattle on a thousand hills." (Ps. 50:10)

In short, everything we have is on loan from Him. *God owns it all.*

John Wesley put it this way: "When the Possessor of heaven and earth brought you into being, and placed you in this world, he placed you here not as a proprietor, but a steward."[5] Stewardship means managing God's treasures in God's way, for God's purposes, and always for God's glory. So, it is pleasing to Him when we live our lives with open hands. We accept what He entrusts to us only as stewards, never as owners.

Paul instructed Timothy: "We have brought nothing into the world, so we cannot take anything out of it either" (1 Tim. 6:7). We dare not think of gripping the things He entrusts to us during this brief span of time between our birth and our death. We must hold everything loosely. We simply maintain the treasures He entrusts to us, investing them wisely but never forgetting that anytime He wants to remove those things from us, it is His sovereign right. That time may be in the middle of our lives when we feel the most prosperous. It may be early in our lives when we think we have earned the right to make a lot and to spend a lot. It may be later in life when the nest egg is broken and we have little to look forward to except an empty nest.

*God owns it all.* You will never be in financial trouble if you remember those four words. They will revolutionize your thinking on finances. I wish "God owns it all" could appear on every checkbook, every pocketbook, every income tax return, every stock transaction, every credit card, every home mortgage, every car title, every real estate contract, and every business deal. I wish all the stuff in our homes—including our houses—were stamped with that reminder in bold letters.

Why don't you consider doing something like this as a reminder? Find a conspicuous place where you pay your bills or regularly plan your finances. Maybe at your desk, your computer, or in your office. Write down those four words: "God owns it all." Post them where you'll continually be reminded of this truth. Then make the decision to live by it for the rest of your days.

## Fanning the Financial Flame

### 2 CORINTHIANS 8:10-24

**NASB**

10 I give *my* opinion in this matter, for
this is to your advantage, who were
the first to begin a year ago not only
to do *this,* but also to desire *to do it.*
11 But now finish [a]doing it also, so
that just as *there was* the readiness
to desire it, so *there may be* also the
completion of it by your ability. 12 For
if the readiness is present, it is ac-
ceptable according to what *a person*
has, not according to what he does
not have. 13 For *this* is not for the ease
of others *and* for your affliction, but
by way of equality— 14 at this pres-
ent time your abundance *being a*
*supply* for their need, so that their
abundance also may become *a sup-*
*ply* for your need, that there may be
equality; 15 as it is written, "HE WHO
*gathered* MUCH DID NOT HAVE TOO

**NLT**

10 Here is my advice: It would be good
for you to finish what you started a
year ago. Last year you were the first
who wanted to give, and you were
the first to begin doing it. 11 Now you
should finish what you started. Let
the eagerness you showed in the
beginning be matched now by your
giving. Give in proportion to what
you have. 12 Whatever you give is ac-
ceptable if you give it eagerly. And
give according to what you have, not
what you don't have. 13 Of course, I
don't mean your giving should make
life easy for others and hard for your-
selves. I only mean that there should
be some equality. 14 Right now you
have plenty and can help those who
are in need. Later, they will have
plenty and can share with you when
you need it. In this way, things will
be equal. 15 As the Scriptures say,

"Those who gathered a lot had
nothing left over,

MUCH, AND HE WHO *gathered* LITTLE
HAD NO LACK."
16 But thanks be to God who puts
the same earnestness on your behalf
in the heart of Titus. 17 For he not only
accepted our appeal, but being him-
self very earnest, he has gone to you
of his own accord. 18 We have sent
along with him the brother whose
fame in *the things of* the gospel *has*
*spread* through all the churches;
19 and not only *this*, but he has also
been appointed by the churches to
travel with us in this gracious work,
which is being administered by us
for the glory of the Lord Himself,
and *to show* our readiness, 20 [a]tak-
ing precaution so that no one will
discredit us in our administration
of this generous gift; 21 for we have
regard for what is honorable, not
only in the sight of the Lord, but also
in the sight of men. 22 We have sent
with them our brother, whom we
have often tested and found diligent
in many things, but now even more
diligent because of *his* great confi-
dence in you. 23 As for Titus, *he is* my
partner and fellow worker [a]among
you; as for our brethren, *they are*
[b]messengers of the churches, a glory
to Christ. 24 Therefore [a]openly before
the churches, [b]show them the proof
of your love and of our reason for
boasting about you.

**8:11** [a]Lit *the doing* **8:20** [a]Lit *avoiding this*
**8:23** [a]Lit *for you* [b]Lit *apostles* **8:24** [a]Lit *in the face of the churches* [b]Or *show the proof...for boasting to them about you*

and those who gathered only a
little had enough."*

16 But thank God! He has given
Titus the same enthusiasm for you
that I have. 17 Titus welcomed our
request that he visit you again. In
fact, he himself was very eager to go
and see you. 18 We are also sending
another brother with Titus. All the
churches praise him as a preacher of
the Good News. 19 He was appointed
by the churches to accompany us as
we take the offering to Jerusalem*—a
service that glorifies the Lord and
shows our eagerness to help.
20 We are traveling together to
guard against any criticism for the
way we are handling this generous
gift. 21 We are careful to be honor-
able before the Lord, but we also
want everyone else to see that we
are honorable.
22 We are also sending with them
another of our brothers who has
proven himself many times and has
shown on many occasions how eager
he is. He is now even more enthusi-
astic because of his great confidence
in you. 23 If anyone asks about Titus,
say that he is my partner who works
with me to help you. And the broth-
ers with him have been sent by the
churches,* and they bring honor to
Christ. 24 So show them your love,
and prove to all the churches that
our boasting about you is justified.

**8:15** Exod 16:18. **8:19** See 1 Cor 16:3-4.
**8:23** Greek *are apostles of the churches.*

It is virtually impossible to get through a day without hearing somebody talk about money. I venture to guess it is one of the most talked-about matters on the planet. Irish playwright and author of yesteryear, Oscar Wilde, once wrote in *The Picture of Dorian Gray*, "Young people, nowadays, imagine that money is everything. . . . And when they grow older they know it!"[6]

As important as money may be, we are all aware that there are some things money can't buy. Consider these examples:

- Money can buy medicine, but not health.
- Money can buy a house, but not a home.
- Money can buy companionship, but not friends.
- Money can buy entertainment, but not happiness.
- Money can buy food, but not an appetite.
- Money can buy a bed, but not sleep.
- Money can buy a crucifix, but not a Savior.
- Money can buy the good life, but not eternal life.

Why is it so difficult even for believers to get a grip on money before money gets a grip on them? Richard Foster gives us a clue: "When Jesus uses the Aramaic term *mammon* to refer to wealth, he is giving it a personal and spiritual character. When he declares, 'You cannot serve God and mammon' (Matt. 6:24), he is personifying mammon as a rival god. . . . Mammon is a power that seeks to dominate us."[7]

If we're not careful, our genuine *need* for money will become a *desire* for money. The *desire* for money will become a *longing for more* money. When that happens, the warning of Paul to Timothy could very well fall on deaf ears: "For the love of money is a root of all sorts of evil, and some by longing for it have wandered away from the faith and pierced themselves with many griefs" (1Tim. 6:10).

Though they had not yet reached the point of lusting after money, Paul felt concerned that the Corinthian Christians had taken a step in that direction. One year after they had first agreed to help ease the financial crisis in Jerusalem by giving from their abundance, the Corinthian commitment had waned. Like an untended campfire, the roaring flames of their original zeal had dwindled to smoldering embers barely noticeable in a pit of smoky ash. In 2 Corinthians 8:10-24, Paul attempts to fuel the flames of financial surrender by pointing out three hindrances to God-honoring giving (8:10-15) and two principles for God-honoring receiving (8:16-24).

## — 8:10-15 —

The Corinthians abounded "in everything" (8:7). They had faith, good teaching, knowledge, sincerity, and love. It seems they also were quite well off financially. Yet in the midst of their surplus, they struggled with focus. They had turned inward, consumed by their own internal problems: factions, false teachers, spiritual gifts, unrepentant sin. These things turned their attention from outward ministry to inward controversy. To realign them with their original God-given mission, Paul pointed to two examples of self-sacrificial giving: the Macedonian

Christians who gave abundantly despite hardship and poverty (8:8) and Jesus Christ, who gave up all his heavenly riches to become poor in order to save us all (8:9). Now Paul seeks to overcome three common hindrances to giving: *procrastination* (8:10-11), *hesitation* (8:11-12), and *exception* (8:13-15). Let's consider how he addresses each of these.

First, *procrastination* plagued the Corinthians. Though the Corinthian congregation was the first church to commit to financial support, a year later it still had not followed through on that commitment (8:10-11). Procrastination involves intentionally and habitually putting off something that should be done. It's not just forgetting; it's forsaking. It is not merely being accidentally delayed; it is intentionally ignoring. The procrastinator's favorite word is *tomorrow*. The Corinthians had fallen into that trap. Tomorrow became next week. Next week became next month. And now, a year later, they still had not followed through on their commitment. The decisive cure to the plague of procrastination is the second word of verse 11: *now*.

Second, *hesitation* paralyzed the Corinthians. Hesitation is sometimes motivated by uncertainty: "Should I give my money to this person or to somebody else?" "Should we give this amount to the church or that amount?" Sometimes hesitation is motivated by lack of readiness (8:11): "If I just wait a little longer I'll have more to give." "My financial situation is *almost* ready to absorb this kind of financial gift, but not yet." Paul responds to these excuses (8:11-12). The Corinthians already had made a commitment to a particular cause: the support of the Jerusalem church. The church's need had not improved during their delay. In all likelihood, it had grown worse. Paul's point in 8:12 seems to be along the lines of the old adage "A bird in the hand is better than two in the bush." Paul says to the Corinthians, essentially, "If you're ready, you can do it. You can complete the project even if you don't think you have the resources. Do what you can now without hesitation; don't worry about what you *can't* do."

The third hindrance to the Corinthians' giving was *exception*. The person hindered by this excuse says, "Since others have it easier financially than I do, I am not responsible. I'm an exception." We can always find people better off than we are. Somebody always has a nicer car, a bigger home, a larger paycheck, more free time. If we simply pass the hot potato down the line, nobody will ever give anything to anybody. The Lord's work will screech to a halt. The Corinthians likely thought others could foot the bill this time; they would catch the next opportunity when it came around.

Paul responds by turning the tables. They should care nothing about the abundance of others that makes their own wealth pale by comparison. Instead, they should focus on the needs of others in contrast to their own abundance (8:14). Instead of worrying about keeping everything "fair and equal," they should simply trust their giving to the providential care of their sovereign God, the great equalizer who has a way of balancing our provisions in the work of His kingdom. When he wrote, the church in Jerusalem needed assistance from the Corinthians. But someday, the burden might shift, and the Corinthians could be the ones in need. Because God alone knows the future, He can be trusted to provide for any need when it arises. We don't need to excuse ourselves from giving now because of the needs we might have in the future.

Procrastination, hesitation, and exception—these hindrances relate to the *giver*. Paul concludes this chapter by focusing on the *carrier* of the financial support, sharing two principles for how those in ministry should handle the giving (8:16-24).

## — 8:16-24 —

The first part of this chapter directly addressed the Corinthians and their need to follow through on their commitment to giving. The second fills in details related to how Paul and his associates were to handle the gifts that would be given. For us today, the principles Paul shares in these last verses apply primarily to the recipients of financial gifts: Christian organizations, evangelistic ministries, missionaries, Christian schools, and local churches.

First, *only qualified people should handle financial responsibilities.* Throughout these verses Paul mentions three men—Titus and unnamed "brothers"—who would handle the collection of the gifts. Note their credentials: earnest (8:16), willing (8:17), approved by the churches (8:19), administratively gifted (8:19), diligent (8:22), cooperative (8:23), and Christ-glorifying (8:19, 23). Also notice that the emphasis isn't on "thrifty," "polished," "business-minded," "focused on the bottom line," or "eager for return on investment." These weren't businessmen, fundraisers, or accountants. They were godly men of unblemished integrity, well-known to Paul and the churches, entrusted as a team to receive and carry out the project with diligence.

This leads to the second principle: *Money matters should be administered honestly and openly.* Paul says that they were "taking precaution so that no one will discredit us in our administration of this generous gift" (8:20). Why must they be so cautious? First, because the money belonged to God. It was not a gift to Titus and his two buddies, but a gift to God for the sake of all the suffering saints in Jerusalem. They were accountable to the Lord Himself for handling the finances. Second, they were accountable to others. When people give money to churches, missionaries, ministries, or charities, they trust that their money will be used wisely and carefully—and in a manner consistent with the ministry's purpose and goals. That sacred trust must be guarded.

Having dismissed the hindrances of procrastination, hesitation, and exception, and having reassured the Corinthians that their hard-earned resources would be treated in a God-honoring way, Paul closes with a final exhortation. With these words, he seeks to fan the flame of their dormant commitment, producing a blazing testimony of giving for all to see: "Therefore openly before the churches, show them the proof of your love and of our reason for boasting about you" (8:24). In other words, "Make us proud and get the job done!"

# APPLICATION: 2 CORINTHIANS 8:10-24

## Giving with Gusto

Think with me about the three hindrances that smothered the Corinthians' passion for giving: procrastination, hesitation, exception. How often we fall into the same casual attitude toward what should be an exciting exercise of faith in a God who owns it all. Rather than a calm, calculated, cold approach to financial contributions, the biblical examples of Spirit-led and God-glorifying giving paint a brilliant picture of joy, exuberance, and *gusto*. Consider the following examples.

When the Israelites gave of themselves and of their belongings to construct the tabernacle in the wilderness, they had to be told not to give anymore (Exod. 36:6-7), showing their gusto. Wouldn't it be great to hear such an announcement from the pulpit some day?

When the people in Jerusalem rallied around Nehemiah and rebuilt that wall, their gusto resulted in the quick realization of what had once seemed like an impossible goal (Neh. 2:17-18; 4:6; 6:15-16). They probably surprised even themselves!

When Jesus challenged His followers to be unselfish, He taught that it is "more blessed to give than to receive," connecting joy with our financial investments in eternal things (Acts 20:35).

Want to bring back the gusto for giving? Want to capture some of the blessing that comes from sharing with others? Consider three simple suggestions that work for my wife and me.

First, *reflect on God's gifts to you*. Consider His blessings in your life. Forget about the things you don't have (a list that could be miles long). Instead, think about what He has given you. Hasn't He been good? Always better than we deserve. Sufficient food, clothing, and safe shelter. Blessings of good health, happy families, growing children, and close friends . . . and so much more. Yes, some of these things have come and gone. Maybe we are struggling with less than we once had. But consider your life as a whole. Then respond to Him with thanksgiving.

Second, *remind yourself of His promises regarding generosity*. Call to mind a few biblical principles that promise the benefits of sowing bountifully. Hebrews 6:10 says, "For God is not unjust so as to forget your work and the love which you have shown toward His name, in having ministered and in still ministering to the saints." We may not be rewarded with material blessings, but we can rest in the promise that He won't forget us. In fact, He will graciously provide all of our needs "according to His riches in glory in Christ Jesus" (Phil. 4:19). So don't fret! Call to mind His promises of provision.

Third, *examine your heart*. Nobody but you can do this. Open that private vault and ask several hard questions, such as:

- Is my giving proportionate to my income? Or have my resources increased while my giving has stayed the same?
- Am I motivated by a stale duty to fulfill a responsibility, or by the joy of ministering to others? Am I treating my giving as a transfer of numbers or an expression of love?
- If someone else knew the level of my giving to God's work, would I be a model to follow, or would I feel embarrassed?
- Have I prayed about giving, or am I an impulsive responder? Do I have a plan? If somebody were to ask me my giving strategy, would I have an answer?

Have you lost the joy of giving? Get it back! Avoid procrastination, hesitation, and exception. Instead, reflect on God's gifts, remind yourself of His promises, and examine your heart. Then give with gusto!

# The Trip to Bountiful Giving
## 2 CORINTHIANS 9:1-6

NASB

1 For it is superfluous for me to write
to you about this ministry to the
[a]saints; 2 for I know your readiness,
of which I boast about you to the
Macedonians, *namely,* that Achaia
has been prepared since last year,
and your zeal has stirred up most
of them. 3 But I have sent the breth-
ren, in order that our boasting about
you may not be made empty in this
case, so that, as I was saying, you
may be prepared; 4 otherwise if any
Macedonians come with me and
find you unprepared, we—not to
speak of you—will be put to shame
by this confidence. 5 So I thought it
necessary to urge the brethren that
they would go on ahead to you and
arrange beforehand your previ-
ously promised [a]bountiful gift, so
that the same would be ready as a
[a]bountiful gift and not [b]affected by
covetousness.

6 Now this *I say,* he who sows spar-
ingly will also reap sparingly, and he
who sows [a]bountifully will also reap
[a]bountifully.

**9:1** [a]Or *holy ones* **9:5** [a]Lit *blessing* [b]Lit *as covetousness* **9:6** [a]Lit *with blessings*

NLT

1 I really don't need to write to you
about this ministry of giving for the
believers in Jerusalem.* 2 For I know
how eager you are to help, and I have
been boasting to the churches in
Macedonia that you in Greece* were
ready to send an offering a year ago.
In fact, it was your enthusiasm that
stirred up many of the Macedonian
believers to begin giving.

3 But I am sending these brothers
to be sure you really are ready, as I
have been telling them, and that your
money is all collected. I don't want to
be wrong in my boasting about you.
4 We would be embarrassed—not to
mention your own embarrassment—
if some Macedonian believers came
with me and found that you weren't
ready after all I had told them! 5 So
I thought I should send these broth-
ers ahead of me to make sure the gift
you promised is ready. But I want
it to be a willing gift, not one given
grudgingly.

6 Remember this—a farmer who
plants only a few seeds will get a
small crop. But the one who plants
generously will get a generous crop.

**9:1** Greek *about the offering for God's holy people.* **9:2** Greek *in Achaia,* the southern region of the Greek peninsula. *Macedonia* was in the northern region of Greece.

If you've ever struggled with how to tackle a seemingly insurmountable task that had to be done, you know the challenges that can present themselves. We can be paralyzed with fear, demoralized by failures, and agonized over decisions. Yet all the while, the clock ticks away as our deadline approaches.

In my experience, there are four essential ingredients for overcoming these kinds of challenges and actually achieving a goal. First, *there must be active participants.* When we face a monumental task, it's no time for one-man bands. Teamwork is necessary. Second, *there must be a clear objective*. We need to know where we are starting, precisely where we are going, and what steps need to be taken. Third, *there must be strong enthusiasm*. The best leaders bring out the best in people. This engenders teamwork and a level of energy that can't be achieved in any other way. Fourth, *there must be the promise of reward*. The reward doesn't need to be material, but there must be some kind of "payoff," even if it's the feeling of accomplishment one gets when reaching a goal.

Back in the first century, there was a job that had to get done. People's lives counted on it. The struggling church in the city of Jerusalem depended on the generosity of people they had never met. The job of financial relief required a leader who could motivate the right people to pursue the right goal with enough direction and enthusiasm to get the job done. This leader, the apostle Paul, had taken on the task of gathering support for the Jerusalem church from people who probably would never in their lives visit Jerusalem.

In this kind of situation, all four ingredients for successfully accomplishing a goal were bound to be challenged. Active participation would be challenged by procrastination; clear objectives, by distractions; enthusiasm, by disinterest; and promise of reward, by the feeling of "having it all." In the opening verses of 2 Corinthians 9, Paul applies a strategy for accomplishing the task that not only motivated the Corinthians to pursue their noble goal but also can help us lead others in an effective ministry of giving.

## — 9:1-5 —

The apostle Paul says that his reminder to them about giving was "superfluous" (9:1). He was likely referring to all of 2 Corinthians 8, where he had been writing "about this ministry to the saints" (9:1), that is, the financial contribution to the Jerusalem church. Why was it "superfluous"? Because Paul had confidence that they would be ready to fulfill their promise at a moment's notice (9:2).

Paul had addressed the issue of giving with the Corinthians earlier in the year (1 Cor. 16:1-3). Since that time he also had received news about their progress from messengers who had visited Corinth (2 Cor. 7:6-7). Therefore, Paul likely had good reasons to believe the Corinthians ran the risk of becoming distracted from their obligation by circumstances they faced in the congregation. Though he had every confidence of their intention, he employed a rhetorical strategy to keep the matter at the forefront of their mind without making it sound like he didn't trust them to follow through.[8]

# Reckless Generosity

## 2 CORINTHIANS 9:5

*My older brother, Orville, now a seasoned and respected missionary, was never a wealthy man, but he was wonderfully generous with what he had. He never held back from the Lord—and that's still true! This overabundance of faith led him to serve the Lord for more than thirty years in Buenos Aires, Argentina. Prior to that, he had done some short-term mission work in Mexico and had come north to gather his wife, Erma Jean, and the kids for the long trip down into the far reaches of South America.*

*Before leaving, they stopped off for a quick visit with our parents in Houston. Now, you have to appreciate the kind of man my father was. Look up the word "responsible" in the dictionary, and his picture is there! To him, risks are for those who fail to plan. Responsible people leave nothing to chance. As far as he was concerned, faith is something you exercise when your three backup plans fall through and you have run out of all other options. My father was a believer, but he never understood the life of faith. Not really.*

*My brother, on the other hand, was stimulated by faith. He has lived his entire adult life on the raw edge of faith. To him, life doesn't get exciting until God, and God alone, can get us through some specific challenge. Let me assure you, that drove our dad nuts!*

*Orville pulled up to the house in an old Chevy sedan on four of the slickest tires I had ever seen. My father always inspected tires when we came to visit. I wondered how long it would take for him to say something. I'm sure Orville did too. Not very is the answer.*

*After a great supper of good ol' collard greens and corn bread, red beans, onions, and sliced tomatoes, my mother and sister went into the kitchen, leaving my father at one end of the table, Orville at the other, and me (only a teenager) sitting on one side. Then it started.*

*"Son, how much money do you have for your long trip?"*

*"Oh, Dad, don't worry about it. We're gonna' be fine."*

*Before he could change the subject, my father pressed the issue, "Answer me. How much money do you have in your wallet?"*

(continued on next page)

*Orville smiled and shrugged as he said, "I don't have any in my wallet."*

*I sat silent, watching this verbal tennis match.*

*"Nothing in your wallet? How much money do you have? You're gettin' ready to go down to South America! How much money you got for that trip?"*

*With that, my brother smiled, dug into his pocket, pulled out a quarter, set it on its edge on his end of the table, then gave it a careful thump. It slowly rolled past me all the way to my father's end of the table and fell into his hand. Dad said, "A quarter? That's all you've got?"*

*Orville broke into an even bigger smile and said, "Yeah. Isn't that exciting!"*

*That was not the word my father had in mind. After a heavy sigh and a very brief pause, Dad shook his head and said, "Orville, I just don't understand you."*

*My brother grew more serious. Looking Dad in the eyes, he quietly answered without blinking, "No, Dad, you never have."*

*I don't know how he actually made the trip to their destination, or how he and Erma Jean took care of all their little kids, but they made it—and they never went hungry. They faithfully served in Buenos Aires and traveled to other parts of the world for more than three decades. My father was a man who lived through the Great Depression, lived in fear of poverty his whole life, seldom took a risk, and, I must add, never experienced the joy of trusting God—the One who made my brother smile so big that day.*

*Jesus never said that having nice things is wrong. By His sovereign choice, He may ordain some to be as poor as Himself and His disciples. Yet He may want others to have an overabundance of money and material goods. Why? So that they might give in abundance. His chief concern is not the issue of wealth; He cares about us and where we turn for security. Whether or not we own nice things, He wants to be sure that they don't own us!*[9]

Paul bounces back and forth between talking about the Corinthians' role and responsibilities in the ministry of giving and his own (9:2-5). He had been boasting about the Corinthians' readiness in contributing to the Jerusalem mission: "Achaia [the region of Corinth] has been prepared since last year" (9:2). In other words, Paul pointed to the Corinthians as the first church to volunteer to give (8:10). Since that time, Paul had been using their eagerness to stir up the zeal of others (9:2).

Can you imagine the conversation?

Paul: "The Jerusalem church is suffering. The light of the gospel is spreading to the Gentiles, but the original source is dwindling under persecution. They need help. Fast."

Macedonians: "But it's so far away. What can we do?"

Paul: "Well, when the Corinthians heard about the need, they immediately volunteered to set aside a portion of their money for a year and send it directly to Jerusalem. They pledged a significant amount. Of course, it was purely voluntary, but . . ."

Macedonians: "We would *love* to help out! We don't have much, but we can do without to keep the flame alive in Jerusalem!"

Now imagine if, after "boasting" of the Corinthians' involvement, Paul arrived in Corinth with some representatives from Macedonia, only to discover that the church that had expressed such an eagerness to be involved had actually copped out (9:4). How humiliating! To prevent this from happening, Paul sent a small delegation ahead of him to Corinth (9:3, 5). In effect, Paul was saying, "Look, guys, I've been telling those Macedonians what kind of people you are, how generous and enthusiastic and willing to give. Can you imagine how you and I are going to feel if we haven't gotten our act together? So, make sure everything is in its place before we arrive."

Paul knew the human-nature tendency to part with only the bare minimum and call the job done. That's found everywhere! The Corinthians' rough year with internal conflicts and problems, however, had made their situation even more acute. Their own fund-raising for the "promised bountiful gift" to Jerusalem could have been affected by "covetousness" (9:5). This verse serves as a gentle yet firm reminder that the Corinthians shouldn't wait until the last minute to collect the money for the gift.

## — 9:6 —

Paul shifts from his specific message to the Corinthians to a general message for everyone, supporting his practical exhortation with an important spiritual truth about giving: "He who sows sparingly will also reap sparingly, and he who sows bountifully will also reap bountifully" (9:6).

Farmers and gardeners know that you will grow only as many plants as you sow seeds for. You can't sow two seeds and reap a full field at harvest. Likewise, there is a correlation between the amount of time, energy, and finances we give to the Lord's ministry and the spiritual blessings we reap in return.

I am aware that there has been a lot of false advertising on this subject over the last several decades. The so-called prosperity gospel has spoiled a perfectly healthy doctrine of sowing and reaping. Those "name it and claim it" preachers have turned God's promise of blessing us in order to bless others into a virtual Ponzi scheme. Let me be clear. God never promises to match you dollar for dollar, or to multiply your financial contribution sent to some TV or radio preacher with a thirty, sixty, or hundredfold return on investment, or to reward your "seed gift" by opening His floodgates of material blessings in the form of guaranteed health and enormous wealth. God promises to supply all of our needs, not all of our greeds (Phil. 4:19). And He promises to reward us with what we might call "incorporeal" blessings—blessings of the heart such as the joy of obedience, the pleasure of inner peace, and the outflow of abundant love for the brethren.

Yes, God promises a bountiful reaping for faithful giving, but don't take this verse out of its biblical context. God may bless a person with riches in order to use that person as a conduit to bless others. If that is you, then use it generously for God's work or risk losing it to the world. If you are blessed in other ways, stay faithful in your ministry of giving—whether that's a gift of your time, your musical ability, your energy, your skills, your intellect, or your more modest—but equally noble—financial contributions.

## APPLICATION: 2 CORINTHIANS 9:1-6

### Making the Most of Ministry Opportunities

Paul commended the Corinthians for enthusiastically volunteering to contribute generously to what we might call the Jerusalem Relief Fund. Because of their eagerness to be involved, Paul launched a yearlong campaign among churches far and wide to contribute to that worthy cause.

We, too, have numerous opportunities for involvement in worthy ministries. Some of them ask for our time and energy—teaching in the children's ministry, singing in the choir, serving in leadership, working behind the scenes as a volunteer for a vacation Bible school, or cleaning the church facility after a big event. Other opportunities require financial support—sending missionaries overseas, contributing to a building fund, providing relief for a region of the world where the church is suffering, purchasing Bibles or ministry resources for believers with nothing. For those willing to open their eyes and ears, an abundance of ministry opportunities will present themselves every day. How can we make the most of them? I glean four ways from the example preserved for us in 2 Corinthians 9:1-6.

First, *become an active participant*. The Corinthians were the first to step up to the plate when they heard of the Jerusalem church's need for relief and, no doubt, numerous other sister churches then got on board. Are you currently a participant in a specific ministry? At what level would you rate your involvement? Weak? Average? Strong? How would others who work with you characterize your commitment to this ministry? Do you often excuse yourself and back out? Show up late? Give a minimal amount of time or money? If you aren't involved as an active participant, I urge you to move out of the passive realm of theory and get into the exciting realm of action. Stop studying about giving and start living it!

Second, *understand the stated objective*. On numerous occasions—in person, in writing, and through messengers—Paul made it clear to the Corinthians the details of the Jerusalem Relief Fund ministry and exactly how he would carry out the stated goal. When you've committed your time or finances to a particular ministry, understand what that ministry is trying to accomplish and how. Understand its ongoing, as well as special, needs and be ready to step up to help meet them. In other words, know the ministry and its leadership. If your involvement goes beyond financial contributions, make sure your participation isn't cross-grained with the purposes of the ministry. And if the ministry suddenly takes a turn contrary to its purpose and objectives, consider whether you want to continue your involvement or focus on a different ministry opportunity.

Third, *demonstrate strong enthusiasm*. Whereas the Macedonian churches overflowed with enthusiasm, reflected in their giving even beyond their reasonable means, the Corinthians seemed to have lost steam. The fact is that lack of enthusiasm can be even more damaging to a ministry than lack of participation. Why? Because lost enthusiasm preserves the illusion that something is being done, while in reality no progress is being made. I have heard people answer legitimate concerns in church with the lame response, "We have a committee taking care of that," only to discover much later that the committee had not met for months. Let me suggest that you don't get involved (or stay involved) in a ministry for which you lack strong passion. I know you might feel like you are abandoning your post, but chances are there is a more enthusiastic person who is being kept from involvement because of your mediocre commitment. Do you demonstrate strong enthusiasm for the ministries in which you are involved? Or do you give of your time and finances grudgingly?

Fourth, *remember the promised rewards*. When the ministry gets tough (and every ministry does) remember that God will honor your active, enthusiastic, conscientious involvement. He will never just use you and toss you aside like a disposable tool. Quite the contrary! Those who are faithful in little things will be rewarded with much—including greater opportunities to be involved in ministry (Luke 16:10; 19:17). Yes, ministry involvement might cut into your precious and carefully guarded downtime—but you will be rewarded with "a Sabbath rest for the people of God" (Heb. 4:9). Ministry may drain your energy—but you'll one day be "raised in power" (1 Cor. 15:43). Ministry will also add to your expenses with no tangible return on investment—but even in material poverty "you are rich" spiritually (Rev. 2:9), and one day we will be rewarded with "riches in glory" (Phil. 4:19).

Consider how Christ Himself exemplified these four principles in His own ministry. He was a voluntary, active participant in God's grand plan of redemption (Heb. 10:7). He always kept sight of His goal (Matt. 20:18-19). He demonstrated strong enthusiasm (John 4:34). And He never forgot the reward (Heb. 12:2). As Christ's followers, called to be involved in ministry (Eph. 4:12), all of these principles apply to us. Are you enthusiastically participating toward a clear goal, with your eyes fixed on the reward?

# Ministry through Giving
## 2 CORINTHIANS 9:7-15

NASB

7 Each one *must do* just as he has pur-
posed in his heart, not grudgingly or
under compulsion, for God loves a
cheerful giver. 8 And God is able to
make all grace abound to you, so
that always having all sufficiency in
everything, you may have an abun-
dance for every good deed; 9 as it is
written,

> "HE SCATTERED ABROAD, HE GAVE
> TO THE POOR,
> HIS RIGHTEOUSNESS [a]ENDURES
> FOREVER."

10 Now He who supplies seed to the
sower and bread for food will supply
and multiply your seed for sowing
and increase the harvest of your righ-
teousness; 11 you will be enriched in
everything for all liberality, which
through us is producing thanksgiv-
ing to God. 12 For the ministry of this
service is not only fully supplying the
needs of the [a]saints, but is also over-
flowing through many thanksgivings
to God. 13 Because of the proof given
by this ministry, they will glorify God
for *your* obedience to your confes-
sion of the gospel of Christ and for
the liberality of your [a]contribution
to them and to all, 14 while they also,
by prayer on your behalf, yearn for
you because of the surpassing grace
of God in you. 15 Thanks be to God for
His indescribable gift!

**9:9** [a]Lit *abides* **9:12** [a]Or *holy ones* **9:13** [a]Or *sharing with them*

NLT

7 You must each decide in your heart
how much to give. And don't give re-
luctantly or in response to pressure.
"For God loves a person who gives
cheerfully."* 8 And God will gener-
ously provide all you need. Then
you will always have everything you
need and plenty left over to share
with others. 9 As the Scriptures say,

> "They share freely and give
> generously to the poor.
> Their good deeds will be
> remembered forever."*

10 For God is the one who provides
seed for the farmer and then bread
to eat. In the same way, he will pro-
vide and increase your resources and
then produce a great harvest of gen-
erosity* in you.

11 Yes, you will be enriched in
every way so that you can always be
generous. And when we take your
gifts to those who need them, they
will thank God. 12 So two good things
will result from this ministry of giv-
ing—the needs of the believers in Je-
rusalem* will be met, and they will
joyfully express their thanks to God.

13 As a result of your ministry,
they will give glory to God. For your
generosity to them and to all believ-
ers will prove that you are obedient
to the Good News of Christ. 14 And
they will pray for you with deep af-
fection because of the overflowing
grace God has given to you. 15 Thank
God for this gift* too wonderful for
words!

**9:7** See footnote on Prov 22:8. **9:9** Ps 112:9. **9:10** Greek *righteousness.* **9:12** Greek *of God's holy people.* **9:15** Greek *his gift.*

Perhaps you recall the parable Jesus told Simon the Pharisee to help him understand why it was appropriate for a weeping woman, known to Simon as a prostitute, to anoint Jesus' feet with expensive perfume and kiss them (Luke 7:36-39). The parable (Luke 7:40-47) frames a simple situation: Two people owe the same creditor, but one owes a lot of money and the other owes only a small amount. If the creditor forgives both debts, which person will be more thankful? Which will love the creditor more? The point Jesus made is that a great amount of forgiveness—the grace Jesus had shown to this weeping woman—results in a great outpouring of love—the woman's response to Jesus. The joy of forgiveness is one that results in lives full of grace towards others.

This principle of acting in response to God's grace with an outpouring of love is one that guides Christian conduct in every area of life. A mindful response to what the Lord has done for us results in a gracious and willing attitude to help those around us, especially fellow believers. It should not surprise us then that this principle of God's overflowing grace underlies Paul's thinking when he speaks to the Corinthians about their giving.

As we turn our attention to the last part of 2 Corinthians 9, where Paul deals with the application of giving, we read a description of the *manner* in which we are to give. It says, in effect, that we need to put into action the principles characterized in others' examples and in response to God's abundant blessings. The one who claims to live obediently by faith in God does not ignore this vital area. In other words, living by faith includes giving by grace. As a response to what God has done for us, we should bountifully and cheerfully give back to Him. In 2 Corinthians 9:7-15, Paul encourages us to pass on God's grace to others in tangible ways.

## — 9:7 —

In 2 Corinthians 9:6, Paul draws upon an agricultural metaphor to illustrate the spiritual truth that scant sowing makes for a scant harvest. Generous sowing, however, makes for an abundant harvest. Paul takes this general principle and makes it personal, even individual (9:7). Notice that Paul addresses "each one." There are no exceptions. Everybody must be involved in financial stewardship and contributing to the ministry in some way.

This giving must also be intentional, not haphazard. The Greek term for "purposed" means to choose beforehand or decide ahead of time. A believer's financial planning should originate not from external pressures but from "the heart." Gracious giving results from heartfelt resolve. If it does not spring from the heart, it is given "grudgingly or under compulsion." But when giving comes from a heart full of cheer, it will not only feel rewarding for the giver, but it will also inspire others with the joy of giving.

Look closely at those five final words: "God loves a cheerful giver." The Greek word for "cheerful" is *hilaros* [2431], from which we get our word "hilarious." This doesn't mean God loves a ridiculous giver, or a funny giver, or a giver who doesn't take giving seriously. It means that God desires our giving to generate the same exuberant joy in our hearts as a lively celebration or a hearty laugh. If you can't give with a smile, then you are not giving from the heart.

When I look at how giving has been treated in the church today, I feel most of us have been ripped off! So many churches have taken the joy out of giving. They have prescribed certain percentages or pushed hard for certain amounts. That sounds more like the drudgery of the Law than the joy of grace. According to 2 Corinthians 9:7, giving should be fun! I don't know about you, but I don't find it fun to be virtually handed a bill and asked for a check. Hard sells aren't fun. High-pressure salesmen aren't fun. Giving to meet some arbitrary goal isn't fun. You know what *is* fun? Giving in response to God's grace, giving to others out of love and joy, and giving to a ministry vision we believe in. That's *cheerful* giving. I know it doesn't make sense that a human being would give like that—generously without prescription, voluntarily without compulsion—but, frankly, that's grace giving.

## — 9:8-11 —

Paul moves the focus from the immediate giver to the ultimate Giver. We can give liberally, without worry, because God can make His grace abound to us so we will always have enough (9:8). Never forget: We can never out-give God. He will never appear to us one day and say, "Well, child, you've tapped Me dry. There's no more left." As regularly as you dispense your resources in generous giving, God can replenish them and refresh you with divine grace. This principle of God's liberal provision creates confidence in the giver.

To undergird his argument, Paul quotes from Psalm 112:9 and alludes to Isaiah 55:10 (2 Cor. 9:9-10). Keener explains Paul's rhetorical strategy here:

> In 9:9, he quotes Psalm 112:9, which in context refers to the generosity and vindication of the righteous; having given to the poor,

> their righteousness endures. Yet God is the supreme benefactor on whom these generous benefactors also must depend; thus in 9:10 Paul recalls Isaiah 55:10, which speaks of God as the one who gives seed to the sower (i.e., to those who scatter in 9:9) and bread for food. As they kept giving, God would keep multiplying their seed so they could give more and multiply their harvest of righteousness.[10]

The storehouse of all good things belongs to God (Jas. 1:17). From that infinite source of blessing, He can replenish all the seed we sow, whether that seed is material or spiritual. God not only will supply the seed, He will also multiply it (2 Cor. 9:10). The ultimate purpose of God's liberal provision to His people is to produce thanksgiving (*eucharistia* [2169]) to God (9:11). Ultimately, everything returns to God's glory, that He would be praised and thanked for His blessings.

Think about the last time you received a wonderful, surprising gift. Your need was great, but you chose not to advertise it. Nobody knew about it except you and the Lord. You waited on God and patiently surrendered to His provision and timing. Then God marvelously supplied through a surprising source. You had never expected it, yet there it was. Remember your response? *Thanksgiving*. "Oh, how I thank You, Lord!" That's the kind of praise the Lord always deserves from us in response to His ministry of grace.

Let's return for a moment to the specific historical situation in Paul's day. The people in Jerusalem were desperate. Cut off from the rest of the world, they had no ability in themselves and no hope of relief from others. They turned their attention to God and God alone, the One who could do miracles. Then one day, as they teetered near the brink of implosion, a delegation arrived in Jerusalem—a small group sent by Paul, representing dozens of churches and hundreds of Gentile Christians unknown to the Jewish believers in Jerusalem. They laid before the elders of the Jerusalem church a large amount of money, enough to purchase food and to supply relief for months to come. What a spectacle of God's astonishing provision! It would be a testimony to the scoffing Pharisees of the wonder-working love among those who comprise the Christian church that this gift should come even from among the "unclean" Gentiles.

## — 9:12-15 —

This bountiful gift naturally would bring a joyful response from the recipients. Paul encourages the Corinthian church to give by helping them see that giving evokes a reciprocal blessing. Those who give joyously and graciously, seeking no credit for themselves, glorify God (9:13). The result? The entire process inundates heaven with a high tide of praise, surging at the feet of the Lord (9:12).

Notice that everybody involved is blessed. First, *the giver* is blessed by the joy inherent in giving and by the promise of reward from the hand of God. Jesus once said, "It is more blessed to give than to receive" (Acts 20:35). One form of blessing to those who give is that they receive the benefit of the prayers of the recipients on their behalf (2 Cor. 9:14). Second, *the recipients* of the gift are also blessed. They receive a solution to their problems and relief for their affliction. Third, *God* is also blessed, as the recipients overflow "through many thanksgivings to God" (9:12). They will glorify God because of the givers' obedience (9:13). They don't fail to attribute to God the ultimate responsibility for the blessing.

Paul closes this chapter with a sudden outburst of gratitude to God for His grace: "Thanks be to God for His indescribable gift!" (9:15). The perfect picture of grace God has placed throughout Scripture is Jesus Christ hanging on a rugged cross. Can you turn away from such a picture of love, such a picture of giving, such a picture of amazing self-sacrificial grace? Can you look at such a picture and not be changed, not be compelled to give yourself to Him, not be compelled to give to others in the way He gave Himself to you?

# APPLICATION: 2 CORINTHIANS 9:7-15

## New Covenant Giving

Stewardship is a key principle in Scripture—stewardship of our time, our gifts and abilities, and our money. The Old Testament prescribed very specific regulations for giving "tithes" and offerings (Lev. 27:1-34; Deut. 14:22-28; Mal. 3:8-10). In the New Testament, Jesus frequently spoke about wealth, riches, money, and stewardship (Matt. 6:24; 13:22; Mark 4:19; Luke 15:12; Luke 16:1-13).

Although the New Testament never prescribes the "tithe" or a mandatory "10 percent" to be given to the church, it does address the issue of generous financial contributions and stewardship of one's possessions. There are four primary passages in the New Testament to consider, and each focuses on a different element of giving.

| |
|---|
| **JUSTIFICATION FOR GIVING**<br>**1 Corinthians 9** |
| **INSTRUCTIONS FOR GIVING**<br>**1 Corinthians 16** |
| **ILLUSTRATIONS OF GIVING**<br>**2 Corinthians 8** |
| **APPLICATION OF GIVING**<br>**2 Corinthians 9** |

*First Corinthians 9*. This passage provides the justification for giving. Those ministers who sow spiritual things through their preaching and teaching have a right to receive material support from those to whom they minister (1 Cor. 9:11). Fair remuneration is explicitly prescribed and encouraged in Scripture (1Tim. 5:17-18). Though Paul chose not to receive money for his spiritual labor, this was his own decision, not a required principle for others (1 Cor. 9:12, 15-18; Acts 20:33-35).

*First Corinthians 16*. At the end of his first letter to the Corinthians, Paul provides instructions for giving (1 Cor. 16:1-2). For all who wonder about proper procedure, these two verses supply us with a good checklist to guide our giving. In these verses we find no pressure, no announcement, no public attention, and no manipulation.

- Systematically—"on the first day of every week"
- Individually—"each one of you"
- Consistently—"put aside and save"
- Proportionately—"as he may prosper"
- Privately—"no collections be made when I come"

*Second Corinthians 8*. This passage gives two illustrations of proper giving: the Macedonians (8:1-3); and Jesus Christ (8:9). Here we see that giving should be done with great generosity (8:1-3) as an overflow of one's devotion to the Lord (8:5). Just as Jesus Christ gave up everything for our sakes—becoming poor so that we might become spiritually rich (8:9)—we, too, should give self-sacrificially (8:3).

*Second Corinthians 9*. The fourth passage reveals the application of giving. Like the rest of the Christian life, giving is not to be done out of grinding obedience to rules and regulations, in response to guilt trips, or because of peer pressure. Giving should come from the heart. Ideally, it should be done with a most free and willing attitude. A person should not be reluctant to give nor regret giving but rather be eager to give and also to receive joy from this kind of stewardship.

May the Lord help us all to strengthen the body and bring glory to God by understanding and practicing the principles taught in these passages.

# THE TRUE APOSTOLIC MINISTRY (2 CORINTHIANS 10:1–13:14)

Many years ago I was going through a time of intense criticism, and no one knew it better than my wife, Cynthia. In the middle of storms like that, we're always tempted to steer toward one of two extremes: to retaliate with the same kind of vitriolic tone leveled at us, or to lie down like an old rug and just let the critics walk all over us.

Cynthia had a wonderful way of helping me steer a straight course between those extremes. While keeping me in the calm eye of the storm, she found a piece written by President Theodore Roosevelt in 1910. She had its text made into a decoupage, a plaque I could hang in my study, and there it hung for years to remind me of a vital truth every pastor needs to learn early on in ministry:

> It is not the critic who counts; not the man who points out how the strong man stumbles, or where the doer of deeds could have done them better. The credit belongs to the man who is actually in the arena, whose face is marred by dust and sweat and blood; who strives valiantly; who errs, and comes short again and again, because there is no effort without error and shortcoming; but who does actually strive to do the deeds; who knows the great enthusiasms, the great devotions; who spends himself in a worthy cause; who at the best knows in the end the triumph of high achievement, and who at the worst, if he fails, at least fails while daring greatly.[1]

I pity the pessimists and cynics who live their lives in the twilight zone between victory and defeat, whose thoughts linger on suspicions, whose eyes constantly look for flaws in those involved in ministry, and whose mouths spew criticism and sarcasm. What a dreadful world such people must live in! I wish there was a combination of words I or somebody else could say to snap them out of their morose moods and put an end to their habit of hurtful words.

My heart goes out even more to the objects of these unfair and

## KEY TERMS IN 2 CORINTHIANS 10:1–13:14

***astheneia* (ἀσθενεία)** [769] "weakness," "frailty"
This word can refer to a variety of physical, emotional, or intellectual disabilities or ailments. These could include sickness or disease (Luke 8:2), incapacity due to our finiteness (Rom. 8:26), or moral weakness leading to temptation and sin (Rom. 6:19). Paul uses the term to refer to personal weaknesses in his ministry that are overcome not by his own strength, but by the grace of Christ working in him (2 Cor. 12:9). In this sense, Paul can "boast" about his weaknesses rather than hide them in shame (12:10).

***metaschēmatizō* (μετασχηματίζω)** [3345] "to change in outward appearance," "to disguise"
The word "disguise," used three times in 2 Corinthians 11:13-15, means "to change in appearance, transform." Though similar in meaning to the Greek word *metamorphoō* [3339], the term *metaschēmatizō* emphasizes the outward appearance or form of something rather than the inward essence or reality. Paul's use of the term for false teachers who deceptively transformed themselves into something they were not indicated that the essence of the person remained the same, but the outward appearance changed. This always has been Satan's strategy—to convincingly appear to be something he is not.

inappropriate attacks. Ministry challenges us enough without all the negativity. When someone lobs a caustic, unjust, and mean-spirited grenade of criticism into the midst of an already difficult ministry situation, it can devastate not only the minister but also the ministry. I've witnessed and experienced the carnage firsthand.

In the final section of 2 Corinthians, a letter written by Paul primarily to address issues of Christian ministry, the apostle addresses the question of authentic authority in ministry. Therefore, I have titled this climactic section "The True Apostolic Ministry" (10:1–13:14). First, Paul defends the genuineness of his apostolic calling against some troublemakers in the Corinthian church who had criticized, ridiculed, and undermined his God-given authority (10:1-18). Fearing that his children in the faith might be led astray by malicious false teachers (11:1-6), Paul directly strikes back at the authority and teaching of his opponents (11:7-15). In a rare moment, Paul chooses to fight fire with fire, taking up the challenge of his adversaries and "boasting" of his superior qualifications as an apostle of Christ in contrast with their empty boasting (11:16–12:21). With a warning that he will soon pay a personal visit to the church as he had intended for months, 2 Corinthians serves as a final call for those in the church to reaffirm their allegiance to the authentic apostolic ministry and thereby to retain a pure apostolic faith (13:1-14).

# In Defense of Paul's Ministry

## 2 CORINTHIANS 10:1-18

**NASB**

1 Now I, Paul, myself urge you by the meekness and gentleness of Christ—I who am [a]meek when face to face with you, but bold toward you when absent! 2 I ask that when I am present I *need* not be bold with the confidence with which I propose to be courageous against some, who regard us as if we walked according to the flesh. 3 For though we walk in the flesh, we do not war according to the flesh, 4 for the weapons of our warfare are not of the flesh, but [a]divinely powerful for the destruction of fortresses. 5 *We are* destroying speculations and every lofty thing raised up against the knowledge of God, and *we are* taking every thought captive to the obedience of Christ, 6 and we are ready to punish all disobedience, whenever your obedience is complete.

7 [a]You are looking at [b]things as they are outwardly. If anyone is confident in himself that he is Christ's, let him consider this again within himself, that just as he is Christ's, so also are we. 8 For even if I boast somewhat [a]further about our authority, which the Lord gave for building you up and not for destroying you, I will not be put to shame, 9 [a]for I do not wish to seem as if I would terrify you by my letters. 10 For they say, "His letters are weighty and strong, but his [a]personal presence is unimpressive and his speech contemptible." 11 Let such a person consider this, that what we

**NLT**

1 Now I, Paul, appeal to you with the gentleness and kindness of Christ—though I realize you think I am timid in person and bold only when I write from far away. 2 Well, I am begging you now so that when I come I won't have to be bold with those who think we act from human motives.

3 We are human, but we don't wage war as humans do. 4 *We use God's mighty weapons, not worldly weapons, to knock down the strongholds of human reasoning and to destroy false arguments. 5 We destroy every proud obstacle that keeps people from knowing God. We capture their rebellious thoughts and teach them to obey Christ. 6 And after you have become fully obedient, we will punish everyone who remains disobedient.

7 Look at the obvious facts.* Those who say they belong to Christ must recognize that we belong to Christ as much as they do. 8 I may seem to be boasting too much about the authority given to us by the Lord. But our authority builds you up; it doesn't tear you down. So I will not be ashamed of using my authority.

9 I'm not trying to frighten you by my letters. 10 For some say, "Paul's letters are demanding and forceful, but in person he is weak, and his speeches are worthless!" 11 Those people should realize that our actions when we arrive in person will

are in word by letters when absent, such persons *we are* also in deed when present.

12 For we are not bold to class or compare ourselves with [a]some of those who commend themselves; but when they measure themselves by themselves and compare themselves with themselves, they are without understanding.
13 But we will not boast beyond *our* measure, but [a]within the measure of the sphere which God apportioned to us as a measure, to reach even as far as you.
14 For we are not overextending ourselves, as if we did not reach to you, for we were the first to come even as far as you in the gospel of Christ;
15 not boasting beyond *our* measure, *that is,* in other men's labors, but with the hope that as your faith grows, we will be, [a]within our sphere, enlarged even more by you,
16 so as to preach the gospel even to the regions beyond you, *and* not to boast [a]in what has been accomplished in the sphere of another.
17 But HE WHO BOASTS IS TO BOAST IN THE LORD.
18 For it is not he who commends himself that is approved, but he whom the Lord commends.

**10:1** [a]Lit *lowly* **10:4** [a]Or *mighty before God* **10:7** [a]Or *Look at...* or *Do you look at...?* [b]Lit *what is before your face* **10:8** [a]Or *more abundantly* **10:9** [a]Lit *so that I may not seem* **10:10** [a]Lit *bodily presence is weak* **10:12** [a]Or *any* **10:13** [a]Lit *according to the measure* **10:15** [a]Lit *according to our sphere* **10:16** [a]Lit *to the things prepared in the*

be as forceful as what we say in our letters from far away.

12 Oh, don't worry; we wouldn't dare say that we are as wonderful as these other men who tell you how important they are! But they are only comparing themselves with each other, using themselves as the standard of measurement. How ignorant!

13 We will not boast about things done outside our area of authority. We will boast only about what has happened within the boundaries of the work God has given us, which includes our working with you.
14 We are not reaching beyond these boundaries when we claim authority over you, as if we had never visited you. For we were the first to travel all the way to Corinth with the Good News of Christ.

15 Nor do we boast and claim credit for the work someone else has done. Instead, we hope that your faith will grow so that the boundaries of our work among you will be extended.
16 Then we will be able to go and preach the Good News in other places far beyond you, where no one else is working. Then there will be no question of our boasting about work done in someone else's territory.
17 As the Scriptures say, "If you want to boast, boast only about the LORD."*

18 When people commend themselves, it doesn't count for much. The important thing is for the Lord to commend them.

**10:4** English translations divide verses 4 and 5 in various ways. **10:7** Or *You look at things only on the basis of appearance.* **10:17** Jer 9:24.

Not all critics seek to demoralize or destroy. Sometimes criticism comes from a sincere heart, like the wife who says, "Not that tie, honey," or the loving father who says, "Son, I know this isn't the best work you can do." Other times, criticisms may be meant well but delivered too harshly, like the instructor teaching a student to drive saying, "If you keep driving like that, you'll kill us both!" (It's probably true, but not the most constructive way to put it.) Even constructive criticism, well-intentioned and well-delivered, can hurt our feelings. Sometimes that's inevitable. But there's a difference between hurting another's feelings and harming another's character and reputation.

The kind of criticism that actually harms a person comes from carping, caustic detractors whose words fly like arrows from bows of opinion or just plain ignorance. Their goal? To take their target down, not to build them up or help them. Like the countless varieties of biting or stinging insects, critics swarm in many species. I'm sure we have all been stung by spiteful criticism's harsh barbs. Such experiences—especially for people involved in ministry—are unavoidable. Since we can't escape it, we might as well learn to expect it, or even better, prepare for it. If we don't prepare ourselves for the vicious onslaught of mean-spirited criticism, we may very well feel like throwing in the towel or switching to sucker punches in retaliation.

I didn't have a class on handling criticism during my years in seminary. To my knowledge, there isn't such a class in any seminary. It's something you learn either by watching your mentors deal with it, or by enduring it yourself, "on the job." This explains why 2 Corinthians 10 is so vital for those involved in ministry. As we work through this chapter, we will see Paul dive headfirst into the subject of ministry-related criticism. A close look at his words reveals several slanderous criticisms that had been hurled Paul's way, and how he dealt with them.

## — 10:1-6 —

Unfortunately, we don't have a specific list of the Corinthians' complaints or the criticisms of Paul's opponents that incited them to treat the man with such coldness and hostility. Paul likely had gotten wind of the slander, misrepresentations, and exaggerations through personal reports from his trusted assistants, Timothy and Titus. His letter doesn't rehearse the charges, but simply sets forth his defense. We can decipher the unfounded criticism leveled against Paul through his response (10:1-2).

The first verse addresses the accusation of two-faced hypocrisy. They criticized Paul for being bold with his letters but lacking courage in person. Paul's language needs to be read with a tone of sarcasm, as he virtually quotes the crowd of critics in Corinth. They were saying, essentially, "You're meek when you are with us, but you write bold letters when you're away from us. You're two-faced! When you actually have to face people, you're Mr. Nice Guy, but when it's just a pen and a piece of paper, you boldly unleash! Would the real Paul please stand up?"

The second verse combats the criticism of fleshly motives. They accused him of walking in the flesh, of harboring impure motives, and of using manipulative methods. The Judaizing false teachers especially would have regarded Paul as an "anything goes" liberal because he didn't follow the Law to a tee. To a legalist, nonlegalists always appear too worldly. They also accused Paul of false motives—grasping for power, prestige, and maybe even money. Those who did not want to follow through on the Corinthians' commitment to the Jerusalem Relief Fund would have tried to characterize the project as a moneymaking scam by the apostle himself. Finally, they would have perceived Paul's multiple letters and messengers as means of manipulating them for his own selfish ends.

Despite the inaccurate defamatory remarks by his critics, Paul approached the Corinthians with "the meekness and gentleness of Christ" (10:1). This tone reflects a calm, controlled response to the Corinthians who had come under the spell of the malicious accusers. Meekness, however, doesn't mean weakness. Meekness isn't rolling over and playing dead as people kick and prod you. Christ used the same term for "meek" to describe Himself in Matthew 11:29, but He didn't hesitate to unleash a tirade of rebuke against Jewish hypocrites (Matt. 23:13-33). Depending on the circumstances and the context, the same person can be meek and humble or angry and severe.

Near the end of the letter, Paul reveals the reason for the difference in tone: "For this reason I am writing these things while absent, so that when present I need not use severity, in accordance with the authority which the Lord gave me for building up and not for tearing down" (2 Cor. 13:10). A reasonable explanation, right? Yet in the minds of unreasonable critics, unwilling to grant Paul the benefit of the doubt, the smallest hint of inconsistency got blown out of proportion.

In an attempt to clear the fog from the minds of the Corinthians, Paul pulls back the curtain of the physical world to persuade them that the battle against the criticism of the false teachers is a spiritual one (10:3-5). It therefore requires methods of spiritual warfare rather than a carnal approach to handling controversy (10:3). Paul knew he couldn't just show up in Corinth and start knocking heads together. Nor could he simply pull rank like a general and give them all a tongue-lashing. Instead, Paul had to do battle in the hearts and minds of the Corinthian congregation, drawing them away from the deception of the false teachers and critics and allying them once again with their founding apostolic teachers. To this end, Paul had to destroy "speculations" and challenges to the "knowledge of God" by "taking every thought captive to the obedience of Christ" (10:5).

In biblical days, cities constructed defenses to protect them from enemy invasion. These included fortresses, elevated places with lookout towers, and lofty, sturdy walls to prevent invaders from gaining easy access. The image of the strongly fortified city stands at the fore of Paul's mind as he compares the spiritual battle with an earthly city siege. The "fortress" is our mind. "Speculations" represent the walls built around that fortress. Thus, the presuppositions, biases, and preconceived notions can shield the mind from the invasion of the truth, while the mind itself stands immovable in the face of the attack. Not until the Lord penetrated that thick wall of defense could Paul hope to attain a victory over the hearts and minds of the Corinthian Christians. They were kept captive under the influence of a handful of manipulative, deceptive false teachers doing everything they could to keep Paul and his apostolic associates outside the wall they had constructed.

So, what was Paul's spiritual strategy in this desperate battle against the false teachers? First, he needed to gain the full allegiance of the true believers in Corinth. To be sure, many already were on his side. Nevertheless, far too many wavered in their loyalty between the orthodox Christians and the false brethren. That group needed to be won back to a fully obedient commitment to Christ (10:6). When that happened, Paul could confront the pockets of ingrown disobedience and rebellion with a united front, resulting in the Corinthian church being liberated from its deceptive oppressors.

## — 10:7-18 —

Unfazed by the trumped-up criticisms of his opponents, Paul responded with four reasonable answers to their unreasonable attacks: *He corrected their perspective* (10:7), *he clarified his motive* (10:8-9), *he confessed his authenticity* (10:10-12), and *he communicated the facts* (10:13-18).

First, *Paul corrected their perspective* (10:7). Very simply, he charged his critics with focusing on the external rather than the internal. The critics revealed their shallowness with this criticism, but its pain cut deep. Of all their complaints, his less-than-impressive physical appearance had a ring of truth, as confirmed by a traditional description of Paul from the second century. Paul was "a man small in size, baldheaded, bandy-legged, well-built, with eyebrows meeting, rather long-nosed, full of grace."[2]

Clearly Paul didn't turn any heads. The crowd wasn't attracted to his physical appearance. Yet the critics who complained against Paul for his less-than-impressive presence had completely forgotten that God loves to demonstrate His power and glory through earthen vessels (4:7). In fact, had those carping Judaizing snobs paid closer attention to their own Old Testament Scriptures, they would have recalled that "God sees not as man sees, for man looks at the outward appearance, but the LORD looks at the heart" (1 Sam. 16:7). People sometimes criticize because they don't look deep enough. They have not peered below the surface or stood in the other's shoes—like the Corinthian critics. Had they looked beyond the surface of Paul's life, they would have seen Christ in him, just as they should see Christ within themselves (2 Cor. 10:7).

Second, *Paul clarified his motives in ministry* (10:8-9). Having turned their attention from the externals to the internals, Paul made sure his opponents understood what was in his heart. Paul had a goal in his apostolic ministry to always build up, never tear down (10:8). Even though he may have had authority as an apostle to rebuke and correct the Corinthians for their sins, he wanted to edify, not terrify (10:9). Here Paul is completely transparent about his motives in ministry. In contrast to his power-hungry opponents who constantly tore Paul down in order to extend their own authority over the Corinthians, Paul assured them that he had a positive ministry of construction, not a negative ministry of destruction.

Third, *Paul confessed his authenticity* (10:10-12). In technological lingo, we often see the term WYSIWYG—an acronym for "what you see is what you get." This is particularly important in desktop publishing with the desire for the layout on the computer screen to look exactly the same as what the printer spits out. As far as Paul's ministry was concerned, it was WYSIWYG. Paul was Paul—whether in their midst or through his letters (10:11). Now, his particular tone might change depending on the situation, but that's to be expected. Paul himself didn't change his views on Christ, his attitudes toward holiness and sin, or his methods of preaching the gospel and calling believers to a committed Christian life.

The critics' accusations that Paul was a heavyweight in his letters but a lightweight in person were unfounded. Paul was just being himself, through and through. But not everyone can make that claim. Not everybody backs up their boasting with reality. Authenticity—WYSIWYG—deserves no criticism. Paul didn't compare, didn't compete. He had no dirty secrets in his life that he needed to hide from the searchlight. Paul had a specific group of people in mind who felt the need to "commend themselves" (10:12)—that is, compare themselves by their own standards, trying to demonstrate their superiority over other ministers.

I have never seen such vicious and ambitious competition in ministry as I see today in North American Christianity. So many pastors—especially younger ones—compete for the limelight, trying to grow bigger, look better, come across as edgier, cooler, more relevant. Ultimately, they won't be able to keep up the charade. It takes an incredible amount of energy to pretend to be something that you are not. People need to be who they are. They need to get out of the way and turn the spotlights back onto Jesus. I would say to any and all in ministry, point your fans in His direction, and model authenticity, even if it means people will no longer embrace you as some sort of semidivine superstar. After all, you're not!

Fourth, *Paul communicated the facts about ministry* (10:13-18). In our legal system defense attorneys sometimes have to provide legal counsel for less-than-desirable clients. When asked how they are going to defend such clients, they often answer, "With the facts. We can only argue the facts." In other words, you can't make things up. You just tell it the way it is, deal with the facts, and let the wheels of justice roll on. You can only argue the facts.

In ministry, there is nothing like facts to help in times of unjust criticism. Paul rapidly rehearsed the facts about his own ministry scope as it involved the Corinthians.

- God had given him the ministry to reach the Gentiles with the gospel (10:13). The Judaizers severely criticized this ministry focus, accusing Paul of trying to spread his own personal kingdom and authority rather than the kingdom of God.
- Within the sphere of his evangelistic calling, Paul reached the Corinthians (10:14). Like parasites, those Judaizers who came after him invaded the church planted by Paul and began to boast of their work as if they had established the church in Corinth themselves.
- He hoped the Corinthians' growth would lead to additional resources to expand his ministry (10:15-16). The Judaizers' strategy involved overhauling churches that already had been planted in order to boast of their conquests; Paul took the approach of preaching where no churches had yet been planted.

Whereas Paul had reason to boast based on the facts, his opponents had no reason to boast. Yet Paul remained meek, humble, and patient in the midst of their criticisms, while they boasted all the more boldly in their hijacking of the churches. In fact, Paul quotes Jeremiah 9:24, "He who boasts is to boast in the LORD," not in their own accomplishments, riches, or strength (2 Cor. 10:17). Ultimately, God alone is the Judge whose commendation counts. Self-promotion and self-approval are meaningless, the hollow words of braggarts. True servants of God present the facts as they are and then let the Lord God sort it out.

# APPLICATION: 2 CORINTHIANS 10:1-18

## Facing Criticism in the Throes of Ministry

One of my favorite questions to ask someone at an ordination council, in an interview for a ministry position, or at the threshold of a promotion to a position of leadership at a company or business, is: "How do you handle criticism?" It is a vital question seldom considered, much less actually asked and answered.

As we reflect on Paul's own response to the mental, emotional, and spiritual attacks that came to him in the form of unjust criticism from unrighteous people, we need to come to terms with the reality of criticism in ministry. Trust me when I say that everybody involved in any level of ministry—full-time, part-time, or volunteer—needs to understand the challenges of criticism and be prepared to handle them in a wise, godly manner. Let me share three facts about criticism that will arm you for the spiritual battle that's coming.

First, *no one is immune to criticism*. Unfortunately, it is an unavoidable part of living among human beings. Do your best not to get paranoid. Expect criticism, but don't obsess over it. Don't run in fear of it. Face it with strong resolve. Since we can't escape it, we might as well ready ourselves for it. Decide beforehand that you will neither lie down and give up nor stand up and engage in an ugly fight over every nitpicking critique.

Second, *criticism can be taken too lightly or too seriously*. If we take criticism too lightly and let every less-than-positive comment bead off of us like rain on a windshield, we might ignore valuable instruction that could help us. Where would we be without our parents' correction? Or without that close friend who lives out Proverbs 27:6 and points out our blind spots? Taking criticism lightly can deprive us of opportunities for personal development and growth. We will remain juvenile and immature, unteachable and stubborn.

On the other hand, if we take criticism too seriously, we could lose heart. If we obsess over every biting comment, every harsh e-mail, every disapproving frown, every anonymous letter, we might shrink back with lack of confidence in everything we do. Second-guessing every decision. Regretting every minor mistake. Crafting our messages or lessons to please individual people. These overreactions will literally demoralize a pastor and paralyze a ministry. We might eventually decide never to dream again. Worse, we might quit before finishing the task.

A balanced approach is to listen to legitimate criticism, but take unjust criticism with a grain of salt. Several things I have learned over the years:

- Ignore the really scathing criticisms as well as the exalted praise. Neither is helpful. You will meet people in ministry who can say nothing good. Others can say nothing bad. Almost without exception, the truth is somewhere in the middle.
- I don't read anonymous criticisms. In fact, anonymous criticisms will never reach me. If individuals won't reveal their names to you, then those persons don't really care about you; their motives are usually destructive, not constructive.
- On the other hand, anonymous compliments can be trusted because the person who shares without recognition is clearly not interested in flattery or softening me up for a favor, which adds to the likelihood that they offer a sincere message of gratitude.
- I keep a few personal family members and friends close at hand to discuss both criticisms and praises to help keep me balanced. My wife is great at this. She can often see through motives like Superman through a wall. She knows when to "toss it in the trash" or "take it to heart" like no one else in my life. We all need somebody in our lives to help guide us through such verbal minefields.

Third, *some criticism needs to be answered; much of it doesn't.* If a criticism is based on a misunderstanding, clear it up as soon as possible. Those are usually easy to dispense with, and once the air is cleared, you will gain not only a sympathizer but a supporter. If at all possible, meet in person; if not, keep the dialogue open to make sure you can avoid further miscommunication.

If it's a matter of minor disagreement, consider a meeting of the minds. If good might come from an exchange of thoughts, put your heads together and think through the major issues. Even if there is no change of mind on either side, it's a noble goal to come to a mutual understanding of each other's perspective. Sometimes you simply agree to disagree.

If responding to the criticism, however, would lead only to more argument, it might be best to let the criticism remain unanswered. You can usually tell by the level of venom involved. If it sounds mean-spirited, it probably is. Or if the critic is known as a chronic grouch, experience already has taught you that engaging in that kind of combat will result only in a stalemate. There is no need to become a pen pal with someone looking for a fight! I repeat: Let it go.

We will all face criticism in ministry (and in life). We need to prepare ourselves so we don't pass it off too lightly or worry over it too seriously. And we need to discern whether the criticism needs to be answered. When we go into ministry situations with our eyes wide open, we will be able to see criticism coming and deal with it wisely.

# Not All "Ministries" Are Ministries
## 2 CORINTHIANS 11:1-15

**NASB**

1 I wish that you would bear with me
in a little foolishness; but [a]indeed
you are bearing with me. 2 For I am
jealous for you with a godly jealousy;
for I betrothed you to one husband,
so that to Christ I might present you
*as* a pure virgin. 3 But I am afraid
that, as the serpent deceived Eve by
his craftiness, your minds will be
led astray from the simplicity and
purity *of devotion* to Christ. 4 For if
[a]one comes and preaches another
Jesus whom we have not preached,
or you receive a different spirit which
you have not received, or a different
gospel which you have not accepted,

**NLT**

1 I hope you will put up with a little
more of my foolishness. Please bear
with me. 2 For I am jealous for you
with the jealousy of God himself. I
promised you as a pure bride* to one
husband—Christ. 3 But I fear that
somehow your pure and undivided
devotion to Christ will be corrupted,
just as Eve was deceived by the cun-
ning ways of the serpent. 4 You hap-
pily put up with whatever anyone
tells you, even if they preach a dif-
ferent Jesus than the one we preach,
or a different kind of Spirit than the
one you received, or a different kind
of gospel than the one you believed.

**NASB**

you bear *this* beautifully. 5 For I consider myself not in the least inferior to the [a]most eminent apostles. 6 But even if I am unskilled in speech, yet I am not *so* in knowledge; in fact, in every way we have made *this* evident to you in all things.

7 Or did I commit a sin in humbling myself so that you might be exalted, because I preached the gospel of God to you without charge? 8 I robbed other churches by taking wages *from them* to serve you; 9 and when I was present with you and was in need, I was not a burden to anyone; for when the brethren came from Macedonia they fully supplied my need, and in everything I kept myself from being a burden to you, [a]and will continue to do so. 10 As the truth of Christ is in me, this boasting of mine will not be stopped in the regions of Achaia. 11 Why? Because I do not love you? God knows *I do!*

12 But what I am doing I will continue to do, so that I may cut off opportunity from those who desire an opportunity to be [a]regarded just as we are in the matter about which they are boasting. 13 For such men are false apostles, deceitful workers, disguising themselves as apostles of Christ. 14 No wonder, for even Satan disguises himself as an angel of light. 15 Therefore it is not surprising if his servants also disguise themselves as servants of righteousness, whose end will be according to their deeds.

**11:1** [a]Or *do indeed bear with me* **11:4** [a]Lit *the one who comes preaches* **11:5** [a]Or *super-apostles* **11:9** [a]Lit *and I will keep* **11:12** [a]Lit *found*

**NLT**

5 But I don't consider myself inferior in any way to these "super apostles" who teach such things. 6 I may be unskilled as a speaker, but I'm not lacking in knowledge. We have made this clear to you in every possible way.

7 Was I wrong when I humbled myself and honored you by preaching God's Good News to you without expecting anything in return? 8 I "robbed" other churches by accepting their contributions so I could serve you at no cost. 9 And when I was with you and didn't have enough to live on, I did not become a financial burden to anyone. For the brothers who came from Macedonia brought me all that I needed. I have never been a burden to you, and I never will be. 10 As surely as the truth of Christ is in me, no one in all of Greece* will ever stop me from boasting about this. 11 Why? Because I don't love you? God knows that I do.

12 But I will continue doing what I have always done. This will undercut those who are looking for an opportunity to boast that their work is just like ours. 13 These people are false apostles. They are deceitful workers who disguise themselves as apostles of Christ. 14 But I am not surprised! Even Satan disguises himself as an angel of light. 15 So it is no wonder that his servants also disguise themselves as servants of righteousness. In the end they will get the punishment their wicked deeds deserve.

**11:2** Greek *a virgin.* **11:10** Greek *Achaia,* the southern region of the Greek peninsula.

After just a few minutes of light-handed haggling, you settle on a selling price: five dollars. Not bad for a pile of clothing that doesn't fit you anyway. After all, this is a yard sale, and the goal is to get rid of as much junk by the end of the day as possible—perhaps you will have a little extra cash in your pocket to boot.

The gentleman snatches the bag of clothes and hands you a piece of yellow construction paper roughly the size of a five-dollar bill. On the front is an attempt at Abraham Lincoln in green crayon, in each corner the number "5." You turn it over and read "Five Dollars" in big block letters that look like they were written with the fist-grip of a five-year-old.

"Um, what's this?" you ask.

"It's five dollars," the man answers, eager to leave.

I'm not exactly sure where this hypothetical conversation might go from there, but I'm confident you wouldn't respond, "Oh, okay. If you say so. Thanks. Have a nice day!"

Nobody but a very small child would be tricked by such a shoddy counterfeit. Professional con artists strive to match the real currency paper's weight and feel. They labor at getting the colors and details as close to perfect as possible. A crayon-marked scrap of yellow paper won't pass anybody's test of authenticity.

For as long as there has been truth, falsehood has never been far behind. Satan himself countered God's simple, straightforward command in Genesis 2:16-17 with a similar-sounding deception in Genesis 3:1. So also, honest ministries always have been surrounded (and sometimes even outnumbered) by fakes: artificial, deceptive, and dangerous. Unfortunately, people often have trouble discerning the difference between the true and the false. On the face of it, they bear a startling resemblance. But start scratching below the surface, and soon you will uncover a dangerous deception.

When the apostle Paul wrote 2 Corinthians, he pulled no punches regarding false, untrustworthy "ministries." His observations and warnings remain as relevant today as in the days of first-century Christianity. Perhaps more so.

## — 11:1-3 —

False teachers abound today. They are organized, well funded, and sometimes well respected. The false teachers that Paul had to contend with came in a couple of main varieties. The first were the Judaizers—those who believed that people could be saved only if they followed the Old Testament Law. In their book, even the Gentiles who accepted Jesus as their Messiah had to be circumcised and accept the old covenant as well as Jesus. The second heresy came from the Docetists—those influenced by Greek philosophy who rejected the full humanity of Jesus, disparaged the physical body and the physical creation, and refused to believe in the bodily resurrection. It is likely that the Corinthians had encountered both heresies—Docetists who rejected the physical resurrection (see 1 Corinthians 15) and Judaizers who desired to contradict Paul's gospel of salvation by grace through faith in Christ alone (see Galatians 1–2).

False teachers from both groups accused Paul of heresy. They suggested he preached a false Christ, a false gospel, and a false hope. So, in 2 Corinthians 11, Paul warns the gullible Corinthians of the trap awaiting them.

Paul first expresses his distaste for what he has to do—"Bear with me in a little foolishness" (11:1). By foolishness he means having to talk about himself, which would appear like boasting about his role as an apostle. In order to put the false apostles and false prophets in their places, however, circumstances forced him to pull out his certificate of authenticity to underscore his credentials as a true apostle. He reminds them that he already had to speak a bit of foolishness, and they already had borne with his folly (11:1). He refers to having to "boast" of his true accomplishments in contrast to his opponents' exaggerated achievements (10:14-18).

### SEVEN SIGNS OF A FAKE MINISTRY

1. Heresy—Failure to adhere to and respect classic essentials of the faith held by all Christians
2. Authoritarianism—Absolute, unchallengeable power resting in one person
3. Exclusiveness—Insistence that their group alone is the One True Church
4. Greed—Manipulation and guilt tactics to get money; no financial accountability or transparency
5. Impurity—Moral looseness, lack of personal restraint
6. Secrecy—Lack of openness in operations, authority structures, and decisions
7. Rationalization—Defensiveness when confronted about wrongdoing

Paul reveals his jealousy for the Corinthians—not stemming from irrational suspicion or unrighteous envy, but godly jealousy (11:2). In the Old Testament, God sometimes described Himself as a "jealous God" when the Israelites worshiped other gods (Exod. 20:5; 34:14; Deut. 4:23-24; 5:9; 32:16, 21). So, when Paul feared that some of the Corinthians were in danger of straying from the "simplicity and purity of devotion to Christ" (2 Cor. 11:3), to whom Paul had betrothed the church in Corinth as a spiritual bride (11:2), he became justifiably jealous. In short, Paul knew that many in the Corinthian church had been "two-timing" the truth with falsehood, the true Christ with a stand-in, the authentic apostles with apostolic wannabes.

Paul was jealous for their spiritual purity, as a father would be jealous for his daughter's sexual purity before he presents her to her groom. Paul wanted to offer to Christ a church with an unadulterated loyalty to, and love for, Him. Yet in light of the recent crises and ongoing trials in the church at Corinth, Paul feared that they would be led astray from the truth, just as Eve had been led astray by the serpent (11:3).

When people get caught up in false teaching, simplicity and purity get lost. All sort of debris seeps in to muddy the waters, cloud their thinking, and make it difficult for them to act on the simple biblical truths of the faith. Those caught up in false teaching get argumentative. They become divisive. They think things are far more complicated than they really are. They try to be nuanced or intellectually and socially respected. Ultimately, they become arrogant. The Bible itself gets marginalized, or it becomes something so subject to competing interpretations that they treat it as if it had no meaning at all.

All of that is the opposite of what Paul means by the "simplicity and purity of devotion to Christ" (11:3). The solution? Get back to, and stay with, the basics.

## — 11:4-12 —

Paul now contrasts the true and the false teachers (11:4-12), showing the Corinthians three ways to know the difference:

- The false teachers proclaimed another Jesus and a different gospel (11:4).
- The false teachers displayed attractive charisma (11:5-6).
- The false teachers were in it for the money (11:7-12).

First, *the false teachers proclaimed another Jesus and a different gospel* (11:4). The term translated "another" (*allos* [243]) means "another of a similar kind." A false teacher may talk about Jesus, he may sound biblical, but he is fooling you. Heretics have historically been very skillful at using Christian terminology but with drastically different meanings. They refer to "Jesus," but if you ask questions about the nature and character of their "Jesus," you will find they have added to or taken away from the biblical portrayal of the Lord Jesus Christ. They talk about "God," but they don't mean the triune God—Father, Son, and Holy Spirit. They speak of "resurrection," but they have redefined the term to refer to a belief that contradicts the biblical teaching and understanding.

The other "Jesus" preached by false teachers is a "Jesus" the apostles didn't preach (11:4). Consequently, the heretics present a "different" spirit and a "different" (*heteros* [2087]) gospel. The Greek word *heteros* means "another of a different kind." The heretics' spirit is contrary to the Spirit of God. Instead of unity, it creates division. Instead of peace, it brings turmoil. Instead of truth, it teaches falsehood. To what other spirit could Paul be referring than to the spirit of antichrist? That spirit is a devilish usurper attempting to displace the genuine work of the Spirit of God.

Additionally, the gospel of the false teachers opposes the gospel of salvation by grace through faith in Christ alone. The false teachers, under the influence of Satan, have added conditions to the free grace of the gospel: good works, circumcision, observing the Law, submitting to their leadership. Sadly, the Corinthian congregation had made room for these false teachers' lies, just as they had once made room in their midst for the adulterer's sexual immorality (1 Cor. 5:1). Paul said with a tone of sarcasm, "You bear this beautifully," meaning they tolerated this heresy as if everything were just fine. But things were *not* fine.

The "Jesus" the heretics preached was not the same Jesus preached by Paul and his fellow apostles (1 Cor. 1:23). The spirit they had received in their midst was an unclean spirit, not the Holy Spirit of God they had received when they believed (1 Cor. 12:13). And the gospel they permitted was *not* the gospel Paul had preached to them in the beginning, which they had received, and on which they once stood (1 Cor. 15:1-5). How were these false teachers gaining a hearing and establishing a foothold in the Corinthian congregation?

It's because *the false teachers displayed attractive charisma* (2 Cor. 11:5-6). The Corinthians were slowly but surely being persuaded to embrace—or at least tolerate—heretical teaching because it came wrapped in appealing charm. Here Paul begins a proper defense of his apostolic authority as he directly squares off against the false apostleship of his opponents. The Judaizing critics were attempting to downplay the authority of Paul's teachings by pitting it against the apparently superior authority of the "most eminent" apostles.

With the term "most eminent", some commentators believe Paul referred to his opponents' false claims of themselves being apostles who surpassed even Paul in grandeur.[3] Others understand this to refer to the "pillars" of the Jerusalem church mentioned in Galatians 2:6-10.[4] In this case, Paul wasn't pitting himself against other authentic apostles, but against false teachers who had illegitimately claimed those apostles for themselves. Lowery writes, "The false apostles hoped to derive authority by claiming to be associated with the Twelve. Without demeaning the Twelve, Paul affirmed his own status as an apostle of similar rank."[5]

It would have been easy for the Judaizers to illegitimately hijack the reputation of Jerusalem apostles like Peter and John as well as James, the brother of Jesus. Why? Because Jewish Christians living in Jerusalem had resolved to live according to the customs of their culture: keeping the Sabbath, following the Law, and observing Jewish festivals. The Jerusalem apostles had made it clear at the Jerusalem council, however, that this lifestyle was not to be enforced among Gentile converts (Acts 15:19-29). Nevertheless, Judaizers still interested in forcing the Law on Gentiles had appealed to the practices of the "eminent apostles," thus denigrating the authority of Paul and discrediting his entire ministry. The actual Jerusalem apostles never would have been involved in such a destructive and deceptive ploy.

Apparently, too, these potent adversaries of Paul possessed great powers of persuasion. Yet keen rhetorical skill without accurate knowledge of the truth had no value. Paul, though not always eloquent in speech or attractive in appearance, excelled in his revelations and knowledge of divine mysteries (2 Cor. 12:1-7). Ultimately, it wasn't the packaging but the contents that mattered. The fakes had outward appeal; Paul had inward substance—a contrast usually found between false and true leaders.

A third contrast between Paul and his opponents was that *the false teachers were in it for the money* (11:7-12), while Paul was in it for the ministry. Craig Keener explains: "Paul defended his 'volunteer' status in 11:7-9. Just as sophists emphasized rhetorical form over content, they charged fees from their students; Paul is truly an 'amateur' rather than a professional (11:6) in this regard."[6] Eloquent orators trained in the best rhetorical techniques could be hired to represent a certain perspective in public, or they could charge fees to give students the privilege of sitting at their feet and acquiring their knowledge.[7] In other words, those who collected fees were clearly *professionals*. Paul didn't charge the Corinthians a dime for his priceless ministry to them (11:7, 9). Therefore, some concluded, Paul must be an amateur compared to the skilled rhetoricians.

Paul had financed his missionary efforts through the support of what we might call "sending churches" (11:8). In fact, even when in financial need while ministering to the Corinthians, Paul refused to take support from them, waiting instead for fresh support from the churches in Macedonia (11:9). What irony! Paul had refused to collect support from the Corinthians in order to demonstrate his sincerity in preaching for the sake of Christ and to remove the possibility that some would accuse him of false motives (1 Cor. 9:5-17). Yet the false teachers had twisted this, making Paul's "freebie" message inferior to their "pay per view" approach to ministry, likely arguing along the lines of "you get what you pay for."

Paul had acted admirably. He never wanted it to be said that he came to the Corinthians for the money they could have amply provided. Ministers of the gospel must never make money their motive. Though "the Lord directed those who proclaim the gospel to get their living from the gospel" (1 Cor. 9:14), Peter said that shepherds of God's church should not engage in ministry "for sordid gain, but with eagerness" (1 Pet. 5:2).

Paul concludes his contrast with the false teachers by providing a personal explanation for his boasting (2 Cor. 11:10-12). We can tell from Paul's tone that he hated having to defend himself by pointing out his own credentials and accomplishments. He was so driven to conform to the image of Christ that when the situation required him to point out facts about himself in order to defeat those who claimed to be superior to him, he felt genuinely embarrassed to do so. Would that ministers today feel ashamed to point out all of their accomplishments! It seems the opposite is now true. Godly, faithful, humble pastors actually feel ashamed when they *don't* have a stunning career with incredible accomplishments like the superstar who delights in grabbing the spotlight.

As much as Paul couldn't stand "boasting" about himself, he resolved that he would continue to point out the deficiencies of those false teachers to "cut off opportunity from those who desire an opportunity to be regarded just as we are in the matter about which they are boasting" (11:12). In order to rip the sheepskins from those wolves in sheep's clothing, Paul needed to meet their empty boasts with the facts from his own ministry.

## — 11:13-15 —

The popularity of those false preachers didn't surprise Paul. He recognized Satan—the archenemy of the church—behind it all. Those men were "false apostles, deceitful workers, disguising themselves as apostles of Christ" (11:13). Just as Satan himself deceives the world by masquerading as an "angel of light" (11:14), so his devilish servants also disguise themselves as "servants of righteousness" (11:15). The word "disguise," used three times in these three verses, is the Greek term *metaschēmatizō* [3345], which means "to change in appearance." Though the essence of the thing remains the same, its outward appearance looks different.

# Deceived by Doctored Delicacies

## 2 CORINTHIANS 11:13

*A friend of mine ate dog food one evening. No, he wasn't at a fraternity initiation, but at an elegant student reception in a physician's home near Miami. The dog food was served on delicate little crackers with a wedge of imported cheese, bacon chips, an olive, and a sliver of pimento on top. It was hors d'oeuvres à l'Alpo.*

*The hostess (a good friend) is a first-class nut! You would have to know her to appreciate the story. She had just graduated from a gourmet cooking course, so she decided the time had come to put her skills to the ultimate test. Did she ever! After doctoring up those miserable morsels and putting them on a couple of silver trays, with a sly grin she watched them disappear. My friend couldn't get enough. He kept coming back for more. I don't recall how they broke the news to him, but when he found out the truth, he probably felt like barking and biting her on the leg! He certainly must have gagged a little.*

*Ever since hearing that true story, I've thought about how perfectly it illustrates something that transpires daily in another realm: religious fakes. Professional charlatans. Frauds. Counterfeit Christians who market their wares on shiny platters decorated with tasty persuasion and impressive appearance. Being masters of deceit, they serve up delectable dishes of bad food camouflaged by spiritual-sounding lingo.*

*This fits perfectly with Paul's description in 2 Corinthians: "For such men are false apostles, deceitful workers, disguising themselves as apostles of Christ. No wonder, for even Satan disguises himself as an angel of light. Therefore it is not surprising if his servants also disguise themselves as servants of righteousness" (2 Cor. 11:13-15). A glance at the silver platter and everything looks delicious: apostles, angels, servants. But if you look a little more closely, you'll see it all*

(continued on next page)

*for what it really is: poisonous doctrine nobody should ingest, false prophets, demonic forces, and spiritual slave drivers.*

*Unfortunately, so long as there are hands to pick from the platter of doctored-up dog food, there will be good-looking, sweet-smelling false teachings available. But some day, some dreadful day, the final Judge will determine and separate the truth from error. There will be a lot of gagging and choking, and the false teachings that pleased the undiscerning palate will no longer taste good.*

The servants of Satan may appear right and good at first. But their "end will be according to their deeds" (11:15). They will fall victim to their own lies and ultimately will perish without Christ. Peter echoes the same warning several years later: "There will also be false teachers among you, who will secretly introduce destructive heresies, even denying the Master who bought them, bringing swift destruction upon themselves" (2 Pet. 2:1).

## APPLICATION: 2 CORINTHIANS 11:1-15

### Don't Fall for the Fakes!

It does us no good to cluck our tongues and shake our heads when we see somebody led astray by a charlatan. We need to recognize that everybody is susceptible to Satan's attempts at deception. He tried to deceive Jesus Christ (Matt. 4:1-10), so what makes us think we can escape his temptations? Instead of pretending we're immune, we need to prepare beforehand for the inevitable deceptions that will come to us through Satan's servants today: false ministers and fake ministries. To keep from falling for the fakes, let me give a couple of suggestions.

First, probe deeply into the doctrinal statement of the organization and listen carefully to the theology of the individual. If the ministry doesn't have a doctrinal statement, back off and don't support them financially. If they produce a doctrinal statement, read it closely with your Bible open and make sure it aligns with the orthodox truths of the Christian faith. Does it proclaim the true, perfect deity and sinless humanity of Christ? Does it acknowledge Christ as the second Person of the Trinity: Father, Son and Holy Spirit? Does it teach the depravity of humanity and the need for a Savior? Does it affirm salvation as a free gift of God, purchased at the cross by Christ alone, and available without works, based on His death and miraculous, bodily resurrection? Usually those areas—the doctrines of God, Christ, and salvation—are the ones that phony ministries tamper with the most.

Second, examine the lives of those in leadership. Jesus says you will know the good from the bad based on their fruit (Matt. 7:20). Are the leaders accountable to anybody beyond themselves? Do they have servants' hearts or do they run the ministry with absolute, unquestioned authority? Are they accessible, open to questions, and willing to hear constructive criticism? Are they free from sexual and moral impurity? Do you find them free of greed and financial impropriety? We shouldn't expect our leaders to be perfect, but we should expect them to be authentic, willing to admit their imperfections. And we should expect them to be accountable to a constitution, a plurality of leaders, and also to the congregation or constituency they serve. Beware of spiritual-sounding Lone Rangers! Peter warned the leaders of the churches in Asia Minor not to lord over their church, but to prove "examples to the flock" (1 Pet. 5:3). Servant-hearted models of humility should be the standard of authentic leadership.

Remember, you have a message of hope based on Jesus Christ and the Word of God. When you come into contact with a fake ministry or a false teacher, share that message but stay on the offensive. Know your Bible, stick to the central issues of Jesus Christ and salvation. Don't entertain their doctrines for one moment. What may look like a pot of gold at the end of a rainbow may really be a coiled rattler waiting to strike.

# The Flip Side of Fruitful Ministry
## 2 CORINTHIANS 11:16-33

NASB

16 Again I say, let no one think me foolish; but if *you do,* receive me even as foolish, so that I also may boast a little. 17 What I am saying, I am not saying [a]as the Lord would, but as in foolishness, in this confidence of boasting. 18 Since many boast according to the flesh, I will boast also. 19 For you, being *so* wise, tolerate the foolish gladly. 20 For you tolerate it if anyone enslaves you, anyone devours you, anyone takes advantage of you, anyone exalts himself, anyone hits you in the face. 21 To *my* shame I *must* say that we have been weak *by comparison.*

But in whatever respect anyone *else* is bold—I speak in foolishness—I am just as bold myself. 22 Are they Hebrews? So am I. Are they Israelites? So am I. Are they [a]descendants of Abraham? So am I. 23 Are they servants of Christ?—I speak as if insane—I more so; in [a]far more labors, in [a]far more imprisonments, [b]beaten times without number, often in danger of death. 24 Five times I received from the Jews thirty-nine *lashes.* 25 Three times I was beaten with rods, once I was stoned, three times I was shipwrecked, a night and a day I have spent in the deep. 26 *I have been* on frequent journeys, in dangers from rivers, dangers from robbers, dangers from *my* countrymen, dangers from the Gentiles, dangers in the city, dangers in the wilderness, dangers on the sea, dangers among false brethren; 27 *I have been* in labor and hardship, [a]through many sleepless

NLT

16 Again I say, don't think that I am a fool to talk like this. But even if you do, listen to me, as you would to a foolish person, while I also boast a little. 17 Such boasting is not from the Lord, but I am acting like a fool. 18 And since others boast about their human achievements, I will, too. 19 After all, you think you are so wise, but you enjoy putting up with fools! 20 You put up with it when someone enslaves you, takes everything you have, takes advantage of you, takes control of everything, and slaps you in the face. 21 I'm ashamed to say that we've been too "weak" to do that!

But whatever they dare to boast about—I'm talking like a fool again—I dare to boast about it, too. 22 Are they Hebrews? So am I. Are they Israelites? So am I. Are they descendants of Abraham? So am I. 23 Are they servants of Christ? I know I sound like a madman, but I have served him far more! I have worked harder, been put in prison more often, been whipped times without number, and faced death again and again. 24 Five different times the Jewish leaders gave me thirty-nine lashes. 25 Three times I was beaten with rods. Once I was stoned. Three times I was shipwrecked. Once I spent a whole night and a day adrift at sea. 26 I have traveled on many long journeys. I have faced danger from rivers and from robbers. I have faced danger from my own people, the Jews, as well as from the Gentiles. I have faced danger in the cities, in the deserts, and on the seas. And I have faced danger from men who claim to be believers but are not.* 27 I have worked hard

nights, in hunger and thirst, often
without food, in cold and [b]exposure.
28 Apart from *such* [a]external things,
there is the daily pressure on me *of*
concern for all the churches. 29 Who
is weak without my being weak?
Who is [a]led into sin [b]without my in-
tense concern?

30 If I have to boast, I will boast of
what pertains to my weakness. 31 The
God and Father of the Lord Jesus,
He who is blessed forever, knows
that I am not lying. 32 In Damascus
the ethnarch under Aretas the king
was guarding the city of the Dama-
scenes in order to seize me, 33 and I
was let down in a basket through a
window [a]in the wall, and *so* escaped
his hands.

**11:17** [a]Lit *in accordance with the Lord* **11:22** [a]Lit *seed* **11:23** [a]Lit *more abundant* [b]Lit *exceedingly in stripes* **11:27** [a]Lit *often in wakefulness* [b]Lit *nakedness;* i.e. lack of clothing **11:28** [a]Or *the things unmentioned* **11:29** [a]Lit *made to stumble* [b]Lit *and I do not burn* **11:33** [a]Lit *through*

and long, enduring many sleep-
less nights. I have been hungry and
thirsty and have often gone without
food. I have shivered in the cold,
without enough clothing to keep
me warm.

28 Then, besides all this, I have the
daily burden of my concern for all
the churches. 29 Who is weak with-
out my feeling that weakness? Who
is led astray, and I do not burn with
anger?

30 If I must boast, I would rather
boast about the things that show
how weak I am. 31 God, the Father
of our Lord Jesus, who is worthy of
eternal praise, knows I am not lying.
32 When I was in Damascus, the gov-
ernor under King Aretas kept guards
at the city gates to catch me. 33 I had
to be lowered in a basket through
a window in the city wall to escape
from him.

**11:26** Greek *from false brothers.*

Several years ago as I traveled to a speaking engagement on the East Coast, a president of a Christian college met me at the airport. As soon as I saw him, I recognized that something wasn't quite right. He looked like the weight of the world had been stuffed into an invisible backpack and placed on his shoulders. He was stooped over and looked a little grim. I called his name, gave him a big hug, and said, "Well, how are you doing?"

He responded, "How am I doing? I'm growing and I am learning. That's how I'm doing. You know, Chuck, several years ago I used to have a glib answer when people asked me 'How are you doing?' To keep things simple, I always responded loudly, 'Fantastic!' But these last few years I have decided to get real—to be honest. The best I can say today is 'I'm growing and I'm learning, but I'm not *fantastic*!'"

I think some of us need to learn what the president of that school was honest enough to admit. When we always answer "Fantastic!" we frequently hide the reality of our pain and leave a false impression that our lives are a colorful bed of roses. Oh, on occasion we do enjoy those wonderful touches of God's favor, times of great joy when we can honestly smile and utter "Fantastic!" But more often than not, the answer really ought to be, "I'm growing and I'm learning."

Life that is lived *realistically* is not lived *fantastically*. Even the "best" Christians are not immune to abrasive and harsh rubs with reality. The painful shoves of disaster, disease, and death jostle the Christian as often as anyone else in this world. These things can leave our lives in shambles, tear apart our families, and leave us reeling for days, weeks, or even years. Real life often is the flip side of "fantastic."

This translates into ministry as well. Like the rest of life, ministry can have its occasional fantastic moments, but more often than not we need to be prepared for the flip side, the day in, day out, during which we are simply growing and learning. Sometimes through pain. At other times through hardship. Always through patience and perseverance found through prayer and faith. *That's* real ministry.

In the city of Corinth in the middle of the first century, the absence of a strong apostolic witness like Paul, Peter, or even the gifted teacher Apollos, created a vacuum of sound leadership that was quickly filled by false teachers. In they marched, looking better than Paul, preaching better than Paul, and touting impressive credentials Paul didn't appear to have. As a result, Paul had to resort to a little boasting of his own qualifications and accomplishments (11:1-6), which he referred to as "a little foolishness." The dazzling impression the false teachers made on the Corinthians forced Paul into the uncomfortable situation of having to assert his own credentials as an apostle (11:16-33).

Some of the marks of Paul's authentic apostleship make up the flip side of fruitful ministry—the realistic picture of suffering, persecution, pain, and pressure that went along with his genuine concern for the churches. The false teachers put on a bright face of "fantastic!" On the other hand, Paul described the real ingredients of growing and learning through the trials of life.

## — 11:16-21 —

Paul could barely tolerate the uncomfortable position in which the false teachers had put him. He had no qualms about writing page after page about Jesus Christ, His saving work, and our faith response to the gospel. He could pen long treatises on grace, practical instructions for the Christian life, and manuals for pastoral ministry. But when it came to pointing to his own accomplishments, Paul would rather hide under a rock than brag about himself. Something tells me that if Paul had to write a résumé today, he would leave so much out about himself that he would never get the job.

In 2 Corinthians 11:16-19, Paul apologizes for his need to go on boasting: "What I am saying, I am not saying as the Lord would, but as in foolishness, in this confidence of boasting" (11:17). In other words, the kind of boasting he did was not Christlike. Jesus wouldn't have done it. The Corinthians had become so enamored with the false teachers who foolishly boasted about their credentials, that Paul had determined to fight folly with folly. He would reluctantly put himself in the role of the foolish (*aphrōn* [878]) boaster, meeting the braggarts on their own turf and defeating them at their own game.

I can hear the disappointment in Paul's words when he points out the abuse the Corinthians willingly endured at the hands of the false teachers (11:20). They enslaved the church to the yoke of legalistic bondage. They devoured them with their false doctrines. They took unfair advantage of their hospitality and financial generosity. They exalted themselves above the truly qualified leaders in the church. And they metaphorically struck the Corinthians in the face. And the worst part? *Not a single one of them had any authority or right to do any of that!* Here we see why Paul would willingly take such desperate rhetorical measures as to boast (*kauchaomai* [2744]) about his accomplishments in the proud manner of his opponents. Such people needed to be stopped.

Compared with the false teachers, Paul describes himself as weak (11:21). He had neither their worldly charisma nor their cultural sophistication. At least Paul never made it a point to display fancy rhetorical footwork or to emphasize his curriculum vitae. He didn't hang his diplomas on his front door or drop names of the famous people he knew or studied under. So, on the surface Paul and his associates appeared "weak." But with a sudden cataloguing of his credentials and accomplishments, the tide turns.

## — 11:22-33 —

The false teachers had their set of impressive credentials. And once Paul decided to open the door to a little foolish boasting about things that didn't really matter to the ministry (11:22), he matched them and even far exceeded them.

| CREDENTIAL | FALSE TEACHERS | APOSTLE PAUL |
|---|---|---|
| Hebrew? | Yes | Yes |
| Israelite? | Yes | Yes |
| Descendant of Abraham? | Yes | Yes |
| Servant of Christ? | So-called | More so |

Paul lingers on the last credential (11:23), because this is the heart of the matter. The Judaizing false teachers had a Hebrew pedigree, but did they have a heart of sincere devotion and sacrificial service to Christ? The Corinthians had become enslaved to these masters of rhetoric and oration. They had become impressed with the external sparkle of their slick, polished presentations. But had they considered the matter of this last credential?

So, were these bona fide Hebrews also authentic servants of Christ? Paul takes his boasting to a new level—except this level isn't what anyone would have expected. Instead of listing his accomplishments, *he highlights his setbacks* (11:23-27)! Scar by scar, Paul shows the Corinthians his battle wounds. Each tells a story of genuine devotion to Christ in contrast to the false teachers' life of comfort and ease. The Judaizers lived in a world in which they would use the word "fantastic!" to describe their ministries. And why not? They showed up in churches already established by Paul's toil, tears, and tribulations. Like thieves harvesting where they hadn't sown, the false teachers performed ministries of ease. On the other hand, Paul's world of ministry was one of growing and learning, filled with pain, heartache, and uncertainty. Paul's uphill, winding road followed Christ to the cross—a life of suffering and sorrow (Heb. 12:2-3; 1 Pet. 2:21). It also traced the steps of numerous saints who had gone before him (Heb. 11:35-38).

If all the crushing circumstances Paul rattled off (2 Cor. 11:23-27) weren't enough to convince the Corinthians of his authentic ministry, Paul also ached with anxiety. He writes, "Apart from such external things, there is the daily pressure on me of concern for all the churches" (11:28). Cumulatively, these pressures had molded Paul into the man he had become. They made him weak and defenseless, but also empathetic. He could therefore strengthen the weak and show his genuine concern for those tempted to sin (11:29).

When you have suffered like Paul—with both external and internal catastrophes, crises, and concerns—your faith moves from the theoretical realm into the practical. This allows for *authentic* spiritual learning and growing and *genuine* ministry as a true servant of Christ. It is true that "fantastic" days become the exception to the rule. But it is also true that a believer lives in the realm of the real rather than the imaginary. When you've been weakened by the trials of ministry, you understand a person in weakness. When you've been there yourself, you're concerned, not condemning. Think about it. When you finally banish the fake "Fantastic!" response to "How are you doing?" you become vulnerable and accessible. Nobody weakened by calamities feels comfortable seeking comfort and understanding from so-called "successful" people who always have it all together. Nobody struggling with sin wants to get counsel from a believer who never seems to battle temptation.

Paul reemphasizes his weaknesses (*astheneia* [769]), not his strengths, as proof of his authentic servanthood (11:30). If he is forced to boast in defense of his ministry, Paul chooses to boast regarding his weaknesses. At the climax of this boasting, he tells the humiliating anecdote of narrowly escaping the city of Damascus in a basket through a window in the city wall (11:31-33). Can you imagine what Paul would have said that evening in response to the question, "So, Paul, how are you doing? Fantastic?"

Paul: "Sure, if 'fantastic' means you had to get dumped into a rickety basket like a sack of salt and lowered out a window like somebody's trash. Thanks for asking, but honestly, I had a really bad day. Unimaginable, in fact. I thought I was going to die in Damascus! But I'm learning and growing from all of this. Always learning and always growing."

I'm not sure how that person would have responded to Paul's transparency, but I know it wouldn't have been, "Oh, that's nice," or "Well, I'm fantastic, myself," or "The sun'll come out tomorrow." Chances are much better that Paul's openness would have granted an opportunity for sharing in another's hardships and heartaches.

## APPLICATION: 2 CORINTHIANS 11:16-33

### Boasting Like Paul

I'm convinced that Paul's credentials for ministry would have driven a pastoral search committee or missionary-sending agency absolutely batty. His was not at all like the pristine and impressive résumés flaunted by his professional opponents in Corinth. The contents of Paul's lengthy curriculum vitae in 2 Corinthians 11:22-33 were written in blood, stained with tears, smeared with dirt, and tattered by enduring too much action in a raging spiritual war that left him stooped over, not standing erect. As I think about how to respond to this remarkable chapter, three things stand out about Paul's descriptions of his credentials, his circumstances, and his character.

First, *Paul doesn't deny the pain and pressures of life.* He doesn't pretend that everything's "fantastic!" when his world is crumbling around him. Never once does he suggest that following Christ is always a problem-free stroll through the park. In fact, take a moment now to ponder all of the hardships Paul endured in ministry. Compare them to the trials you have experienced in church life, outreach, discipleship, or other kinds of ministry in which you've been involved:

| | | |
|---|---|---|
| Labors | Frequent travels | Danger from false brethren |
| Imprisonments | Dangers from rivers | Hardship |
| Beatings | Dangers from robbers | Sleepless nights |
| Death threats | Danger from Jews | Hunger and thirst |
| Lashings | Danger from Gentiles | Starvation |
| Canings | Danger in the city | Coldness |
| Stoning | Danger in the country | Lack of clothing |
| Shipwrecks | Danger on the sea | Worry for the churches |

Chances are, neither you nor anybody you know has experienced even half of these things in ministry. As we consider our own ministry plights, fears, frustrations, and challenges, however, we would do well to call to mind the lyrics of that great hymn by John Newton:

> Thru many dangers, toils and snares,
> I have already come;
> 'Tis grace hath brought me safe thus far,
> And grace will lead me home.[8]

Second, *Paul doesn't market the misery of his ministry.* Paul shared his litany of hardships only because he had to. You get the distinct impression that he found it awkward to talk about himself in these terms. He would much rather talk about the sufferings and triumph of Christ than about his own trials and buffetings. But in telling his story, he didn't seek pity or consolation. He didn't share war stories for public applause. He didn't increase his fame as "the apostle who spent a day and a night adrift at sea" or "the minister who endured beatings, canings, and stoning." I'm sure Paul easily could have marketed his experiences into an opportunity to increase his own renown as a bona fide hero.

We can learn much from this man. Candidly, we need to take care about talking too much about ourselves. It is a fine line between legitimately sharing a testimony of how God has worked in our lives in spite of hardship and becoming either a complainer or a braggart for our own gain. Our stories of agony and ecstasy can help comfort and encourage others. But we must always ask ourselves: Am I actually doing this because I want everybody to know what I've suffered in this life of faith? Are my reasons for telling this pure or tainted? What's my motive?

Third, *Paul doesn't even try to explain why these things happened.* So many people claim to be "fantastic!" because they believe that to confess anything negative would reflect poorly on their Savior. But God never promised smooth sailing. On the contrary, He promised a bumpy ride (John 16:33). In his account of suffering for the sake of the gospel, Paul makes no attempt at analyzing or moralizing. Though he could confess with all of us that he grew and learned from these experiences, he didn't attempt to defend God by explaining exactly *how* he grew and what new things he learned. Most of the time, we can't put such lessons into words. We, too, should learn to endure the suffering without obsessing over the "why" questions. They may never come this side of glory. And then, we won't need an answer.

# Gloves of Grace for Handling Thorns

## 2 CORINTHIANS 12:1-10

**NASB**

1 Boasting is necessary, though it is
not profitable; but I will go on to vi-
sions and revelations [a]of the Lord. 2 I
know a man in Christ who fourteen
years ago—whether in the body I do
not know, or out of the body I do not
know, God knows—such a man was

**NLT**

1 This boasting will do no good,
but I must go on. I will reluctantly
tell about visions and revelations
from the Lord. 2 I* was caught up
to the third heaven fourteen years
ago. Whether I was in my body or
out of my body, I don't know—only

**NASB**

caught up to the third heaven. 3 And
I know how such a man—whether
in the body or apart from the body
I do not know, God knows— 4 was
caught up into Paradise and heard
inexpressible words, which a man is
not permitted to speak. 5 On behalf of
such a man I will boast; but on my
own behalf I will not boast, except
in regard to *my* weaknesses. 6 For if I
do wish to boast I will not be foolish,
for I will be speaking the truth; but I
refrain *from this,* so that no one will
credit me with more than he sees *in*
me or hears from me.

7 Because of the surpassing great-
ness of the revelations, for this
reason, to keep me from exalting
myself, there was given me a thorn
in the flesh, a messenger of Satan
to [a]torment me—to keep me from
exalting myself! 8 Concerning this I
implored the Lord three times that it
might leave me. 9 And He has said to
me, "My grace is sufficient for you,
for power is perfected in weakness."
Most gladly, therefore, I will rather
boast [a]about my weaknesses, so that
the power of Christ may dwell in me.
10 Therefore I am well content with
weaknesses, with [a]insults, with dis-
tresses, with persecutions, with dif-
ficulties, for Christ's sake; for when
I am weak, then I am strong.

**12:1** [a]Or *from* **12:7** [a]Lit *beat* **12:9** [a]Lit *in*
**12:10** [a]Or *mistreatment*

**NLT**

God knows. 3 Yes, only God knows
whether I was in my body or outside
my body. But I do know 4 that I was
caught up* to paradise and heard
things so astounding that they can-
not be expressed in words, things no
human is allowed to tell.

5 That experience is worth boast-
ing about, but I'm not going to do
it. I will boast only about my weak-
nesses. 6 If I wanted to boast, I would
be no fool in doing so, because I
would be telling the truth. But I won't
do it, because I don't want anyone to
give me credit beyond what they can
see in my life or hear in my message,
7 even though I have received such
wonderful revelations from God. So
to keep me from becoming proud,
I was given a thorn in my flesh, a
messenger from Satan to torment me
and keep me from becoming proud.

8 Three different times I begged
the Lord to take it away. 9 Each time
he said, "My grace is all you need.
My power works best in weakness."
So now I am glad to boast about my
weaknesses, so that the power of
Christ can work through me. 10 That's
why I take pleasure in my weak-
nesses, and in the insults, hardships,
persecutions, and troubles that I suf-
fer for Christ. For when I am weak,
then I am strong.

**12:2** Greek *I know a man in Christ who.*
**12:3-4** Greek *But I know such a man, [4]that he was caught up.*

Ours is the age of the self-made person who is *more* than adequate. Not only do we want to appear as though we have our lives together, but we want it to appear that we have put our own lives together better than most. The word "adequate" originally comes from Latin and means "make level to" or "being equal to a requirement." The common colloquialism "I'm equal to the task" would be a good way to put it in today's idiom. But the idea of *more* than adequate brings with it a touch of conceit, doesn't it? "Not only can I do it, but I can do it better than most. I'm self-sufficient." The sense is that we can measure up to *any* task. We dislike the thought that we might be *un*equal to any challenge . . . or that someone else might be more "equal" than we are! This kind of thinking tends toward competition, rivalry, and even open conflict.

In our era of self-sufficiency, three kinds of people appear to have it all together. First, the *highly intelligent* seem to have an edge on everybody. With keen wits and a couple of academic degrees to boot, the intellectuals try to stay on top of every situation with a cascade of golden phrases meant to outdo the competition. Second, the *greatly gifted* tend to dominate pop culture. Talented musicians produce smash hits. Sports icons rake in an obscene amount of cash. Good-looking orators can demand a huge honorarium or draw votes in the political realm. For the gifted, winning comes so easy. Third, in our Christian circles the *deeply religious* appear to glide through life with an appropriate Scripture on their tongues and an abundance of faith to move mountains and create joy in their hearts. They describe their prayer and devotional lives as rich and rewarding and they exude a sense of calm and tranquility. They seem to be so aligned with the Holy Spirit that nothing could pull them off course.

What we don't often see among the highly intelligent, greatly gifted, and deeply spiritual, however, are the great gaps of inadequacy that they live with. Paul wrote in 1 Corinthians 4:7, "For who regards you as superior? What do you have that you did not receive? And if you did receive it, why do you boast as if you had not received it?" That verse should cut every one of us down to size. Nobody gave themselves their smarts, talents, or spiritual devotion. Everything we have—from ability to opportunity—comes to us as a gift from God. James said, "Every good thing given and every perfect gift is from above, coming down from the Father of lights" (Jas. 1:17).

So how does God remind us to acknowledge His generosity and to rely on His strength when He's given us such marvelous abilities? How does God prevent the arrogance of more-than-enough adequacy and the sin of self-sufficiency? *He gives us a thorn in the flesh.* Let's look closely at 2 Corinthians 12 to gain more insight into this significant—and often overlooked—reality.

## — 12:1-6 —

At the time of Paul's writing, as we have learned, Corinth had been invaded by Judaizing false teachers who wished to compel everybody, including Gentiles, to observe every detail of the Law of Moses in the very same manner that they did. Many had impressive credentials,

## THE THREE HEAVENS

### 2 CORINTHIANS 12:2

The various ways people perceive the universe in the twenty-first century differ from the ways people understood the cosmos in the first. Today, many scientists believe all existence is simply matter and energy; the difference between "heaven" and "earth" is one of location, not levels of existence. Those who believe in a spiritual dimension of the universe often view the supernatural dimension as existing alongside of or within the present material universe, or perhaps existing on a completely separate plane of reality.

In the ancient world in which Paul preached and wrote, a number of cosmologies competed for adherents. The Gnostics viewed the universe as comprised of dozens or even hundreds of levels of being, each inhabited by distinct ranks of creatures. Others viewed the world as having two basic realms, the spiritual and the physical, constantly in conflict as good versus evil or light versus dark.

The biblical Jewish and Christian view of the cosmos reflects a moderately hierarchical and mildly dualistic worldview. Unlike much religious and philosophical literature of the time, the Bible doesn't precisely spell out details of cosmology. It rather utilizes categories and concepts of the day, leaving much to mystery and speculation.

What is this biblical view of the cosmos? The Bible understands three basic "levels" of the universe—the heavens, the earth, and below the earth.[9] The term "heavens" may be further divided into three levels. The "first heaven" includes the sphere surrounding the earth. Today we call this the "atmosphere" or "sky," in which birds fly and clouds drift. The "second heaven" includes everything in the cosmos above the earth's atmosphere—the moon, sun, planets, stars, and galaxies. From a modern worldview perspective, both the first and second "heavens" are technically still part of the physical universe. Not so with the "third heaven." In the biblical sense, the "third heaven" was the term used to describe the dwelling place of God, the angels, and any other spirit beings. Paul says that he was "caught up to the third heaven. . . . into Paradise" (2 Cor. 12:2, 4). We might call this today the "spiritual realm," a plane of reality accessible only by heavenly invitation, like the one the apostle John received in Revelation 4:1.

The realm of existence "below the earth" also has both a physical and spiritual dimension. Physically, it may refer simply to the grave or to underground spaces from which water may flow or lava may spew. Or it may refer to the place of spirits who have departed from the earthly plane but have not been admitted into the presence of God. In both cases the same terms often are used—*sheol* [H7585] in the Old Testament or *hadēs* [86] in the New. Context helps determine whether the text is referring to the physical or the spiritual realm.

So, when Paul described being caught up "to the third heaven. . . . into Paradise," he referred to his own, personal translation into a place in the spiritual realm, not to another planet or even another galaxy.

**Paul's Cosmology**

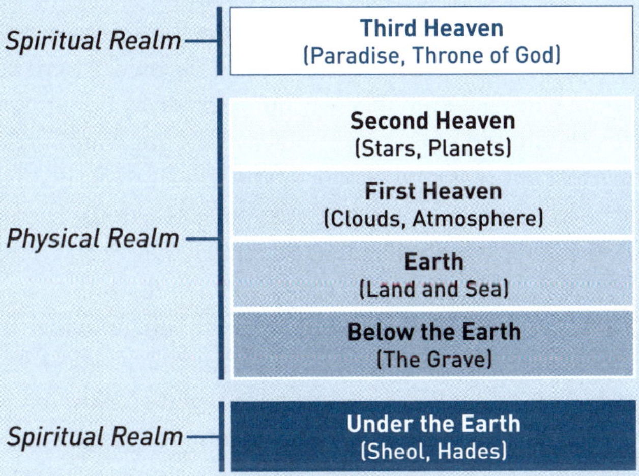


gifts, skills, and holier-than-everybody-else lifestyles that drew the attention of a fair percentage of the Corinthian congregation. Some of the impressionable believers were beginning to be swayed by all the testimonies of great ability. So Paul, although he hated boasting, found it necessary to remind the Corinthian church that his own credentials could stand up against anybody's (2 Cor. 11).

Uncomfortable with trumpeting his gifts and experiences, Paul adds a brief explanation of his view on boasting: "Boasting is necessary, though it is not profitable" (12:1). David Lowery explains, "He did it . . . in the hope that it would silence his critics and enable him to minister freely. He also neatly turned his readers' attention from these irrelevant credentials to those that were an apostle's authentic marks."[10]

I know all of us can think of circumstances in which we are expected to talk about ourselves, our gifts, training, experiences, and accomplishments. Job interviews, political campaigns, promotional media interviews—all of these require some kind of establishment of authority or qualifications. When such necessary self-promotion crosses the line into selfish braggadocio, however, it accomplishes nothing. People are put off by it, and God is never impressed. It neither edifies others nor honors the Lord.

And yet the crisis in Corinth required that Paul re-establish his authority among the church. Therefore, Paul adds a postscript to his résumé. He snags their attention with a credential that he has never revealed. He tells his readers of an experience he had fourteen years earlier when he was taken to paradise (12:1-4).

Although in this passage Paul writes in the third person, most commentators believe he's indirectly describing his own experience.[11] It's likely that he chose to write this way out of modesty or perhaps out of reverence. The timing of the event places it during Paul's wilderness experience just after his conversion, a time when he was not in contact with anyone (Gal. 1:17-18). Imagine that! Paul had actually been "caught up" into the highest spiritual realm, much like the apostle John would experience about fifty years later (Rev. 4:1). There, in the presence of angelic beings and the Lord Himself, he heard things "which a man is not permitted to speak" (2 Cor. 12:4). The experience was so extraordinary that he couldn't tell if it had occurred while still in his physical body or outside his body (12:2-3). All he knew was that his experience was "inexpressible" (12:4).

This brief account of the most astounding of Paul's "visions and revelations of the Lord" (12:1) packs a powerful rhetorical punch. Against his boastful, arrogant opponents who loved to draw attention to themselves with their accounts of spiritual experiences, Paul trumps them all with an account he kept secret for over a decade. The fact that he had never shared this experience is itself part of his rhetorical strategy. Think about this for a minute. Whereas false teachers trying to boost their perceived authority point to every little personal experience they can to toot their own horns, Paul seems to have sat silently on his indescribable experience for fourteen long years. And even at this writing, he seems reluctant to let people know about it.

Unlike the media-grabbers of today, Paul didn't capitalize on his experience. We see no vying for speaking engagements or book contracts. No plans for a made-for-TV movie. No magazine articles, blogs, or websites. Paul's profound visit to "the other side" stayed where it belonged—in Paul's own heart and mind. It personally empowered him with unparalleled knowledge and confidence in the face of his apostolic ministry, but instead of exploiting his experience, he kept it under wraps. He waited until circumstances required him to reveal it.

Uncomfortable with sharing the extreme nature of his "visions and revelations of the Lord" (12:1), Paul suddenly shakes his readers out of their mode of the thrilling and supernatural. Yes, such heavenly encounters would be perfect grist for those who love to boast, but from Paul's perspective he would be much better off boasting about his weaknesses (12:5). Paul wants to make sure no one gives him credit for the glory he experienced, so he doesn't describe it in detail. He speaks not a word about his interaction with the Lord. In fact, it wasn't even permissible to do so (12:4). Instead, Paul makes sure his readers know he told the truth, and he refuses all temptations to boast further. Why? So no one could put him on a pedestal or canonize him into supersainthood. He would rather people pay attention to his lifestyle and his preaching—both of which point people to Jesus Christ instead of to himself (12:6).

## — 12:7-10 —

Shifting from the sublime heights of heavenly bliss to the mundane depths of earthly suffering, Paul draws attention to the flip side of his unparalleled spiritual experience. To keep him from succumbing to pride "because of the surpassing greatness of the revelations," God gave Paul a constant reminder of his inadequacy: a "thorn in the flesh, a messenger of Satan" (12:7).

Commentators have speculated without end on what the "thorn" represents because Paul gave no specific details. Some have suggested that it represented spiritual temptations—the urge for Paul to doubt and waver in his faith when things got hard. Others suggest the thorn refers to suffering and persecutions (like those described in 2 Cor. 11). Some have narrowed it to one specific kind of enticement: sexual temptation that tested Paul's commitment to remain celibate (cf. 1 Cor. 7:7). Still others have guessed some kind of physical handicap, disfigurement, or disease: perhaps a speech impediment, poor eyesight, a hunchback, epilepsy, malarial fevers, or even migraines.[12] Though we cannot be dogmatic, it may very well be that Paul suffered from failing eyesight. In light of his statement in Galatians 4:15—"if possible, you would have plucked out your eyes and given them to me"—many conclude that Paul suffered from some affliction of his eyes. Poor eyesight may also explain the reason Paul pointed out the "large letters" he used to write with his own hand (Gal. 6:11). In any case, so severe was the sting of this thorn that three times he pleaded with the Lord to take it away from him (2 Cor. 12:8). But each time the request was denied. The Lord, however, didn't leave him without comfort.

The Lord Himself explained to Paul why he allowed the affliction to remain: "My grace is sufficient for you, for power is perfected in weakness" (12:9). The word "perfected" is the Greek term *teleō* [5055], meaning "finished" or "fulfilled." The idea seems to be that just as Christ could cry out "It is finished" when the power of God was demonstrated through the extreme weakness of the Son's death on the cross, so in Paul's life God's all-sufficient grace demonstrated its power through the thorn in his flesh. What a paradox! Paul never forgot that "God has chosen the weak things of the world to shame the things which are strong" (1 Cor. 1:27).

Because of this truth, Paul determines to boast about his weaknesses rather than his strengths. Through those weaknesses "the power of Christ may dwell" in him (2 Cor. 12:9). You see, if Paul had it all together and had been miraculously and wonderfully healed at his first or second request, then people might be able to point to Paul's intelligence, giftedness, and devotion as the source of his adequacy. But because Paul had debilitating physical struggles as well as countless external trials, the astounding success of his ministry can be attributed only to the grace of God. No wonder, then, Paul could say, "Therefore I am well content with weaknesses, with insults, with distresses, with persecutions, with difficulties, for Christ's sake; for when I am weak, then I am strong" (12:10).

# APPLICATION: 2 CORINTHIANS 12:1-10

## When Thorns Rip at Your Adequacy

The thorns that humbled Paul and allowed him to glow with God's empowering grace are still around today. They come in various forms: trials, sickness, tragedies, difficulties, persecutions, temptations, and the stressors of life. Each of us has at least small, prickly thorns scratching at our hearts, minds, and bodies, irritating and influencing us. Yet we, too, can learn to handle these thorns with the gloves of grace.

First, *look within*. Instead of praying that the thorns would be removed, I suggest you look within and remember that God has permitted these things not for our punishment or our harm, but for our good. The thorns are not in and of themselves good. But the good that God brings out of painful situations is worthy of praise. As you think about your own trials, be careful what you call "thorns" in your life. Spouses, children, and parents aren't thorns, though they may bring opportunities to test your patience! Those relationships certainly bring about spiritual growth. But they aren't thorns. Remember that "thorns" in Paul's sense involve physical ailments, painful experiences, emotional trauma—something that will be removed in the resurrection and the new world, but are nevertheless a nagging, unavoidable presence in your life today.

What thorns are you dealing with today? Depression? A chronic illness? The effects of an accident? Emotional scars? Post-traumatic stress disorder? The aftermath of addiction? Physical debilitation? Some kind of handicap? Let me encourage you to ask the Lord to make His grace sufficient for you. If He wants to remove this thing, of course He can. But Paul's example teaches us that His strength can flow through you in the midst of your weaknesses. So embrace the weakness. Don't *love* the bad, but have faith and hope in the good that He can fashion from it.

Second, *look beyond*. Instead of staring at the stinging thorns, focus on the fragrant grace that will give you hope, strength, peace, and joy in the midst of the pain. This requires us to periodically close our eyes to the suffering around us and let our biblically informed imaginations travel to the future world. Can I suggest you memorize the following passage so you can call it to mind in the midst of dealing with the sharpest thorns?

> And I heard a loud voice from the throne, saying, "Behold, the tabernacle of God is among men, and He will dwell among them, and they shall be His people, and God Himself will be among them, and He will wipe away every tear from their eyes; and there will no longer be any death; there will no longer be any mourning, or crying, or pain; the first things have passed away." And He who sits on the throne said, "Behold, I am making all things new." And He said, "Write, for these words are faithful and true." (Rev. 21:3-5)

Paul himself caught a glimpse of the "paradise" reserved in the third heaven (2 Cor. 12:2-4). What we can only imagine, he saw. Yet we can know with confident hope that Christ will one day restore this perfect dwelling place when He returns in glory to establish His kingdom on the earth. In that day, the original curse of "thorns and thistles" will be lifted (Gen. 3:17-18; Rev. 22:3), and in paradise we will be free from all pain and suffering forever.

# Honesty Wrapped in Humility
## 2 CORINTHIANS 12:11-21

**NASB**

11 I have become foolish; you yourselves compelled me. Actually I should have been commended by you, for in no respect was I inferior to the [a]most eminent apostles, even though I am a nobody. 12 The [a]signs [b]of a true apostle were performed among you with all perseverance, by [a]signs and wonders and [c]miracles. 13 For in what respect were you treated as inferior to the rest of the churches, except that I myself did not become a burden to you? Forgive me this wrong!

14 Here for this third time I am ready to come to you, and I will not be a burden to you; for I do not seek what is yours, but you; for children are not responsible to save up for *their* parents, but parents for *their* children. 15 I will most gladly spend and be expended for your souls. If I love you more, am I to be loved less? 16 But be that as it may, I did not burden you myself; nevertheless, crafty fellow that I am, I took you in by deceit. 17 *Certainly* I have not taken advantage of you through any of those whom I have sent to you, have I? 18 I urged Titus *to go,* and I sent the brother with him. Titus did not take any advantage of you, did he? Did we not [a]conduct ourselves [b]in the same spirit *and walk* in the same steps?

19 All this time [a]you have been thinking that we are defending ourselves to you. *Actually,* it is in the sight of God that we have been speaking in Christ; and all for your upbuilding, beloved. 20 For I am afraid that perhaps when I come I may find you to be not what I wish and may be found by you to be not what you wish; that perhaps *there will be* strife, jealousy, angry tempers, disputes, slanders, gossip, arrogance, disturbances; 21 I

**NLT**

11 You have made me act like a fool. You ought to be writing commendations for me, for I am not at all inferior to these "super apostles," even though I am nothing at all. 12 When I was with you, I certainly gave you proof that I am an apostle. For I patiently did many signs and wonders and miracles among you. 13 The only thing I failed to do, which I do in the other churches, was to become a financial burden to you. Please forgive me for this wrong!

14 Now I am coming to you for the third time, and I will not be a burden to you. I don't want what you have—I want you. After all, children don't provide for their parents. Rather, parents provide for their children. 15 I will gladly spend myself and all I have for you, even though it seems that the more I love you, the less you love me.

16 Some of you admit I was not a burden to you. But others still think I was sneaky and took advantage of you by trickery. 17 But how? Did any of the men I sent to you take advantage of you? 18 When I urged Titus to visit you and sent our other brother with him, did Titus take advantage of you? No! For we have the same spirit and walk in each other's steps, doing things the same way.

19 Perhaps you think we're saying these things just to defend ourselves. No, we tell you this as Christ's servants, and with God as our witness. Everything we do, dear friends, is to strengthen you. 20 For I am afraid that when I come I won't like what I find, and you won't like my response. I am afraid that I will find quarreling, jealousy, anger, selfishness, slander, gossip, arrogance, and disorderly behavior. 21 Yes, I

am afraid that when I come again my God may humiliate me before you, and I may mourn over many of those who have sinned in the past and not repented of the impurity, [a]immorality and sensuality which they have practiced.

**12:11** [a]Or *super-apostles* **12:12** [a]Or *attesting miracles* [b]Lit *of the apostle* [c]Or *works of power* **12:18** [a]Lit *walk* [b]Or *by the same Spirit* **12:19** [a]Or *have you been thinking...?* **12:21** [a]I.e. sexual immorality

am afraid that when I come again, God will humble me in your presence. And I will be grieved because many of you have not given up your old sins. You have not repented of your impurity, sexual immorality, and eagerness for lustful pleasure.

Deception and arrogance—these things usually characterize false teachers. Because they have rejected the truth, they must concoct false doctrines and weave questionable narratives. As Paul explained to Timothy, they are "always learning and never able to come to the knowledge of the truth" (2 Tim. 3:7). They "oppose the truth" and are "rejected in regard to the faith" (2 Tim. 3:8). Such imposters will "proceed from bad to worse, deceiving and being deceived" (2 Tim. 3:13).

Besides deception, false teachers exude arrogance like a bad odor. In fact, the arrogant "lie against the truth" (Jas. 3:14). Peter writes, "Speaking out arrogant words of vanity they entice by fleshly desires, by sensuality, those who barely escape from the ones who live in error" (2 Pet. 2:18). Because the one identified as the Antichrist of the end times will be characterized by "a mouth speaking arrogant words and blasphemies" (Rev. 13:5), it should not surprise us that the spirit of antichrist today manifests itself in the same way.

What is the antidote to this devilish deception and arrogance? *Honesty and humility*. Paul exhibits both of these marks as an authentic minister of Jesus Christ in 2 Corinthians 12:11-21.

## — 12:11-14 —

In this passage, Paul returns to the subject of his relationship with the Corinthians. False teachers in Corinth had verbally assailed Paul (2 Cor. 10–11), but rather than defending their founding apostle who had invested himself on their behalf, many of the Corinthians said nothing, and some of them actually sided with Paul's opponents (12:11). Contrary to his usual style, and against his desire, Paul wrote back in self-defense, engaging in the same kind of "foolish boasting" that had been a hallmark of his adversaries rather than of his own ministry (12:11).

For marks of his authenticity in contrast to their fraudulence, Paul pointed to his willingness to suffer extreme hardship for the gospel (11:23-33). As proof of his authority, he recounted a spiritual journey to paradise fourteen years earlier that contained revelations he could not articulate to others (12:1-6). Now Paul turns to a specific demonstration of his equality with the "most eminent apostles" (12:11). Here he likely refers to the heroes of the Judaizers—those apostles to the Jews, such as Peter. We should not take this as Paul setting himself up against Peter, but rather as a means to correct the Judaizers' attempt to create a wedge between the unified apostles. Paul argues that he is just as much an apostle as those that the Judaizers were illegitimately claiming as their own.

To demonstrate the truth of his apostleship, Paul points to the "signs" performed among the Corinthians (12:12). He implies that only those truly sent by God in the power of the Spirit could do these things. This function of signs and wonders as verifying the apostles' gospel message is confirmed in Hebrews 2:3-4, when the author recalls, "After it [the gospel] was at the first spoken through the Lord, it was confirmed to us by those who heard, God also testifying with them, both by signs and wonders and by various miracles and by gifts of the Holy Spirit according to His own will."

Paul reminds them that during his stay with them they received all of the works of an authentic apostle. All those reading or hearing this letter would have instantly remembered many of the miracles—the healings, the revelations, the mighty signs that only a true prophet of God could do. What a powerful and persuasive argument for his authority! Yet at the same time, Paul mockingly apologizes that he refused to become a burden to them (2 Cor. 12:13). To what was he referring? A statement in 1 Corinthians 9 clarifies this:

> My defense to those who examine me is this: Do we not have a right to eat and drink? Do we not have a right to take along a believing wife, even as the rest of the apostles and the brothers of the Lord and Cephas? Or do only Barnabas and I not have a right to refrain from working? . . . If we sowed spiritual things in you, is it too much if we reap material things from you? If others share the right over you, do we not more? Nevertheless, we did not use this right, but we endure all things so that we will cause no hindrance to the gospel of Christ. (1 Cor. 9:3-6, 11-12)

In other words, he had every right to expect them to provide his living expenses for preaching the gospel, but he refused to rely on their support. Whereas other authentic ministers of the gospel—such as Peter, James, and John—*did* rely on the churches in which they ministered for their support, Paul did not. This, Paul says, was the only difference between his own apostolic ministry and that of the Corinthians' "favorite" apostles. With biting sarcasm, Paul ironically asks the Corinthians to forgive him for not letting them have the full apostolic experience (2 Cor. 12:13)!

Despite their extremely unkind behavior toward him, however, Paul says he wants to visit them (12:14). How could he overlook their disrespect and disloyalty? Why wasn't he angry and resentful? Because he had deliberately set aside his pride. His ministry experiences taught him how to handle abuse, rejection, persecution, and hatred. He could handle a little Corinthian confusion and waffling. Pride produces anger, resulting in resentment and retaliation. His thorn in the flesh and his confidence in the Spirit's empowerment replaced his pride with humility, his anger with forgiveness. He had no pristine public image to project or to protect; he was a "nobody" (12:11). He had no greedy desire for material goods; he wanted only a loving relationship with his children in the faith (12:14). Clearly, he was a man of honesty and humility.

### SEVEN WAYS GOD TEACHES HIS CHILDREN

1. By meeting our needs when we are helpless, He teaches us trust.
2. By making us wait for what we need or want, He teaches us patience.
3. By stretching us beyond the realm of the familiar, He teaches us vision.
4. By taking us through the consequences of wrong choices, He teaches us values.
5. By allowing us to fail and make periodic mistakes, He teaches us wisdom.
6. By permitting pain and affliction, He teaches us humility.
7. By involving us in the lives of difficult people, He teaches us unselfishness.

## — 12:15-18 —

Like any loving parent, Paul is willing to give everything he has for his spiritual children, even to "spend and be expended" for the souls of the Corinthians (12:15). What Christlike humility! Christ didn't come to be ministered to but to minister to others. He didn't come to be served but to serve (Mark 10:45). He didn't come to take but to give (Matt. 20:28). Yet this absolute surrender to the service of the gospel among the Corinthians had led to a gross inequality. Paul had poured himself out for them, but they failed to reciprocate. Here Paul returns to a theme he first introduced earlier in this letter: "O Corinthians, our heart is opened wide. You are not restrained by us, but you are restrained in your own affections. Now in a like exchange—I speak as to children—open wide to us also" (2 Cor. 6:11-13).

Another aspect of Paul's honesty and humility is his refusal to take unfair advantage of the Corinthian believers. Everything he did in his conduct remained aboveboard. His words and actions were honest and open. The language Paul uses (12:16) may be designed to directly counter the claims of his critics, who likely suggested that Paul's apparent honesty and sincerity—as well as his extreme sacrificial service to them—were all part of an elaborate, clever plot to lure the Corinthians in by deceit. False teachers will always twist the simple facts with a complex explanation to make themselves look better and their opponents look worse.

He refuses to take this insidious strategy lying down. He asks them to think for themselves: Had any of Paul's companions, such as Titus or Timothy, ever taken financial advantage of them, even long after they had been "reeled in" by Paul's alleged trap of deception (12:17-18)? Both Paul and his assistants—the pioneer church planters and those continuing the work—lived by the same standard, walked the same walk, while conducting themselves with honesty and humility during their entire ministry among them. If Paul had been deceptively fishing for converts to a devious falsehood in order to cash in later, surely the hook would have snagged them, or the net would have fallen by now. Yet instead, Paul and his associates continued to live with integrity.

## — 12:19-21 —

Paul concludes this chapter with brutal honesty regarding his hopes and fears. Though he had been defending his apostolic authority, he had done so not for selfish reasons but with honesty before God for the sake of the Corinthians (12:19). Yet he fears that when he comes, he will find the Corinthians still in disarray, that his efforts at confronting their wrongs will have fallen on deaf ears, that he will be utterly disappointed to the point of open mourning in their presence (12:20-21).

If that were to happen, then they would find an apostle Paul they didn't expect—and one they would not like (12:20). They would not find an open-armed father beaming with pride over his children, but a stern-faced disciplinarian ready to deal out justice. From the beginning of this letter, Paul had been trying to preempt such a sorrowful visit. He wrote, "But I determined this for my own sake, that I would not come to you in sorrow again" (2:1). What things would make Paul sorrowful?

He rattles off a brief sampling of what have become typically Corinthian problems: "strife, jealousy, angry tempers, disputes, slanders, gossip, arrogance, disturbances, . . . impurity, immorality and sensuality" (12:20-21). Add to this their potential failure to follow through on their promise of financial support for the Jerusalem church (9:3-4), and Paul's visit to them would be nothing short of a disaster!

By the end of 2 Corinthians 12, the apostle has made his expectations clear. He has openly shared both his fears and his hopes. He has exhibited complete honesty in a spirit of true humility. Now the ball is in the Corinthians' court. Would they pick it up and play by the rules on Paul's team? Or would they pass it to Paul's rivals and join them in their unfair opposition?

# APPLICATION: 2 CORINTHIANS 12:11-21

## Responding with Honesty and Humility

In our churches, as in our families, people will hurt us. This is the reality of any close and meaningful relationship built on honesty and humility. In the close-quarters living to which we are called, we can easily offend others, and be easily offended. We can hurt each other's feelings, harm each other's reputations, and break each other's relationships. I wish I could say that among brothers and sisters in Christ who genuinely love each other, these things are an exception rather than the rule. But the truth is, the closer we allow ourselves to get to each other, the more the sharp edges of our personalities jab and scrape each other.

How do we respond when someone has offended or mistreated us? What do we do when we've been wronged, slighted, or humiliated? Paul's parental response to the Corinthians, who had belittled, betrayed, and berated him, gives us a great example to follow. His model of honesty and humility in 2 Corinthians 12:11-21 produces several questions we can ask ourselves.

First, *Is my image a little too important to me?* In humility, Paul wrote, "I am a nobody" (12:11). Can we approach ridicule and mistreatment with the same attitude? Or is our knee-jerk reaction to respond in defense of our reputation? Is responding for the sake of our public image a pursuit of honesty?

Second, *Am I falling into the trap of keeping score?* Paul said he wouldn't take a penny from the Corinthians (12:14). He had given sacrificially but never demanded or expected anything in return. In fact, he remained willing to "spend and be expended" for their sakes. Though they should have responded with love and respect, he did not make these a condition for his love for them. Are your own relationships built on a give-and-take desire for equality, or are you willing to give repeatedly, even if you see no signs of a "return on investment"?

Third, *Do I flatter other people for my own advantage?* Paul made it clear that he never took advantage of the Corinthians—either personally or through his representatives (12:16-18). He didn't say or do just enough good to string them along in feigned friendship, only to load them down with a list of hefty demands. He didn't have ulterior motives when dealing with those believers in Corinth. People with such motives engage in flattery, not friendship. Friendship doesn't try to manipulate others for personal gain.

As we try to develop authentic, vulnerable relationships with those in our church body, we are wise to do so with honesty and humility. And when those brothers and sisters in Christ inevitably let us down, we need to remember these characteristics of Christlike love.

# Passing the Test of Faith
## 2 CORINTHIANS 13:1-14

**NASB**

1 This is the third time I am coming
to you. EVERY [a]FACT [b]IS TO BE CON-
FIRMED BY THE [c]TESTIMONY OF TWO
OR THREE WITNESSES. 2 I have previ-
ously said when present the second
time, and though now absent I say
in advance to those who have sinned
in the past and to all the rest *as well,*
that if I come again I will not spare
*anyone,* 3 since you are seeking for
proof of the Christ who speaks in me,
and who is not weak toward you, but
mighty in you. 4 For indeed He was
crucified because of weakness, yet

**NLT**

1 This is the third time I am coming
to visit you (and as the Scriptures
say, "The facts of every case must be
established by the testimony of two
or three witnesses"*). 2 I have already
warned those who had been sinning
when I was there on my second
visit. Now I again warn them and all
others, just as I did before, that next
time I will not spare them.

3 I will give you all the proof you
want that Christ speaks through me.
Christ is not weak when he deals
with you; he is powerful among you.
4 Although he was crucified in weak-
ness, he now lives by the power of

He lives because of the power of God.
For we also are weak [a]in Him, yet we
will live with Him because of the
power of God *directed* toward you.
5 Test yourselves *to see* if you are
in the faith; examine yourselves!
Or do you not recognize this about
yourselves, that Jesus Christ is in
you—unless indeed you [a]fail the
test? 6 But I trust that you will real-
ize that we ourselves [a]do not fail the
test. 7 Now we pray to God that you
do no wrong; not that we ourselves
may appear approved, but that you
may do what is right, even though
we may [a]appear unapproved. 8 For
we can do nothing against the truth,
but *only* for the truth. 9 For we rejoice
when we ourselves are weak but
you are strong; this we also pray for,
[a]that you be made complete. 10 For
this reason I am writing these things
while absent, so that when present I
*need* not use severity, in accordance
with the authority which the Lord
gave me for building up and not for
tearing down.
11 Finally, brethren, [a]rejoice, [b]be
made complete, be comforted, be
like-minded, live in peace; and the
God of love and peace will be with
you. 12 Greet one another with a holy
kiss. 13 All the [a]saints greet you.
14 The grace of the Lord Jesus
Christ, and the love of God, and the
fellowship of the Holy Spirit, be with
you all.

**13:1** [a]Lit *word* [b]Lit *shall be* [c]Lit *mouth*
**13:4** [a]One early ms reads *with Him* **13:5** [a]Lit *are unapproved* **13:6** [a]Lit *are not unapproved*
**13:7** [a]Lit *be as* **13:9** [a]Lit *your completion*
**13:11** [a]Or *farewell* [b]Or *put yourselves in order*
**13:13** [a]Or *holy ones*

God. We, too, are weak, just as Christ
was, but when we deal with you we
will be alive with him and will have
God's power.
5 Examine yourselves to see if your
faith is genuine. Test yourselves.
Surely you know that Jesus Christ is
among you*; if not, you have failed
the test of genuine faith. 6 As you test
yourselves, I hope you will recognize
that we have not failed the test of ap-
ostolic authority.
7 We pray to God that you will not
do what is wrong by refusing our
correction. I hope we won't need to
demonstrate our authority when we
arrive. Do the right thing before we
come—even if that makes it look like
we have failed to demonstrate our
authority. 8 For we cannot oppose
the truth, but must always stand for
the truth. 9 We are glad to seem weak
if it helps show that you are actually
strong. We pray that you will become
mature.
10 I am writing this to you before
I come, hoping that I won't need to
deal severely with you when I do
come. For I want to use the authority
the Lord has given me to strengthen
you, not to tear you down.
11 Dear brothers and sisters,* I
close my letter with these last words:
Be joyful. Grow to maturity. Encour-
age each other. Live in harmony and
peace. Then the God of love and
peace will be with you.
12 Greet each other with a sacred
kiss. 13 All of God's people here send
you their greetings.
14*May the grace of the Lord Jesus
Christ, the love of God, and the
fellowship of the Holy Spirit be with
you all.

**13:1** Deut 19:15. **13:5** Or *in you.* **13:11** Greek *Brothers.* **13:14** Some English translations include verse 13 as part of verse 12, and then verse 14 becomes verse 13.

From pop tests to blood tests, from bar exams to eye exams, testing is a regular part of life. Aside from medical, academic, and professional tests, we also encounter personal tests of faith: sickness, affliction, broken dreams, failures, peer pressures, moral temptations, and even doubts and fears.

Did you know you can prepare for these tests before they come? We can all "study" for these exams by turning to God's Word for the answers to the most important questions in life: Who is God? What does He expect from us? What should I believe? How should I live in light of that? As we carefully work our way through these questions, we will become increasingly better prepared to handle life's unannounced personal tests when they arrive.

In the last several chapters of 2 Corinthians, Paul has been building up to a final comprehensive exam for the wayward Corinthian church. Not only would there be objective outside evaluation (13:1-4), but the Corinthians would be called on to analyze themselves (13:5-6). If they would follow through on this and shore up their shortcomings, they would be complete in Christ, built up in their holy faith in the triune God.

## — 13:1-4 —

Every examination must have a grader, somebody who can judge whether a person has passed or failed, and to what degree. In the case of the Corinthian church, Paul reveals the standard by which they would be critiqued and the seriousness of the evaluation's outcome. Rather than sending assistants, messengers, or observers, Paul would visit the church *personally*. In fact, it would be the apostle's third visit (13:1).[13]

Paul attaches significance to his third visit. The Old Testament Law required that final judgment in a matter could be rendered on the basis of "two or three witnesses" (Deut. 19:15). The background of this text points to a subtle threat: Judgment was imminent. If the Corinthians did not heed his first and second warnings, he would "not spare anyone" (2 Cor. 13:2). Paul is strenuously exhorting them to clean up their lives to avoid a basement-to-attic housecleaning upon his arrival. In other words, a test was coming. Paul would slip on white gloves, open the doors to the dark corners of their lives, and run his fingers over every shelf.

The Corinthians had criticized Paul for seeming strong in his letters but being weak in person (10:10). In previous visits, he had not

## PAUL'S MYSTERIOUS SECOND VISIT

### 2 CORINTHIANS 13:1

A major question of chronology has left many commentators of 2 Corinthians perplexed: How many times prior to writing 2 Corinthians did Paul visit Corinth? Everybody agrees that Paul founded the church in Corinth during his first visit between AD 50 and 52. About a year after that, he wrote a very brief letter to the Corinthian church now lost to us (1 Cor. 5:9). Then around AD 54 Paul wrote 1 Corinthians from Ephesus to address a series of major problems in the church reported to him by messengers and travelers from Corinth (Acts 19:1; 1 Cor. 1:11; 16:17). Though he intended to travel to Corinth by land after making his way north through Macedonia (1 Cor. 16:5), he received troubling news from Corinth.

At this point the question of an "interim visit" surfaces. In 2 Corinthians 2:1, Paul mentions that he didn't desire to come to them "in sorrow again." Then in 2 Corinthians 12:14; 13:1 he mentions that his next visit to them would be his "third." Therefore, many scholars propose an unrecorded brief second visit from Ephesus to Corinth and back again.[14] Following this visit, Paul wrote 2 Corinthians from Macedonia, having heard the latest update about the Corinthians from Titus (7:5-6).

Some commentators, however, see the idea of a second visit between 1 and 2 Corinthians as unlikely: "Paul had carefully avoided visiting Corinth for some time. The whole tenor of the Epistles, moreover, implies that he had not been to Corinth since his long stay there, since it would have been hardly possible, had such a visit been paid, that some more distinct notice of it should not appear in letters so overflowing with personal details as these."[15] To solve this problem, some have proposed an unmentioned second visit shortly after his very first departure from Corinth but before writing the original lost letter (prior to 1 Corinthians).[16]

Another solution suggests that Paul's "painful visit" was not made personally, but through a proxy bearing a letter from him—a reference either to 1 Corinthians or to the "sorrowful letter" mentioned in 2 Corinthians 7:8, "For though I caused you sorrow by my letter, I do not regret it; though I did regret it—for I see that that letter caused you sorrow, though only for a while." Paul used the same Greek term for "sorrow" in reference to both his interim letter and the theorized visit in 2 Corinthians 2:1-4.

> But I determined this for my own sake, that I would not come to you in sorrow again. For if I cause you sorrow, who then makes me glad but the one whom I made sorrowful? This is the very thing I wrote you, so that when I came, I would not have sorrow from those who ought to make me rejoice; having confidence in you all that my joy would be the joy of you all. For out of much affliction and anguish of heart I wrote to you with many tears; not

so that you would be made sorrowful, but that you might know the love which I have especially for you. (2:1-4)

Therefore, it is possible that Paul counted the letters he had written (1 Corinthians or the "sorrowful letter" or even both) as a "second visit" to the Corinthian Christians. That Paul regarded the letters read by his authoritative delegates like Timothy or Titus as somehow mediating his presence is confirmed when he wrote, "For I, on my part, *though absent in body but present in spirit*, have already judged him who has so committed this, *as though I were present*" (1 Cor. 5:3, emphasis mine). Calvin wrote, "He came the first time in sadness by an Epistle, that they might not have occasion to feel this severity when he was present with them."[17]

I find it unlikely that Paul made a quick trip to Corinth between 1 and 2 Corinthians for two main reasons: 1) During this time, he wrote the "sorrowful letter" in order to avoid a painful visit (2 Cor. 2:1-4); and 2) In 2 Corinthians he had to defend his delay in coming to them against the charge of failing to follow through on his intention as expressed in 1 Corinthians (2 Cor. 1:15-17). Had he made an interim personal visit, this explanation for why he did not visit them wouldn't make sense. Therefore, I prefer either a) an unmentioned second visit after his original departure but before writing 1 Corinthians; or b) a "visit by proxy" or presence "in spirit" in order to deliver Paul's judgment on a particular issue and to make sure his strong instructions in 1 Corinthians were being followed.

appeared particularly authoritative, commanding, or strong. His gentle demeanor had raised doubts about his apostolic authority—that Christ was actually speaking in and through him (13:3). Paul explains that his impending severity would erase all misguided judgments about his authority. When he came, they would have no further questions regarding whether Christ spoke through him. Paul's apparent waffling between "weakness" and "power" reflected Christ's own ministry—"He was crucified because of weakness, yet He lives because of the power of God" (13:4). Likewise, the apostles sometimes appeared "weak" for the sake of preaching the gospel, but when the situation called for it, they could direct the authority of God toward those who needed it.

## — 13:5-10 —

Paul was coming to test the Corinthians soon, and therefore he vigorously urged the Corinthians to prepare themselves for the exam: "Test yourselves to see if you are in the faith; examine yourselves!" (13:5). As law school graduates hoping to pass the bar exam will drill themselves with practice tests in anticipation of exam day, so also the Corinthians should drill themselves to be ready for Paul's return.

Underscore the word "yourselves" (13:5): It occurs three times in this verse. Not only is the term emphasized by repetition, but it is emphasized in Greek by being placed out of the normal order of the sentence structure. A more literal rendering might be: "You yourselves test . . . you yourselves prove . . . that Jesus Christ is in you." The emphasis is on each one of us examining ourselves to see whether Jesus is, in reality, in us. Admittedly, this relates to our initial conversion and salvation, but it can also refer to Christ working in and through us in our daily walk with Him. This test doesn't ask how faithful we are to church attendance, how well we say mealtime prayers, or how many Bible verses we have memorized. The essential exam determines whether we genuinely stand within the circle of faith with Jesus Christ.

The self-examination has three parts: a test, a proof, and a perception.

| EXAM PART | GREEK WORD | QUESTIONS TO ASK |
|---|---|---|
| Test | *peirazō* [3985], "test" | Do you have a personal relationship with Christ? Have you experienced any significant changes in your life through knowing Him? Do you experience His leading, His presence, His peace, His joy? |
| Proof | *dokimazō* [1381], "examine" | Can you show any evidence that you have really experienced the new birth? How different are your thoughts, habits, goals, relationships, and feelings from the world around you or from the way you used to be? |
| Perception | *epiginōskō* [1921], "recognize" | Do you recognize the work of the Spirit in your life? Do others recognize this? Are you growing in knowledge, confidence, and peace? Are you producing the fruit of the Spirit (Gal. 5:22-23)? |

Please note that Paul isn't urging the Corinthians to doubt their salvation, although this passage is often taken that way. Yes, Paul believed that false teachers among the Corinthians lacked true faith in Christ, so for them such a test would demonstrate their lack of salvation. But for the most part, he regarded the Corinthians as brothers and sisters in Christ. The whole context of 2 Corinthians 13 pertains to their willingness to respond positively to Paul's correction—that is, spiritual growth or "sanctification." They would demonstrate the authenticity of their relationship with Christ when they responded positively to Christ's commands through Paul. When Paul encouraged the Corinthians to examine whether they were "in the faith," it was his way of saying, "Show me that you are a believer. Live like it! Obey the words of Christ! Do those things that demonstrate without a doubt the sincerity of your faith!"

Paul hoped that after all his evidence and arguments authenticating the genuineness of his ministry, the Corinthians would realize that he and his fellow apostles "do not fail the test" (13:6). Because they clearly exhibited the attitudes and actions of devoted servants of Christ, they had the right to turn the spotlight on the Corinthians and ask them to demonstrate their own authenticity.

Like parents praying for their children prior to a big test, Paul prays that the Corinthians will pass the test, that they will "do no wrong," regardless of their attitudes toward the apostles (13:7). He is concerned that his students learn, not that he gains a reputation as a good teacher. It is for their sake, not his, that he hopes they pass the test. Like all good teachers, Paul is committed to the pursuit of truth (13:8). This is why he could never lower the standards, overlook accountability, or let the Corinthians get away with their slapdash attitudes and actions.

Paul is like those excellent teachers who beam with delight at their students when they "get it," when they become "complete" or "mature" in their learning (13:9). Like any caring instructor, Paul wants his disciples in Corinth to step up. He does not want to show up with a rod of correction. He wants to build them up, not tear them down (13:10). The manner of his coming, however, would completely depend on how well the Corinthians prepared themselves for the examination of their lives and their church.

## — 13:11-14 —

As Paul nears the end of this strong, firm, and convicting letter to the Corinthians, he first provides six rapid-fire practical commands for how all believers are to conduct their lives (13:11-12). As you read through these, consider that Paul associates these six brief exhortations with a powerful promise that "the God of love and peace will be with you" (13:11):

*Rejoice.* This joyous response to life's often trying circumstances could come only if the Corinthians heeded Paul's warnings and admonitions. If they heeded him, they would find freedom from the legalism of the Judaizers, liberty from the consequences of unrepentant sin, and laughter from the deep-down joy of the Holy Spirit.

*Be made complete.* The Greek word *katartizō* [2675] refers to being ready or prepared, supplying what is missing to bring about full usefulness. The Corinthians were to be ready for anything—especially ready to change false beliefs and repent of wrong practices.

*Be comforted.* On the use of the Greek word *parakaleō* [3870] here, Philip Hughes writes, "It seems preferable to translate it here in its other sense, namely, 'be admonished' . . . that is, respond to the plea which this epistle conveys."[18] In other words, comfort would come when they heeded Paul's exhortation.

*Be like-minded.* Literally, the Corinthians were to "think the same thing." This excludes outright rebellion and conflict, and it also eradicates schisms, factions, parties, and harsh controversies. When we are like-minded toward Christ, we will be like-minded toward others—unselfish, transparent, and supportive.

*Live in peace.* This was Paul's goal for all the churches—that they bear with one another without conflict. Sadly, neither the church in Corinth nor most churches throughout history, even into our own day, have completely modeled this. Yet we must all strive for peace in our relationships with fellow members of the body of Christ.

*Greet one another with a holy kiss.* Paul desires that the Corinthians concretely express their affection for each other, not merely feel or say it. In today's culture, a "holy kiss" might take the form of a comforting embrace, an arm around another's shoulders, a reassuring pat on the back, or a tangible gift of our affection and appreciation.[19]

After extending a greeting from the fellow saints with him (13:13), Paul ends this grand epistle with a beautiful triune blessing. What a fitting way to conclude our journey through this second letter to the Corinthians, recalling the grace, love, and fellowship we enjoy through an eternal relationship with the one true God, through His Son, Jesus Christ, by the power of the indwelling Holy Spirit (13:14):

> The grace of the Lord Jesus Christ,
> and the love of God,
> and the fellowship of the Holy Spirit,
> be with you all.

# APPLICATION: 2 CORINTHIANS 13:1-14

## Two Reminders to Retain the Message

Paul's second letter to the Corinthians ends with wonderful words that remind us that the entire Godhead—Father, Son, and Holy Spirit—is involved in our salvation and Christian lives. In fact, the whole book has given us timely reminders of timeless truths regarding the precious calling we have in ministry to one another. We've learned so much from 2 Corinthians that it's hard to put our arms around it all. Let me share two reminders to help us retain the message of this book.

First, *release the love of God, wherever you may be.* Paul did that with the Corinthians. When they were going astray, he lassoed their wayward hearts and corralled them back into the fold. Yet he did it in love. Yes, there were some sharp words of confrontation, but even these were inspired by his deep love for, and devotion to, them. When you release the love of God, it will serve as a magnet, drawing even the most hardened, cynical, or rebellious sinner back to the heart of God.

Second, *remember the love of God, whatever may happen to you.* Many reading this have gone through some extremely tough times. Your life has imploded, and you've had to face trying circumstances you're not sure you can endure. Paul, too, passed through these stages of life and ministry. And God was with him every step of the way. Never forget this vital fact: God is there in the midst of your struggles. He knows your pain. He loves you with such depth that He gave His Son to redeem you from sin, death, and despair. And He sent His Spirit to draw you closer into fellowship with Him and to unite you to His body, the church. If you can remember the light of His love when darkness closes in, the message of 2 Corinthians will have done its work in your life.

# ENDNOTES

## 1 CORINTHIANS

### INTRODUCTION

1 F. W. Grosheide, *The First Epistle to the Corinthians*, The New International Commentary on the New Testament (Grand Rapids: Eerdmans, 1953), 13.
2 Marion L. Soards, *1 Corinthians*, New International Biblical Commentary (Peabody, MA: Hendrickson Publishers, 1999), 3–4.
3 Wendell Willis, "Corinth," in *Eerdmans Dictionary of the Bible*, ed. David Noel Freedman (Grand Rapids: Eerdmans, 2000), 279–280.
4 See a brief summary and description in Rivka Gonen, *Biblical Holy Places: An Illustrated Guide* (Jerusalem: The Jerusalem Publishing House, 2000; published for North America by Mahwah, NJ: Paulist Press, 2000), 31–33.

### OPENING GREETING AND PRAYER (1 CORINTHIANS 1:1-9)

1 See Craig S. Keener, *1–2 Corinthians*, The New Cambridge Bible Commentary, ed. Ben Witherington III (Cambridge: Cambridge University Press, 2005), 20.
2 Compare the three names in 1 and 2 Thessalonians (Paul, Silvanus, and Timothy), as well as those letters' use of the first person plural, indicating the entire apostolic team stood behind the contents of the letter, regardless of which of the three actually penned the words of the letter on behalf of Paul. The letters to the Corinthians, on the other hand, come directly by Paul's authority.
3 F. F. Bruce, ed., *1 and 2 Corinthians* (Greenwood, SC: The Attic Press, 1971), 30.
4 After the Reformation, theologians would relate this initial "setting apart" to the one-time experience of "justification," reserving the term "sanctification" for the believer's subsequent experience of being progressively made more holy. Though distinguishing these terms in theological discussion helps to avoid confusion, the New Testament does not use these terms in the same way as later theologians. The Bible does express salvation in terms of a one time past conversion, an ongoing present process of spiritual growth, and a future experience of resurrection and glorification, but the terms and images used for these three "tenses" of salvation vary in Scripture.
5 See Gary Smalley and John Trent, *The Blessing* (Nashville: Thomas Nelson, 1986), 104–107.
6 David Prior, *The Message of 1 Corinthians: Life in the Local Church*, The Bible Speaks Today (Downers Grove, IL: InterVarsity, 1985), 23.

### REBUKING DIVISIONS AND FOLLY (1 CORINTHIANS 1:10–3:23)

1 William Barclay, *The Letters to the Corinthians*, The New Daily Study Bible, 3rd rev. ed. (Louisville: Westminster John Knox, 2002), 20.

[2] Helen H. Lemmel, "Turn Your Eyes upon Jesus," in *The Hymnal for Worship and Celebration*, ed. Tom Fettke (Waco, TX: Word Music, 1986), no. 335.
[3] Michael P. Green, "The Meaning of Cross-Bearing," *Bibliotheca Sacra* 140 (April 1983): 124–27.
[4] See S. G. F. Brandon, *Jesus and the Zealots* (New York: Scribner's, 1967).
[5] Tertullian, *On the Flesh of Christ* 4.
[6] Ibid., 5.
[7] Robert Jamiesen, A. R. Fausset, and David Brown, *A Commentary, Critical, Experimental, and Practical, on the Old and New Testaments,* vol. 3 (Grand Rapids: Eerdmans, 1984), 287.
[8] Keener, *1–2 Corinthians*, 34–35.
[9] Donald W. Burdick, "*Oida* and *Ginōskō* in the Pauline Epistles," in *New Dimensions in New Testament Study*, eds. Richard N. Longenecker and Merrill C. Tenney (Grand Rapids: Zondervan, 1974), 344–356.
[10] Gregory the Great, preface to *Moralia* vol. 1, 4.
[11] Ralph Earle, *Word Meanings in the New Testament* (Grand Rapids: Baker, 1986), 221.
[12] Keener, *1–2 Corinthians*, 43.
[13] Barclay, *Letters to the Corinthians*, 42.

## CORRECTING ILLS AND IMMORALITY (1 CORINTHIANS 4:1–6:20)

[1] Keener, *1–2 Corinthians*, 43.
[2] A. T. Robertson, *The Epistles of Paul*, vol. 4, Word Pictures in the New Testament (Nashville: Broadman, 1931), 106.
[3] Prior, *The Message of 1 Corinthians*, 65.
[4] We know that Paul had committed to a single life, but we can't be sure whether he was never married or a widower (1 Cor. 7:8). In any case, it seems that if Paul had had any children, he would have made mention of them somewhere in his relatively large collection of writings.
[5] John White and Ken Blue, *Healing the Wounded: The Costly Love of Church Discipline* (Downers Grove, IL: InterVarsity, 1985), 66.
[6] See 1 Cor. 4:6, 18, 19; 5:2; 8:1; 13:4. The seventh occurrence is in Col. 2:18.
[7] Barclay, *Letters to the Corinthians*, 53.
[8] Ibid., 58–59.
[9] Gustav Friedrich Hertzberg and William Nickerson Bates, *Ancient Greece*, A History of All Nations, vol. 3 (Philadelphia: Lea Brothers, 1905), 326.
[10] Keener, *1–2 Corinthians*, 52.
[11] W. Harold Mare, "1 Corinthians," in *The Expositor's Bible Commentary,* vol. 10., ed. Frank E. Gaebelein (Grand Rapids: Zondervan, 1976), 221.
[12] Prior, *The Message of 1 Corinthians*, 107.
[13] Keener, *1–2 Corinthians*, 57.

## STRENGTHENING FAMILY AND FELLOWSHIP (1 CORINTHIANS 7:1–10:33)

[1] Keener, *1–2 Corinthians*, 62.
[2] Johannes P. Louw and Eugene A. Nida, eds., *Greek-English Lexicon of the New Testament Based on Semantic Domains,* vol. 1, *Introduction and Domains,* 2nd ed. (New York: United Bible Societies, 1988), § 13.141. The word appears only here in the New Testament.
[3] See 4 Maccabees 16:9.
[4] Mike Mason, *The Mystery of Marriage: As Iron Sharpens Iron* (Portland: Multnomah, 1985), 45.

5 Keener notes that the identity of the men and their virgins in this passage "was undoubtedly clearer to the Corinthians than to subsequent interpreters" (see Keener, *1–2 Corinthians*, 71).
6 Ittai Gradel, *Emperor Worship and Roman Religion*, Oxford Classical Monographs (Oxford, UK: Oxford University Press, 2004), 16; Kathryn Hinds, *Everyday Life in the Roman Empire* (Tarrytown, NY: Marshall Cavendish, 2010), 231; William Smith and Charles Anthon, eds., *A Dictionary of Greek and Roman Antiquities*, 3rd ed. (New York: Harper and Brothers, 1843), 845.
7 Frederic Louis Godet, *Commentary on First Corinthians* (1889; repr., Grand Rapids: Kregel, 1977), 401.
8 Earle, *Word Meanings*, 230.
9 In a sacrifice fly, the batter hits the ball high into the air to the outfield, where it's sure to be caught by an outfielder. But the ball is hit so far away from third base and home plate that it takes longer for the outfielder to throw the ball to home than it takes for the third-base runner to score a run. The result? The hitter gets an out, but the third-base runner races home and wins the game. The batter sacrifices himself for the team.
10 Barclay, *Letters to the Corinthians*, 95.
11 Pausanias, *Description of Greece* 5.2.4.
12 Polybius, *Histories* 2.12.8.
13 Strabo, *Geography* 8.6.20.
14 John S. Howson, *The Metaphors of St. Paul*, 2nd ed. (London: Strahan, 1869), 153.
15 Alexander Solzhenitsyn, *One Day in the Life of Ivan Denisovich* (New York: E. P. Dutton, 1963), 158.
16 Grant R. Osborne, *The Hermeneutical Spiral: A Comprehensive Introduction to Biblical Hermeneutics*, 2nd ed. (Downers Grove, IL: InterVarsity, 2006), 328.
17 Mare, "1 Corinthians," 249.
18 Godet, *Commentary on First Corinthians*, 487–88.
19 R. C. H. Lenski, *The Interpretation of 1 Corinthians*, Lenski's Commentary on the New Testament (Minneapolis: Augsburg Fortress, 2008), 415.

## ORDERING CHURCH AND WORSHIP (1 CORINTHIANS 11:1–14:40)

1 Keener, *1–2 Corinthians*, 90.
2 David K. Lowery, "1 Corinthians," in *The Bible Knowledge Commentary*, vol. 2, ed. John F. Walvoord and Roy B. Zuck (Wheaton: Victor Books, 1983), 529.
3 For an accessible discussion on both the essential equality and role distinctions between men and women, see Alexander Strauch, *Men and Women, Equal Yet Different: A Brief Study of the Biblical Passages on Gender* (Colorado Springs: Lewis and Roth, 1999).
4 Keener, *1–2 Corinthians*, 94.
5 For historical treatments of the relationship between the Lord's Supper and the Love Feast, see Everett Ferguson, "Lord's Supper and Love Feast," *Christian Studies* 21 (2005–2006): 27–38; and Marcel Metzger, *History of the Liturgy: The Major Stages*, trans. Madeleine M. Beaumont (Collegeville, MN: Liturgical Press, 1997), 21–22.
6 See Ralph P. Martin, *Worship in the Early Church* (1964; repr., Grand Rapids: Eerdmans, 1975), 110–129.
7 Metzger, *History of the Liturgy*, 41.
8 Paul uses the Greek phrase *peri de* ("now concerning") six times in 1 Corinthians, each indicating an abrupt transition away from one topic to another (7:1; 7:25; 8:1; 12:1; 16:1; 16:12).
9 Louw and Nida, *Greek-English Lexicon*, 57.91.

[10] These essential truths include major doctrinal issues such as the Trinity, the full deity and full humanity of Christ, the Virgin Birth, the atoning death of Christ to pay for our sins, the miraculous bodily resurrection of Christ, the promise of His future return, salvation by grace alone through faith alone in Christ alone, the inspiration and inerrancy of Scripture, and similar orthodox, non-negotiable truths.
[11] Though 1 Corinthians 14:39 urges the church to "desire earnestly to prophesy," this corporate exhortation must be read in light of the whole teaching of 1 Corinthians 14, which clearly acknowledges that not all are prophets and therefore not all will be able to prophesy (1 Cor. 12:29). The idea seems to be that the attitude of the church as a whole (not individuals within the church) should be to desire the presence of prophesying in the congregation.
[12] Prior, *The Message of 1 Corinthians*, 211.
[13] See feature "Gift, Gifts, and Fruit" on page 183 for further distinctions between the baptism of the Holy Spirit and being filled with the Holy Spirit.
[14] Ray C. Stedman, *Body Life*, 2nd ed. (Glendale, CA: Regal, 1979), 56.
[15] Robertson, *The Epistles of Paul*, 176.
[16] Gerhard Kittel, ed., *Theological Dictionary of the New Testament*, trans. and ed. Geoffrey W. Bromiley (Grand Rapids: Eerdmans, 1987), 1:37.
[17] Keener, *1–2 Corinthians*, 108; Lowery, "1 Corinthians," 535.
[18] Earle, *Word Meanings*, 239.
[19] Keener, *1–2 Corinthians*, 110.
[20] Barclay, *Letters to the Corinthians*, 148.
[21] John Godfrey Saxe, "The Blind Men and the Elephant," in *The Poems of John Godfrey Saxe: Complete in One Volume* (Boston: Ticknor and Fields, 1868), 259.
[22] Ibid., 260.
[23] For more information see John F. MacArthur Jr., *Charismatic Chaos* (Grand Rapids: Zondervan, 1992); Robert G. Gromacki, *The Modern Tongues Movement* (Phillipsburg, NJ: P&R, 1972); Spiros Zodhiates, *Speaking in Tongues and Public Worship: First Corinthians*, Exegetical Commentary Series (Chattanooga, TN: AMG Publishers, 1997).
[24] The Bible lists spiritual gifts in only four passages (Rom. 12; 1 Cor. 12; Eph. 4; 1 Pet. 4). The gift of tongues is listed only in 1 Corinthians 12, and it is placed last or next to last each time. Note especially the order of priority in 1 Corinthians 12:28.
[25] John F. Walvoord, "Contemporary Issues in the Doctrine of the Holy Spirit Part IV: Spiritual Gifts Today," *Bibliotheca Sacra* 130 (1973): 319.
[26] Though the longer ending of Mark was likely not an original part of Mark's inspired Gospel, it is used here as an early Christian historical testimony to the nature of the signs and wonders as confirming the apostles' message.
[27] See *1 Clement* 5.3–4; 42.1–3; Ignatius *Magnesians* 13.1; Ignatius *Romans* 4.3; Polycarp *Philippians* 9.1; Tertullian, *Against Marcion* 4.5.
[28] "The Muratorian Fragment," in Bruce M. Metzger, *The Canon of the New Testament: Its Origin, Development, and Significance* (Oxford: Clarendon Press, 1987), 307 (italics mine).
[29] See Acts 2:1-13; 10:46-48; 19:6.
[30] Prior, *The Message of 1 Corinthians*, 259–261.
[31] Neil Babcox, *A Search for Charismatic Reality* (Portland, OR: Multnomah, 1985), 69.

## CONCERNING DEATH AND RESURRECTION (1 CORINTHIANS 15:1-58)

[1] Louw and Nida, *Greek-English Lexicon*, 23.55.
[2] John R. W. Stott, *Basic Christianity*, 2nd ed. (Downers Grove, IL: InterVarsity, 1971), 21.
[3] Prior, *The Message of 1 Corinthians*, 265.

[4] William Barclay, *The Letters to the Corinthians*, 2nd ed., The Daily Study Bible Series (Philadelphia: Westminster, 1956), 167–68.
[5] See Mare, "1 Corinthians," 287–88.
[6] Keener, *1–2 Corinthians*, 128; Lowery, "1 Corinthians," 544.
[7] Jim Elliot, *The Journals of Jim Elliot*, ed. Elisabeth Elliot (Old Tappan, NJ: Fleming H. Revell, 1978), 174.
[8] Ignatius, *Ephesians* 7.1; *Romans* 5.1; *Smyrnaeans* 4.1.
[9] Barclay, *Letters to the Corinthians*, 2nd ed., 158.
[10] Louw and Nida, *Greek-English Lexicon*, 79.2.
[11] Keener, *1–2 Corinthians*, 133.
[12] Paul alludes to the full realization of passages in the Old Testament that speak of God's victory over death (e.g., Isa. 25:8; Hos. 13:14).

## CONCLUDING INSTRUCTIONS AND WARNINGS (1 CORINTHIANS 16:1-24)

[1] Keener, *1–2 Corinthians*, 136.
[2] Fritz Rienecker, *A Linguistic Key to the Greek New Testament*, ed. Cleon L. Rogers Jr. (Grand Rapids: Zondervan, 1980), 448.
[3] It is likely that Paul received some of his information about the spiritual and moral condition of the church at Corinth from these men.
[4] Prior, *The Message of 1 Corinthians*, 283.
[5] We find it in the very early Christian writing *The Didache* (dated by recent historians at about AD 50–70) at *Did.* 10.6, indicating that its use had spilled over from Jewish communities into Greek Christian writings quite early.
[6] Keener, *1–2 Corinthians*, 141.
[7] Larry W. Hurtado, *At the Origins of Christian Worship: The Context and Character of Earliest Christian Devotion* (Grand Rapids: Eerdmans, 2000), 44.
[8] John Chrysostom, *Homilies on the Epistles of Paul to the Corinthians* 44.4. Nicene and Post-Nicene Fathers, Series 1, vol. 12, ed. Philip Schaff (Grand Rapids: Eerdmans, 2009), 265.

# 2 CORINTHIANS

## INTRODUCTION

[1] Some commentators propose a brief visit directly from Ephesus to Corinth and back, not mentioned in Acts 19, which failed to end the controversy (David K. Lowery, "1 Corinthians," in *The Bible Knowledge Commentary, New Testament Edition*, ed. John F. Walvoord and Roy B. Zuck [Wheaton: Victor Books, 1983], 551–552). This would have been Paul's original "painful visit" (2 Cor. 2:1, NLT). There's no reason to reject this theory as a possibility. It seems better, however, to reconcile his inability to come to Corinth prior to Macedonia (described in 2 Cor. 1:15-23), as an indication that he had not yet visited them between 1 Corinthians and 2 Corinthians. Reference to another "painful visit" may, in fact, refer to the hardships he endured during his very first visit to Corinth (Acts 18:9-18), or it may refer to his presence among them "in spirit" through the reading of his letter that had caused them sorrow (2 Cor. 7:8; see 1 Cor. 5:3).
[2] Craig S. Keener, *1–2 Corinthians*, The New Cambridge Bible Commentary, ed. Ben Witherington III (Cambridge: Cambridge University Press, 2005), 162.

## THE CRUCIAL CONCERNS OF MINISTRY (2 CORINTHIANS 1:1–3:18)

[1] John Keith, "How Firm a Foundation," in *The Hymnal for Worship and Celebration* (Waco, TX: Word Music, 1986), no. 275.
[2] See Joni Eareckson Tada, *Joni: An Unforgettable Story*, 25th anniversary ed. (Grand Rapids: Zondervan, 2001).
[3] See Joni Eareckson Tada, *A Place of Healing: Wrestling with the Mysteries of Suffering, Pain, and God's Sovereignty* (Colorado Springs: David C. Cook, 2010).
[4] Murray J. Harris, "2 Corinthians," in *The Expositor's Bible Commentary*, vol. 10, ed. Frank E. Gaebelein (Grand Rapids: Zondervan, 1976), 321.
[5] Washington Irving, *Rip Van Winkle* (New York: Doubleday, 1905), 13.
[6] David K. Lowery, "2 Corinthians," in *The Bible Knowledge Commentary*, vol. 2, ed. John Walvoord and Roy B. Zuck (Wheaton: Victor Books, 1983) 556.
[7] C. K. Barrett, *The Second Epistle to the Corinthians*, Black's New Testament Commentaries (New York: Harper and Row, 1973), 79.
[8] Lowery, "2 Corinthians," 559.
[9] William Barclay, *The Letters to the Corinthians*, The New Daily Study Bible, 3rd rev. ed. (Louisville: Westminster John Knox, 2002), 218.
[10] Richard Baxter, *The Reformed Pastor* (London: James Nisbet, 1860), 77.
[11] Augustus M. Toplady, "Rock of Ages, Cleft for Me," in *Hymnal for Worship and Celebration* (Waco, TX: Word Music, 1986), no. 204.

## THE MINISTRY OF RECONCILIATION (2 CORINTHIANS 4:1–5:21)

[1] Barclay, *Letters to the Corinthians*, 236.
[2] Ibid., 234.
[3] Keener, *1–2 Corinthians*, 175.
[4] C. S. Lewis, *The Weight of Glory* (Grand Rapids: Eerdmans, 1965), 14–15.
[5] The death of Enoch is unrecorded in Scripture. We are told that "Enoch walked with God; and he was not, for God took him" (Gen. 5:24). This mysterious passage is explained for us in Hebrews 11:5—"By faith Enoch was taken up so that he would not see death." During the time of the prophets, Elijah is described as departing from this world not by death, but by "a chariot of fire" that appeared from heaven, and "Elijah went up by a whirlwind to heaven" (2 Kgs. 2:11). Both of these are obviously exceptions to the general rule, supported by Scripture, that "it is appointed for men to die once and after this comes judgment" (Heb. 9:27).
[6] Joseph Bayly, *The Last Thing We Talk About*, rev. ed. (Elgin, IL: David C. Cook, 1973), 11.
[7] David Steinmetz, "Purgatory," in *The New International Dictionary of the Christian Church*, rev. ed., ed. J. D. Douglas (Grand Rapids: Zondervan, 1978), 814.
[8] Paul Barnett, *The Second Epistle to the Corinthians*, The New International Commentary on the New Testament (Grand Rapids: Eerdmans, 1997), 275.
[9] Adapted from Charles R. Swindoll, *Great Days with the Great Lives* (Nashville: W Publishing Group, 2005). Copyright © 2005 by Charles R. Swindoll, Inc. All rights reserved. Used by permission.
[10] A. W. Tozer, *The Root of the Righteous* (Camp Hill, PA: Christian Publications, 1986), 156.
[11] R. V. G. Tasker, *The Second Epistle of Paul to the Corinthians* (Grand Rapids: Eerdmans, 1958), 89–90.

## THE REALISTIC PORTRAIT OF MINISTRY (2 CORINTHIANS 6:1–7:16)

[1] Lowery, "2 Corinthians," 568.

[2] Barclay, *Letters to the Corinthians*, 252.
[3] Cited in Tony Campolo, *Who Switched the Price Tags?* (Dallas: Word, 1986), 7–8.
[4] Lowery, "2 Corinthians," 570.
[5] Though Paul refers to an individual's physical body as the "temple of the Holy Spirit" (1 Cor. 6:19), his temple image is also used of the corporate body, the church (1 Cor. 3:16-17; Eph. 2:21-22). The context and grammar in 2 Corinthians 6:16 show that Paul has the corporate idea in mind.
[6] No single Old Testament passage contains all of these terms and images. Paul seems to be drawing from several passages, such as Exod. 29:45; Lev. 26:11-12; Isa. 22:21; 43:6; Jer. 31:33.
[7] Barbara Walters, *How to Talk with Practically Anybody about Practically Anything* (New York: Dell, 1970), 142.
[8] Johnny Lee, "Lookin' for Love," by Wanda Mallette, Bob Morrison, and Patti Ryan, *Urban Cowboy Soundtrack*, Full Moon, 1980, LP.
[9] Adapted from Charles R. Swindoll, "The Value of a Mentor, Part 1," *Encouraging Words for Pastors from Chuck Swindoll* (blog), June 2009, http://insightforliving.typepad.com/insight_for_living_blog/2009/06/the-value-of-a-mentor-part-1.html.
[10] Lowery, "2 Corinthians," 570.

## THE SELF-SACRIFICIAL MINISTRY (2 CORINTHIANS 8:1–9:15)

[1] Philip Edgcumbe Hughes, *Paul's Second Epistle to the Corinthians* (Grand Rapids: Eerdmans, 1962), 284.
[2] Hans Dieter Betz, *2 Corinthians 8 and 9*, ed. G. W. MacRae (Philadelphia: Fortress, 1985), 43.
[3] Tasker, *Second Epistle*, 111.
[4] See Ron Blue, *Master Your Money* (Nashville: Thomas Nelson, 1986), 19–20.
[5] John Wesley, "The Use of Money," in *Sermons on Several Occasions* (New York: Lane & Tippett, 1845), 446.
[6] Oscar Wilde, *The Picture of Dorian Gray* (New York: Barnes and Noble Classics, 2003), 35.
[7] Richard J. Foster, *Money, Sex & Power: The Challenge of the Disciplined Life* (San Francisco: Harper & Row, 1985), 25–26.
[8] Keener, *1–2 Corinthians*, 211.
[9] Adapted from Charles R. Swindoll, "Ragged-Edge Faith and Reckless Generosity," *Insights* (May 2007): 1–2.
[10] Keener, *1–2 Corinthians*, 213–214.

## THE TRUE APOSTOLIC MINISTRY (2 CORINTHIANS 10:1–13:14)

[1] Theodore Roosevelt, from the speech "Citizen in a Republic," given at the Sorbonne, Paris, France, April 23, 1910, as quoted in John Allen Gable, ed., *The Man in the Arena* (Oyster Bay, NY: Theodore Roosevelt Association, 1987), 54.
[2] "Acts of Paul and Thecla" in *Fathers of the Third and Fourth Centuries*, vol. 8 of Ante Nicene Fathers, American repr., ed., Alexander Roberts, James Donaldson, and A. Cleveland Coxe (Grand Rapids: Christian Literature Publishing Company, 1886), 487. Though this account comes to us from a document written about a century after Paul's death, it likely preserves an accurate memory of Paul's general visual appearance because the tendency would have been to paint a more glorious picture of the highly revered apostle. This less-than-flattering account has a ring of truth, because it goes against what we would expect from a later fictional, legendary description.

[3] Barrett, *Second Epistle*, 277.
[4] Lowery, "2 Corinthians," 578.
[5] Ibid.
[6] Keener, *1–2 Corinthians*, 227.
[7] On the history of ancient rhetoric see Thomas Habinek, *Ancient Rhetoric and Oratory,* Blackwell Introductions to the Classical World (Oxford, UK: Blackwell, 2004).
[8] John Newton, "Amazing Grace," in *The Hymnal for Worship and Celebration* (Waco, TX: Word Music, 1986), no. 202.
[9] All three are reflected in Psalm 139:7-10, which indicates that God is everywhere present and active. We are told that Christ's sovereignty also extends to all spheres of existence, as one day every knee will bow to Him "in heaven and on earth and under the earth" (Phil. 2:10). These same three levels are reflected in the book of Revelation as well (Rev. 5:3, 13).
[10] Lowery, "2 Corinthians," 582.
[11] Harris, "2 Corinthians," 395.
[12] See Hughes, *Paul's Second Epistle*, 442–448.
[13] See historical feature, "Paul's Mysterious Second Visit," on page 481.
[14] Ernest Best, *Second Corinthians*, Interpretation: A Bible Commentary for Teaching and Preaching (Louisville: John Knox, 1987), 2, 124; Lowery, "2 Corinthians," 552.
[15] John James Lias, *The Second Epistle to the Corinthians,* The Cambridge Bible for Schools and Colleges, ed. J. J. S. Perowne (Cambridge: Cambridge University Press, 1897), 130.
[16] Robert B. Hughes, *Second Corinthians,* Everyman's Bible Commentary (Chicago: Moody Press, 1983), 16–17.
[17] John Calvin, *Commentary on the Epistles of Paul the Apostle to the Corinthians,* vol. 2., trans. John Pringle (Edinburgh: Calvin Translation Society, 1849), 146.
[18] Hughes, *Paul's Second Epistle*, 487.
[19] On the ancient custom of the "holy kiss" see the application section, "Keep Your Kisses! How about a Holy Hug?" on page 274.